Other Books by John Scarne

SCARNE'S NEW COMPLETE GUIDE TO GAMBLING

Fully Revised, Expanded, Updated Edition

by John Scarne

A FIRESIDE BOOK
Published by Simon & Schuster
NEW YORK LONDON TORONTO SYDNEY TOKYO SINGAPORE

Copyright © 1961, 1974 by John Scarne

All rights reserved
including the right of reproduction
in whole or in part in any form

First Fireside Edition, 1986

Published by Simon & Schuster, Inc.

Rockefeller Center
1230 Avenue of the Americas
New York, New York 10020

FIRESIDE and colophon are registered trademarks of Simon & Schuster, Inc.

Designed by Jack Jaget

Manufactured in the United States of America

10 9 8 7 6 5
20 19 18 17 16   Pbk.

Library of Congress Cataloging in Publication Data

Scarne, John.
    Scarne's new complete guide to gambling.

    "A Fireside book."
    1. Gambling. 2. Gambling systems. I. Title.
II. Title: New complete guide to gambling.
GV1301.S355   1986   795   86-13734

ISBN: 0-671-21734-8
ISBN: 0-671-63063-6 Pbk.

To the 81,500 men and women gamblers and to the 15,000 professional gamblers throughout the world who helped me gather the necessary information contained in this book by answering the questions I asked them during my many gambling surveys over the past twenty years.

Contents

4. *Betting on Sports Events*   109

5. *Lotteries, Sweepstakes, Pools and Raffles*   141

11. *Correct Odds in Dice Games Using Two, Three, Four or Five Dice*   337

12. *Black Jack, or Twenty-One: Casino Style*   342

13. *Black Jack Strategy*   366

14. *Roulette*   393

15. *Slot Machines: The One-armed Bandits*   430

SCARNE'S NEW COMPLETE GUIDE TO GAMBLING

Scarne dealing himself four aces at an Army camp demonstration during World War II. (Wide World)

Senators Karl Mundt (R., S.D.), Sam Ervin (D., S.C.), Chairman John Mc-Clellan (D., Ark.), and subcommittee counsel Jerome Adlerman watch John Scarne demonstrate the use of marked cards during the Senate Investigation subcommittee hearings in Washington on August 22, 1961. Mr. Scarne also testified before the subcommittee, giving the facts and figures which he gathered in his five-year nation-wide gambling survey. (Wide World)

Introduction

How does one get to be the world's foremost authority on games and gambling? The answer is simple: you need to be a magician. It helps even more, of course, if you are also a magician's magician, a reputation John Scarne acquired when he first appeared on the magic scene at the age of seventeen. Nate Leipzig, who was starred for many years in vaudeville as the International King of Cards, saw an exhibition of the young Scarne's skill and said, "He is the most expert exponent of wonderful card effects and table work that I have ever seen in my life." Howard Thurston's advance man and press agent, John Northern Hilliard, the author of a classic treatise on conjuring, said, "Scarne has a technical mastery that is unsurpassed. I have yet to see anyone who surpasses him in originality and sheer skill of hand."

Scarne's ability to make a deck of playing cards jump through hoops naturally attracted the notice of professional gamblers, who are always on the lookout for anything new in that line. The honest gamblers must always know the angles in order to protect themselves from cheats, and the card sharps wanted to find out how John did his magician-bafflers for obvious reasons. It wasn't long before Scarne was calling these gentlemen by their first names and they had given him the monicker "the Professor"—originally because it used to be a term applied to top-ranking magicians and later because of his encyclopedic knowledge of gambling.

But proficiency in sleight of hand is not the whole answer. Scarne is also a natural mathematical genius, and since all games of chance have a mathematical basis, this helps. Early in his career, not knowing that mathematicians Daniel Bernoulli, Laplace, Gauss and others had worked out the probability formulas that are used to figure odds and percentages—about a hundred and fifty years earlier—Scarne started from scratch, worked out his own methods and, in effect, redid the work for himself.

Scarne's curiosity and his triple interest in sleight of hand, games and mathematics led to a lifelong study of gambling, which has culminated in this book. His fame as an authority dates from World War II, when he saw that the gambling demonstration he gave as part of his magic performance was stealing the show whenever he played before a GI audience. He realized then that the stories he had heard about the big winnings made by gamblers and hustlers in World War I were not just tall stories. The questions his audiences asked indicated that they knew so little about the basic facts of gambling that they were sitting ducks for any halfway smart hustler. The next thing John knew, he was fighting a one-man war against the Panzer divisions of card sharps and dice mechanics who were staging a blitzkrieg directed at GI Joe's pay. Other evidence he gathered showed that the cheats and hustlers were enjoying a gold rush nearly as lucrative as anything that ever hit the Klondike.

John gave hundreds of gambling demonstrations for thousands of members of the Armed Forces and for gatherings of the top brass, but he was outnumbered; there were millions of men in the Armed Forces. Then the press began to help. *True Detective* magazine, the first to assist in Scarne's clean-up campaign, ran a series of six articles in which John told how players could protect themselves from cheaters. *Life* followed with a picture story, and then *Yank, the Army Weekly* signed him to do a continuing series of articles. The next step was John's first book, *Scarne on Dice.* It was hailed on its publication as the definitive work on the subject. Published in 1945, it is still selling. After twelve printings it has just been reissued in a completely revised edition. The full story of Scarne's campaign to protect GI Joe has been told in John's two autobiographies, *The Amazing World of John Scarne* and *The Odds Against Me.*

Here we will simply quote General Hap Arnold, Commanding General of the U.S. Army Air Force, as to its success. He said: "John Scarne's one-man crusade against crooked gambling in the Armed Forces during World War II saved servicemen tens of millions of dollars a month in potential gambling losses when he practically cleaned up crooked gambling in the Armed Forces singlehanded." Admiral Ernest J. King, Commander-in-Chief of the U.S. Navy, told John: "You have done a great service, both to your country and to the members of the Armed Forces."

Shortly after the war, John's second book was published—*Scarne on Cards.* This, like the dice book, was a comprehensive, definitive work, and it clinched Scarne's reputation as the world's leading gambling authority. No one before or since has ever done anything so complete and so authoritative. Both books became the bibles of the trade in Nevada; many casinos bought copies for their employees to use as manuals. Later, the reviewers, gaming experts, mathematicians, gamblers and millions of ordinary game enthusiasts said the same thing of the first publication of *Scarne's Complete Guide to Gambling.* These three books without a doubt proved Scarne to be the world's foremost gambling authority.

Scarne's books are the only ones that leading makers of professional gaming equipment, Ewing Manufacturing Company, B. C. Wills & Company and others, list in their catalogues, which say in essence that no casino employee or operator should be without any of Scarne's books. Magazine writer and editor Sidney Carroll has said, "To call Scarne an outstanding expert on gambling is to praise him with a faint damn. He is by all odds the world's greatest."

John has also been called into consultation as an expert on games and gambling by the U.S. Senate, the Federal Bureau of Investigation, the British Home Office, the Puerto Rican government, the government of Panama, the government of the Netherlands Antilles and numerous other government and hotel agencies throughout the world. He is also game consultant to the *Encyclopaedia Britannica* and to the *World Book Encyclopedia.* In addition to the books already mentioned, he has written more than twenty books on magic, games and gambling.

For the past twenty years, he has been retained by the Hilton International Hotel chain to oversee their global casino operations. In this capacity he screens prospective casino administrators, helps install new casino operations, selects and buys the proper gaming equipment, helps set up and supervises training programs and croupier schools to teach new employees and makes frequent inspections of these casinos to ensure that both management and patrons continue to get an honest deal. In fact, making certain that everyone gets an honest deal is John's main business. The casinos hire him for this purpose and he carries on the work in his books, magazine articles, lectures and demonstrations which expose crooked gambling and explain how to detect crooks at work. Law-enforcement agencies, casino operators and gamblers have praised him, and countless cheats have damned him, for having done more to combat dishonesty in gambling than all the other efforts toward this end combined.

The once universal phrase "according to Hoyle" is now obsolete among gamblers. They say, "According to Scarne." Such a change could only be achieved by a man who has spent a lifetime of constant study and research into every phase of games and gaming.

But Scarne not only writes game rules; he invents them. John has invented more than 200 games, among them the skill board games of Teeko, Scarney and Follow the Arrow, the card games of Skarney, Skarney Gin and Scarney Baccarat, and the dice games of Scarney Craps, Scarney Dice and Scarney 3000. He has his own game company (John Scarne Games, Inc., 4319 Meadowview Ave., North Bergen, N.J. 07047) to market them. His newest book, *Scarne's Encyclopedia of Games,* analyzes in detail the winning strategy and rules of play for most of these games. This new revised edition of *Scarne's Complete Guide to Gambling* contains the rules of play and winning strategy for Scarney Baccarat, Scarney Craps, Scarney Dice, Scarney 3000, Skarney Gin and other Scarne games.

Games are never static; they continually evolve and change, and many rule books continue to reprint out-of-date rules long after they have become antiquated. Scarne, unlike other game-book authorities, is on the inside of the gambling business. He sees the changes and variations of play as players and casinos adopt them; he revises his Official Rules regularly and incorporates the new variations; and he often recommends new rules of his own which make the games mathematically more sound.

Scarne is, by far, the foremost authority on odds, percentages and the mathematical structure of gambling games. He has, time after time, calculated the precise mathematics of gambling problems where other rule writers and even professional gamblers, operators and mathematicians have failed. The present book analyzes in detail the underlying mathematics of several games for the first time, notably Black Jack, Bingo, Baccarat, Scarney Baccarat, Trente et Quarante and Racehorse Keno. Casino operators, pit bosses and other gamblers of long experience told him that Black Jack could not be analyzed mathematically because of the great complexity of the betting and method of play. The newly revised edition of *Scarne on Dice* gives for the first time in print anywhere the exact house percentage on the Twenty-Six game, a figure that the operators themselves have been guessing at for years. They have only known about what to expect in earnings but have never obtained an exact mathematical answer. John has now figured it to three decimal places.

Guesses never satisfy Scarne. He is a perfectionist. This also applies to his ability to manipulate cards, dice and other gaming devices. Today, fooling magicians and professional gamblers is still his hobby. I have seen some of the best card men in the country sitting around the luncheon table at The Magicians Club in New York watching

John do card tricks and gambling moves and heard them saying, "I see it, but I don't believe it; it's impossible!" John delights in doing the impossible.

No card or dice cheat anywhere can perform as many different cheating moves as can John Scarne. There's a reason. A skilled card mechanic or dice cheater can make a good living if he is expert at one method of executing a smooth and indetectable second deal or dice switch. That's all he needs to know and all he bothers with. But there are many different methods, and every time John spots a new one he isn't satisfied merely to know how it is done. He doesn't sleep until he has practiced it so that he can do the move as well or better than the cheat he caught using it. This comprehensive knowledge enables him to detect cheaters quickly and surely.

His knowledge of playing strategy equals his skill. In fact, he knows so much that he is barred from playing in Las Vegas and Reno. He knows, for instance, that Black Jack is the only casino game in the world in which, during play, the odds sometimes favor the player rather than the house, and in this book, in the chapter on Black Jack strategy, he explains why. Casino operators know that it is dangerous to give players an even break because in the long run they would break even, and giving players an edge is suicide because the house would be bound to lose. "Hi, John," they tell him when he walks in. "Nice to see you again, but you can't gamble in this casino."

Scarney Baccarat is the first really new casino banking game in the past century. It combines the principles of Baccarat, Chemin de Fer, Bank Craps and Black Jack. This fantastic new banking card game is featured in dozens of casinos the world over and is destined to become the number one banking card game in the near future.

Skarney, based on several entirely new game principles, is the most bizarre, exciting and charmingly exasperating card game in history. It has the bluff as in Poker, scores like Canasta and is played like no other card game. Skarney Gin is the game that is rapidly displacing regular Gin Rummy as America's favorite two-handed card game.

Teeko, a two-handed board game which makes use of only four pieces to a side, surpasses Checkers as a skill game. It can be played in more than twenty different ways, with or without point scoring. Teeko's scope is so great that John wrote a 257-page book, *Scarne on Teeko*, explaining its playing strategy. On one occasion he challenged ten of the nation's top-ranking Chess, Checkers and Bridge masters to Teeko in simultaneous play, and he offered to pay $1000 for each game he lost. He played ten players simultaneously, including Chess champion Larry Evans, who was three times United States Open Chess Champion, World Checkers Champion Tom Wiswell, and John Crawford, Contract Bridge Master and winner of many national tournaments. There were three rounds of Teeko play, a total of thirty games. John risked a possible loss of $30,000, and he didn't have to pay a nickel. He won all thirty games.

John's other great skill board game creation is Scarney, which by the way is how "Scarne" is pronounced. It is so simple that a child can learn it in a few minutes and at the same time so complex in its possibilities that it surpasses chess in scope. Scarney can be played in many different ways. It is not only a true solitaire game, but a true singles game that can be played by two, three, four or more players each playing for himself. It has an inner world and logic of its own, taxing the capacity of the most skilled gamester. There is almost no chance that you will ever play two games alike because the starting positions alone number nearly 21 trillion; to be precise, 20,822,789,880,000!

Scarne has also developed a new casino-type Craps layout known as the "Scarney Craps," plus an entirely new type of dice called "Scarney Dice." There are more than forty new home, club and casino-style games including Scarney 3000 that can be played with these dice.

Scarne watches checker champion Tom Wiswell make a move in Teeko match in which Scarne played ten players simultaneously and won all games. Other players shown are Judy Holliday, Jim Braddock, Patty McCormack. (United Press International)

In 1962, John Scarne at the offices of John Scarne Games, Inc., of North Bergen, N.J., with his wife, Steffi, and his son, John Teeko, who is holding a Teeko game, one of the 200-odd games invented by the author.

Scarney 3000, America's new hit dice game, has been acclaimed by game experts as the most fascinating family and club dice game on the market today. I tell you this about these games so you will understand why famed sports columnist the late John Lardner once wrote: "Scarne is to games what Dr. Einstein is to advanced physics."

This new revised edition of *Scarne's Complete Guide to Gambling* is the most all-inclusive, up-to date and authoritative book on gambling ever written. It is a book that only John Scarne could have written.

SIMON AND SCHUSTER

1.
Gambling: America's Biggest Industry

AMERICA'S $500 BILLION GAMBLING HANDLE

Gambling in the United States, despite all the Federal and state restrictions against it, is the leading industry in the country, both in the number of participants and the amount of money involved. Its handle surpasses the combined total money volume of the 100 largest industrial organizations in the country, including such giant corporations as U.S. Steel, General Motors, General Electric, Metropolitan Life, Ford Motor Company and any others you care to name. Today about 90 million adult Americans—of whom 43 million are men and 47 million are women—are gambling the astronomical sum of $500 billion annually.

Almost 90% or $450 billion of this huge amount is wagered illegally; only $50 billion legally.

The number of illegal gambling operators in America, race bookies, operators of Poker and dice games, etc., has been reduced with the enactment and enforcement of additional Federal interstate antigambling laws. This loss of gambling revenue has been more than made up by gigantic increases in other forms of gambling: (1) The Numbers game, despite Federal and state police harassment, has increased considerably in participants and money wagered. (2) The huge national interest in sports generated by television (football, basketball, hockey, etc.) has resulted in billions of fresh dollars being bet among gamblers and with illegal sports bookies. (3) The legalization of many state race and dog tracks, lotteries, raffles, Bingo games and off-track betting has contributed hundreds of millions more to the national betting handle.

Gambling, in general, is a constant growing industry, increasing the number of participants and gambling handle, except for some occasional economically "bad" years. There is no doubt in anyone's mind, that is, if he gets around at all, that gambling is *big business*. How big? Nobody knows exactly. As for me, I'll stick with my nationwide gambling survey of a few years ago, which revealed a yearly gambling handle of over $500 billion, a figure which has since been accepted by the U.S. Senate Subcommittee on Gambling Investigations, the Department of Justice and the Internal Revenue Service.

Note that this $500 billion handle does not represent gambling industry income or profits; it is the annual gambling exchange. It is all the money handled; it is the total amount wagered. Many of the dollars in the $500 billion are duplications because they are bet and rebet back and forth many times between players, and between players and gambling operators, before they are finally won or lost.

Of the $500 billion handle, the actual cost to the betting public for their yearly gambling pleasure—the annual gambling revenue from all forms of gambling—amounts to about 10% of the $500 billion, for a gross revenue of $50 billion. Of this, an average of 60% or $30 billion goes for building and maintenance of gambling establishments. Examples: upkeep of racetracks, Las Vegas hotel casinos, Poker rooms and Bingo parlors. This leaves $20 billion as the nation's net gambling revenue. The $20 billion is divided almost equally between (1) professional or organized gambling and (2) private gambling. The $10 billion yearly net revenue from all forms of organized gambling includes betting, both legal and illegal, at the various types of banking games such as Craps, Black Jack, slot machines, Roulette, casino side games, carnival games, and punchboards; with race and sports bookies; in lotteries, Bingo, baseball and football pools, Keno, raffles, Numbers and all other forms of gambling in which a professional operator or banker is involved. The $10 billion yearly net revenue of private gambling entails illegal betting among friends, acquaintances and strangers at all kinds of card games (Poker, Gin Rummy, Black Jack, Skarney, Pinochle, Bridge, Canasta, etc.), at Craps, Scarney Dice and other dice games, at guessing games and sports and at any other form of illegal gambling in which a professional operator or banker is not involved.

The recipients of this $20 billion annual net gambling income include the millions of male and female gamblers who possess some sort of edge over the others. They are the operators of gambling schemes, the experienced or skilled gamblers, gambling hustlers and cheats and racketeers and their henchmen who are the behind-the-scenes bosses of most of the illegal and some of the legal gambling activities in this country. Also included among this group, since they derive income from gambling, are the unscrupulous law-enforcement agents and politicians who accept graft to permit illegal gambling to operate free of police interference.

Strange but true, most of the above group including the so-called "smart gamblers" have one thing in common with the average gambling chump. They can't resist gambling at someone else's game, or even their own, and in turn they recontribute several billions of their annual new gambling profit to the $20 billion annual take.

DOES THE MAFIA CONTROL GAMBLING IN AMERICA?

My lifetime of study of all forms of bigtime illegal gambling operations reveals that it is *not* controlled by the mythical Mafia or by any single mob or syndicate. This is, of course, contrary to what many racketeers, Federal and state law-enforcement agencies, Federal and state district attorneys, judges, legislators, politicians, television programs, books, magazines and newspapers keep saying. What rubbish! First, there is no such an animal as the *Mafia*. Secondly, such statements by these sources—some of which are ill advised, others for ethnic reasons and some for personal gain—are welcomed by the real mobster bosses, especially when their names appear in print as Mafia figures. It's good for their business. It puts fear in the hearts of people they deal with and makes their money deals and collections much easier to achieve.

Most major news sources and many book authors in this country seem to have a policy of labeling every arrested gambler big or small who has an Italian name as a member of the Mafia, and those gamblers who do not possess Italian names as non-voting Mafia members. But the truth of the matter is that most towns and hamlets have their own racket bosses who control the local gambling and seldom team up with any outside operators. Occasionally a few racket bosses using fronts may become partners in purchasing a casino in Europe, the Caribbean or elsewhere, but there is no single mob or syndicate that controls gambling throughout the United States. Las Vegas, Nevada, the biggest gambling bonanza in history, is the best example of the non-existence of the Mafia. Check the names of the old and the present-day operators and you find very few so-called "Mafia names." The same holds true for the casino managers, shift bosses and other major casino employees.

Professional gamblers and race and sports bookies should not be confused with mobsters or racket guys. Generally speaking, race and sports bookies or operators of Poker rooms are local sportsmen who break the law by giving the local populace a place or chance to gamble. Many of the new breed of bookmakers are college graduates. In fact, mobsters or racketeers are as different from the bookies or Poker room operators as night from day. These "animals," as they are commonly called by bookies and gamblers, think nothing of torturing a victim by breaking his legs, head, and even killing him when it serves their purpose.

Today illegal race and sports bookies are constantly being arrested by the FBI and other state law-enforcement agents. But as soon as one bookie is jailed, another takes his place. It's an endless chain that never seems to stop. As to the employment of FBI agents in tracking down bookies all over the country, I agree with my friend, the late J. Edgar Hoover, former Director of the Federal Bureau of Investigation, who said, "The FBI has much more important functions to accomplish than arresting gamblers all over the country." In spite of Mr. Hoover's opinion, today FBI agents are constantly playing the cat and mouse game with bookies all over America.

THE LAW VS. GAMBLING

From early 1950 to May 1951, the U.S. Senate Committee to Investigate Organized Crime in Interstate Commerce, headed by Senator Estes Kefauver, conducted the greatest anti-gambling crusade in this country's history, with the end result that Congress enacted several Federal anti-gambling laws, including the one that requires the operator of a race or sports book, lottery, policy or Numbers game, baseball or football pool, etc., to purchase a $50 Federal occupational stamp and pay a 10% Federal excise tax on the operation's gross betting handle. Failure to buy the stamp is a misdemeanor punishable by a term of imprisonment for one year or less and a minimum mandatory fine of $1,000. Failure to pay the 10% excise tax is a felony punishable by imprisonment for five years or less and fine of not more than $10,000.

The immediate result was for the next two or three years illegal organized gambling almost came to a standstill. Most of the nation's bigtime gambling operators and race bookies closed shop and were either in hiding, jailed or being investigated by Federal or state authorities. Those who continued to operate retained only a small percentage of their former business.

This situation didn't last long. In 1954, a bolder and much less law-abiding generation of gambling operators made their appearance. Most of them were former employees of the retired operators. They picked up where their predecessors left off, and one of the greatest gambling binges in American history took place.

Then came 1961 and another U.S. Senate Subcommittee Investigation of Organized Gambling, headed this time by Senator John McClellan. This probe resulted in Federal enactment of the most severe anti-gambling statutes in our history. Under the new law it became a Federal crime to travel interstate to promote or participate in illegal gambling (this, for example, handicapped agents or "collectors" in carrying money for gamblers from one state to another).

Another portion of the Federal law prohibits the interstate transportation in whole or in part of slot machines, Roulette wheels, wheels of fortune and various other kinds of gambling equipment. Still another Federal interstate law prohibits transmitting bets by wire or telephone, or transporting betting paraphernalia (policy slips, sports parlay cards, etc.). But a great increase in gambling occurred in spite of the Federal anti-gambling laws and the thousands of local and state gambling probes throughout the country. The result of the Senate Committee's exposures and its various other "witch hunts" was the enactment by state legislatures of many stiff anti-gambling laws.

While anti-gambling campaigns, which usually take place for obvious reasons just before national or state elections, may result in additional anti-gambling legislation, the publicity that accompanies these crusades also focuses the attention of the average citizen on gambling activities. The net effect often is that he begins to gamble more frequently and in greater numbers than before. Today, in spite of all the additional anti-gambling laws, the United States is the largest gambling nation—both legal and illegal—in the world.

It's a curious situation when the greatest part of a country's biggest business is conducted outside the law. Only one state, Nevada, legally permits casinos (as does Puerto Rico). However, debate on casino gambling is attracting considerable interest in several eastern states. Two states, New York and Nevada, and Puerto Rico, permit off-track betting. There are 30 states in which pari-mutuel betting at racetracks is legal; 9 permit betting at dog tracks, 25 or more have legalized Bingo or raffles or both; 5 states allow slot machine operations in varying degrees of activity, and 1 permits the operation of carnival games. The fastest-growing form of legalization is, of course, the state lottery. More than a dozen states operate or are in the process of legalizing their own lotteries. Puerto Rico, which bars slot machines in its casinos, has the oldest legal operating lottery on American soil. Incidentally, New Jersey's successful state lottery, upon which most other state lotteries are patterned, was developed from the Treasury

Ticket information in this book with additional information by your author.

ANOTHER SCARNE GAMBLING SURVEY

My work as a gambling authority takes me into every type of place where Americans gamble: the plush legal gambling casinos of Las Vegas, Reno, Puerto Rico, Curaçao, the Bahamas, Latin America, Europe and North Africa, also the plush and dingy illegal gambling dives that are spread all over this country. Recently on one of my periodical visits to Las Vegas, I was impressed by the crowded casinos. A closer look, however, revealed that most players were so-called "average Americans." Generally speaking, they placed minimum limit bets and their play appeared amateurish. Gone were most of the "high rollers" (big-money gamblers) of yesteryear who lined the dice and Black Jack tables placing maximum limit bets of $500, $1,000 or more on each decision. Even the Baccarat–Chemin de Fer tables had reduced their $20 minimum limit bet to $5. It became obvious to me that with the recent acquisition of most of the big casinos by giant corporations and syndicates a new breed of small gamblers had taken over the Strip casinos. The high roller, if not dead, was fast on his way to extinction.

This drastic change in Las Vegas casino gambling habits led me to the decision to undertake another gambling survey—to determine just what was what in the gambling world. I wanted, among other things, facts and figures about the new breed of players. I wished to know why they gambled and what kind of gambling they preferred. To avoid any bias in these results I carefully avoided questioning anyone I saw gambling and did not include in my survey count anyone I knew in advance to be a gambler. This survey was made from a random sampling of our populace.

My questionnaire included, among many others, such questions as: "Do you gamble?" "What is your favorite gambling activity?" "Why do you gamble?" "If you do not gamble, why not?" "Are you in favor of legalized casinos?" Answers were obtained from people in all walks of life and in varied urban and rural areas throughout the United States.

I found as in earlier surveys that most people were interested in the subject and the questions and eager to supply answers. Aided by several assistants, I obtained replies from 10,000 women, 10,000 men and 5,000 professional gamblers, a total of 25,000 adults. Here were my findings from the answers to the questions above:

1. Do you gamble? "Yes" was the answer given by 80% of the women and 76% of the men.

2. What is your favorite gambling activity? The replies show that the various types of gambling rank in order of number of participants as follows: (1) card playing; (2) lotteries, raffles, Numbers and Bingo; (3) horse racing; (4) betting on sports events; (5) dice games; (6) carnival games; (7) slot machines and consoles; (8) punchboards and sales cards.

The majority stated that they did not confine themselves to the one form of gambling they listed as their favorite but also indulged in one or more other gambling activities.

3. Why do you gamble? The big majority, 75%, replied that they gamble primarily to win money. Another 20% said that they gamble for pleasure, and, of this group, one-fifth put it in stronger terms by saying that they had found nothing more exciting or thrilling. The remaining 5% gamble for reasons that have nothing to do with the nature of gambling itself, such as the character who goes to the Poker parlor to watch his girl friend dealer, or the lady who plays Bingo just to get away from her husband.

4. If you do not gamble, why not? Half of this group said they could not afford it; 30% said they do not believe it is possible to beat the game; 10% said they used to gamble but had stopped because they usually went broke; 4% said they know nothing about gambling; 2% stated that they believe all forms of gambling are sinful; and the remaining 4% gave assorted other reasons, such as the woman who replied, "My husband said he'd leave me if he ever caught me gambling. I love my husband, so I don't gamble."

5. Are you in favor of legalized casinos? I received 10,401 "Yes" votes and 5,199 "No" votes for a favorable edge of about 2 to 1.

In the field of private card playing I found that 70% of my sample stated that they played cards regularly. The proportion of men to women in this group is about 50–50. I found that Poker had more devotees than any other card game. Rummy was a close runner-up as the favorite game, and Bridge was in the number three spot. Here is how the card players voted on their favorite game.

BY SEX	POKER	RUMMY	BRIDGE	OTHERS
Men	36%	35%	8%	21%
Women	38%	32%	22%	8%

Most card players, of course, play more than one card game; this table shows only how they voted on their favorite game.

With reference to all money wagered in private card games, Poker led with 51%, Gin Rummy was second with 30% and Bridge ran far behind with less than 1%. The remaining 19% was wagered at all

other card games: other forms of Rummy, Pinochle, Skarney, Crib-
bage, Hearts, Canasta, Skarney Gin, etc.

Why is this country now experiencing the greatest gambling boom in
its history? The reasons I give below are based not only on the results
of the surveys but also on a lifetime of observation and study of every
facet of gambling.

1. The legalization in some states of horse racing, lotteries, off-track
betting, greyhound racing, casino games, Bingo, raffles, etc., has
created new opportunities for gambling legally. The fact that these
operations are under state supervision gives reasonable assurance that
they are honestly run, and because of this, millions who did not gamble before now do so.

2. A great many people have more money today than ever before
and can for the first time afford to gamble.

3. The constant daily publicity which the nation's newspapers and
television give to horse racing—their listing of the daily entries, results,
payoff mutuels, ratings and handicappers' selections—have induced
millions of people who never before bet on a horse race to visit the
tracks. Once there, they begin betting and become horse bettors.

4. The front-page newspaper stories about the million dollar winners in the recently legalized state lotteries such as New Jersey, New
York, etc., with their pictures of the jubilant winners induce millions
to purchase lottery and raffle tickets.

5. The enormous popularity of Bridge created new millions of
women card players, most of whom began for the first time to play for
money. Because any card game eventually loses interest when no financial stake is involved, many also began to gamble at simpler and faster
games such as Poker, Gin Rummy, Canasta and Black Jack.

6. Most illegal casino operators have learned over the years (and
the Nevada operation is proof of it) that more money can be made
with an honest percentage game than with a *flat store* (crooked game).
As the illegal casinos operated more honestly they acquired new customers, many of whom had not previously gambled for fear of being
cheated.

7. Since casino gambling was legalized in Nevada, Puerto Rico, the
Bahamas and elsewhere, the constant publicity given to its casinos by
word of mouth, in motion pictures, television, national magazines and
newspapers has attracted tens of millions of tourists who previously
knew little or nothing about casino games. They visited the casinos,
learned to play Roulette, Black Jack, Craps, the Wheel of Fortune,
slot machines and other casino games, enjoyed them and, when they
returned home, looked for action in other casinos.

TYPES OF GAMBLERS

There are seven different kinds of men and women gamblers. Which category are you in?

1. *The occasional gambler* who knows little or nothing about the hard mathematical and psychological facts of the games on which he now and then wagers some money. The vast majority of America's gamblers fall into this class, and it is their losses which make gambling our biggest industry.

2. *The degenerate or habitual gambler* who plays constantly and who knows considerably more about gambling but is not smart enough to know that he can't beat adverse odds. He craves action, any kind of action, and he lives in a dream world in which he hopes someday to make a big killing and then quit gambling forever. When he does win a bit, he almost always gambles it all back and, like most players, winds up broke.

3. *The skilled gambler or gambling hustler* who knows a lot more about any sort of gambling than the occasional or the habitual gambler, plays a much better game than they do and consequently wins more often than he loses. He is usually on hand to start the game, and he specializes in games which contain some element of skill, such as Poker, Gin Rummy, Bridge or Black Jack. The hustler plays for blood: he seldom gives another player a break because he believes that is no way to earn money at gambling. He usually knows where the favorable percentage lies in most private games of chance, such as Craps, and he makes the most of this by offering the occasional and habitual gamblers sucker odds, which, not knowing any better, they usually accept.

4. *The professional gambler or gambling operator* who earns his living, or most of it, by operating some gambling scheme. He is called a gambler because he runs a gambling operation, but he doesn't really gamble. He is a businessman (or woman) who runs a gambling operation and understands his trade, and either makes direct levies on the play or receives a percentage because the odds are in his favor. The professional gambler, like the legitimate banker and insurance operator, acts as a middleman in risks which the players voluntarily take or wish to be rid of, charging a commission for the service. He is not betting against the players; they are actually betting against each other. His top aides are also in this category.

5. *The gambling cheat or crook* who makes money by cheating at cards or dice, running a fake lottery or raffle, operating a fixed carnival game, punchboard, slot machine or any other *gaffed* (crooked) gambling device. Also included in this category are any employees of a

crooked gambling house or any participants in crooked schemes, whether or not they do the actual cheating themselves. The cheat's gamble is not so much in winning or losing as in whether or not he will get away with it.

6. *The gambling chiseler* who is really only a petty crook and sneak thief. He knows that he needs an edge to make money by gambling, and he gets it by inducing a friend at a racetrack or casino game to give or loan him money with which to gamble. He usually bets only part of the money and pockets the rest, and if he wins, he conceals all or part of the winnings. This is a favorite racket of women chiselers.

In a Poker game the chiseler often forgets to put up his ante at his turn of play, and he is quick to grab any *sleeper* (money belonging to another player which the latter has forgotten about). He will borrow money during a private game and forget about paying it back.

The chiseler—and there are millions of these characters—preys mostly on the habitual, chronic gambler. He is often caught, but that doesn't deter him, since he considers it an occupational hazard.

7. *The system gambler* who lives in a dream world all his own, believing that it is only a question of time until he finds an infallible betting system which he can use to amass a fortune. He is a perfect *mark* (sucker) for racetrack touts. He buys tips and most of the advertised systems, and although they fail, one after another, he buys more, always hoping to find the one that is perfect. The system horse player usually spends as much money on worthless tips and systems as he bets on the horses, and he wastes many hours trying to figure out a system of his own.

Legalized gambling's annual $50 billion handle is completely overshadowed by the huge illegal gambling handle of $450 billion. Illegal gambling flourishes in one form or another in every city and hamlet from coast to coast. It can escape the notice of police, district attorneys and politicians who are sworn to enforce the anti-gambling statutes in only one way. It pays $5 billion annually to these officials for their passive permission to operate. This graft or protection money, known as *ice,* enables some police chiefs to own rows of apartment buildings and some county sheriffs to retire early to fancy estates in Florida. Illegal gambling will, I believe, continue to thrive in spite of whatever future investigations may be made by well-meaning Federal and state committees and in spite of any new laws that may be enacted in an attempt to suppress it.

GAMBLING AND THE FEDERAL TAX PROBLEM

The most bewildering topic among gamblers who make a big hit is the tax procedure employed by the Internal Revenue Service in the collection of income taxes on a player's gambling winnings. From a technical and legal standpoint, the IRS regulation states "that a gambler's total yearly winnings must be included in his income. However, he is permitted to deduct his gambling losses incurred during the same year, but only to the amount of his winnings." That is the law, but since all consistent gamblers who buck adverse odds are losers over the long run, where does that leave the poor sucker who happens to be lucky enough one day to win $1,000 or more in a Las Vegas Keno game or a state lottery or to hit a $2 daily double ticket for $600 or more?

To begin with, few gamblers (and none that I know of) keep a record of every bet they make during the year. So even assuming that in early December in any given year, a Craps shooter in Las Vegas gets lucky and manages to get a hot hand at the dice table and wins $1,000 or more, who is to say whether this puts him in the winner's circle for the year? To further complicate matters, no legal casino, racetrack or legal gambling operation keeps records of an individual's gambling transactions—especially those on a cash basis. Therefore, the matter of what to report is up to a gambler's conscience. Sure, there are many cases where gamblers report winnings of $25,000 or more made at a racetrack or at a gambling casino, but many of these individuals are racket guys who list their alleged winnings as earnings rather than reveal illegitimate sources of revenue.

At racetracks, any $2 ticket whose payoff is $600 or more means that the winner must fill out tax forms at the track which in turn will deliver them to the Internal Revenue Service. The same holds true for winners of state lotteries.

From a practical standpoint there is only one game played in Nevada today where the Internal Revenue Service requires that a report be made of any sizable wins. This is Keno. Some of the Keno lounges, in fact, post a detailed schedule citing the size of the winning tickets that the casino must report to the IRS. The schedule is as follows:

COST OF TICKET	MINIMUM WINNINGS WHICH MUST BE REPORTED
.00– .59	$600
.60– .89	1,200
.90–$1.19	1,800
$1.20–$1.79	2,400
$1.80–$2.39	3,000
$2.40–$2.99	3,600
$3.00–$3.59	4,200
$3.60–$9.99	6,000
$10.00 and over	10,000

The IRS policy creates for winning Keno, lottery and horse players, etc., as many questions as it does answers. For example, a horse player buys several $2 daily double or exacta tickets and gets lucky and wins $2,000. In accordance with racetrack policy, a report of the winnings is made to the Internal Revenue Service, whom we will assume expects the $2,000 winnings to be added to the taxpayer's gross income for that year. The trouble is that during the same year the player lost more than $2,000 at Las Vegas and at various racetracks. However, since no records were kept of these betting transactions, the player has no way of proving this except by his own statement—which the IRS will not accept unless it is documented. At the racetrack such documentation is possible by evidence of losing bets. The player can produce losing tickets on horse races, Keno and lotteries, canceled checks to casinos, etc.

On the basis of the above information, we would have to conclude that anyone who plays the horses, buys lottery tickets, plays Keno, or gambles in Las Vegas, and intends to apply gambling losses against potential gambling winnings, better start keeping records of his gambling transactions—the more comprehensive the records are the better. Because based on past performances, it's a sure bet that your word and undocumented records won't carry much weight with the Internal Revenue Service. But, on the brighter side, there are probably 50 million gamblers in America who just for once would like to make a big winning of $2,000 or more and be faced with the problem of whether or not the IRS will permit them to deduct their gambling losses on their income tax returns.

In concluding this first chapter I want to point out that this book, the first of its kind—for gamblers of both sexes and covering all the major forms of gambling in America—was not written to encourage gambling. You will see, as you read, that it does just the opposite. The more knowledge a person has about the mathematics and the inside workings of gambling the less likely he is to become a habitual gambler. I firmly believe that if the gambling information in this book is read and studied by enough people it will do more to cut down the annual betting handle in this country than all the sermons that have ever been preached on the evils of gambling.

The moral question aside, habitual gambling is still an undesirable economic activity. For any person who is already a habitual addict inoculated with gambling fever, I am convinced that the best medicine anyone could prescribe, the one most likely to cure the patient, would be a copy of this book.

This book contains the most extensive mathematical analysis of gambling ever written, and yet it can be read and clearly understood by anyone who knows simple arithmetic. This book is the first attempt in the history of gambling to correct the sucker or chump situation in all phases of gambling in America. It is the first book to tell what makes every gambling operation tick, and to give the up-to-date rules and methods of play of each gambling scheme. It is the first book that explains how to gamble sensibly, that gives the player's best bet at each game and the adverse odds or percentages each player must buck at his favorite form of gambling, as well as the methods by which the player can detect those wily and affable crooks who try to cheat him, and thus avoid cheating himself.

You will also find here considerable evidence to prove that gambling against adverse odds is not one of the more trustworthy methods for reaching and staying on Easy Street.

2.
The Mathematics and Science of Gambling

WHAT IS GAMBLING?

Gambling consists in risking something one possesses in the hope of obtaining something better. No one can avoid gambling, because life itself forces us to make bets on Dame Fortune. In business, education, marriage, investment, insurance, travel, in all the affairs of life we must make decisions which are gambles because risk is involved.

Many people, for pleasure or gain, also risk money on games of chance, games of skill and games which combine both chance and skill.

Games of chance are those in which there is no element of skill. Gamblers call these "mechanical games." There are hundreds of such games, and they are the most popular form of gambling. They include lotteries, raffles, policy numbers, Bingo, wheels of fortune, slot machines, most dice games (Craps, Chuck-a-Luck, Hazard, Under and Over Seven, Beat the Shaker, etc.), and some card games (Faro, Baccarat Las Vegas style, etc.).

Games of skill are those in which the element of chance is completely or nearly nonexistent, such as Scarney, Teeko, Checkers, Chess, bowling, horseshoe pitching, tennis and golf.

Games of chance and skill combine both elements and include most games played with cards: Poker, Gin Rummy, Bridge, Black Jack, Pinochle and many others. Sports contests such as horse racing, baseball, football, basketball and prizefights are usually thought of as contests of skill. But we must include them in this category because, from a gambling viewpoint, they all involve a certain amount of chance which sports fans know as "the breaks of the game." In baseball, for example, a bad hop of the ball may lose the game for either team. Also, present-day bookies' methods of handicapping or laying the odds on national sports contests are such that the element of skill plays little part in helping a bettor pick a winner.

GAMBLERS AND SCIENTISTS

Dice are the oldest of all gambling devices. Man's earliest written records not only mention dice and dice games but crooked dice as well. Dice of one sort or another have been found in the tombs of ancient Egypt and the Orient, and in the prehistoric graves of both North and South America.

The earliest gamblers thought that the fall of the dice was controlled by the gods, and although a few of them tried to outwit divinity by loading the cubes, most of them probably considered that any prying into the matter was sacrilegious.

In the sixteenth century at least one gambler began to wonder if the scientists who were beginning to make valid predictions about other matters might not also be able to foretell how the dice would fall. An Italian nobleman asked Galileo why the combination 10 showed up more often than 9 when three dice were thrown. The great astronomer became interested in dice problems and wrote a short treatise which set forth some of the first probability theorems. His reply to the gambler was that $6 \times 6 \times 6$ for a total of 216 combinations can be made with three dice, of which twenty-seven form the number 10 and twenty-five the number 9.

In France, in 1654, the philosopher, mathematician and physicist Blaise Pascal was asked a similar dice question by one of the first gambler-hustlers on record. The Chevalier de Méré had been winning consistently by betting even money that a six would come up at least once in four rolls with a single die. He reasoned from this that he would also have an advantage when he bet even money that a double-six would come up at least once in 24 rolls with two dice. But he had been losing money on this proposition, and he wanted to know why.

Pascal worked on the problem and found that the Chevalier had the best of it by 3.549% with his one-die proposition. Throwing a double-six with two dice, however, would theoretically require 24.6+ rolls to make it an even-money proposition. In practice it can't ever be an even-money bet, because you can't roll a pair of dice a fractional number of times: it has to be either 24 or 25 rolls. Here is a calculation I have never seen in print before: The exact chances of rolling two sixes in 24 rolls are: 11,033,126,465,283,976,852,912,127,963,392,284,191 successes in 22,452,257,707,354,557,240,087,211,123,792,674,816 rolls.

This means that dice hustler De Méré had been taking a beating of

1.27+% on the bet. If he had bet that two sixes would come up at least once in 25 rolls he would have enjoyed a favorable edge of .85%.

Pascal corresponded with mathematician Pierre Fermat about this and similar gambling problems, and these two men formulated much of the basic mathematics on the theory of probability.

History doesn't state how many francs Chevalier de Méré lost on his double-six betting proposition before Pascal explained why he was getting the worst of it, but I do know that nearly 300 years later, in 1952, a New York City gambler known as "Fat the Butch" lost $49,000 by betting that he could throw a double-six in 21 rolls.

Fat the Butch, although a smart gambling-house operator who has made millions booking dice games, went wrong on the bet because he figured it this way: There are 36 possible combinations with two dice, and a double-six can be made only one way—so there should be an even chance to throw a double-six in 18 rolls. Consequently, when "The Brain," a well-known bigtime gambler, offered to bet $1,000 that a double-six would not turn up in 21 rolls, Fat the Butch thought he had the best of it and jumped at the opportunity.

After twelve hours of dice rolling, Fat the Butch found himself a $49,000 loser, and he quit because he finally realized something must be wrong with his logic. He was, later, part owner of the Casino de Capri in Havana, and when I told him it would need 24.6 rolls to make the double-six bet an even-up proposition, and that he had taken 20.45% the worst of it on every one of those bets, he shrugged his massive shoulders and said, "Scarne, in gambling you got to pay to learn, but $49,000 was a lot of dough to pay just to learn that." "That is for sure," I agreed.

Although most of the odds and percentage problems you will encounter in this book can be calculated simply, a few, like the double-six problem above, are more complex. Here is the formula for figuring problems of this type. To find out when the chances are *approximately* equal in any single event, multiply the "odds to one" by .693, the co-log of the hyperbolic log of 2. This will give the approximate number of chances, trials, rolls, guesses, etc., needed to make any event an even, or fifty-fifty proposition.

For example: the odds are 35 to 1 against throwing double sixes with two dice in one roll. Multiply 35 × .693 and you find that a double-six can be expected to appear in the long run once in approximately 24.255 rolls. (The figure of 24.6+ given earlier is more exact.) To calculate the approximate number required for a double event such as throwing double-sixes twice, multiply the "odds to one" by 1.678. For a triple event multiply by 2.675; a quad event, by 3.672; and a quint event, by 4.670.

CHANCE AND HOW IT WORKS

Chance and the way it works is a subject on which schools should place more emphasis. Their mathematics courses today barely mention it. The average educated citizen should know and understand some of the basic facts in this area of study. If he did, many gambling enterprises, particularly the banking games of chance, would collect from our gambling population billions of dollars less in annual profits than they now do.

I am talking about that branch of mathematics known as probability theory. The principles formulated by Galileo, Pascal, Fermat and Newton formed the groundwork of probability mathematics; Daniel Bernoulli, Laplace and Gauss developed it further. Many other mathematicians have since added refinements and found a great many very important uses for it which are far removed from the gaming tables. The modern physicist uses probability theory in studying the behavior of electronic particles within the atom; the biologist and bacteriologist use it in heredity studies; the whole insurance business depends upon mortality tables that are based upon probability theory; and any businessman who uses statistics or combinatorial analysis owes a debt to the gamblers who first asked science to consider the problem.

Probability theory supplies mathematical methods for discovering what can be expected to happen when the results depend upon chance.

It states, for instance, that each player in a game of chance has an equal chance to win in the long run. If, during a long evening of play at Poker or Bridge, you never get a decent hand, or when you do get a halfway decent hand someone else always gets a better one, you may doubt this. But your experience does not contradict the theory of probability, because the theory does not pretend to state that you and the other players will get an equal number of good hands in one evening of play. It states that the longer you play the more likely you are to get approximately the same number of good hands.

And be careful that you don't misunderstand that last statement, as many gamblers do. They think that results *must* "even up" in the long run. This is true in one sense, but not in another. Probability theory says, for instance, that when you toss a coin, heads will turn up *about* half the time in the long run. It doesn't say that in a very long run heads and tails *must* come up exactly the *same number* of times.

Coin-tossing experiments have shown that the deviation between the actual numerical results and the expected results sometimes increases in long runs. In a series of 100 tosses you may get 45 heads or 55 heads instead of the expected 50, a deviation of 5 heads from the expectation. In a series of 10,000 tosses the difference between the actual result and the expected result may have increased to 50 over the expected 5,000.

But consider this deviation from the percentage standpoint. In a series of 100 tosses the difference of 5 heads over or under the expected 50 is 10%. In a series of 10,000 tosses the difference of 50 heads from the expected 5,000 is only 1%. The percentage of difference does tend to decrease in the long run. It is only in this sense that results tend to "even up."

We must also keep in mind just what constitutes a long run or a long series. In one respect it differs for different people. A long run for an occasional gambler may consist of the total number of bets he makes in a lifetime; to the habitual gambler, it may be the number of bets he makes in a week; and to the operator whose casino is patronized by hundreds of players daily, a long run may consist of the total bets made against the house in a single day or night shift.

This means that the casino operator's results tend to conform more closely to the expected results much sooner than that of any individual gambler, because the operator's long run occurs in a much shorter space of time.

WHAT ARE ODDS?

We cannot predict whether heads or tails will be thrown on the next toss of a coin, but since heads can be expected to come half the time, we can say that its chance of appearing is ½, or that it has a probability of ½. With a symmetrical die of six sides, each side has an equal chance with each of the others and we can expect any one side to be thrown an average of once in 6 times. Its probability is 1/6.

With two dice, each of the six sides of one die can be combined with each of the six sides of the other to form 6 × 6, or 36, combinations. The chance that any combination of two like numbers, such as two sixes, two fives, etc., will appear is 1 in 36, or 1/36.

When an event has a probability of 0 it is an impossible event; when the probability is 1, the event is certain. All other probabilities are expressed by fractions falling between 0 and 1. When the probability is ½, we say the chances are fifty-fifty, or even. A probability of 1/6 is less an an even chance. The fraction is the mathematical way of saying an event has 1 chance of happening in a total of 6 possible chances.

We use the fraction when calculating probability problems, but for betting purposes we express the probability differently. We state it in terms of the advantage that the unfavorable chances have over the favorable chances, or in terms of the *odds* against the event's happening. Any specific side of a die has a probability of 1/6, and the odds against that side being thrown are the 5 chances that some other side will appear against the 1 chance that the specified side will be thrown. The odds then, are 5 to 1 that the specified side will not appear. When the probability is 1/36, the odds are 35 to 1. When the probability is 2/36, the odds are 34 to 2, or 17 to 1.

If I bet $35 to your $1 that a double-ace will not be thrown on the next roll, the betting odds are the same as the true odds. In the long run I can expect to win at the rate of 35 out of every 36 bets, and you can expect to win at the rate of 1 out of every 36 bets. In the long run neither of us win or lose but will come out even. Gamblers call such a bet at true odds an *even-up proposition*. In general, odds may be defined as the advantage one bettor or competitor gives to another in proportion to the assumed risk, so that each has an equal chance.

PERCENTAGE AND HOW IT WORKS AGAINST THE PLAYER

The professional operator of any organized gambling scheme cannot offer bettors even-up propositions. He cannot pay off at the true or correct odds. As he says: "There is no percentage in that." He must in some way gain an advantage or edge over the player; he must have a better chance to win every single bet. A crooked gambler obtains this by cheating. The honest gambling operator obtains it either by levying a direct charge or by extracting a favorable P.C. (percentage) on each wager. He does this last very easily: he simply pays off winners at less than the correct odds.

Most of the 90 million gamblers in America know that every gambling operator has the advantage of a favorable percentage over the player. But as most of them can't calculate it, they never know how powerful it actually is, and because it works so smoothly and quietly, they forget most of the time that it is even there.

Here is a simple example that shows how the P.C. operates and why it shouldn't be forgotten. Suppose you walk up to a carnival wheel with $15 in your pocket. This wheel, let us say, has 15 betting spaces on its layout numbered from 1 to 15, and the operator pays winners at odds of 10 to 1. You place a $1 bet on number 6. Since the probability is 1/15, you can expect in the long run to lose 14 bets for each one that you win.

Let's also suppose that the wheel acts exactly this way in the first 15 spins. You lose the first 14 bets and you are out $14. You have only one buck left. Now you bet that. Number 6 pops up and you win. If the operator paid off at correct odds of 14 to 1, he would return the $1 you bet plus $14 which you won; you would break even with the $15 you had at the start.

But no carnival or any other gambling operator ever does this. In our example, since he pays off at 10 to 1 your win gets you $10. This, with the $1 bet which is returned to you, adds up to $11. You have $4 less than at the start. This $4 out of $15 is the operator's favorable percentage, his charge for operating the game. It is what makes gambling operators rich and most players poor.*

Now let's forget probability theory for a moment and look at it in another way. Suppose you bet your $15 all at once by placing $1 on each of the 15 betting spaces. You must win one of these bets on the next spin because you have all 15 numbers covered. In this situation, spinning the wheel is unnecessary. The operator might just as well scoop up your $15, retain $4 for himself and hand you $11. You say that only a nitwit would gamble in this fashion? I agree. But, in the long run, this is no different, percentagewise, from betting a single number 15 times in succession.

Today, even most of the novice and inexperienced gamblers are aware that this house P.C. exists in all organized forms of gambling, but most of them believe it to be much less than it is. In spite of the fact that the methods for figuring it are usually neither complicated nor difficult, very few gamblers know precisely what it is. You may be surprised to learn that most operators don't know either.

The general rule for figuring the percentage is simply this: the operator's favorable percentage (or the player's disadvantage) is the amount the player is short divided by the total amount he would have collected if paid off at the true odds. In the carnival wheel example above the player is $4 short and he would have collected a total of $15 if paid off at the true odds. Divide 4 by 15 and you get a percentage of 26⅔% in favor of the operator.

If you make 100 such $1 bets, the probability is that you will end up with a loss of $26.66⅔. But don't make the common mistake of supposing that if you start with $100 and place $1 bets on number 6 all

---

* Would you be surprised to learn that in most gambling games you do not pay a percentage to the house for the privilege of using its facilities when you lose? Look at the carnival wheel example above. Notice when the operator collected his percentage: he got it when the player won—because he paid off at less than the correct odds. It is the winners who pay for the privilege of gambling, not the losers.

If you make forty bets at Roulette and lose them all without the 0 or 00 appearing, the casino hasn't really earned anything on this action. It has the money you lost, but that money hasn't yet been earned by the house; it may have to be used to pay off winning bets. The player next to you, however, may make one bet, win and walk off, and the house earns money on this transaction because it keeps a percentage of his winnings.

Usually the winner doesn't even think about the charge he pays when he collects; even if he does, he is so pleased at winning that he doesn't care. The loser may beef about losing, but he can't object that the house is charging him a percentage on his losing bets. The house P.C. can only be subtracted from the payoff made on winning bets.

evening that you will lose *only* this amount. The $26.66⅔ is not your total loss for the evening; it is your *average rate of loss*. Old Man Percentage is in there grinding away on every bet made. You are losing *at the average rate of* $4 on every 15 bets of $1 each.

You can start with $100 and place more than 100 bets because you can also bet the money you win. The more bets you place the more you lose in the long run, and at the end of 375 spins of the wheel your average rate of loss will have reduced your $100 bankroll to zero. The operator will have earned it all.

Let's carry this further. Suppose you start with $100 and find at the end of the evening that you have made a total of 750 bets of $1 each and have finished with the same amount of $100 with which you started. You haven't come out ahead, but you are pleased because the evening's gambling entertainment has cost you nothing—so you think. Actually, that 26⅔% you were bucking cost for you $200 in winnings, because if your winning bets had been paid off at correct odds you would have walked away from the carnival wheel with $300 instead of $100.

Now let us suppose that the wheel operator's favorable edge was only 3⅔%. On $750 worth of action you would have walked away with $272.50 instead of breaking even. If the operator's P.C. was only 1⅔% you would have walked away with $287.50. This should make it obvious that your chances of winning are better when you buck a smaller house percentage than when you buck a bigger one.

I said earlier that the methods for figuring the P.C. are usually not complicated or difficult. Note that word *usually*. It all depends on the game; sometimes it can be really tough. One example: for over thirty years dozens of top mathematicians have tried in vain to calculate the bank's favorable P.C. at the game of Black Jack as it is played in the Nevada casinos. Their writings on the subject indicate clearly why they have failed: they simply don't know enough about the way the game is really played—the problems they work out are never those which are of any practical use to the Black Jack player. They usually suffer from the same handicap when they try to analyze other gambling games.

The author takes pride in stating here that after months of difficult analysis he has succeeded in being the first person to calculate the bank's favorable percentage at Black Jack (see Chapter 12).

GAMBLING OPERATORS ALSO HAVE HEADACHES

The bank's favorable percentage is what enables the gambling operation (legal or illegal) to pay its expenses and still make a handsome profit. If it paid winners off at the correct odds, the operation would be gambling with the players—something it avoids like the plague. If it did this it would sometimes win and sometimes lose, and could expect, in the long run, to come out with about the same bankroll it had at the start. After the *nut* (expenses) was deducted, the final figure on the profit-and-loss sheet would have to be written in red ink, a shade of writing fluid no businessman or gambling operator likes to use.

The operator's percentage take is the price you pay for making use of his gambling facilities. In a private or friendly game of cards or dice, when a more experienced player has a favorable percentage working for him because you accept his sucker bets, it is the price you pay for your ignorance of the game's mathematics.

The percentages vary with different bets and in different games. Players who don't know what percentages they are bucking don't realize that they are often paying much more for the privilege of gambling than they need to. The smart gambler avoids bets and games having a stiff percentage against him.

The average gambler, making all sorts of bets and bucking various unknown percentages, often bucks such stiff ones that even when he has a lucky streak and should win, he ends up a loser. His chance to win is chopped down to less than nothing simply because he doesn't know what he is doing.

Since the house percentage guarantees that the operators can't lose, because they are not really gambling, you might think that the life of a bigtime gambling operator, a sports or horse bookie or a casino operator is a bed of roses. Nothing could be further from the truth. The headaches encountered by the bigtime businessman are minor compared to those that plague the gambling operator. Many of them live on milk diets because the constant tension gives them ulcers.

The greater part of the time most operators act more like players; they are always rooting against the bigtime bettors. And the illegal operator is under even more tension; he knows that the best police and political connections can often go wrong, and he worries about arrests and raids even though he is paying protection money. I know of one bigtime operator who waited a year to get an okay to run a casino in a resort spot for a four-month tourist season. He invested $50,000 to furnish the casino, paid another $50,000 in advance for protection for the season and, on opening night, was raided by state troopers. He was arrested and the casino bankroll and equipment confiscated. He lost everything: the $50,000 original investment, the $50,000 protection money, the year's time he had spent in preparation plus another six months which he spent in jail.

Clergymen are also bad medicine and often raise such a fuss at a moment's notice that a cleanup of gambling follows. Elections are headaches because gambling is often a major issue. Many politicians have risen to great heights by backing gambling investigations and sending bigtime gamblers to jail. One was eventually a candidate for President of the United States and another ran for Vice President.

Other headaches are the uncertainty of steady, continuous business, fights with rival operators, crooked employees who steal from the house and crooked players who try to beat the house (even the Monte Carlo casino was cheated a few years ago by dice sharps).

The tensions and uncertainties of the gambling business are so great that most operators always wear a glum look; few ever smile, at least when they are working. As a rule, the dough they drag down isn't enough to compensate for the worry and the ulcers, especially when most operators gamble a great part of it away at some other game.

HOT AND COLD PLAYERS

Probability theory states what can be expected to happen in the long run. A gambling operator makes so many more bets than any individual player in a single gambling session that he experiences a much longer run, and his wins and losses thus conform much more closely to what probability says he can expect. For the individual player, even an extended series of sessions is still a short run. His winning and losing, therefore, may vary considerably from his long-run expectation; he experiences winning and losing streaks.

A player on a winning streak is said to be *hot;* on a losing streak he is *cold*. I have often seen a player get so hot that no matter what game he plays, or how he places his bets, he continues to win. Such winning streaks sometimes continue for weeks at a time. Since the odds are against the player, however, he experiences more losing than winning streaks, and they last longer.

At Craps, I have seen a player bet the dice to win for an hour or so and win nearly every bet, then turn around, bet the dice to lose and continue to win nearly every bet. I have seen a player run a measly $20 into $56,000 at Roulette over a two-week period. I have seen a Craps player, bucking the house odds for about five hours of play each night, run a $10 bill into $125,000 in a month's time.

Gambling-game operators insure themselves against risk inherent in these hot streaks by putting a minimum and a maximum limit on the size of the wagers they accept. This prevents a hot player from winning too much in too short a space of time. It means that the player who tries to make a big killing when he is hot must play longer and make many more bets. The more bets he makes the less chance he has of walking away with the operator's bankroll because there is more chance that his winning and losing streaks will balance out.

The maximum limit also prevents the progressive-system player

from doubling up his bets each time he loses and continuing indefinitely until he finally wins one bet that recoups all his losses plus a
profit. As for the player who doubles when he wins, trying for that one
big killing, if there were no limit to stop him, and if his capital was
large enough, he could eventually bet such huge sums that he might
eventually break the bank. The minimum and maximum betting limits
are usually so designed that a player who bets the minimum limit at
the start can double the size of his previous bet no more than seven
times before he is stopped cold by the maximum limit.

The maximum limit also makes it impossible for a bigtime gambler
to walk into a casino, ask the size of the house bankroll and then bet
the full amount. The casino would go broke at once if he won, and if
he lost and decided to bet the full amount of the house bankroll again,
he would have another shot at closing the casino. Casinos and bookies
would all have gone out of business long ago if there were no betting
limits.

Gambling operators do not operate on the hope that they will win
money from the players; their business depends on the fact that their
favorable percentage earns them money on every bet made. The
greater the volume of bets the more income they receive. This is why
all gambling-game operators prefer long sessions. It is also why the $2
horse bettor is the "ace in the hole" with most horse bookies—there are
so many of them. For the same reason, the consistent $1 or $2 bettor in
Nevada casinos is commonly referred to by house men as an "unpaid
shill."

The maximum betting limit and the operator's percentage edge are
the two most important reasons why gambling schemes earn fortunes.

LUCK AND HOW IT WORKS

Paradoxically, however, the gamblers who are the godfathers of a
whole branch of mathematical science today know little about it. They
got lost by the wayside when the professors began answering their
questions in an argot even stranger than the gambler's own—the language of mathematical symbols. As a consequence, although modern
man has tossed the superstition that dice can divine the future into the
discard, many gamblers still believe that the fall of the dice or the
turn of a card is controlled by some supernatural force.

Many Numbers players bet on numbers seen in dreams; many lottery
purchasers shy clear of tickets which bear certain "bad luck" numbers;
many Poker players insist on a certain spot at the table. Most Craps
players, when losing, insist that the dice, and sometimes even the
dealer, be changed; some gamblers walk around the Bridge table to

change their luck, others carry good-luck charms; some avoid betting on Friday. One racetrack gambler I know shaves in the track's washroom before the first race because when he doesn't he loses—or so he thinks. Many gamblers bet only when they feel lucky, and abstain when they feel unlucky.

I'm superstitious about gambling, too. I won't gamble against adverse odds!

Many gamblers don't realize that the correct answers can all be obtained with figures—and that the mystic symbols having to do with black cats and four-leaf clovers can be thrown out the window. As a class, gamblers are superstitious for the usual reason—ignorance. They don't understand how chance operates or know what luck really is.

The dictionary defines luck as a person's apparent tendency to be fortunate or unfortunate. Most people who use the word, however, forget that this tendency is not real but only apparent. Anyone who believes that one player has a better chance of winning a bet because he is luckier than another is no smarter than the customers of the sorcerers and witches of the Middle Ages, the African voodoo doctor or the gypsy fortuneteller who reads tea leaves.

If you gambled and won yesterday, you may correctly say that you were lucky, because you are merely stating that you placed your bets in such a way that they agreed with the fall of the dice or the turn of the wheel. But the fact that you were lucky yesterday or that you have been consistently lucky in your affairs does not guarantee you a better break than the next guy tomorrow. The odds on dice, cards, Numbers, Roulette or any other gambling game are not different for different people at different times. If your past luck has any effect on your future luck, then some supernatural force is working for you because you carry a rabbit's foot.

The supernatural will continue to get a foot in at the door just as long as we try to investigate chance as it applies to a single person. But if we consider chance as it applies to a large group of players and a long series of wagers, then we begin to make sense, and superstition gets a quick brush-off.

One of the first things we discover is that the marvelous run of luck you had yesterday or last week isn't always as astonishing as it seems. At Bank Craps, the gambler who puts his money on two aces and takes 30 to 1 that they will appear on the next roll feels that he is a very lucky guy indeed when the two aces are thrown four times in a row, and he bets on each roll, especially if he happens to know that the odds against such a thing happening are 1,679,615 to 1. He is amazed that some mysterious fate has singled him out for such a favor. But the guy who was betting the limit on the front or pass line and lost four big bets when those two aces appeared four times in succession would consider himself as being the champion hard-luck guy in the world.

Both players forget that the statement that the odds are 1,679,615 to 1 against such an event also means that the event can be expected to occur on the average once in every 1,679,616 times. They forget that on the night when that succession of double-aces appeared there were thousands of other Craps games in progress and several millions of dice throws were made. It would have been more amazing if someone somewhere had *not* thrown a double-aces four times in a row. If you had stayed at home with a good book or a blonde, the run of double-aces would probably have happened just the same in some game somewhere, and someone else would have exclaimed over his remarkable luck or, if he was betting the front line, his bad luck.

Prolonged winning or losing series in various forms of gambling are not unusual for individual players. And every few years a gambling record of one sort or another is established in some casino at some gambling activity by someone, somewhere. Here are several examples to prove the point.

The longest successive single number of wins at Roulette witnessed by this author occurred on July 9, 1959, at the El San Juan Hotel in Puerto Rico. I watched the little ivory Roulette ball drop into the number 10 pocket six times in succession. The chance of this happening is 1 in 133,448,704.

The longest color win recorded at the game of Roulette in an American casino occurred at the Arrowhead casino in Saratoga, New York, in August 1943, when the color red won 32 consecutive times. The odds against this happening are 22,254,817,519 to 1. You may call it a miracle, but remember that the odds are exactly the same—22,254,-817,519 to 1—against a series of 32 alternate wins of blacks, odd, even or any other arbitrary series of 32 wins that pay off even money. If you consider the 32 red wins to be a miracle, then any series of 32 even-money wins is also a miracle. It is only the spectacular effect of a long series of wins of one color that attracts attention and makes it seem remarkable.

On the evening of January 18, 1952, at the Caribe Hilton casino in San Juan, Puerto Rico, I was thunderstruck to see a woman set a world's record at the Craps table by making 39 consecutive passes. When I came out of my fog, I calculated the lady's chance of making those 39 passes to be 1 in 956,211,843,725. This record still holds today.

When we remember that millions and millions of players rolled the ivories billions and billions of times in hundreds and hundreds of gambling joints in America during the past fifty years, we realize that 39 passes is not as miraculous as it sounds. And I was thunderstruck, not because this world's record was established, but because I was on hand to witness it. The odds against that are many times greater.

More astonishing than any of these is the feat of the Englishman who, some years ago, won first prize in the British weekly football pool and, ten weeks later, again struck gold when he once more copped first prize. Since 20 million Britons play the pool each week, and our English friend made ten plays in order to hit the second jackpot, it can be calculated that he had 1 chance in about 40,000,000,000,000.

Anything may happen to a single individual when gambling, odds or no odds, but don't expect to walk up to a Craps table tomorrow and throw 39 straight passes. The odds are still 956,211,843,724 to 1 that you won't.

GAMBLER'S FALLACY

Many inveterate gamblers who are constantly fighting the adverse odds at banking games go broke faster than the house percentage would ordinarily dictate because of a basic misunderstanding about the theory of probability. Their first mistake consists in calling it the "law of averages," and then forgetting that the important word in that phrase is not "law" but "averages." The theory of probability is a mathematical prediction of what may be expected to happen on the average or in the long run, not a law that says that certain things must inevitably happen.

If the color red appears on several successive spins of a Roulette wheel these gamblers bet that black will appear next. They think that black is more likely to turn up than red because they think the "law" says that black and red *must* eventually come up an equal number of times. In a Bridge, Poker or Gin Rummy game these players, when losing steadily, insist on sticking it out because they believe the "law" states that the longer they lose the more certain they can be that their luck will change. And if they hit a winning streak, they are afraid to ride with it because they believe the chances of a losing streak's setting in are constantly increasing.

This belief, known as the doctrine of the Maturity of Chances, has lost fortunes for many gamblers. In spite of the fact that mathematicians have for years called it the "gambler's fallacy," there are still many otherwise well-educated gamblers who argue heatedly in its favor.

They don't, or won't, understand the basic principle that *every chance event is absolutely independent of all preceding or following events*. If you toss a coin and get ten successive heads, it does *not* follow that tails are more likely to come up on the next toss in order to help even things out. The coin doesn't know what happened earlier and couldn't do anything about it in any case. The chance is still 50–50 and is always 50–50 on any single throw, no matter what happened on previous throws.

THE "GUESSER'S DISADVANTAGE"

There is another curious belief held by many educated and uneducated people, including a lot of gambling operators and bookmakers who have spent the greater part of their lives in bookie rooms, at gaming tables and at racetracks and who, of all people, should know better. They say: "The player who does the guessing as to his betting selection has the worst of it. Even when you toss a coin and the chances are fifty-fifty, the guy who cries heads (or tails) is more likely to be wrong and will lose more bets than the guy who keeps his mouth shut and just covers the bet."

This "guesser's disadvantage" theory originated back in the days when the players had no clear notion of why it was that operators of games always showed a profit. They noticed that the operators never expressed any opinion as to the result of the next throw of the dice or turn of the wheel but merely covered the players' bets and let the latter do all the guessing. They jumped to the conclusion that this explained the operator's advantage.

The theory was repeated so often and gained such wide acceptance among gamblers that even today players who know the odds and have some knowledge of the operation of percentage still insist "there is something in it."

If anyone ever tries to give you such an argument, here's the way to stop him. Just say, "Okay, suppose we bet on the toss of a coin and suppose I do all the guessing. And suppose I always guess heads. Are you trying to tell me that the coin is going to land tails oftener than the laws of probability say it can be expected to just because I have a stubborn habit of guessing heads?

"And how does the coin know what I'm guessing? Does it have ears? And suppose it's a Chinese coin, and I make my guesses in English; would the coin be hep to what I am saying or would it have to send out a hurry call for a translator? And even if it did know, how does it manage to make that extra half turn part of the time so it lands tails more often and crosses me up? Maybe it's part jumping bean and part acrobat? Or maybe it's haunted?"

If the guy still wants to argue that his "guessers have the worst of it" theory is right, you should phone the nearest newspaper and tell them you have discovered a freak who believes that a fifty-cent piece is so smart it should have the right to vote!

GAMBLING SYSTEMS

In the gambling casinos where I am a consultant, players often come up to me and say, "Hey, Scarne, give me a system so I can beat this game." They all get the same answer: "If I knew any system that would overcome the house percentage, I would keep it strictly to myself. If you had a surefire winning system you would do the same." There is nothing more futile than the attempt to cook up betting systems that will overcome adverse odds.

The oldest and commonest betting system is the Martingale or "doubling up" system, in which bets are doubled progressively. This probably dates back to the invention of dice, but every day of the week some gambler somewhere re-invents it, or some variation of it, and believes he has something new. Over the years hundreds of "surefire" winning systems have been dreamed up, and not one of them is worth the price of yesterday's newspaper.

The reason is simple. When you make a bet at less than the correct odds, which you always do in any organized gambling operation, you are paying the operator a percentage charge for the privilege of making the bet. Your chance of winning has what mathematicians call a "minus expectation." When you use a system you make a series of bets, each of which has a minus expectation. There is no way of adding minuses to get a plus, or adding losses to show a profit.

Add to this the fact that all gambling operators, including race and sports bookies, limit the size of the player's wagers so that it is impossible to double up bets indefinitely. This and the house percentage make all gambling systems worthless.

The sole exception is in games of both chance and skill when the player has some special skill or knowledge that enables him to make most of his bets with a plus expectation. As an example, suppose a certain ball club is a 2 to 1 favorite to win today's game because the team's star pitcher is scheduled to be in the lineup. If you obtain inside information that he has suffered an injury which will keep him out of the game, and if you then get 2 to 1 odds on the underdog, you would have a plus expectation.

The system player believes his system will overcome the operator's favorable edge. He couldn't be more wrong. Systems actually work against the player and for the house because they are all based on a combination or series of bets, and the more bets the system player makes, the more he increases the operator's percentage take.

Gambling operators also love system players because they have to bet a specified amount of money, usually more than the average player bets, in order to back up the system. The system demands that the player bet it all, and the gambling operator knows he is going to get it all.

If a casino player with $100 wants merely to double it, the soundest plan is to risk it all in one bet on the "don't pass" line on the Craps table. When he splits his $100 into smaller bets, as he would have to do playing most systems, he merely reduces his chance of doubling his money; the smaller the bets the less chance he has.

SKILL VS. CHANCE

In card games combining chance and skill, the more skillful player enjoys an advantage over the player with less skill which is sometimes even stronger than the operator's favorable percentage in banking games such as Craps or Roulette.

Two equally skilled players playing Poker, Gin Rummy, Pinochle, etc., every night for a year will proably win and lose an approximately equal number of hands or games. Over a long period, a more skilled player will outdistance his less skilled opponent in games or money won. The more pronounced his advantage in skill is, the sooner the difference will show up.

In the long run, the element of chance cancels out and the element of skill, like the casino's favorable percentage, is what really determines the final outcome. The more skillful player is eventually bound to win. If you lose consistently at card games in which skill is a factor, don't blame it on that fickle, blind, perverse and cold-bloodedly impartial old baggage Lady Luck. Blame the superior card-playing skill or knowledge of your opponents.

HOW TO BETTER YOUR CHANCES OF WINNING

What are your chances of winning at your favorite gambling game? This depends on what kind of a gambler you are. The sucker or chump gambler has little chance of winning. The experienced gambler of the sort who the operator wishes would take his business elsewhere has a much better chance.

The mathematicians and most writers on gambling say: "If the percentages are against you and you make hundreds of bets over a long, long time, you must eventually lose." This is good advice, except that it doesn't apply to most of the new breed of American gamblers today because they don't gamble that much or that long; they are occasional gamblers, many of whom gamble only a few times a year. They don't all lose; some of them win.

If all players always lost, organized gambling would have folded up long ago. All operators know that they have to send out winners to get business. The more winners there are, the more business is stimulated, and the greater the operator's profits.

The fact that some gambling operations are *rigged* (crooked) in itself proves that players can and do win in an honest game, even against the adverse odds. If no player ever won, no operator would ever need to resort to cheating. Although there are tens of thousands of crooked gambling operations, they are smalltime operations compared to the honest bigtime gambling games and schemes in operation today. The reason is obvious—crooked operations are sooner or later exposed and go out of business, while the honest game stays in business and prospers year after year. The various methods of cheating peculiar to each kind of gambling operation will be explained for your protection later in these pages.

One proof that some people do win is seen in the announcements of the $50,000 and $1 million winnners in state lotteries in New York, New Jersey and various other states. But the Irish Hospitals' Sweepstakes still holds, I believe, the all-time lottery money winning record set when a London candy-store proprietor, Emilio Scala, took home $1,-773,660 in 1931. Your author personally knows a man who won $500,000 at the Craps table in a three-month period of play, and a woman who won $200,000 in six weeks of play at Baccarat. You yourself can probably name one or more people you know who have won considerable amounts. The advice "Don't gamble; you can't win" is not true for everyone all the time. There are thousands of players who have won, and thousands more who will win, thousands of dollars gambling.

It is true, of course, that most players lose. It is also true that they lose much more often than they should because they know little or nothing about gambling. Of the 90 million American gamblers today, about seven out of eight are inexperienced men and women who are making fools of themselves by indulging in a gambling venture they know little or nothing about.

If, after reading this book, you continue to play the part of a chump and let adverse odds or sucker bets reduce your winning chances to less than nothing, or if you let some cheat clip you, don't say you had no way of knowing any better.

The best way to improve your chance of winning is to have a good working knowledge of the correct odds and percentages in the games you play. You will find this information, on all the bets in all the most popular forms of private and organized gambling in America, in this book.

3.
Horse Racing:
The King of Sports

THE HISTORICAL BACKGROUND OF RACING

Horse racing is more than 6,000 years old, and harness racing is some 3,000 years older than flat racing. The horse was only 13 hands high (4'4") when first domesticated by man in prehistoric times, and for thousands of years was used only as a draft animal. A carved shell cylinder which dates from 4000 B.C. or earlier shows Assyro-Babylonian warriors using horse-drawn chariots in battle; it is a safe bet that these soldiers also staged chariot races. Inscriptions on tablets found in Asia Minor that date from 1500 B.C. or before prove that chariot racing was then already very old because the racing stables of the Assyrian Kings which are described were elaborate ones.

Sometime during the first millennium B.C., selective breeding brought the horse up to a size that was useful for equestrian purposes; the first formal mounted race of record was one that took place in the 33rd Olympiad in Greece, about 624 B.C.

In England, where modern "organized" racing began, the earliest formal description we have is of the races that took place at the weekly Smithfield horse fairs during the reign of Henry II, about 1174 A.D. King John (1199–1216) had "running horses" in his royal stables. James I helped establish racing at Epsom and Newmarket early in the seventeenth century, and his grandson Charles II (1660–85) was such a great patron of the sport that he came to be known as "the father of the British turf."

While the records are few and frequently contradictory, it is generally accepted that America's first racetrack with regularly scheduled meetings and stake races was founded in 1665 by New York's first Eng-

Racing scene on Hempstead Plain, Long Island, where New York's first English governor, Richard Nicolls, established the first American race course in 1665 near the present Belmont Park. (Bettmann Archive)

lish governor, Colonel Richard Nicolls. The lack of good horses in New York prompted Governor Nicolls to sponsor racing as a proving ground. The site of the first racetrack was the Newmarket course on Hempstead Plain, Long Island, not far from the present location of Belmont Park. Another early track was "Race Street" in Philadelphia, which is evidence that some of the earliest "racecourses" were down the main streets of the early settlements.

All thoroughbred horses racing in the United States today can trace their ancestry to one of three sires, the Byerly Turk, the Godolphin Bard and the Darley Arabian. These were the only three thoroughbreds listed in the studbook of 1793 that perpetuated themselves.

Standardbred or harness horses likewise trace their ancestry back to these three sires. The standardbred horse is a pedigreed animal originally so called because he had to race up to a certain set standard of speed. This standard has steadily decreased time-wise as faster horses were produced through improved breeding methods.

The obvious difference between standardbred and thoroughbred horses is in their appearance. Standardbreds possess longer bodies, have heavier legs and are of less height. Therefore, they are not as attractive as thoroughbreds. Thoroughbreds can go faster in a race, but do not possess the stamina of the harness or standardbred horse. Standardbred horses can warm up for five or six miles on the morning of a race, while thoroughbred horses are rested and relaxed to a point of drowsiness. Harness horses can run many races in one day if necessary, thoroughbreds are through after one race. Another difference between the thoroughbred and the standardbred is that thoroughbreds run or gallop and are ridden by a jockey in a saddle. Harness horses are guided by a driver seated on a sulky and during the race must maintain a specified gait. Hence, the start of the race and its continued strategy are naturally different. Due to these differences, harness racing appeals to a particular breed of racegoer. Harness racing due to its night-and-day operation may soon equal or surpass thoroughbred racing attendance.

The thoroughbred horse travels the mile faster than the standardbred. Harness horses race at speeds averaging 25 to 30 miles per hour for the mile distance; in the homestretch, speeds of up to 35 miles an hour are attained by the best horses. A good thoroughbred races the mile at 38 to 40 miles per hour. As for the difference between pacers and trotters, little more than a second separates the world pacing and trotting records (the pacing record is faster). A pacer is usually considered slightly faster within a specific race classification, and can get away faster at the start.

Horse racing owes much to the patronage of royalty and has long been called the "Sport of Kings." But kings these days are in short supply, and this term seems antiquated. There is even considerable doubt that horse racing can still be called a sport; it has degenerated into a purely commercial operation. Track owners, horse owners and state officials are far more interested in the dollar than in developing the breed.

Because horse racing now attracts the greatest crowds in sports history and because betting on the horses is the most popular form of gambling in the United States today, it might be called the "King of Gambling." I hesitate to try to change the speech habits of horse players that much, so let's call it the "King of Sports."

My recent survey shows 40 million bettors, of whom 10 million were women, wagered yearly the enormous sum of over $48 billion on the outcome of one or more races in the United States. This includes legal and illegal race betting. Although in 1972 horse racing (thoroughbreds and harness) retained its position as the country's number one spectator sport for the 21st successive year with a total attendance of 74,015,395, it suffered its first box office setback since 1967. A variety of problems—strikes, date conflicts, extended seasons and New York State's off-track betting—contributed to the decline of 2,938,893, down 3.8%

from the 1971 record of 76,954,288. The "trots" were hurt the most at the box office, experiencing a decline of 1,778,278 from the 1971 total of 30,203,645. The "flats" slipped 2.5% in attendance, attracting a total of 45,590,028 spectators, a decline of 1,160,615. Although 1972 national race attendance dropped 2,938,893, the combined pari-mutuel wagering at the flats and trots reached an all-time high of $6,293,999,976, divided as follows: thoroughbred wagering, $4,211,575,277; harness wagering, $2,082,424,699. Purse distribution reached an all-time high of $305,096,049.

Included in the total of paid admissions to tracks there are, of course, many repeaters—thousands of people who attended every day of a meet, and tens of thousands who went to the track several times during the year. My racetrack survey indicates that during 1972 at least 20 million different Americans, of whom 8 million were women, visited a track at least once and made a legal bet of at least $2 at the pari-mutuel windows.

In order to get an approximate figure for the money wagered off-track with the hundreds of thousands of illegal bookies in this country, I interviewed 3,000 horse players at and away from the tracks in different parts of the country—every kind of player from the $2 bettor to the bigtime bettor who bets $100 to $20,000 on a race with a horse office (a bookmaking syndicate made up of three or four or more bookies who are grouped together so that they can handle the bigtime bettors' horse action).

I asked these questions: How many times during the year did you visit a racetrack? How much did you bet per visit? Did you place off-track bets with illegal bookies? If so, how often and in what amounts? The answers I collected indicate that at least $7 is wagered illegally away from the track for every $1 wagered legally at the track. Multiplying the more than $6 billion average pari-mutuel figure by 7 gives us a total of approximately $42 billion of illegal betting, and a grand total for all wagers of $48 billion.

I suspect that last figure is not only conservative but quite low, because I believe the ratio of illegal to legal betting must be considerably higher than 7. But let's use the $42 billion illegal off-track figure, to be on the safe side.

The reader must remember that the term "handle" always means the total amount of money in circulation in a betting operation. If you bet $2 and win $5, your wager, plus the money paid to you by the bookie, a total of $7, is the handle for that one bet. The $42 billion illegal off-track handle is the total sum that moves back and forth from player to bookie and bookie to player.

Bookies, on a national average, have about a 10% edge on their customers, which means that an average of 10¢ of each dollar bet with them is lost by the players. I calculate that the bookies' gross revenue for 1972 was $4.2 billion. And here is how that is split up:

40%	$1,680,000,000	bookies' net profit
30%	$1,260,000,000	paid to runners and agents (this is 30% and not 50% because, although bookies pay runners and agents half of their monthly winning action, bookies also handle considerable player action which does not come through runners or agents)
15%	$630,000,000	paid as ice (protection money) to politicians, law-enforcement officers and racket bosses
15%	$630,000,000	for operating expenses: rent, salaries for office help, handouts to broke players, phone bills and incidentals
Total	$4,200,000,000	

My survey reveals that while approximately 40 million Americans— 30 million men and 10 million women—made at least one $2 bet, either legal or illegal, on a horse race during the year, of the over 74 million paid admissions at the tracks about 60% were men and 40% were women, with the men doing more betting: the ratio of men to women bettors was 3 to 1. Of the $42 billion off-track handle, $6.6 billion, or about 15%, was wagered by women.

The average bettor (both on and off track, male and female) is more often than not a church member who is married and who bets an average of $4 each day he bets. But I know of at least fifty big horse bettors who have each bet a million dollars or more on the horses in one year.

The age of 90% of the horse bettors is from 25 to 65. Among the men, 50% are businessmen, professional men, judges, politicians; 45% are factory, office and other salaried employees; 5% are bookies, gambling operators, gamblers, touts, hustlers and other easy-money characters. Among the women, 88% are housewives and salaried employees, 10% are businesswomen, professional women or retired, 2% are gamblers, operators, bookies, hustlers, and other easy-money gals.

BOOKMAKING AS AN INDUSTRY

Many changes have taken place in the illegal bookmaking industry since the first publication of this book. For example, in 1949 the most popular place for the inveterate horse player to bet his money was the *horse room* or *wire room*. Here he could listen to the loudspeaker announce the fluctuations of the odds, last-minute jockey changes, late withdrawals of entrants, a running description of the race as it happened and, finally, the names of the *in-the-money* horses and the official track payoff price on each horse.

At that time the biggest wire-service supplier for bookies was the Continental Press Service, which had leased 23,000 miles of telegraph circuits from Western Union and had 20,000 bookie customers. Other wire-service suppliers had another 10,000 bookie subscribers. Since each subscriber, depending upon his location, had to pay the wire service from $150 to $500 per week, a great many bookies joined forces and subscribed as a group. Such a combine was called a *horse office*. Sometimes as many as 40 bookies shared the same information, but the national average was probably about three bookies for each subscription. This gives us a total of 90,000 bookies. Since there were at least twice that many bookies operating without benefit of a wire service, we have a total figure of 270,000 bookies.

If we now add the army of full-time and part-time employees working for these bookies—the grafting cops and politicians, runners, clerks, accountants, collectors and muscle men, and the vast number of agents who solicited bets, such as the operators of cigar and newspaper stands, restaurants and shoeshine parlors, and the soliciting agents in factories, office buildings, etc.—we find that the total number of people engaged in the illegal horse-booking industry in 1949 was well over 700,000.

In that year the bookmakers' national handle was close to the $18 billion mark. (Note: The track pari-mutuel turnover that year was $1,598,533,974.)

The steady growth of the bookmaking industry had a major setback in the years 1951 through 1953. This was due to the Kefauver and countless other Federal and state crime investigations and to the enactment of two Federal laws which were designed to drive the bookmaker out of business. One required bookies to buy a $50 gambling stamp and pay a Federal 10% excise tax on gross receipts. The other, aimed at eliminating the racing-wire services, outlawed the interstate transmission of gambling information before or during the races by telegraph, telephone, radio, television or other interstate communication.

In those years hundreds of bookies were either jailed for Federal income-tax violation or for breaking some state anti-gambling statute. Police pressure put many others out of business. Others quit booking horses because of the wire-service ban and turned their attention to sports booking and other gambling activities. Some moved to the race track clubhouse and accepted illegal bets at the track.

Early in 1954 the pendulum began swinging back again. Millions of horse players needed someone to book their action, and a younger, hungrier generation of new bookies replaced the old-timers who were in jail or out of business. Former runners, agents, subagents and horse players became bookies almost overnight, and by 1956 there were more bookies at work than ever before. There were not as many big-time bookies as before but by now these newcomers have had time to fatten their bankrolls and are booking the high-rolling action.

My survey at the time revealed that approximately 300,000 bookies with 1,300,000 employees were required to handle the sum of $50 billion wagered in 1960 by 30 million horse bettors. Shortly thereafter, the number of illegal bookies in America took a sharp drop because of the enactment of additional Federal interstate anti-gambling laws and their strict enforcement by agents of the Federal Bureau of Investigation.

My latest survey reveals that approximately 200,000 illegal race bookies with 800,000 employees are required to handle the sum of $42 billion wagered yearly by 40 million horse bettors.

Even the most casual reader of the sports pages must admit that thoroughbred and harness racing have undergone the greatest expansion in their history during the past two decades. A look at the figures proves it. The annual racetrack attendance in 1960 was 47 million. In 1972 it was 74 million. Several factors have caused this expansion, among them the growth of population and personal income, and the building of many new racetracks. Another very important factor is the millions of women who in years since 1960 have joined the men at the racetrack to become horse bettors.

Racing and pari-mutuel betting are now legal in 30 states, which possess more than 150 tracks. Of these, about 100 are major thoroughbred and harness tracks. This is big business: hundreds of millions of dollars are invested in tracks, breeding farms and horses. If the rate at which racetrack officials are currently engaged in enlarging their tracks and building new and bigger ones continues, the present attendance figure may be doubled in another two decades.

The annual salaries now paid to employees of this vast industry— the track officials and employees, state employees, racing writers, jockeys, trainers, breeders, grooms, stable boys, veterinarians, handicappers, etc.—total tens of millions of dollars, but this is small when compared to the billions of dollars wagered by the millions of bettors on thoroughbred and harness races.

Baseball was once America's number one national spectator sport, but today despite baseball's team expansion to 24 major league teams and 20 minor league teams, its total annual attendance including World Series and play-offs totaled 38,891,479 for 1972. While the annual attendance at other sports has jumped, baseball has suffered a severe decline and is third to racing and football. Horse racing, as it

A *typical race day at the Big A, the $50 million Aqueduct Race Track,
America's largest thoroughbred track. (Wide World)*

has been for years, is still the king of spectator sports in which gambling is a key factor.

The increasing public interest in horse racing over baseball and
other sports has little to do with the horses. The great majority of race
fans know nothing about horses and care less. Watching the gee-gees
circle the track soon becomes monotonous; the excitement in the stands
is due to the financial stake the spectators have in the race. This is also
why the 35 dog tracks in the nine states that permit greyhound racing
are today almost always jammed to capacity. Elephant races would
draw the same crowds if they offered the same opportunity for getting
a bet down.

WIN, PLACE, SHOW AND EXOTIC BETS

There are three *money pools* in each race (except in rare instances
such as stake races): the win pool, the place pool and the show pool.
The payoff prices that the horses pay to win, place and show depend
entirely on the total amount of money wagered in each pool and the
amount wagered on the horses that finish first, second and third.

The present pari-mutuel betting system provides for wagers being
made on any horse in a race in one or all of the following ways:

1. **To win:** The bettor collects if the horse he bet to win finishes first.

2. **To place:** The bettor collects if the horse he bet to place finishes either first or second.

3. **To show:** The bettor collects if the horse he bet to show finishes either first, second or third.

A wager of the above three—win, place and show—is called a *combination ticket* or *across the board.* Many major tracks call a bet on win and place a combination ticket since the win, place and show combination or across the board ticket has been abolished.

4. **Daily double:** The bettor collects if the horses he bet in the first and second races (or the fifth and sixth races) both finish first.

5. **Twin double:** The bettor collects if the horses he bet in the first and second races and the fifth and sixth races all finish first. The trick is to bet the horses you believe will win the first and second races. If they both win, you go to the betting window and exchange your winning ticket for your choices to win the fifth and sixth races.

6. **Quiniela:** The bettor collects if the two horses he bet in one race finish first and second, without regard to the order in which they do so.

7. **Exacta** (also known as a **perfecta**): The bettor collects if the two horses he bet in one race finish first and second in the order selected.

8. **Triple** (also known as a **trifecta**): The bettor collects if the three horses he bet in one race finish first, second and third in the order selected.

9. **Superfecta:** The bettor collects if the four horses he bet in one race finish first, second, third and fourth in the order selected.

10. **The 5–6 sweepstake pool:** The bettor collects if the six horses he selected, one in each race, all finish first. There are consolation prizes for picking 4 or 5 out of 6 winners, etc. This 25¢ bet, which can be placed in Puerto Rico at the track or at an off-track betting shop, was first introduced on the island back in 1913 and is still growing in popularity.

The above described *exotic bets,* as they are sometimes called, are not offered at all tracks: some tracks just feature the daily double, quiniela and exacta, while others go with a daily double, quiniela, exactas and a triple. I don't know of any track, at present, that offers the twin double or superfecta.

Racetrack betting procedure is simple enough, but many track bettors know almost as little about the betting system as they do about horses. At Belmont Park one day, after the fifth race, I saw a woman tear up her tote ticket as she said to a friend, "Grace, I'm the unluckiest person in the world. When I bet a horse to place it wins. If I bet it to show it places or wins."

I picked up the torn halves of the ticket, looked at them and returned them to the woman. "This is a winning ticket," I said.

"It couldn't be," she said. "I played the horse to place and it came in first." When I explained that a ticket to place collects when the horse comes in first or second, and a show ticket collects when the horse comes in either first, second or third, she groaned. "I've been tearing up winning tickets ever since I started coming to racetracks."

This woman isn't unusual; there are thousands of bettors in the same boat. Many bettors throw away tickets as soon as they see that their horse did not finish in the money. They don't realize that the horse that ran fourth, or even fifth, may pay off if it is later announced that one or more of the first three horses was disqualified. The state of New York has had as many as $400,000 in uncashed valid tote tickets in one year. At least an equal amount must be picked up by *stoopers* or *ticket pickers* who make a practice of hunting for discarded winning tickets which they cash at the windows.

Track bettors who can't recognize a winning ticket when it stares them in the face pay at least a million dollars a year for their ignorance. They are, in effect, making a gift to the state treasury, which is hardly the horse bettors' favorite charity.

There was more than $52,535 in uncashed tickets on the Super Horse, Secretariat, in his three races, the Kentucky Derby, Preakness and Belmont, that crowned him the first triple winner in a quarter of a century. Secretariat paid $5 to win in the Derby, $2.60 in the Preakness and $2.20 in the Belmont. Naturally some uncashed tickets at

Bettors purchasing tickets at the $2 tote windows. (Wide World)

Tote tickets for Win, Place, Show, Daily Double, Exacta, Triple, and Quiniela.

Belmont were kept as souvenirs on the first triple crown winner in 25 years—but most of the 10,231 uncashed winning tickets were either thrown away or torn up as losing tickets.

TYPES OF RACES

Maiden race: Horses entered in a maiden race are those that have never previously won a race. In racing lingo, a horse who wins for the first time has broken its maiden and cannot again compete in a maiden race at any track.

Claiming race: Each horse is entered at a certain claiming price and any horseman may *claim* (buy) the horse after the race, provided he has deposited an amount equal to the claiming price with the racing secretary's office in advance. If two or more horsemen put a claim on the same horse, they draw lots to decide the claim.

Optional claiming race: Some states permit claiming races in which the owner of a horse has the opportunity of protecting himself against losing it. He simply does not file a claim form for his horse with the racing secretary's office; this prevents any claim from being made.

Maiden claiming race: As the name implies, it is a claiming race for maidens.

Maiden special weight race: This is a race for maidens who the owners or trainers feel are too good to be entered in claiming races. All horses in the race run at the same weight.

Handicap race: In this type of race any owner paying the required entrance fee may run his horse. But to ensure a real contest, the track handicapper (usually the track secretary) assigns a certain weight to each horse in an attempt to adjust matters so that each horse, in the handicapper's opinion, has an equal chance to win. He assigns the heaviest weight to the horse he thinks has the best chance, the lightest weight to the horse with the poorest chance, and other weights to the in-between horses in such a way that, if his judgment were infallible, all the horses would finish in a dead heat. If the weight of a jockey and his gear total 108 pounds and the weight assigned to his horse for this race is 113 pounds, five pounds of lead are inserted into the *bag* (saddle cloth) to make the prescribed weight.

Allowance race: This is similar to a handicap race except that the amounts of weight to be carried by the horses are not assigned by the track handicapper but are determined by the rules set down by track officials in the condition book.

Stake race: These races are for the better horses, and the purses and entrance fees are much higher than in other races. The race almost always is for two- and three-year-olds only. The weights carried by the horses are adjusted so that all horses carry the same total weight. The theory here is that since the owner has paid a high entrance fee he is entitled to test his horse against the others without any weight handicap. Small racetracks sometimes run stake races in the same manner as handicap races when they lack the better horses.

Match race: This is usually a race between two of the country's outstanding thoroughbreds and the conditions of the race are arranged by the owners and trainers. Usually "winner takes all," meaning that the entire purse (sometimes more than $100,000) goes to the winning horse.

Since the totalisator at all recognized tracks has a maximum of 12 keys connected to the tote board in mid-field, only the names and information concerning 12 horses can be flashed on the tote board. But since there are often more than 12 entries in a race, the racing secretary of each track has the authority to group any two or more horses in excess of 11 into a *field*. If 17 horses are entered, 6 would be grouped as a field. The secretary groups each field with horses he believes have the poorest chance of winning. A player who bets on a horse in the field collects if any of the field horses win. Always check your program to see if your horse is entered as a field horse. Bettors who don't do this may see the name of some other horse on the tote board as the winner, think their horse has lost and tear up their winning tickets.

Also check *to see if your horse is part of an entry,* because if any horse of the entry wins you also collect. *Entries* are two or more horses from one or more stables that employ the same trainer. The racing secretary may reject or accept entries.

THE TRACK LINE AND THE MORNING LINE

The questions I have been asked most often over the years by horse players are these: How are the track line and the morning line calculated, and who does it? Who decides that a certain horse should be rated at odds of 2 to 1 and another at odds of 40 to 1, hours before track time?

The track line is calculated as follows: After the track's handicapper or secretary completes his racing card for the following afternoon, he sends the card with the names of the horses entered in each race and other necesary data to the track's pricemaker. This is the man who evaluates each horse's chances of winning and states it in terms of probable odds. He is not trying to pick winners; he is trying to judge as closely as possible each horse's chances of winning in terms of odds. He must know the horses, their past performances, track conditions and other factors. The odds he arrives at are based on this knowledge and incorporated in the track line.

In order to make a true line the pricemaker should base the combined opening odds of a race on the 100% figure, plus the percentage revenue cut taken by the state and track—but this seldom happens.

In New York State races the state takes a 10% cut and the track takes 5%, a total of 15%. The pricemaker should base his odds on a total of 115% plus an additional 2% or 3% for breakage, for a total of 117% to 118%. In some states the combined state and track cut is 12%, and the pricemaker should then use a figure of 114% to 116%; a figure of 120% or thereabouts should be used in a state where the combined state and track cut is 17%. But pricemakers aren't that exact; their lines usually run from 125% to 140% or more.

The track pricemaker and the pricemakers or handicappers on the daily racing sheets operate in the same fashion. They all figure the horses' winning chances in terms of percentages, then transpose into odds. The reader who wants to turn the odds given back into percentages can do so by referring to the following table. This table is also used by smart, bigtime race bettors.

PRICEMAKER'S AND BETTOR'S PERCENTAGE TABLE

Odds	Percent	Odds	Percent	Odds	Percent
1–1	50.00	19–1	5.00	2–3	60.00
6–5	45.45	20–1	4.76	2–5	70.42
7–5	41.67	25–1	3.85	2–7	77.77
8–5	38.46	30–1	3.23	2–9	81.81
9–5	35.71	35–1	2.77	3–4	57.14
2–1	33.33	40–1	2.44	3–5	62.50
11–5	31.25	50–1	1.96	3–7	70.00
12–5	29.41	60–1	1.64	3–10	76.92
13–5	27.78	75–1	1.32	4–5	55.55
14–5	26.31	80–1	1.23	3–11	71.42
3–1	25.00	100–1	.99	8–15	65.27
16–5	23.81	150–1	.66	9–10	52.63
17–5	22.72	200–1	.50	11–10	47.62
18–5	21.73	250–1	.39	13–10	43.47
19–5	20.83	300–1	.33	15–10	40.00
4–1	20.00	350–1	.28	17–10	37.04
21–5	19.23	400–1	.25	19–10	34.47
22–5	18.51	450–1	.22	3–20	86.95
5–1	16.67	500–1	.20	7–20	74.07
11–2	15.39	1–100	99.00	9–20	68.97
6–1	14.29	1–50	98.04	11–20	64.52
7–1	12.50	1–40	97.56	13–20	60.60
8–1	11.11	1–30	96.77	15–20	57.14
9–1	10.00	1–20	95.23	17–20	54.05
10–1	9.09	1–10	90.91	19–20	51.28
11–1	8.33	1–9	90.00	15–100	86.95
12–1	7.69	1–8	88.89	35–100	74.07
13–1	7.14	1–7	87.50	45–100	68.97
14–1	6.66	1–6	85.71	55–100	64.52
15–1	6.25	1–5	83.33	65–100	60.60
16–1	5.88	1–4	80.00	75–100	57.14
17–1	5.55	1–3	75.00	85–100	54.05
18–1	5.26	1–2	66.67	95–100	51.28

If you want to change any odds not given above into percentages, simply add the odds digits and divide the total into the digit or digits which comprise the last half of the number forming the odds.

Examples: Odds on Horse A are 1 to 1, so you add $1 + 1 = 2$, then divide 2 into $1 = 50\%$. Odds on Horse B are 19 to 1, add $19 + 1 = 20$, divide 20 into $1 = 5\%$. Odds on Horse C are 2 to 3, add $2 + 3 = 5$, divide 5 into $3 = 60\%$.

What happens to these probable odds when the pari-mutuel windows open and betting begins depends upon the amount of money wagered on each horse. Sometimes the bettors don't like the track-line favorite and they bet so heavily on some other horse that by the time the windows close the odds have changed, and their horse is now the favorite. The pricemaker merely tries to predict the payoff odds, but in the long run it is the track bettors themselves who finally make the winning payoff odds.

The morning line made up by the newspaper pricemakers is even more out of line than that of the track or racing-sheet pricemakers.

Before the enactment of the 1951 Federal law prohibiting interstate transmission of racing information, most off-track bookies received their price lines from the racing-wire services. This law is difficult to enforce 100%, and many bookies still manage to get wire information in one way or another by phone or coded telegram, but the majority, like most horse players, take their morning line from the daily racing sheets, such as the *Daily Racing Form,* which all have their own price-makers and handicappers. (Note that the term "handicapper," which in its strict sense means that man who assigns weights in a handicap race, is now widely used to mean "pricemaker" as well.)

Soon after the track secretary announces the *scratches* (withdrawals) in each race, most racing sheets print a later edition which carries their revised odds. This is called the *revised line* or the *late line.* Small four-page papers called *scratch sheets* are also published which give late scratches (except the last-minute ones), together with other racing information and their own listing of the probable odds.

ORIGIN OF BOOKMAKING AND THE PARI-MUTUEL BETTING SYSTEM

Betting in colonial America consisted largely of private wagering between men of means who raced their horses against those of their neighbors, and of wagering between the partisans of the horse owners. As this type of betting flourished, the stakeholders who held the amounts wagered and paid off the winner began to charge a fixed fee or commission, usually 5%.

After Governor Nicolls of New York built the first American racetrack on Long Island in 1665 and race events were programmed in which more than two horses were entered, this method of private race betting became inadequate, and a new method, the *auction pool,* began to be used. Auction pools, usually held in hotel rooms and lobbies near the track the night before the races were to be run, were mostly patronized by competing horse owners and their friends. The general public seldom participated.

The pool operated as follows: The operator or auctioneer displayed a slate bearing the names of the entries in each race. He began by

Bettors bidding on horses at an auction pool in 1888. (Culver Service)

asking for bids on the favorite in the first race. After this bidding closed and the price bid was known, the second choice horse was auctioned off, and so on. Poorer horses were sometimes auctioned off as a group; this was the forerunner of today's *field*. The top bid on a favorite seldom exceeded $100. The holder of the ticket on the winning horse received the total sum in the auction pool less a 5% deduction taken out by the auctioneer for services rendered.

Later, the holders of tickets on horses that ran second or third were also allowed to share in the pool. This is the origin of today's win, place and show pools.

By 1858 racing attendances had increased to the point where a majority of the betting public insisted on backing their selections with cash. This led to the development of the *Pricemaker's Percentage Table* (see page 45). It also signaled the beginning of bigtime betting at and away from the track and was the beginning of today's $48 billion legal and illegal bookie business.

When the Saratoga, New York, track opened in 1860, many bookmakers were on hand to accept bets from the public on any horse entered in the races. At that time they also worked on a 5% margin of profit. Later they increased this to 10%, 15% and sometimes 20%. Many also began working the crooked angles by becoming horse owners themselves, racing their animals under other names and bribing jockeys and trainers. Eventually they almost dominated racing, up until the advent of the pari-mutuel betting system.

The Saratoga books were successful and soon were imitated, and race books began to replace private race betting, stakeholders and auction pools at other tracks.

In 1871 James E. Kelley of New York City became the first bigtime professional bookmaker on record in this country when he ran a winter book on the Belmont stakes at Jerome Park, Long Island, New York.

The bookies preferred the flats rather than the harness tracks for their operations, and private betting and auction pools remained with the trotters until the pari-mutuel system was legalized.

At most of the thoroughbred tracks, before the pari-mutuel betting system came into use, the books were licensed by the track and paid the track a fixed fee for the privilege of accepting bets within the track enclosure. Each bookie was his own handicapper and pricemaker and usually quoted his own payoff odds. These often varied from one bookie to another; the price lines usually totaled from 110% to 120%. Smart race bettors, consequently, shopped around hunting the best odds. Rival bookies sent scouts to other books, looking for one who would overlay a horse or post an odds line that totaled up to a *Dutch book* (an odds line which totaled less than 100%). If he found a Dutch book, the smart bettor or rival bookie would win money by betting each horse in the race. The bookie with the Dutch book very quickly became an ex-bookie.

An example shows how it worked. Suppose it is a six-horse race and the bookie has the following "odds to 1" posted on his board. Horse A, 4 to 1; B, 19 to 1; C, 4 to 1; D, 9 to 1; E, 4 to 1; and G, 4 to 1. The rival bookie knows by heart that 4 to 1 odds transposed into percentages equals 20%, 9 to 1 odds, 10%, and 19 to 1 odds, 5% (see *Pricemaker's and Bettor's Percentage Table,* page 45), for a total of 95%. If he bets his money correctly he will win an amount equal to about 5% of the money he wagers, and the more money he bets, the more he will win, and the bigger the percentage difference, the bigger the bookie's rate of loss. Suppose the rival bookie bets $100 on each of the 4 to 1 shots, $50 on the 9 to 1 shot, and $25 on the 19 to 1 shot. He has bet a total of $475, and no matter which horse wins, he collects $500 for a profit of $25, about 5% of the money he wagered.

Crooked races were common before the pari-mutuel system and the most widely used method of rigging a race was to have a jockey hold back the favorite. The bookie in the know took as much action on the favorite as he could without arousing suspicion of rival bookies. Then he would send his runners to the rival bookies to bet all the horses in the race except the favorite; they would bet their money as described above in the Dutch book. Suppose a rival bookie's odds line totaled 113⅓% and the *favorite* who was rigged to lose was listed at 2 to 1 odds, which transposed into percentages is 33⅓%. If we subtract 33⅓% from 113⅓%, we get a balance of 80%. Rigging a race turned a true odds line into a Dutch book.

Track bookies in those days, unlike today's illegal bookies, had to know their racing angles, odds and percentages to stay in business. I recall many would-be racetrack bookies whose $50,000 and $100,000 bankrolls didn't even last a day. And, as one old-time hep race bettor recently said, "Scarne, those were the good old days when a man who really knew his odds and percentages could go to the track and win money by simply working the angles."

The pari-mutuel (Paris mutuel) system was invented in Paris, France, in 1865 by Pierre Oller. There are various stories as to why he conceived the system. One is that Oller devised it to keep his money and that of his friends among themselves. But the story that sounds most convincing to me concerns the bookmaker who went broke quoting his own odds. He asked Oller if he could figure out a system that would enable the bookmaker to make money no matter which horse won. Oller suggested that tickets be sold on each horse and that the payoff price of each winning ticket be determined by the amount of money wagered on the winner in relation to the amount wagered on all the horses in the race. This meant that the bettors would be wagering against each other rather than against the bookmaker, and they could get back only the amount wagered minus a percentage which the bookmaker retained as his commission. This is exactly what happens today.

When Pierre Oller's betting system was first put to use in Paris, a hand-operated tally machine was used to register and tabulate the wagers. Soon afterward a mutuel ticket-dispensing machine made its appearance in France. This machine became known to American track operators under the name of the "French Clicker Machine." Four of these were purchased by Colonel Lewis Clark, founder of the Kentucky Jockey Club (later changed to Churchill Downs) and installed in the Jockey Club for the running of the first Kentucky Derby in 1875. Colonel Clark installed the machines and the pari-mutuel system in order to drive the bookies from the track so that all betting profits would go to the track. He was successful until 1890, when the bookies again took over. During the first ten years of their operation, these French Clickers dispensed only $5 win tickets. In 1885, place and show tickets, also priced at $5, were added. Colonel Clark was the first to group two or more horses from one or more stables that were handled by the same trainer to run as a *coupling* (entry). The now popular $2 win ticket was first sold in 1889.

The bookies forced the Kentucky Jockey Club to drop the mutuel system in 1890, and Pierre Oller's innovation was forgotten for eighteen years until Colonel Matt Winn, then head of Churchill Downs, in an effort to get around a state anti-gambling law, renovated six old Clickers and used the mutuel system again for the 1908 Derby. The results were gratifying. Two of these machines dispensing $5 mutuel tickets handled $18,300 on the Derby alone and about $67,000 for the day. Racing fans began referring to the Clickers as "iron men" as they began making their appearance in other racing centers. But it wasn't until the advent of the automatic ticket-issuing machines and the electrically controlled totalisator in 1933 at Arlington Park in Chicago, which eliminated the danger of human error and dishonesty, that state officials realized the potential pari-mutuel revenue to the state, and the pari-mutuel system came into general use.

The first completely electrical totalisator was designed and built in the United States in 1927–28, but its first use was in England in 1930, following the legalization of pari-mutuel wagering by the British government. During 1930, 1931 and 1932, electric Odds Results and Payoff Display Boards were installed at Bowie, Hialeah and Pimlico.

The now popular $2 win, place and show tickets were first sold in the United States in 1911. Today there are, in addition, $5, $10, $20, $50 and $100 tickets, and they can be purchased in various combinations: win, place and show, win and place, etc. The price of these tickets and their combination arrangements are designed to accommodate individuals who like their action small, big or bigger. The daily double came from Canada in 1930.

The 5–6 sweepstake pool under the name of "Cinco-Seis" first made its appearance in Puerto Rico in 1913. The exacta is none other than the "perfecta" wagered at the Spanish game of jai-alai. The triple and superfecta are simply variations of the perfecta. The twin double is nothing more than two daily doubles combined.

HOW THE TOTALISATOR AND THE PARI-MUTUEL SYSTEM WORK

The totalisator is a portable assembly of especially designed electrical equipment. Its basic elements consist of:

1. Standard (win, place and show), daily double, quiniela, exacta, triple and superfecta ticket issuers, which register and total each ticket as it is issued;

2. Adding machines which total the sales registered by the standard issuers;

3. An automatic odds computer;

4. Electric indicators which show on the display boards the approximate odds during wagering and the order of finish of the first four entries (result) by program number, entry and pool totals obtained by the adding machines, the prices paid on a $2 winning mutuel ticket, race numbers, time of day, post time, etc.

Today, when you buy your ticket at the pari-mutuel window, the *operator* (seller) pushes a button and his ticket-issuing machine prints and delivers the ticket. At the same time it registers the amount of the bet with the totalisator, which is an adaptation of the dial phone system. This electronic brain adds, sorts, and transmits the totals of all bets to the infield tote board at intervals of about 90 seconds until the closing of the pari-mutuel windows.

The totalisator simultaneously sends the information to the infield tote board and to indicator boards in the mutuel department, or calculating room, which show in a progressive manner the total amount wagered in each pool and how much has been wagered on each horse in the win, place and show pools. Calculators in the mutuel department figure the changing odds on each horse and the new odds are flashed to the tote board. The calculators' method for figuring the mutuel payoff prices for win, place and show are quite complicated. The simplest example I can give follows:

We will suppose the race is run at a New York track where the combined mutuel take of state and track is 15% and the track "breaks to a nickel." We will assume that $129,400 was bet on all the horses in the win (straight) pool, and the red-hot favorite and eventual winner was backed to the amount of $100,000 by the betting public. The

The infield tote board, which flashes odds, results, pool totals, payoff prices, and other information. (Culver Service)

A typical tote room in which a system of parallel checking automatically verifies all data and functions at each step before the issuer permits a ticket to emit. Pictured are a console or desk, two printers in the right foreground and computers in the right background. (American Totalisator Co.)

calculators go through the following steps to determine the mutuel payoff price for a $2 win ticket.

1. Immediately after the betting windows close and the final betting totals have been flashed to the mutuel department, the calculators deduct the combined state and track percentage take from the gross win pool, in this instance 15% of $129,400, or $19,410. This leaves a net of $109,990 in the win pool. No other calculations are made until the race is over and the results have been flashed to the mutuel department.

2. Then they deduct from the net win pool the amount wagered on the winner—in this instance $109,990 minus $100,000—leaving a balance of $9,990. This is the amount to be divided as earnings among the holders of winning tickets. The $100,000 bet on the winning animal is set aside so that it may be returned to the winners.

3. The calculators next figure the dollar odds (earnings on each $1 unit bet on the winner). They simply divide the remaining amount in the win pool by the amount bet on the winning horse; in this instance, $9,990 divided by $100,000 gives a dollar-odds figure of 9 99/100¢.

4. But racetracks don't like to pay off in odd cents and can't pay

The Yonkers, New York, Raceway tote room and personnel, where bets are registered as tickets are purchased. Electronic computers add, sort and transmit bet totals and final payoff odds to the tote boards. (Yonkers Raceway)

off in fractions of a cent, so whenever the last cent digit of the dollar odds is any other figure than a 5 or 0 or a fraction thereof, the calculators subtract or break off that digit to the last nickel by making it a 5 or 0. In this instance there is a 4 99/100¢ breakage on each dollar odds, so the 9 99/100¢ becomes 5¢, giving the state and track an additional take of $4,990 for a total profit to the state and track of $24,400 in the win pool.

5. Since all mutuel prices are based on a $2 wagering unit, the calculators multiply the dollar-odds figure by 2, in this instance 5 cents times 2, and get a net winnings of 10 cents, and the 4 99/100¢ breakage doubles and becomes 9 98/100 ¢.

6. Finally, the $2 wagered is added to the net winnings, in this instance $2 plus 10¢, for a win payoff mutuel of $2.10, the figure that is posted on the track's board and printed in the newspapers under the heading of race results. If the track had not deducted breakage, and if the Treasury minted 1/100¢ pieces, the win mutuel would have paid $2.1998 instead of $2.10.

The mutuel payoff price on *place bets* is calculated in much the same way as the win mutuels, except that two horses share in the place pool, the one that finished first and the one that finished second. I should mention here that no horse goes to the post at a set price to place because the mutuel he will pay to place depends on two factors: (1) how much money is bet on the animal, and (2) how much is bet on the animal that happens to run first or second with him. Calculators use several methods to compute place mutuels. The following is a common one:

1. From the total amount of money (gross place pool) bet on all the horses to place (run first or second), the calculators deduct the combined percentage take of state and track.

2. From the remainder (net place pool) they deduct the money bet on the horses which ran first and second.

3. This remainder is then divided by 2 because half the money in

The console or desk is used to control all the input and output functions of the computer. The television cameras are used to monitor the odds, prices, probable Daily Double, Exacta and Triple prices and the race or races. Mikes are used to communicate with the tote and mutuel people throughout the plant. (Yonkers Raceway)

the net place pool goes to holders of place tickets on the horse who finished first, and half to the holders of place tickets on the horse who finished second.

4. The result (half the net place pool) is divided by the amount bet to place on the horse whose place payoff is being calculated.

5. The percentage breakage is then subtracted by rounding off the last cents digit, making a 5 or 0.

6. The result of this deduction, usually a dollars-and-cents figure, is multiplied by 2.

7. Adding $2 (the sum paid for the mutuel place ticket) to the remainder gives the mutuel payoff price on a place bet.

This procedure is repeated for the second horse who shares in the place pool.

The method used by the calculators to compute *show mutuels* are the same as for calculating place mutuels except that three horses who finished first, second and third share in the show pool.

The method used by the calculators to compute the daily double, quiniela, exacta, triple and superfecta payoffs is the same as calculating the pari-mutuel payoff for win, place and show. Each of these exotic wagers goes into a pool which is held separate from all others.

HOW NICKEL AND DIME BREAKAGE WORKS

The rounding out of the last cent digit or fraction thereof to a 5 or 0 is called *breakage to a nickel,* and with very rare exceptions when the last digit is a 5 or 0 and rounding out is unnecessary, the state or track or both, as the case may be, receive an additional percentage take.

Most tracks in America break off or round the last cent digit or a fraction thereof to the nearest dime by reducing it to a zero; this is called *breakage to a dime.* When the track breaks to a dime, however, the calculators round out the last cent digit of the net earnings of a $2 unit, rather than a $1 unit as is done when the track breaks to a nickel. Because of this track rule, the player pays exactly the same amount of percentage breakage in both instances.

However, there is one rare exception. I must report that the player pays a wee bit more breakage when the track breaks to a dime. Example: With nickel breakage, whenever the amount wagered on a horse whose mutuel is to be figured divides evenly into the amount of the net pool and gives a last-digit result of a perfect 0 or 5 (minus a fraction) the track deducts no percentage. This will occur about twice in every several thousand mutuels. But in dime breakage this will only happen when the perfect 0 shows. And for that reason the player pays an infinitesimal amount more breakage when the track breaks to a dime instead of a nickel.

You can easily learn if a track breaks to the dime or nickel simply by consulting the race results in your local paper. If you find that the 10-cent figures shown in the mutuel payoff prices in each of the nine races run at that track end in an even number of dimes such as .00, .20, .40, .60 and .80, it's a trillion to one that the track being studied breaks to a dime. If, however, you find among these figures one or more odd dime figures, such as .10, .30, .50, .70 or .90, it's a cinch bet that the track breaks to a nickel.

This extra tax gimmick called breakage is imposed on the bland assumption that a horse player doesn't want to be bothered with pennies or nickels when cashing his winning ticket. But this money, extracted from the horse player, also reduces a winning player's payoff price when betting with off-track bookies.

These pennies and nickels add up to millions per year. The state of New Jersey's take in percentage breakage from a recent 50-day meet at the Camden track totaled $1,145,674.31, which is quite a chunk of breakage dough. Yet this amount is small compared to the tens of millions in breakage earned by illegal bookies.

Most writers on racing and most track owners say that the track breakage averages about 2%, but they have never explained how they arrived at this figure. I am going to analyze the problem and find out exactly what this breakage amounts to in percentage.

There are two ways to figure the percentage. This is how the track calculator does it—we'll use the example given on page 51. There we found that $129,400 was the gross amount wagered in the win pool and $100,000 of this amount was bet on the winner. The calculators deducted $19,410 as the legal take-off, plus $4,990 in breakage for a combined state and track profit of $24,400. When this is divided by $129,400, the total amount bet on the race, we get an answer of .1880+ or 18.80+%. From this we subtract the combined state and track take of 15% and find that the breakage deduction comes to 3.80+%.

Now let's figure it according to the method I gave on page 51. In the race problem we are using a $2 win ticket which would have paid $2.1998 if there had been no breakage deduction, and if the U.S. Mint made 1/100¢ pieces. But, since the calculators did deduct 9 98/100¢ from $2.1998, they arrived at an actual payoff price of $2.10. To find the bettor's disadvantage, divide the amount of breakage deduction by the total amount the bettor would have received if the breakage had not been deducted. In this instance, $.0998 divided by $2.1998 gives an answer of 4.536+%. This is .73% more than the 3.80+% answer which was obtained using the calculator's method of figuring.

This is the strangest percentage problem in racing, and one which I am sure has never before been discussed in print. We have obtained two different answers and yet, for all practical purposes, both can be considered to be correct because they add up to the same amount in dollars and cents. The track mathematicians are wrong if they figure their percentage of breakage on the gross win pool instead of the net win pool, because the 15% legal take was deducted from the gross win pool before the race was run and therefore has no bearing on the breakage percentage.

Since it makes no difference moneywise to the track, the calculators will continue to use their method rather than mine. Besides, from their viewpoint, figuring it my way sounds confusing when it is stated: The combined state and track take of 15% of the gross win pool added to the 4.536+% breakage take of the net win pool gives the track and state a total percentage of 18.80+% of the gross win pool.

It all adds up to the fact that a so-called smart player who bets on favorites usually pays a greater percentage in breakage than the player who likes long shots. Example: If a hot favorite wins and the mutuel payoff price is $2.1999 before the breakage-to-a-dime deduction, the actual mutuel payoff will be $2.10, and the favorite bettor has been charged the maximum breakage possible, 4.541+%.

But if a long shot wins, and the mutuel payoff price without the breakage deduction is $40.19, the mutuel payoff price will be $40.10, and the long-shot player has only been charged 1/5 of 1% for breakage.

The men and women who play favorites believe they have the best deal. Few realize that the shorter the payoff price, the greater the possible breakage percentage in favor of the track and against the players.

My analysis proves that the track's nickel or dime breakage deduction will take 2.23% from each winning mutuel ticket in the long run. However, not to complicate matters, let us go along with the 2% figure used by most racing experts.

The shortest odds on record are the 1 to 100 odds offered three times against Man o' War in 1920. The great horse won all three races, and in each of the three races the track had to add money to the win pool rather than deduct its takeoff and breakage. (See *minus pools*, page 60.)

In any of the 30 states where racing is legal, the total deductions for state taxes and the track's cut, including breakage, cannot run less than 12% nor more than 21.036%.

In Puerto Rico, Panama and other Latin American countries, however, the total deductions run from 22% to 43%!

If you desire to transpose the mutuel payoff price as shown in the race results of your newspaper into "odds to 1," simply subtract $2 from the mutuel payoff price and divide by 2. Suppose the mutuel price was

$5.40; subtracting $2 leaves a balance of $3.40. Dividing this by 2 leaves an odds to 1 figure of 1.70 to 1.

A player can amuse himself at the track by computing the approximate mutuel win payoff price on any horse simply by multiplying the final odds to 1 figure as shown on the tote board by 2 and then adding $2. Let's suppose a horse shown on the tote board is quoted at odds of 8 to 1. Multiply 8 by 2 and add 2, and you get a result of $18, which amount will be the approximate mutuel price if the horse wins. Naturally if the posted odds are way off, the result of your calculation will also be way off.

The disposition of the total state and track deduction differs from state to state. Examples: Of Rhode Island's 15% total take-off, 8% goes to the state. Of Maine's 17% total take-off, 7% goes to the state. Of New York's 15% total take-off, the state demands 9% to 10% at the flats and 5% to 11% at the harness tracks.

The states also differ in the way they handle disposition of breakage. In Arizona, Colorado, Kentucky, Louisiana, Maine, Nebraska and Oregon, the tracks get all the breakage. In Florida the state gets it all. In New Jersey the harness tracks keep all the breakage, and the state takes all the breakage at the flat tracks. The remaining states usually divide the breakage 50–50 between state and track.

HOW THE STATE AND TRACK CUTS BEAT DOWN THE PLAYERS

Nearly all racetrack bettors believe that the legal state and track take (15% plus 2% breakage in New York) is the only handicap they must overcome to have a winning day at the races. This is true provided the bettor only bets on one horse in one race, but when he and other bettors re-bet winnings, and the nonwinners bet fresh money, the 17% handicap jumps to about 30% for the daily double and the nine races.

For example, let us say at New York's Long Island Aqueduct track the mutuel turnover for the day totaled $6,033,585. The bettors actually risked about 57% of this total because, except for the first race and the daily double, in which only fresh money was bet, about half the winnings on previous races was re-bet.

On the opposite page is a table that shows how the 17% bite really works on the daily double, three exactas, triple and all nine races.

On this racing day at Aqueduct, the track bettors won back only 70% of the calculated sum risked, which means that track and state really took out a 30% bite of the money risked rather than the 17% which nearly all bettors believe they take.

RACE	BETTING HANDLE	FRESH MONEY	83% RETURNED TO WINNERS	17% TAKE-OFF
Daily double	$ 343,814	$ 343,814	$ 285,367	$ 58,447
First	261,561	261,561	217,095	44,466
Second	329,560	164,780	273,534	56,026
Third	422,002	211,001	350,261	71,741
Fourth	456,616	228,308	378,991	77,625
Exacta 4th race	360,218	180,109	298,981	61,237
Fifth	499,028	249,514	414,193	84,835
Exacta 5th race	390,006	195,003	323,705	66,301
Sixth	531,730	265,865	441,335	90,395
Exacta 6th race	410,012	205,006	340,310	69,702
Seventh	611,477	305,738	507,525	103,952
Eighth	464,795	232,392	385,779	79,016
Ninth	452,138	226,069	375,274	76,864
Triple 9th race	500,628	250,314	415,521	85,107
	$6,033,585	$3,319,474	$5,007,871	$1,025,714
SUMMARY	$6,033,585	Betting handle for nine races, daily double, exactas and a triple		
	$3,319,474	Calculated sum risked by bettors		
	$1,025,714	State and track take including breakage (17%)		
	$2,293,760	Total sum returned to winners		

If you still don't believe that pari-mutuel betting is a sure way to lose money in the long run, let me try to convince you with this hypothetical case. Suppose a factory owner who employs 1,000 workers wants to give them a day's outing at a New York racetrack. Suppose the track owners allow them the exclusive use of the track for that day, and suppose they can bet odd change. The benevolent factory owner gives each employee $10 on the condition that he bets the entire amount in the first race on any horse he likes and in any manner (win, place or show).

It is also stipulated that the 1,000 bettors are to be partners, dividing their winnings and sharing their losses after each race. The winners always turn their winnings back to the factory owner and he redivides the money equally among all the bettors. He wants everybody to have a good time. They all agree, and it sounds like fun.

They're off! Everybody has his $10 riding in the first race. After the finish the winners turn their tickets in to the factory owner, who cashes them and finds that, after the 15% state and track cut plus 2% breakage has been deducted, he has $8,300. He redivides this sum, and each of the 1,000 employees has $8.30 to bet on the second race. The winning tickets this time total $6,889, and when this is redivided each employee gets $6.88. This betting and redividing procedure is continued through all nine races. After the ninth race and the final redivision, each happy employee finds that his original $10 has shrunk to $1.86.

The state and track cut has taken $8,140 in legal deductions from the original $10,000. If the track had run 18 races, each player would finally be left with a grand total of 35¢. No comment needed.

MINUS POOLS

A minus pool is a pool in which the payoff would be less than $2.10, and the track has to make up the difference.

In all states where racing is legal, the law says that the track must pay the player a profit on a winning bet which must be at least 10¢ on each $2 win, place or show bet. A $2 winning ticket must pay off at least $2.10. It sometimes happens that there is so much action on a red-hot favorite that, after the track and state's percentage is taken out, not enough money remains in the pool to pay the winning mutuel. The track loses money in this instance because it has to make up the difference. This explains why when only three horses are going there is no show mutuel. In a match race, where only two horses run, there are, of course, no place or show mutuels.

RACE TOUTS AND THEIR METHODS

A *tout* (also called *tipster* or *chiseler*) is a person who makes a living at or away from the track by trying to convince anyone who will listen that he has useful inside information.

Touts can be found wherever there are horse bettors. A successful tout must have plenty of savvy and a wide repertoire of alibis for use when his selections don't finish in the money. He must also have a good memory for faces so that he doesn't make the mistake at some later date of trying to clip the same mark the same way. Like an actor, the tout's chief stock in trade is the sincere conviction he manages to convey to strangers, especially so-called gamblers and wise guys. He usually pretends to have close friends among the top trainers, jockeys and owners. He also begins calling you by your first name seconds after he meets you.

What he doesn't have is the inside information he talks so much about; he makes his selections just as anyone else does. Some touts print their selections on tip sheets, usually one-page mimeographed sheets, and sell them at $1 apiece as the horse players enter the track. If the tipster had a good day and managed to pick a few winners, as you leave there will be a dozen barkers passing the sheets out free and shouting out the big winner—"Today's daily double paid $328.80!" or something of the sort. This is the come-on that tries to sell you on his tip sheet and induce you to buy it on your next visit. If the tipster had a bad day, there is no shouting and no free sample sheets are passed out.

Although touting is not supposed to be permitted at the track, it has almost come to be accepted by officials as an unavoidable petty-larcenous evil of racing. A smart bettor steers clear of any bearer of Greek gifts at the racetrack, especially if he offers a tip on a horse.

Some of these information-loaded chiselers charge a fixed fee for their worthless information; others ask you to place a bet for them on their horse (using your money, of course). A tout may be anyone—a gambler, bookie, horse player, small horse-owner, ex-jockey, stable hand, racetrack employee, ex-horse trainer, or the wife or girl friend of any of these. You may even be touted by one of your own friends who is innocently passing on a tout's tip.

Female touts usually team up with a man who poses as a husband or boy friend. Here is one routine used by an attractive, good-looking couple in their middle thirties who usually work Aqueduct and Belmont Park. They are adept at making friends rapidly with nearly anyone. Their angle for clipping the suckers is good; it can take several chumps at once.

The wife—let's call her Peggy—excitedly offers the information to likely prospects that she and her husband, Joe, have a confidential tip on a horse in the next race which they just received from a trainer. She is sorry she can't name the horse because the tip cost $50, and if too many players bet on the horse the odds will drop.

Just before the race is run, Joe fades, leaving Peggy with the *marks* (suckers, chumps). As soon as the horses cross the finish line Peggy screams, "We got him! We got him!" And she names the winner. A few minutes later Joe reappears counting a fat handful of bills. "Honey," he says, "we just won seven hundred bucks!" The marks are impressed.

A race or two later the same thing happens again. This is usually sufficient and the marks are ready to *spring* (put up some money). Again Joe wanders off, and when he returns he says glumly, "He has a terrific horse in the next race, but he's asking a hundred dollars, money in hand, before he'll talk. Do you think we should go for a hundred?"

This is Peggy's cue. She turns to her new-found companions. "There are five of us here," she says brightly. "If we each put up twenty dollars we can all share in the winner." She makes it sound as though she was doing them a great favor. Since they have been praying for a break like this, it's in the bag. They put up $20 apiece and Joe goes to buy the information. He comes back with the name of a horse which he has probably selected by closing his eyes and poking a finger at the program. Everybody except Joe and Peggy, who haven't made even a $2 bet all day, gets some money down on the horse. If the nag loses, Peggy and Joe alibi the loss and lose themselves in the crowd. If the horse wins, they try to hustle a bonus from the winners. They usually succeed because the suckers figure they have a real good thing, and they want to keep Peggy and Joe happy so they'll share the tips they get the next day.

The touting racket is much more vicious away from the track because the chiselers don't have to worry about being spotted by track detectives or cops and can use a greater variety of techniques. They run newspaper ads, contact players by phone or letter, send telegrams to prospective suckers, fake long-distance calls, and make use of stooges who pretend to have won big on the tout's tips. Touts often manufacture sucker bait by sending themselves telegrams signed with the name of a prominent horse owner or jockey and giving the names of winners. The wires, of course, are sent after the races and the times of sending erased or changed.

BETTING RINGS

There are several gambling syndicates of a type which few bookies or bettors know anything about. They represent themselves as a group of bookmakers but are, to insiders, known as *betting rings*. They earn their money by actually betting on horse races!

The betting ring accepts bets from certain horse owners, bigtime gamblers, bookies, racket guys, jockeys and other people who are in the know and whose reputations are on the shady side. They do this in order to learn if and when some horse is to be held back or some other form of crookedness is to take place in a race. They accept bets from these shady sources and if, in their opinion, the information is solid, they then bet money of their own and lay off all the action among other bookmakers throughout the country.

The shady characters who know the race is going to be crooked prefer to place their bets with a betting ring because the ring is in a position to move a *big order* (big bet), and because they know the ring will keep the information confidential, since it is also to the ring's advantage to do so. The betting rings also accept bets from honest high rollers as a cover to keep their real operation secret.

I know one such betting ring which has, in the past few years, won millions of dollars wagering on races in which inside information of this sort gave them an edge and sometimes even a sure thing. The members of this ring own about a dozen racehorses and thus know many horse owners, jockeys and trainers; they know which ones can be bought, and sometimes bribe them.

A few years ago one of America's top ten biggest bettors and the owner of a racing stable was taken by a New Jersey betting ring for the $450,000 he had bet on his own horse to win. The ring *got to* (bribed) the jockey, who saw to it that the horse did not finish in the money. It ran fifth.

Because the ring knows it can't trust the shady characters who place crooked bets, it insures against the possibility that it will be given a phony crooked-race tip by charging a 2½% commission whenever the information fails to hold up.

Since this situation exists in racing, touts and tipsters take advantage of it and call their own selections *hot horses* or *information horses*.

All touts follow the same rule: Never give a sucker an even break. What the sucker should ask himself and seldom does are these questions: Why, if this guy's selections are so good, doesn't he have a fat bankroll? Why is he trying to get money by giving me winners? Why doesn't he use his own money to bet on these surefire tips? The answer, of course, is that the tout doesn't really believe in his own selections.

Your selection is actually better than any he gives you because you don't have to pay extra for the privilege of betting on it.

Touts sometimes ensure themselves a winner by touting every horse in the race, each one to a different player. But, winners or losers, touts seldom run out of customers even when they give out loser after loser to the same chump.

If you have been listening to touts, perhaps this story will cheer you up. Two touts met at a track just before the last race. One said, "I've got a real good bettor. He's loaded and he's been betting a hundred bucks for me on each horse I've given him. So far I gave him seven losers in a row. What should I do now?"

"Give him up," the second tout replied. "He's hard luck!"

CROOKED HORSE RACING

The history of racing is replete with stories of bigtime betting swindles, crooked races and ringed horses. Some of the most fantastic stories are true, some are tragic, others are so greatly garbled after being told and retold that even a magician couldn't discover the real truth.

The largest wager by a single bettor on a crooked horse race in which a ringer was planted was a $300,000 bet made by Arnold Rothstein, whom I first met back in the Roaring Twenties when I was nineteen years old. Rothstein was the biggest racket guy of his day, and the shrewdest, crookedest gambler; he would bet or back any gambling proposition that involved chicanery. I met him shortly after his big $300,000 bet. This time, crime didn't pay; the ringer lost.

Rothstein got it back, however. Not long afterward he again bet $300,000, distributing it with dozens of bookmakers throughout the country—this time on a horse of his own, Sporting Blood. The horse won and paid even money, and a lot of raised eyebrows in sporting circles indicated that this race may not have been on the level either.

Today, racing in this country is probably as clean as it ever will be because of the constant vigilance of the State Racing Commissions, the Jockey Club and the Thoroughbred Racing Protective Bureau. All running horses racing on flat tracks in America must be registered thoroughbreds. This means that their ancestry can presumably be traced back to one of three stallions: the Byerly Turk, the Godolphin Bard, or the Darley Arabian.

One of the Jockey Club's most important functions is keeping the American Stud Book up-to-date. This book lists all registered thoroughbreds, and no horse may run at any recognized track unless he is listed. All thoroughbreds now have a registry number tattooed on the inside of the upper lip. This makes it much more difficult than it once was to put a ringer in a race. Most often, a ringer is a good horse entered under a fictitious name in a cheap race against inferior horses. This gives the owner or trainer a really good chance of winning the race and purse, and he bets big on the ringer with the unsuspecting bookies.

The most common shady trick in racing today, one that is hard to eliminate, consists in holding back a horse for a few races until the odds on him go sky high, then letting him go all out to win. A horse who has run badly in his last few races gets little betting support from the public, the pricemakers' odds indicate that he has little chance to win, and the boys in the know who bet on him win heavily if he finishes in the money.

Every now and then a new drug menace to honest racing makes its appearance. Racing crooks may induce a veterinarian to dope a horse with one of the many new drug combinations. One is an adrenalin preparation in oil which is injected into the horse's bloodstream several hours before the race and followed by a booster shot of Benzedrine about a half hour before post time. This and some of the other wonder drugs can make a 50 to 1 shot into an almost sure winner. Just recently the Pennsylvania State Horse Racing Commission suspended the licenses of a state veterinarian, a horse owner, a trainer and a specimen collector accused of having participated in or having had knowledge of the fact that drugs had been administered to horses entered in races at a major racetrack in Pennsylvania. The urine sam-

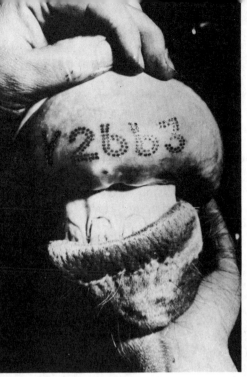

Registry number tattooed on a race-horse's upper lip as a safeguard against the introduction of ringers into races.

ples taken from the drugged horses after races at this track were switched and replaced by other samples so as to indicate a negative result.

Even though the state and its protective affiliates take every precaution to deter crooked horse racing, such as the Film Patrol and stewards watching for rough or suspicious riding, post-race chemical testing for illegal drugs, lip tattoos to prevent the use of ringers, the introduction of such exotic bets as exactas, triples, twin doubles and superfectas has introduced a new menace to honest racing. Racing crooks induce a shady veterinarian to dope a number of horses with a drug called acepromazine, a depressant capable of turning a 40-mile-an-hour potential winner into a 32-mile-an-hour certain loser. Example: In an eight-horse superfecta race four horses are injected with this tranquilizer; then the crooks bet on the four *live* horses, covering all the possible (24) four-horse combinations, and no matter in what order these live horses finish, the crooks are sure to have one winning (1–2–3–4) superfecta ticket. Twenty-four different combination bets of $3 for a total of $72 assures these crooks of a $3 winning superfecta ticket, which will almost certainly pay off more than $72.

This trick can succeed because, until recently, tracks generally haven't done urine analysis on or taken saliva samples from also-rans, but only from winners. The use of depressants must surely result in broader testing. The racing fan need not be too alarmed: it is getting harder and harder to dope horses these days as investigative agencies are working around the clock to rid racing of its drugging problem.

HUNCH AND FORM PLAYERS

The majority of horse bettors are students of neither racing nor betting. They go to the tracks for recreation and to satisfy their gambling urge. Most of them bet a couple of bucks on each race and on the daily double. Their methods of selecting horses are primitive. They pick horses because of some emotional association with the name of the horse or jockey, or the colors of the jockey's silks. They like the way the horse switches his tail on the way to the starting gate, or they have a psychic hunch, usually having to do with numbers. The occasional bettor is almost always a *hunch player.*

I know one woman who won several hundred dollars on a 50 to 1 shot because a flock of birds flew over the track and she counted them and chose the jockey whose number matched.

The biggest daily double payoff in history was won on July 4, 1954, by a San Diego widow, Mrs. Ottillia Alexander, who held the only daily double ticket on Slick Trick and Rocklite at Agua Caliente. It paid $12,724.80. When reporters asked her how she had picked the two winning horses she said, "It was easy. The post position of the two horses were the same as the first two digits of my home street address."

Although most bettors are hunch players, the largest percentage of money is bet by the *form players,* or so-called *smart bettors,* who believe themselves to be handicappers. Fortunately for the track and the bookies, their calculations seldom give many of them the same answer. Actually their calculations are minimal; most of them follow very simple systems. Some are *chalk players* who bet only on favorites, others bet only on long shots, others only on second- or third-choice horses. Some bet only on a horse who won his last race. Some bet only front-running horses, others on strong finishers. There are almost as many such systems as there are form players.

The player who really tries to select his horses on the basis of studying form finds that there is too much information available in the innumerable racing and scratch sheets, and much of it is contradictory. Even the professional handicapper, skilled as he may be, has a real job on his hands. These experienced men spend considerable time every day studying the past performance sheets of one or more daily racing papers. To them each race is a complex problem involving the mathematics of odds, furlongs, fractional times, track conditions, age of horses, past performance, weights carried, post positions and a dozen other contributing factors.

No matter how carefully they have weighed and divided and multiplied and compared these factors, fate still deals most of the cards. Once the bell clangs and the fillies spring from the barrier anything can happen—an unruly horse, a bad start, interference, a jockey's mismanagement of distance, a horse's nervous reaction. These unpredictable factors often make the best handicappers and pricemakers look pretty silly. A few years ago at Saratoga the favorites picked by these professionals lost 22 successive races!

Throughout one entire year I followed the racing selections of three of the nation's outstanding handicappers. One lost 4% of his yearly gross betting handle, another 5%, and the third 6%—an average loss of 5%. And this is far better than the 12½ to 20% loss suffered by the average hunch player. It boils down to this: Even if you are a form player of professional caliber, the best you can expect to do is cut down your yearly losses.

Any banking game—horses, dice or cards—that can be beaten by an application of skill or knowledge must eventually go out of business. I see no sign that form or hunch players will ever bring that about in racing.

SYSTEM PLAYERS

Like all other forms of organized gambling, racing also has its *system players*—bettors who are convinced that there is some mysterious method which will enable them to win consistently. System players are prime marks for the boys who advertise and sell systems. These keys to fortune always look fine on paper and always come a cropper in practice because one or more important factors have been overlooked.

Of the hundreds of systems I have analyzed over the years the most popular is the *double-up, progressive* or *Martingale* system. Some players who have used this for years and lost money still insist that the only reason they haven't retired wealthy is because they don't have enough money to back up the system and make it work.

The theory is that if you have enough money to double your bet each time you lose, you will eventually win one bet that will retrieve all previous losses plus a profit.

For example: you bet $2 to win on a horse. If you lose, you bet $4 on a horse in the next race. If you lose again, you bet $8, then $16 and so on. Whenever you win, if the payoff price is even money or better, you get back all your losses plus $2 or more. What is wrong with that?

The double-up system would work very nicely in any casino banking game that did *not* have a maximum betting limit. But try to find one. Why do you suppose the house limit is there?

"How to Win" advice and past-performance information for the form player are published in dozens of tip sheets and other racing guides. (Ilse Mayer from Monkmeyer Press)

There is no house limit in racing; the sky (or your bankroll) is the limit. So why doesn't it work here either? The double-up system players always claim that the reason they didn't get rich playing this system is because they were limited by the size of their bankrolls. They are wrong; they could start with all the gold in Fort Knox and they would still lose.

There are two big monkey wrenches in the machinery; the pari-mutuel betting system, and the fact that losing streaks will eventually send even the million-dollar bankroll player to the cleaner's. You can't tell when your losing streak will come, but you can only be absolutely certain that it will arrive if you continue to place bets. Suppose you start with a $2 bet, double your bet each time you lose, and you lose 15 successive bets. When you lose the 15th bet of $32,768 you have lost a total of $65,534. The system says that you must double your bet again and place a wager of $65,536. If you win this you'd get back all your losses plus a $2 profit.

But you find you have a problem. The $65,536 question now is: Where do you place a bet of this size? With a bookie? Sure, you can find one who would take it. But if you won and if you aren't a regular bigtime customer and don't know your way around in gambling circles, could you find the bookie the next day? The answer to that is a large NO.

There is only one place you can safely get down a bet of this size—at the track itself. Of course, you would need about a dozen assistants to help you bet this much at the windows in the time allotted between races. And you'd have to keep hiring assistants; ten more losses, which includes the $65,536 wager, and you'd be commanding a small army of helpers madly trying to place bets totaling $33,554,432.

Let's assume you do succeed in wagering the $65,536 and your horse comes in a winner. It is highly doubtful, after the state, track and breakage deductions, that your horse would pay as much as $3, even if it was a 50 to 1 shot before you made your bet. The system worked, but you still lose $32,766 and you still haven't paid off all those assistant bettors.

You now know how to save yourself thousands of dollars: forget the double-up system.

Betting on the favorite is a popular system because it offers such a high percentage of winners. But payoff prices on favorites are low; and when you consider the additional P.C. in breakage taken out on winning favorites, it should be obvious that you aren't going to win any big sum of money very fast.

Betting on the jockey as a system sounds good, because a few of the better jockeys win from 15% to 25% of their races. But you need a first-class crystal-gazing ball in good working order to know which jockey is going to get hot when—and the state and track P.C. is still grinding you down. The same is true of all the other systems such as betting post positions, betting horses who have won previous races and betting on the selections of certain handicappers. Old Man Percentage is always there working quietly and efficiently against you.

Let's daydream a bit and suppose you really do cook up a system that works. How long do you think it will be before the track and bookies get wise to what is going on? And how soon after that will they rule out the kind of bet your system depends on? This would probably happen so fast you wouldn't yet have won enough money to pay for all the time you spent devising the system—so you still lose!

Another proof that systems don't work is that track operators and bookies never discourage a system player. They like them; the system keeps them betting. And if anyone tries to sell you a book titled *How to Beat the Horses*, you might hesitate just long enough to wonder why the author is to eager to tell everyone all about it instead of keeping it a secret and using it himself.

And now, having said all that, I'll give you a system that could work.

My friend Vincent Brennan, an avid turf enthusiast, tells me that when this system first made its appearance, about 1921, a well-known New York bookie lost $150,000 before he realized what was happening.

Here it is. Give your bookmaker $60 and a betting slip that contains the names of your favorite handicapper's first, second and third choices in the same race. The conditions of your bet are these: $10 is to be bet on the favorite. If the favorite loses or is scratched, $20 is to go on the second choice in the same race. If this horse loses or is scratched, $30 is to go on the third-choice horse. The only possible way you can lose is when all three horses lose, or when the first and second choice lose and the third choice pays less than even money. When any one of the three horses wins and the payoff price is better than even money, you come out ahead.

This is what happens. If the favorite wins, the bookie pays you for your $10 winning bet and returns your $50 *if money*. If this horse loses or is scratched, you have $20 riding on the second choice. If he wins you collect on the $20 bet and get back $30 *if money*. If the second choice loses or is scratched, you have $30 riding on the third choice. If he wins, you collect on the $30 winning bet and get back either $10, $20, $30, or just your winning bet, depending on whether the first two horses lost or were scratched. If all three lose, naturally, you are out $60, but you will, in the long run, win more bets than you lose and you will eventually break the bookie *if* he continues to take your action.

The difficulty is to find a bookie who is so dumb he never heard of this gimmick and can't dope it out. Actually, this disadvantage isn't as great as you might think—there are some pretty dumb bookies in the business.

There is only one system that really works all the time—buy a race-track or become a bookmaker so that the P.C. works for and not against you. Even the best of handicappers can't pick enough winners to come out ahead of the game; that's why they are working for tracks or newspapers. As Pittsburgh Phil once said, "You can beat a race, but not the races."

PORTRAIT OF A BOOKMAKER

Most bookies and betting handicappers today still match the picture of them that Damon Runyon painted in "Guys and Dolls" and other stories. If you think the names he gave his characters were exaggerated, here are a few monickers of present-day bookies and betting handicappers: Florida Louie, Richie the Crutch, Joe the Weeper, Pick Your Nose Willie, Big John, Jake the Plumber, Tommy the Owl, Melon Head Abe, Squinty Eye Joe and Ragamuffin Pete. I could go on and on.

My survey shows that 5% of the bookies never graduated from grammar school, 31% had one to three years in high school, 42% graduated from high school but had no further schooling, 18% matriculated at college, and 4% graduated. There may even be a Phi Beta Kappa or two, but they didn't show up in my sampling.

The majority are married and are between the ages of 25 and 60. Most of them own their own home and a flashy automobile. Ninety percent gamble on horses, sports, dice, cards or some other game—a percentage that holds true for all gambling operators. Seventy percent, before becoming bookies, were players, runners or agents who discovered the earning power of the bookie and decided to go into business for themselves. Better than twenty percent are sons of former bookies. Fifty percent of the bookies now operating have been arrested for gambling or bookmaking one or more times. Fifty percent of the married ones have a mistress, and 5% are married to former showgirls. Twenty percent either work for racket guys or must split their winnings with them.

Let's take a look at a real big bookmaker. I recently interviewed a New York bookie who is retired and who, not so long ago, ran the biggest book in the country. During his big years he thought nothing of accepting a $50,000 bet on a horse. You'd know his name if I mentioned it because he's had more than his share of front-page publicity.

"Why is it," I asked him, "that when anyone asks a bookie, 'How you doing?' the answer is almost always, 'Bad. I lost today, took a beating, lost big, got moidered.'"

"Scarne," he said, "bookies are a very queer lot. They are the only people in the world who can afford to buy Cadillacs, send their kids through college, own their own homes, buy a lot of luxuries and still lose money every day."

"So all bookies are liars?"

He grinned. "No, not all—but if you want to bet me that ninety-nine out of a hundred are damned liars, you'd have to give me real big odds." As we talked, he had this to say about his business.

"I was in a very rough business. I had a dozen or more run-ins with the law, and it cost me thousands to square myself. I did a couple of short stretches in the can. When I was handling a couple of million dollars' worth of action a day, I had to overcome a lot of hazards to stay in business. When a race was fixed, the thieves wanted me to accept their big bets. My runners often stole money on me by pocketing collections from losing players and telling me the players had run out. My clerks and sheet writers stole thousands by doctoring the daily run-down sheet. Many players, knowingly or unknowingly, *past-post* me [betting on a winner after the race is over].

"I canceled gambling debts owed me by hundreds of broke players. Hundreds of others borrowed money from me and damned few paid me back. Winning players who were always sure to show up the next day to collect were hard to find when they lost heavily; some I never did find. Cops and charity collectors bombarded me with tickets and requests for dough every day. I had to pay thousands in ice to cops and politicians for protection, and I had to pay back to my runners fifty percent of their winning monthly handle. Add in salaries to clerks, accountants and sheet writers and you can see that the nation's biggest book had a real fancy overhead.

"I won't give you the bookies' stock answer and say I lost money every day; you know better. When I retired and took inventory, I found I had five million in cash, not counting real-estate buildings and other investments."

Does this prove you can't beat the races by *betting* on horses?

WOMEN BOOKIES

Since there are approximately 7,000 female bookies doing business in America today, you might be interested in knowing how members of the fair sex become bookies. I've met at least a hundred bigtime women bookmakers; but let me tell you about the first one I met. The only name I knew her by was Cleo. She operated in a southern resort city and employed about twenty girl runners, mostly showgirls and waitresses. When I asked her how she became a bookie, I got this story:

"Several years ago I was working as a waitress in one of the top restaurants in town and, like the rest of the girls, I used to bet a few bucks each day on the horses. I was giving my horse bets to one of my customers, a guy named Charlie who was a bookmaker. I also got the other waitresses to give me their bets, and passed them on to him. I wasn't getting paid for picking up these other bets, but Charlie seemed to be a nice guy and almost always left me a two-dollar tip every day with his cup of coffee. So, you see, I didn't mind doing him a favor.

"Then one day Charlie didn't show, and I couldn't give him the girls' horse bets. When I got through work that afternoon, I went looking for him and couldn't find him. I was worried. I wondered what I should do with the money and betting slips I had collected. I was scared, too. What if the horses the girls bet on won and paid a big price? I couldn't pay off. And I was sure the girls wouldn't believe me if I told them the bookie had disappeared.

"Well, that night I listened to the race results on the radio and checked my slips. Out of the twenty horses the girls bet on, not one horse won. It was the first time I was happy that the girls lost. I had collected a hundred and eighty dollars. Well, I just figured that if the girls had won I would have had to pay them, and since they lost, the money belonged to me.

"The next day I collected the bets again, and Charlie didn't come in again. As a matter of fact, he still hasn't showed up, and this happened five years ago. At the end of the first year I made a ten-thousand-dollar profit by just collecting bets from the waitresses. So I decided to quit my job as a waitress and go into the bookie business, and here I am. Today I buy a new Cadillac car every six months and have more money than I ever dreamed I would have, thanks to my Charlie, the book-maker who never showed up."

Cleo's *book* (total sum wagered) is now one of the biggest books in this southern city and averages about $25,000 a day. She employs about 40 runners, mostly women. Hundreds of players have become bookmakers in much the same manner as Cleo did, and it's still as simple as that today. It wasn't quite that easy before the introduction of the pari-mutuel system of betting, when the bookie had to know how to make his own payoff prices before the race. But now anyone can become a bookmaker, provided he gets an okay from the local political or racket boss and is willing to run the risk of being arrested. All a woman needs is the okay to run and a few hundred dollars to start her book, a number of horse bettors and an elementary knowledge of arithmetic.

My survey shows not only that there are at least 7,000 women bookies in business today but that this figure is rapidly increasing. Widows of bookmakers who are used to the easy money often carry on the book when their husbands die.

These bookies all employ at least one runner who picks up the bets from the players, pays off the winners and collects from the losers the following day. I estimate that in the city of New York there are at least 5,000 women who are part-time runners or agents. They are employed as waitresses, receptionists in office buildings, elevator operators, fac-tory workers, salesladies and so on. They simply collect bets from their co-workers and other horse players and telephone them in to the book-makers. For this service, the runners receive 50% of the weekly profit which is made from the bets they call in. If the runner's total bets show a loss for the week, she receives nothing.

A bigtime male bookie recently told me that he paid a girl agent who was employed as a $125-a-week secretary the sum of $20,000 just for calling in her boss's horse bets. Her boss is the owner of one of the nation's largest firms manufacturing men's clothing. The girl thought she was smart. She insisted on 10% of her boss's losses, which amounted to $200,000 in one year. "It was a good deal for the secretary," the bookie explained, "and as for me, well I just wish I had a couple of more 'smart' gals like that working for me. If she hadn't insisted on that ten percent, she would have gotten the usual fifty percent and made a hundred thousand dollars profit for the year!"

HORSE MOBS WHO CHEAT BOOKMAKERS

For years bookmakers have been cheated out of large sums of money by crooked horse bettors working in groups of two, three or more cheaters. They are known to the trade as *horse mobs* or *past posters*.

Such betting cheats are not as common today as they were before the passage, in 1951, of the law prohibiting the interstate wire-service transmission of last-minute racing information. This law closed a great many horse rooms, but there are still thousands in various sections of the country which receive wire-service running descriptions of the races run at one specified track in the country, and last-minute racing information (such as the results, off time, mutuels and post time) from the races run at other major tracks in the United States. Posted on the walls of many of these horse offices you'll see the Federal $50 yearly license stamp which, with the payment of 10% of the amount of each wager made, is in accordance with Federal laws enacted in 1951. Establishments possessing stamps, as a rule, compel the winning player to pay the 10% Federal tax. They pay the tax on the players' losing bets.

Although track officials do not send out race results until all the races have been run or permit anyone else within the track's enclosure to do so, horse mobs and racing services manage to get the information and supply bookmakers with the results a few minutes after a race. Some racing services even supply a running description of each race to bookmakers by making use of the facilities of Western Union Telegraph Company and the American Telephone and Telegraph Company.

A few years ago, the Florida State Racing Commission suspended the license of Tropical Park, one of the country's outstanding racetracks, because its operator allegedly made over a hundred phone calls from his office at the track to a Midwestern bookmaker during racing hours. Later that year the Florida courts lifted the suspension. Reason given: The penalty for such a violation was too severe.

The racing services and horse mobs have many ingenious methods of getting this valuable information fast. Here are a few.

1. They use a miniature radio-broadcasting set small enough to be carried in a woman's handbag or on an agent's body. A confederate with a receiving set is parked in a truck or car just outside the track, and the broadcast information is relayed by phone to a central office from which it is forwarded by coded wire or telephone to its final

destination. Many persons have been arrested at racetracks for signaling. Frequently someone is arrested simply for carrying a miniature radio-broadcasting set. In nearly all such cases which have come to my attention a woman was involved.

2. Visual signaling systems are also used to transmit the information to a confederate who watches from outside the track with powerful binoculars.

3. One of the commonest methods, and one that is difficult to stop, is for a runner to leave the track with the information immediately after each race and relay it to a confederate on the outside.

Horse mobs try to beat the racing services to this information and, when they succeed, can often beat the bookmaker for large sums of money. If they can't get the information first, they use other methods. Here is the way the Whitey Mob, which operated in and around Chicago, worked.

The mob rented a room as near as possible to a horse room, located the phone wire going into the horse room and tapped into it, running a wire back to their own room. When the race results began coming in, the mob diverted the call to themselves and made a tape recording of it. The race results were then relayed by courier, telephone or prearranged signal such as the blowing of an automobile horn to a member of the mob posing as a horse bettor in the bookmaking room. Upon receipt of the race result, the confederate put a sizable bet on the winner. A few minutes later the mob played the tape recording into the telephone and let the horse room have the results. The delay made a sure-thing bet possible and the bookie lost a tidy sum of cash.

These mobs are always on the lookout for races which are run off several minutes before the scheduled time listed in the racing sheets. This sometimes happens on rainy or foggy days when the weather is threatening to get worse. Racing officials, trying to beat the bad weather, may allow a race to start a few minutes before the advertised starting time.

The same situation occasionally occurs before a stake race which is to be nationally televised. The previous race may have to be run off a few minutes before scheduled time to ensure that the televised race isn't late for the cameras.

Thousands of bookmakers have been fleeced out of hundreds of thousands of dollars by accepting bets on races that have been run off a minute or more before the time listed in the racing sheets. Bookmakers who don't subscribe to a racing service are the most probable victims. Smart bookies, when they accept a bet at post time, protect themselves by giving the player a *time bet*. This is an agreement that the bet is valid at the exact time of making. Thus, if the player gives a bookie a bet at 3:15 P.M. on Teeko at Bowie, and later information shows that the race was run off earlier, the bet is off.

The most ingenious system for fleecing bookmakers that has come to my attention was employed by the Blondie Mob, so called because the members were five attractive-looking girls, all blondes, ranging in age from twenty-three to thirty-five. How much money these girls stole is anybody's guess. Some gamblers place the figure at a million dollars, others at two million dollars. I know for sure that they fleeced one bookmaker out of $100,000.

As a gambling authority and consultant, I am sought after by law-enforcement agencies, governments where gambling is legal, private clubs and organizations, and individuals who have lost large sums of money and believe they have been cheated but don't know exactly how. My policy is not to accept assignments from gamblers who operate illegally, but I did accept this one because of its peculiar circumstances and the challenge it offered.

The incident goes back a number of years, I was in Los Angeles, having just returned from a tour of Army camps in Alaska, where I had been lecturing to GIs. The telephone in my hotel room rang one day and a voice said, "Mr. Scarne, my name is ———. I wonder if you are available to take on a gambling assignment?" (Let's call the man Mr. Quinn, since that wasn't his name.)

I told him I might be if the price was right and if it interested me. An hour later, I entered a penthouse apartment in one of Hollywood's most fashionable districts. A butler opened the door, and I followed him into the study where Mr. Quinn waited. I recognized him instantly as one of the top bookmakers on the West Coast. He was far more intelligent than most bookies. I guessed by his speech that he had had an accountant's training but had realized that he could make more and easier money as a bookmaker.

"Scarne," he said, "I handle one of the biggest books on the West Coast. My daily handle is seldom less than $30,000 and I think I know the ins and outs of the business, but I have a question. Do you think it is possible for a woman horse bettor to be so lucky she can overcome a bookmaker's percentage and win $100,000 within a four-week period?"

"A woman horse player has beaten you for $100,000 in four weeks?"

"That's correct. After she won $50,000, I began to think that maybe it wasn't just luck. Maybe she's just plain smart and has some angle for beating the races that really works, and maybe not. I have a special room in this apartment, but only big bettors are ever invited into it—and the girl is one of them."

I followed him across the large living room and through a door into a well-equipped bookmaking room. It had all the standard paraphernalia: an adding machine, betting slips, racing sheets, ledger, telephone, table and several comfortable chairs. Quinn said, "This room is on the top floor of the building. It's air-conditioned and soundproof and has no windows. What's more, my players must arrive here before post time. After post time, no one is allowed off the elevator at this floor until after the last race. I don't see how anyone in this room can get any information from outside. The bettors are not permitted to make or receive phone calls while they are here, and the phone number is not listed. If Blondie is getting information, I want to know how."

I told Quinn that my policy is not to make investigations for gamblers or gambling casinos operating outside the law. "But," I said "I'm as curious now as you are, so I'm going to try to find out what's happening. If Blondie is cheating, she may be the smartest cheater I've ever seen."

The next afternoon found me scanning a scratch sheet in Mr. Quinn's luxurious bookmaking parlor. Several of his bigtime customers were there, including the smartly dressed and attractive Blondie. I could see at once that she didn't have a radio-receiving gimmick on her; the low-necked dress she wore was a tight fit and no room to spare.

When the races were over, Blondie was a $2,000 winner. After she and the other bettors had gone, Mr. Quinn turned to me and asked, "Well, is she lucky or smart?"

I smiled. "She's smart. She's been past-posting you, and the guy who has been tipping her off is you!"

"Me?" he exclaimed. "That's impossible!"

"I don't think so. When Blondie gave you that $300 straight win bet on High Noon in the third race at Hialeah Park it was already a couple of minutes after post time."

"So what? I let my bettors put bets down a few minutes after post in this room all the time. As a matter of fact, I don't even bother to look at the clock. When I get the results of a race over the telephone from my main office, I stop taking bets, but not until then. How could she get the name of the winner in this soundproofed room? If a bomb exploded across the street, you couldn't hear it in here."

"Like this," I replied. "Blondie knew that the third race at Hialeah Park had been run and she got a coded signal from a confederate on the outside. A confederate who relayed the dope through you. Her confederate is the person who called in the bet on Snow Shoes in the eighth race at Hialeah."

Mr. Quinn immediately turned to the table and scanned his ledger.

"That was May, another blonde! But I still don't get the whole gimmick."

"May called in quite a number of bets, didn't she?"

"Yes, but what has the Snow Shoes bet in the eighth got to do with the bet on High Noon in the third race?"

"May is operating from a room that has a direct line from one of the wire services. She gets the results of the race a minute or so after the race is over. As soon as she knew High Noon had won the third race she phoned and gave you a bet of 50, 20 and 10 on Snow Shoes in the eighth, and she asked you to repeat it, which you did. Blondie heard you say, 'You bet me 50, 20 and 10 on Snow Shoes in the eighth at Hialeah.' And Blondie simply added the first digits of the amount of the bet, got an answer of 8 and knew that the horse listed as number 8 on her scratch sheet had won the third race. What is number 8 on Blondie's and your scratch sheet?"

Quinn looked at it. "It's High Noon! Okay, that's it."

I learned from Quinn that there were five blondes in the mob and that before they took him many of the other bookies in the Los Angeles area had gotten the same treatment.

I don't know what happened to the Blondie Mob; I do know that they had a real sweet gimmick and worked it more expertly than any male mob of cheaters that has ever come to my attention.*

THE INSIDE OPERATION OF A BOOKMAKER

If you are betting at the track, it makes no difference to the track operators which horses you bet or which horses win. The pari-mutuel scheme of betting always guarantees the state and the track operators their legal percentage. It isn't that simple for the bookie. If too many of his customers bet on the horse that wins, he loses money on that race. If most of his customers bet on losers and nobody bets on the eventual winner, the bookie cleans up.

In general, a bookie pays the winner of a win, place or show bet exactly what he would have collected if he had placed his bet at the racetrack. But this doesn't mean the off-track bookie collects the same percentage of profit the track does. That would happen only if the bookie had wagers on all horses in a race in the same proportions as the wagers made at the racetrack.

In theory, that is the basis of a successful bookie operation. In practice, it seldom happens, because the bulk of the off-track money is rarely bet on more than one, two or three horses in the same race. This

---

* High Noon and Snow Shoes were not the actual names of the horses involved.

brings up a question which, to this author's knowledge, has never before been discussed in print.

How does an off-track bookie's percentage edge compare with the track's total percentage deduction from the gross betting handle of a race? And which is greater?

We cannot get this answer by using probability theory math as we can with questions concerning dice or cards. Racing is a horse of another color. Every horse race is different, and there are too many unknown and variable factors to consider.

Off-track bookmaking also has many variable factors that affect the bookie's percentage of profit. He may take a bet on a horse that is eventually pulled by the jockey. In such an instance the bookie keeps 100% of the bet. Or he may accept a bet on a horse that has been heavily overplayed by the track bettors; if the horse wins, the bookie's profit may run as high as 80%.

What takes place in a race can't change the percentage take at the track, but it can change the bookie's P.C.

A $2 bet can't hurt a bookie, but a $500 bet may knock him out of business. The track welcomes both bets with open arms. It doesn't care how good a handicapper a bettor may be; he is treated the same as a dub or a hunch player. They both supply an equal profit to the track. The average horse player or hunch player holds no danger for the bookie, but he must be extra careful in handling a good handicapper's bet. The inexperienced horse bettor pays the bookie a greater rate of profit than does a good student of horse racing. Most smart bigtime bettors place their big action with bookies rather than at the track, because they don't want to lower the mutuel payoff price.

Since this author never says die, I set out to solve this bookmaking percentage problem in the only way possible—by making use of the old, reliable clocking system.

My clocking experiment consisted of studying the yearly bookkeeping records of 300 bookmakers operating in various sections of the country, one third belonging to the smalltime bookies, one third to the fair-sized bookies and one third to the bigtime bookies. I found that the average smalltime bookie retains about 18% of his yearly gross handle as winnings; the average fair-sized bookie retains about 10%; and the average bigtime bookie retains about 5% of his yearly gross handle as winnings.

This sampling indicates that the off-track bookie's average percentage of winnings in this country is 10%. The cut deducted by the parimutuel system of betting in the 30 states where track betting is permitted is as follows: The combined state and track percentage take at thoroughbred racing runs from a low 12% in the states of Delaware, Maryland, Nebraska and South Dakota to a high of 17% in the state of Maine. At harness racing it runs from a low 12½ to 15% in the state of Oregon to a high of 20% in Kentucky. At quarter-horse and fair racing it runs from a low 12% in Maryland to a high of 17½% in Ohio. And so it goes from state to state.

A bookie always hopes that all his customers will place bets on each horse in the same race in such a way that his total payoff to the winners will be the same, no matter which horses finish in the money.

This will assure the bookie his expected percentage because he is bound to pay out less than he collected. I am assuming that a favorite won and the bookie pays off at track odds and doesn't have to resort to his maximum payoff limit. When this occurs, his cut is much greater on the race than that of the track and state.

Of course, the bookie's favorable percentage always earns money for him over a period of time even if all customers bet the same horse in each race, or even the same horses in every race at every track. The bookie loses money to one race, wins to another, but, in the long run, his favorable P.C. is sure to earn money.

The smart bookie, however, tries to protect himself against heavy losses on any one race by putting a limit on his possible losses. This is known as his *extension* and is determined by the size of his book or bankroll, or the way he happens to feel that day. It may run from a low $50 to a high of $25,000 or more on a single horse. The bookie uses two methods of staying within his extension.

1. Once the bookie's betting extension has been reached on a horse, he can refuse any further wagers on that horse merely by informing would-be bettors that he is loaded and won't take any further action on the horse, or, for that matter, on the race.

2. He can accept all wagers and lay them off with a rival or larger book. This layoff process continues until it reaches a top-level bookie who has a representative at a phone near the track. He phones his man and tells him to bet the excess action at the mutuel windows. This does two things: it keeps the top-level bookie within his own extension and, if the amount bet is big enough, it brings the price down, so that if the horse wins, all the bookies pay a smaller mutuel price on the winner.

The small bookie can't always lay off his action with a big book. Sometimes the big bookie is also loaded with bets on the same horse and he may refuse to accept the action. When this happens, the small bookie can do only one thing. He prays that the horse which has the excess action loses. Prayers on a matter of this kind don't always get results, which is still another reason for those stomach ulcers mentioned earlier.

In other gambling activities the operator usually takes a greater P.C. from the small or inexperienced bettor than from the big or experienced gambler. A smart bookie, on the other hand, arranges his maximum payoff limit on a win, place and show bet so that the big bettor gets a lower maximum payoff limit than the small bettor. The bookie is not doing this just to be nice to the small bettor. The bookie figures it this way. A $2 or $5 bettor is almost always a hunch player and a sucker. He knows little or nothing about racing and makes his same $2 bet day after day. His bets are so small that they can't hurt the bookie. But the big bettor is too often a spot bettor who has some sort of inside information, and the bookie protects himself by shortening his maximum payoff limit.

Here are the standard payoff limits most bookie in the United States offer. If you bet $2 to $25 on a horse to win, place or show, the bookie's maximum payoff limit is 30, 10 and 5. This means that the limit payoff is 30 to 1 on a win bet, 10 to 1 on a place bet and 5 to 1 on a show bet. It makes no difference how much higher the track odds may be— 30, 10 and 5 is all the bookie will give you. If your bet is $100 to win, place or show, the bookie's limit payoff will shrink to 20, 8 and 4. Should you bet anywhere from $200 to $20,000 to win, place or show, you are lucky if your bookie quotes you a payoff limit of 15, 6 and 3.

The payoff limits of 30–10–5, or whatever they happen to be, apply to all bets, straight or contingents. These 30–10–5 limits cut down the player's winnings. Suppose the results and the track payoff prices for a race which was won by a long shot are as follows:

	WIN	PLACE	SHOW
Teeko	$66.00	$26.40	$16.20
Moko		10.40	6.50
Scarney			5.60

If you placed your $2 bet on Teeko at the track to win, you collected $66. If you bet the $2 with an Eastern bookmaker, you would only get $62. For a $2 place bet on Teeko, the track payoff would be $26.40 against the bookmaker's $22. On a $2 show bet the track payoff would be $16.20 against the bookmaker's $12. On Moko and Scarney, the track's and the bookmaker's payoff would be the same.

This proves that the bookie often takes a greater P.C. than the track. He says he is justified because he runs the risk of being arrested and jailed.

Many bookmakers will pay you the track mutuel on winning long shots if you insure your bet by paying an additional 10% of the total bet.

Straight betting and betting the daily double, quinielas, exactas, triples and other exotic bets are permitted at the pari-mutuel windows; the totalisator is not mechanically geared to handle anything else.

The bookie has no such mechanical limitations; he will also handle parlays, round robins, "if" money bets, reverse and back-to-back bets and insurance bets. I analyze these below. I don't consider the ability of the horses, but merely discuss the mathematical and deceptive aspects of these bets.

1. The parlay: This involves betting two or more horses with one stake. The horses are in different races and may even be at different racetracks. There are win, place and show parlays. To play a *win two-horse parlay*, the bettor picks two horses to win, Horse A in any race or on any track, and Horse B in any race or on any track except the race in which the first horse is entered. If either horse fails to win, the parlay is lost. If both horses win, the parlay is won. The same holds true for a place or show parlay.

One reason I consider the parlay to be a sucker bet is because I doubt that there is a horse player in the country so successful in picking winners that he is justified in trying to pick two winners at the same time. The more horses in the parlay, the more foolish the bet. Three-, four- and five-horse parlays are simply ridiculous.

Now look at the mathematics of a parlay. Bookmakers in the East state that they pay odds of 50 to 1 across the board on any parlay, win, place or show, and their maximum payoff odds are 50 to 1, or $102 for a $2 bet. Do they pay off as advertised? Well, not all the time. Hidden in that "50 to 1 across the board" statement is some misdirection and some chicanery.

Let us recall the fact that the straight payoff prices on any winner cannot exceed 30–10–5. How then can a two-horse show parlay ever figure to pay odds of 50 to 1? The best price a bookie will pay off on a show bet is 5 to 1. If the payoff price on one or both horses exceeds the 5 to 1 odds, the best the bettor can collect is 25 to 1 plus his original bet. The "50 to 1 odds across the board" statement is pure misrepresentation.

Compare a $2 wager on a three-horse parlay to win with three straight bets to win—Teeko in the first race, Scarney in the third race and Moko in the fifth race. Suppose these three horses came in the money. The track mutuel payoffs are as shown on page 83.

If you had $2 riding on the above three-horse win parlay at odds of 50 to 1 you would collect $102 for your $2 bet. Not bad. But suppose you wagered $2 on Teeko in the first race to win. You would collect $20 for your $2. And if you bet the $20 on Scarney in the third race to

	WIN	PLACE	SHOW
1st Race			
Teeko	$20.00	$18.40	$ 8.40
Merlini		4.40	2.40
Lucky Stiff			4.60
3rd Race			
Scarney	16.00	8.40	4.40
Hal Leroy		10.60	5.40
Prince Charmer			8.80
5th Race			
Moko	10.00	8.20	3.20
Peaches		9.60	4.60
Ripe Apple			10.40

win, you'd collect $160. If you wagered the $160 on Moko to win the fifth race, your winnings would total $800. Isn't this better than the $102 you collected for picking the same three winners in a three-horse parlay?

If you still insist on playing parlays after reading this, you should at least know how to calculate your own payoff prices to avoid being short-changed by a bookmaker or some friend you ask to figure the parlay for you. To get the payoff price on a two-horse parlay, simply multiply the individual mutuel payoff prices together and divide the total by 2. Example: If Horse A pays $10.40 and Horse B pays $6.40, the correct payoff is $10.40 × $6.40, divided by 2, or $33.28. To calculate a three-horse parlay, multiply the three mutuel payoff prices together and divide by 4, and on a four-horse parlay, multiply the four payoff prices together and divide by 8.

If you wish to avoid some division, do as most bookies do. Multiply one mutuel price by half the payoff price of the other. Example: Horse A pays $10.40 and Horse B pays $6.40; multiply $10.40 by $3.20 (half of the payoff price of Horse B); result: $33.28. To figure the payoff price of a three-horse parlay, halve two of the mutuels and multiply the two results by the third mutuel price, etc.

2. Round robin: This involves the playing of all possible two-horse parlays on three or more horses. Thus, a three-horse round robin is three two-horse parlays. A four-horse round robin is six two-horse parlays. If a parlay is foolish, this is more so.

3. "If" money bets: Here you place a fixed amount unconditionally on a horse, then stipulate that if this horse wins, another fixed amount shall be wagered on another horse or horses. This type of bet, as in the case of parlays, round robins, etc., is an attempt by the player to multiply the winnings of a small stake. Actually you are simply making two bets instead of one and giving the bookmaker more profit percentage-wise.

4. Reverse and back to back: This is merely a double "if" bet and the player must put up two cash bets on two horses instead of one. Example: A player wagers $2 on Horse A, then "ifs" $4 on Horse B, then wagers $2 on Horse B and "ifs" $4 on Horse A. You could call it two "if" bets in reverse. Again the bookmaker earns more percent-agewise than on a single bet.

Although round robins and back-to-back bets give the bookie a greater P.C. than a straight win, place or show bet, many bookies re-fuse to handle such bets because they prefer to limit a player's winnings and don't want to risk a big money payoff.

5. Daily double: Since the daily double is the best bet at the race-track because the daily double pool is a separate entity and the track and state percentage deductions are taken off the entire pool rather than individual races, one would think that the bookies would pay bigger odds on a daily double than on a two-horse win parlay.

Most bookies know that the track and state take a smaller cut out of a daily double than a bookie gets from a two-horse win parlay. But they ignore this and, as a rule, pay 75 to 1 on daily doubles and only 50 to 1 on two-horse win parlays.

Bookies figure it this way: in a daily double, players must pick the winners in the first and second races at the same racetrack—races usually run by poor horses. In a two-horse parlay the player may pick two horses from any race at any racetrack and thus has more chance to pick better horses. As you can see, bookies don't overlook anything in their favor.

Bookies as a rule refuse to accept bets on quinielas, exactas, triples and similar one-race horse parlays. The reason is that they know of many single races that have been fixed.

SCARNE'S ADVICE ON BETTING THE RACES

It should be obvious by now that "beating the horses" or rather "beating the state and track percentage deductions" is an impossibility in the long run. Track officials I interviewed all agreed that the track-goer should get a better run for his money. There isn't anything they can do as long as racing remains the country's most heavily taxed sport or gambling activity. The heavy taxation, in turn, helps the illegal off-track bookie to earn billions of dollars annually because when he pays off at track odds he is also collecting a similar heavy tax.

The state of New York demands a 10% tax cut (9% at the Saratoga track) plus 60% of the breakage (50% at Saratoga) at flat tracks and from 5% to 11% plus half the breakage at harness tracks within its borders. From the flat track's cut of 5% plus 50% to 60% of the breakage, plus part of the paid admissions, the operators must invest millions of dollars to build tracks, spend thousands daily for upkeep and maintenance and pay out thousands daily in purses. If you want to blame someone other than yourself for losing your shirt on the horses, you could blame the state.

If you are one of the millions who go to the tracks to bet the horses for fun, remember that you must pay for the privilege. How much you pay is entirely up to you. If you want to keep the price down to what you think the entertainment is worth and what you can afford, here is a good system: Before leaving home, decide how much you want to spend (bet), add the track admission price, the price of a program, an allowance for refreshments and the price of your transportation. The total is your budget. Take this amount with you and no more, so that if you lose you won't be tempted to recoup your losses and lose more than you planned.

Then bet the favorite to *show*. Forget about *win* and *place* bets. I don't say that this advice will win you any money, but it will cut down your losses.

I don't recommend off-track betting with a bookmaker, but if you can't resist the urge, also add these rules:

1. Bet cash only, never on credit; the temptation to bet beyond your means in trying to recoup your losses is too difficult for most people to resist. Credit betting ruins more gamblers than anything else. Remember that "money you don't have on you, you can't lose."

2. Bet on a horse running at a track where the state and track percentage cut is the smallest, because if you win, the mutuel payoff price will be more.

3. Make as few bets as possible so that the money wagered, if lost, won't disturb you mentally.

4. Bet your horse to show if you can. (Some bookie won't accept a show bet unless it is accompanied by a win or place bet of equal money.)

5. Stay away from parlays, "if" money and back-to-back bets.

6. Always remember that when you pick a winner, you were lucky; it wasn't good handicapping. And don't forget that "you can beat a race, but not the races."

SCARNE'S ADVICE ON "EXOTIC" PARI-MUTUEL BETS

Most racetracks in America have eliminated the combination win, place and show ticket and have replaced it with a combination win and place ticket. This confirms what I have been saying for years, that a show bet is the best possible race bet. However, you still can find a show betting window at the track if you look around.

Many new signs are posted above the betting windows advising you of the many exotic wagers available at the track: the daily double, exacta, triple and similar wagers called various other names at different tracks. I would not consider these two- and three-horse combination bets displayed at modern track betting windows as sucker bets if the player makes just one such bet on any specific race because each of these exotic wagers goes into a separate pool and the state and track's take including breakage (17% in New York State) are taken off the pari-mutuel handle. In short, a player pays the same percentage charge when making an exotic bet as making a win, place or show bet. But when the player starts "wheeling" these exotic bets by making six or more combination bets in one race, then he's placing sucker bets because he is paying 17% on each multiple bet made. For example, a bettor might "wheel" the daily double. That is, he will take a horse listed 1 on his program in the first race that he rates as a possible winner and combine it with every other horse in the second race. Thus, if the second race is made up of eight horses, he makes the following bets:

1ST RACE	2ND RACE	1ST RACE	2ND RACE
Horse 1—Horse 1		Horse 1—Horse 5	
Horse 1—Horse 2		Horse 1—Horse 6	
Horse 1—Horse 3		Horse 1—Horse 7	
Horse 1—Horse 4		Horse 1—Horse 8	

If he purchases eight $2 daily double tickets, the "wheel" will cost him $16.

On the other hand, if a bettor "criss-crosses" the daily double, he is taking several horses in each race and betting every possible combination of those horses. For instance, if a bettor likes Horses 2, 3, 4 in the first race at Aqueduct and horses 4, 5, 6, 7 in the second race, he can "criss-cross" these horses and get the following bets:

1ST RACE	2ND RACE	1ST RACE	2ND RACE	1ST RACE	2ND RACE
Horse 2—Horse 4		Horse 3—Horse 4		Horse 4—Horse 4	
Horse 2—Horse 5		Horse 3—Horse 5		Horse 4—Horse 5	
Horse 2—Horse 6		Horse 3—Horse 6		Horse 4—Horse 6	
Horse 2—Horse 7		Horse 3—Horse 7		Horse 4—Horse 7	

If he buys $2 daily double tickets, the "criss-cross" will cost him $24.

Many race bettors feel they can pick the two most likely winners in a given race but are not certain which will beat the other; thus, they will often "put one horse on top" and then "reverse" this, putting the other horse "on top." That is, if a bettor has narrowed his choices down to Horses 4 and 6 in the exacta in the fourth race at Aqueduct and isn't sure which horse will win, he can "reverse" the exacta and get the following bets: Horse 4—Horse 6 and Horse 6—Horse 4. If he buys $2 exacta tickets, the "reverse" will cost him $4.

If a bettor "boxes" an exacta, he is taking several horses in the race and betting every possible combination of those horses. In other words, if a bettor likes Horses 1, 2 and 3 in the exacta in the fourth race at Aqueduct, he can "box" the exacta and get the following bets:

Horse 1—Horse 2	Horse 2—Horse 1	Horse 3—Horse 1
Horse 1—Horse 3	Horse 2—Horse 3	Horse 3—Horse 2

If he buys $2 exacta tickets, the "box" will cost him $12.

Of course, it is possible to "wheel" a horse in the exacta. You can either wheel a horse "on top" (that is, to win) or on the "bottom" (that is, to come in second), or both. For example, if a bettor likes Horse 2 in the exacta in the fourth race at Aqueduct, but doesn't think he will quite win, he can "wheel" him "on the bottom" with every other horse is the race and get the following bets:

Horse 1—Horse 2	Horse 6—Horse 2	Horse 10—Horse 2
Horse 3—Horse 2	Horse 7—Horse 2	Horse 11—Horse 2
Horse 4—Horse 2	Horse 8—Horse 2	Horse 12—Horse 2
Horse 5—Horse 2	Horse 9—Horse 2	

If he buys $2 exacta tickets, the "wheel" will cost him $22.

Another exotic track wager is the triple. The smallest triple wager permitted at the track is $3. A special track betting window accepts a triple three-horse box. A triple three-horse box permits the player to select three horses in the race and should the three run win, place and show, in any order, he collects the winnings allocated to one $3 parimutuel ticket. This triple three-horse box is nothing more than a track gimmick to get the player to bet the six possible combinations for a total of $18. Example: A three-horse box combination made up of horses 2, 3 and 7 is as follows:

Horses 2–3–7	Horses 3–7–2	Horses 7–3–2
Horses 2–7–3	Horses 3–2–7	Horses 7–2–3

The most costly gimmick bet is to "box" a superfecta. This is nothing more than to bet on several combinations of the same horses. First the player selects the horse to finish first and "wheels" it with all combinations of three other horses to come in second, third and fourth. That is, if the bettor likes Horse 2 to win in the superfecta race and he likes Horses 3, 6 and 9 to finish in some order of second, third and fourth, he can bet Horse 2 as the key horse. The bettor purchases tickets on:

Horses 2–3–6–9	Horses 2–6–3–9	Horses 2–9–3–6
Horses 2–3–9–6	Horses 2–6–9–3	Horses 2–9–6–3

If the bettor plays $3 superfectas, this bet will cost him $18. If however, he wants to bet all combinations of Horses 2, 3, 6 and 9 with one of them winning and the others finishing second, third and fourth, he can "box" all four for $72. This, of course, is the same as four separate boxes.

If you wished to bet on all possible winning combinations in an eight-horse race, you would have to make 1,680 possible bets at $3 each for a total of $5,040 wagered. This would ensure your having a $3 winning ticket on the superfecta.

A recent grand jury investigation of a major New York harness track intimated that considerable skulduggery was taking place in superfecta betting by horse owners, trainers and jockeys. For example, if four horses in an eight-horse race are held back, the number of possible winning tickets is reduced from 1680 to $4 \times 3 \times 2 \times 1 = 24$. At $3 a ticket, $72 will ensure a superfecta winner. (The largest superfecta payoff for a $3 ticket was $111,912 on April 21, 1972, at Yonkers Harness Raceway in New York.)

Another group of racing crooks are called *10 percenters*. Since winnings of $600 or more for a $2 winning ticket must be reported to the Internal Revenue Service, there are mobsters or mob members who will collect a player's big race winnings for a 10% charge. The 10 percenters have scouts at the track who try to ascertain the big winner or winners of daily doubles, exactas and superfectas. They then try to make a deal to collect, let's say a $65,000 superfecta win for $6,500. They have a stooge sign his name and social security number when collecting the superfecta winning. They pay him $1,000 or so, and keep the remainder of the 10% due them. However, I know of a number of instances where the superfecta winners were foolish enough to hand over their winning tickets to one of these mobsters, only to find that instead of the agreed upon deal, the mobster scrammed with the entire superfecta winnings. Should you be one of the lucky ones to win a large sum of money at the track and some 10 percenter approaches you to make a deal, tell him in no uncertain terms to get lost. It is to your advantage to report your winnings and race losses to the Internal Revenue Service when filing your annual income tax return. Most major tracks, in order to aid the Internal Revenue Service and rid the tracks of these 10 percenters, have ruled that any winning daily double, exacta, triple or superfecta ticket whose payoff is $5,000 or more will be paid by check.

One of my main objections to superfecta and twin double wagering is that these bets are a simple and sure way to encourage and reward dishonesty at the track. Scandalous revelations about the activities of twin double and superfecta betting syndicates at Florida and New York tracks have made that particular pari-mutuel wrinkle persona non grata at most major racetracks. This also holds true for superfecta wagering.

The 5–6 sweepstake pool is the only exotic racing wager that cannot be rigged. It's impossible, no matter how many racing crooks are involved, to rig six consecutive races and get away with it.

My advice, therefore, is *not* to wheel, box or key bet the exotic bets. Play these bets one at a time, betting only on your number one selection.

LEGALIZED OFF-TRACK BETTING VS. THE ILLEGAL BOOKIE

The persistent growth of the illegal bookmaking industry, in spite of the recent all-out efforts of Federal and state governments to suppress it, is definite proof that the millions and millions of Americans who bet the horses are not in sympathy with the present anti-bookmaking statutes.

The public's disregard for these prohibitory gambling laws is understandable when we consider that 30 states, by virtue of their participation in the track's profits, seem hypocritical to the general public, especially the horse player. When the horse bettor places a wager at the track he is a good guy who is helping the state financially; his action is not only legal but encouraged. But as soon as he places an off-track bet with an illegal bookie, he is a crook and a bum. If you want to draw conclusions from that double morality situation, go ahead; I'm just giving you the facts.

Department of further confusion: In 1951 the Federal government, which has taken a stand against off-track bookies, joined them as a business partner when Congress passed the law that requires horse and sports bookies and other gamblers to buy a $50 gambling stamp and pay a 10% excise tax on their gross receipts.

All previous Federal and state attempts to suppress illegal bookmaking have failed. Twenty million horse players continue to bet with their bookies whenever they feel like it, just as millions of Americans patronized their bootleggers during Prohibition. That crime problem was solved by making the sale of liquor legal, but illegal bookmaking is a horse of a different color, which can't be easily changed.

If society really wants to eliminate illegal off-track race betting, a simple but drastic way would be to enact legislation prohibiting horse tracks; an illegal horse track would be tough to operate because it would be much too big to hide. The possibility that this will ever be done is very remote.

The solution for illegal bookmaking most often suggested is that the American bookie should be legalized and his business taxed. Would this work? A good many legislators are asking themselves this question, and it may be you, as a voter, who will have to make the decision. Most legislators and voters simply do not have enough facts about gambling at hand to make an intelligent decision. I have an opinion which, since I have studied gamblers and gambling all my life, is, I believe, an informed opinion. Before I state it, let us look at some of the factors on which it is based. Let us take a closer look first at the present relationship between the politicians, the law-enforcement agencies, the bookies and the racket guys; and then let us examine legalized bookmaking in the countries where it now exists.

PROTECTION AND GRAFT

No other form of illegal gambling in this country enjoys so much and such effective police and political protection as illegal bookmaking. A weekly payment buys protection that allows the bookie to operate most of the time without interference by law-enforcement agencies. It also ensure that the cops pay no attention to complaints of irate non-paying competitors, reform groups and state watchdog committees. This protection is more efficient than it is in most other forms of gambling activity because a bookie operation can be more easily hidden from public view. A small room and a telephone are all most bookies need to conduct business; some operate without even that.

The amount of ice paid by the bookie and the number of recipients of such graft vary considerably according to the size of the town. In small towns and villages where the political machine dominates the scene, the machine boss has his *iceman* who collects protection pay-offs. Sometimes the ice is only split two ways—between the political boss and the chief of police—but the county boss, sheriff and county prosecutor usually get their cuts. Even if they don't collect in cash they close their eyes to the situation for political reasons.

Small communities near big cities are favorite locations for the big-time bookies. The protection is stronger in the small town because there are fewer law-enforcement agencies to bother the bookie, and the smalltown iceman doesn't demand as much weekly protection money. During the late forties, a bookie's weekly protection cost was about $450 per phone in New York City as against $250 per phone in suburban areas like Bergen and Passaic counties in New Jersey.

This is why these New Jersey counties became the mecca of New York bookies. A check I made at that time showed about 5,000 New York bookies, plus 1,000 local bookies, were *sitting* in these two counties and accepting bets by phone. Most of the towns had their own local icemen. If the *pollies* (politicians) of the party in power happened to be against the bookie operation, then the okay came from the police department, which had its own iceman. It was the iceman who secured the spot and the phone for the bookie. He'd approach someone who had a phone in his home or shop and give him this pitch: "Joe, you don't use your phone much in the afternoon. If you let one of my bookies use it from one until six P.M. you can pick up an extra fifty dollars per week." Since Joe was picked because his weekly income was only $50 or less, this was always a tempting proposition. If the illegality seemed to worry him, the iceman added, "Forget it. If town officials bother you report to me. The okay comes right from the top." Joe, of course, had to be smart enough not to ask who the top was; if he did the iceman would simply forget the matter on the theory that anyone that nosy couldn't be trusted.

The amount of ice the bookie paid was based on the number of phones he had, at $250 per phone. For years, because about 6,000 phones were being used by bookies, the average citizen in Bergen and Passaic counties found it next to impossible to get a phone installed in his home. Today, judges in Bergen County are trying to atone for its past sins by sending convicted gamblers and bookies to state's prison for one to three years. However, bigtime Bergen County bookies who can afford to pay $450 per phone per week operate in other nearby New Jersey counties in comparative safety.

In large cities throughout the country it is usually the vice squad that collects ice. In New York City the price per week once ran as high as $1,000 per phone, in Chicago $750, in St. Louis $500. And whenever the *heat was on* (pressure by the public, newspapers or politicians) the price of ice jumped. The ice for a horse room ran as high as $5,000 per week, depending on location.

Today as before, there is no good way to beat the ice. Those who try to *sneak* (operate without protection) find themselves being arrested with annoying regularity, and some judge finally assigns them to a rent-free spot in a nice, cool jail. Eventually they either quit the game or pay the ice. Even then the protection sometimes goes sour and the ice-paying bookie winds up in the cooler.

Don't think you can simply contact a member of a big-city vice squad, offer to pay the required ice, and get a bookie okay. You need a real good recommendation that you are a *stand-up guy,* meaning that you won't *squeal* as to who is getting the ice in case you are arrested. From whom does the vice squad find out that you are or are not a stand-up guy? That's right—the local mobsters.

I believe that this situation will continue to exist for a long time—so many people like it the way it is. The corrupt politicians and law-enforcement agencies view legalization with alarm because then there would be no more graft money. Even many politicians and district attorneys who are not on the graft are against legalization, because they would lose the lovely headlines they now get when they make or promise to make drives against gambling at election time—drives which invariably fizzle out.

As soon as one of these drives begins, the cops on the take get word to the bookies that the heat is on. The bookies lay low, that is, go into hiding, or even quit temporarily. The press prints fat headlines announcing the big cleanup on the front pages, runs editorials backing the drive and continues to print the daily racing charts back in the sports section.

There is a shake-up in the police department, a few cops take the rap by being demoted, dismissed or occasionally jailed. There are a few raids and bookie arrests; the bookies play along with the politicians and help make the drive look kosher by agreeing to stand-in arrests, an occupational hazard they know they have to put up with.

When the election is over, the gambling story slips from the front pages, gets lost in the later pages, and finally disappears. The heat is off, and the bookies are open for business again at the same old stands.

Do you think the bookie himself wants legalization to make him an honest citizen? The answer is no. Most bookies, due to prior gambling arrests, would not be able to qualify as state-licensed bookmakers. Those who could would also vote against legalization because it would mean that their records would be open to Federal and state scrutiny—a prospect that no bookie cares to think about.

LEGALIZED OFF-TRACK BETTING IN VARIOUS COUNTRIES

Any reader, before deciding whether off-track betting should be legalized in his state, should know how it works in Great Britain, Australia, New Zealand, France, Ireland and Puerto Rico, and in Nevada and New York City. Here are some facts and figures.

Great Britain: It is estimated that 2% of Britain's gross national product is legally and illegally wagered on horses each year. Off-track bookies in Britain are called *turf accountants* or *betting commissioners*. Prior to May 1, 1961, when the new Betting and Gaming Act of 1960 went into effect, transactions between English bookies and bettors were only permitted by mail or telephone. Bettors could not enter a bookmaking room because such a visit would class it as an illegal "gaming house." The players' betting was all done on credit accounts which were opened with the turf accountant just as we open a charge account with a department store; credit and bank references were required. Non-paying *punters* (bettors) were blacklisted by other bookies and could be ruled off all tracks in England. Cash betting was legal only with bookmakers at the racetrack or at the track betting windows operated by the Racecourse Betting Control Board, which used all its profits for the improvement of racing.

Since millions of British punters did not have credit standings with turf accountants and liked to do their betting privately, they looked up Peter, the illegal bookie who, like his American cousin, would accommodate them.

Even though bookies were licensed and off-track betting was legal, and there was no direct tax on betting, London police, during 1957, arrested 6,405 illegal street bookies, many more than in the city of New York, where protection instead of legalization is the controlling factor.

On July 29, 1960, Queen Elizabeth signed a new Betting and Gaming Act which repealed many of the previous antiquated gaming laws and is designed to come to terms with British gambling as it exists today. The first major British anti-gaming act, part of which was still in force, was passed by Henry VIII in 1541, after bow-and-arrow makers reported that their workers were so addicted to dice and Backgammon that they were not turning out longbows in sufficient numbers. The law Henry authorized was called "An Acte for Mayntenance of Artyllerie and Debarring of Unlawful Games." Since that date, all games of chance have technically been illegal, but "many subtle and crafty persons," as Henry's act called them, continued to evade the law. During the next 400 years a succession of laws was passed aimed at curbing the British passion for gambling, with little effect. During World War II and since, gambling in Britain, law or no law, reached new highs.

The 1960 act endeavors to face this situation realistically and to bring gambling under control by legalizing much of it. Street betting is still illegal and the penalties have been increased, but off-track betting offices, into which anyone over eighteen may go and place bets on horse and dog races, were opened in England, Scotland and Wales as of May 1, 1961. The authorities grant licenses to operators who establish reasonably good character and pay $280 for a bookmaker's permit and $2.80 for a shop license. In London 290 betting shops were opened and 409 in Scotland. A month after the act went into effect, it was reported that the total number of betting shops in Britain was between 5,000 and 10,000.

Gambling in private dwelling houses with cards, dice and other gambling devices is also permitted, provided no professional game operator is involved and the player is not charged for making use of the gambling facilities. The act also specifies that all players must have an equal chance of winning. This last obviously refers to banking games of chance and means that payoffs must be made at the correct odds so that there is no favorable percentage for the house. In card and dice games in which skill is an important factor the less skilled player obviously cannot have an equal chance to win against expert players.

Gambling in clubs is also permitted by the new act except that the club's gaming facilities are available only to club members. The club may charge a fixed sum of money for their use, and the charge must be determined in advance. This per-hour or per-session fee is similar to the fee per hour charge levied on Poker players at the Poker clubs in Gardena, California (see page 670).

Slot machines, called "fruit machines" by Britons, are legal provided that not more than two machines are available in any one spot, that the stake hazarded does not exceed sixpence (7¢), and that all stakes are applied either in payment of winnings or for purposes other than private gain. Carnival and bazaar games are legal provided that the price of each chance does not exceed one shilling (14¢), that the total worth of the merchandise prizes in one determination of winners, if any, does not exceed 50 shillings. No money prize may exceed one shilling.

This law has cut down illegal gambling and graft payments considerably and contributed respectable amounts of money to charitable organizations and the government. It has been interesting to see how this has worked out after several years of operation.

Australia: Strict government regulations keep the legal off-track racing handle in Australia down to a minimum because placing a horse bet is like depositing or withdrawing money from a bank. The legalized bookies are found mostly in West Australia and Tasmania; women bettors and loiterers are discouraged from frequenting a bookie office. Illegal bookies are also found in Australia.

New Zealand: Off-track betting has been legal in New Zealand since 1950. Betting shops in New Zealand provide only the minimum of racing information, such as the entries and probable odds. No last-minute jockey changes or other pertinent racing data are permitted by law. All horse bets must be made in cash or against cash deposits in the betting agent's possession. Wagers made with these off-track betting agents go through a sort of off-course totalisator called TAB, which stands for Totalisation Agency Board. There are over 300 legalized betting agents in New Zealand. All off-track bets must be made with the agency 90 minutes before race time, and they relay their bets to TAB's central office. Five percent of the gross totalisator off-track handle goes to the state, plus a tax of 2½% on TAB's dividends.

France: In the home of pari-mutuel betting, this system of off-track betting was legalized in 1933. At the time of writing, France has 760 subsidiary pari-mutuel agencies in shops and cafés where off-track bettors place their horse wagers.

All betting, at or off the track, goes through the pari-mutuel machine. Bets must be placed the morning before the race, and each of the subsidiary shop and café agencies has a teletype whose operator relays the bets to the track.

The subsidiary pari-mutuel agencies are controlled by a combine of private racing interests operating under government regulations. Each agency receives as its share 1% of its total betting handle. The take of the government and the private interests from the combined betting handle is 13½%. Of this the government takes 4%. The off-track bettor also has to pay a government stamp tax of 1⅗% to 1⅘% on each wager of 100 francs or more. Illegal bookies are also found in France.

Ireland: The passage of Ireland's 1926 Betting Act made it one of the first countries in the world to legalize off-track betting. Ireland has over 600 licensed off-track bookies operating about 1,700 horse offices. Up until 1955, the government placed a 7½% tax on each bet made with an off-track bookie; then it was upped to 10%. Both bettors and bookies protested that this was excessive, and the increase has caused many former licensed bookies to go underground and operate illegally.

PUERTO RICO'S TRACK AND OFF-TRACK BETTING

Puerto Rico's off-track race betting is limited to betting on the daily double, exacta and cinco-seis or 5–6 pool. El Comandante Racetrack in Rio Piedras, a few miles from San Juan, is the only track in operation in Puerto Rico. There are eight races run at the track on Wednesdays, Fridays, Sundays and legal holidays all year round. The pari-mutuel betting system is used at the track, but no show betting is permitted.

In 1971, during El Commandante's best year of racing, the total racing handle was $63,385,148. Of this, $31,930,743 was bet on the 5–6 pool and $10,021,600 on the daily double and exacta, with over 95% of these amounts being bet off-track. Ten percent went for agents'

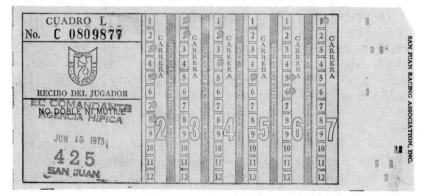

A cuadro ticket used in the 5–6 pool and sold at Puerto Rico's El Comandante track and at more than 500 Agencias Hípicas throughout the island.

commissions, 7.65% to the Commonwealth and 25.65% to the track for a total take-off of 43.3%. The 5–6 pool off-track handle has increased at the rate of $1½ million per year for the past 13 years.

The pool started in 1913 in Puerto Rico and has been operating continually for over 59 years. Various forms of pools operate at racetracks in Mexico, Venezuela, Peru, Great Britain, Germany and the United States. In the early days of the pool in Puerto Rico it was sorted by manual methods; today, at El Comandante, the pool is computed by a modern electronic method.

Betting tickets in the 5–6 pool are called *papeletas* and *cuadros* and are based on the selection of the winning horse in each of the last six of the eight races run at El Comandante Racetrack. These ticket bets are placed through 545 Agencias Hípicas (race agencies) operated by contractors and licensed by the track and government. A papeleta costs 33¢ at an off-track race agency and 28¢ at the track windows. The purchaser picks a combination comprised of six horses, one in each race. It is really a six-horse parlay. If it wins, the buyer shares in 70% of the 6 pool (after legal deductions) with any other winners. The remaining 30% is awarded as a consolation to the person or persons picking five winners. In the event that no one picks six winners, then the pool pays off on 5–4 or 4–3, and so on.

When a last-minute scratch takes place, it is a *nula race* (void race). A ticket holder of five winners, when there are five valid races and one void race, participates in the 70% of the 6 pool as many times as he selected horses in the void race. Thus, if the fourth race is void and a winning player has selected five horses in that race, he gets five shares of the 6 pool. If there are two void races on the program, the number of horses bet in the first void race is multiplied by the number of horses bet in the second void race. The total is the number of shares in the 6 pool a selector of four winning horses receives. Naturally, when two void races are on the program, the 6 pool pays very little.

A cuadro is the same as a papeleta except that the purchaser can select as many six-horse combination bets as he desires, all of which are registered on the same ticket, paying 25¢ for each combination plus a 15¢ charge for the cuadro ticket.

A bettor making a papeleta or cuadro bet is given a selection card by the off-track agent or track seller. He writes the number of the horses he selects beside the number of each race and the seller, using an electrical machine, punches the player's selections on two identical cards. The purchaser is given one and the other is taken to the track to be processed in a glass-enclosed room in the pool building.

The electronic system in use at El Comandante was the first of its kind in the world. The electronic room has sorters, tabulators and four Univac machines which tabulate, register, sort the winners and even make out the payoff checks.

The electronic sorters in the pool room at El Comandante handle 800 cards a minute. The tabulators which handle the papeletas register the cards at the rate of 120 a minute. The Univac electronic computer-tabulator combination makes a permanent record of each cuadro at the rate of 150 a minute.

Also unique in the pool operation are the airplane and boat pick-ups of cards from agencies in the outlying parts of the island. Cards from Ponce, Mayaguez and distant points are picked up every racing day by plane and brought to the track for processing. An agency on the island of Vieques, located 18 miles off the coast of Puerto Rico, sends its cards in by launch.

Few cuadro players are content with the minimum purchase of two combinations. The majority of them buy four or more combinations, and there are those who buy them in the dozens. There is one cuadro purchaser in Puerto Rico who stands above all the rest; I can describe him best by relating the following incident.

One afternoon several years ago, at El Comandante Racetrack, I ran into Bill Barondess, known in Puerto Rico as its biggest cuadro bettor. He handed me his day's betting card and I observed that his race selections involved two horses in the second race, one in the third, three in the fourth, seven in the fifth, seven in the sixth, and four in the seventh and last race. The number of betting combinations listed on the card read 1,176. Bill's Cuadro for that day cost him $294 plus a 15¢ charge for the card.

He was lucky that day since one of his 1,176 combinations had a winner in each race. That afternoon, however, the favorite or second-choice horse won each of the six races and the 70% of the net pool

John Scarne scanning the day's race results in the Hialeah Turf and Sports Club on the Las Vegas Strip. (Las Vegas News Bureau)

was divided among 1,000-odd winners, so Bill's share of the 6 pool, the smallest ever, amounted to $36.40.

One share in the 6 pool usually averages from $2,000 to $15,000. There have been many 6-pool winners who have collected more than $30,000, and several who have won more than $50,000. The record payoff to date for a 25¢ winning combination is $101,033.

LEGAL OFF-TRACK BOOKMAKING IN NEVADA

Nevada is the only state in the U.S. where off-track race and sports books are legal. The race books are usually run in conjunction with sports books. Nevada gambling officials exercise a very strict control over off-track race books. It's much easier to get a state casino license for a $50,000,000 hotel than to get a race-book license for a small office with one telephone. This is done to prevent violations of the Federal ban on transmission of illegal racing information over interstate lines. The state also requires strict adherence by the bookie to the Federal law requiring him to purchase the $50 Federal bookie stamp and pay the 10% excise tax.

A horse or sports book in Nevada must be operated in a building separated from all other forms of gambling. Race bets may not be accepted over the phone but must be made in person, and each appli-

Nevada gaming licenses and Federal Tax stamps posted in the Hialeah Turf and Sports Club. (Las Vegas News Bureau)

cant for a race or sports-book license must sign a waiver allowing the state to tap the bookie's telephone at will. Race bookies in Nevada must pay an annual 3% state tax on gross winnings under $250,000, a slightly higher tax on a gross over that. So far, no Nevada book has reported exceeding $250,000.

During 1973, the 23 race and sports books operating in Nevada reported a gross taxable revenue of approximately $3.8 million. This breaks down to a yearly gross handle of a mere $130,000 for each race and sports book. This means that Nevada's yearly tax revenue from this source is very small, $90,000 to be exact, a figure that has not been exceeded in any previous year. Off-track or sports betting in Nevada is such a minor operation not because their gamblers are any different. They aren't; they love to bet horses and sports. It is due to the insistence of gambling officials that all Nevada race and sports books must operate in accordance with the Federal bookie laws.

Nevada, the gambling mecca of the world, has only a handful of race books—less than half the number of illegal bookies who operate in one of the large industrial plants in my neck of the woods. It is obvious that the high rollers don't place their big action with the legalized race and sports bookies but give it to illegal bookies in or out of the state.

Since my survey shows that an illegal bookie or a state-licensed off-track bookie cannot pay the 10% Federal excise tax on his gross receipts and operate a successful race or sports book, it is ridiculous for state legislators even to think about legalizing the off-track bookie. The state won't derive a large revenue from this source until the present Federal bookie laws are made more realistic.

Without blowing a cop's whistle and without naming names, I reiterate that no bigtime bookie in America, whether he is a licensed bookie in Nevada or an illegal bookie in my home town of Fairview, New Jersey, can operate a successful race or sports book and still pay the 10% Federal excise tax on a bookie's gross receipts.

NEW YORK CITY'S OTB OR OFF-TRACK BETTING

New York is the first state in the country to operate legalized off-track pari-mutuel betting on horses. (Nevada has legalized off-track race and sports bookies.) The bill which gave New York City the Off-Track Betting Corporation, better known as OTB, was passed in April 1970. OTB is a public benefit corporation, operating under New York State statutes which allow New York City to operate off-track betting offices. The OTB's gross take permitted by law is 17% of the amount wagered plus breakage. After deducting the commission to be paid to participating tracks within the state, OTB's annual net revenue is divided between the state and city, 80% or $160 million of the first $200 million going to the city, and 20% or $40 million to the state. Net revenues in excess of $200 million are divided equally between New York City and New York State. Breakage and unclaimed winning tickets are paid to the state as tax.

OTB has 100 or more branch offices located throughout New York City. As at the track, the smallest bet permitted is $2. OTB designates the horses by letter rather than by number in order to avoid the confusion of having the horses carry a "track number" and an "OTB number." In addition to win, place and show betting, OTB offers the daily double and such exotic bets as the exacta, triple and superfecta. At present, OTB regularly handles the NYRA (New York Racing Association) tracks—Aqueduct, Belmont Park and Saratoga. These tracks run on a rotating schedule and OTB handles whichever NYRA track is open. OTB handles New York harness racing at Roosevelt, Monticello and Yonkers raceways. OTB also handles bets on tracks in other states, such as Maryland, and it schedules special events such as the Kentucky Derby, the Preakness, the Washington D.C. International and the Colonial Cup. These special events are determined at

Agencia Hípica, one of the 500-odd off-track betting offices in Puerto Rico.

A typical opening day at one of New York City's 100 or more Off-Track Betting offices. (New York OTB Corporation)

			WRITE IN THE AMOUNT OF THE BET. THEY CAN BE $2.00, $5.00, $10.00, $50.00 and $100.00 OR MULTIPLES THEREOF							
OTB NEW YORK CITY OFF-TRACK BETTING CORPORATION	TRACK	RACE NUMBER	WIN	PLACE	SHOW	DD	QUINIELA	EXACTA	HORSE LETTER	2nd HORSE OF DAILY DOUBLE OR EXACTA
FIRST BET										
SECOND BET										
THIRD BET										
FOURTH BET										
FIFTH BET										

THIS IS ONLY A WORKSHEET. PLEASE CHECK YOUR BETS CAREFULLY. YOUR TICKET IS YOUR ONLY RECEIPT.

IN PLACING A BET THE BETTOR AGREES TO BE BOUND BY THE RULES AND REGULATIONS OF THE CORPORATION CURRENTLY IN EFFECT.

TOTAL $ ___ 00

A copy of New York City's Off-Track Betting worksheet.

the discretion of the corporation. The OTB, however, is not permitted by the Federal government to combine its pools with out-of-state tracks.

Whenever OTB takes bets on an in-state race, it attempts to combine its pools with those of the track. In the event that technical breakdowns result in a failure to combine pools, OTB has the option of paying at track prices, refunding all bets or creating its own pool at a separate payoff rate. OTB usually pays winners at track prices with the exception of the Belmont Stakes, which is usually run as a "separate pool" event.

The OTB accepts bets by telephone provided the bettor is a resident of the state and has on deposit with the Telephone Deposit Betting Center of OTB an amount at least equal to his wager. There is *no* credit given. Telephoning bets from outside New York State to place a bet with OTB is prohibited by Federal law.

Back in 1961 with the first edition of this book, I stated, "I am sure that the track's racing attendance and betting handle would take a big drop with the legalization of off-track pari-mutuel betting." My recent OTB survey agrees with the study conducted by a group from City University of New York which indicates that for every dollar wagered at OTB branches, there was a resulting 85¢ decline at the major tracks in New York State. And again, as I predicted, OTB has not been effective in taking customers away from bookmakers. In fact, my survey reveals that due to the vast publicity generated by OTB, illegal bookmakers in the New York area have increased their betting customers by approximately 15%. Plus this, bookmakers offer credit, phone service without a mandatory "bank account," they'll book parlays, reverses and "if" wagers and, in some cases, even offer a 50% rebate on total losses at the end of a month's time.

If you were to ask my opinion as a gambling expert if OTB has proven to be a success, I would have to answer "No," for reasons already stated. But, despite the pros and cons about the success or failure of OTB in New York City, it has inspired California, Delaware, Maryland, Missouri, New Hampshire, New Jersey, Connecticut, Pennsylvania and Rhode Island, among others, to consider legalized off-track betting. However, any politician advocating pari-mutuel off-track betting for a state which has a short racing season had better forget it. And if anyone thinks that off-track pari-mutuel betting will eliminate the illegal bookie, he has another guess coming. Every country in the world with legalized off-track betting is still plagued with illegal bookies. One reason is the many restrictions that legalization usually places on the horse bettor. Since he can't understand them and can't see why it is necessary to follow so many rules when he just wants to put a couple of dollars on some nag, he bets with the illegal bookie because it is simpler.

At the time of writing, New York City's two major harness tracks (Yonkers and Roosevelt) are suing OTB for $45 million, blaming OTB for recent losses in attendance and handle. It takes about $150,000 a day to operate Yonkers Raceway (Roosevelt's costs are the same). The OTB, which makes use of the track's facilities, and does about 40% of the track's handle, pays only about 5% of the $150,000 daily operational cost. Track officials are demanding a greater share of OTB's earnings for the use of their facilities. With the recently appointed state three-man super-racing agency, which has the last say over both track and off-track betting in New York State, I'm sure the tracks' demands will be resolved.

WHAT CONGRESS SHOULD DO ABOUT THE 10% FEDERAL EXCISE GAMBLING TAX LAW

Enacting laws that prohibit gambling is easy; enforcing such laws is next to impossible. Anti-gambling laws promote police and governmental corruption. The illegal gaming operators buy protection from the very people responsible under the law for stamping them out.

Ironically, attempts at suppression also exempt illegal gambling operators and prizewinners from taxation. Legally they are supposed to report this illegal income, but this is just another law which the operator and winning players disregard.

The many Federal and state anti-gambling laws on the books today do not reflect the view of the 90 million adult Americans who indulge in gambling of one kind or another and who do not consider it morally wrong. The existence of these laws, however, makes it legally wrong and classes these people as lawbreakers. Because these laws are neither supported nor obeyed by a majority of the public, they engender an increased disrespect for law and result in greater corruption among officials whose duty it is to enforce the law.

I believe that the most ludicrous gambling statute ever enacted is the Federal law requiring any organized gambling scheme, legal or illegal, to purchase a $50 stamp and pay a Federal 10% excise tax on its gross handle (gross receipts). Gambling schemes affected by this tax are race and sports books, policy numbers, football and baseball pools and all forms of lotteries. The lone exception to the Federal tax is race betting in the 30 states where pari-mutuel wagering is legal. Other Federal statutes prohibit the interstate transmission and acceptance of race bets.

When I was a consultant to the U.S. Senate Subcommittee on Organized Crime which sponsored the law, I learned that the subcommittee honestly believed that most illegal race and sports bookies, numbers operators and various lottery-type operators, fearing Federal prosecution, would fold up their tents and quit. Although today we have fewer race bookies, we have considerably more sports bookies and Numbers and lottery operators than ever before. Therefore, it is obvious that the law did not achieve its intended result.

I have talked to dozens of illegal bookmakers about the 10% Federal excise tax on their gross earnings. A bigtime Florida bookie says, "I'd like to abide by the Federal ten percent bookie tax, but how can I when I only earn six percent on my handle? I have to sneak and take my chances of being pinched." When I asked a Numbers operator in California if he had paid his Federal gambling tax, he replied, "It is hypocritical for the Federal government to expect to get a revenue from the Numbers racket when other state and Federal laws are dead set against the policy numbers."

As mentioned earlier, the only form of organized betting that is exempt from the 10% Federal excise tax is pari-mutuel race betting. I doubt that Congress at the time of the enactment of this law ever gave it a thought that state lotteries would soon be legalized and would be affected by the law. Not only do illegal operators of race and sports books, Numbers games and lottery operators avoid the tax like a plague, but state governments operating lotteries do the same. These states, including New York, New Jersey, Massachusetts and Pennsylvania, have concocted a gimmick basing their prize awards on previously run pari-mutuel races in order to avoid the payment of the excise tax to the Federal government.

What can be done? I suggest that the Federal government should amend this law and abolish the 10% excise tax on all legalized state operated gambling operations such as race and sports books and all forms of lotteries, and at the same time amend the Federal law which prohibits the interstate advertising on television, radio and newspapers of any state operated lottery scheme. This would eliminate the subterfuges employed by the states in order to avoid payment of the Federal 10% excise tax.

What can be done about the legal and illegal bookie? I suggest that if the Federal government is really serious about obtaining revenue from the thousands of racehorse and sports bookies in this country, it should try lowering the 10% excise tax on race and sports bookies' gross receipts to a more realistic 10% on the gross winnings. I firmly believe that tens of thousands of bookies who are now operating without paying the 10% tax (as well as those making only a token payment because they can't pay this 10% tax and stay in business) would immediately pay a tax on their gross winnings.

I predict that if this bookie tax is reduced as described above, our Federal treasury will collect $500 million more per year in race bookie taxes, and an additional $300 million from sports bookies and football and baseball pool operators.

Some people object that if the tax is lowered, the bookies still will not pay the tax because the Internal Revenue boys will pass on the bookies' names and business addresses to state law-enforcement officials who would then make raids and arrests for state violations. The answer to that is that any bookmaker now doing a profitable business is already buying protection from these sources and will continue to do so.

While I'm on the subject of gambling laws, I believe that card playing for money (Poker, Bridge, Rummy, etc.) in private homes should be legalized by the states. However, no professional game operator should be involved; the player should not be charged for making use of the gaming facilities; all players should have an equal chance of winning, and no banking card games should be permitted.

Card playing in clubs should also be legalized with the club's gaming facilities available only to club members. The club could charge a fixed sum of money for their use, the charge being determined in advance. The charge should be a per-hour or per-session fee similar to the per-hour charge levied on Poker players at the legal Poker clubs in Gardena, California.

Revision of private gambling laws is taking place in most countries today. (See Great Britain, page 92.) Our state laws need such revision. We also need a change in our attitude toward card playing, which is one of widespread hypocrisy. Our hypocritical, confused and inconsistent legal situation is politically unhealthy. It is time that legislators and voters recognize the fact that a majority of our citizens want to gamble at cards and are doing so in greater numbers each year in spite of the existing prohibition. It is time they realized that anti-quated and unrealistic laws against private card playing do not prevent gambling but instead give racketeers the opportunity to organize and control card games.

SCARNE'S STATE OFF-TRACK BETTING PLAN

Since the legalization of off-track bookies such as those operating in Nevada, England and Australia would serve no useful economic purpose for the state, and the French, New Zealand and New York City type of off-track pari-mutuel betting scheme reduces racetrack attendance and revenues, that leaves only one form of legalized off-track betting as a solution: Scarne's State Off-Track Betting Plan.

My Off-Track Betting Plan with several additional variations works something like Puerto Rico's off-track betting system (see page 95) which has been in successful operation since 1913. The basic rules of my plan are as follows:

1. The off-track betting offices will handle only such exotic wagers as the daily double, exacta, triple, and the 5–6 sweepstake pool (similar to Puerto Rico's cinco-seis pool) which allows a player to wager as little as 25¢. Each pool will be combined with an in-state track pool. A separate pool will be run for special races run in other states.

2. No win, place or show betting will be permitted.

3. The off-track betting offices will be privately owned and each office will receive a commission based on its gross handle.

In my opinion, the off-track betting plan outlined above will achieve the following results:

1. Because a player can select his own numbers (horses) and can wager as little as 25¢ at the 5–6 pool, it will cut down the play at the Numbers game, something that state lotteries and New York City's off-track betting system have failed to accomplish. Most of the off-track players who would patronize such an office, like those in Puerto Rico, would for the most part not be horse players, but people who play the Numbers racket, spending 25¢, 50¢, $1 or more daily. Puerto Rico's off-track 5–6 betting pool has all but eliminated the illegal "Bolita" (Latin America's Numbers racket).

The main reason for the Bolita's decline is that a player has the chance to win $80,000 or more by purchasing a 25¢ ticket at the track or from any off-track agency. Since there are no handicappers so perfect that they can pick all the winners in six straight races, the hunch player has just as much chance of hitting the 5–6 pool as anyone else, and more people, consequently, participate. Two big 5–6 pool winners I recently interviewed in Puerto Rico said they had never visited a racetrack or placed a $2 bet on a horse. The smallest bet permitted at any of New York City's off-track betting offices is $2, which automatically eliminates the majority of New York City's Numbers players. The seasoned horse player may place his $2 or more on the daily double, exacta, or triple, as well as wagering on the 5–6 pool.

2. Legalization of my betting plan will increase rather than cut into the track's racing attendance and betting handle since the 5–6 pool will introduce many non-horse players to racing, and they will become horse players and visit the track. My study of racing in Puerto Rico has revealed that over the past 16 years the off-track betting system has steadily increased the attendance and revenue of El Comandante (Puerto Rico's only racetrack). Puerto Rico's racing revenue for 1957 was approximately $22 million, of which $11 million was bet at El Comandante Racetrack and $11 million was placed through 320 off-track betting agencies. In 1971, El Comandante Racetrack's revenue increased to about $21 million and the off-track bets placed through 545 betting agencies jumped to $42 million.

3. Private ownership will save each state millions of dollars. By licensing off-track betting agencies as was done in Puerto Rico, the state saves the gigantic cost incurred by New York City's OTB. The betting agencies will be set up according to state design by the licensee. This will save the state millions of dollars, as the state will not be responsible for equipment, maintenance, salaries, etc., which will be the responsibility of the licensee. The closing of an agency and/or the opening of a new one will not cost the state one penny.

I see no reason why my off-track betting plan operating in densely populated racing states such as New Jersey, New York, California, Illinois and Pennsylvania wouldn't at the least equal that state's track pari-mutuel turnover. Actually it should do much better because most of the millions of dollars bet off-track would involve the 5–6 sweepstake pool: the total deductions from this pool would be about 50%, similar to the deductions from state lotteries. The state would receive 30% of the deduction and the off-track agents, track officials and horsemen the remaining 20%.

The 5–6 sweepstake pool winning payoffs should be as follows. The person or persons selecting the most winners from the third to the eighth races receives 50% of the net pool; 30% goes to the person or persons picking the second greatest number of winners from the third to the eighth races. The remaining 20% is awarded as consolation prizes to the person or persons picking the third greatest number of winners from the third to the eighth races.

With my plan there are no void races or small payoffs such as occur in Puerto Rico's 5–6 pool due to nula (void) races. A player who has selected six horses one of which is scratched automatically becomes the possessor of the next highest post position horse. If, for example, Horse 5 is scratched, all holders of Horse 5 become holders of Horse 6. If Horse 6 is also scratched, they become holders of Horse 7. If the highest post position horse is scratched, holders of this horse become holders of Horse 1.

A prize award of $1 million or more for a 25¢ winning ticket comprised of six horses in a combined track and off-track 5–6 sweepstake pool run in a heavily populated state would occur fairly often.

The state's revenue derived from the 5–6 sweepstake pool plus the revenue received from the off-track daily double, exacta and triple pools, would in my opinion surely double the track's pari-mutuel revenue without reducing the track's pari-mutuel handle. Scarne's Off-Track Betting Plan is designed to work in any of the 30 racing states. On second thought, the 5–6 sweepstake pool by itself could also be made to work in non-racing states. It certainly would net more millions for the state than the present state lotteries.

4.
Betting on Sports Events

My sports survey shows that betting on the outcome of local and national sporting contests is the number one illegal form of gambling in the United States—illegal off-track race betting is second. This great upsurge in sports betting is due primarily to extensive television sports coverage on all sorts of sporting events and the great team expansion of professional football, baseball, basketball and hockey. Today about 60 million Americans are wagering approximately $30 billion yearly on all sorts of amateur and professional sporting contests. My New York City sports survey agrees with the one conducted by the Oliver Quayle organization for the city of New York. Both estimates state that New York City's sports fans bet over $1 billion yearly.

About half, or $15 billion, of the total national sports handle was wagered with friends and acquaintances in bets ranging from a dollar to several thousand dollars. These private wagers on sports and other events rank in volume as follows: football, baseball, basketball, hockey, boxing, golf and political elections, and such skill contests as bowling, horseshoes, Checkers, Chess, billiards, pool and Teeko.

The remaining $15 billion is wagered each year by countless millions of Americans with thousands of sports bookmakers and hundreds and hundreds of horse bookies. The books retain about 4¢ of each dollar they handle, a gross revenue on the $15 billion of $600 million. About 60% of this goes for operational expenses—salaries, gamblers' losses not collected, phone charges (one such bookie is known to spend $10,000 a month on phone calls in order to operate his trans-country sports business) and graft paid to corrupt police officers and politicians. This leaves a net profit of $240 million.

One example of how important sports betting in this country has become is a Federal investigation and trial of the operators of a sports office in Terre Haute, Indiana. The government subpoenaed 175 of the country's bigtime bettors—a list which included several multimillion-aires, movie people, hotel owners and other business tycoons. The evidence indicated that some of these bettors wagered as much as $25,000 on a single football game.

SPORTS OFFICES AND BOOKMAKERS

There are now about 4,000 bookmakers in America who handle sports wagers exclusively, most of whom will not take horse-race bets. Two of these, both big ones, are women.

In addition, there are more than 300 *sports offices*. A sports office is a combine or syndicate of three or more of the top sports bookmakers who have joined together so as to be able to handle the betting of the nation's biggest bettors. As a rule, the smallest bet these offices will accept is $100 on a single contest, the largest, $20,000. But this $20,000 maximum limit is sometimes upped for special customers; and for the Super Bowl and World Series play the sky is the limit.

The day's handle for one of these offices may run from a low $50,000 to a high of $500,000 or more.

Baseball betting accounts for about 40%, or $6 billion of the bookies' yearly sports handle; football, about 45% or $6.75 billion, and basketball, hockey, prizefights and state and national political elections, 15% or $2.25 billion.

The bettors who patronize the bigtime bookies or sports offices are tens of thousands of people in all walks of life: industrialists, politicians, judges, lawyers, stock brokers and manipulators, oil and movie magnates, as well as Numbers operators, bookmakers, casino operators, racketeers and other easy-money boys.

Most of the betting involving the big bettor and the bookie or sports office is conducted by phone and courier. The courier, or runner, merely collects from the losers and pays the winners. This is done strictly on a cash basis—"No *maps* (checks) accepted." If the sports office and the bigtime bettor are in different states the winner of a big wager (bookie or player) must travel to the loser to collect.

Betting conversations by phone are usually in code, and no names are ever mentioned. The necessary bookkeeping is also coded, numbers representing the names of superstars, teams, etc. These codes are used primarily to make it tough for Federal law-enforcement agencies to get evidence. Formerly, bookies operating within the borders of a single state had no fear of Federal prosecution, but the enactment of the 1951 Federal gambling law requiring a bookie to purchase a $50 license stamp annually and pay 10% of his gross handle as a Federal tax changed that.

The 10% tax is highly unrealistic. As one bookie told me disgusted, "I would go broke in one day if I paid the 10% Federal bookie tax. Look what would happen when a player bets me $1,050 to $1,000 on a Pick 'em ball game and he wins. I lose $1,000 and must still pay Uncle Sam $105 for accepting the bet. If I take a $1,050 baseball bet on each of two opposing teams, I'd earn only $50 on the $2,100 worth of action, and would have to pay Uncle Sam $210. That would put me out of business in short order—so I don't buy the stamp. I just pay Uncle Sam what he rightfully has coming when I file my income tax."

The nation's number one sports betting contest is the annual Super Bowl. The runner-up is, of course, the World Series, with the Kentucky Derby running third. Approximately $600 million changes hands on the Super Bowl game and about $500 million is wagered on the outcome of the World Series plus the single games. The largest single bet to this author's knowledge was made by a Midwestern betting combine with a number of western sports offices. They wagered $825,000 on the outcome of a World Series game. A $200,000 wager is the largest single wager known on a Super Bowl game.

MISCONCEPTIONS ABOUT BETTING SCALPERS

Many bookies who handle baseball action believe that *scalpers* (bettors who wager on two opposing teams in order to minimize their losses through some mysterious mathematical formula unknown to the bookies) have a sure-fire winning proposition when they scalp a World Series. As one New Jersey bookie told me, "Scarne, these baseball scalpers bet big on the Series favorite, then turn around and bet the underdog in each single game. They are sure to win money. How they do it I don't know, but, believe me, they do it." This is like the old joke about the woman who thinks the department store loses money on every item it sells, but makes millions yearly because it sells so many thousands of each item.

This misconception about scalpers arose years ago when a sports office considered its pricemaker, or handicapper, not only a baseball whiz and a mathematical genius but a prophet to boot. They would quote a price and accept bets weeks before game time not only on the outcome of the Series, but also on each of the seven scheduled games. With this betting setup a sports scalper with a fair knowledge of simple arithmetic would seek a sports line on the World Series and the individual games from as many bookies and sports offices as possible.

He would then select the best price on the outcome of the Series and the best price on each of the individual games. This could involve selecting as many as eight prices each from a different bookie or sports office. By comparing the World Series price with the combined price line of the individual games, he could easily determine if the difference resulted in a minus or plus expectation. If it was minus he forgot the matter. If plus, he would bet his money with the different bookies, laying the shortest price on the Series favorite and taking the longest odds on the underdog in the individual games. This would guarantee him a profit, no matter what happened.

But the scalper can't do this today because he can't get a bet down on any single game until the day of that game; bookies only quote prices day by day on World Series games. The only sure thing about scalping the Series today is that the scalper is paying the bookie a greater profit because he is making a greater number of bets.

RACE BOOKIES AND SPORTS BETTING

In addition to the sports bookmakers, some horse bookies will accept wagers on national sporting events. Some do it merely to accommodate their horse bettors; others do it as a business. As a rule, the small curbstone horse bookies won't accept a fair-sized sports wager unless they know they can lay the bet off with a sports bookie and earn a profit in so doing.

One reason many horse bookies won't take sports bets is that horse-race wagers give a greater percentage of earning power than most sports bets. Another reason is that the bookie lacks the necessary knowledge and ability for taking such bets. The horse bookie who accepts horse bets exclusively merely accepts bets within his *extension* (the limit he has placed on the amount of his losses) and doesn't need to calculate the bets because the pari-mutuel payoff system does that for him. The track totalisator calculates the payoff prices for win, place and show bets and enables the horse bookie, as a rule, to earn the same percentage of profit as the state and track combined.

Booking sports bets isn't that easy. The sports bookie needs to have considerably more ability and ingenuity. A successful bigtime sports bookie must also be a sports handicapper and pricemaker, because the odds or price may change several times before the contest takes place. If the sports bookie can't do this himself he hires a clerk who can.

Take a ball game as an example. A major-league ball team's star pitcher is slated to pitch today's game. The quoted odds are 8 to 5 that his team will win, and this price is based solely on the announcement that the team's ace pitcher will be the starting pitcher. Then, a few minutes before game time, the manager decides to start someone else.

Since time is short and bettors are on the phone trying to get bets down before the game begins, the bookie must make up his own price line. If the line he quotes is not a true one, and he is dealing to smart bettors, it's a safe bet that he'll take a good beating on the action.

Even though the sports bookie must know more than the horse bookie to stay in business, he still can't figure some types of baseball odds. I proved this and had some laughs doing it during my sports-bookie survey, when I offered most of them a proposition bet. I asked them to calculate the payoff price on a winning parlay which I pretended I had made and won. I said I had bet $4.93 on a three-team parlay, laying odds of 7 to 5 on the first team, and taking odds of 9 to 5 and 6 to 5 on the other two teams. (Remember, when you *lay* odds of 6 to 5, you are betting $6 to win $5, or some multiple of these figures. When you *take* odds of 6 to 5, you are betting $5 to win $6, of some multiple.) The proposition bet was that if the bookie could figure the correct payoff price of the parlay to the first two decimal places, I would pay him that amount. If he failed he would pay me the correct sum.

Most of the bookies admitted that they didn't know how to calculate it because they always work with round-figure bets ($5 and $10, etc.) and refuse to accept wagers involving cents. The few bookies who did accept my proposition came up with wrong answers. The correct payoff price for this parlay to four decimal places is $52.0608. The formula for computing it can be found on page 83.

THE SPORTS LINE AND HOW IT IS MADE

The true sports line, or prevailing betting odds on sports events used by bookies, unlike the morning line in horse racing, is not made by the so-called sports handicappers and pricemakers, but by sports offices and the big layoff bookies (who take bets from each other as a hedge against heavy losses). The bigtime sports offices and layoff bookies control the handicappers and pricemakers who in a sense simply parrot this bookie information and sell it to newspapers (or to whomever will buy it) as their own sports line.

Included among these sports handicappers is the self-proclaimed nation's foremost oddsmaker and mathematical genius—Jimmy "the Greek" Snyder. A former newspaper columnist, now a publicist, Snyder's "sports line" appears in newspapers coast-to-coast. But of the 20 or more so-called "sports lines" that I have investigated over the past few years, "the Greek's" has the poorest win record of them all! I took time out a few years ago to carefully study his winning average for the first five weeks of the National Football League campaign. It was a dull .547, based on 35 wins out of 64 selections. But this was one of Snyder's better records! To prove how really "good" Jimmy's fantastic record of 35 winners out of 64 selections is, just take a list of 64 football games. Close your eyes and stick a pin in 64 game selections. According to the laws of probability, your win percentage should be .500—32 wins out of 64 selections. Of course, with a little luck, you could easily beat Jimmy (the Greek) Snyder's record blindfolded. This is the same sports handicapper who in 1973 could not see Secretariat, the superhorse of the century, winning the triple crown.

Although Las Vegas is the casino gambling mecca of the world, it possesses only about 14 licensed sports-betting parlors (Nevada possesses 23), each of which makes its own sports line. This is, of course, dictated by the bets they have accepted. The combined $3.8 million yearly race and sports handle of the 23 Nevada race and sports books does not equal the sports handle of one illegal bigtime bookie: that is, one who accepts single wagers of $10,000, $20,000, $50,000 or more. The reason is that the Federal excise tax compels a legalized bookie in Nevada to charge each sports bettor 10% extra on each bet. What bigtime gambler would place a $20,000 bet in a Las Vegas sporting parlor and pay a fee of $2,000 for so doing? None that I know. Therefore, any sports line including Jimmy (the Greek) Snyder's emanating from Las Vegas is only a newspaper line and is not used by bookies or smart bettors.

Although most bookies in America open with the same sports line, it doesn't remain that way for long. Like the changing odds at a racetrack, the bookies' odds change as bets are placed.

Although made on what appears to be a sound basis, the odds quoted by a bookie or a sports service are often not the true odds, and the bookies, in this situation, can lose considerable cash. One night some years ago the ace pitcher for the Giants (when they still belonged to New York, before moving to San Francisco) was drinking heavily in a New Jersey night club; he left at 4:00 A.M., pie-eyed. He was to pitch the same day. A bookie client of a sports service was in the club at the time, and on his information the service made the opposing team a 2 to 1 favorite. These were the true odds up to this point; but the sports office spy system missed out on some front-line news. They failed to discover that our hero woke up the next morning without the expected hangover, feeling as fit as a fiddle. If they had gotten such a report they would have changed their odds again. That afternoon the Giant hurler pitched a two-hitter, one of the best games of his career, shutting out the opposition and winning. Since the sports service information failed to hold up, their bookie clients lost plenty.

As the money wagered at a racetrack changes the race odds, the money bet with bigtime layoff bookies controls the betting odds. A $20,000 bet placed on an underdog baseball team can change the odds and make the underdog a favorite, and a $50,000 bet on a big football game can move a spread by one point or more and in some instances make the underdog the favorite. Handicappers call the big bookies during the period before events to learn how money is being wagered on a contest, and the handicappers set their sports line according to what they are told. Very often the bookies, to serve their own purposes, give the handicappers the wrong information. This information ends up as the sports line you find in your local paper. Newspaper odds are seldom true odds, and bookies have no respect for them because newspaper sports handicappers do not have access to the vital information available to bigtime bookies. If you mention newspaper odds to a bookie, his answer is always: "Let the newspapers book your bet."

BETTING ON BASEBALL GAMES

How does a bookie manage to make money by accepting wagers on ball games? The sports bookie, like the operator of any gambling game, must obtain a favorable percentage on every bet he accepts, no matter which team the player puts his money on.

Like the operators of most gambling establishments, the sports bookie or office takes as great a favorable percentage as his betting clientele will permit. If his customers are inexperienced or in the sucker class, his percentage is high. If they are smart baseball bettors he has to content himself with a much smaller margin of profit. The odds are 50 to 1 that you fall in the former category, and here's how you can tell.

The bookies deal four different price lines, depending on the type of clientele they have, as follows:

1. The 40¢ line. This is dealt by the curbstone bookie to inexperienced baseball bettors and to the rank-and-file gambling sucker.

2. The 20¢ line is dealt by a fair-sized horse bookie to the small-time, but more experienced, baseball bettors.

3. The 10¢ line, called the "dime line," is dealt by the bigtime bookies and sports offices to experienced big-money bettors.

4. The 5¢ line, the "nickel line," is dealt by sports offices and big-time bookies as an inducement to rival bookies to accept their layoff bets.

The above is customary practice but there are occasional exceptions. A big bettor, for instance, may ask for a price line that will give him a better break and the bookie may give it to him because he wants to continue to get the customer's business.

BASEBALL'S 40¢ LINE

When two ball teams are rated as having an equal chance of winning a game, this is, in gambling lingo, an *even-money* bet, or a *Pick 'em* affair. When you read or hear of odds quoted as "even money" or "You Pick 'em," it means that the sports-service handicappers have rated both teams as having an equal chance to win.

But don't think that when the bookie takes your bet on an even-up proposition he will put up an equal amount of money. When a baseball game is quoted as even money by a sports handicapper, the bookie quotes a price of 6 to 5 Pick 'em. He will accept wages on either team but the bettor must lay or give odds of 6 to 5.

If the New York Yankees are playing the Cleveland Indians and it is a Pick 'em affair, the bookie will accept bets on either team, but $6 of your money must be bet against the bookie's $5. Suppose the bookie were to accept only two wagers of $6 each. Steffi, a Yank supporter, bets $6 on the Yankees, and Evelyn, a Cleveland enthusiast, bets $6 on the Indians with the same bookie. The total bet with the bookmaker is $12. It doesn't matter which team wins, the bookie pays off the winner at $11 (the $6 wagered plus the $5 profit). The bookie retains as his profit $1 (1/12 of the money wagered). His favorable percentage with this 6 to 5 bet on an even-money game is, therefore, 8⅓% of all money wagered with him.

Since only two 6 to 5 bets give the bookie a $1 profit, you can see how lucrative accepting sports bets is for a bookie dealing a 40¢ line to a sucker trade. Especially so if his clients insist on playing baseball parlays, round robins or back-to-back bets.

If the game is called off due to rain, darkness or curfew before being completed, and the score is tied, some bookies do even better. They pocket the entire $12. The bettor has two defenses against this. He must either be smart enough to have inquired beforehand whether tied games are no contest or he must be able to beat the bookie in a fist fight.

When one baseball team is favored over another the bookie's strategy is the same as with a Pick 'em game; his tactics are a bit different. He gains his favorable percentage by quoting two different prices. If the Yankees are an 8 to 5 favorite to beat the Baltimore Orioles, the bookie quotes his price as "7–9 Yanks favorite." This means that if you want to bet on the Yanks you must lay or give the bookie odds of 9 to 5, and if you want to bet on the Orioles the bookie will lay you odds of 7 to 5. When you bet the favorite you must give the bookmaker bigger odds than he will give you when you bet the underdog.

This differential of two points between the bookie's take and lay price gives the bookie a two-point spread in his favor on each bet made, no matter whether the bettors lay the odds or take the odds.

In the above instance, if one player laid $9 to $5 on the Yankees and another took $7 to $5 on the Orioles, the bookie would break even if the favorite won and earn $2 if the underdog won. This is why bookies prefer the underdog as the winner.

When a bookie operating on a two-point spread quotes a price of 7–9 so-and-so the favorite, the bettor should realize that the true odds on the favorite are 8 to 5. If the bookie quotes 8–10 so-and-so the favorite, the true odds are 9 to 5. The middle figure between the two prices the bookie quotes is the first odds figure, and the second odds figure is always 5.

The bookie who deals in a two-point spread receives little if any action from experienced or smart baseball bettors.

Here's another sound bit of advice for the inexperienced bettor: Don't mention the name of the team or teams on which you wish to bet until after the bookie has quoted his price on the game or games. If you say, "I want to place a bet on the Yankees against the Orioles; what are your payoff odds?" the bookie, knowing you want to bet on the Yankees, who are, let us assume, the favorites, may quote you a price of 9–11 instead of his prevailing price of 7–9. If you place the bet, you are laying odds of 11 to 5 instead of 9 to 5.

You may ask, "After the bookie has quoted 9–11 Yankees the favorite, wouldn't it be smart to turn around and say, 'I'll take the Orioles at nine to five'?" The shrewd bookie has an out for this. He says, "Let me check and see what the present odds on the sport line are first." He then makes a fake phone call to the sports-service office and reports back that the sports line on this game has changed and is now 7–9 Yanks favorite, which means that a bet on the Orioles will receive 7 to 5 odds from the bookmaker. This, of course, was the bookie's real price all along. This shows how tricky sports bets can be for the inexperienced player.

As I have said, bookies who deal in a two-point spread cater largely to suckers or inexperienced sports bettors. Some of these bookies falsely call their line a "20¢ line" instead of a "40¢ line" to mislead their bettors; others call it a "20¢ line" because they themselves do not know the difference.

Bookies who deal a 40¢ line, or, for that matter, those who deal a 20¢ line, quote their price line in terms of odds like 6 to 5 Pick 'em, or, 7–5, 7–9, 8–10, etc., because it is difficult for the average baseball bettor to spot the 40¢ spread. But if we transpose these price odds into a dollar price line, the 40¢ spread becomes obvious. A 6–5 Pick 'em becomes $1.20 to $1, Even 7–5 becomes $1 to $1 and $1.40 to $1, 7–9 becomes $1.40 to $1 and $1.80 to $1, 8–10 becomes $1.60 to $1 and $2 to $1.

Not only most baseball bettors but most bookies haven't the slightest idea what the bookie's favorable percentage is when dealing a 40¢

line. Some bettors think the different price quotes give the same percentage; others think it is to their advantage to take the bookie's odds rather than lay the odds; others never give the percentage angle a thought.

Since the bookie's percentage varies with each quotation, the smart baseball bettor should know what the percentages are. This will enable him to obtain a slightly better percentage break—if he still insists on betting the 40¢ line.

Here is a 40¢ price line table, listing its most popular price odds and the bookie's favorable percentage on each. Each percentage has been calculated to two decimal places.

BASEBALL'S 40¢ LINE

Correct Odds on Favorite	Bookie Lays the Odds	Bookie's Favorable Percentage *	Bookie Takes the Odds	Bookie's Favorable Percentage *
5 to 5	5 to 6	8.33%	6 to 5	8.33%
6 to 5	5 to 5	9.09%	7 to 5	6.46%
7 to 5	6 to 5	8.33%	8 to 5	5.17%
8 to 5	7 to 5	7.69%	9 to 5	4.24%
9 to 5	8 to 5	7.14%	2 to 1	3.53%
2 to 1	9 to 5	6.66%	11 to 5	3.03%
11 to 5	2 to 1	6.25%	12 to 5	2.57%
12 to 5	11 to 5	5.88%	13 to 5	2.22%
13 to 5	12 to 5	5.55%	14 to 5	1.96%
14 to 5	13 to 5	5.26%	3 to 1	1.72%
16 to 5	14 to 5	9.52%	18 to 5	2.62%
3½ to 1	3 to 1	11.11%	4 to 1	2.76%

* NOTE: These percentages have been calculated to only two decimal points; the third figure was dropped whenever it appeared.

Note that the bookie's favorable percentage varies with each betting quotation, and that his percentage of profit runs from a high of 11.11% to a low of 1.72%. Note also that a bettor who lays the odds to a bookie by betting on the favorite pays a lesser percentage to the bookie than the bettor does who takes the odds by betting on the underdog.

BASEBALL'S 20¢ LINE

As I have said, the bettor who accepts a 40¢ line payoff is either an inexperienced baseball bettor or a rank gambling sucker. But let me warn the $5 and $10 bettor that he will have to be content with the 40¢ price line because no present-day bookie in his right mind is going to lower his price line for the small $5 or $10 gambler.

If you place bets of $50 or more on the outcome of a ball game, you deserve and can get better odds than the 40¢ sucker line. Insist that your bookie quote the true 20¢ line. He'll argue loud and hard that that is what he is dealing, but you'll know by the time you finish this chapter whether or not to believe him. If the 20¢ line he claims he's dealing is really a 40¢ line and he insists on being stubborn about wanting to steal your money, take your baseball business elsewhere. A new bookie won't be too hard to find.

The 40¢ line, as we have seen, is based on a two-point differential between the bookie's lay and take odds. The 20¢ line is based on a one-point odd spread, or a 20¢ spread when figured on a $1 take price. The bookie's favorable percentage, therefore, when he deals a 20¢ line is approximately half the 40¢ line percentage.

To get this one-point spread the bookie has to resort to the use of fractions in his price line. Where the 40¢ line bookie quotes odds of 6 to 5 on a Pick 'em or even-money game, the 20¢ line bookie will quote odds of 5½ to 5. The player must lay $1.10 to the bookie's $1, no matter which team he bets on.

BASEBALL'S 20¢ LINE

Correct Odds on Favorite	Bookie Lays the Odds	Bookie's Favorable Percentage	Bookie Takes the Odds	Bookie's Favorable Percentage
5 to 5	5 to 5½	4.54%	5½ to 5	4.54%
5½ to 5	5 to 5	4.76%	6 to 5	3.93%
6 to 5	5½ to 5	4.54%	6½ to 5	3.44%
6½ to 5	6 to 5	4.34%	7 to 5	3.06%
7 to 5	6½ to 5	4.16%	7½ to 5	2.72%
7½ to 5	7 to 5	4.00%	8 to 5	2.50%
8 to 5	7½ to 5	3.84%	8½ to 5	2.24%
8½ to 5	8 to 5	3.70%	9 to 5	2.02½
9 to 5	8½ to 5	3.57%	9½ to 5	1.82%
9½ to 5	9 to 5	3.44%	2 to 1	1.70%
2 to 1	9½ to 5	3.33%	10½ to 5	1.58%
10½ to 5	2 to 1	3.22%	11 to 5	1.41%
11 to 5	10½ to 5	3.12%	11½ to 5	1.31%
11½ to 5	11 to 5	3.03%	12 to 5	1.22%
12 to 5	11½ to 5	2.94%	12½ to 5	1.12%
12½ to 5	12 to 5	2.85%	13 to 5	1.09%
13 to 5	12½ to 5	2.77%	13½ to 5	1.01%
14 to 5	13 to 5	5.26%	3 to 1	1.71%
3 to 1	14 to 5	5.00%	16 to 5	1.54%
3¼ to 1	3 to 1	5.88%	3½ to 1	1.66%

If the New York Yankees are an 8½ to 5 favorite over the Detroit Tigers, the 20¢ price line would read: 8–9 Yankees favorite, which means that the bookie will lay the Yankees at $1.60 to $1 or take the Tigers if the player lays $1.80 to $1.

These two examples show the one-point differential and the 20¢ difference between the bookie's take and lay price.

Remember, however, that many bookies who deal a 20¢ line, like the 40¢ line dealers, knowingly or unknowingly misrepresent the situation and claim to be dealing a 10¢ line, quoting their price in odds which helps mislead the player.

To realize just how big a sucker the bettor is who accepts the 40¢ line when he should be getting the 20¢ line, compare the tables on pages 118 and 119.

The bookie's percentage of profit, which varies as before, runs from a high of 5.88% to a low of 1.01%. Again note that his favorable percentage is less when he takes the odds, more when he lays the odds. Two decimal places only have been used, the third figure being dropped when it appeared.

BASEBALL'S 10¢ LINE

Bookies or sports offices who deal the dime, or 10¢, line cater only to bigtime bettors and smaller bookies. Their customers are located from coast to coast; a New York bookie may have customers in Chicago, Texas, Nevada or even California.

Bookies who deal the 10¢ line seldom accept baseball wagers of less than $100. (If the bet is under that amount the same bookie will deal the bettor a 20¢ line.) Most bets run from $100 to $20,000 on a single ball game, and as high as $40,000 on parlays, back-to-back bets and round robins.

The 10¢ line operates on a ½-point differential between the bookie's lay and take price. On a Pick 'em or even-money game the bettor must lay the bookie odds of 5¼ to 5, instead of the 5½ to 5 odds demanded by the 20¢ line bookie. If a team is a 6 to 5 favorite, the bookie will lay the player odds of 5¾ to 5 and insist that the player lay him odds of 6¼ to 5.

Unlike the bookies dealing 40¢ and 20¢ lines, the 10¢ line bookie has nothing to hide, and he runs down his price line in dollars and cents rather than in odds. This makes it easy to see the 10¢ differential in the take and lay price.

Examples: 5¼ Pick 'em becomes $1.05 to $1 Pick 'em; 6¼ to 5 and 6½ to 5 become $1.20 to $1 and $1.30 to $1; 7¾ to 5 and 8¼ to 5 become $1.55 to $1 and $1.65 to $1, etc.

BASEBALL'S 10¢ LINE

Correct Odds on Favorite	Bookie's Price Line	Bookie Lays the Odds	Bookie's Favorable Percentage	Bookie Takes the Odds	Bookie's Favorable Percentage
5 to 5	105 Pick	5 to 5¼	2.38%	5¼ to 5	2.38%
5¼ to 5	Even 11–10	5 to 5	2.43%	5½ to 5	2.14%
5½ to 5	105–115	5¼ to 5	2.38%	5¾ to 5	2.00%
5¾ to 5	110–120	5½ to 5	2.32%	6 to 5	1.87%
6 to 5	115–125	5¾ to 5	2.27%	6¼ to 5	1.73%
6¼ to 5	120–130	6 to 5	2.22%	6½ to 5	1.70%
6½ to 5	125–135	6¼ to 5	2.17%	6¾ to 5	1.59%
6¾ to 5	130–140	6½ to 5	2.12%	7 to 5	1.47%
7 to 5	135–145	6¾ to 5	2.08%	7¼ to 5	1.36%
7¼ to 5	140–150	7 to 5	2.04%	3 to 2	1.34%
3 to 2	145–155	7¼ to 5	2.00%	7¾ to 5	1.25%
7¾ to 5	150–160	3 to 2	1.96%	8 to 5	1.21%
8 to 5	155–165	7¾ to 5	1.92%	8¼ to 5	1.11%
8¼ to 5	160–170	8 to 5	1.88%	8½ to 5	1.09%
8½ to 5	165–175	8¼ to 5	1.85%	8¾ to 5	1.00%
8¾ to 5	170–180	8½ to 5	1.81%	9 to 5	.97%
9 to 5	175–185	8¾ to 5	1.78%	9¼ to 5	.90%
9¼ to 5	180–190	9 to 5	1.75%	9½ to 5	.88%
9½ to 5	185–200	9¼ to 5	1.72%	2 to 1	1.70%
2 to 1	190–210	9½ to 5	3.33%	10½ to 5	1.58%
10½ to 5	2–1 11–5	2 to 1	3.22%	11 to 5	1.41%
11 to 5	210–230	10½ to 5	3.12%	11½ to 5	1.31%
11½ to 5	220–240	11 to 5	3.03%	12 to 5	1.22%
12 to 5	230–250	11½ to 5	2.94%	12½ to 5	1.12%
12½ to 5	240–260	12 to 5	2.85%	13 to 5	1.09%
13 to 5	250–270	12½ to 5	2.77%	13½ to 5	1.01%
14 to 5	260–300	13 to 5	5.26%	3 to 1	1.71%
3 to 1	280–320	14 to 5	5.00%	16 to 5	1.54%
3¼ to 1	3–3½	3 to 1	5.88%	3½ to 1	1.66%

Ten-cent-line bookies, however, employ their own argot when running down their price line. "One twenty" means a price line of $1.20 to $1 with the take price of $1 being taken for granted and not mentioned. "One forty" means $1.40 to $1, "One fifty" means $1.50 to $1, etc.

Many bookies use further abbreviations. If the price line reads "Yankees favorite 120–130," they merely say "Yankees 20–30." This tells the experienced bettor that the bookie will lay $1.20 to $1 on the Yankees, and if the player wants to bet on the Yankees he must lay the bookie $1.30 to $1.

Also, since the 10¢ line is based primarily on the past performances of the starting pitcher, most bookies call the name of the pitcher rather than the team he represents. If the Chicago Cubs are 115–125 favorite over the Philadelphia Phillies and the announced starting pitchers are Ferguson Jenkins for the Cubs and Steve Carlton for the Phillies, the bookie quotes his price line as Jenkins 15–25 over Carlton.

This also means that the bookie is stipulating that if either Jenkins or Carlton fails to start the game the bet is off. If the bettor wants his bet to ride despite a starting pitcher substitution, he says, "Action." When he does this the bettor agrees to accept the bookie's new opening price line if a pitcher substitution takes place.

When the sports service computes its price line, it usually gives a team playing on its home grounds an edge of 20¢ to 30¢. For example, the Chicago Cubs with Jenkins pitching are playing away from home and the price line reads "Jenkins 20–30 over Joe Doe." If the same game were being played in Chicago, the price line might read "Jenkins 50–60 over Joe Doe." By the same reasoning, the sports service might make Chicago the favorite on its home grounds, but away from home Chicago might be made the underdog against the same team.

The sports services give the home team a 20¢–30¢ spot in the price line because (1) the visiting team must come to bat first, and (2) the home team is playing on its home grounds.

I have interviewed hundreds of bettors and bookies without finding one person who knew the bookie's favorable percentages when dealing the 10¢ line. The correct percentages shown on page 121 appear in print here for the first time.

The bookie's favorable percentage runs from a high of 5.88% to a low of .88%. Note that the percentages for the last ten quotations above are the same as the last ten on the 20¢ line table. Only two decimal places have been used, the third figure having been dropped when it appeared.

BASEBALL'S 5¢ LINE

Many horse bookies and smalltime sports bookies refer to their 20¢ line as the "5¢ line" or, more commonly, the "nickel line." Many bettors accept this terminology and believe they are being dealt a nickel line. Some of the bookies who miscall their 20¢ line a nickel line know what they are doing; some don't.

The true 5¢ or nickel line is, with very rare exceptions, dealt only by top sports offices and top bookies as a means of price-line changing or as an inducement to accept the sports office or bookie's layoff action.

The true nickel line works on a ¼-point differential between the price lines of the two opposing teams. Example: In a Pick 'em or even-money game the bettor must lay the bookie odds of 5⅛ to 5 no matter which team he bets on. Since the nickel line is quoted in dollars and cents rather than odds terms, the bookie quotes a Pick 'em game as "$1.02½ Pick." The bookie's favorable percentage on this wager is 1.21%.

Note the 5¢ spread between the bookie's take and lay price in the following examples: 102½ pick, even–105, 102½–107½, 122½–127½, 152½–157½, 162–167½, 172½–177½, etc. The bookie's favorable percentage in these examples runs from a high of 1.23% on the bookie's take price of even–105 to a low of .51% on his lay price of 172½–177½.

One would think that since the bookie's favorable percentage in dealing a nickel line is about half that of a dime line, the bigtime bettors would all insist on being dealt the nickel line. This is not true, because the bookie who deals a nickel line specifies that players who ask for a run-down of his price line must make at least three separate bets, none of which can be less than $1,000 or more than $3,000. For this reason most bigtime bettors prefer the dime line.

WHY SOME SPORTS BOOKIES GET ULCERS

Most writers on gambling seem to believe that a baseball bookie seldom, if ever, gambles. If they had the faintest idea of the number of sports bookies who have gone broke gambling, they'd stop writing such books and articles as "Gamblers Don't Gamble" and "Bookies Aren't Gamblers." These writers labor under the impression that a baseball bookie can make a fortune merely by sitting in his office and accepting bets over the telephone. They think that if the bookie happens to get excessive action on a certain team, he simply phones a layoff bookie, gets rid of the undesired action and earns a profit by doing so.

I agree that if the bookie is a small curbstone operator taking small action he can lay off his excess action to a bigger sports bookie. If he is taking horse bets he can easily work within his extension. A small horse bookie can call a bigger bookie and lay off his excess action, and this process can continue until it reaches the top-level bookie. Even the top-level bookie, in turn, has a place to lay off his excess action; he simply phones his representative at the track and tells him to get rid of it by betting it at the $100 pari-mutuel window.

But the baseball bookie has no sure out for his layoff bets, and his operation, therefore, requires considerably more ingenuity than a horse bookie's. A baseball bookie's dream would be to have all his bigtime customers bet equal amounts on opposing teams. Suppose his price line on a Boston-Chicago game reads "1.05 Pick 'em." If his customers bet him $21,000 on Boston and another $21,000 on Chicago, the bookie would earn $1,000 no matter which team won. Since this rarely happens, he has to resort to a few artful dodges to stay in business.

One thing he does is to keep a running check of the total monies wagered on each ball club. If there are large sums wagered on one team and very little on its opponent, the bookie jockeys his price line in an effort to get more action on the underdog.

This doesn't always work. Here's an example which illustrates the bookie's price-line changing and shows what can happen if the bigtime bettors ignore such changes. The speaker is a sports bookie operating in Florida.

"Scarne," he said, "a year or so ago the Yankees were scheduled to play Cleveland. The game was 105 Pick. An hour before game time a customer of mine, who has been named by Congressional investigating committees as one of the top ten racket guys in the country, phoned and bet me $21,000 on the Yankees. I immediately changed my price line to read 'Yanks favorite, even 11–10.'

"Fifteen minutes later the same racket guy called and layed * me $22,000 on the Yankees. I changed my price line to read 'Yanks 105–115.' The racket guy called again and this time layed me $23,000 on the Yankees. When he called a fourth time I informed him I wasn't taking any more action on the Yankee-Cleveland game. Scarne, I found myself with $66,000 worth of action on the Yankees and not a quarter's worth on Cleveland.

"I called a couple of small bookies, but they dealt a twenty-cent line and refused to take ten-cent-line action even when I told them they could have it free. So I called a few of my rival bookie friends who deal in a ten-cent line. Even for free they wanted no part of it."

"What did you do then?" I asked.

"Well, I went home and watched the game on TV and prayed every time a Yankee batter got up to the plate that he'd strike out. Lucky for me my prayers were answered and Cleveland won. I did not have any sixty grand to pay off this racket guy, and if the Yanks had won I would not be around to relate this story."

"Why did you take the action when you didn't have money to cover your loss if the Yankees won?"

"Well, Scarne, when I upped the price on the Yankees I thought the racket guy would bet Cleveland and I could not get hurt. After I upped the Yankees twice and the racket guy still kept betting the Yankees I knew my only salvation was to pray."

---

* Since most gamblers spell the past tense of "lay" as "layed" rather than "laid," I will follow their custom.—J.S.

This story happens to have had a happy ending, but some of them don't. I know of a midwestern sports office that lost $550,000 to its bigtime bettors during a recent baseball season.

The running of a bigtime dime-line baseball book also calls for a surprising degree of ingenuity in order to conceal the betting and financial transactions from the prying eyes of Federal, state and local law-enforcement agencies. On the phone, for instance, a bookie has to talk in code. Here is a typical phone conversation between a bigtime New York bookie and a bettor who, for security reasons, is calling from a public phone booth in Miami. Incidentally, many bigtime bookies, prior to the enactment of the Federal anti-gambling laws, made use of the WATS (an abbreviation for *wide area telephone service*). This is a telephone company service whereby the customer is given a flat rate for long-distance telephone calls to limited areas at specific times of the day. This service is favored by bigtime bookies because of the special rates and because the telephone company does not keep records of the long-distance calls for this service. Now, let's get back to our phone conversation:

BOOKIE (into phone): Hello, Dave speaking.

BETTOR: Hello, Dave. This is Number Thirty-two calling. Check bottom figure.

BOOKIE: Hold on, Thirty-two. (Pause) Bottom figure is 1–29–55 in our favor.

BETTOR: That's correct, Dave. Run me down.

BOOKIE: Okay, Thirty-two. Here goes the run-down. American League: Hunter and Blyleven 105 Pick; Stottlemyre 15–25 over Tiant; Palmer 70–80 over Bell; Wood 15–25 over Bosman; Lolich 10–20 over Dumming; Ryan 25–35 over Busby. National League: Gibson 60–70 over Blass; Marichal 25–35 over Gullet; Lonborg and Seaver 105 Pick; Pappas 50–60 over Torres; Roberts 15–25 over Gentry; Sutton 10–20 over Kirby. That's it, Thirty-two.

BETTOR: Okay, Dave. Give me Stottlemyre to win, 18 big ones.

BOOKIE: You got Stottlemyre to win, 18 big ones.

BETTOR: Give me Wood to win for 16 small ones.

BOOKIE: You got Wood to win for 16 small ones.

BETTOR: Give me Blass to win for a big nickel, with action.

BOOKIE: You got Blass to win for a big nickel with action.

BETTOR: Give me the Yankees and Mets in a parlay for a big nickel, with action.

BOOKIE: You got the Yankees and Mets in a parlay for a big nickel with action.

BETTOR: Give me the Yankees, Mets and Pittsburgh in a round robin for 6 small ones with action.

BOOKIE: You got the Yankees, Mets and Pittsburgh in a round robin for 6 small ones with action.

BETTOR: One more, Dave. Give me Torres to win for 3 small nickels. That wraps it up, Dave. Call you tomorrow.

BOOKIE: You got Torres to win, 3 small nickels. Okay, Thirty-two, lots of luck. Talk to you tomorrow.

The preceding text concerning sports and horse bookies should enable you to decode most of this phone conversation, and the following definitions of terms will clarify the rest.

Bottom figure: Money owed to bookie by player, or player to bookie, involving previous betting transactions. The bookie's quote of "1–29–55 in our favor" means that the bettor owes the bookie $12,955 to date; figures of 3–6–25 would indicate $3,625, etc.

Run me down: The bettor is asking the bookie to quote his price line.

One big one: $1,000. A "small one" is $100, a "big nickel" is $500, a "small nickel" is $50.

Other bookies may use these code words differently. A "big one" might mean $100, a "small one" $10; a "big nickel" could mean $5,000, a "small nickel" $500. A "big dollar" might mean $1,000, a "small dollar" $100.

Similar coding of conversations is also used by bookies dealing in football, basketball, hockey, horse racing, etc.

HOW TO FIGURE YOUR WINNING BASEBALL BETS

Many sports bettors don't know how to figure two- and three-team winning parlays, and take it for granted that the bookie's payoff price is correct. Many bookies, knowing this, pay off less than they should.

Hundreds of sports bookies compute their odds payoff on the basis of a $1 price line and, knowingly or unknowingly, cheat their customers of thousands of dollars yearly merely by dropping a penny fraction or the third decimal place when it appears.

For example, suppose you made a $50 bet by parlaying two ball teams and layed odds of 6 to 5 on each game. You win, and your bookie converts the 6 to 5 odds into a money price of $1 to 83⅓¢, which is correct. The fraction is awkward, so he drops it and pays you $167.44. This fraction-dropping has cost you 61¢ because the correct payoff price figures out as $168.05. Don't be a chump for a bookie; learn to do your own figuring.

It is not difficult to figure parlays of single-game payoffs if you use the following method especially devised by the author for the readers of this book.

Computing the payoff odds on a single game sounds simple enough

—but is it? Suppose you made a $5 bet at 6 to 5 odds, and you won. How much money must your bookie pay you? If you had made a $6 bet you would not need to do any pencil work; at 6 to 5 odds you'd expect to receive $11. But the fact that you bet $5 makes it harder to figure, at least it is for most inexperienced sports bettors.

Here's how to do it. First put down the amount of your bet, in this case $5; then put a multiplication sign after it.

Now add the odds figures (in this case, 6 plus 5) and use the answer (11) as the bottom part (denominator) of a fraction. One of the odds figures is used as the top part (numerator) of the fraction. Which one? That depends on whether you were laying or taking the odds. When you lay the odds the complete fraction will be more than ½, when you take the odds it will be less than ½. If you lay odds of 6 to 5, the fraction will be 6/11; if you take to 6 to 5 odds, the fraction will be 5/11.

And here's my gimmick. Reverse the fraction by transposing numerator and denominator so that 6/11 becomes 11/6. Then multiply this by the amount of your bet as follows:

$$\$5 \times \frac{11}{6} = \$9.16\tfrac{2}{3}$$

This $9.16⅔ is the correct amount due you on a $5 bet which you layed at 6 to 5 odds.

If you wagered $55 and took the 6-to-5 odds your arithmetic would be as follows:

$$\$55 \times \frac{11}{5} = \$121$$

This gives you $121 as the correct amount due you on your $55 winning parlay.

Parlay payoffs are figured with the same mathematical formula. First put down the sum of your wager, then reduce the price odds of each game to fractions. Reverse the fractions and multiply your wager by the fractions. Example: You bet $65 on a three-team parlay. You layed the odds of 7 to 5 on the first team and took the odds of 9 to 5 and 6 to 5 on the other two teams. Your parlay won and you figure the correct payoff this way:

$$\$65 \times \frac{12}{7} \times \frac{14}{5} \times \frac{11}{5} = \$686.40$$

There is still one wrinkle to consider. If the bookie's price odds involve a fraction such as 6¼ to 5 or 8¾ to 5, you must add another gimmick to the formula.

Suppose you parlayed a $50 bet on three winning teams. You layed odds of 9½ to 5 on the first team, and took odds of 8¼ to 5 on the second team and 6½ to 5 on the third team. You must convert the price odds into a money line on the basis of a $5 take. Odds of 6¼ to 5 become $6.25 to $5, 8¾ to 5 becomes $8.75 to $5, etc. You use the formula as explained above and get this:

$$\$50 \times \frac{\$14.50}{\$9.50} \times \frac{\$13.25}{\$5.00} \times \frac{\$11.50}{\$5.00}$$

Now you reduce your $5-take line figure to terms of cents simply by dividing by a common divisor 25. This gives you:

$$\$50 \times \frac{58¢}{38¢} \times \frac{53¢}{20¢} \times \frac{46¢}{20¢} = \$465.14$$

On this three-team winning parlay your bookie owes you $465.14. But you might not get that much unless you knew how to figure it yourself.

BASEBALL'S RUN SPREAD BET

To stimulate interest in baseball betting and to make a few extra bucks, modern bookies have stolen a page from hockey betting (see page 133) and introduced the now popular ½—1, 1½—2 or 2—3 run spread. This means that if the player bets the underdog team, he is given a ½-, 1½- or 2-run handicap or spot, making the game an even-money bet. Most bookies who handle this kind of baseball action will accept wagers on either team but the bettor must lay or give odds of 6 to 5, which gives the bookie an 8⅓% advantage.

To illustrate, let's say the New York Yankees are playing the Cleveland Indians and the bookie's price line reads "Yankees favorite 1½—2 runs." If you bet Cleveland and the Yankees win the game by a score of 3 to 2, you win. For you to lose, the Yankees must outscore the Indians by three runs or more. If the Yankees score two runs more than Cleveland, the game is a tie—no one wins, no one loses. For this bet to be valid, bookies insist that it be a full nine-inning game or longer.

If you are one of the millions of baseball bettors who go for run spread bets, shop around and try to get the best price line available, such as 11 to 10 Pick 'em instead of 6 to 5 Pick 'em.

BETTING ON FOOTBALL

More money is bet on the outcome of college and professional football games than on any other sport. Many more tens of millions of dollars are wagered on gridiron contests each Sunday during the professional football season than in any one week of baseball, except during the World Series.

The biggest bettor on football games in 1973 was a Texas oil man who is also well known for his big casino betting in Nevada. His bets during the professional football season averaged $2 million each Sunday. He usually bet between $50,000 and $100,000 with a single bookie office, and spread his day's business among about 20-odd bookies operating in widely separated cities. During the closing week of the college football season this bigtime bettor wagered $1,100,000 on 23 different football games. He won $50,000 on the day's play. This same bigtime bettor wagered $500,000 on the Minnesota Vikings to beat the Miami Dolphins in the 1973 Super Bowl game. Three sports offices booked this $500,000 losing wager.

The scouting systems and methods used by the sports services in obtaining real inside information would make any group of investigators working for a U.S. senatorial or congressional committee look like a pack of Cub Scouts. Dozens of fake injuries to football stars may be announced during the season without any change in the price line. But should a real injury occur, even though unannounced, the price line changes immediately.

If the bookies who handle football action gave their customers a price line like baseball's 40¢, 20¢ or dime lines, they would have gone broke long ago. It is much easier to pick the winner of a college football game by studying past performance than it is to pick a major-league baseball winner, especially since there are 30 or more colleges from which to select.

There have been hundreds of incidents during the past year or two in which teams—both college and professional—put out phony injury reports to key personnel in hopes of throwing off the game plans of their opponents. They may have convinced the opponents that something was wrong but the sports offices and layoff bookies are not taken in by these phony reports since they have access to inside information on most teams.

Note that when it is announced in the press that the team's star quarterback is not going to be in the starting lineup for a big game because of an injury, the gamblers' pipeline already had this information 15 minutes after the injury happened—maybe even before the owner of the team knew. This information could have come from a team physician, a coach, a locker-room attendant, a player, a member of the front-office staff, a secretary or even a newspaperman covering the team. There is absolutely no way to hide this information from the pipeline. Bookies have been known to pay as much as $5,000 for such information.

The sports office's or layoff bookie's opening line (not to be confused with the Las Vegas line, the newspaper line, etc.) is not made without accident. When it fluctuates, there is a reason. The big bookie takes many things into consideration in making his opening line. After the betting begins, a $20,000 bet can increase or diminish the spread a point or two on a particular team; a $50,000 bet can make the favorite team the underdog, etc.

The football information services or sports offices use the football "spread" or handicap gimmick which tends to make every game a Pick 'em or even-money contest. The pricemaker arranges a suitable point spread or handicap which he believes will equalize the teams' chance of winning, as far as bookie and bettor are concerned.

Example: Suppose Army is slated to tackle Navy this coming Saturday. After considerable handicapping, the pricemaker decides that Army should beat Navy by 9 points. He makes the game an even-money contest by quoting a price line of "Army 9 points over Navy." This means that bettors who put their money on Army win their bets if Army beats Navy by a margin of 10 points or more. If Army wins by exactly 9 points the game is considered a tie (no contest) and the bettor neither wins nor loses. If Army beats Navy by 8 points or less, or if Army ties or loses to Navy, then all bets on Army are lost.

Bookies don't like to have to return players' bets on tie games, so they eliminate the possibility of ties by adding an extra half-point differential, quoting a price line like this: "Army 9½ points over Navy." This half-point is also used as a means of price changing and as a come-on to induce bettors to bet on the underdog. If, for instance, the price line reads: "Princeton 6-point favorite over Yale" and the bookie receives a rush of Princeton money, he tries to balance his book and induce the customers to bet on Yale by changing his price line to read: "Princeton 6½ points over Yale."

When the bookie believes that two opposing teams are evenly matched, his line will read: "Army-Navy Pick 'em 6–5" or "Army-Navy Pick 'em 11–10."

When the bookie decides that two opposing teams are evenly matched, neither team receives a spot or handicap. But the bet is not made at even money. The bookie will take action on either team and you must always lay him odds. His price line will read either "Army-Navy Pick 'em 6 to 5" or "Army-Navy Pick 'em 11 to 10." The small bookie deals the 6 to 5 Pick-em line and you must lay him odds of 6 to 5 no matter which team you wager on. If you do business with a sports office or bigtime bookie you get a much better break; you put up odds of 11 to 10.

The bookie who deals a 6 to 5 Pick 'em line has a favorable edge of 8⅓%. The 11 to 10 line gives him an advantage of only 4 6/11%. Don't be a chump when betting on football games; insist on the 11 to 10 Pick 'em price line. If your favorite bookie won't oblige, find a bookie who will.

BETTING ON BASKETBALL

Today there is little bigtime betting with sports books on either college or professional basketball games. I questioned more than fifty bigtime sport bookies and found the largest single bet any of them accepted was $2,000. The bookie who accepted that bet told me he did so only because the bettor was a $20,000-a-game football bettor whom he didn't want to lose as a customer.

Most bookies who handle baseball and football action refuse to handle basketball bets. Those bookies who do deal in basketball and who will handle a $20,000 bet on a baseball or football game will seldom accept more than $1,000 basketball bet. If you want to place a $5 or $50 bet on a basketball game you'll have to do it with the curbstone horse bookie. He's easy enough to find; there are thousands and thousands throughout the country.

The bookie's basketball line, like the football line, uses a point differential between the price line of the opposing teams. If Fordham is a 12-point favorite over Columbia and you bet on Fordham, you collect only if Fordham beats Columbia by 13 points or more. If Fordham wins by exactly 12 points the game is considered a tie and the bet is off. If Fordham wins by 11 points or less, or if Columbia wins, all bets on Fordham are lost.

The basketball line also emanates from the Middle West, but the sports services don't have the same confidence in it that they do in their baseball and football lines. The daily basketball line usually has one or more games "circled" and, occasionally, one or more called "off the board."

The service may circle a game for a number of reasons, such as a tip from one of its basketball scouts that a man whom the service eyes with suspicion will referee the game. Circling the game tells the bookie that for his own protection he should cut his extension per player in half. If his extension on a game is $300, it drops to $150.

When the service calls a game "off the board" it means that one of the scouts has reported that he believes the game will be crooked. This warns all bookies not to accept any action on the game. The service gives neither details nor the source of its information to the bookies, especially when the information has to do with a possible fix.

The sports services' suspicion of crookedness in basketball games and the bigtime bookies' refusal to handle big basketball bets is the result of college basketball scandals in which many top college stars were found to have thrown games. The bookies can't forget the financial beatings they suffered.

Here's what one bookie who refuses all basketball action told me: "Scarne, every basketball team has one or two stars who score most of the baskets; the other three players are merely fill-ins. So some punk offers one of these kid college stars a bribe of a new automobile. The punk says he doesn't want the star to betray his classmates or his college by throwing the game. Nothing of the sort. The kid's team will still win but not by as big a margin of points. 'What's the difference,' the punk says, 'if your team wins by nine or eleven points instead of fifteen or twenty? It still wins.'

"Let's suppose Squedunk is a ten-point favorite to beat Sowats. Joe Doe, Squedunk's star, is a thirty-point basketball player, and one of those rats who specialize in bribing kids has gotten to Joe. Joe plays his game so that Squedunk wins by nine points or less. Joe is still the college hero because Squedunk won, but those extra baskets he purposely missed would cost me a bankroll. Most of the kids won't go for this, but maybe one will, and I'm not taking chances. A bookie who handles big-money bets on basketball is begging to be taken, and believe you me, that's what happens to him sooner or later."

Bookies who deal a basketball line also have two price lines: the 6 to 5 Pick 'em and the 11 to 10 Pick 'em. If you are a small or inexperienced bettor it's a safe bet you'll be dealt the 6 to 5 Pick 'em line; if you're a smart sports bettor you'll probably be dealt the 11 to 10 line. Just remember the 6 to 5 line gives the bookie a favorable percentage of 8⅓% and the 11 to 10 line gives him only a 4 6/11% edge.

BASKETBALL'S UNDER AND OVER BET

Sports bookies in order to increase their basketball action and to protect themselves against a possible fix have introduced a new innovation in sports betting—it's known as basketball's Under and Over bet. It really is a simple bet. The bookie quotes a figure which indicates the possible combined number of points that will be scored by both teams. Let's say the bookie's basketball line (quoted figure) is 200 points. The player may bet that the teams will score over or under 200 points and must lay or give odds of 6 to 5 for a bookie advantage of 8⅓% of all money wagered with him. If the combined scores total exactly 200 points, it's a standoff or push and no one wins, no one loses. Example: Let's say the New York Knicks are playing the Boston Celtics and the bookie's point line is 200. The Knicks score 126 points, the Celtics score 112 for a combined score of 238 points. Players betting "over" win, players betting "under" lose their bets. Should the combined team scores total less than the 200, players betting "under" win and players betting "over" lose. Try to get your bookie to accept the bet at 11 to 10 odds.

Some bookies' basketball lines quote three figures—for example, 200, 201 and 202 as the combined team scores. If the player bets "under" and the score is 199 or less, he wins. If it is exactly 200, it's a push. If he bets "over" and the score is 203 or more, he wins, exactly 202 it's a push. Should the score total the in-between figure, in this instance 201, the bookie wins both the under and over bets—and the players must lay the bookie 11 to 10 odds. Some bookies accept even money on such a wager. The single quote figure is a much better bet. Naturally the bookie's point line varies with each game and at times when he can't make up his mind on the line number, he takes the game off the board (no bets accepted). This is another indication that bookies don't gamble.

BETTING ON HOCKEY

Hockey is one of the most popular betting sports with American sports gamblers. My survey shows that $200 million was bet on the outcome of hockey games during 1973. The biggest single wager made during 1973 with a New York bookie was a $25,000 bet made by a Canadian sportsman on the Toronto Maple Leafs. Most bets on hockey accepted by bookies range from $50 to $500.

The hockey sports line emanates from Cincinnati, Minneapolis and Montreal. Few bookies, however, subscribe to the line, and even those seldom bother to check it.

There are a number of reasons why hockey has become the fourth most popular betting sport. These are the two principal ones:

1. The team expansion to four leagues with their many championship playoffs that are constantly being shown on television.

2. Today's bookies offer the hockey bettor the point differential used in baseball, football and basketball price lines in which the bettor lays odds of 6 to 5 or 11 to 10, or the bettor may accept the bookies' hockey price line based on a differential in goals, in which case he must also lay the odds of 6 to 5 or 11 to 10. The hockey price line based on the differential in goals works as follows.

Example: The Chicago Black Hawks are favored to beat the Boston Bruins and the bookie's price line reads: "Chicago favorite 1–1½ goals." This means that if the bettor puts his money on the Chicago Hawks he wins only if they beat Boston by 2 goals or more since it's impossible to score half a goal. If he puts his money on the underdog, the Boston Bruins, he loses if Chicago beats Boston by 2 goals or more.

A few bookies do use a goal differential of from ½ to 2 goals between teams and demand that the player lay odds of 6 to 5 or 11 to 10 on either team.

BETTING ON GREYHOUND DOG RACING

Greyhound racing is popular the world over with at least 300 dog-racing tracks in operation, including those in the United States, most countries in South America, Ireland, England, France, Italy and China. The greyhound dog racing handle in the United States today exceeds $800 million per year. Greyhound racing is permitted in nine states, Florida, Arkansas, Alabama, Colorado, Arizona, Massachusetts, New Hampshire, Oregon and South Dakota. Florida, with its 17 dog tracks, leads all other states in race attendance and betting handle. The Derby Lane dog track in St. Petersburg, Florida, rates as the oldest in America, having been in operation since early 1925.

Since the introduction of the mechanical rabbit, greyhound racing has become big business and as a result greyhound breeding has become an important industry in this country. Prices range from about $500 for unknown puppies to $25,000 or more for top racers.

All major greyhound tracks operating in the United States use the pari-mutuel betting system. At most tracks there are 12 races a night, featuring daily doubles, exactas, quinielas, superfectas or Big E's. (For explanations of these wagers, see page 39.) In addition to these, several Latin American countries use an imitation of Puerto Rico's 5–6 pool in which a bettor or bettors picking 6 winners from the fourth through ninth races divide 75% of the pool, the remainder being distributed to those picking 4 or 5 winners.

SCARNE'S ADVICE ON BETTING THE DOGS

If you are one of the many thousands who go to the track to bet the dogs for fun, remember that you must pay for the privilege. If you want to keep the price down to what you can afford, here is a good system: Before leaving home, decide how much you want to spend (bet), add the track admission price, the price of a program, allowance for refreshments and price of transportation. Take this amount with you and no more, so that if you lose you won't be tempted to recoup your losses and lose more than you planned. Then bet the favorite to *show*. Forget about win and place bets. I don't say this advice will win you money, but it will cut down your losses. Always remember that when you pick a winner, you're lucky; it isn't good handicapping. Don't forget that "you can beat a race, but not the races."

BETTING ON JAI ALAI, THE WORLD'S FASTEST GAME

Jai alai, regarded as the fastest game in the world, originated in Spain from a form of handball played by the Basques more than 200 years ago. In Spain it is known as *pelota vasca*. Jai alai was first imported to this hemisphere by way of Cuba in 1900; today it is played in Spain, France, Italy, China, the Philippines, Mexico, Cuba and other Latin American countries. In 1935, Florida legalized jai alai with a pari-mutuel betting system. Jai alai was recently introduced at the M.G.M. Grand Hotel in Las Vegas, Nevada.

Jai alai is played with a basket hand covering (cesta) and a hardened goatskin covered virgin rubber ball (pelota) in an enclosed auditorium (fronton). The object of the game is to throw the ball with such speed and spin that it rebounds into fair territory so that the opposition is unable to catch it either in the air or on the first bounce, or to return it to the back wall.

The game can be played either single or doubles. The skill of the game lies in placing the ball out of reach of the opposition, or imparting an incredible amount of spin on the ball so that the opposition cannot return it. Balls travel at speeds up to 150 miles per hour, making the game all action as the players must catch and throw without stopping the motion of their arms.

Betting in Florida at jai alai is the same as pari-mutuel race betting: each player or team is given a number and wagers are taken on where the players will finish. In addition to the standard win, place and show betting there is exotic wagering. There are two daily doubles on the 3rd and 4th events and the 10th and 11th. There is quiniela and perfecta wagering on each match.

To win the quiniela the bettor must select the players of the teams that finish first and second in a given game. Either team may win, the other must finish second. Perfecta wagering is actually a quiniela in which the bettor must select the exact order of finish for the first two places. Payoffs can be high in the perfectas—a $1,314.60 perfecta was hit at Dania, Florida's finest jai alai palace. $100 payoffs on the perfecta are common.

The Big Q was introduced several years back and was an instant success. The trick is to wager $2 before the start of the first game on two teams you think will finish first and second. If they win you exchange your winning ticket at no additional cost for your choice of the win and place finishers in game two. If you're a winner you can collect as much as $4,168.20 or as little as $171.80—those are the biggest and smallest Big Q payoffs at Dania, Florida, last season.

One final note. Bet the favorite to show. Forget about the win, place, daily double, quiniela, perfecta and Big Q bets. I don't say this advice will win money, but it will cut down your losses.

BETTING ON ELECTIONS

My survey shows that approximately $200 million is wagered annually with bookies on the outcome of national, state and local elections. The biggest single wager on record placed with a bookie was made by a racetrack owner when he took $1.2 million to $1 million that Richard Nixon would beat John F. Kennedy for the Presidency of the United States. This huge wager was placed with a dozen of the nation's bigtime sports offices.

The bookies' price line in election betting is usually 6 to 5 Pick 'em. From then on the money wagered with the bookie has the price line jumping up and down.

Most bookies act as their own pricemakers in election betting, so it's most unusual for several bookies in the same area to have different price lines. They usually operate on a two-point spread as in the 40¢ line in baseball. In a Pick 'em contest, the bettor must lay the bookie odds of 6 to 5 no matter which candidate he puts his money on.

When one candidate is so pronounced a favorite that his election is almost certain, the bookies use a vote differential in order to stimulate business. For example, a bookie in my home town of Fairview, New Jersey, will make Candidate Battaglia a 2,000-vote favorite over Candidate Reme for Mayor. The bookie will accept odds of 6 to 5 on either candidate, but Battaglia must win by at least 2,001 votes for his supporters to collect. A 2,000-vote majority by Battaglia is not considered a tie, and the bookie pockets all. Reme supporters win their bets if Battaglia wins by a 1,999-vote majority or less or if Reme is elected or ties. The bookie has an 8⅓% advantage riding for him.

When you bet against a bookmaker in elections, you can win provided you have an edge in information that will overcome the bookie's percentage. If you are aware, and the bookie isn't, that a political leader who formerly supported Battaglia is going to switch his backing to Reme at the last minute and carry enough votes with him to cut Battaglia's expected 2,000-vote majority down to 1,000, you have a solid bet that could beat the bookmaker.

Because the vote differential in state and national elections often runs into hundreds of thousands the bookmakers have no bed of roses when they accept action on political elections.

BETTING ON PRIZEFIGHTS

In 1946, $500 million was bet on prizefights in the United States. My recent survey shows that this figure has dropped to an all-time low of approximately $75 million in an average year. The decline of boxing is largely responsible for this decline in betting, plus the fact that most bookies refuse to handle the fight action that is available. Their reluctance is due to the continual exposures of crooked fights. Most sports bookies agree with a top sports bookie whom I interviewed. He said, "Any bookie who takes fight action is out of his mind. Sure, he earns a few bucks on fights that are on the square. Then along comes a tanker and wham! The bookie is taken for a bundle. I want no part of any fight action."

The few bookies who do handle fight action do it to accommodate their customers, but the biggest wager they'll accept is $500 unless it is a championship fight.

The biggest betting fight in the past ten years was the 1971 heavyweight championship match between Muhammad Ali (Cassius Clay) and Joe Frazier; about $100 million was wagered with sports bookies. The bigtime bookies' opening price line read "Clay, Frazier 6 to 5 Pick 'em." If you bet on Frazier you had to lay the bookie odds of 6 to 5; if you bet on Clay you still had to lay 6 to 5.

Most bookies, however, who handle fight wagers quote a two-point spread price line. Example: 7–9. If you bet the favorite you have to lay 9 to 5, if you bet the underdog you take 7 to 5. If a fighter is a 4 or 5 to 1 favorite the bookies usually refuse to take action on the underdog.

The bookies' opening fight price line emanates from a Washington, D.C., sports office.

BETTING ON GOLF GAMES

My survey shows that gambling on golf is now big business. Gamblers and golfers wagered approximately $700 million on golf games, matches and tournaments in 1973.

The biggest loser of record is an American sports bookie who was taken for $300,000 on a rigged Calcutta sweepstake in Florida.

As evidence of the large sums of money bet on golf matches let me cite the Las Vegas Annual Tournament of Champions. This is not only golf's biggest gambling extravaganza but also its biggest Calcutta pool. Unlike the Calcutta pools at most golf clubs, the tournament players are not given point handicaps. Since participating players must have won a Professional Golfers Association-sponsored tournament during the year, the field is small and strictly class.

After the participants are chosen, the Calcutta pool opens with a player auction in which gamblers bid for individual golfers. The bids for the privilege of "owning" a player usually range from $2,000 to $25,000. After 10% of the pool's total handle is taken off the top for the Damon Runyon Cancer Fund the rest is usually divided as follows: 50% to the holder of the winning player, 20% to the holder of the second place, 15% to the holder of third place, and 10% and 5% to the holder of fourth and fifth place. It is customary for the owners of a winning player to reward him with 10% of his winnings.

As the tournament progresses the gamblers who own players resort to hedging and scalping their man in an attempt to make money on him no matter how he places in the tournament. Sometimes they are able to sell shares in their golfer which add up to three times the price of the auction bid. I know of one Nevada gambling-house operator who paid $20,000 for a top golfer and sold shares in him that totaled $60,000.

In 1959 the total initial bids in the Calcutta pool of the Las Vegas Tournament of Champions reached their highest total—$285,000. Carl Anderson, a Los Angeles business executive, collected $95,760 by backing Stan Leonard, the winner of the first prize.

During the tournament there is much side betting among the high rollers around Las Vegas. If you can't get a side bet down you can find a sports bookie who will accommodate you, provided you accept his price line. Nevada bookies make their own price lines on golfers and will accept bets up to $5,000 on individual golfers. Approximately one million dollars is wagered each year in Nevada on the outcome of this tournament.*

Hundreds of Calcutta pools are run yearly in golf clubs throughout the country. Most of these, however, operate on the basis of a player's handicap, the purpose of the handicap being to try to give each player an equal chance to win first prize.

Many of the first-prize awards in these contests are won by golf hustlers who join the club solely in order to participate in the Calcutta tournament. They pose as poor golfers, are given a high handicap, and then on the day of the tournament play top-grade golf and walk off with the first prize. It's usually a good idea to look suspiciously at a recent golf-club joiner who is involved in the club's Calcutta pool: he may be a ringer.

---

* Since the above was written the Calcutta pool has been discontinued because the Professional Golfers Association refused to cooperate. It was rumored that some players had been bribed.

This gimmick is used all the time. There are hundreds of golf hustlers who prey on club golfers. Some have won as much as $100,000 in one year by masquerading as poor golfers, then betting big on a certain game in which they suddenly show top form and win. Golf hustlers sometimes work two or three clubs in the same area at the same time.

In concluding this sports chapter my advice can be summed up like this: If you must bet on sports:

1. Learn how to figure your winning payoffs.
2. Insist on being dealt the best price line available.
3. Avoid bets that have a high percentage in the bookie's favor.

SCARNE'S LEGALIZED STATE SPORTS BETTING PLAN

Several state committees in New York and New Jersey are studying possible state legalization and operation of sports betting offices which will handle bets on football, baseball, basketball, hockey, etc. There are many hazards that will be encountered by the state in operating its own sports betting offices, and I will discuss the most important ones here. I will also discuss my state sports betting plan that will eliminate these hazards. This is the only plan that is workable; it will save the states untold millions of dollars which would be lost or stolen by sports betting slickers and cheats.

Before the installation of the first electrically controlled pari-mutuel betting totalisator in 1933 at Arlington Park in Chicago, books were licensed by the track and paid a fixed fee for the privilege of accepting bets within the confines of the track. Each bookie was his own handicapper and pricemaker and quoted his own payoff odds when accepting a bet. What happened to most of these licensed legal race bookies of yesteryear? They went broke. If a state or city were to operate sports betting offices in the same manner—being handicapper and pricemaker—it too would lose money.

A state or city can't operate in the same manner as today's illegal sports bookie because the illegal book can refuse to accept any sports bets it wishes. The state betting office, on the other hand, would have to accept all bets listed. The state would also have difficulty in doing as the illegal sports bookie does, quoting new price lines as the betting continues. And just one sports event fixed by a syndicate of crooked sports bettors could cost the state operators untold million of dollars plus a major sports scandal.

My recommendation is that sports betting should be done along the lines of racetrack betting using the pari-mutuel system. Each game or event would have its own separate pool, and the money wagered on each event would determine the payoff odds. Ten percent, plus breakage, would be taken off the top by the state.

Here's how it works: A morning sports line similar to a track line is posted at all betting offices. For example, let's suppose the Yankees are playing Detroit at Yankee Stadium and the morning line opens showing the Yanks 6–5 favorites, which is only an indicator prior to the purchase of pari-mutuel tickets. What happens to these probable odds when the pari-mutuel windows open and betting begins depends upon the amount of money wagered on each team. Sometimes the bettors don't like the favorites so they bet heavily on Detroit; by the time the windows close the odds have changed, and Detroit becomes the favorite. The morning sports line merely tries to predict the payoff odds, but the bettors themselves make the actual payoff odds.

Betting would continue up to game time. Then the exact payoff would be determined as follows: In our example, let's say $300,000 is bet on the Yankees and $200,000 on Detroit. The total handle on the game, of course, is $500,000. After the state's cut of 10% is taken (breakage in this instance has not been deducted), there is a pool of $450,000 to be paid to the winners. If New York wins, we simply divide 300,000 into 450,000 and find that for every $2 wagered, a Yankee bettor is paid off at a price of $3 including the original bet. If Detroit wins, a Tiger bettor receives $4.50 for a $2 bet. I would suggest that state's breakage be kept to a nickel on each dollar (the rounding out of the last digit or fraction to either 0 or 5).

This pari-mutuel sports betting plan has insurance—the state cannot lose. The same plan can be employed for any sports events—football, basketball, hockey, fights, etc. The only hazard this plan does not eliminate is the Federal 10% excise tax on its gross betting handle. Repeal of this Federal law is the best solution to this problem.

5.
Lotteries, Sweepstakes, Pools and Raffles

My survey indicates that 67 million Americans, of whom 40 million were women, wagered the gigantic sum of $20 billion in 1973 at various forms of lotteries such as Policy Numbers, Bingo, Keno, raffles, baseball and football pools, Treasury Tickets, the Irish Hospitals' sweepstakes and other foreign and domestic lotteries.

Since their first appearance lotteries have been and still are the number one gambling activity for the greatest number of people the world over. Government lotteries or government-supervised lotteries are conducted today in more than 50 countries, among them the Latin-American countries, Ireland, England, France, West Germany, Italy, Spain, Turkey, Russia, China, plus 12 states in this country. These lotteries vary in methods of determining winners, ticket prices and amounts of prize awards, but essentially they all consist of the chance selection of tickets or numbers, or the prediction and selection of results of sporting events.

Lotteries are ancient. The casting of lots to divide up the land is mentioned a number of times in the Bible. St. John, writing of the crucifixion of Jesus, mentions the prophecy concerning His garment when he says, "They said therefore among themselves, Let us not rend it, but cast lots for it, whose it shall be: that the scripture might be fulfilled, which saith, They parted my raiment among them, and for my vesture they did cast lots. These things therefore the soldiers did."

Door-prize drawings, a form of lottery, are at least a couple of thousand years old. This type of drawing was an entertainment feature of the dinner parties given by many of the Roman emperors. Nero gave his guests presents by letting them draw for such prizes as a slave or a

Detail from relief sculpture (about A.D. *1175) showing soldiers throwing dice for Christ's cloak.*

fashionable villa. Heliogabalus added a touch of humor by mixing among the valuable prizes such odd and worthless ones as six dead flies, several ostriches or a dead dog. Augustus Caesar sometimes sold his guests tickets and gave out articles of very unequal value; it was he who sponsored the first known public lottery in order to raise funds to repair the city of Rome.

The next clear record of this sort of commercial lottery is found in the town records of the Burgundian town of L'Ecluse, where, in 1420, a lottery was used to raise money to strengthen the town's fortifications. Similar lotteries were held at that time in the Low Countries; the town records of Bruges, Belgium, show that on February 24, 1446, the widow of the painter Jan Van Eyck won two *livres.* Lotteries were also used in those times as a means of selling land, livestock, works of art and other commodities.

THE FIRST PUBLIC MONEY LOTTERY

The first public lottery paying money prizes was *La Lotto de Firenze,* which began in Florence, Italy, in 1530, and was soon followed by similar drawings in Genoa and Venice to raise funds for various public projects. This custom spread throughout Italy, and when the Italian republics were consolidated in 1870 the Italian national lottery came into being. Except for a few interruptions due to wars, this lottery has been in constant operation ever since. Today, five numbers between 1 and 90 are drawn every Saturday from each of ten wheels identified by the names of ten Italian cities. Players may wager as little as a penny on their selection of some or all five of the numbers to be

A late 17th-century royal lottery at the court of Louis XIV. The King is seated at the center of the upper table facing the kneeling figure of the royal valet, who holds a bag of tickets. The valet counts out the tickets as the King watches, and they are distributed to the players who place them in small boxes and use the lighted tapers to seal them with wax. The great Bishop Bossuet (lower left) reseals each box, and they are put aside until the drawing. In the lottery shown, the King won three prizes, one of 100,000 francs, and the Queen and the Dauphin also won. The King returned his large prize to be drawn again in smaller amounts, and this picture was engraved in honor of his liberality. (Culver Service)

Oh, yes! Oh, yes! Oh, yes!
Perhaps you all can guess
The news I've now to tell
Is sure to *bear the bell*.
The Fourteenth of June is nigh,
Then if your luck you try,
Dame Fortune you may nap her,
A *belle* without a *clapper*.

TWO of £20,200!
BESIDES 3,000 OTHER PRIZES;
Will all be decided
14ᵗʰ of JUNE.
No Classes!—Every Ticket drawn out singly, each
deciding its own fate and no other.

** Ticket and Share Chances are selling at all the
Lottery Offices in London; and by all their Agents in
the Country.

Handbill advertising one of the many English lotteries which were drawn in the 18th and early 19th centuries. (Culver Service)

drawn from a specified wheel. A player who correctly guesses all five numbers drawn from a named wheel is paid off at odds of 1,000,000 to 1. His chance of doing it is 1 in 43,949,268. Other winning selections are paid off at lesser odds.

My research shows that our early nineteenth-century policy shops and our present-day Numbers game, Lotto, Keno and Bingo are all derived from the Italian national lottery. For further information on this lottery see Chapter 8, pages 207–209.

THE BRITISH LOTTERY MANIA

Italians who accompanied Catherine de Medici to France at the time of her marriage to King Henry II in 1533 introduced lotteries into France. The first government-sponsored lottery in England was one which Queen Elizabeth announced in 1566 and advertised as "A verie rich Lotterie Generall, without any blancks . . ." The money raised was to be used "towardes the reparation of the havens [harbors] and strength of the Realme and towardes such other publique good workes." The first prize was worth £5,000—partly cash, partly silver, tapestries and the like. There were 400,000 tickets available at ten shillings each, and since there were no blanks, each buyer received back at least one-fourth of his investment. The Queen also promised that for seven days any ticket buyer would be safe from arrest for anything except major crimes. The ticket sale did not go well, and high-pressure selling methods had to be used, some of the towns being forced to appropriate public money to buy tickets. The drawing, postponed once, finally began in January 1569, at the west door of St. Paul's Church.

British colonization of America was financed partly by royal lotteries; the first, authorized by James I in 1612, raised £29,000 for the Virginia Company, which was sending settlers to the New World. In 1694 Parliament began using a state lottery as a means of floating a £1 million loan, tickets selling at ten pounds each and the prizes in the form of 16-year annuities. Private lotteries in the next few years were so numerous and there were so many abuses and outright swindles that they were abolished in 1699 by an act of Parliament. They were permitted again in 1710 and again suppressed (except for government lotteries) in 1721. Lotteries in other European countries have a similar history of alternate legality and attempted suppression. A lottery in 1753 raised money that founded the British Museum, and by 1755 the lottery mania was so great that mobs of ticket buyers broke down the doors of ticket offices on opening day in their eagerness to buy.

In those days before income taxes, and up until 1826, the British government used national lotteries as a means of raising funds. It was in this period that something very like the present Numbers game got its start. Called "insurance betting," it consisted in making side bets on

A Bluecoat Boy draws a number from a drum in a British government lottery in 1770. After it was found that numbers were sometimes switched, the boys were required to hold one hand behind the body, as this one is doing.

the numbers to be drawn in the national lottery, and illegal insurance betting houses were operated on the speakeasy principle. Runners, called morocco men because they kept records of the bets in red morocco leather notebooks, did business all over England, even in the smallest villages, and their employers paid them a small weekly salary when they went to jail, as Numbers operators do for their runners today. Government informants whose business it was to search out the insurance houses often collected protection money for keeping quiet; and sharpers made use of carrier pigeons to get word of the numbers drawn so they could bet on them before couriers reached the betting offices with the news.

GREAT BRITAIN'S PREMIUM BOND LOTTERY

In 1956 Prime Minister Harold Macmillan of Great Britain initiated a national lottery to bolster the public interest in English bonds. Britons quickly dubbed him "Mac the Bookie." A player buys a £1 premium bond which has a number attached, and six months later his bond number is put into an electric machine called an "Ernie." The player is eligible for a prize in the monthly drawing as long as he holds his bond. The prizes are tax-free. The bond's interest earnings of 4% all go into the monthly lottery pool. The bond can be cashed at any time for its face value, only the interest being wagered. For every $28,000 in the pool, there is one tax-free prize of $2,800, two of $1,400, four of $700, ten of $280, twenty of $140 and two hundred of $70. This premium-bond scheme was not so successful as had been expected. During the first year of its operation only $308 million worth of bonds was purchased, mostly during the first six months, and the total prize awards amounted to only $11,200,000. In 1959 the bond pool received very little action. One reason for these disappointing results was fear on the part of purchasers that inflation would decrease the value of their bond investments. Another was that the premium-bond scheme, with a top payout award of only $2,800, couldn't compete with the ever more popular football pools in which prizes of more than half a million dollars could be won for a two-penny wager.

THE BRITISH FOOTBALL POOL

No betting activity in the history of Great Britain has ever fired the imagination of the British public so much as the legal football (soccer) pools. The handle of the eight major privately run British football pools in 1972 was $339,360,000. Half this amount, or $169,680,000, was returned to the players in so-called "dividends," or prize money. About 30%, or $101,808,000 went to the government in taxes, and the remaining 20%, $67,872,000, paid salaries, printing costs, advertising and other expenses, and the promoters' profits, which are limited by law to 3%.

About 20 million Britons spend at least one evening a week hoping to acquire sudden and fabulous fortune by trying to select from 50 or more football matches 8 that will end in a tie. The bettor of 2¢ or more is not compelled, as in the premium-bond lottery, to purchase a £1 bond. The record award was won by an English mechanic, Colin Carruthers, in 1973, when his 2¢ bet won $1,574,502.50.

In heavily taxed Britain the football pools are one of the very few roads to quick and big money because there is no tax on winnings.

There are several methods of betting the pool, the treble (triple) chance pool being the most popular. In this pool the ticket buyer tries to pick 8 tied soccer games from a pool coupon list of 45 or more soccer matches. A point scoring system allots 3 points for a tied game, 2 points for a win by the visiting team and 1½ points for a win by the home team. If no one scores the magic 24 points by picking eight tied games, the jackpot (top award) goes to the holder(s) of the next highest total. If two or more players tie, the jackpot is divided equally among them. There are several other types of bets which can be made, such as picking three tied matches, six winning scores, twelve winning scores or the correct scores of various matches. But it is the treble chance that pays the really big money.

Factory, store and office workers form groups in a joint effort to cop the big awards. Every Saturday evening at 5:00 P.M., in hundreds of thousands of homes, people cluster around their radio sets listening to the sportscast which gives the afternoon football results. For ten minutes or so there is no sound except the noncommittal voice of the announcer, and tension mounts as the scores of the winning teams are announced. Failure to win is only a spur to another attempt the following week.

Newspapers devote entire pages to the pool, and handicappers list their selections forecasting the results of 45 or more matches. The advertising of the rival pools is prodigious, and even the sides of buses bear posters with photos of the smiling winners and lists of the dazzling six-figure jackpots which have been paid.

SMALL BRITISH LOTTERIES

The premium-bond lottery and the football pools are not enough to satisfy the Briton's gambling urge. In August 1956, the Small Lotteries and Gaming Act came into force and legalized the broad use of lotteries, Bingo and similar games by organizations established for charitable, sporting and cultural purposes not connected with private gain. Expenses are limited to 10%, prizes to 50%, and the balance

YOU can win £250,000 PLUS

FOR 1D 1/4

TOP DIVIDEND ON LITTLEWOODS

TREBLE CHANCE

FEB.11TH NOW 9 ONLY 4 — RESULTS / AWAYS

ARSENAL	CARDIFF	1
ASTON VILLA	TOTTENHAM	2
BOLTON	BLACKBURN	3
BURNLEY	SHEFF. WED.	4
CHELSEA	BLACKPOOL	5
LEICESTER	NEWCASTLE	6
MAN. CITY	WEST BROM.	7
NOTT'M F.	BIRMINGHAM	8
PRESTON	FULHAM	9
WEST HAM	EVERTON	10
WOLVES	MAN. UTD.	11
BRISTOL R.	DERBY	12
CHARLTON	LINCOLN	13
LIVERPOOL	LEYTON O.	14
NORWICH	PORTSMOUTH	15
PLYMOUTH	HUDD'FIELD	16
ROTHERHAM	SCUNTHORPE	17
SHEFF. UTD.	LUTON	18
SOUTH'PTON	IPSWICH	19
STOKE	SWANSEA	20
SUNDERLAND	MIDDLESBRO	21
BARNSLEY	BRADFORD C.	22
BRENTFORD	CHEST'FIELD	23
COLCHESTER	NOTTS C.	24
GRIMSBY	Q.P.R.	25
HALIFAX	SHREWSB'RY	26
HULL	BRISTOL C.	27
NEWPORT	BOURN'M'TH	28
READING	COVENTRY	29
SWINDON	SOUTHEND	30
TORQUAY	PORT VALE	31
TRANMERE	WALSALL	32
WATFORD	BURY	33
ALDERSHOT	MILLWALL	34
BRADFORD	GILLINGHAM	35
CHESTER	CREWE	36
CRYSTAL P.	ROCHDALE	37
DARLINGTON	MANSFIELD	38
DONCASTER	CARLISLE	39
HARTLEP'LS	WREXHAM	40
NORTH'PTON	BARROW	41
OLDHAM	ACCRINGTON	42
PETERBORO	EXETER	43
SOUTHPORT	STOCKPORT	44
WORK'GTON	YORK	45

12 MATCH 1D POINTS POOL

3 DIVIDENDS 50% - 30% - 20%

HOME 1 pt.(1) AWAY 2 pts.(2) DRAW 3 pts.(X)

ASTON VILLA	TOTTENHAM	1
BOLTON	BLACKBURN	2
PRESTON	FULHAM	3
WEST HAM	EVERTON	4
BRISTOL R.	DERBY	5
SOUTH'PTON	IPSWICH	6
COLCHESTER	NOTTS C.	7
TRANMERE	WALSALL	8
WATFORD	BURY	9
CHESTER	CREWE	10
HARTLEP'LS	WREXHAM	11
SOUTHPORT	STOCKPORT	12

FORECAST ALL 12 MATCHES

THE POPULAR FIVE

ASTON VILLA	TOTTENHAM	1
PRESTON	FULHAM	2
COLCHESTER	NOTTS C.	3
TRANMERE	WALSALL	4
CHESTER	CREWE	5

Min. 3d. Max. 20/- Per Col

LITTLEWOODS POOLS LTD., LIVERPOOL · Managing Director: Cecil Moores
Directors: Nigel Moores . L. Brierley-Jones · Executive Director: A. A. George

If your name or address has altered, please enter previous name or address here

When remitting your total stake money FRACTIONS OF A 1d. SHOULD BE IGNORED

12 Attempts 1/- | 18 Attempts 1/6 | 24 Attempts 2/-

ALWAYS ENTER YOUR FULL ADDRESS PLEASE

I have read and Agree to Littlewoods Football Pool Rules, 1960/1961 which govern this entry and agree that this transaction is binding in honour only. (Copies of the Rules can be had on request). I am not under 21 years of age.

I ENCLOSE P.O. NUMBERED

TO COVER THE AMOUNT STAKED ON THIS COUPON Make your Postal Order payable to Littlewoods Pools Ltd., and cross it with two heavy lines //

Mr. Mrs. Miss

FULL Postal Address

Block letters please

VALUE £

STAKES
Treble Chance......
3 Draws......
4 Aways......
1D Points......
Popular 5

REFERENCE NUMBER FOR CLAIMS AND CORRESPONDENCE

Winning clients who prefer no publicity put a 'X' here ......

FEB.11 27

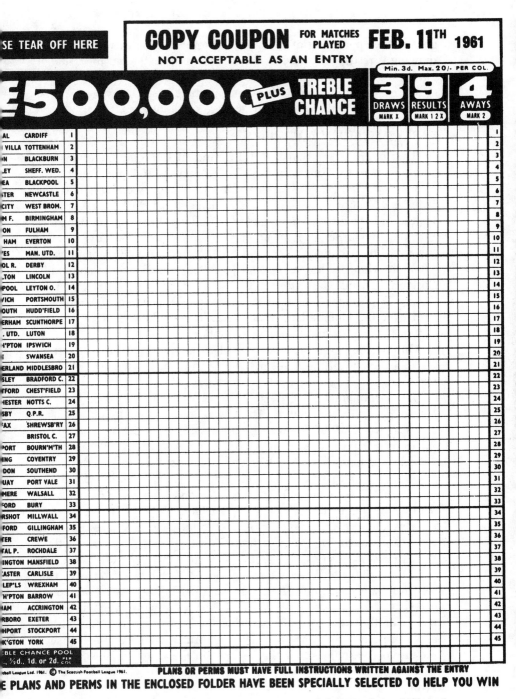

Coupon used by players to make their selections in the British football pools. (Littlewoods Organization)

goes to the sponsoring organization. The total value of tickets in any drawing is restricted to £750, the first prize to £100 and the value of any ticket to £1. Before legalization one British newspaper in 1950 estimated that there were 20 million participants who wagered £50 million, or $140 million, annually at these small lotteries.

EARLY AMERICAN LOTTERIES

The lottery craze that swept England in Georgian times had its counterpart in the American colonies. As early as 1665 the Dutch held a lottery for the poor in New Amsterdam. There were a half dozen lotteries operating in each of the 13 colonies most of the time preceding the American Revolution, and it was all very respectable. Benjamin Franklin and other prominent citizens sponsored a lottery to raise funds to buy a battery of cannon for the defense of Philadelphia. In 1762 John Hancock helped managed a lottery to raise money to rebuild Boston's Faneuil Hall after it had been damaged by fire; in 1768 George Washington managed a lottery for the purpose of building a road over the Cumberland Mountains. These, like the early English lotteries, were a form of voluntary taxation.

One contemporary account says that in 1672 there was "a lottery wheel in every city and town large enough to boast a court house and a jail."

The Continental Congress in 1776 voted a lottery to raise $10 million to finance the Revolution. There were to be 1 million tickets selling at prices from $10 to $40 with prizes ranging from $20 to $50,000, all prizes over $50 to be paid in government notes redeemable after five years. The scheme was abandoned when it was realized that the population was less than 4 million and most people couldn't afford the minimum $10, let alone $40. The wealthier ones who could were mostly Tories who had no desire to aid the rebellion.

This abortive Continental Congress lottery and a congressional act of 1823 permitting a group of professional operators to run a lottery whose proceeds were to be used to beautify the city of Washington, D.C., were the only lotteries ever authorized by the U.S. Congress. One reason may be that the 1823 Grand National Lottery, as its promoters called it, sold thousands of tickets, held the drawing, announced the names of the winners—and never paid off. The promoters vanished and were never apprehended. The top prizewinner of $100,000 sued the city of Washington for that amount in the United States Supreme Court and was the only winner to collect when the Court ruled in his favor.

The many other legal lotteries which were advertised as "government-sponsored" were not national but were authorized by state legislatures for a variety of worthy causes. The Virginia Legislature granted Thomas Jefferson permission to run a lottery in 1826—he was then 83 years old, land poor and in debt—so that he could by this means dispose of some of his property, including Monticello. Tickets had already been printed at the time he died, but his heirs abandoned the scheme. Between 1765 and 1806 Massachusetts authorized four lotteries to build dormitories and supply equipment for Harvard; many other colleges in those days—Dartmouth, Yale, Columbia, William and Mary, Union,

Early American lottery tickets from lotteries sponsored by George Washington and John Hancock, and one from a lottery to raise funds for Harvard College. (New-York Historical Society)

Brown—profited from lotteries. Money for many church building funds was also raised through lotteries.

By 1800 that early form of the Numbers game, insurance betting, was well established in this country. In 1831 a major drawing was held on an average of once a week in New York City alone; by 1832 the *Boston Mercantile Journal* published the results of a study of lotteries held the previous year which showed that 420 lotteries were operated in eight Atlantic seaboard states—and this is incomplete because some states were omitted. Even so, it means that there was more than one drawing for each day of the year, and the total sum spent for lottery tickets for the year was calculated to be $66 million—five times the expense of running the Federal government. Since many of these lotteries were now privately owned, some were bound to be crooked—with the usual result that public opinion turned against them. By 1840, most of the states had passed legislation barring lotteries, but tickets were still shipped in from states that had not done so. The anti-lottery groups then began to lobby for Federal legislation, and, in 1890, Congress barred the distribution of lottery tickets through the mails. This was also ineffective because the lottery operators used other means of distribution.

The legal lottery drawings of this period were conducted with elaborate ceremony in large halls before crowds of spectators. The most popular form of drawing was to use cards numbered from 0 to 99. A frock-coated operator placed 100 cards in a glass cylindrical drum mounted on a center spindle. The drum was turned for several minutes to mix the cards; then a blindfolded boy reached into the drum and removed one card. The operator read its number aloud; it was verified by a public-appointed watchdog committee and then written on a blackboard.

Grand National Lottery ticket issued in an attempt to raise money to beautify the city of Washington. (New-York Historical Society)

Ticket from the Louisiana lottery, last of the great legal lotteries in this country, 1869–1894. (Culver Service)

This was repeated twice more, and the three drawn numbers were combined to form the winning number. If 25 was the first drawn number, 35 the second and 10 the third, the winning number would be 253510. Some lotteries used the present raffle-draw principle of placing ticket stubs bearing the buyer's name and address into the drum.

POLICY SHOPS

Most of the clandestine lotteries during the 1800s used as their winning number the same ones which were drawn in one of the more popular legal lotteries. This made it unnecessary to hold illegal public drawings, which would be raided by the police.

Like the clandestine operators of the Italian national lottery, many illegal operators also allowed players to select their own numbers, and wager as little as a penny that the one, two, three, four or five numbers selected would be among the first five or ten numbers drawn. These illegal operations were known as *policy shops*. Most of them went out of business when the last of the legal lotteries were abolished in 1895, although a few continued in the early 1900s by claiming to employ the winning numbers drawn by foreign lotteries. There was little public enthusiasm for these, and they did not last long.

THE LOUISIANA LOTTERY

Prior to the introduction of the state legalized lottery in New Hampshire in 1963, the Louisiana lottery was the last of the great legal lotteries in the United States. It ran monthly drawings with prizes ranging up to $250,000, and twice a year ran a big special in which the top award was $600,000, a magnificent sum for those days. It had agents in every city and hamlet in the country. In 1894, after 25 years of the lottery, the Louisiana Legislature refused to extend the promoter's charter because of the congressional act of 1890 forbidding the sending of lottery tickets through the mails.

When the company was disbanded the public discovered that its operators had earned millions of dollars. Louisiana legislators began accusing each other of bribery, and it was widely claimed that the promoters had almost taken over the government of Louisiana. It is anybody's guess why the lawmakers and the press waited 25 years to make these accusations; I suspect it was because the ice had ceased to flow.

In 1895, when Congress realized that the 1890 laws forbidding the sending of lottery tickets through the mails had not solved the problem of preventing their sale, it passed laws forbidding the interstate transportation of tickets in any manner. This killed the legal lotteries and increased the number of illegal and crooked lotteries.

THE PUERTO RICAN LOTTERY

The first legal lottery under the American flag still in operation is the government-sponsored lottery of Puerto Rico. The Puerto Ricans, deprived of their old Spanish provincial lottery shortly after the Spanish-American War, in 1898, when it was abolished by the United States Military Governor, took to the clandestine Bolita and bought Santo Domingo lottery tickets. The lottery was reestablished by the Puerto Rican legislature in 1924, and the U.S. Congress, which has the power of veto over territorial legislation, did not use this power.

The Puerto Rican lottery, like most of those in Latin America, has a weekly drawing. The top prize, *El Primero*, is $100,000. Twice a year, near Christmas and the Fourth of July, there are big drawings in which El Primero is $480,000 and is called *El Gordo* (the Fat One). The lottery prize money is all tax-free.

While casino gambling is a tradition in Puerto Rico, the lottery is both a tradition and a ritual. Puerto Rico's lottery has grown considerably in the past decade. There once were 50,000 tickets distributed weekly, each possessing 60 pieces or parts worth 25¢ each for a total of $15 per ticket. Now there are three series (A, B, C) each of which is comprised of 45,000 tickets for a total of 135,000 tickets. Each ticket is comprised of 80 pieces worth 25¢ each for a total of $20 per ticket. There are thousands of prizes drawn each week ranging from $100,000 first prize, $36,000 second, $16,000 third, $10,000 fourth, and so forth down to your money back if the last number on your ticket is the same as the last digit of the winning number. The purchase of 1/80 piece of a top winning ticket in the regular weekly drawing costs 25¢ and the winner collects $1,250; a 1/80 piece of a top winning ticket in one of the two special drawings costs $1 and pays off $6,000.

Since most Latin-American lotteries are similar, here is a description of the Puerto Rican lottery operation. Every Wednesday morning a good-sized crowd gathers in front of the Lotería building in Santurce, tickets in hand. Sidewalk vendors sell refreshments and everyone expectantly watches the huge electric sign which will flash the winning numbers as they are drawn. The first drawing begins at 10:30 A.M. and the last number is usually called by noon.

The men enjoy waiting in the warm sunlight; many of the women prefer to sit in the air-conditioned auditorium which seats about 250, where they can watch the little balls drop from the big silver machine and hear the winners called. The crowd usually disperses after the big weekly prize is drawn, and the players obtain the other results from Thursday's newspapers, which carry full-page listings of all winning numbers. The miscellaneous prize numbers are determined by number approximation, sequence and relation of ending numbers to the first-prize number.

The drawing is made on the auditorium platform, where there is a large, electrically operated machine having one large and one much smaller mesh drum. The larger drum contains 45,000 balls somewhat larger than marbles, which possess five-digit numbers matching those on the tickets sold. The small drum contains as many balls as there are prizes and the numbers on these indicate the value of the prize.

Both drums are rotated the same number of times and then one ball is released from each drum simultaneously. If the ball numbered 17187 drops from the large drum when ball number 1 drops from the small drum, then number 17187 wins the week's big prize, El Primero. The drawing is continued until all the balls have been drawn from the small drum.

On the Lotería's second floor, among the offices, is a kind of farmers' cooperative—a bank from which the *agentes,* the top class of licensed ticket sellers, can borrow money. They buy their tickets from the government and often need money to tide them over until ticket sales pick up as the day of the drawing approaches. These loans are always repaid because, if not, the borrowers would immediately cease to be *agentes.*

CROOKED LOTTERIES

Before 1895, in states where lotteries were legal there were usually regulations demanding that lottery operators be of unquestionable character and reputation before being issued a license. There were then no such restrictions on the many illegal operators, who often set up business with scarcely enough money to print their first batch of tickets. Hundreds of lotteries of various sorts sprang up overnight operated by crooks, confidence men and cheats who did a booming business.

Many, in an attempt to avoid Federal prosecution, followed the practice of their English contemporaries and called their lotteries by other names: Keno, raffles, pools, sweepstakes and the like. Some foreign lotteries also now began selling their tickets in the United States.

The American operators seldom held any drawings and those they did hold were almost always rigged, especially when they advertised cash awards of $50,000, $100,000, $300,000 and sometimes more. I can't imagine an illegal lottery of that period actually paying anyone a cash prize of more than $100.

As an illustration of how these crooked lotteries were run, let me tell you about a lottery operator I met during the early 1920s at a time when this country was being flooded with millions of crooked lottery tickets.

In 1923, I was playing a four-month engagement as a magician at a Mexican night club in Tijuana, where I became well acquainted with a man who called himself Doc Peters and who often sat at a ringside table watching my act. Everyone, including the Doc himself, told me that he was the operator of the Tijuana lottery, the foremost of the day, and that Doc's offices on the second floor of the club were where his American agents came to turn in their cash and obtain another month's supply of tickets. I stuck close to Doc because I knew that I might never again have the opportunity to get the real inside story of crooked lotteries from one of the masters.

One evening, after my last show, Doc invited me upstairs and asked me to do some card tricks for a group of about 20 men. I did these for an hour or so and stayed on until the others had gone. As I was about to leave the Doc said, "Wait a minute, I want to show you something," and he took me into an adjoining room lined with shelves which were filled with stacks of lottery tickets.

"You must have at least a hundred thousand tickets there," I said.

"Yes," he replied, "but that's nothing. The boys who just left took the big bulk with them. They are my top promoters in the States—from New York, Chicago, Los Angeles, all the big cities. They cover the country for me. But that wasn't what I wanted to show you. I've got a proposition for you. You've entertained my friends and business associates several times and I want you to know I appreciate it."

"That's okay, Doc," I said. "I enjoy it and besides it keeps me in practice."

Doc went to a big safe, opened it and took out a large suitcase. He placed it on a table and threw back the lid. It was quite a sight. The case was filled to the brim with unstacked greenbacks.

"That," Doc said, "is the money those boys just turned in from ticket sales in the States. Can you guess how much is there?"

I shook my head. "I have no idea." I was a bit worried trying to figure out why he was putting on this show for me. I knew he wasn't afraid of being held up because the Mexican cops, who were probably also on his payroll, were always hanging around the club.

"Take a guess," he insisted. "Go ahead."

"Okay. $50,000.

"Scarne, you know it's more than that. There's about $200,000 there, and that case gets refilled every month. Some racket, eh? A lot more profitable than doing card tricks. Scarne, I want you to reach in there quickly with your left hand, grab as many bills as you can and come out fast. I'll give you three seconds."

I didn't know what he was getting at, but I obeyed. I reached in, grabbed as many bills as I could and brought them out quickly. A few dropped and fell back into the suitcase as I asked, "What do I do now?"

"Put them in your pocket," Doc said. "That's your pay for a fine evening's entertainment."

I didn't give him an argument; I did as he asked. When I counted up in my hotel room I found that I had $630, not bad pay for doing a few card tricks, but not as much as I expected. Doc was a man who figured the angles and I suspect he had put the smaller denominations on top covering the fifty- and hundred-dollar bills below.

During the four months that I knew him I learned a lot about Doc and his operation. Although he was known as the biggest lottery operator in the States during the twenties and early thirties, he never actually ran a real lottery. Like most such operators at that time, he was merely selling fancily printed fake tickets to about 30 crooked American lottery promoters. He also sold a four-page result sheet which was printed days before the alleged drawing was supposed to take place. Each ticket was marked to sell for $1 and Doc received $2.40 for each booklet containing 24 tickets. The printed matter on the tickets stated that 2000 prizes were awarded each month: a top prize of $300,000, second prize of $75,000, third prize of $50,000, 1000 consolation prizes of $100 each and 997 of $50 each.

The Doc told me that in March 1923, his banner month up to that time, he hald sold 100,000 booklets or 2,400,000 tickets. At his price of 10¢ each, this brought him $240,000. His expenses, including the lavishly printed tickets and the result sheets, came to only about one eighth of this amount, leaving him a net profit of 700%.

The promoters who purchased tickets from Doc distributed them to thousands of agents throughout their territory, who in turn sold them to an unsuspecting American public. The agents who were in the know sometimes received as much as 70% commission on each dollar ticket sold. Most of the agents didn't know they were selling tickets in a fake lottery, and received about 40%. The promoters told them—and they in turn told the public—that the Tijuana lottery was run by several wealthy Mexican horse owners and that the drawings were held each month in a different Mexican city. Since lotteries were also illegal in Mexico, the drawings had to be held secretly, but the ticket purchaser would receive a result sheet after the drawings which named the winners and the city where the drawing had been held.

In order to avoid suspicion that the lottery was crooked, and to stimulate sales, each promoter would give out a few small prizes in spots where he thought they would do the most good. He simply gave the Doc the names of the winners and the numbers of the tickets they held and the Doc printed them in the result sheet. The promoter, of course, paid off these small winners himself; occasionally, he pretended to pay off a top award of $100,000 or more. The winning name he gave the Doc was, of course, the name of a confederate.

No one will ever know how much money the American public lost to hundreds of such lottery operations, but it must have totaled billions of dollars. Eventually the public became suspicious because there were so few big prize winners, and ticket sales dropped off.

TREASURY TICKETS: FATHER OF TODAY'S STATE LOTTERIES

In early 1969 I informed the New Jersey Lottery Commission (who at that time were in the midst of setting up the workings of a state lottery) that in my opinion the Commission should pattern the state lottery after the illegal Treasury Tickets, which are thoroughly described in this book. The New Jersey Lottery Commission read the Treasury Ticket copy that follows; I met with the Commission; and the New Jersey State Lottery was born. (See Chapter 6, pages 176–179.)

About 1925, Treasury Tickets began sweeping the country. The public knew it was honest and, although its prizes were small, it got a big play. It was called the Treasury Ticket because the last five digits of the United States daily Treasury balance were used as the winning number. Tickets cost 25¢, 35¢, 50¢ and $1. A five-digit number was printed on each ticket, which was made of heavy colored paper, folded several times in such a way that the number was hidden, and its ends intricately sewed together. No stub was required. After buying a 50¢ ticket, the purchaser ripped away the thread, unfolded the ticket and the number he found beneath the words "Treasury Number" was his number for the week. If it corresponded at any time during the week with the last five digits of U.S. Treasury balance figures which are printed in most newspapers, the holder won the top prize. For a $1 ticket this was usually $1,000 on Monday, $1,500 on Tuesday, $2,000 on Wednesday, $2,500 on Thursday and $3,000 on Friday. Consolation prizes were also usually awarded as follows: $200 if the last four digits matched, $5 for the last three digits, and $1 for the last two digits. If the U.S. Treasury balance for the day was $135,645,365, the top award would go to the holder of 45365, and the minor awards to the holders of numbers ending with 5365, 365 and 65. Some Treasury Ticket operators also paid a daily $1,000 award if the player's number was the reverse of the winning five-digit number. A 25¢, 35¢ or 50¢ Treasury Ticket paid out smaller prizes.

Treasury Tickets enjoyed their greatest popularity during the late twenties and thirties, although there are still a few in operation. The operators were usually local sporting figures who went about the business of selling tickets, each in his own way, satisfied with a net profit that was rarely more than 10%. They earned a comfortable living but never made any really big money. The mobsters and racketeers, busily making big money at bootlegging, paid little attention to this operation. The Treasury Ticket operators seldom resorted to strong-arm methods to prevent competitors from moving into their territories; their agents often handled as many as ten different Treasury Tickets at the same time. I knew a number of these operators in my home town who were respected citizens of the community and didn't know what the word "racket" meant.

There was at least one agent selling tickets in most of the factories and office buildings throughout the country. If you missed seeing what the winning Treasury number was in the papers, a Treasury result sheet listing the winning numbers was available the following week. Since the prizes were small, most Treasury operators were honest and paid off, although now and then you would hear of an operator who had to pay off a big prize in installments, and more rarely of one who couldn't pay off because he had gone broke.

It was the Treasury Ticket operators themselves who were fleeced more often than the players—by crooked agents. I knew a woman ticket agent in my home town of Fairview, New Jersey, who put several local operators out of business. There are 100,000 different possible arrangements of the five digits in a Treasury number, and if an operator sold a tenth of these, or 10,000 tickets, each week, he could make a good living provided he didn't have too many dishonest agents. Mae Smith, as I'll call her, used to take 1,000 tickets a week and sell about 600. As was customary, the 400 unsold tickets were returned to the operator, usually after the winning numbers had appeared in the papers. The operators thought that the agent couldn't know the numbers on the tickets that were returned because of the way they were sewn shut—but paper dampened with carbon tetrachloride becomes fairly transparent while it is wet. Mae dipped each ticket in this chem-

ical, separated the edges of the ticket along one of its sides—which are
not sewed together—so that only one or two layers of paper covered
the Treasury number, held it before a strong light and was able to
read the heavily printed number. Since she already knew the winning
numbers for the week, she removed all the winners from this group
and returned the others, after they had dried and become opaque
again. When her customers who had won turned their winning tickets
in to her for collecting, she added the winning tickets she had found
and collected for herself too.

An operator who had a couple of cheats like Mae working for him
couldn't stay in business long; he found himself paying out too many
winners in proportion to the number of tickets sold. This cut down the
small profit margin so much that the operators found it difficult to
make a living, and Treasury Tickets were soon hard to find. Today,
only a few operators remain.

BASEBALL AND FOOTBALL POOLS

A form of lottery which capitalized on the public's interest in sports
also began to achieve popularity during the late twenties and thirties
—the baseball and football pools. Of the baseball pools the most successful was the Albany baseball pool, which will serve as a good example to explain their operation. Numbers were used to represent the
teams in the three biggest baseball leagues: the American, National
and International. Since at the time there were only eight teams in
each league, the numbers ran from 1 to 24.

Participants paid $1 and selected five numbers representing the
teams they thought would score the greatest number of combined runs
for the week. The ticket holder whose five teams scored the most runs
received the top award, usually about $25,000. The sizes of the awards
varied, depending on the number of tickets sold. The ticket holder
whose five teams scored the next highest number of runs usually received about $10,000, and so on down to a small $50 consolation prize.

The Albany baseball pool paid out about 40% of its gross handle
in prizes, the other 60% taking care of agents' commissions, police
graft and operators' profits. This was one of the few honest baseball
lotteries then in operation, and to make sure that the customers were
aware of this the operators distributed a player's sheet listing all the
five number selections sold for the week. These were available at the
start of the week's baseball play, and it was evident that the operators
could not later ring in fake winners. I have a player's sheet that contains 123,265 selections, which means that at $1 per ticket $123,265
worth of tickets were sold in that week.

Most of the hundreds of other baseball pools in the late twenties

TIES LOSE UNLESS PICKED

3 WINS IN 3.. 4 for 1	8 WINS IN 8.. 100 for 1
4 WINS IN 4..10 for 1	10 WINS IN 10.. 250 for 1
5 WINS IN 5..15 for 1	12 WINS IN 12.. 500 for 1
6 WINS IN 6..25 for 1	15 WINS IN 15..2500 for 1
7 WINS IN 7..50 for 1	16 WINS IN 16..5000 for 1

CONSOLATION PRIZE

9 Out of 10....15 for 1	14 Out of 15....200 for 1
11 Out of 12....25 for 1	15 Out of 16....300 for 1

College Football—Saturday, Sept. 19, 1970

KANSAS U		TEXAS TECH + 3
MICHIGAN ST.		WASHINGTON U + 3
OREGON ST.		IOWA U + 3
COLORADO U		INDIANA U + 7
U. C. L. A.	(R)	PITTSBURGH + 7
GEORGIA U		TULANE + 7
GEORGIA TECH	(Reg.TV)	FLORIDA ST. + 7
CLEMSON		VIRGINIA U + 10
NO. CARO. U	(Reg.TV)	NO. CARO. ST. + 10
OREGON U		ILLINOIS U + 10
SO. CALIFORNIA		NEBRASKA U + 10
MISSOURI U	(Reg.TV)	MINNESOTA + 13
DUKE		MARYLAND U + 14
KANSAS ST.		KENTUCKY U + 14
PURDUE		T. C. U. + 14
ARMY	(R)	BAYLOR + 14
FLORIDA U		MISSISSIPPI ST. + 14
ALABAMA		VIRGINIA TECH + 14
OKLAHOMA U		WISCONSIN + 16
TENNESSEE		S. M. U. + 16
L. S. U.		TEXAS A&M + 17
SO. CAROLINA U		WAKE FOREST + 17
PENN STATE	(R)	NAVY + 21
NOTRE DAME	(R)	NORTHWESTERN + 21
TEXAS U		CALIFORNIA U + 21
ARKANSAS U		OKLAHOMA ST. + 21

Pro Football—Saturday, Sept. 19, 1970

N.Y. GIANTS	(R)	CHICAGO BEARS + 3

Pro Football—Sunday, Sept. 20, 1970

ATL FALCONS		N.O. SAINTS + 3
G.B. PACKERS		DET LIONS + 3
S.F. 49ers		WASH RED SKINS + 3
MINN VIKINGS	(TV)	K.C. CHIEFS + 3
BALT COLTS		S.D. CHARGERS + 6
D. BRONCOS	(TV)	BUFFALO BILLS + 6
PITTS STEELERS	(TV)	HOUST OILERS + 6
MIA. DOLPHINS	(TV)	BOST PATRIOTS + 7
OAK RAIDERS	(TV)	CINCI BENGLES + 10
D. COWBOYS	(R)	PHIL EAGLES + 14

Pro Football—Monday, Sept. 21, 1970

CLEVE BROWNS	(R-TV)	N.Y. JETS + 3

NAME_____ AMT_____
(PLEASE CIRCLE ALL SELECTIONS)

N⁰ 32927

TIES LOSE UNLESS PICKED

3 WINS IN 3.. 4 for 1	8 WINS IN 8.. 100 for 1
4 WINS IN 4..10 for 1	10 WINS IN 10.. 250 for 1
5 WINS IN 5..15 for 1	12 WINS IN 12.. 500 for 1
6 WINS IN 6..25 for 1	15 WINS IN 15..2500 for 1
7 WINS IN 7..50 for 1	16 WINS IN 16..5000 for 1

CONSOLATION PRIZE

9 Out of 10....15 for 1	14 Out of 15....200 for 1
11 Out of 12....25 for 1	15 Out of 16....300 for 1

College Football—Saturday, Sept. 19, 1970

KANSAS U		TEXAS TECH + 3
MICHIGAN ST.		WASHINGTON U + 3
OREGON ST.		IOWA U + 3
COLORADO U		INDIANA U + 7
U. C. L. A.	(R)	PITTSBURGH + 7
GEORGIA U		TULANE + 7
GEORGIA TECH	(Reg.TV)	FLORIDA ST. + 7
CLEMSON		VIRGINIA U + 10
NO. CARO. U	(Reg.TV)	NO. CARO. ST. + 10
OREGON U		ILLINOIS U + 10
SO. CALIFORNIA		NEBRASKA U + 10
MISSOURI U	(Reg.TV)	MINNESOTA + 13
DUKE		MARYLAND U + 14
KANSAS ST.		KENTUCKY U + 14
PURDUE		T. C. U. + 14
ARMY	(R)	BAYLOR + 14
FLORIDA U		MISSISSIPPI ST. + 14
ALABAMA		VIRGINIA TECH + 14
OKLAHOMA U		WISCONSIN + 16
TENNESSEE		S. M. U. + 16
L. S. U.		TEXAS A&M + 17
SO. CAROLINA U		WAKE FOREST + 17
PENN STATE	(R)	NAVY + 21
NOTRE DAME	(R)	NORTHWESTERN + 21
TEXAS U		CALIFORNIA U + 21
ARKANSAS U		OKLAHOMA ST. + 21

Pro Football—Saturday, Sept. 19, 1970

N.Y. GIANTS	(R)	CHICAGO BEARS + 3

Pro Football—Sunday, Sept. 20, 1970

ATL FALCONS		N.O. SAINTS + 3
G.B. PACKERS		DET LIONS + 3
S.F. 49ers		WASH RED SKINS + 3
MINN VIKINGS	(TV)	K.C. CHIEFS + 3
BALT COLTS		S.D. CHARGERS + 6
D. BRONCOS	(TV)	BUFFALO BILLS + 6
PITTS STEELERS	(TV)	HOUST OILERS + 6
MIA. DOLPHINS	(TV)	BOST PATRIOTS + 7
OAK RAIDERS	(TV)	CINCI BENGLES + 10
D. COWBOYS	(R)	PHIL EAGLES + 14

Pro Football—Monday, Sept. 21, 1970

CLEVE BROWNS	(R-TV)	N.Y. JETS + 3

NAME_____ AMT_____
(PLEASE CIRCLE ALL SELECTIONS)

N⁰ 32927

A college and pro football lottery ticket.

were not this honest. They were run by crooks and fly-by-night lottery operators who disappeared when there was a big winner, moved to some other locale and set up shop there with the same ticket.

Baseball pools as large as the Albany pool do not exist today because government agents more or less enforce the law forbidding the transportation of lottery tickets across state lines. They once used the teams in the American and National Leagues, a total in 1961 of 16 instead of the Albany pool's 24, and they used the total winning runs of four, rather than five, teams. The player was not permitted to select his number but received a sewed-together ticket, usually priced at 50¢, which contained a hidden number designating the teams the buyer had for the week. The number of possible four-team combinations was only 1,820 and the top weekly prize award was therefore small, seldom more than $200. Today baseball pools still use the American and National League teams and thus have numbers 1 through 24.

Most of these small pools are run by individuals who think that such an operation will net them thousands of dollars until, having found out differently, they fold up after a few weeks of the baseball season, leaving unpaid winners behind.

Football pools were originally conducted in the same manner as the Albany baseball pool, the ticket holder trying to pick a group of teams that would score the most points. Today, football-pool players try to name the winners of each game. The operators offer odds to the player for picking 3 winners, 4 winners, or as many as 10 winners. In order to eliminate the possibility that a team's past performance will be too much help to the player in picking winners, the operators, like the professional sports bookmakers, use a sports line (see page 113) and give inferior teams a *spot*, or handicap in points.

Football-pool operators pay off winners at ridiculous odds. In an evenly matched game or one reduced to equality by a logical spot, the chance that a selected team will win is 1 in 2. A participant trying to select three winners in three games has 1 chance in 8, four winners in four games, 1 chance in 16. The operators pay 4 to 1 for picking three winners, and 9 to 1 for picking four, etc. You have 1 chance in 1024 to pick ten winners in ten games, and the payoff odds are only 200 to 1. It's a bad deal from any angle: the more winners you try to pick, the less chance you have of winning. And if you had a couple of bucks riding and did happen to pick ten out of ten, it's an even bet that you'd never get paid.

In 1928, a concentrated drive by police throughout the country put the Albany baseball pool and many of the smaller baseball and football pools out of business, and the lottery-buying public was again victimized by crooked foreign lotteries, mostly Canadian and Mexican.

THE IRISH HOSPITALS' SWEEPSTAKES

In 1930 the Irish Dail, or Parliament, passed an act permitting the running of a sweepstakes for the benefit of Irish hospitals; since then

Americans have been able to buy tickets in an honest lottery whose top prize has been well over a million dollars.

The Irish Free State government knew that a sweepstakes operation limited to Ireland could not be successful and that tickets would also have to be sold in foreign countries, particularly the United States. Since the government could not itself participate in violation of other countries' anti-lottery laws, a private company, Hospitals Trust, Ltd., was formed to operate the Sweepstakes, and John McGrath, a former Minister of Industry and Minister of Labor in the Free State government, was named managing director. His first partner was a professional bookie, Richard Duggan.

The Sweeps promoters set up their first headquarters at 13 Earlsford Terrace in Dublin, and their clerical staff originally consisted of one typist. Today, the Sweepstakes is easily Ireland's largest and most profitable business enterprise. It has about 1,500 permanent employees and adds about 2,500 part-time employees during the drawings, which occur three times each year. The plush Sweeps headquarters with its teakwood floors is now one of the principal tourist sights in Ireland.

Since the Sweeps is legal only in Ireland, the operators cannot use paid advertising to promote ticket sales in other countries and have had to invent promotional gimmicks. One of the most effective, in the early days, was the floating ashore along our Atlantic coast of a great many fish-shaped bottles, each containing a paper entitling the finder to a drink of his choice at any tavern and asking him to drink to good luck in the Irish Sweepstakes. Jack Dempsey honored some of these papers at the Eighth Avenue bar he then operated in New York City. The bottles created much talk and received a great amount of newspaper publicity because most people believed the bottles had floated all the way across the Atlantic. Actually the Sweeps promoters had arranged to have them dumped by the thousands into our offshore coastal waters.

Then, in 1931, when the press reported that Emilio Scala, a London candy-store proprietor, had won $1,773,660 to become the biggest money winner in the history of the Irish Sweepstakes and, for that matter, in any lottery ever held, the American public began begging for Sweepstakes tickets.

Initially all correspondence and money transactions between ticket purchasers and the Dublin headquarters were conducted by mail. Each year American ticket purchasers mailed millions of letters containing ticket stubs, checks, currency, money orders, bank drafts, etc., to the Irish Hospital's Sweepstakes headquarters. The U.S. Post Office made an attempt to stop these flagrant violations of our Federal anti-lottery laws in 1935, when they stopped nearly a million of these letters and returned them to the senders. About the same time the British Home Office banned all mail addressed to the Dublin Sweepstakes office.

The Sweeps promoters, hard hit by these actions, knew that if they continued the Sweepstakes was doomed, and they took immediate steps to set up a smuggling operation. Today they employ agents in the United States who receive smuggled shipments of tickets in bulk. They have devised many ingenious smuggling methods, and naturally also pay considerable amounts of graft money to ensure safe delivery. Federal agents now and then find such shipments disguised as legitimate foreign imports. The largest was confiscated in 1948, when 82 cartons containing over 2 million tickets were found aboard the transatlantic ocean liner *America*. The most recent big Federal confiscation of tickets was in 1950, when six men were arrested for bringing in over a million Sweeps tickets.

Today, such seizures do not throw a monkey wrench into the ticket sales for that drawing, contrary to what one might think; the attempt to smuggle the tickets in is made months before the scheduled drawing so that there is time to replace any confiscated shipment. All the promoters lose is the manufacturing and shipping costs.

The trusted agents who receive these large shipments redistribute them to agents throughout the country, who, in turn, distribute to sub-agents and sellers in their territory. The ticket stubs and cash pass back through this organization setup to the major agents, who again smuggle the ticket stubs back to Dublin and send the money either by personal check or by means of some international money transaction which makes it impossible for U.S. postal or Customs authorities to confiscate the cash.

Upon receipt of stubs and cash the Sweeps promoters send to the ticket purchasers, through the same smuggling and distribution organization, official receipts or counterfoils.

The mails are also still used by thousands of American Sweeps agents and ticket purchasers, who avoid arousing the curiosity of U.S. postal authorities by addressing letters not to the Sweeps headquarters in Dublin but to the hundreds of Sweeps depots in Ireland run by Sweeps agents using many different names and addresses. Ticket stubs are mailed in opaque or lined envelopes, and payment is made in currency, bank drafts, Express money orders—anything except U.S. postal money orders. If you ask an American ticket seller getting his tickets from an agent in Ireland what his source of supply is, the answer is nearly always, "A relative."

Sweeps tickets today are sold in most countries that do not have their own national lotteries. Governments which run lotteries somehow manage to discourage the sale of Irish Sweepstakes tickets; very few are sold in the Latin-American countries, and none in countries behind the Iron Curtain.

Having solved the promotion and distribution problems, the Sweeps promoters then came up with a new angle which more than any other led to the spectacular worldwide success the Irish Sweepstakes enjoys today and a distinction no other lottery has ever attained.

The innovation did away with the system of having one group of winners by dividing the money for prize awards into £100,000 units, later changed to £120,000, the present practice. At the present rate of exchange of about $2.80 to the pound, this is a payoff total of $336,000 for each group of winners. After the amount of money available for prizes is divided into £120,000 units, any remaining sum is divided into 50 cash prizes of equal amounts called residual prizes. Here are the amounts of the prizes for each group as advertised for the third drawing in 1957:

Winning horse	$140,000
Second horse	56,000
Third horse	28,000
Drawers of unplaced horses	84,000
70 consolation prizes of $280 each	19,600
150 consolation prizes of $56 each	8,400
Total prizes	$336,000

This procedure has changed the Irish Sweepstakes into a true lottery because the value of the prize awards is fixed and known in advance to the ticket purchaser. In the usual sweepstakes the value of the awards is not known in advance because it is determined by the sum of money in the pool when it closes.

Irish Hospitals' Sweepstakes Drawings

Most of the millions of Americans who buy Sweeps tickets have no idea how the winners are determined. This is how it is done: There are three Irish Sweepstakes drawings each year coupled with the running of the famed English horse races: The Grand National Steeplechase, the Epsom Downs Derby and the Cambridgeshire Stakes. After you buy a ticket and have received an official receipt, your chances of winning are as good as those of any other ticket buyer. Your stub, bearing your name (or nom de plume) and address, is held with millions of others under lock and key at the Dublin headquarters. About ten days before the running of the determining race, a government

Irish Hospitals' Sweepstakes ticket and a counterfoil for the 1961 Grand National race at Aintree.

watchdog committee headed by the superintendent of the Garda Siochana Irish Police places the tickets in a number of the huge pneumatic machines that shuffle and reshuffle them with blasts of compressed air for three days.

On the day of the drawing the tickets are placed in a giant drum which has 48 portholes giving access to its interior. Nurses of hospitals which are Sweeps beneficiaries take their places at the drum before an assembly of government officials and members of the press who represent numerous papers all over the world. As the great drum revolves, a nurse reaches through one of the portholes and draws out a ticket stub. Simultaneously another nurse draws from a nearby smaller drum the printed names of the horses entered in the race. The number of the stub and the name of the horse are announced, recorded by auditors of the watchdog committee and microfilmed to prevent any error or switching. Example: Stub No. R.P.V. 26115 is drawn from the giant drum at the same time that the name of the horse Fairy Stone is drawn from the small drum. The owner of the ticket whose name is on the stub thus has Fairy Stone as his horse in the race to be run the following week.

This procedure is repeated until the names of the horses in the small drum have all been drawn. Then more stubs are drawn from the large drum to determine the winners of the smaller consolation prizes.

In the third Sweeps draw of 1957, the small drum contained the names of 85 horses, each duplicated 21 times for a total of 1,785 because there were 21 prize units of £120,000 or $336,000. The 21 holders of tickets whose number was drawn with that of the winning horse each received $140,000. The 21 holders of tickets on the horse which ran second each received $56,000, and the 21 holders of the ticket on the horse who ran third each received $28,000. Holders of the remaining 1,722 tickets on the remaining 82 horses which were also-rans and nonstarters each received $1,024.39 1/41. The promoters inform all overseas winners of their good fortune by cable.

The 91st Irish Hospitals' Sweepstakes (the third drawing of 1957) paid 6,455 winners $7,170,800, the second largest total in its history. This sum was paid as follows:

	EACH	TOTAL
21 prizes on the winning horse	$140,000	$2,940,000
21 prizes on the 2nd-place horse	56,000	1,176,000
21 prizes on the 3rd-place horse	28,000	588,000
1,722 prizes on also-rans and nonstarters	1,024	1,764,000
1,470 consolation prizes	280	411,600
3,150 consolation prizes	56	176,400
50 residual prizes	2,296	114,800
		$7,170,800

* Prize amounts which figure out to odd cents or fractions thereof are rounded out to the nearest dollar.

Have you ever wondered whether you should reward the person from whom you purchased a Sweeps ticket that won a top award? The answer is that unless you feel really philanthropic it is not necessary. The promoters found that big Sweeps winners almost never gave the seller any decent amount, so the prize fund now provides bonuses for the sellers. The 63 sellers of the big winning tickets receive bonuses of $2,800, $1,680 or $1,120, depending on whether the ticket was on a horse that ran 1st, 2nd, or 3rd.

This total of $117,600 in bonus money added to the prize awards in the 91st running of the Sweepstakes gave a grand total of $7,288,400 paid out by the promoters.

TAXES ON SWEEPS TICKETS

Although the whole Sweepstakes operation is illegal in this country, the Internal Revenue Bureau and state tax collectors aren't a bit hesitant about taking a big bite out of any prize money you win. If the head of a family of four whose annual income is $5,000 wins one of the top Sweeps prizes of $140,000, Uncle Sam's cut is about $85,000, leaving the winner a net of about $55,000. In New York the state takes another $9,500 in income tax, leaving the lucky winner with about $45,000, or less than one-third of his prize.

A few winners have tried keeping their good fortune secret, hoping to avoid the tax by not reporting it: but the Internal Revenue boys notify them of their tax burden before they receive the cash. There is one legal gimmick by which a Sweeps purchaser can reduce the tax bite: he can divide the ownership of the ticket by signing more than one name on the ticket stub. If the head of a family of four who won $140,000 had listed his wife and two children as co-owners each would be entitled to 25%, or $35,000. Filing four separate returns would cut the total $85,000 tax down to about $63,000, a saving to the family of $22,000. This is legal, provided the partnership is in good faith and not just a tax-evasion scheme.

Many winners have gone to Dublin to collect, mistakenly believing that this would avoid the U.S. tax bite. Some have even established themselves as bona fide residents of Ireland only to discover later that the Internal Revenue Bureau takes the position that the prize money was won while they were living in the U.S., and that later foreign residence of whatever duration does not exempt them from taxes. Uncle Sam has a good memory and a lot of patience, and a winner who doesn't return for years will still find a Treasury man waiting to greet him.

Irish or English betting commissioners such as England's biggest betting-commission house, Douglas Stuart Ltd. (commonly known as "Duggie's"), manage to siphon off a healthy percentage of Sweeps winnings. It's a safe bet that if you draw a favorite horse to win in the Grand National Steeplechase, the Epsom Downs Derby or the Cambridgeshire Stakes, an overseas betting commisioner will contact you a day or so before race time and make you an offer to buy at least a half interest in your ticket. In the 91st drawing they were paying from $10,000 to $15,000 for a half interest on the horse favored to win the Cambridgeshire.

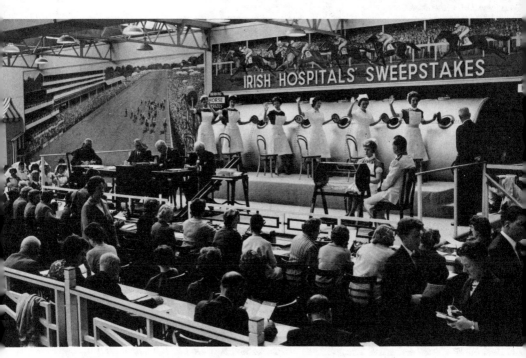

A 1961 drawing of the Irish Hospitals' Sweepstakes. Six nurses draw tickets from giant drum which has forty-eight portholes in eight rows of six each. (Derrick O. Michelson, Dublin)

A nurse selects a slip bearing the name of a horse from the small glass drum. (Derrick O. Michelson, Dublin)

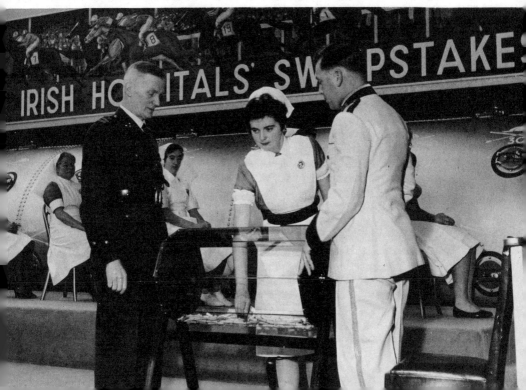

Mr. J. O'Sheehan, Director of the Draw, reads a drawn counterfoil and announces a winner's name. In the background Chief Superintendent Creagh collects more counterfoils which the nurses have just drawn. (Derrick O. Michelson, Dublin)

WHAT ARE YOUR SWEEPSTAKES CHANCES?

How many Sweepstakes tickets are sold annually throughout the world? What are a Sweeps ticket buyer's chances of drawing a horse that wins? These are questions that no one in the Sweeps organization will answer. A study of the Sweeps rules and regulations printed on each ticket plus some deduction and calculation will, however, supply answers which I believe are very close to the correct ones:

This copy appears on the back of each ticket:

> The amount of money received from sale of tickets under the Public Hospital Act of 1933 to 1940 will be distributed as follows—25 per cent will be paid to the hospitals. The balance after deduction thereout of the expenses as sanctioned by the Minister for Justice under the scheme for the Sweepstakes will be distributed in prizes. The amount provisionally certified by the Auditors on the day preceding the draw to be available for prizes, if exceeding 120,000 pounds, will be divided into as many prize units of 120,000 pounds as the sum admits. The remainder of the money available for prizes will be distributed into 50 cash prizes of equal amount.

The Public Hospital Act of 1933 to 1940 states that commissions paid to ticket sellers and agents are deducted prior to any distribution of money received from ticket sales. What percentage of the gross income from sales is paid in commission is a matter of speculation. But since the small ticket seller receives two free tickets for each ten sold (a booklet contains 12 tickets), this is a commission of 16⅔% or more. The top agent or wholesaler receives from 10% to 15% commission on each ticket sale; the combined commissions probably average about 30% of the gross.

The hospitals receive 25% of the remaining 70%, or 17½% of the gross. This leaves 52½% of the gross from which the promoters take their running expenses. Because the Sweepstakes is Ireland's biggest industry and requires thousands of employees, and because I assume that some government officials in countries where lotteries are illegal must be receiving ice, I estimate that the promoters deduct about 12½% of the gross handle to cover their expenditures.

This leaves 40% for prize money. The prize fund for each unit of £120,000 plus £200 for the sellers' bonuses totals in American money $341,600. Figured as 40%, this means that 305,000 tickets with a gross retail value of $854,000 are sold to form each prize-award unit. Taking as an example the 91st Sweeps drawing, which had 85 horses listed as possible starters, and using the above figures, we can calculate the ticket buyer's chances as follows:

1　in 305,000 of winning the top $140,000 prize award;
1　in 101,666 of drawing a horse that places 1st, 2nd or 3rd;
1　in 3,470 of drawing a horse listed as a possible starter;
1　in 1,000 of winning a prize of any size (except residuals) from $56 to $140,000.

This third Sweeps drawing of 1957 paid out a total of $7,288,400 in prize awards and sellers' bonuses. If this is 40% of the gross handle of all ticket sales it means that 6,507,500 tickets were sold for a gross retail price of $18,221,000.

The Sweeps promoters reported that the total receipts for 1957 were £12,752,000 or $35,705,600. If we call this 70% and add the 30% we've calculated for agents' commissions we find that the gross retail price paid for the tickets the world over in 1957 was about $51 million. From this figure we get an approximate total ticket sale of 18,200,000. I estimate that about 70% of the total, or almost 13 million tickets, were sold in the United States.

The first drawing of 1959, the 95th Sweepstakes, listed 25 prize-award units and a ticket sale increase of 1,420,000 over the 91st drawing. More Irish Hospitals' Sweepstakes tickets are sold each year. From 1960 to 1970 the sales of Sweeps tickets in the United States averaged about 20 million per year. Then came 1973 and with the legalization of state-run lotteries in New York, New Jersey, Pennsylvania, Massachusetts, Michigan, Iowa, Washington and several other states, the Sweeps sales in the United States dropped to an all-time low of 5 million for the year.

Compared with the hundreds of other lotteries, raffles, pools and the many weekly state-run lotteries with their 1 in a million chance of winning a top prize of $50,000, I believe that the best $2.80 lottery buy today is an Irish Hospitals' Sweepstakes ticket. The only criticism I can make is that seller and buyer are violating our anti-lottery laws. Otherwise the operation is an honest one.

If you happen to purchase a counterfeit ticket or if the character who sells you your ticket fails to turn in your money, this is not the fault of the Irish operators. They print warnings on each genuine ticket against counterfeits, although this isn't really much help, since the counterfeit tickets bear the same warning. Your best protection against counterfeits and the crooked seller who fails to turn in your stub and money is to buy from someone who you know has handled ticket sales for at least a year and has previously supplied Sweeps buyers with official stub receipts.

Although you have only 1 chance in 305,000 of winning a top prize of $140,000, your chance of winning a prize award of some sorts is 1 in 1,000, which is exactly the same as the 1 in 1,000 chance the Policy Numbers player has of hitting his three-digit number. And when you consider honesty, odds, size of awards and purchase price, a Sweeps ticket is the best lottery buy in the United States today.

RAFFLES

The oldest, and still very popular, form of lottery in America is the raffle, or local drawing. Next to Bingo, raffles are the country's biggest fund raisers for charity. Fraternal organizations, veterans' groups and almost every other kind of organization in the country have benefited at some time from a raffle of some sort. Many raffles have automobiles valued at $2,000 to $15,000 as prizes, with the raffle tickets selling from a low of 10¢ to a high of $100. Some drawings have $50,000 and $125,000 homes as their top awards. And, I have known of some raffle tickets on estates that have sold for as much as $1,000 each.

The only advice I can give you on local raffle-ticket buying, whether it is legal or illegal in your state, is: Be careful from whom you buy. There are a great many crooked and counterfeit raffle tickets floating around.

To sum up, there are hundreds of variations on the general lottery patterns. Depending on the type of lottery and its clientele, the operators return to the winners in prizes somewhere between 10% and 55%

of the ticket money collected. Most of the foreign lotteries now selling tickets in this country which list top prizes of $100,000 or more are out-and-out frauds which have no drawings and which give the crooks operating them 100% of the total take. So, be careful.

6.
State Lotteries
and How They Work

When the state of New Hampshire voted to go into the gambling business with a statewide lottery in 1963, it broke a 70-year precedent and became the first state since the abolishment of the Louisiana Lottery in 1895 to operate a legalized lottery in the United States. (Puerto Rico has had a national lottery since 1934.) The moralists wailed that the plan would fail and go down in history as New Hampshire's fool tax experiment.

Nothing could have been further from the truth because by 1973, 12 states—New Hampshire, New York, New Jersey, Connecticut, Michigan, Maryland, Pennsylvania, Massachusetts, Iowa, Washington, Montana and Virginia—had authorized state lotteries to raise public funds and several other states are prepared to get their lotteries rolling in the near future. Before 1963, when moral considerations outweighed financial needs in the public's mind, the states' legislators moved slowly in their efforts to legalize and operate state lotteries. But, having studied the lottery returns in states where the lottery question was on the ballot and learned that in all cases the public voted overwhelmingly in favor of a statewide lottery—legislators in other states are saying, "Me, too."

In 1963, the day New Hampshire voted a statewide lottery, I predicted that New York and all states adjoining New Hampshire would quickly adopt statewide lotteries. My reasoning was obvious. If only one state has a legalized lottery, this takes away large sums of lottery money from residents of adjoining states. In order to keep that money for their own needs, ever increasing numbers of states are legalizing state lotteries—and now that these lotteries have started to operate, I

174

believe they will spread across the country. By 1980, every state in the country with a fair-sized population will operate its own statewide lottery.

State lotteries have cut deeply into the ticket sales of the Irish Hospitals' Sweepstakes and similar foreign lotteries. However, state-run lotteries have not hurt the illegal Numbers game, for a very good reason: the Numbers racket pays better odds than the state lotteries do.

Numbers players are a breed by themselves. They like to pick their own three numbers; they like daily action; they like to bet in private, and they like credit action when they are broke. Legally, the Numbers players are supposed to pay taxes on their winnings, but they seldom if ever do.

When the original New Hampshire state lottery was introduced in 1964, it was patterned after the Irish Hospitals' Sweepstakes. It combined a lottery with horse races. There were only two drawings a year, one in July, the other in September, both keyed to horse races at Rockingham Park, New Hampshire. Tickets sold for $3. The purchaser wrote down his name and the tickets remained in the machine. The tickets were collected and placed in bank vaults. They were taken out before the two horse races on which the sweepstakes were run.

The sold tickets were mixed in a drum and matched to 400-odd horses nominated for the races. Small prizes of $125 or slightly more were paid on the first matching. At post time, tickets matched to the entries in the two deciding races were paid some $3,000. The big prizes were two of $50,000, two of $25,000 and two of $12,500, paid for win, place and show in each of two races. In addition, there were monthly bonus prizes totaling $5,000, designed to keep interest alive during the long period between drawings, from September to July. These small prizes were based on computerized selections of numbers and the winners got another crack at the next drawing. The New Hampshire lottery later was patterned after the New Jersey lottery.

The New Hampshire lottery gave back to the winning players 35¢ of each dollar they invested. Though it did not achieve the financial bonanza expected by many of its backers, it was responsible for getting the lottery ball rolling in New York. On June 1, 1967, lottery tickets went on sale in New York, making it the second state in the country to get into the legalized lottery business.

New York state lottery tickets first sold for $1. Drawings took place once a month. For each million tickets sold, there were 15 grand prize winners plus 225 consolation prizes. First prize was $100,000; second, $50,000; third, $25,000, and fourth, $10,000. Then there were 11 prizes of $5,000 each. Consolation prizes included 15 prizes of $1,000, 15 of $700, 15 of $400, 15 of $250 and 165 of $150. This adds up to 240 winners splitting up $300,000 in prizes for each million tickets sold. In addition to the monthly drawings, the New York State Lottery Commission ran a $250,000 once-a-year free drawing to stimulate year-round interest. Payments to the $250,000 winner were spread over a ten-year period to lessen the income-tax impact. In addition to this prize there were a number of consolation prizes ranging up to $7,500. To prepare for the special drawing, 200-odd tickets were drawn and set aside from each million tickets sold monthly.

As in the Irish Hospitals' Sweepstakes, the original New York state lottery monthly winners were chosen by a combination of fishbowl-type drawings and the results of a horse race. But, unlike the Irish Hospitals' Sweepstakes, the New York state lottery winners were chosen according to the results of a race run *before* the drawing.

The original New York state lottery did not achieve the financial results expected by its original backers, due to a poor distribution arrangement. The buyer had to go to a hotel, local government agency or bank to buy a lottery ticket and once there he had to write his name and address on a duplicate ticket, keep the carbon and drop the original into a box. Imagine a laborer, dirty from work and perspiration, walking into a bank and standing an hour in line to purchase a lottery ticket. To add to the problem, Congress passed the 1967 Federal banking statute which prohibited the sale of lottery tickets by banking institutions insured by the Federal government. Fortunately, the distribution problem was solved. Of course, statewide lotteries, like all other legalized gambling ventures, have to go through a period of trial and error before the correct format is found.

The best arrangement to date began on December 16, 1970, when the first of New Jersey's statewide lottery tickets went on sale. The basic format of the ticket was fashioned after the illegal Treasury Tickets popular during the 1920s and '30s (see page 158). All winners are based on a six-digit number obtained from several drawings and the result of a previously run horse race. Tickets sell for 50¢ and the lottery has one weekly drawing. Like the illegal Treasury Ticket, the New Jersey lottery does not require the name or address of the ticket buyer. Tickets are identified simply by number.

In addition to weekly drawings, the New Jersey State Lottery Commission runs a semifinal drawing whenever the members decide that revenue from the sale of weekly tickets warrants it. Winners of the semifinal drawing are entered in what is known as the 50¢ Millionaire drawing.

While the prize awards of New Jersey's lottery have gone through several changes, here are the ones in use at the time of printing. The commission awards prizes on a million-ticket base. Tickets show a six-

John Scarne and Ralph F. Batch, Executive Director of the New Jersey State Lottery Commission, shown discussing new ways to improve the New Jersey State Lottery during a weekly lottery drawing in southern New Jersey. (Ralph F. Batch)

digit number between 000,000 to 999,999. If 5 million lottery tickets are sold per week, the six digit numbers from 000,000 to 999,999 are repeated five times. The weekly cash prize awards plus 18,999 entrants into the 50¢ Millionaire semifinal drawing per million tickets are as follows. If all six digits on the ticket match the drawn number, the holder wins $50,000 in the weekly drawing. The last five digits receives $4,000; the last four $400; and the last three $40.

For example, if the Weekly Winning Number is 123456:

123456	(all 6 digits match)	wins $50,000	1 winner
X23456	(last 5 digits match)	wins $4,000	9 winners
XX3456	(last 4 digits match)	wins $400	90 winners
XXX456	(last 3 digits match)	wins $40	900 winners
XXXX56	(last 2 digits match) "50¢-Millionaire" Semifinal Drawing	wins entry into the	9,000 entries
12XXXX	(first 2 digits match) "50¢-Millionaire" Semifinal Drawing	also wins entry into the	9,999 entries

There are on the average 1,009 cash winners each week for every million tickets sold. And, there are approximately 18,999 entrants into the semifinal drawing.

To most lottery-ticket buyers, the methods of determining the winners in the New Jersey lottery (and other state lotteries) are most confusing. This is because several drawings are required before the ultimate winners are determined by a *gimmick* supposed to represent the results of a previously run horse race. The gimmick is purely a subterfuge to avoid the 10% Federal excise gambling tax. That is, since horse racing is exempt from this tax, the ultimate winners are supposedly decided by the results of a horse race, and payment of the tax isn't necessary.

Here is how the six-digit basic winning number is arrived at. Again, for example, 123456 is the winning number. First, the last four digits are selected. This is done by pushing a button to stop four rotating cylinders. Each sealed transparent cylinder contains a large rubber ball and ten equally spaced positions numbered from 0 through 9. When the motor is stopped suddenly, each ball bounces around in its cylinder and comes to rest in one of the numbered positions. These four numbers become the last four digits of the winning number. Cylinder 1 determines the third number of the six-digit number, cylinder 2 the fourth number, cylinder 3 the fifth, and cylinder 4 the sixth. Now the horse-race gimmick is used.

On the auditorium platform at the drawing site is a giant chart marked "Post Position Finalists." This chart depicts 10 post positions marked 1 to 10. Alongside each of these 10 post positions are placed the same four selected numbers. In the example I used earlier, these numbers would have been 3456. Next, the memory bank of a giant computer is asked to reveal the unsold tickets ending with XX3456. Because there are only 100 possible combinations of the first two digits (00 to 99), the information can be obtained instantaneously. Next, a fishbowl-type drawing takes place. One hundred balls numbered from 00 to 99, with the exception of the balls bearing the first two digits of unsold XX3456-form numbers, are placed in a clear bowl and are rotated to mix them up. From this, ten balls are selected at random, one at a time, and as each ball is drawn, its number is noted and placed before the previously selected four numbers and given a post position on the chart. For example, the first ball drawn from the bowl is numbered 33; it is assigned post position No. 1. Number 33 is placed into the empty space next to post position No. 1 and is followed by the last four winning numbers—333456. The second ball is drawn and its number, say 55, is placed in the empty space next to post position No. 2, followed by the previously four selected numbers. Post position No. 2 will show as 553456. And so it goes until each of the ten post positions contains a six-digit number.

The final step is as follows: Ten envelopes are placed in a bowl and thoroughly mixed. Each contains a program sheet from a previously run horse race at a specified track and the post position of the winning horse. In the ten envelopes, naturally, all ten post positions are represented. The winning post position of the first envelope selected (say 2), determines the weekly winning number, namely 553456.

The semifinal drawing is accomplished as follows: The tickets which contain the first 2 and/or the last two correct digits in a weekly drawing are automatically entered in the next announced semifinal drawing. For example, let's say that out of 20 million tickets sold in a period of several weeks, about 379,980 ticketholders will enter the semifinals. A three-digit number is drawn at random and published in most New Jersey papers as the result of the semifinal drawing. Should the last two digits of an entry's serial number match the last two digits of the three-digit semifinal winner, he receives $100. Should the last three digits of an entry's serial number match the winning three-digit number of the semifinal drawing, he becomes eligible to enter the 50¢ Millionaire drawing where the prizes are as follows: $1 million first prize (payable $50,000 a year for 20 years), $200,000 second prize ($20,000 a year for 10 years), $100,000 third prize ($10,000 a year for 10 years), and seven fourth prizes of $10,000 each. All other finalists receive $500 each.

Ralph F. Batch, Executive Director of the New Jersey State Lottery Commission, exhibits drawn ball which determines the first two winning digits in a South Jersey weekly lottery drawing as John Scarne and his son, John Teeko, look on. (Ralph F. Batch)

New Jersey's weekly ticket sales have taken a sharp drop since the neighboring states of New York, Pennsylvania and others have copied the New Jersey lottery format in their own lotteries. Ralph F. Batch, the former executive director of the New Jersey Lottery Commission, had instituted a daily lottery in an attempt to replace the lost sales of the weekly lottery. Daily tickets, like the weekly tickets, are sold through agents and special coin-vending machines. These vending machines dispense tickets on a daily basis only, with tickets for each day's 4:00 P.M. drawing available until 3:55 P.M. All prizes are based on a five-digit winning number with a maximum of 3,816 cash winners for every 100,000 tickets sold. The $2,500 first prize goes to the ticket with the five digits in order. Prizes of $250 go to ticketholders with the five digits in exact reverse order, the first four numbers in proper order, and the last four digits in reverse order. Prizes of $25 go to ticketholders with the first three numbers in exact order, the middle three, the last three, and all five numbers in any scrambled combination. A $2.50 prize is paid to anyone with the first two numbers, the second and third, the third and fourth and the last two. In addition, lottery bonus drawings are held periodically in which all daily losing tickets are eligible to participate. Prizes range from a station wagon and automobiles filled with groceries to many other valuable items manufactured or produced in the Garden State.

The daily state lottery, due to its small capital prize of $2,500, is a dismal failure. My friend and former lawyer Charles C. Carella, the present executive director of the New Jersey Lottery Commission, and other Commission members are now studying "Scarne's Proposed State Numbers Plan" to raise additional state revenue (see pages 203–204).

YOUR CHANCES OF HITTING THE NEW JERSEY STATE WEEKLY LOTTERY

1 chance in 1,000,000 of winning the $50,000 "Grand Prize"
1 chance in 100,000 of winning $4,000 to $50,000
1 chance in 10,000 of winning $400 to $50,000
1 chance in 1,000 of winning $40 to $50,000
1 chance in 52 of being entered in the semifinal drawing

YOUR CHANCES OF HITTING THE 50¢ MILLIONAIRE LOTTERY BASED ON THE SALE OF 25 MILLION TICKETS

1. About 18,999 out of every million tickets sold will be entered in the semifinal drawing. The odds of this occurring is about 1 chance in 52.

2. About 189 out of the 18,999 tickets entered will receive $100 for having the last two digits of the serial number match the last two digits of the three-digit semifinal number. The odds of this occurring is about 1 chance in 5,200.

3. The chances of being entered in the 50¢ Millionaire Lottery are about 1 chance in 52,000.

4. The chances of winning the $1 million grand prize in the 50¢ Millionaire Drawing is based on the number of tickets eligible. If 25 million tickets are eligible, the chance is about 1 in 25 million.

5. The chances of winning $100,000 to $1 million is about 1 in 8,333,333.

6. The chance of winning $10,000 to $1 million is about 1 in 100,000.

7. The chance of winning $500 to $1 million is about 1 in 47,428.

In all other state lotteries making use of the New Jersey format, the odds are about the same.

Most of the states that have lotteries now follow a version of the New Jersey plan. For example, early in 1972, New York switched its lottery format to that of New Jersey's. Prizes are: $50,000 for matching all six digits, $5,000 for matching the last five digits (this is $1,000 more than New Jersey pays), last four digits wins $500, last three digits wins $50; and tickets matching the last two digits automatically become eligible for a later bonus drawing, somewhat similar to New Jersey's 50¢ Millionnaire drawing. Under New York State's lottery law, receipts are divided up in the following manner: 45% for the state, 40% for prizes, and 15% for administration costs.

SCARNE'S PROPOSED TRIPLE-ACTION LOTTERY PLAN

What follows is my proposed triple-action lottery plan, the first such lottery plan in the world, which will greatly increase and possibly double a state's yearly lottery revenue. My original Twenty Numbers, a lottery-type contest produced by Marden-Kane, Inc., was the first lottery-type ticket printed by computer. Twenty Numbers preceded New Jersey's successful state lottery by several years. In fact, the basic format of the New Jersey state lottery appeared first in the original edition of my *Scarne's Complete Guide to Gambling* in 1961.

In spite of its early success, the state prize award structure used by New Jersey and copied by various other states can stand considerable improvement to help increase ticket sales. The faults I find with the present-day state lotteries are as follows:

1. There are too few big prize awards (winners) to satisfy the average ticket buyer.

2. A $50,000 first prize is fine, but the 90% drop from $50,000 to $5,000 for second prizes and the 90% drop from $5,000 to $500 for third prizes and still another 90% drop from $500 to $50 for fourth prizes does not make for a good lottery. In most foreign government-run lotteries, the percentage drop from one prize to the next lower prize is seldom more than 50%. My proposed weekly prizes are: $50,000 first prize, $20,000 second prize, two $15,000 third prizes, two $10,000 fourth prizes, etc.

3. In addition to the weekly drawings and in an attempt to stimulate ticket sales in the state lottery, states run an additional drawing every several weeks at the discretion of the state lottery commission. These are called "Bonus drawings," "50¢ Millionaire drawings," or "Super drawings," depending on the state in which the lottery is held. These additional Bonus drawings fail to achieve their purpose of promoting additional ticket sales because the method of determining the tickets eligible for these drawings eliminates about 98% of the tickets at the very outset. Here is an example of what a lottery-ticket buyer must go through in order to enter a Bonus drawing. To enter a Bonus drawing, a ticketholder must first match the first two digits or the last two-digits of the six-digit weekly winning number. Then he must watch the newspaper for an announcement of the semifinal drawing in which a three-digit number randomly drawn will appear. If his last three digits match the semifinal number, and if his first or last two digits make him eligible in the first place, he is eligible to enter the Bonus drawing. This is a complicated procedure for the average lottery-ticket buyer to follow and results in player lack of interest. Under my proposed triple-action lottery plan, weekly tickets still sell for 50 cents and a state may make use of its own format in determining the winning prize awards. Each 50-cent ticket has a chance to win three different prize awards in three different drawings. In short, it is possible for a 50¢ ticket to win (1) the weekly $50,000 top prize; (2) to win the monthly top prize award of $5,000; and (3) the giant sweepstakes with a top prize of $250,000 to $500,000 or more, depending on the total number of tickets sold during the month.

In my triple-action lottery plan, each 50¢ lottery ticket carries a six-digit number as a weekly lottery ticket number which is eligible for the prize awards for the date marked to the right of the weekly lottery ticket number. In addition, there's a second six-digit number, the monthly lottery ticket number, and the date of that drawing is noted at the right of the monthly lottery ticket number.

Under the proposed plan, the state lottery and sweepstakes would pay back to the ticket buyers 50% of the gross take. The Puerto Rican lottery, the oldest legal lottery under the American flag, returns 68%

Ticket from New Jersey's successful 50¢ weekly lottery, a forerunner of present-day state lotteries.

of its gross take in prize awards. The illegal numbers racket pays back 50% of its take. In order to be competitive, a state should pay back 50% of its gross take. Lottery ticket buyers, like all other gamblers, are a realistic lot. They care little who runs the game or who gets the profits; all they are interested in is winning and getting a fair shake for their money. All other considerations, such as helping the elderly, education, and state institutions are irrelevant.

1. For each million weekly 50¢ triple-action lottery tickets sold, the gross take is $500,000. Based on this figure, Scarne's proposed lottery system would pay back 1,009 weekly cash awards for every million tickets sold, for a total payback to winners of $200,000 or 40% of the gross take.

2. Out of the remaining 10 percent or $50,000 for each million lottery tickets sold weekly, Scarne's proposed lottery system would pay back ten monthly winners, divided as follows: One $5,000 winner and nine $500 winners for a total of $9,500.

3. In addition, all winners of the monthly lottery are to be entered in the giant sweepstakes, whose top prize award may total $250,000 to $500,000, or more.

Now, let us say the winning six-digit number selected at the official weekly lottery drawing is 123456. The 1,009 weekly lottery prize awards totaling $200,000 for every million tickets sold would be divided as follows:

WEEKLY LOTTERY PRIZE AWARDS

Winning six-digit number	123456	receives $50,000	1 winner
Reverse of winning number	654321	receives $20,000	1 winner
One above winning number	123457	receives $15,000	1 winner
One below winning number	123455	receives $15,000	1 winner
Two above winning number	123458	receives $10,000	1 winner
Two below winning number	123454	receives $10,000	1 winner
Three above winning number	123459	receives $ 8,000	1 winner
Three below winning number	123453	receives $ 8,000	1 winner
Four above winning number	123460	receives $ 5,000	1 winner
Four below winning number	123452	receives $ 5,000	1 winner
Last five digits correct	X23456	receives $ 2,000	9 winners
Last four digits correct	XX3456	receives $ 200	90 winners
Last three digits correct	XXX456	receives $ 20	900 winners

At the end of four weekly lottery drawings, the monthly lottery drawing takes place and the following prizes are awarded for each one million weekly tickets sold:

MONTHLY LOTTERY PRIZE AWARDS

Winning six-digit number	123456 receives $5,000	1 winner
Last five digits correct	X23456 receives $ 500	9 winners

This adds up to $9,500, leaving $40,500 per million tickets sold for giant sweepstakes prizes.

Each of the above monthly lottery prize winners is automatically entered in the giant sweepstakes, which follows the monthly drawing by a week or two. The holder of a winning monthly lottery ticket of either $5,000 or $500 brings his winning ticket to the specified state lottery agency. The state claim agent will hand him a notarized receipt and forward his ticket to the State Lottery Commission, which will mail him a check for $5,000 or $500 and enter his name in the giant sweepstakes drawing. The same procedure is followed with winning weekly lottery tickets.

THE GIANT SWEEPSTAKES AND HOW IT WORKS

Let's say a state sells 4 million weekly lottery tickets for a four-week total of 16 million tickets. Each of these 16 million tickets participates in the monthly lottery drawing, which is a sort of semifinal for the giant sweepstakes drawing. Under Scarne's proposed lottery plan, 160 winners out of 16 million tickets will be selected in the monthly lottery. Each of these will receive $500 or $5,000 and be eligible to enter the giant sweepstakes drawing which should take place a week or two after the monthly lottery drawing. The gross sales revenue for 16 million tickets totals $8 million from which 10 percent or $800,000 must be placed in a special monthly and giant sweepstakes pool. Out of this $800,000 special pool, $154,000 is used to pay prize awards of $500 or $5,000 to each of the 160 monthly lottery winners. The remaining $646,000 left in the special pool will be distributed as prize awards to the ten lucky winners in the giant sweepstakes drawing.

These prize awards are as follows: 50% of the pool's $646,000 or $323,000 goes to the first-prize winner, 20%, or $129,200, goes to the second-prize winner, 15%, or $96,900, goes to the third-prize winner and 15%, or $96,900, to be divided equally among the seven fourth-prize winners.

GIANT SWEEPSTAKES PRIZE AWARDS
When 16 Million Tickets Are Sold

First Prize Award	$323,000
Second Prize Award	$129,200
Third Prize Award	$ 96,900
Fourth Prize Awards (7)	$ 13,843

The cost of operating such an enterprise should total no more than 10% of the gross revenue. This would include computer costs, advertising and a 5% commission for sales agents—plus a special bonus of $10,000 to the store or agent that sells the winning ticket for the top giant sweepstakes award, $2,000 each to the sellers of the three runner-up tickets, and $2,000 to the seller of the weekly $50,000 prize ticket. This leaves the state with 40% of the gross take, which in our example is a net profit of $4 million for the four-week period.

7.
The Numbers
Game

The most popular form of lottery played anywhere in the world today is our own Numbers game. My survey shows that during 1973 almost three out of every eight persons who gamble in this country played the numbers. These 36 million Americans, of whom 15 million were women, wagered the gigantic sum of $10 billion in an effort to hit the elusive three digits that would pay off.

The Numbers game has different names among various segments of the population: Policy game, Mutuel Numbers, Negro Numbers, Policy racket, Numbers racket and others. Foreign-born Latin Americans call it Bolita; the winners in this Latin-American lottery are usually determined by drawing small numbered balls from a box. The operators and their employees and the majority of players refer to the game simply as "the Numbers." Most journalists, law-enforcement agents and government officials call it the Numbers racket or the policy racket.

Today's Numbers game is a variation of the Italian national lottery (see page 207) which has been in existence since 1530. In America, during early colonial days, clandestine lottery operators, like their English contemporaries, permitted players to wager on two or more numbers of their choice, the winning numbers being determined by the last two or three numbers of the first-, second- and third-prize numbers drawn in some legal lottery. Since most players played a combination of digits derived from the five-figure number on their weekly lottery ticket, this illegal wagering was called "insurance betting" and the operation itself was known as "policy shop," both terms deriving from "insurance policy."

In 1973, the $10 billion numbers handle in the United States was greater than the total handle of all the combined foreign government-sponsored lotteries in Europe, Asia and Latin America plus the privately operated Irish Hospitals' Sweepstakes and the legally run football pools in England and other European countries.

The largest handle of any type of lottery outside the United States, contrary to the statements made by some so-called gambling experts, is grossed by the British football pools. The eight major pools took in $339,360,000 in 1972. The players got back 50% of this ($169,680,000) in prize money, called "dividends." About 30%, or $101,808,000, went to the government in taxes, 17%, or $57,691,200, went for overhead, and the legal limit of 3%, or $10,180,800, to the promoters as profit. The top prize award for a twopence wager can run as high as $1,500,000 or more.

The $10 billion U.S. Numbers handle for 1973 broke down approximately as follows: 47% came back to players as prize money; 40% paid salaries, operational expenses, lawyers' fees and fines: 7% ($700 million) was retained by the operators as profits. The final 6%, or $600 million, went to corrupt politicians and law-enforcement agents as the illegitimate tax called graft or ice. It is called ice because it is used to cool off the officials so the heat won't go on.

The state and Federal share in taxes was: 0%.

OPERATION

We'll begin our description of how the Numbers game works by defining some terms and listing the personnel.

Agent: A person who solicits bets on the Numbers. A storekeeper, shoeshine boy, newsstand operator, or an employee of a hotel, office building, industrial plant, etc. In some sections of the country the agent is called a *runner*.

Runner: A person who picks up the daily Numbers business from several agents. He is also the payoff man when a player hits a number. Some runners also solicit business from bigtime Numbers players. The runner is so called because he is always on the go, trying to avoid arrest.

Controller: A head runner or branch or area manager who has other runners working under him and who receives their daily collections. He is called a controller because he has to keep the runners in line—not always an easy job.

Spot controller: A controller who operates without runners. He takes big action from a select clientele of bigtime Numbers bettors, usually soliciting his business in the bars and clubs they frequent.

Drop: The place from which the controller operates for a few hours each day and to which his runners bring their day's business. It is usually a room in a private home or an apartment and the tenant is paid from $25 to $100 per day for its use, depending upon the size of the drop. There are thousands of such drops in our major cities.

Bank (sometimes called the *big drop*): The headquarters to which the controllers bring their day's receipts.

Banker: The operator of a bank. Most banks are controlled and financed by a syndicate of bankers. They must have access to a large bankroll—as much as $500,000 in a large city—so that they can pay off when players make big hits.

Inside men: Employees who use computing machines and other modern office equipment and make up a list of all the bets made and their payouts. The bankers themselves oversee this operation.

Numbers service: A service which supplies Numbers bankers with each official winning number as it appears. The number is based on the payoff prices at a specified racetrack. The service office in each large city has a man at the track who reports by phone as the races are won. The service sells the information to bankers throughout the country. Each client pays from $100 to $250 per week plus phone charges.

Avoiding police raids where protection is weak or nonexistent requires considerable ingenuity. Here's a method used by an upstate New York bank:

One runner distributes the number books to agents, another runner picks up the money and a third gets the money slips from the agents. Each of these runners does business with a different controller and each controller operates from a different drop or money bank. Since each phase of the operation is separate, a single police raid can't wreck the organization, and the cops never get more than a part of the cash receipts even if they raid one of the money banks. Conviction without the slips is impossible; money alone is not considered sufficient evidence.

The police are behind the eight ball in this constant Numbers game of hide-and-seek. Here's an incident my friend Patrick Sullivan, former police commissioner of North Bergen, New Jersey, told me a few years ago.

"Scarne," he said, "I was once tailing a runner whom I wanted to arrest with as many slips as possible in his possession, so I tailed him all over town. Finally I saw him come out of an Italian restaurant carrying a two-gallon pot. He'd made about ten pickups by now, so I grabbed him.

"I expected to find the number slips and the money in the pot, but it was filled with *pasta e fagioli* [a bean-and-noodle soup]. The man denied being a Numbers runner, and since we found no evidence on his person or in his car we had to release him. About a year later I met the suspect at a political rally. He admitted he had been a runner but claimed he had quit. 'Commissioner,' he said, grinning, 'remember the day you stopped me with the pot of *pasta e fagioli?* You didn't dig deep enough. The slips and cash were there. The pot had a false bottom.' "

Pat added, "If some of those characters only used as much ingenuity in some legitimate business, they'd go far."

In order to get the information you'll find in this chapter I had to talk to hundreds of runners, controllers and bankers throughout the country. I found that Detroit and Chicago have a Numbers syndicate which controls most of the banks in those cities. New York City, as one of the biggest bankers told me, can't ever be controlled by one combination or mob; it's too big. New York has about six major banks, the largest ones being the Harlem bank, the Brooklyn bank and the Bronx bank. Each one does about $200,000 worth of business per day. In addition there were at least a thousand small banks in New York City, many operating on the sneak without paying protection money. This includes several hundred runners who work for the big banks but hold out some of the action and bank it themselves.

As proof of that daily handle figure per bank, here's what the police found in a raid on a Numbers drop in Brooklyn a few years ago. They confiscated thousands of Numbers slips, and a count showed a total of 1,500,000 bets, ranging from a low nickel bet to a high $100 on a single number. The total at that drop for one day's business was $200,000. If all six banks did as well that day the grand total comes to $1,200,000—and this doesn't count the bets gathered by all the small bankers.

The police found no money at this drop. A Numbers bank of this size employs about 30 controllers, each with about 20 runners working under him, and each runner may have as few as 5 or as many as 100 agents soliciting bets.

In another raid, at about the same period, New Jersey police had even better luck. They raided a Numbers drop in a North Arlington private home and seized not only Numbers slips, tapes and adding machines but $281,283 in cash as well. Numbers operators whom I talked to later said, "Those boys were real dopes to have their drop and the bankroll in the same place."

Why has the Numbers game grown to such huge proportions? It is illegal in every state, including Nevada, and yet you can always find a spot to get down a bet: the corner bar, a candy store, gas station, grocery store or barber shop, your office building or factory, the apartment hotel where you live. The Numbers solicitors who used to hang around poolrooms, barbershops and bars looking for nickel and dime action have left that business to the owners and employees of those places and have gone on to greener pastures. They work as bellboys, messengers, elevator operators in large hotels and office and apartment buildings where the traffic flow is greater and the potential players are wealthier. One of the best spots for a runner is a job in a large industrial plant. If he doesn't take a job there himself, he gets an employee to act as an agent.

Twenty years or so ago, the Numbers was largely a poor man's game. Since many operators still permit bets of as little as 10 cents, it is still the number one lottery for the poor man. Today, however, everyone plays Numbers. Many bettors have been known to wager as much as $1,000 on a "hot number."

ORIGIN OF TODAY'S NUMBERS GAME

My survey indicates that about 50% of the adult black population of our large cities plays the Numbers regularly. One reason for the game's popularity among Negroes may be the fact that, like the game of Craps, they invented it.

In the spring of 1921, in New York City's Harlem, a predominantly Negro section, a group of Negro lottery operators were selling Treasury Tickets at 50¢ and $1. Realizing that there were many prospective customers who couldn't afford the price, they added a 10¢ weekly ticket to the line. It immediately began selling so big that a few weeks later they had to discontinue the 50¢ and $1 tickets because everyone was buying the dime tickets.

The demand was so great that many additional agents and subagents had to be hired. It was the biggest lottery ticket-selling boom Harlem had ever seen. But a bug developed: a year later the dime ticket had to be withdrawn because it cost just as much to print tickets and result sheets for the 10¢ ticket as for the 50¢ and $1 tickets. After the printing bills were paid, there were no profits left to speak of.

TREASURY TICKETS

Although the dime ticket was a financial failure, it did prove that Harlem wanted a low-priced ticket. If the high printing costs could somehow be reduced or eliminated there were plenty of profits to be made. The operators solved the problem a year later. They began marketing a "You Pick 'em Treasury Ticket." In effect, this brought back the old policy-shop lottery which had disappeared after legalized lotteries were abolished by Federal law in 1895. The new scheme was similar. Players were permitted to select any five-digit number from 00000 to 99999 as their playing number for the week. This cut down printing costs to next to nothing; all that was required was small sheets of paper with the heading. *You Pick 'em daily Treasury Ticket.*

The player merely wrote down his or her name, the selected number and the date of purchase. The winning numbers, as with the other Treasury Tickets, were the last five digits of the daily report of the U.S. Treasury balance as published each day in the newspapers. A player who had picked five digits in the right order received $300. If he got the last four right he won $30; the last three paid $3.

CLEARINGHOUSE NUMBERS

Another Harlem lottery group soon eliminated printing costs completely with a daily lottery known as "Clearinghouse Numbers." The player simply wrote his selected number and the amount of his bet on a slip of paper which bore no printing—the method which is used today. Players selected only three digits and made bets from one penny to a quarter. The winning numbers were the last three digits of the Cincinnati Clearinghouse daily balance. The payoff was 500 to 1, or $5 for each 1¢ wagered.

This was an immediate success, and other Negro treasury and lottery operators in various sections of the city began booking the clearinghouse numbers. Most of them dropped their other tickets altogether.

This type of operation not only saved the big printing costs of printing tickets and the fancy result sheets which carried many winning weekly numbers; it also minimized the chances of arrest, since agents no longer had to carry valises or bulky packages of tickets and result sheets. Another big advantage was that it was a daily rather than a weekly operation, and even though most players were wagering pennies the weekly handle was greater than before.

The players liked the new setup because they could select their own numbers and put their money on their favorite lucky number. This made them feel that the game was more honest. These advantages for both operator and player soon made the Numbers the world's biggest lottery.

In 1923, a few months after the clearinghouse numbers began to be used, the game became known to the white population as "Nigger Numbers," to the Negroes as "the Numbers" and to law-enforcement officials and journalists as "Policy Numbers." By 1927, as many whites as Negroes were playing the game and they, too, began to call it simply "the Numbers." It was now firmly entrenched in all the poorer sections of our big cities, particularly New York, Philadelphia, Chicago, Detroit and Los Angeles.

THE RACKET BOYS MOVE IN

When Prohibition was repealed in 1933 the now out-of-work hoodlums, bootleggers and racketeers turned to illegal gambling operations,

and many of them picked the Numbers as their new racket. They took
over simply by moving in and beating up or killing off any Numbers
operator who objected. By 1935, these tough boys were in control, and
the game came to be known as the Numbers racket.

Before the racketeers moved in, most of the operators, known as
policy kings or *bankers*, were usually well-known, small-time neighborhood sportsmen, politicians and bar and restaurant owners who tried to
avoid trouble by keeping on good terms with everyone. They would
lend money with a smile, cash checks for customers and pass out tur-
keys to the needy on Thanksgiving. The racketeers were a different
breed: they carried machine guns.

The local operators were either forced out of business or had to be
content with being runners for the mob. Some who had strong political
connections or were tough eggs themselves became controllers or even
bankers, but they had to join the organization. After several gang wars
and considerable bloodshed the Numbers game in each principal city of
the United States became geographically organized, with different
mobs or combinations controlling different territories in and around the
cities. Strong-arm methods were, and still are, used to keep each mob
in its own territory.

THE $6 MILLION NUMBERS SWINDLE

There were more than a thousand banks in operation in New York
City by 1930. Then something happened which cut that number
down. A confidence mob succeeded in bribing a Cincinnati Clearinghouse clerk to rig the last three digits of the daily balance for December 11. He agreed to round the next day's figure off so that the three
final digits were 000. Scores of agents hired by the con men began
betting heavily on 000 with all the banks. When the rigged number
appeared in the papers the following day many bankers found themselves unable to pay off. The Numbers boys estimated at the time that
$10,000 had been wagered on 000. At the then prevailing odds of 600
for 1, the banks owed $6 million. Hundreds closed up and the bankers
made themselves scarce. Others agreed to pay off the winners on the
installment plan. The swindlers probably collected about $500,000 of
the $6 million. How much money was won and how much collected
throughout the rest of the country is anybody's guess. This Numbers
episode ended with several murders and the disappearance of the
clearinghouse clerk.

THE PARI-MUTUEL HANDLE NUMBER

Some of the New York City banks that survived switched to using
the last three digits of the summary of the Stock Exchange as the

winning number and, afraid that this could also be rigged, limited single bets to $1. A few years later most banks throughout the country began basing the winning number on the payoff prices at a specified racetrack.

It works this way: Let's say the six combined payoff totals of the horses finishing 1st, 2nd and 3rd at New York's Belmont track were $81.60 for the first three races, $192.20 for the first five and $315.10 for the first seven. If you drop the cents and take the last dollar digit of each of the three totals, the winning number for the day is 125. This complicated system made rigging unlikely.

Today, since all major racetracks use ticket-vending machines and electrically controlled totalisators, there is very little chance of rigging, and many operators now use a simpler system. They take the last digit of the handle wagered on the 3rd, 5th and 7th races. If the total sum wagered on the 3rd race at Belmont Park was $113,261, on the 5th race $97,208, and on the 7th, $108,302, the day's winning number would be 182.

Some banks simplify the system even more and take the last three digits of the total handle at a specified track. If all bets total $2,118,332 at Belmont, for instance, the winning number is 332. The Numbers players get the winning number from their newspapers, most of which carry both the individual race handle and the total handle.

PROTECTION AND THE LAW

The Numbers racket, by 1939, had blossomed into a billion-dollar national industry. And in that year it received nationwide front-page publicity when Jimmy Hines, a prominent Tammany Hall bigwig, was convicted and imprisoned for his participation in a Numbers bank operated by the notorious ex-bootlegger "Dutch" Schultz. Thomas E. Dewey, then a special rackets prosecutor, rose to fame through his prosecution of Hines and later became Governor of New York State and twice ran for President.

If you think the publicity on the Hines case was bad for the Numbers, think again. It gave added impetus to the play. Numbers players are only interested in getting paid off when they win, and the bigger the racket and political names behind the bank, the more secure they feel! People who had never before played Numbers read about the Hines case and then, out of curiosity, began to play.

Horse players, dice and card players also pay little attention to gambling exposure headlines. They merely shrug and say, "Some politician is looking for publicity," or, "Some newspaperman needs copy so he picks on gambling." The only time these exposures disturb them is when there's so much heat on that they can't get a bet down.

Things haven't changed much since the day of Jimmy Hines. A gigantic illegal industry like Numbers couldn't operate for a day without protection. The racketeer operators now have a working arrangement with politicians and cops that enables them, for the most part, to operate without fear of arrest. They even employ the police to discourage rival Numbers runners from soliciting business outside their specified territory.

When this happens the old underworld code "Never squeal to the cops" is overlooked. The mob gives the cops on their payroll the runner's name and the addresses of his number pickups. The cops pull him in. The arrest serves two purposes: it eliminates competition and it makes the police who are taking graft look good in the eyes of the public and the honest government officials. The mobsters I've talked to alibi their squealing by saying, "We pay for protection, so why should some other mob's runners muscle in?"

The cops on the mob's payroll usually demand a certain number of arrests per month. When the supply of rival runners fails to meet the quota, the mob selects one of their own runners to take the rap. This is known as an *accommodation* or *stand-in* arrest. In the big cities a runner, on conviction, will be fined anywhere from $100 to $1,000; the mob picks up this tab. One out of ten arrested runners gets a jail sentence; while he is in jail, the mob pays his salary and an amount approximating his commissions to his family.

NEW YORK CITY'S NUMBERS GAME

A conservative estimate of the 1973 daily handle of New York's six biggest Numbers banks is $1,200,000. The 1,000 small banks in the city did another $800,000 worth of business daily. This is a combined business of $2 million per day, $12 million for a six-day week, and over $600 million for the year. 1973 is also the year in which the national gross handle topped the $10 billion mark.

How many runners and agents were required to handle this $600 million annual gross in New York City? Naturally, you can't get official statistics from any law-enforcement body; they haven't got them. I got an estimate this way: I asked 200 runners and agents in different parts of the city how often they had been arrested on a Numbers charge during the year, and I found a total of 17 arrests, a ratio of about 1 in 12.

The Magistrate's Courts that year reported 14,103 Numbers arrests. If the 1:12 ratio holds, then about 170,000 runners and agents made their living or part of their living from Numbers. This many runners and agents would need about 30,000 bankers, office workers, controllers, crooked cops, politicians and lawyers on the Numbers payroll, a total of 200,000 people in the numbers racket.

My New York City Numbers handle figure was confirmed by a recent study conducted by the city of New York. This study, undertaken by the polling organization of Oliver Quayle, revealed that New Yorkers gamble over $600 million a year at the Numbers games—just as I have been saying for years.

LUCKY NUMBERS

Most people today wouldn't bet money on a fortuneteller's prediction based on a layout of cards or tea leaves, or the juggling of some astrological figures. But most Numbers players believe that the sight or mention of any three-digit number is a psychic sign and that some supernatural force has brought it to their attention. Millions of dollars are bet by numbers players every day on what they consider is their lucky number for the day: their street address, the last three digits of their birth year, the sales total of a purchase, the license number of a passing car . . .

The favorite reading matter of millions of Numbers players is (1) the newspapers that report the winning numbers; and (2) dream books and numerology pamphlets which give interpretations of dreams, daily happenings, birthdays, etc., in terms of three-digit numbers. *Know Your Dream, Lucky Star, King Tut* and *Gypsy Queen* are among the best sellers in New York City.

The system is simple: If you dreamed last night that you took a trip on a bus, look under *Travel*. You are told that "travelling means you will change jobs (213)." If you dreamed of visiting a lawyer, this means "you will suffer from a cold (165)." Dreaming of money: "Your luck will change (381)"; dancing girls denote "happiness and you will come into money (814)." A doctor denotes pregnancy (119) for a woman and illness for a man (415). Oddly enough, although many of these books are published by the same company, they all give different interpretations and numbers.

For a somewhat higher fee you can get information at first hand from palmists, numerologists, astrologers, dream analysts and other purveyors of sixth-sense and psychic information. I visited a Madame Zonga who ran a dream parlor on Lexington Avenue in Harlem and whose advertisement in the Harlem papers guaranteed that she would interpret your dream and tell you what your lucky number was. Her dream parlor was a small store, its street display window covered with a loud multicolored curtain. Sheets of paper tacked to the walls inside bore crudely drawn three-digit numbers with the legend below:

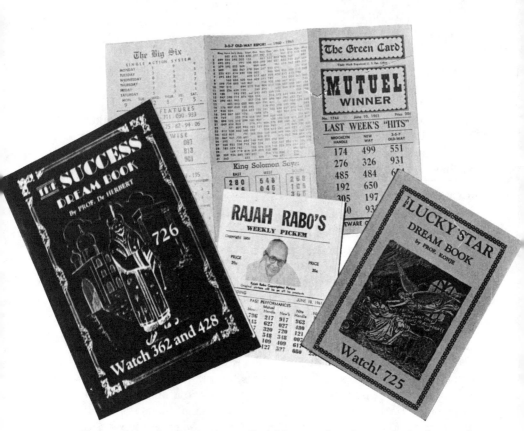

Harlem dream books (foreground) and hot number sheets which claim to be able to predict winning numbers. (Stanley Einzig)

"These are just a few of the Lucky Numbers Madame Zonga predicted in the last month."

There were six women customers ahead of me, and I waited nearly an hour before Madame Zonga invited me into the inner sanctum, which was separated from the rest of the room by long curtains suspended from the ceiling. It contained two chairs and a small table. The first order of business was to give her my age, date of birth, date of marriage, wife's birth date, child's birth date and an assortment of other personal figures.

Then I had to relate my dream, and she cautioned me that she must know as much about it as possible since one important detail overlooked might result in a wrong interpretation. I made up a dream as I went along, injecting numbers wherever possible. She jotted down all the figures. When I reported seeing a man and a girl in the dream, Madame Zonga insisted that I try to estimate their ages. I guessed 30 and 36. She added these figures to those previously noted, added the lot, and got a total of 9,463. I think there's an undeveloped market here that adding-machine salesmen should know about; she didn't have one. From this total she picked the combinations 394, 946 and 463 as my lucky numbers and told me I should play them daily until they hit.

I asked her what her fee was for this valuable advice and she replied that there was no charge (there's an ordinance against fortune-telling), but if I cared to donate a dollar to a worthy cause (Madame Zonga?) it would be appreciated. I gave her the dollar and as I left asked, "Do you play the Numbers yourself?"

She smiled slightly and shook her head. "No, I don't gamble. I'm unlucky."

In addition to the dream books, at least a dozen weekly number sheets are published and sold in all major American cities. They are priced from 25¢ to $1 and give you the winning numbers for the previous year or so, plus a list of numbers which they claim are due to come up soon.

Dream books have been around a long time. This Chinese dream book has long been used by players in the Chinese Word-Blossoming lottery. (Stewart Culin, from Chess and Playing Cards)

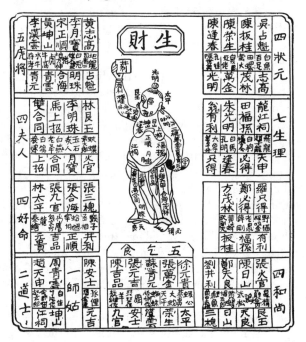

NUMBER 614

Here's a Numbers game incident which happened right under my nose not so long ago. I was having breakfast with my friend Jack Reme in Jack's Diner in Fairview, New Jersey, when a woman patron whom we'll call Jane sat down at the counter and began telling about a dream she had had the night before. Dramatically, she emphasized the fact that one of the most important features of the dream was a vivid impression in bright lights of the number 614.

"In my dream," she went on, "I gave Gimp [the neighborhood runner] two bucks to bet on 614 and I remember seeing a lot of other people betting on the same number. Gimp picked up thirty dollars' worth of bets and 614 won. Gimp brought in a grip full of money and paid everybody off."

There was only one thing to do about a dream as definite as all that, and Jane did it. She phoned Gimp, who made his headquarters at Abe's newsstand across the street. He came to the diner, Jane gave him a $2 bet on number 614, and other patrons of the diner began betting quarters, halves and dollars on 614. Within an hour Gimp had collected $30 worth of action. The betting stopped at that point because the bettors figured that if they exceeded the amount in Jane's dream they might put the hex, or evil eye, on the number.

Believe it or not, that afternoon the winning mutuel number at Belmont was 614. All the bettors were happy, and those who hadn't believed in dreams before were converted.

The next morning Gimp arrived at the diner to pay off. The payoff price at that time was 600 for 1, and runners did not collect the 10% commission on winning numbers. A bettor who wagered $2 received $1,200, a 50¢ bet collected $300 and a dime bet got $60. It was a big day at Jack's Diner. Gimp paid off a total of $16,800. Another $1,200 should have been paid to Jane but she didn't come in all day. Was she ill? If so, it must be something real serious; Jane would have left her own funeral to collect that $1,200.

A friend of Jane's told me later that she had gone to visit friends in Chicago, but I got the straight story from Gimp shortly after.

"John," he said, "you'll never believe this one. I•wasn't getting any business out of Jack's Diner so I got Jane to shill for me with her dream story. The 614 number I just picked up out of the air. If my boss, the head runner, knew I touted all those people on 614, I'd be out of a job."

"And just where," I asked, "is the missing Jane?"

"Scarne, she's really sick. She's at home but she's staying under cover. She owes a lot of money to people around town and they expect to get paid since they heard about the $1,200 she won on the number she dreamt."

"So, why doesn't she pay off from her winnings?"

"That's why she's sick. She didn't bet a penny on 614. I gave her that two dollars to bet to make it look good. And I didn't put that bet into my book. It makes me sick, too."

This story leaked after a while and Jane left town. One memory of Fairview I'm sure she'll always have is number 614.

NUMBERS BETS AND PAYOFF ODDS

When you place your numbers bet the seller gives you a small pad which contains two carbon sheets. You write down your selected number and the amount of your wager like this: 125—$1. The seller takes your dollar, tears off and gives you the top sheet. The two carbon copies remain in the pad. The seller retains one copy and turns the other in to the Numbers bank before the races start.

The banks and runners advertise their payoff odds as "500 to 1," or "400 to 1," but since they retain the money you wagered they are actually only paying off at 499 to 1, or 399 to 1. The player who hits is so pleased at winning that he doesn't notice, or doesn't mind, the small holdback, but that one small unit really adds up during the year for the bank. It amounts to $1 in each $1,000 wagered. On the total national handle, this holdback averages $10 million.

Also, you never get the full $500 that you are led to expect from the 500 for 1 odds: you get 450 for 1. At odds of 400 for 1, you get 360 for 1. Today your payoff is cut down by 10% because the runner takes this out as his commission. On a $5 billion total national handle this amounts to $500 million in commissions.

There is another cute gimmick known as *boxing* which results in more winners and, consequently, more business for the bank. When you write your number on the betting slip you may *box* it by drawing a square around it. This indicates that you are betting on all combinations of the chosen number and is known as a six-way combination bet. If you select number 125 and box it you are betting on 125, 152, 215, 251, 512 and 521. This, of course, reduces the payoff to about one-sixth. If the bank pays 500 for 1 on a straight bet, a six-way box payoff is 80 for 1. The bank is making a little extra on this box bet, because the payoff corresponding to 500 for 1 on one number is 83⅓ (not 80) for 1 on six numbers.

Any *straight* or *head* number which contains two identical digits (such as 121, 323, 556) is known as a three-way combination because only three different combinations can be made with it. If you box

Number 121, for instance, you are betting on 121, 112, and 211. Since many banks pay only 80 for 1, the same as on a six-way combination, it is sheer lunacy to box numbers of this sort.

A number composed of the same three digits, such as 111, 222, 333, etc., is known as a triples number.

Most banks insist that the player bet on a straight number with each combination or box-number bet.

In the past few years banks have added still another wrinkle, known as *single action,* to produce additional winners. The banks permit you to bet on a single digit in any slot. This means that you can bet that a single number of your choice will appear in the position you specify in the winning three-digit number. Example: you can bet that a 3 will appear as the second digit, or a 5 as the first digit, and so on. On single-action bets you receive odds of 8 for 1, 7 for 1 or 6 for 1, depending on the bank. Since the true single-number odds are 9 to 1 or 10 for 1, the bank takes a hefty cut of 20%, 30% or 40% on a single number.

Whenever business slows down because there have been too few winners, the bankers and controllers go into a huddle to cook up some new type of bet which will stimulate business. There aren't many possibilities left which use only three numbers. One variation would be betting on the first two or last two digits; the odds would probably be about 60 for 1. Or you might be allowed to pick one digit and win if this digit appears anywhere in the winning number. The bank would probably pay off this bet at 2 for 1.

Although the Numbers game came into being because it gave the poor man a gamble he could afford, even the rich play it now. A player can still wager as little as a dime on a number if he can find a runner who will accept such action; most of them won't. They don't like to bother with bets under 25¢. The average player's daily bet amounts to 50¢ or $1. Many wager $5 to $10 daily. A $100 bet is common with a great number of players, and I know of several instances when a combination of players have wagered $1,000, the limit that some banks have set. Most banks have a $100 limit on a straight number and a $200 limit on a three- or six-way combination.

THE ECONOMICS OF THE NUMBERS BANK

Here's a breakdown on the financial operation of the bank, showing what happens to your $1 bet. Commissions to runners range from 10% to 25%. If your runner receives 25% he turns over 75¢ of your dollar to the controller, who takes a 5% commission and passes on 70¢ to the bank. If the bank pays off 500 for 1, the winners will get back 49% or 49¢ as prize money. This leaves the bank with 21%.

This 21% gives the average bank handling a gross business of about $6,000 a day a daily income of $1,260, or $7,560 per six-day week. Weekly expenditures for a bank with this handle would come to about $5,560. Of this, approximately $1,560 is paid for protection; $2,000 for salaries of auditors, strong-arm men and other employees; $1,500 to the bank's lawyers and bondsmen for services rendered in springing arrested runners or agents, and another $500 for incidental expenditures such as handouts to hard-up players, entertaining runners and players at bars and restaurants and contributions to local charities.

Deduct the $5,560 weekly expense from the $7,560 gross revenue and you find that the bankers earn $2,000. If the bank is controlled by four bankers, each gets $500 a week, or $26,000 per year—which is not bad, as these boys pay little or no income tax. The bigtime Numbers banks that gross $200,000 a day earn the bank as much as $15,000 a day, or about $4,500,000 per year.

The Numbers game has one advantage to the player in that, unlike dice, cards or horses, the Numbers seldom cause serious financial damage to the millions who play daily. In all my years spent around gamblers and gambling I have never known of a gambler going broke playing the Numbers. This is true even though the addict plays daily and even though there is no restriction on how many different bets he can make or the amounts which can be wagered.

Listen some time to a group of Numbers players looking for the winning number in the daily paper. The fascination the game holds for them will be obvious. Many of these people lead dull, dreary lives, and the Numbers add a dash of spice and of hope. They spend hours dreaming of what they will do with the money when their lucky number hits. A win of $45 or $90 will make them happy for weeks. They feel they've accomplished something.

THE NUMBERS GAME ODDS

What chance does that lucky number of yours have of hitting and paying off? No complicated mathematics is needed to figure this answer. There are 1,000 numbers from 000 to 999 and one of them wins. You have 1 chance in 1,000, which means that the odds are 999 to 1 against you. Every player has an equal chance and the odds remain the same for any number selection, whether it is a repeat of yesterday's winning number or one that hasn't appeared in years.

Some banks pay off at less than the usual odds on *cut numbers*. These are numbers that get much play because too many players believe they are lucky numbers. Some numbers banks issue a cut-number sheet listing nearly 200 cut numbers. Craps players believe that 711 is a lucky figure; in some sections of Chicago this is a cut number with the payoff cut to 400 for 1. Most New York City banks specify that triplets

(000, 111, 222 and on up to 999) and hundreds (100, 200, 300 and on up to 900) are cut numbers, and some banks even refuse to accept action on them. This is not because the bankers believe these numbers have a better than 1 in 1,000 chance of hitting. The odds are cut because these numbers get such heavy play and the bankers want to reduce it. And at the same time the bankers earn more money with their 400 for 1 payouts. If 711 should hit when several hundred players had bet on it, the bank might find itself in financial difficulty when paying off.

During the baseball season, the banks catering to a predominantly Negro trade announce at the beginning of the season that any winning number which is the same as the current daily batting average of Hank Aaron, or whichever Negro star is prominent this season, will be considered a cut number paying 400 for 1 odds.

The Numbers game operators give various dubious reasons as to why they cut as many as two hundred numbers, but the real reason is that it reduces the players' winnings considerably and gives the operators an additional take of several hundred million dollars a year.

THE NUMBERS BANK PERCENTAGE TAKE

When the bank adds up its day's business and finds that a cut number or any other number has been heavily played, it balances the day's handle by laying off part of these bets with a "layoff bank." The layoff bank pays odds of 500 for 1 to the regular banks and they in turn pay 400 for 1 to the bettor. The layoff bank also pays a 20% commission of all the money they pay to the regular bank on cut-number winners.

It should be obvious by now that the only people who consistently make a profit at the Numbers racket are the bankers, their employees and the politicians and cops who sell protection.

There's not much point in advising a Numbers player to forget about his favorite game, and gamble, if he must, at some game whose unfavorable percentage isn't so high. Especially the many women players: those I know just don't listen to such advice. If you want to play because it's fun, and are willing to pay the price, that's your business, but if you play because you figure to come out ahead, baby, you can forget it. If you include the standard 10% runner's commission, the unfavorable percentage you are trying to buck is 51% to 61%, depending on the payoff odds of the bank you do business with.

Let me show you just how fast you can lose. Suppose you decide to gamble exactly $1,000 on the Numbers during a certain week. You decide to bet an equal amount on each of the 1,000 possible numbers. Your bank pays 500 for 1, and the runner decides not to take his 10% out of the winnings. On Monday you bet $1 on each of the 1,000 numbers, and you know for sure one of them will win. The last three digits of the total day's handle at the Belmont track turns out to be 225, and your runner pays you $500.

Since your $1,000 bankroll has already shrunk to $500, the most you can bet on each number on Tuesday is 50 cents. You win again, and collect $250. Your loss for two days' play is $750. You should realize by now that you are on a one-way street and headed for the cleaners. On Wednesday you bet $250 on the 1,000 numbers, 25 cents on each. This time the winning number pays you $125. On Thursday you bet $120, 12¢ on each number, and pocket the remaining $5. The winning number pays you $60. On Friday you bet $60 by putting 6¢ on each number. You're lucky again—if that's what you want to call it—and your runner pays off with a smile—a big $30. You now take inventory, but it isn't likely that you are smiling. You have winnings of $30 plus the $5 you pocketed for a total of $35. You stick with the plan and bet $30 on Saturday with a 3¢ bet on each of the 1,000 numbers. You win $15 and add it to the $5 you pocketed for a total of $20. Subtract this from the $1,000 you started with, and the price you have paid for a week's fling at the exciting game of Numbers is $980. If the runner had taken his 10% winning commission you would have got down to small change all the sooner.

Is the game all that exciting? Do you think you can beat the Numbers and come out ahead?

SCARNE'S PROPOSED STATE NUMBERS PLAN

Because the operation of the state lotteries has not reduced the action on the Numbers game and its criminal activity, Charles C. Carella, executive director of the New Jersey Lottery Commission, is studying the possible state legalization and operation of the Numbers game. I met with Mr. Carella to discuss this matter and gave him the following recommendations.

1. That the state numbers betting plan should operate somewhat like the pari-mutuel system of racetrack betting.

2. That each of the three basic Numbers bets, straight (one number), three-way (three numbers) and box (six numbers) should have its own separate pool.

3. Betting should continue until the start of the first race. Then the payoffs would be based on how much was bet on the winning number. Let's say $200,000 is wagered on the 1,000 straight or head numbers, which illegal Numbers operators pay off at 500 for 1, and the day's winning number is 123. The computer shows that only $100 was bet on 123. The state deducts 30% of the $200,000 as its share, leaving $140,000 to be paid to the players who bet the winning 123. $100 divided into $160,000 shows a payoff price of $1,600 for every dollar

wagered on number 123; $400 for a quarter bet, and $160 for a dime bet. The same procedure is used to determine the payoffs on winning three-way combinations and box numbers.

4. Special agents or runners would be hired to solicit Numbers action (like today's illegal runners) throughout a specified area. Lottery agents could also be used for this purpose. These runners would operate from one of a number of central banks in the prescribed area. Numbers bets must be delivered to the central bank before the first race is run at the designated racetrack.

5. Rather than use the last three digits of the day's total handle as the winning number at the track, the state should take the last digits of the handle of the 5th, 7th and 9th races to determine the day's three-digit winning number. This makes it considerably more difficult to rig the winning number.

8.
Bingo:
The $3 Billion
National Pastime

Bingo, that great American gambling game, is the favorite weekly pastime of millions living in cities, towns and hamlets throughout the United States. My survey reveals that each year 22 million Bingo players, of whom 18 million are women, wager approximately $3 billion at Bingo legally and illegally. Since the average Bingo operator returns about 50% of his handle in prizes, these 22 million players paid $1.5 billion for the pleasure of playing the game, an average annual cost of $68 each.

Bingo and proposals to legalize it have caused more debate and controversy in the American press than any other form of gambling. It is now legal in about half our 50 states and a number of other states will bring the issue to the voters in the near future.

My survey also shows that when a state legalizes Bingo the annual handle usually drops to about one-third of its previous illegal handle. This is partly due to the fact that the state places so many restrictions on the game's operation that many of the former illegal promoters throw up their hands and quit. Business also drops off because the sizes of the jackpot prizes permitted by the state are much smaller. In New Jersey, for example, before legalization the top jackpot prize was often as much as $10,000, with several brand-new automobiles as lesser prizes. The present law limits the top jackpot prize to $250.

LEGAL VS. ILLEGAL BINGO

Before legalization, New York State, with its many $2,500, $5,000, $10,000 and $15,000 jackpot prizes, topped all other states with its illegal Bingo handle of $200 million. The New York State Lottery Con-

A typical Bingo parlor in New Jersey, where Bingo playing is legal. (United Press International)

trol Commission reported that the gross Bingo handle during New York's first year of legalization, with a jackpot prize limit of $250, was $41,390,243, and paid admissions were 12,046,474. Remember that, like other businessmen, few gambling promoters, legal or illegal, report all their winnings to state and Federal authorities.

The action of the 22 million players throughout the United States in recent years was handled by about 130,000 Bingo parlors, some of which operated daily, many weekly, others only once or several times during the year. About 60,000 of these were operating within the law in the states where Bingo was legal. The remaining 70,000 Bingo parlors, at church, club and civic affairs, at casinos and carnivals, fairs, amusement parks, arcades and other amusement centers, operated in direct violation of state gambling laws.

Legalization doesn't solve all law-enforcement problems because many of the 60,000 legal Bingo parlors often violate the Bingo laws of their state. The players, of course, don't object, and the local politicians and law-enforcement agencies don't want to buck hundreds of thousands of Bingo players who vote, especially when the Bingo sessions are run under the auspices of churches, synagogues and patriotic, fraternal and charitable organizations, with the profits going toward the support of hospitals, parochial schools and social-welfare programs.

Legalization doesn't end the Bingo controversy either; it remains a point of dispute between Catholic and Protestant clergy, and the split between these religious groups is as wide as on any point of doctrine. There can, however, be no argument that Bingo has raised more money for more charitable groups than any other form of fund raising. It largely supports thousands of veterans' groups, uncounted Catholic grade schools, hundreds of volunteer fire departments; it has aided scores of welfare organizations, raised funds for hospitals and needy families, and given GIs here and abroad trips home to visit their families. Many synagogues and parishes owe their very start to Bingo. Most U.S. military installations throughout the world have weekly Bingo games, the proceeds going to some worthy charity. Bingo is rapidly becoming popular in Asia, Africa, Europe, South America and wherever GIs are stationed. It is now played in every part of the world and is obviously here to stay.

THE ORIGIN OF BINGO

Some writers on Bingo say it is of English, Swedish or Dutch origin. My research shows that it is actually a more complicated version of the still-popular Italian parlor game of Lotto, which is in turn derived from the more than 440-year-old Italian national lottery.

Other writers say that Lotto is a direct descendant of Keno, a form of lottery popular in the gambling dives in and around New Orleans in the early 1840s. (Keno, in a revised form, is still played in many American casinos today, particularly in Nevada, where the maximum payoff odds are 25,000 to 1 for picking 10 correct numbers out of 20 called numbers from a group of 80. A $1 winning bet will get you $25,000 in many Nevada casinos.)

The truth of the matter is the reverse: Keno is a descendant of Lotto, because the latter was played in Italy centuries before Keno made its appearance in New Orleans saloons.

The Italian Lotto is patterned after *Lo Giuoco del Lotto del Italia* (the Italian national lottery), which has been in almost constant weekly operation since it began in 1530. This was the first money lottery to be operated anywhere in the world. (See page 142.)

The resemblance of Bingo to the Italian national lottery becomes obvious when a Bingo card and a result sheet of the lottery are compared. The lottery uses the numbers 1 to 90, Bingo the numbers 1 to 75. The lottery heads each line of its five numbered squares with the name of an Italian city; Bingo heads each line of its five numbered squares with the letters B-I-N-G-O. Here is a listing of the lottery results as published in the Newark, New Jersey, *Star Ledger* several years ago:

RESULTS OF THE GIUOCO DEL LOTTO OF THE REPUBLIC OF ITALY
(BY DIRECT CABLE FROM ROME)

Bari	60	10	63	22	3
Cagliari	14	41	66	69	15
Florence	2	18	22	70	10
Genoa	38	18	39	19	80
Milan	36	34	80	35	39
Naples	74	79	77	7	88
Palermo	85	69	23	34	17
Rome	34	51	48	65	24
Turin	83	58	6	54	13
Venice	29	33	82	15	16

Before the legalization of state lotteries, many American newspapers carried these results each week because it sold newspapers. At that time, about 2 million Americans, mostly of Italian extraction, wagered about $25 million annually in this illegal lottery, and they depended upon the papers for news of the correct results.

Although on a smaller scale, this lottery is still in operation today, and is controlled by the racket boys as is Policy Numbers. Most players wager pennies, nickels or dollars and select either three, four or five numbers under one or more city headings. Some banks permit wager-

ing one or two numbers under any city's heading. A player who succeeds in picking three winning numbers out of five receives $42.50 for
each penny wagered. A correct selection of four out of five pays off
$600 for each penny wagered and five out of five pays $7,200 for each
penny wagered. If you picked five out of five and had a dollar bet riding, you should collect $720,000—but don't count on it. It's a cinch that
no illegal lottery operator in this country would or could pay off that
amount. It's safe to stick to betting pennies—at least you collect.

As further proof that Bingo is an offspring of Lotto and the Italian
lottery, go back to 1925, when our motion picture houses ran raffles to
stimulate business. In order to get around state gambling laws, which
often prohibited such activity, theater managers did not call their drawings raffles but gave them such names as Lucky Night, Lucky Screen,
Bank Night, Banko, Beano, Bombo, Bango and Bingo. Laws were later
passed banning all movie raffles regardless of the name.

Theater Bingo as played then had no resemblance to present-day
Bingo. When he purchased his ticket the moviegoer was given a numbered slip of paper. Duplicates of these slips were mixed in a paper
bag and a member of the audience was asked by the manager to come
on stage and draw the winning number. Sometimes a wheel was spun
to determine the winning number. The manager called it and the holder
of the corresponding number shouted "Bingo!" and was declared the
winner. Prizes were as high as a couple of hundred dollars.

The unknown inventor who turned the parlor game of Lotto into a
gambling game may have taken the name Bingo from this source. I
have traced the word back as far as the 1863 American edition of
Hoyle, but it was then the name of a quite different game played with
dominoes.

THE MECHANICS OF THE GAME

It was not until the spring of 1928 that I saw a Bingo game played
using cards as they are used today. After a performance of magic I
gave for a group of women at a church social and card party in Jersey
City, New Jersey, I heard the entertainment chairman announce,
"Ladies and gentlemen, for your additional pleasure this evening, we
are going to introduce a new and fascinating game called Bingo. It is
played much like Lotto and we use cards similar to Lotto cards, which,
in order to speed up the game, bear only the numbers 1 through 75.
We also use seventy-five balls bearing the numbers 1 through 75."

He placed the balls in a bowl, closed the lid and added, "I will spin
the bowl several times, then press its lever. One ball will drop from the
opening in the bowl and I will call the number of each ball so drawn.
The first player who covers all the numbers on his or her Lotto card is

to shout 'Bingo!' and will receive a brand-new five-dollar bill. You will find kernels of corn on your table to use in covering the numbers on your card."

The bowl used was a regulation Keno bowl mounted on a wooden base, although only 75 balls instead of the 90 employed in Keno were used.* The playing of the game reminded me of my early boyhood when my father, mother and relatives sat down on Christmas Day to play Lotto.

After about 65 numbers had been drawn, a woman shouted "Bingo!" and the game was over. I asked the chairman where he had obtained his equipment and why he called the game Bingo when the principle was Lotto and a Keno bowl was used. He knew nothing beyond the fact that he had purchased the Keno bowl and Lotto cards from a carnival man who had operated a Wheel of Chance at a recent church bazaar.

A few years later casino equipment manufacturers in Chicago began manufacturing Bingo equipment similar to that used today, and the fascination of the game, especially among women, soon attracted the millions of players who have made it the number one charity fund raiser.

Bingo as it is played today is actually a form of lottery except that the cards cannot be purchased or played outside the Bingo premises; each player must be present to cover the drawn numbers on the Bingo card with markers while the actual drawing is taking place.

BINGO EQUIPMENT

Bingo cards are made of either cardboard or paper and the playing surface bears a printed design of five rows of five squares each—25 squares in all. The letters B-I-N-G-O appear above this design, each letter above one of the vertical columns. All the squares contain numbers except the center square, which is considered a free play. The following number arrangement is standard and appears on most Bingo cards.

The first vertical row on the left under the letter *B* contains any five numbers from the group 1 through 15. Under *I* there are any five numbers from the group 16 through 30. Under *N*, the center vertical row, there are only four numbers from the group 31 through 45. The middle square of this row is the center square of the card, and it is either blank or bears a printed *O* or *X* or the words "Free Play." This is always considered a *covered square* or *free play*. Under *G* in the fourth vertical row there are any five numbers from the group 46

---

* Nevada casinos today use 80 balls in Keno.

through 60, and under *O* in the fifth row any five numbers from the group 61 through 75.

In many Bingo parlors one, two or three Bingo cards are pasted to a larger heavy cardboard called a *lapboard*. This prevents the players from taking the cards home as souvenirs and the board serves as a table.

The latest innovation, popular in casino night clubs, is "finger-tip" Bingo cards which require no markers. Slides can be moved to cover each of the card's 25 squares.

The most popular device for selecting numbers is the *Bingo bowl*, often called the *Bingo cage*, a spherical wire-mesh cage about 9½ inches in diameter in which the Bingo balls are placed. It is mounted on a wooden or metal base and has a crank-turning ball-selecting device. There are 75 Bingo balls, each of which bears one of the letters of the word "Bingo" and a number. The B balls bear numbers from the 1 through 15 group; the I balls, from the 16 through 30 group, and so on—the same grouping arrangement as the cards.

Bingo cards. An ordinary card (LEFT) and a finger-tip card (RIGHT) with slides for covering the numbers so that counters are not needed.

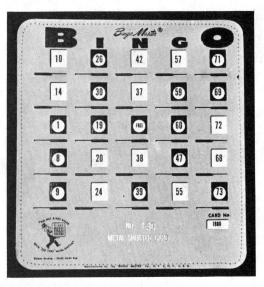

Bingo blower mixing the numbered balls during a game in a Jersey City, New Jersey, church. Young man at right is recording number just called. (Wide World)

When the operator turns the crank the wire cage revolves and the players can see the balls being mixed. When he stops turning the crank, an opening at the bottom of the cage releases one ball.

Another popular device for mixing and selecting the balls is the *Bingo blower*, which consists of a glass enclosure into which 75 lettered and numbered Ping-Pong balls are placed. An electric air compressor sends a stream of air into the glass case which agitates and mixes the balls until one ball falls into a small pocket and then drops out of the enclosure.

THE PLAY OF THE GAME

An announcer, known as the *caller*, calls the letter and number of the released ball over a loudspeaker. If, for example, B5 is drawn, players whose cards bear a 5 in the B column place a cardboard or plastic marker over it. This is called *covering the number*. The caller then places the drawn ball on a master board, which is often connected to an electrically operated panel that lights up the number on a large flashboard so that it can be seen as well as heard. The master board is also used as a check on the drawn numbers.

As soon as any player succeeds in covering five numbers in a straight line on her card, vertically, horizontally or diagonally, she shouts "Bingo!" A *floor man* or *floor woman* goes to the player and reads the covered numbers on the player's card aloud to the caller or a tally man for verification. If the caller confirms that these five numbers have been drawn, the player is declared the winner of the game and the prize.

In many Bingo parlors the jackpot game is a *two-way play.* Some parlors have added three- and four-way plays, although the jackpot is the important factor. The player who first covers a straight-line combination wins a prize, but the big prize, or jackpot, goes to the player who first covers her entire board. This is called a *cover-all* or *blackout.*

If two or more players get a winning position at the same time, the prize money is divided equally.

Many Bingo parlors also feature a *four-way play,* or *round robin,* in which there are four winning positions:

1. The covering of five numbers in a straight line in any direction.
2. The covering of the four numbers at the four corners of the card.
3. The covering of the eight numbers which surround the center "free play" square.
4. The covering of all the numbers on the card.

Some Bingo parlors consider as winning plays the covering of two or three straight lines when they cross or intersect so as to form the letters X, U, L, H or T. Some parlors give a double bonus for specific straight-line positions of five numbers such as the top line or the bottom line.

Recently some Bingo operators have added an extra ball which is distinctively colored and bears no letter or number. It acts as a wild number. In some games, when this ball is drawn, a player can cover any desired number on her card at any time during the game; sometimes it can only be used to cover the last number completing the winning position.

At the end of each game, after the awarding of the prize or prizes, all players clear their card or cards of markers and either retain them or exchange them for the next game. They may also purchase additional cards.

Bingo operators have also created a number of special features to stimulate business, such as *early-bird tickets,* which are sold at a special discount to induce players to come to the parlor early. Sometimes *intermission tickets* are also sold at a discount in the hope of continuing the Bingo action throughout the intermission period. There are also *junior jackpot tickets* which pay off a smaller jackpot. Actually all these specials have the same purpose: to relieve the Bingo player of more cash.

The admission ticket to a Bingo parlor usually costs $1, and the player gets one card called an *all-night board*. Additional single-game cards usually cost 25¢ each. Most players play more than one card at a time, and it is not uncommon to see a woman playing as many as 21 cards at once, a total cost to her of $6. If you think that playing 21 cards simultaneously is a relaxing way to spend an evening, just try it. I have, and you can't relax for a second! It's hard work. But the women love it.

Many large Bingo parlors have a special jackpot which must be won in a specified number of plays. Example: A jackpot winner must be declared within the first 50 numbers drawn. If there should be no winner at one session, an additional $200 or more is added to the jackpot the following week. Jackpots of this kind starting with $500 have been known to reach $10,000 and more before being won.

After clocking a great many Bingo players in different parts of the country, I found that in halls having jackpots of $250 or more the average player spends $4 per session. Some women spend as much as $7 per session; very few as little as the $1 admission fee. Mrs. Edreth Videtti, an avid Bingo player from my neck of the woods, summed it up this way: "A person would look awfully cheap to sit through thirty Bingo games with just the admission board."

THE BINGO DEBATE

Bingo's great popularity is due primarily to two factors: the game is simple to play, and every game must produce one or more winners. Since 30 to 35 games are usually played in one evening, the game obviously supplies lots of fun and tension. Only a game like Bingo could produce the phenomenon of a hall full of several hundred women who seldom say a word except for the cries of jubilation or disappointment at the end of each game.

This impressed an Englishman who visited this country and later told a friend at home: "American women play a very strange game. Can't recall its name, but it's played in a large hall by several hundred women seated at tables with a number of small cards before them. A man on an elevated platform constantly calls out numbers to which the women listen attentively, never saying a word. Then suddenly one woman shouts at the top of her voice: 'Bingo!' and all the others exclaim, 'Aw nuts!'"

I can't see why some reformers call Bingo a "growing national problem." None of the players loses a great sum. At an average cost of $4 per session (actually only $2 over the long run, because half of the money wagered is returned in prizes) millions of women, mostly middle-aged and elderly women who have few, if any, other outlets for their gambling urge, buy hours of sociability, excitement and fun playing a game that also provides considerable sums for worthy causes and community projects.

The main opposition to the legalization of Bingo in many states comes from Protestant ministers who are against it even though legalization would insure that only charitable organizations would benefit. Recently Bob Vancelette and former heavyweight boxing champion James J. Braddock, both of whom assisted me in my survey, went with me to a number of Bingo sessions sponsored by fraternal organizations in and around Philadelphia and found that most of the players were women from local Protestant churches.

Many Catholic churches and Jewish synagogues run weekly Bingo games to raise funds. Occasionally some leading rabbi asks Jewish organizations to refrain from raising money with Bingo, but not all rabbis subscribe to that view. The Catholic hierarchy has never either approved or disapproved of Bingo playing for charitable causes, leaving it solely up to the discretion of the parish priests.

BIGTIME GAMES

Many luxury gambling casinos in this country now run free Bingo parties in order to attract customers to their gaming tables. Some charge a fee, usually $1 for each Bingo card. These games, with attractive $1,000 to $10,000 jackpots, do draw the crowds. One Nevada casino operator told me: "Bingo is a much better draw for us than any name act from movies or television."

Because of the interest of Bingo, many Las Vegas casinos have initiated interesting Bingo gimmicks. For instance, the Aladdin Hotel casino has come up with a form which can best be described as "Super Bingo" for high rollers. The cost to each participant is $25 and the game session is limited to 400 players. The Bingo session consists of ten games with a guaranteed payout of $7,500. The tenth and final game is a giant cover-all prize with $6,000 guaranteed payout to the winner regardless of how many numbers must be drawn to cover all or black out the entire card. This guaranteed cover-all payout is a great deal better for the player than a $6,000 payoff for a $1 ticket in which you must cover the entire board in 50 or less drawn numbers. If 400 players participate in a game of cover-all in 50 or less drawn numbers, the chance of one of the players winning the $6,000 is rather remote—the odds are 529 to 1 against such an occurrence.

Bingo has also spread into the Caribbean and Latin-American countries. During Batista's regime in Cuba, Havana's famed Tropicana nightclub and casino ran nightly Bingo sessions. The charge for each Bingo card, which was good for the whole session, was $2. In addition to the regular big prizes of from $100 to $500 for half a dozen games, the night's jackpot prize for a cover-all in 50 draws was $10,000. The jackpot prize for a cover-all in 51 draws was $5,000, $4,000 in 52 draws, $3,000 in 53 draws, $2,000 in 54 draws, $1,000 in 55 draws, and if no cover-all was made in 55 draws or less, $500 was paid to any player who made a cover-all no matter how many draws were required. The Bingo jackpot prizes in Havana's Sans Souci nightclub were mink coats, Cadillacs and other expensive merchandise.

Bingo operators in states where the game is illegal have invented various gimmicks to circumvent the law. A simple one is to advertise the Bingo session as "socials" or "game nights" and charge a fixed admission fee, usually from $2.50 to $3.50. After a few minutes of entertainment, often merely canned music, or playing some nongambling game, the crowd gets down to the serious business of playing a nameless game that you would immediately recognize as Bingo. The New York State Court of Appeals okayed this gimmick years before the state legalized Bingo when they ruled, that Bingo, Lotto and similar games were permissible if they were provided free during a paid entertainment. I suspect this would work in any state, even in states where Bingo is legal, for operators who do not have Bingo licenses.

BINGO MATHEMATICS

What chance does a Bingo player have of covering all 24 numbers on his card in 50 or fewer drawn numbers? For years I have asked this question of Bingo operators and equipment manufacturers. Not one of them knew. Many replied: "How should I know, when the 'Bingo King' [a Midwestern editor of a national monthly Bingo magazine] has been asked that question hundreds of times and never yet come up with an answer?"

I decided that here was another unsolved gambling problem I would have to break down. I knew the computations would be arduous, and several friends who volunteered to assist on the computation gave up when they found out what a laborious job they had undertaken. One, a neighbor, Evelyn Martinetti, spent six hours multiplying and adding and often getting different results when she checked her figures, and she gave up in disgust. She told my wife, Steffi, "I've got a headache and furthermore I no longer give a damn what the player's chances are of going Bingo in fifty or less drawn numbers."

If you like to dabble in arithmetic, have plenty of time and don't mind headaches, you can check the following figures but it's a 100 to 1 shot you'll also quit and decide that the answer isn't worth all that work.

Here's what you have to do. First find the number of possible ways that 75 Bingo balls can be arranged in groups of 24. The mathematical formula for discovering the number of combinations of n things taken r at a time is written like this:

$$\frac{n(n-1)(n-2)\ldots(n-r+1)}{r!}$$

Substitute 75 for n and 24 for r and you begin to see how much work is involved:

The numerator becomes this: $75 \times 74 \times 73 \times 72 \times 71 \times 70 \times 69 \times 68 \times 67 \times 66 \times 65 \times 64 \times 63 \times 62 \times 61 \times 60 \times 59 \times 58 \times 57 \times 56 \times 55 \times 54 \times 53 \times 52$. This multiplication results in a product of 15,-994,352,952,548,504,498,502,271,753,960,292,352,000,000.

The denominator $r!$ (factorial r) becomes: $24 \times 23 \times 22 \times 21 \times 20 \times 19 \times 18 \times 17 \times 16 \times 15 \times 14 \times 13 \times 12 \times 11 \times 10 \times 9 \times 8 \times 7 \times 6 \times 5 \times 4 \times 3 \times 2 \times 1$, which equals 620,448,401,733,239,439,360,000.

Divide the larger of these answers by the smaller, and you find that 75 Bingo balls can be arranged in groups of 24 in the following number of ways: 25,778,699,578,994,555,700.

A simplified method which saves considerable multiplication is to set up the formula as a fraction and cancel out before multiplying.

$$\frac{75 \times 74 \times 73 \times 72 \times 71 \times 70 \times 69 \times 68 \times 67 \times 66 \times 65}{24 \times 23 \times 22 \times 21 \times 20 \times 19 \times 18 \times 17 \times 16 \times 15 \times 14}$$

$$\frac{\times 64 \times 63 \times 62 \times 61 \times 60 \times 59 \times 58 \times 57 \times 56 \times 55}{\times 13 \times 12 \times 11 \times 10 \times 9 \times 8 \times 7 \times 6 \times 5 \times 4}$$

$$\frac{\times 54 \times 53 \times 52}{\times 3 \times 2 \times 1} = 25,778,699,578,994,555,700$$

Since we want to find out the number of cover-alls that can be formed with the first 50 drawn numbers, we must next find out how many ways 50 numbered Bingo balls can be arranged in groups of 24. We substitute 50 for n and 24 for r in the formula and get this:

$$\frac{50 \times 49 \times 48 \times 47 \times 46 \times 45 \times 44 \times 43 \times 42 \times 41 \times 40}{24 \times 23 \times 22 \times 21 \times 20 \times 19 \times 18 \times 17 \times 16 \times 15 \times 14}$$

$$\frac{\times 39 \times 38 \times 37 \times 36 \times 35 \times 34 \times 33 \times 32 \times 31 \times 30}{\times 13 \times 12 \times 11 \times 10 \times 9 \times 8 \times 7 \times 6 \times 5 \times 4}$$

$$\frac{\times 29 \times 28 \times 27}{\times 3 \times 2 \times 1} = 121,548,660,036,300$$

Finally, we divide the total number of ways 75 balls can be arranged in groups of 24 by the number of ways 50 balls can be arranged in groups of 24.

$$\frac{25{,}778{,}699{,}578{,}994{,}555{,}700}{121{,}548{,}660{,}036{,}300} = 212{,}085$$

That's the answer: if you purchase only one card for the jackpot or cover-all game, your chance of winning by covering all the 24 numbers on your card in 50 or less drawn numbers is 1 in 212,085. It does not matter how many other players there are; you and each of the other players have the same chance of 1 in 212,085. If you use two cards your chance will be 2 in 212,085; if you use three cards, 3 in 212,085, and so on. (Actually, multiplying by 2, 3 and so on is an approximation to the mathematically exact method; but for any practical number of Bingo cards the approximation is more than accurate enough.)

The Bingo operator will be interested to learn that if he sells a complete set of 3,000 Bingo cards for a session his chances of *not paying* the jackpot in 50 or less drawn numbers are 212,085 divided by 3,000, or about 70 to 1 in his favor.

Here in tabular form are the chances a one-card holder has of making a cover-all in 50, 51, 52, 53, 54 or 55 drawn numbers:

Total Numbers Drawn	Chances of Making a Cover-all with One Card
50 or less	1 in 212,085
51 or less	1 in 112,284
52 or less	1 in 60,458
53 or less	1 in 33,081
54 or less	1 in 18,379
55 or less	1 in 10,359

Just for curiosity, while we are on this subject, let us calculate how many Bingo cards could be printed without having two cards on which the number arrangement is duplicated. Each card bears 5 of a group of 15 numbers under each four columns headed by the letters B, I, G and O, and 4 out of 15 numbers under the letter N. The formula that supplies the answer is this:

UNDER B $\qquad$ UNDER I $\qquad$ UNDER N

$$\frac{15 \times 14 \times 13 \times 12 \times 11}{5 \times 4 \times 3 \times 2 \times 1} \times \frac{15 \times 14 \times 13 \times 12 \times 11}{5 \times 4 \times 3 \times 2 \times 1} \times \frac{15 \times 14 \times 13 \times 12}{4 \times 3 \times 2 \times 1} \times$$

UNDER G $\qquad$ UNDER O

$$\frac{15 \times 14 \times 13 \times 12 \times 11}{5 \times 4 \times 3 \times 2 \times 1} \times \frac{15 \times 14 \times 13 \times 12 \times 11}{5 \times 4 \times 3 \times 2 \times 1} = 111{,}007{,}923{,}832{,}370{,}565$$

This is the number of cards it is possible to print without duplicating a single card. And remember that Bingo card manufacturers usually print only 3,000 different cards to a set.

Now let me ask a hypothetical question: What would you think of a promoter's running a Bingo game, charging 1¢ for each card and agreeing to pay a jackpot prize of $1 million to any person who succeeded in covering his or her entire card in the first 24 drawn numbers? Crazy? No. He's real smart, because your chance of winning that million bucks is only 1 in 25,778,699,578,994,555,700. If the same Bingo promoter succeeded in selling every possible different Bingo card he would collect, at 1¢ each, the astronomical sum of $1,110,079,238,323,-705.65! $1 million compared to this sum is truly a drop in the bucket. He would have a tough time doing this, however, because with a world population of 3,860,000,000, every single person on the face of the earth would have to buy 28,758,528 cards and each pay $287,585.28.

CHEATING AT BINGO

When run by charitable organizations, Bingo is relatively free of the crookedness that accompanies many other forms of gambling. A few professional operators who run Bingo games at fairgrounds, amusement centers and other public places are not always satisfied with their percentage take and cheat the players of the big jackpot prizes which they have advertised.

It's a simple dodge. They plant a house player, usually a woman, in the crowd who wins the big prize and later returns it, receiving only a fee for her day's or night's work. She wins because she is given a couple of Bingo boards whose numbers have been recorded on a sheet of paper which the announcer keeps within view. Or sometimes identifying marks are placed near the numbers on the master board which correspond with those on the house player's cards. Then, as he draws the balls from the cage, the announcer miscalls one or more numbers. If, for example, he sees that the house player needs B-8 and G-47 to go Bingo he pretends to read these two numbers from the next two balls drawn. The house player shouts "Bingo!" The announcer goes through the motions of confirming the numbers as the usher checks the player's card and then nonchalantly replaces the miscalled balls in the Bingo cage. The plant collects the jackpot and the other players are none the wiser.

Bingo players can protect themselves from this method of cheating by selecting one player to sit beside the announcer and check the numbers on the balls as they are drawn. A random choice of a player could easily be made by having the announcer, his back to the audience, throw out a Ping-Pong ball, the person catching it being the one to act as checker. This checking would only be necessary when the Big Special or Big Jackpot is being played. If you suggest this procedure to your Bingo operator and he welcomes your recommendation, he's honest. If he doesn't, then you would be wise to find yourself another Bingo parlor.

Another method employed by cheating Bingo announcers to sneak the jackpot is accomplished as follows: The announcer's woman plant takes a front seat as close as possible to the announcer, making sure that no other player will be between them. To help facilitate the scheme, the woman plant plays ten or more Bingo cards. The announcer continues drawing and calling numbers until his plant cues him by lifting and turning her head toward him. This is the signal that informs the announcer that the plant requires one number to hit the jackpot. Once contact is made between the announcer and plant, the plant inaudibly calls the desired number. This is strictly a lip expression. The announcer, accustomed to the plant's lip movements, gets the message, and miscalls the next drawn number by calling the signaled number. The plant then shouts, "Bingo!" and the suckers are left holding the bag.

Some Bingo players, too, have dishonest methods of beating the game. They don't actually beat the operator because he loses nothing; they are cheating the player who would have won the prize that the cheat manages to get.

Like many honest women players, these cheats carry their own transparent plastic markers, plus an extra set of 75 markers which are gaffed. Each gaffed marker has a piece of paper bearing one of the numbers 1 through 75 pasted to the marker's underside. The numbers match the printing of the Bingo card. When one of these gaffed markers is placed on a Bingo card square it hides the legitimate number on the card and substitutes a different one. When the cheat requires one or two numbers to complete Bingo, she reaches into her handbag under the pretense of getting a cigarette, selects the markers bearing the needed numbers, places them on the card and calls "Bingo!" Since the checker merely reads the numbers through the transparent marker, he sees nothing wrong. It has, however, become more difficult to get away with this gimmick because most Bingo cards now carry a serial number which is keyed to the numbers on the card and indicates whether any of them have been changed.

This keyed serial number was responsible for the retirement of Bingo's number one cheat, a gray-haired woman in her seventies whom we shall call "Grandma." She haunted Bingo parlors from Maine to Florida and New York to California and, without any doubt, won more money at the game than any other player, honest or dishonest. I know personally that she robbed several Bingo parlors around New York City of at least $20,000. One of the operators told me that he had considered suing her for ten grand in an effort to get back some of the dishonestly won money, but he dropped the idea when he realized that he wasn't the injured party; it was the players who might have won whom she had cheated. I managed to trace her and by promising not to reveal her right name got her to tell me her story.

"I had a sweet angle," she said, "before they began putting those serial numbers on the cards. My husband, Leo, having been a Bingo operator himself, knew the ropes, and we bought a set of three thousand cards from each of the dozen main Bingo suppliers in the country. On our first visit to a Bingo parlor, one of us would steal one card. If this wasn't possible because the cards being used were pasted down on lapboards, we made a drawing of one of the cards. At home we would match the stolen card or drawing against the cards we had bought and find the set which was an exact duplicate because it had been bought from the same supplier.

"We would put about one thousand of the duplicate cards into an index arrangement which Leo had fitted into the inside of a grip. At the next Bingo session Leo entered the parlor with the grip and I followed just behind him and got a seat next to him. My daughter came in later and took a seat some distance away. We pretended to be strangers and never spoke to each other. Leo wrote down the numbers called by the announcer during the games and when he came to the big special in which the jackpot was to be awarded, this list of called numbers told him whether he had a winning card filed in his grip. If he did, he went into it to get one of the sandwiches he also carried there, and got the winning card at the same time.

"I held one of my cards on my lap under the table and Leo took it and substituted the winning card. As soon as my daughter saw my husband reach down under the table it was her cue to ask the announcer to repeat the calling of the numbers drawn. This gave me time to put the winning card on the table and put my markers on the called numbers of the winning combinations, or cover the entire card if it was a cover-all.

"As soon as the announcer repeated calling the last drawn number I would shout 'Bingo.' While the checker was coming over to verify this, Leo got up and walked out with the grip. And I collected the jackpot. It was as simple as all that."

"Practically foolproof," I said, "except that there was a small chance someone else would also have a winning card."

She nodded. "If someone else hollered 'Bingo' first I'd keep quiet. But one night at a cover-all game in Brooklyn, another woman and I both shouted 'Bingo!' at the same time. When our cards were checked they were found to be identical. And when they announced that the payment of the prize money would be delayed until the following day, it had me worried. But an hour later, after a lot of checking, one of the operators told me, 'Grandma, the other winner says she won't consider two identical cards to be a tie because no two are supposed to be alike. Apparently the manufacturer slipped up and put two identical cards in this set; we'll have to take the matter up with him. So instead of splitting the money you each get $1,000. Please accept our apologies for the delay.'"

I asked the old lady how much money she had beat the parlors for over the years. "Oh, I don't know," she said, and then began rattling off various amounts she had won in different parts of the country. I added them mentally and when I passed the $100,000 mark I said, "Altogether maybe $200,000?"

She smiled and said modestly, "Could be. But when those serial numbers began showing up on the cards, I knew the jig was up." Grandma is retired now, living very comfortably at a fashionable address, with no financial problems in her old age.

YOUR BEST BET AT BINGO

Compared to other gamblers, even the inveterate Bingoist (a term I coined) never loses more than a very moderate amount of money. My survey shows that she spends an average of $4 per session, and since 50% of this is returned in prizes, it costs the inveterate player in the long run only $2 per session. Since she plays 27 to 35 games in the usual 8:30 to 11:00 P.M. session, a $2 charge for this much entertainment is very small. No other gambling game supplies this much entertainment for so little.

Many Bingoists buy six to ten cards at a time because this increases their chances of winning. It does, but not nearly as much as they think. Here's how it breaks down. Suppose there are 299 players, each with only a single $1 card (the admission card) at a session when you join in. If you buy only the one card, the management has taken in a total of $300. Each player has 1 chance in 300 of winning a prize award in a single game (a probability of .0033). The odds against winning for each player are 299 to 1.

Now, suppose you buy three additional cards for $1; you have four cards at a total cost of $2. Each of the other players now has 1 chance in 303 of winning while you have 4 chances in 303. The probability that you will lose with four cards is 299 in 303, and the probability a player with one card will lose is only slightly greater: 302 in 303.

Your chance of winning is four times greater than that of a player with only one card, but your chance of losing is approximately the same. The purchase of the extra cards certainly hasn't increased your winning chances enough to make it worth the extra $1 cost. We must conclude that mathematically the wisest bet at Bingo is to buy and play only one card.

Since the total prize awards for each game remain the same whether 300 or 500 cards are sold, it is the Bingo operator who really profits when players buy extra cards. If every Bingo player read this proof that playing only one card is the best bet at Bingo, and then did just that, the game would soon become less interesting for another reason. The amounts of the prize awards are based on the expectation that most players will buy extra cards. If they didn't, then the prize awards would have to be reduced.

It is very unlikely that this will happen. Playing one card all evening can become very monotonous, especially when the drawn numbers are running against you; it is much more fun to play several cards. Just remember that when you buy extra cards you are buying more excitement and entertainment but are not appreciably increasing your chances of winning.

9.
Gambling Casinos:
Carpet and Sawdust Joints
Yesterday and Today

Casino gambling is illegal in all states except Nevada, and yet the sum of money earned by its operators is exceeded only by the earnings of state and track in betting on the horses.

Although second to horse betting in earnings, the gross casino gambling handle of about $100 billion in 1973 in the U.S. was almost twice the race betting handle of $46 billion. My survey shows that about 31 million Americans, of whom 13 million were women, visited one or more gambling houses during this year, and that there are more than a million men and women who earn all or part of their living directly or indirectly from gambling casinos.

If we add to the U.S. gross handle another $5 billion which Americans gamble in the legalized casinos of Puerto Rico, Bahamas, Netherlands Antilles, Haiti, other Caribbean countries, England, Panama, Monte Carlo, France, Italy, West Germany and other foreign countries, we find that in 1973 they wagered the gigantic sum of $105 billion in casino gambling.

The five banking games in American and Caribbean casinos that get the most action, listed in order of their popularity, are: Craps, Black Jack, Slot Machines, Roulette and Baccarat–Chemin de Fer and Scarney Baccarat. These games handle about 85% of all money wagered in casinos catering to American gamblers. The remaining 15% is bet at casino side games such as the dice games—Hazard, Klondike, Chuck-a-Luck, Under and Over Seven, Beat the Shaker; the wheels of chance—Big Six, Money Wheel, Racehorse Wheel, and Keno.

This over-all U.S. gross handle of $100 billion was estimated as follows: Take the official figures on legalized gambling first. In 1973,

Behind this sign lies the Las Vegas strip, gambling mecca of the world. (Las Vegas News Bureau)

the 100-odd Nevada gambling establishments reported to the State Tax Commission a combined gross revenue of $804 million. If we add to this the fact that millions of dollars are stolen each year from the casinos by professional cheats and casino employees, I am sure that the men and women who gambled in Nevada in 1973 paid out at least $849 million for their gambling pleasure. However, to simplify our mathematics, let's just take a round figure of $800 million as our basis for further calculations.

After clocking the five most popular casino games a great many times, I have found that on an average 4¢ out of each dollar wagered is retained by the house. If this seems low because most casino games have a house P.C. greater than 4%, remember that there are several bets in Bank Craps, the game that receives the most action, on which the house percentage is considerably less. This is also true of Baccarat-Chemin de Fer.

If the $800 million is 4%, then the gross handle for legalized gambling in Nevada in 1973 comes to $20 billion. If this seems high, remember that more than 18 million tourists visited the state, most of whom placed bets ranging from 5¢ to $1,000 and more, gambling in more than 100 casinos which were open for business 24 hours a day.

Also bear in mind that the dollars in any gross-handle figure are counted a good many times before they are won or lost. Let me illus-

226 SCARNE'S NEW COMPLETE GUIDE TO GAMBLING

trate this with a clocking experiment I made at the swank Havana Hilton casino shortly before Castro took it over. I sat on a ladder overlooking the dice table, paper and pencil in hand, and kept track of all wagers for five hours. During that period $3 million went back and forth across the table from players to dealers to players. This was the gross betting handle, and yet only $40,000 actually changed hands by the end of the five-hour period.

In order to get an approximate figure as to the yearly gross handle of the illegal casinos in the United States, I interviewed about 200 operators and employees of illegal gambling houses, large and small, in various sections of the country. I found that for every dollar wagered in the 100-odd legal casinos in Nevada, $4 was wagered in the thousands of illegal casinos in the country. With a $20 billion legal gross handle, this 4 to 1 ratio means that the illegal gross handle was $80 billion, on which the illegal operators earned about 4%, or $3.2 billion.

While the legalized casino betting handle has risen in the past ten years, the illegal casino betting handle like the illegal off-track race handle has declined. This is due, primarily, to the strict FBI and police enforcement of federal and state anti-gambling laws. But, chances are, as in the past, every twenty years sees a drastic drop in the illegal gambling handling of all sorts—then a few years later the illegal take again begins its upward climb.

CARPET JOINTS

Casinos are divided by the inveterate gambler into two groups. The plush luxury casinos, like those on the Las Vegas Strip, are known as *carpet joints* or *rug joints*. Unpretentious casinos without all the fancy decoration, such as those found on Fremont Street in downtown Las Vegas, are called *sawdust joints*.

A carpet joint is usually an annex to a hotel or night club. It contains flashy modern casino equipment, brocade drapes, wall-to-wall carpeting and other expensive décor, and it caters to a mink-stole-and-dinner-jacket clientele. The carpet joint's casino and credit managers dress formally and are as suave and sleek as their most distinguished guests, soft-spoken and apparently full of good will. A small carpet joint may have four to six gaming tables; a large one, legal or illegal, may have twenty or more.

Most of the larger rug joints here and in the Caribbean, except those in Puerto Rico, are operated by gambling syndicates of former illegal gambling operators. These gamblers seldom appear in the limelight as the owners and, in the case of legal casinos, not even on the gambling licenses issued by the state or Federal Government. The apparent owner or front man is usually an *easy-money guy* (a wealthy speculator) without a police record. He may be a lawyer, politician, businessman or anybody.

Before big business bought out most of the Las Vegas Strip casinos, the front man formed a corporation issuing 100 shares of stock, called points, which sold, depending on the size and potential of the casino, for $25,000 to $50,000 per point, or even more. A few years back, a one-point interest in the plush Sands Hotel casino, of which my friend Frank Sinatra owned nine points, was selling for $92,000. Shares in Caesar's Palace once sold for only $50,000. The professional gambling operators, under various fronts, usually took the controlling interest and sold the other points to friends, some of whom were legitimate businessmen. The floorwalkers and pit bosses usually purchased one or two points (known as working points) on the understanding that they were to be employed at the customary weekly salary, and casino managers and shift bosses usually found it difficult to get jobs without buying in.

SAWDUST JOINTS

Most of the legal gambling establishments are rug joints, and most illegal ones, because they must move around in order to evade the law, are sawdust joints. The latter cater only to men and usually favor dice games such as Money or Bank Craps, or both; and the operators are usually a *combination* (syndicate) of neighborhood toughs, one of whose members is the racket boss of the area. The sawdust joint is also a meeting place and gambling rendezvous for the racket guys.

In a big city, a sawdust joint which has five or six dice tables often grosses more money annually for its operators than do some of the carpet joints of Nevada, but it pays much more in protection money than the Nevada operators have to pay in license fees and taxes. The ice demanded of a sawdust joint in and around New York City once ran as high as $7,500 per week, in the Chicago and Los Angeles areas $5,000, and in the St. Louis area $3,000. Compare these weekly payments with the annual $30,000, plus 1% of gross revenue, Puerto Rican casino tax which such plush rug joints as the Caribe Hilton Hotel casino and the El San Juan Hotel casino pay, and you see why the professional casino operator prefers to run a legal casino and why some politicians and police officials get rich.

Big-city sawdust joints usually rent two or three locations at once so they can make quick overnight moves when the protection man tips them off that law-enforcement agents not in on the graft have learned the location and intend to make a raid. The sawdust joint is usually a floating Craps game or floating gambling joint which moves from place to place and is often located in a warehouse or large garage.

THE BARN

The most successful of all sawdust joints, one which played a prominent part in the Senate crime probe in the fifties, was located in Bergen County, New Jersey, and was called the Barn. It started in 1937 about eight blocks from my home in Fairview, in the cellar of a local gambler. It housed one Money Craps game, and the gambler booking the game was known as the Baron. The game grew in size so fast that the Bergen County racket boys pushed the Baron out and took control. The joint moved from Fairview to Cliffside Park, back to Fairview, to Little Ferry, to Fort Lee and to Lodi, where it was when it folded as a result of the Kefauver probe.

Lodi is only a few miles from where I live, but when I visited the Barn there in 1945 I first had to go to New York City; local patronage was discouraged. A Cadillac limousine picked me up outside the swank Sherry-Netherland Hotel (a service that extended to all the first-rate New York hotels) and took me to a used-car lot in Little Ferry, New Jersey, where I met other men with the same destination. Another car took us to the Barn.

We entered a large rectangular bulding, formerly a taxi-repair garage, and found ourselves in a small anteroom just about big enough to contain four men. A sliding panel in an inner door moved aside and a pair of eyes gave us the once-over through the small glass window. Then this opened and we passed into another small room, where we were searched for weapons. This was not just a formality; I saw that several pistols and revolvers had already been checked in the "frisk room" by their carriers. It was done to minimize the possibility of the casino's being held up by gunmen.

Leaving the frisk room, we entered the Barn itself. There were six dice tables, four Black Jack tables and a Shimmy (Chemin de Fer) table. It was in this sawdust joint that I saw the biggest dice gambling of my career. Seven of the biggest gamblers and casino owners in the country were present: Bugsy Siegel, New York and West Coast gambler and racketeer; Willie Moretti, then racket boss of Bergen County; his brother, Sally Moretti; a wealthy shirt manufacturer, a celebrated New York lawyer, a well-known movie star and a Chicago department store owner. The wagers made that night were all in the thousands of dollars and few bets were made with the bank. The biggest single bet was on the point 4. Willie Moretti took $120,000 to $60,000 from the other big-time gamblers. P.S.: Willie missed the 4. At the end of the evening the shirt manufacturer, now long retired, had won $800,000—in cash, not chips or IOUs.

The Barn's annual gross during its 15 years of operation was greater than that of any casino in the world. Its monthly gross profits averaged more than the annual gross profit of Monaco's Monte Carlo Casino during its best years. The largest single night's take by the Barn's operators was that of September 1, 1946, when the 11 gaming tables showed a gross profit of $1,250,251.

The largest number of illegal gaming tables in a single casino at one time in America were in operation during the early forties at the Devon Club, a sawdust joint in Toledo, Ohio. It catered largely to Detroit horse bettors who were transported the intervening 50-odd miles in Greyhound buses at the club's expense. The Devon Club had 20 Bank Craps tables, 25 Black Jack tables and 8 casino side games—53 gaming tables in all.

THE RACKET BOYS MOVE IN

Casino operations in America prior to 1932 were on a small scale. Every city and town had its back-alley dice games and smoke-filled card rooms, run usually by well-known local political figures or sportsmen. Most towns were wide open for gambling but, except for a few of the larger sawdust joints and a few elegant rug joints with a well-to-do clientele, the gambling was not really organized. Each operator was on his own, and the cops and politicians had little or no idea of the earning power of casino gambling. If you ran a Craps game, paying the cop on the beat a few bucks would buy all the protection you needed.

Racketeers paid little attention to the business; the big racket money was all in bootlegging. In fact, it was the bootlegging crowd who were the sawdust joints' biggest suckers; they wagered their bootlegging profits with abandon. They were the sawdust-joint operator's delight. Then the repeal of Prohibition left the racket boys without their customary source of revenue, and they turned their attention to gambling operations.

Little by little the bootleg mobs began to move in on the casino business and other forms of gambling such as the Numbers game; former owners like the Barn's original owner, the Baron, were pushed out. By 1934 the mobs had control and the business was organized. The politicians with their icemen were put on the *pad* (payroll) and the cops, at the request of the local mob, began raiding all the small dice and poker games. Organization to a mob means monopoly. The politicians were put on the payroll, and one of their duties was to see that the cops raided all the small private dice and card games and put the competition out of business. By 1935 the country was divided into geographical sectors ruled by different mobs.

It was also during this period, from 1933 to 1935, that rug and sawdust joints sprouted everywhere like mushrooms. It was the biggest casino boom America had ever known. Every major nightclub had its back-room casino. The Miami area of Florida had more than 50 rug and sawdust joints; Saratoga Springs in New York State had 8. Every resort area and large city had at least a couple.

The racket boys had their own ideas about how gambling should be operated. I visited a great many rug joints during that period and I doubt if more than 30% were operated on the up and up. There was nearly always a *dice mechanic* (a cheat skilled at switching) around, ready to go into action if any big money showed. The Roulette wheels were rigged and the Chuck-a-Luck cages wired.

But there was usually at least one game in town that was honest—a sawdust joint that operated honestly not because of any integrity on the part of the operator but because this was the joint patronized by a very discriminating clientele: the racket boys themselves, and all the dice and card cheats, professional crooks, pimps, easy-money guys and some legitimate businessmen.

Dice mechanics were at a premium. Con Baker, the greatest of them all, could switch phony dice into a game with either his right or his left hand. His fees, 10% of the winnings, netted him over a million dollars in his best year. He didn't retire wealthy, however; he died at the age of 37, dead broke.

EARLY CASINOS

There was gambling in this country long before the American continent was discovered by Europeans; the American Indians were inveterate gamblers. European games of chance arrived with the English, French and Spanish explorers. There were apparently a few sawdust joints in operation among the American colonists very soon after the landing of the Mayflower, because only four years later, in 1624, the Virginia Assembly passed a law stating that "Mynisters shall not give themselves to excess in drinking or yette spend their tyme idelie by day or by night playing at dice, cards or any unlawful game."

Charles Cotton in his *Complete Gamester*, published in 1674, says that the most popular casino game at that time in England was Hazard, the ancestor of modern Craps. Hazard, Faro, Macao, Quinze, Trente et Quarante and Rouge et Noir were the major English casino games of the seventeenth, eighteenth and nineteenth centuries. French casinos of the same periods featured Roulette and Trente et Un.

The members of the famous English gambling clubs, White's and Brooks in the eighteenth century and Crockford's in the nineteenth,

A carpet joint in 1843, the famed Crockford's Club. (Culver Service)

were the titled nobility; accounts of their enormous losses are numerous. The Crockford rug joint (1827–44), with a nightly bankroll of £5,000, is said to have netted about £300,000 in its first two seasons. The first issue of the *Gentleman's Magazine* in 1731 printed the following list of gambling-house employees and their functions; many of these jobs still exist, under other names, in present-day casinos.

A Commissioner, always a Proprietor, who lookes in of a Night, and the Week's Accompt is audited by him, and two others of the Proprietors.

A Director, who superintends the Room.

An Operator, who deals the Cards at a cheating Game, called Faro.

Two Crowpees, who watch the Cards and gather the Money for the Bank.

Two Puffs, who have Money given them to decoy others to play.

A Clerk, who is a check upon the Puffs, to see that they sink none of the Money that is given them to play with.

A Squib, is a Puff of lower Rank, who serves at half Salary, while he is learning to deal.

A Flasher, to swear how often the Bank has been stript.

A Dunner, who goes about to recover Money lost at Play.

A Waiter, to fill out Wine, snuff Candles, and attend in the Gaming Room.

An Attorney, a Newgate Solicitor.

A Captain, who is to fight a Gentleman that is peevish about losing his money.

An Usher, who lights Gentlemen up and down Stairs, and gives the word to the Porter.

A gambling saloon in Cripple Creek, Colorado, in 1895. Faro is being played at the left, Keno at the right, a Wheel of Fortune in the background. Note the harp combo on the right. (Culver Service)

A Porter, who is, generally, a Soldier of the Foot Guards.

An Orderly Man, who walks up and down the outside of the Door, to give Notice to the Porter, and alarm the House, at the approach of the Constables.

A Runner, who is to get Intelligence of the Justices meeting.

Linkboys, Coachmen, Chairmen, Drawers, or others, who bring the first Intelligence of the Justices meetings, or, of the Constables being out, at Half a Guinea Reward.

Common Bail, Affidavits, Ruffians, Bravoes, Assassins, and many others.

The first casino operator in America to endow a sawdust joint with elegance and make it a rug joint was John Davis of New Orleans, owner of the Theatre d'Orleans and of the famous Orleans Ballroom. In 1827 he built the first lavishly decorated casino in this country. Its furnishings and gaming tables, and Mr. Davis's wines and liquors, were imported from England and France. The buffet suppers he served his customers have become standard practice in many American carpet joints. But the luxury casinos of today not only serve free drinks and sandwiches to patrons but often spend considerable amounts to get high rollers into the casinos (see page 252).

John Davis's first American carpet joint, like the Nevada casinos, was open for business 24 hours a day, and his Roulette and Hazard tables were well patronized by the wealthy plantation owners of Louisiana. Eight years later, in 1835, when the Louisiana Legislature enacted a law making the operation of a gambling house a felony, Davis quit the casino business and returned to theater management.

In the meantime other operators had noted the success of the Davis casino and established other rug joints in the principal cities of the country. The most famous was the one which Edward Pendleton opened in 1832 on Pennsylvania Avenue not far from the Capitol in Washington, D.C. He called it the Palace of Fortune, but after a year of operation so many players had lost so much at its Roulette, Faro and Hazard tables that Washingtonians referred to it as "the Bleeding Heart." Cabinet members, Senators, Congressmen and other Federal officials were attracted by its gaming tables and its free expensive wines and liquors. President James Buchanan, it was rumored, occasionally visited the private gaming room for a fling at Faro. The Palace of Fortune operated without interruption until Pendleton's death in 1858; President Buchanan attended his funeral, and several Congressmen were pallbearers.

Bucking the tiger in a Western sawdust joint. The Orient Saloon in Bixbee, Arizona, 1903.

The carpet joints of the East offered Faro facilities for the fair sex in 1879.

FARO

By 1850 there were carpet and sawdust joints throughout the country, and Faro was the big game. Plantations and slaves in the South, and in the West, many a poke of gold, were won and lost at the Faro bank. The Western sawdust joints advertised that Faro was available with a sign outside bearing the likeness of a tiger, and playing against the Faro bank came to be known as *bucking the tiger*. The legendary stories of the crooked gamblers of the Mississippi River boats and the Western mining-town saloons mostly concerned individual card cheats and confidence men who traveled from place to place hunting suckers. In one respect they were no different from the gambling cheats of today who usually go broke trying to beat a banking game in a *square* (honest) joint: The old-timers did the same bucking the tiger in some sawdust joint.

Many of the Faro banks of that day were crookedly run, but this was not because Faro is a dead-even game which cannot be dealt honestly and still make money, as some writers have stated. The Faro bank has a 16⅔% edge on the *last turn*, approximately 2% on *splits*, and is dead even on *cases*. The bank requires that a player must make at least one split bet before he can bet on cases.

Many people believe that the game has now disappeared, but at the time of writing there are about seven games in operation in Nevada, one of them at the plush Star Dust Hotel Casino on the Las Vegas Strip.

MONTE CARLO

The year 1858, which saw the closing of the Palace of Fortune, also saw the opening of a European casino that was destined to become the most famous in the world. Some 15 years earlier a young Parisian, François Blanc, along with his brother Charles, began speculating on the Paris Bourse. They displayed such an uncanny foreknowledge of the rise and fall of stocks that the brokers became suspicious and hired detectives to investigate. They found that the brothers had set up a system of signaling by semaphore which brought them news of closing prices elsewhere before they were known on the Bourse. The brokers demanded that they be sentenced to penal servitude but the fraud was so novel that the French Criminal Code had no penalty for it and the judge had to stretch a point to give the Blanc brothers seven months' imprisonment. Although they had returned large sums to some victims so that they would not appear as witnesses, they still had 100,000 francs left. With this stake, François obtained a gambling concession

John Scarne sits in on one of the remaining half dozen Faro games in the country, in Las Vegas.

François Blanc, founder of Monte Carlo. (Monte Carlo Casino)

in Homburg, Bavaria, in 1842, and in a few years transformed the town into such a world-renowned resort that Lord Brougham, high chancellor of England, called him the most brilliant financier of his time.

Since the oftener you play, the more likely you are to lose, any gambling casino that allows local residents to patronize its tables will eventually absorb so much of the local capital that the town may be pauperized. This began to happen in Homburg, and by 1863 Blanc saw that a mounting wave of adverse public opinion would eventually force him to leave. So he prepared a line of retreat. Prince Charles, of the royal family of Grimaldi, desperately in need of funds to run his principality of Monaco, had in 1858 sold a gambling concession to a French combine which had erected a small imitation of Blanc's Homburg casino. After passing through several hands, it was about to fail when Blanc appeared and purchased the concession for 1,700,000 francs.

He spent more millions rebuilding the casino into a showplace which began to attract thousands of visitors from Nice. Residents of

Roulette players at Monte Carlo in 1890. (Monte Carlo Casino)

The Schmidt Salon at Monte Carlo today. (Monte Carlo Casino)

Monte Carlo were not allowed to play. It operated for seven years as a branch office of his Homburg casino on a touch-and-go basis. When the latter closed, in 1870, Blanc transferred his headquarters to Monte Carlo and by 1872 had sunk the whole of his capital, plus large amounts borrowed from Paris bankers, into the operation. Under his personal management the casino prospered so greatly that on his death in 1877 he left a fortune of 200 million francs.

Under the management of the Blanc family and especially François's son Camille, Monte Carlo became, as it still is, the world's most famed casino, although its annual betting handle today is small compared to that of a top Nevada casino.

Of the many stories about Monte Carlo, the one which brought the operators their greatest publicity bonanza began on a July day in 1891 when an English thief and con man, Charles Wells, sat down to play with a £4,000 bankroll of swindled money. He faced exposure and imprisonment if he lost, but after 11 hours of play he had won 250,000 francs (about $50,000). Two days later he broke the bank a dozen times. This is not as profitable as it sounds because it was not the casino bank, but merely the 100,000-franc bank at the Roulette table. Wells claimed his success was due to an infallible system, and he became famous overnight. His phenomenal luck persisted, and at the season's end he returned to England a winner, although grossly exaggerating the profits, which he soon spent. His fame and his ability as a con man enabled him to acquire another bankroll from backers who swallowed his system story, and he returned to Monte Carlo in 1892. He again broke the bank six times before his luck deserted him and he lost everything. On his way back to England he was arrested on charges of fraud, was tried in Old Bailey and sentenced to an eight-year prison term. Later swindles got him another three-year stretch in England and one of five years in France.

Even if the casino had never regained in 1892 any of the money he had won the season before, the operators would still have profited enormously, because Charles Wells became the hero of an international song hit that advertised the casino throughout the world: "The Man Who Broke the Bank at Monte Carlo." Shortly before his death in 1922 he admitted that he had played strictly according to a system only during the second season when he had lost.

CANFIELD AND BRADLEY

The best-known casino operator in any period of American history was Richard Canfield. He operated rug joints in New York City and Saratoga, New York, from 1890 to 1905 and had the most distinguished clientele in the country. His three best-known casinos were the Madison Square Club and the gambling house at 5 East 44th Street next to Delmonico's in New York City, and the Saratoga Club House which ran during the racing season in Saratoga. To minimize the possibility of police raids, many casinos of this period were incorporated as private clubs and issued membership cards. But Canfield still had the iceman to deal with; he paid $100,000 a year as protection money in order to be able to run his two New York City rug joints without police interference.

In 1898 a soft-spoken 39-year-old man, Edward Riley Bradley, later famous as Colonel Bradley, opened the Beach Club in Palm Beach, Florida. In strange contrast to Canfield's expensively decorated casinos the Beach Club was in an ordinary frame house costing perhaps $4,000 to build. It housed four Roulette tables and one Hazard game. No women or Floridians were admitted, or men not wearing evening clothes, or anyone under the influence of liquor. The no-women rule was rescinded in later years. A new building containing an octagonal gaming room was built in 1912. This, too, was an unpretentious frame house, distinguished from its neighbors only by the initials B.C. lettered in white on the wide lawn in front.

I visited the Beach Club in 1932, had a pleasant chat with the colonel, who was then about 73 years of age, and did some card tricks

Exterior view of Monte Carlo casino. (Monte Carlo Casino)

Studies of Richard Canfield

Drawings made of Richard Canfield in the courtroom after police raided his New York casino in 1906. (Culver Service)

for him. At this time the club had nine Roulette tables and one game of Hazard. The Roulette limits were $25 on a straight number and $1,000 on an even-money payoff such as red, black, odd or even.

I asked what the house percentage was at Roulette (the tables had both the 0 and 00). "Young man," Colonel Bradley said, "it's 5 5/19%, no matter how you bet."

This surprised me a bit. "Colonel," I said, "are you saying that every wager made at your Roulette table has the same 5 5/19% house percentage?"

"That's correct, young man. I've been watching these wheels for about 50 years and I ought to know."

The colonel wasn't far wrong. The house percentage on all bets at Roulette is 5 5/19%—except for one. I walked over to an unoccupied table and put a stack of chips on a five-number bet.

"Colonel," I said, "that bet has a percentage of 7 17/19% against the player."

He didn't take my word for it; I had to prove it, but after I had explained the mathematics (see page 403), he said, "How do you like that? A kid walks into my casino and tells the old colonel something about a wheel he never knew before." The gracious old gentleman treated me to a wonderful dinner at the Beach Club restaurant.

Colonel Bradley's Beach Club had the longest run of any illegally operated casino in America—from 1898 until he died in 1941. And that is ample proof that he ran a percentage game, not a crooked one.

NEW CASINO GAMES

About 1915 the sawdust joints began banking two new games: Fading Craps and Black Jack. These were both popular private games and they met with immediate favor among casino players. About 1917 a version of Fading Craps called Bank Craps entered the picture although some gamblers objected at first, not liking the rule that all bets at Bank Craps must be made against the bank. In Fading Craps (today called Money Craps or Open Craps) players could also wager among themselves and bet with the bank. But this resistance vanished, and in a few short years Bank Craps could be found in most of America's sawdust and carpet joints. By 1918 the Faro bank had been replaced by Bank Craps as the number one banking game. Colonel Bradley didn't go along with this trend. His answer when I asked him in 1932 why he had no Craps tables was, "Can you imagine the Vanderbilts and Astors playing a back-alley game?" The colonel at this point was 73, a millionaire several times over, and was thinking of retiring.

More new banking games made their appearance in the early twentieth century than at any other period in American gambling history; among them Bank Craps, Money Craps, Black Jack, slot machines, Chuck-a-Luck, Klondike, Keno and Under and Over Seven. Since the casino's favorable percentage in each of these games was considerably greater than in Faro, their introduction marked the beginning of the casino boom and of gambling as an organized, bigtime national business.

THE HISTORY OF THE LAS VEGAS STRIP

In 1931 the Nevada Legislature passed a bill making gambling legal in the state. Actually, it merely put the stamp of approval on the gambling which was already there. In the rest of the country a good many sermons were preached on the pitfalls of gambling, and most of the nation's press called the bill an experiment that was doomed to fail as did the legalized gambling experiment in Louisiana in the nineteenth century.

The growth of Nevada's gambling industry for the first 15 years was slow. The gambling houses were all sawdust joints patronized mostly by Western gamblers and the gambling there was small time

Downtown Las Vegas at night. (Las Vegas News Bureau)

compared with the gambling that took place in the illegal luxury
casinos and larger sawdust joints in Florida, Illinois, New Jersey, New
York and elsewhere. In 1946 things began to happen that were destined
very soon to make Nevada the gambling mecca of the world.

The Las Vegas sawdust joints were on downtown Fremont Street,
and the now famed Strip on the road leading to Los Angeles had only
two casinos: the Last Frontier and El Rancho Vegas, both designed in
Western style and not in the carpet-joint class. Then on December 26,
1946, Benjamin (Bugsy) Siegel opened the Flamingo Casino, the first
of Nevada's plush rug joints.

I visited it two weeks after its opening, staying at El Rancho Vegas
because the Flamingo hotel accommodations were not yet completed.
The Flamingo opened with six Bank Craps tables, six Black Jack tables,
three Roulette tables and one Hazard game. I didn't meet Siegel on
this trip, but shortly after I checked in again, a couple of months later,
an assistant manager phoned and said that Benny wanted to see me.
No one called him Bugsy if he was likely to overhear it; it was a nickname he hated. I went to his suite and found him playing Gin Rummy
with Monk Schaefer, the casino manager, and several other men.

"I've seen your *Scarne on Dice* book and your magazine publicity and I'd like to see some of your card tricks," Bugsy said. "Would you show me and the boys a few?" Gamblers are always a good audience for card magic, and I did tricks for an hour or so, getting quite a laugh out of Bugsy's baffled reaction.

The next afternoon I looked for Bugsy in the casino and found him talking to Monk near one of the dice tables. "Thanks for the tricks," he said. "They're the best I ever saw; they have all the boys dizzy."

"Glad you liked them," I told him. "Maybe you'll do something for me? Why did you put up a five-million-dollar casino and hotel in the middle of the desert?"

He grinned. "I had a little trouble with Governor Earl Warren. I owned a piece of all those gambling ships that were getting plenty of action three miles off the coast of southern California. Business was so good we had plans to add a dozen more boats. And just when I thought I had it made, Governor Warren came along and closed gambling up tight as a drum, not only in the state but on the boats too. Overnight my dream of a Monte Carlo in the ocean is killed.

"So I'm thinking about where I can find another spot away from any other casinos—a place like the ocean so that when people come to gamble they can't go any place else but have to stick with me. There were too many sawdust joints in Vegas, Reno and other Nevada towns, but I figured it this way. If people will take a trip out into the ocean to gamble, they'll go to a desert, too—especially if it's legal and they don't have to worry about being pinched. So one day I drive into Nevada looking for a nice desert spot and I picked this one because the price was right and it's on the main road to L.A. Then I took a trip around the country and tried to interest some of the boys in the proposition. Some of them thought I was nuts. But I dug up the dough, and here I am with a five-million-dollar hotel and a casino full of customers."

And then Bugsy made a prediction. "Scarne, what you see here today is nothing. More and more people are moving to California every day, and they love to gamble. Since it's legal here in the desert, and not very far away, they'll come here. In ten years this'll be the biggest gambling center in the world."

Bugsy was wrong on only one count: it didn't take ten years. One reason, I believe, was that his murder at the home of a friend, Virginia Hill, in Beverly Hills, California, several months after I saw him, gave his Flamingo so much nationwide publicity that everybody heard about it. Even in death Bugsy Siegel helped turn a chunk of Nevada desert into the now famous Las Vegas Strip, with its blaze of multicolored neon lights, its plush hotels, its carpet gambling joints with their mink-stole clientele, and its live entertainment that is unmatched anywhere in the world.

By 1950, only three years after Bugsy's assassination, the Strip was well on its way to fulfilling his prophecy. Gambling combines from New Jersey, New York, Michigan, Texas and Ohio had already located on the Strip or were planning to do so. Three additional multi-million-dollar casino hotels had been built, and three others were being constructed. There were 25 large gambling houses in Nevada and scores of smaller ones. Their revenue for 1949 was about $41 million.

In November 1950, the U.S. Senate Crime Committee made an on-the-spot study of gambling in Las Vegas to find out whether nation-wide legalized gambling would be a deterrent to organized crime. The committee reported that "Nevada's system of licensed gambling casinos has not resulted in excluding undesirables from the state, but rather served to give gambling a cloak of respectability." They concluded that "as a case history of legalized gambling, Nevada speaks eloquently in the negative."

This opinion came as no surprise to me nor to anyone sophisticated in the ways of casino gambling. As one Strip operator said, "Who did the Senate Committee expect to find running the games here in Vegas? Father Flanagan?" Only an experienced casino operator who has learned his trade in the illegally operated joints can protect a casino bankroll of hundreds of thousands of dollars. It's a sure bet that he was arrested a time or two while getting this experience. Anyone who tries to run a casino without such experience would be quickly driven into bankruptcy by predatory casino employees, larcenous players, dice and card cheats and *agents* (player cheats working in collusion with house dealers).

Even an experienced operator with a half dozen or more trusted and skilled pit bosses must be constantly on his guard against cheating. Some Nevada casinos have hired ex-card and dice cheats as pit bosses or house spotters in order to help protect the casino bankroll. Some of the larger Nevada casinos have observation posts concealed behind one-way glass in the walls and in the ceilings above each gaming table, known as "eyes in the sky."

One would think that the unfavorable publicity from the Senate Committee would have cut down the Nevada gambling handle, but, like the publicity from Siegel's murder, it brought more tourists to the state and the gambling handle increased. The Kefauver probe had another result. Most state and county officials in states visited by the committee clamped down the lid on most of their illegal bigtime casinos, particularly in Florida, New York, New Jersey and Ohio—and the operators began moving to Nevada. One of the most successful recently told me, "Scarne, I love that man Kefauver. When he drove me out of an illegal casino operation in Florida and into a legalized operation in Nevada, he made me a respectable law-abiding citizen and a millionaire." Other Nevada operators have told me the same.

IS GAMBLING IN NEVADA HONEST?

In 1973, as the revised edition of this book was being prepared to go to press, I made an on-the-spot study of most of Nevada's gambling establishments. I was looking for the answer to the all-important question asked daily by the millions of Americans (gamblers and non-gamblers alike): "Is gambling in Nevada honest?"

To get the answer I spent one month visiting casinos all over the state. I scouted all the plush carpet joints on the strip, including the Sands, Flamingo, Star Dust, Tropicana, Dunes, Sahara, Caesar's Place, Las Vegas Hilton, Riviera, Frontier, Aladdin and Desert Inn. In downtown Las Vegas I checked such sawdust joints as the Fremont, Horseshoe Club, Mint, Pioneer Club and California Club. In Reno I visited Harold's, Riverside, Harrah's, Holiday and a number of spots around Lake Tahoe, ending my survey at the Nugget in Sparks. I also scouted several smaller gambling establishments on the highways leading to Las Vegas and Reno.

The only cheating I saw was in the game of Black Jack at several small sawdust joints on the outskirts of Las Vegas and Reno. This cheating consisted of the dealer's either glimpsing the top card of the deck and then resorting to dealing a second, or reversing the undealt cards in his hand.

These instances of cheating are trivial when you consider that $20 billion passes back and forth over Nevada's gambling tables each year.

I believe that the governor, the State Legislature, the members of the Tax Commission and the Gaming Control Board, and the casino operators are to be commended for doing their part in giving the millions of Americans who gamble in Nevada an honest shake for their money. Ironically, I found this does not hold true in any of our other states in which casinos or banking games are run despite anti-gambling laws.

When this book first went to press in 1961, all casinos in Nevada were dealing single deck Black Jack from the hand and complaints of cheating were constantly being heard. At that time, I informed the Nevada Gaming Control Board that in order to eliminate most Black Jack cheating, a state ruling should be enacted that Black Jack must be dealt from a shoe (card dealing box). No such ruling was ever passed. I am happy, however, to report that just as I predicted, most Nevada casinos today deal Black Jack from a shoe and make use of my anti-card casing gimmick. (For further information, see page 474.)

GOVERNMENT SUPERVISION OF PUERTO RICAN CASINOS

Other than Nevada, Puerto Rico is the only place under the Stars and Stripes where casino gambling is permitted by law. Many U.S. legislators and foreign officials who are considering legalized gambling for their own states or countries credit the big American tourist boom in Puerto Rico to its government-supervised casinos. Only 8% of the patrons of the island's casinos are residents of Puerto Rico; the other 92% are tourists. Here, for these legislators and the reader, is a report on how that supervision operates.

The casino rules and regulations of Puerto Rico which, as gambling consultant to the Puerto Rican government, I helped write, were formulated with several objectives in mind. The principal aim, to attract tourists to the island, has met with more success than anyone dreamed.

Another objective was to discourage visits from professional and bigtime bettors; the government wanted casino gambling on a small scale so that the tourists would not be hurt too badly at the gaming tables. This aim was partly achieved by setting a low maximum betting limit of $100 and keeping the casinos open only seven hours a day. Today the maximum betting limit is $200.

Here is a summary of the important Puerto Rican casino regulations. Before gambling was legalized on the island in 1949, authority for regulating games of chance was vested in the Economic Administration, an agency of the Commonwealth government. Within this administration, gambling regulations are specifically handled by the Office of Tourism and an appointed advisory committee. The Office of Tourism insists on painstaking investigations to show that applicants for casino licenses are bona-fide businessmen who will comply with the gambling laws. The laws require that there be other hotel facilities in conjunction with the casino, and an unblemished character and reputation on the part of all owners, stockholders, operators and employees. Croupiers, dealers and floormen must be licensed, and only after careful inquiry as to their desirability. Equipment such as Craps, Roulette and Black Jack layouts must be of a standard and approved type and quality. All Puerto Rican casinos must adhere to standardized approved procedures, rules of play, maximum and minimum betting limits and payoff odds. Only the banking games of Bank Craps, Black Jack, Roulette and Chemin de Fer are permitted in the island's casinos. Slot

John Scarne with casino employees in the El San Juan Hotel casino in San Juan, Puerto Rico. (Conrad Eiger)

machines are barred, and I have heard a good many disappointed comments from women visitors who come in to find that the one-armed bandits are not available.

Trained government inspectors on the administration payroll must be on duty in the casinos from opening until closing time. They test the equipment used before each night's play, and also during the play, if this action seems warranted. The casinos are not considered to be public rooms; admittance is at the discretion of the management, and the casino manager or the government inspector may ask a disorderly or otherwise undesirable person to leave. Except on special occasions, the casinos do not open earlier than 8:30 P.M., and they close at 3:30 A.M. on weekdays, 4:00 A.M. on Saturdays. Soft drinks, coffee and sandwiches are served in the casinos, but no alcoholic beverages. The rules for each game are prominently posted on the walls in English and Spanish. Only chips may be wagered—coins and bills may not.

At the time of writing, the Commonwealth Government is considering the introduction of slot machines and my game creation of Scarney Baccarat in their casinos.

CASINO OPERATION

Most of the bigtime illegal gambling establishments in the United States are controlled by gambling combines. In Nevada, although former illegal operators are responsible for opening most of the casinos on the Vegas Strip, many law-abiding businessmen have bought in. Few of the old-time professional gamblers who helped make Nevada the gambling mecca of the world are in the state today. Most have passed away or retired.

It is a tribute to Nevada's law-enforcement agencies that in spite of some underworld infiltration in the casinos, and despite the fact that gambling draws thousands of undesirables to the state each year, there is little crime in Las Vegas and Reno, and no gangland violence has occurred in Nevada for several years. Even when you add the 18 million tourists who visit Nevada annually to the state's population, it still has one of the lowest percentage crime rates in the United States.

You can find among Nevada casino employees a good many veteran dealers and croupiers who learned their trade in illegal joints and have police records to prove it, but this picture is changing. Dealer and croupier schools are turning out hundreds of formally trained dealers who are *clean* (without police records). It is probable that the next generation of casino employees will be indistinguishable from an equal number of bookkeepers or salesmen. It is also probable that the great majority of the owners and operators will eventually be businessmen without police records like those in Monaco, France, Italy and other countries where legalized casinos have been in operation for half a century or more.

Most of the carpet joints on the Strip have no windows in their gaming rooms to remind a player whether it is day or night, and there are no clocks to indicate the hour. From the casino point of view, day or night means nothing—it is all gambling time. The wheels never stop, the cards are always being dealt and the dice continue to roll. Spectators have no place to sit, except at the Black Jack and Roulette tables, and anyone who sits there becomes a player because the chairs are reserved for that purpose.

The average Strip casinos has eight Bank Craps tables, twelve Black Jack tables, three Roulette tables and one side game such as the Big Six. Around the walls are hundreds of one-armed bandits ranging from nickel to dollar machines. Maximum betting limits at the tables run from $200 to $500, although the casino will raise this for high rollers.

A Strip rug joint has the following employees who, except for the dealers, croupiers and a few others, work a total of six hours of each eight-hour shift—each hour is divided into 40 minutes on and 20 minutes off.

Casino manager: He is in charge of the operation and supervises the shift bosses on the three working shifts. Salary: $40,000 to $100,000 per year, plus bonus.

Casino host: He acts as a good-will ambassador to outstanding high rollers and their wives; he takes them to dinners, shows, makes their hotel and plane reservations and generally keeps them happy. He sends the women orchids and candy and even gives them money to play the slots when their husbands are high-rolling at the tables. Salary: $30,000 to $50,000 per year; he also usually owns a couple of points in the casino.

Credit manager: The next most important employee. He screens your credit cards and has the authority, if they prove satisfactory, to extend whatever credit you require—$500, $1,000, $5,000 or more. Salary: about $30,000 to $50,000 per year.

Since few people carry thousands of dollars in cash around with them, high rollers pay big losses by check. But don't just walk into a Nevada casino and ask to have a check cashed. None of them will do it unless you have filled out a casino credit form and have been issued a casino credit card. The credit manager, whose responsibility this is, checks on you by telephoning your bank; don't expect him to okay you for credit unless you ask during banking hours. If you already have a credit card from another casino it's simpler; the manager makes a phone check with them, and casinos are always open. Ordinary credit cards to most credit managers don't even rate $50 in credit.

Old-time casino operators have considerable patience with broke credit players. They will make a deal with a loser who has lost more than his checking account holds, allowing him to pay off on the installment plan. But they don't like welshers. If, after returning home, you put a stop on checks signed in Nevada because you remember that gambling debts are by law uncollectible in your state, you will first get a firm letter demanding payment, then a phone call, and finally a couple of tough-looking visitors. At this point or shortly thereafter, the would-be welsher pays up. One casino manager told me: "We had a character here last year who took $5,000 worth of credit, won $10,000 at Craps the last night, walked out without picking up his 'hold checks,' and later when we put the checks through he stopped them. Some character, eh? But he changed his mind later."

Big corporations, which now own most of Nevada's major hotel casinos, resort to legal methods rather than strong-arm tactics to collect long-time unpaid gambling debts. A New Jersey Superior Court judge

The Las Vegas Hilton Hotel casino in Nevada. The mirror around the wall near the ceiling is a one-way mirror from which the play can be observed by lookout men. A roving television camera hidden in the ceiling can monitor the action of any desired gaming table to the control room. (Allen Photographers, Inc.)

recently ruled that a Las Vegas gambling casino cannot collect a gambling debt in New Jersey through a civil suit because Nevada laws specify that gambling debts may not be collected in that state. If other states adopt this ruling, Nevada casinos are in real trouble. As I see it, this Nevada law will soon be changed.

Shift boss: He acts as casino manager during his working shift. Salary: $100 per day plus bonuses.

Cashier: He counts the casino bankroll and makes a chip inventory before and after each work shift. He supplies each gaming table with the necessary number of chips at the beginning of the game and more when required. Some casinos allow players to cash their chips at the main cashier's cage. In others, the pit boss pays off winners at the table where the money was won, and in this case the pit boss makes three copies of a cash-out slip. A runner takes two of these to the cashier, who initials the slips and exchanges one of them for the cash amount. The cashier is the employee who does all the casino's bookkeeping.

Larger casinos have a main cashier's office and a pit cashier at a small desk in the ring formed by the circle of Roulette and Black Jack tables. There are usually three cashiers to each working shift. Salary: $350 per week each.

Pit boss: He acts as a floorman or inspector over a Black Jack or Roulette table, makes out and signs cash-out and fill slips, and watches constantly for any errors the dealer or croupiers may make and for any cheating on players' or dealer's part. Salary: $80 to $100 per day.

Spotter or lookout: An employee who observes the play secretly when the house wants to check on the honesty of the dealer. He does this either from behind a one-way mirror glass, usually located in the ceiling, or by acting as a player at the table. Salary: $60 per day.

Black Jack dealer: He deals at the Black Jack table, collects losing bets and pays off winning bets. Salary: $26 per day plus *tokens* (tips) which may total considerably more than his salary.

Croupier: He deals the game of Roulette, collects losing bets and pays off winning bets. Salary: $26 per day, plus tokens.

Craps dealer: He collects and pays off bets at the Craps tables, and alternates with other Craps dealers as a *stickman* (one who calls the numbers thrown). Salary: $26 per day plus tokens.

Shill: A male or female employee who poses as a player in order to stimulate the action. Salary $12.50 to $15 per day.

Runner: He runs errands between the cashier's cage and the pit bosses or box men, carrying cash-out and fill slips and money. Salary: $17.50 per day.

Boxman: He has charge of a dice table and handles all cash and chip transactions between the table and the cashier's office. Salary: $60 per day. When a player gives the Craps dealer money in exchange for chips, the dealer passes the paper money to the box man seated at the center of the table. He is called a boxman because, using a paddle, he pushes the paper money into a slot in the table and it falls into a locked *drop box* underneath. *Cash-out slips* and *fill slips* which he writes and signs go into the same box. Fill slips indicate how many additional chips have been brought to the table from the cashier's cage.

At Black Jack and Roulette tables, money and duplicate slips are pushed into the drop box by the dealer, but the slips must be written out by the cashier or pit boss and signed by the pit boss and the dealer and a copy returned to the cashier. At the end of each eight-hour shift, the locked boxes are taken from each table to the *count room*, where they are unlocked and the contents counted by three or four casino part owners or their representatives.

Ladderman: He sits on a high stand overlooking the dice table just above the dealers and boxman, corrects any mistakes the dealers may make that go unobserved by the boxman, and watches for dice cheats. He usually alternates as a boxman. Salary: $60 per day.

Side game dealer: He deals Big Six, Money Wheel, Race Horse Wheel, Hazard, Chuck-a-Luck or sometimes others. Salary: $26 per day plus tokens.

In addition to the above employees there are also floorwalkers, house spotters, slot machine attendants and mechanics, waitresses, Keno runners, busboys, bartenders, porters, doormen, bouncers, publicity agents, lawyers, tax experts and accountants. The busy swing shift requires about 100 employees to keep the action rolling and about half that number during the slower day and graveyard shifts.

The casino payroll is small compared to the tens of thousands of dollars spent weekly for the live entertainment in the casino's nightclub as a lure to bring in the customers. These shows have made Las Vegas a capital of live entertainment. More television, motion-picture and nightclub stars perform there nightly than in Hollywood and New York City combined. The top-notch casino nightclub shows cost hundreds of thousands of dollars to produce and feature stars sometimes receive as much as $250,000 per week. All this is paid by the casino management, and when you add in state taxes, employees' salaries, rent, free drinks for customers and other incidental expenses, the annual cost runs into the millions.

GAMBLING JUNKETS

A group of gamblers solicited to travel to a casino for the sole purpose of gambling is called a gambling junket. The organizer of such a group is known as the junket leader or junketeer, and the gamblers are called junketers. To the best of my knowledge, the first gambling junket came to Benjamin (Bugsy) Siegal's Flamingo in Las Vegas in early 1947. It came from Hollywood, California, and was comprised mainly of movie moguls and their wives. The gambling junkets for the next decade or so were, as a rule, put together by the casinos. They involved a host of certified gamblers who loved to gamble and had the cash to do so. In return for their business, these invited guests received everything free—room, food, drinks, plane transportation. The only charges were tips and phone calls. Therefore, Bugsy Siegel not only was the "father of the Las Vegas Strip," he also fathered the gambling junket.

With the building of more Strip hotel casinos, the bigtime gambler became the casino's invited guest and to this day, he still is "comped" any time he visits his favorite casino. That is, providing he does not owe the casino money. However, in the late sixties, many small travel agents and gamblers, who were once on junkets, became junketeers. They knew little or nothing about the gambling business and most of the people they put on junkets as gamblers had never been in a casino before. By 1969, there were over 2,000 junketeers in the United States and most of the so-called "gamblers" on their junkets were vacation seekers and free loaders. To discourage this practice, casino operators now insist that "front money" of $1,000 be put up for each man on the junket—wives must pay their plane fare, usually $250 or more as front money. Out of the $1,000 front money, the male gambler receives $750 in non-negotiable chips . . . upon arrival at the casino. In addition, each gambler has to fill out a credit form in advance, and has to state the full amount of credit he wishes to be granted by the casino.

Most junketeers rarely, if ever, collect all the monies due the casino and if they do, they hold out a considerable sum and swear on a stack of Bibles that the player never paid them. In all my casino experience, I have still to meet one junketeer who is honest and does not owe one or another casino thousands of dollars. Their system is first to load a casino with stiffs and then to cop a plea that the players they put on the junket failed to pay their markers. In old days, the airlines and the junketeers were the only ones who made money with the junkets. The airline sold plane tickets. The junketeer got $50 or $75 a head from the casino for each male gambler on his junket, plane commissions from the airline, and at times 10% of all monies lost by gamblers on his junket. In addition, the junketeer and his wife, or mistress, received room and board as guests of the hotel casino.

I must point out to the reader that when a casino fails to collect its gambling debts, it loses not only what is owed to them but monies that these same gamblers received from the casino—so for every $10,000 owed the casino, it is a sure bet that $5,000 in cash was lost by the casino. These characters give chips to their friends and wives to cash in and at times sell their chips to other players at a reduced price. For example, they'll take $400 for $500 worth of chips.

Today most casinos in Nevada, to avoid such skullduggery, insist the junketeer must put up $2,500 in cash for each gambler and his wife, and all gamblers must pay their markers on leaving. This sort of thing helps a bit, but does not completely eliminate stiffs (non-gamblers). Believe me, junkets are not the bonanza many people believe them to be. Several casino operators in the Caribbean Islands remarked to me that they do not know if a junket they have okayed will be loaded with stiffs or not, but since they have little business otherwise, they have to take that chance. "Our only hope is to beat one or two high rollers on the junket real big—that will pay our hotel expenses, plane fares, junket commission, and so on, and all the small amounts lost by the stiffs will be profit. If we don't beat one or more gamblers big, we are sure to have a losing junket."

Recently one gambling operator returning from Europe said, "Scarne, you know we ran dozens of junkets to *blank blank* and we cheated every person on the junket—and you know what, we still couldn't meet our plane and hotel expenses. We went broke simply because most of these junkets carried too many non-gamblers and free-loaders."

I predict that organized junkets will be a thing of the past in the top casinos in the near future. Individual high rollers, of course, will always be welcomed by the casino and receive everything free except for tips and phone calls. However, I doubt if there are enough high rollers around to satisfy the countless number of casinos springing up throughout the world. Thus, then, a toast: "To the millions of small-time gamblers who are the kings of gambling."

NEVADA GAMBLING AND BIG BUSINESS

The old-time gamblers and mobsters who built and operated most of the luxury casinos in Las Vegas and Reno have either gone public or sold their interests to big corporations. Today, the fathers of the Las Vegas Strip, experienced gamblers who made Las Vegas the en-tertainment capital of the world, have little or no say in the internal operations of any of the luxury casinos on the Las Vegas Strip. Gone with these operators are their friends—the bigtime gamblers, the boys who could lose or win $20,000 to $250,000 in one session of play. As I have stated, the high rollers, although not quite dead, are fast becom-ing extinct. Absent from Las Vegas Strip casinos are most of the illegal race bookies who operated in every hamlet and city in our country and made up the bulk of Las Vegas's high rollers. Due to recently enacted Federal and state anti-gambling laws, most of the country's top illegal race bookies are either in jail, indicted, retired, laying low or on the lam. And most who are still operating avoid Las Vegas as if it were a plague since it is rumored that Nevada is infested with more FBI and Internal Revenue agents than any other state in the union. When ex-perienced gamblers ran the Strip's casinos, high rollers seldom welshed on paying gambling losses. Today, one casino group has more non-collectible outstanding debts than all the combined casinos on the Strip during the regime of the old-timers.

Big business practices, in fact, are making Las Vegas a prissy, penny-pinching old lady. Gone is bigtime gambling excitement, the glamour ignited by high rollers and the fantastic round-the-clock cocktail lounges with their star-studded entertainment. Cocktail lounges in most of the Strip's luxury casinos are a thing of the past. In their place are Keno lounges. I predict it won't be long before the $100,000 and $200,000 weekly salaries of headline acts will also be a thing of the past.

In short, big business is changing the gambling character of Nevada—it plans to cater to the average tourist who visits Nevada. In fact, the businessmen have already eliminated the high roller in their plans and cater to the new breed of gamblers: the average man and woman. It's a big gamble on the part of big business. In my opinion, take the glamour and bigtime gambling out of Las Vegas and it will become just another tourist town. Then why should anyone from the East Coast patronize Nevada? And with the legalization of casinos in either New York or New Jersey, which is almost a sure thing in the near future, big business in Nevada had better take a second look at their casino operations. At the time of writing, I have been requested to formulate a series of casino and gaming rules for Charles C. Carella, executive director of all gambling activities in the State of New Jersey.

HONEST CASINOS VS. STEER JOINTS

The millions of people who gamble today are much less likely to be cheated than they were 25 years ago, and I think I can claim that this is due in great part to my efforts. I began writing early during World War II about the cheats who were clipping the GIs, and from then until the end of the war I served as gambling adviser to the United States Armed Forces and gave hundreds of lectures and demonstrations to military personnel here and abroad. I wrote a series of articles exposing cheating methods and explaining how to detect and guard against them for *Yank, the Army Weekly*—articles which were highly praised by such military leaders as Admiral Ernest J. King, chief of naval operations, and General Hap Arnold, commanding general of the Army Air Force.

Articles about my crusade against cheating in the Armed Forces giving the general public my anti-cheating information appeared in most of our national magazines: *Life, Saturday Evening Post, The New Yorker, Time, Newsweek, American Magazine, The New York Times Magazine, Parade, Science Digest* and others. Syndicated feature services carried my articles to newspapers throughout this country and they were published in Canadian, Australian, Indian and South American magazines and newspapers.

Then, in two big, definitive books, *Scarne on Dice* (1945), *Scarne on Cards* (1949), which are still selling today, and in *Scarne's Encyclopedia of Games* (1973), I included thorough exposés of the cheating methods in use. Gambling cheats, knowing that so much of this previously secret information was available to the public, became more and more hesitant about using the exposed methods.

Curiously enough, these exposures of cheating have been a blessing to some crooked casino operators. As the players wise up, the operators find that they have to run their games honestly, and when they do that they discover something that should be obvious: an honest percentage game makes more money for its operators than a crooked game. For one thing, honest casinos get more customers with less trouble. A *steer joint* (crooked casino) has to hire dice and card mechanics and sometimes install rigged gaming tables. It isn't long before the casino help are telling their friends not to patronize the joint, and they in turn tell their friends, and in a very short time hundreds of people know all about it. At this point, the only way to get action is to hire a flock of *steerers* or *agents* to locate and bring the suckers in to be fleeced. A steerer may be anyone: a show girl, an entertainer, a cab driver, a bartender, a business associate, a friend. And steerers are expensive; they sometimes have to be cut in for as much as 50% of the amount lost by the victim or victims brought in. The crooked casino is pretty empty most of the time until a sucker is steered in, and then all the shills and steerers have to put on an act and make it look as if there was a lot of action going on.

Steer joints are mostly located in resort areas, usually have a short season, and are seldom in the same spot the next season. The operators have to depend on taking big sums from a few victims to make a profit; after giving the steerer 50% and paying the mechanic, the shills and all the other people involved, the *touch* or *score* (money won dishonestly) must be real big to make the remaining sum amount to much.

An honestly run casino gets action from everyone: the owners themselves, dealers, croupiers' friends, local townspeople, even rival casino owners. Everyone takes a shot at an honest game even when he knows he can't beat the percentage in the long run. The honest casino has continuous action, and the crooked casino, when the steerers don't have a mark in the place, looks like a morgue.

The casino at Monte Carlo is proof that honest operation is more profitable than dishonest operation. This casino has always been known for its honest operation, and it not only makes a handsome profit for its owners but pays a tax that supplies the government of Monaco with its only source of revenue. It has been in continuous operation since 1858; the largest crooked gambling house known to the author lasted only eight months before folding.

TIPS ON HOW TO SPOT A CROOKED CASINO

Is there any simple, sure-fire method by which you can be sure your favorite casino is on the level? No, it's not that easy. But it can be done. Your best protection is to have in your head the information on cheating at casino games which you will find in this book. In addition, ask yourself the following questions:

1. How long has the casino been operating? The fact that a casino is crooked leaks out faster than you think, and only the honest ones stay in business year after year.

2. Is the casino lavishly decorated or is it a makeshift affair? The bigger the casino's investment in its quarters and furnishings, the more likely it is to be honest. Crooked dice, Roulette and card games are usually found in small casinos, hotel rooms, private homes, at charity balls and conventions behind closed doors.

3. Is the casino well patronized and doing good business, like the legal casinos in Nevada and Puerto Rico? If so, you can almost be sure the operators aren't out to take you for every nickel they can get. A crowded casino is the best proof that it is honest. Don't be the only player or one of a few players in a nearly empty casino whose operators have worried faces!

If you are a high roller and are betting as if you are trying to win the casino—pardner, you're on your own!

As in many other things, your best protection lies in knowing what you are doing. If you know the cheating methods explained in these pages, you have a chance of spotting crooked work. And then, give yourself the best possible chance of winning by sticking to those casino bets which have the smallest house percentage against you. You'll find all that information here, too.

CASINOS' EARNING POWER

As a gambling consultant, casino figures are very important to me. When I visit a casino where I'm employed, my first duty is to check the hold (win) percentages at each table. A table's hold percentage is the percentage expected to be earned by each table. This is the difference between the cash and credit slips dropped into the cashbox under each table minus the payout slips (money paid to winning players). The cashbox has a slot opening on top where the dealer pushes the player's money for chips purchased. If the actual win percentage equals or exceeds the expected hold percentage, I have had an easy visit—if it falls far below, I have to check out the reason. If the payouts to winners are greater than the money and credit slips in the box, the table is a loser. If the money and credit slips total a greater amount than the winner's payouts, the table has won money.

There is no mathematical formula that can be used to compute the overall earning power for a given period at any casino game. This is especially true for Bank Craps Nevada style, simply because there are dozens of different Craps bets made at the dice table, each having a different favorable house percentage. Also, players are very unpredictable as to the type of bets they prefer. However, I have standardized a percentage that each Bank Craps table is expected to earn in a month. This earned percentage, based on my study of daily, weekly, monthly and yearly financial records of Bank Craps tables in a number of major casinos in Nevada and the Caribbean for over 25 years, is about 20%. This means that when a player hands a boxman at a Bank Craps table $100 to purchase chips, the house is expected to earn $20 of the $100, on the average. Even though some players win, some lose and some break even, the table will not depart much from this average in a month.

At times, for days and even for weeks, a Bank Craps table may lose. At other times, the table may win heavily and hold a much higher percentage, but in the long run, the 20 percent figure is the approximate hold percentage of each and every Craps table that is run honestly both from the inside and the outside.

My study of casino records at Black Jack over the past 25 years shows a hold percentage of about 26% over a month. Roulette's hold percentage under the same conditions is about 30%; Baccarat's hold percentage amounts to about 10% over a month's period. The casino side games, such as the Big Six or the Money Wheel, where the house's advantage is 20% or more, have a hold percentage of about 80%.

These percentages should convince the reader that the house's overall percentages will knock out even the best player in the long run.

10.
Craps:
The World's Fastest
Gambling Game

Craps, history's biggest and fastest-action gambling game, is undoubtedly the most widely played game of chance in the United States today; more money is won and lost at Craps every day than at any other form of gambling, with the exception of sports betting and betting on horse races.

Each year about 40 million Americans, of whom about 5 million are women, wager approximately $70 billion at the Craps tables in hundreds of legal casinos and thousands and thousands of illegally operated carpet and sawdust joints in hamlets and cities throughout the United States. Most of the illegally operated gambling joints house only Craps tables; the other banking games (Roulette, Black Jack, Baccarat–Chemin de Fer, slot machines, etc.) are prominent by their absence.

The $70 billion includes only the monies handled each year at Bank Craps and Money, or Open, Craps; it does not take into consideration the additional $60 billion I estimate is wagered each year at Private Craps throughout the country. If we add to this $130 billion Craps handle an estimated $10 billion bet in all other forms of dice games (Backgammon, Barbouth, Four-Five-Six, Beat the Dealer, Under and Over Seven, Chuck-a-Luck, Hazard, Hooligan, Scarney Dice, Poker Dice, etc.), we find the total dice betting handle in the United States is the gigantic sum of $140 billion yearly. The yearly loss suffered by America's dice-shooting gentry is estimated at about 4%, or $5.6 billion, of the $140 billion yearly handle.

The popularity of the American game of Bank Craps has spread in the past two decades to the four corners of the globe. Today, Bank

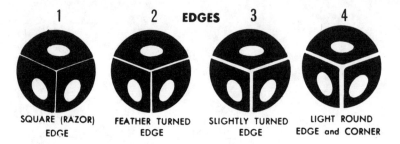

1	2	**EDGES** 3	4

| SQUARE (RAZOR) EDGE | FEATHER TURNED EDGE | SLIGHTLY TURNED EDGE | LIGHT ROUND EDGE and CORNER |

The four most popular edge-style transparent casino dice in use in major casinos.

Craps tables can be found in the plush legal gambling casinos of Monte Carlo, England, Puerto Rico, Turkey, Haiti, Bahamas, Curaçao, Aruba, St. Maârten, Panama, Dominican Republic and other Caribbean islands that cater to American tourists. And wherever American servicemen are stationed, at home or overseas in Europe, Africa and Asia, the galloping dominoes are in action.

Bank Craps and Money (or Open) Craps has not only replaced Faro as the favorite casino game of millions of Americans, but has far outdistanced all other casino games in popularity. Private Craps is the big favorite in the field of friendly or unorganized gambling.

CASINO AND CANDY STORE DICE

Dice have been fascinating people and deciding fates for over 2,000 years. Even the language of dice echoes history. When Caesar made the critical decision to take his victorious army across the Rubicon against the edict of the Roman Senate, he took his retort from the lexicon of the dice player: "Iacta alea est." *The die is cast.*

Primitives all over the globe—the American Indian, the Aztec, and Maya, the South Sea Islander, the Eskimo, the African—have gambled with dice of many curious shapes and markings. Dice have been made from plum and peach stones; seeds; buffalo, caribou and moose bone; deer horn; pebbles; pottery; walnut shells; beaver and woodchuck teeth. In Greek and Roman times, most dice were made of bone or ivory; others were bronze, agate, rock crystal, onyx, jet, alabaster, marble, amber or porcelain.

Almost all modern dice are made of cellulose or some other plastic material. The standard die is marked with a number of small dots (called *spots*) from one to six. The spots are arranged in conventional patterns and placed in conventional relative locations. The spots on the opposite sides always total seven: one opposite six, two opposite five and three opposite four. When the visible vertical sides are two and three and the top side is one, six must be the bottom number while five and four must be on the opposite vertical sides. The combinations of the six spots (sides) plus the number of dice in play determine the mathematical probabilities.

In most games played with dice, the dice are thrown (rolled, flipped, shot, tossed or cast) from the hand or from a receptacle called a *dice cup* in such a way that they will turn at random. The spots that face upward when the dice come to rest are the deciding spots. The sum of the numbers on the top surfaces decides, according to the rules of the game being played, whether the thrower (called the *shooter*) wins, loses, continues to throw or loses possession of the dice.

There are two kinds of dice. *Perfect dice* or *casino dice*, made by hand and true to a tolerance of 1/5,000 inch (dice manufacturers inaccurately advertise perfect dice as true to a tolerance of 1/10,000 inch), are used to play casino Craps. Round-cornered imperfect dice, called *drugstore* or *candy-store* dice, are fabricated by machine and are generally used for social and board games.

Modern casino dice are sawed from extruded rods of cellulose. The spots are drilled approximately 17/1,000 inch into the faces of the die. Then the recesses are filled with a paint the same weight as the celluloid that has been drilled out. The dice are then buffed and polished and, since no recesses remain, are known as *flush-spot dice* or *bird's-eye spot dice*. Most casinos use red flush-spot dice which are transparent and come in sets of five. The standard size used in Nevada, the Caribbean, and most casinos the world over is .750 inch. The dice edges are generally either square and known as *razor edge* or slightly turned and known as *feather edge*. Casino dice usually carry a special monogram and coded serial number as a means of thwarting dice cheats. Perfect dice used in various other dice games range from a .250-inch cellulose or bone "peewee" die to an extra large .770-inch die. Perfect concave-spot dice, although still in use, are rarely seen in the best casinos. Besides drugstore, round-cornered dice, pyramidal, pentahedral and octahedral dice, with all sorts of face designs, have been used.

The three most popular forms of transparent spot dice in use in major casinos.

CONCAVE SPOT   BIRD'S EYE SPOT   FLUSH SPOT

John Scarne teaching Caribe Hilton Casino employees how to detect crooked dice. (Conrad Eiger)

Dice in their various forms are the oldest gambling instruments known to man, and countless games have been played with them. Craps, the most popular gambling house game, is played with two dice. In more social play, Poker Dice and Scarney 3000 are played with five dice; various counter and bar games, such as Twenty-Six, are played with ten dice. In Backgammon and hundreds of "board games," two or more dice are thrown to determine the moves.

MEN AND WOMEN DICE DEGENERATES

Although Bank Craps and Money Craps give the player a better shake for his money percentagewise than any other casino game, more money is lost at Craps than at all other casino games combined. I know a man, one of Nevada's top casino owners, who had saved a cool $6 million during his gambling career. He added another $8 million by selling his casino when he retired. Then, with plenty of time on his hands, he became a Bank Craps player, and in three short years of retirement lost all his fortune trying to beat the game on which he had made it. Casino owners and employees call compulsive Craps players who can't control their urge to gamble *dice degenerates*.

This man's story is not unique. Curiously, a great many casino owners and employees lose most of their gambling earnings at Bank or

Money Craps. One would think that people who earn fortunes in the gambling business would know better than to try to beat any casino banking game, but when it comes to Craps, with its fast action and big-money wagers, these characters lose all common sense, and many of them become suckers at their own game.

The fair sex has its quota of Craps degenerates, too. The most notable one I met was a 72-year-old widow known to Nevada casino operators as "Ma." I saw her last one day in Vegas in the mid-1950s when she entered the downtown Horseshoe Club and asked the owner if he would ante up his $300 Craps limit for her. "Ma," he said, "you can have any limit you want, but your maximum will be determined by the amount of your first bet." Ma didn't bat an eye. "I understand. My first wager is $10,000 on the front line."

She took her place at the table, began putting ten-grand bets on the layout, and within 30 minutes had won a cool $70,000. About a year later, after having lost more than $2 million, she disappeared from the Nevada casinos. The owner later told me that she was the fastest woman Craps degenerate he had ever seen and that as a bigtime bettor she held her own with the outstanding male high rollers.

I know of at least 50 players who have lost a million dollars or more at Craps, but I can name only a couple who have, in the long run, won more than $250,000—and they did it at either Money or Private Craps, where they were not bucking house percentages. Bigtime winners at Bank Craps over the long run are few and far between.

THE UNFINISHED CRAPS HAND

To my knowledge, the biggest sum of money lost by any casino operator in America at a single Bank Craps table in a one-night session was the $300,000 lost by the operators of the 86 Club in Miami, Florida, in late February 1947. Bigtime gamblers all over America still talk about the "unfinished hand" that night at the 86 Club's $1,000 maximum limit Bank Craps table.

The Craps table was crowded with about 30 bigtime gamblers and racketeers from all over the country who were vacationing in Florida, when, at precisely 2:00 A.M., the stickman chanted "Next shooter" as he pushed the five dice in front of an automobile dealer from Detroit. The shooter selected a pair of dice and, after all bets were placed, threw them across the elastic string stretched across the center of the table. What occurred then made Craps history. At 3:30 A.M., the same automobile dealer still held the dice when Charley Thomas and Jack Friedlander, the casino owners, walked over to the dice table and announced, "Gentlemen, that's all for tonight. The bank is broke." In that 1½ hours of Craps shooting, the Detroit car dealer had shot the owners of the 86 Club out of almost $300,000 in cash.

The shooter pleaded with Jack Friedlander to permit him to finish his hand, but Jack shrugged his shoulders and said, "Gentlemen, it will have to end as an unfinished hand," and it did. I was there, and since I knew that the casino carried a $500,000 nightly bankroll, I later asked Jack Friedlander his reason for stopping the game in the middle of a shot. He grinned. "John, after losing nearly $300,000 on that hot hand I figured that as soon as the shooter threw a miss-out all the players would quit. They had their bundle. All the money I could win back would be on that one miss-out—and who knows how many more point, proposition and place bets these characters were still likely to win if this hot hand continued?"

Despite this $300,000 loss, and after paying all expenses including the ice, which at that time in Florida was high, the operators of the 86 Club divided $1,200,000 in profits for their 11-week season.

Most high rollers or so-called smart gamblers prefer Craps to any other casino game because the percentage favoring the house is much less than at nearly all other casino games. These high rollers, however, lose considerably more at Bank Craps than they lose at any other casino game with a greater house percentage; as a rule they find it is just as impossible to beat the front line bet at Bank Craps with its 1.41% disadvantage as it is to beat a game with a much greater house P.C. against the player. As a matter of fact, a front line Craps player bucking the house percentage of only 1.41% is just as big a chump as the racetrack frequenter who bucks the track's favorable percentage of 12% to 20%. This doesn't sound right? I know. But there's a good reason.

The answer is that the major racetracks run only nine races each day, whereas hundreds of front line decisions are made at the Bank Craps table in the same period of time.

If you add the total house percentages you pay at a Craps table in the time it takes to run off nine races and compare this sum with the total percentages you pay for the privilege of betting a horse in each of the nine races, you will find that the smart Craps player is paying a bigger overall percentage than the horse player.

As my good friend Elmer West, one of Nevada's smartest gambling operators, once told me, "The only difference between bucking a game with a house percentage of one percent or less compared to bucking a game which has a much higher percentage is that the player bucking the bigger percentage goes broke much sooner."

The main reason why Craps has outdistanced all other games of chance, both in number of devotees and amount of money wagered, is that it offers the players more personal participation. In other casino games the player can only bet that an event will occur; he cannot bet that it will not occur. In Roulette, the croupier spins the ball and wheel, and the player can only bet that the ball will fall in a certain numbered space or in one of a certain group of numbers; he can't bet that the ball will *not* fall into a certain numbered space. In Craps, the players bet with or against the dice, and also have the opportunity of throwing the dice themselves. The thrill they get when they match their luck against the banker or other players is more personal than the one they get when they simply wait and hope that the Roulette ball will drop into their number.

BANK CRAPS, MONEY (OR OPEN) CRAPS, NEW YORK CRAPS, SCARNEY CRAPS AND PRIVATE CRAPS

Very few men have not played a game of Craps at some time or other. Women, however, seldom played Craps until the 1950s. The game was considered undignified before it appeared in Nevada casinos in the form of Bank Craps. My survey shows that today approximately 5 million women have become Craps players.

Let us look at the differences among the five modern variations of Craps: Private Craps, Bank Craps, New York Craps, Scarney Craps and Money (or Open) Craps.

Private Craps is a friendly social game which does not use a casino, Craps table or banker. The only requisites for Private Craps are two or more persons with cash in their pockets and a pair of dice. It can be played on a street corner, in a back alley, private club, army barracks, living room—anywhere the players have room in which to roll the dice.

Bank Craps is the version of the game found in Nevada casinos and other carpet joints throughout the United States, and in foreign countries where American tourists patronize casinos. Bank Craps is played on a specially constructed dice table which has a special betting layout depicting the types of bets permitted. Chips or checks are used instead of cash when wagers are placed on the layout. Players are not permitted to gamble against each other; all bets are made against the bank.

New York Craps is a version of Bank Craps found in most illegal gambling houses in the eastern part of the United States and in the legal casinos of the Bahamas, Yugoslavia and in England. The game is played on a dice table somewhat similar to a Bank Craps table in which place betting is prohibited and the house takes 5% of the amount wagered on the point numbers (4, 5, 6, 8, 9, 10).

Scarney Craps, a recent creation of the author, is a version of Bank Craps and New York Craps combined. The game is found in casinos in Europe, Curaçao, Aruba, St. Maarten, Turkey and South America. The game is played on a Bank Craps table.

Money (or Open) Craps is so called because, as the inveterate Craps player would say, it is an "open" game and played mostly with cash. It is played on a dice table, and there is a banker called the *book*. The game is found in most illegal sawdust joints and makeshift casinos. The rules permit the players to gamble with each other on the shooter's point number. Players, however, must place all center, flat, off and box-number bets with the book. When he bets the book, the player must pay a charge to him, usually 5% of the amount wagered. Seasoned gamblers, racket guys and other easy-money guys prefer Money Craps to Bank Craps.

ORIGIN AND HISTORY

Craps is of American Negro origin. Their colorful slang is still used in the game and dice are still called "African Dominoes." Around New Orleans, some time after 1800, the Negro tried his hand at the English game of Hazard, which the French sometimes called Craps. But the intricacy of the rules and betting odds of this game led him to simplify the playing procedure so greatly that he ended by inventing the present game of Private Craps.

Private Craps moved up the Mississippi and then out across the country, its habitat the steamboats, the river wharfs and docks, the cotton fields and the saloon. About 1890 the game appeared in the form of Bank Craps in a number of American carpet and sawdust joints but made little progress because the layout permitted only one-

Sixth-century painting on Greek vase shows Achilles and Ajax playing dice.

way action and the maximum limits (usually a top of $25) were very low. Players could only bet right on such layout spaces as win bets, come bets, field bets, and 6 and 8. Because of this one-way action, many gambling house operators used *six-ace flats*, crooked dice which gave a favorable percentage to the wrong bettor—in this case, the casino. Smart dice players, naturally, avoided these games.

The big banking casino games in those days was the card game Faro, originally known as Pharaoh or Pharoo, which had been played in France since the middle of the seventeenth century. Faro entered this country by way of New Orleans in the eighteenth century, and shortly after the Louisiana Purchase (1803) became the most widely played gambling-house game in the United States—a position it held until the game of Craps became a successful casino banking game in the early part of the twentieth century.

THE FIRST CRAPS BOOKMAKER

Because of its one-way action Bank Craps remained a small-time banking game until John H. Winn, a dicemaker by trade, decided to book the Craps game by permitting players to bet against him, either right or wrong, for a charge on each $5 bet made. This innovation made him the world's first Craps bookmaker. After several years of intensive searching for him throughout the United States, I finally located him in New York City early in 1944—many years after he had retired as a professional bookmaker—and heard his firsthand story of

Pre-Winn Bank Craps layout which was used at the turn of the century.

Scarne demonstrating dice moves to John H. Winn, inventor of the Bank Craps layout, in 1945.

how he transformed Private Craps into today's successful casino games of Bank Craps and Money (or Open) Craps.

In New York City, in 1907, he began to book the first Craps game—in a back alley near 14th Street and Broadway. He charged both right and wrong bettors a quarter for a $5 bet and 50¢ for a $10 bet. This improvement gave Winn plenty of business and a handsome profit, and other smart dice players, noticing this, began booking Craps games instead of playing. A couple of years later, hundreds of Craps bookies were operating in the principal cities of the United States. The innovation of allowing players to bet both ways demanded that operators use honest and perfect dice and practically eliminated crooked percentage dice in casino games.

THE ORIGIN OF VIGORISH

John Winn invented the Craps book, the quarter charge that developed into the 5% charge, and he is initially responsible for the games of Bank Craps and Money (or Open) Craps. Eventually, because the 5% charge brought in the money so dependably and was so strong, gamblers took the word *vigor*, added a syllable of jargon—as they often do when they would rather the layman couldn't follow their conversation—and called it *the vigorish*. Some gamblers later trimmed the word down to *vig*. Today both are used.

Shortly afterward, Winn also improved the banking layout of Bank Craps in much the same way. He drew a space on the layout "just a little piece off on one side," and lettered in the words *Don't Pass*. This was done in Philadelphia, to which Winn used to commute weekends, and the layout came to be famous as the "Philadelphia layout," the first Bank Craps layout to give the players an opportunity to bet the dice to lose. Winn also charged a quarter for a $5 bet and 50¢ for a $10 bet on the don't pass line.

Later, a gambler who remembered the *bar* on the zero and double zero in the early French-style Roulette, eliminated the direct charge on the don't pass line and substituted the ace-deuce bar (for explanation of the term "bar" see page 396) on the don't pass space. And, finally, when the wrong players' constant complaints that the ace-deuce appeared too often on the come-out became insistent, the bar on the two aces or on the two sixes was substituted and became standard, although there are still a good many gambling houses which, because their clientele is not *dice smart*, still carry the ace-deuce bar. The dice table at Monte Carlo is an example.

A few years later, chips were substituted for cash and, to add dignity, most Bank Craps layouts dropped Winn's 25¢ charge and paid off at less than the correct odds instead. Winn's original quarter charge still exists at Money and New York Craps and in a few Bank Craps games, and is known as the 5% charge. It was Winn's 25¢ charge for each $5 bet, no matter whether the player bet right or wrong, that eventually made Craps the biggest casino gambling game in the world.

By 1910 Bank and Open Craps had replaced Faro as America's number one casino game. There are today probably not more than a dozen Faro games doing business in the United States, and seven of them are in Nevada. Bank Craps is played today in all major American casinos and in many Caribbean and South American casinos. I was partly responsible for its introduction at Monte Carlo.

Since Bank Craps and Money (or Open) Craps are simply variations of Private Craps, the reader will more readily understand our later analysis if he first takes a look at the official rules for Private Craps.

SCARNE'S OFFICIAL RULES FOR PRIVATE CRAPS

Equipment

1. Two dice numbered from one to six in such a way that the spots on opposite sides add to seven.

2. A wall or backboard against which the dice are thrown.

Players

1. Any number may play.

2. The player throwing the dice is the shooter. Any player, by consent of the others, may start the game by becoming the shooter.

3. A new player may enter the game at any time, provided there is an opening in the circle. If no player objects at the time the new player takes his position, he becomes the shooter at his proper turn, even though he may take a position directly at the left of the shooter.

4. The dice pass around the circle of players to the left—clockwise.

5. Players may leave the game at any time (without regard to their wins or losses).

The Play

1. The dice are thrown and the two numbers, added together, that face skyward when the dice come to rest are the deciding numbers.

2. The shooter's first roll and each roll after a decision has been effected is a *come-out*.

3. If, on the come-out, the shooter throws a natural (7 or 11), it is a winning decision called a *pass;* a crap (2, 3 or 12) is a losing decision called a *miss-out*. If he throws a 4, 5, 6, 8, 9 or 10, that number becomes the shooter's *point* and he continues throwing until either:

(a) he throws his point again, which is a winning decision or pass, or

(b) he throws a SEVEN, which is a losing decision or miss-out.

4. When the shooter misses out on the point, the dice pass to the next player on his left, and it becomes his turn to shoot.

5. The shooter may, if he likes, pass the dice to the next player on completion of any decision without waiting to miss-out on the point.

6. Any player may, if he likes, refuse to shoot in his turn, and pass the dice to the next player.

7. When more than one pair of dice are employed, players may call for a box-up or change of dice at any time; the change takes place immediately after the next decision.

John Scarne explaining Scarney Dice layout to casino personnel at the Curaçao Hilton Hotel Casino where the layout was first introduced.

The Throw, or Roll

1. The shooter shakes the dice in his closed hand and must try to throw them so that both dice hit and rebound from the backboard.

2. If only one die hits the board, the roll counts, but the players may reprimand the shooter.

3. If this occurs a second time, the other players may designate someone else to complete the shooter's turn at throwing. If they wish, they may also bar him from shooting for the duration of the game.

4. If neither die hits the board, or if, when playing on a table or elevated surface, one or both dice fall off the playing surface, the roll is *no-dice:* it does not count and the dice must be thrown again.

5. If the dice hit any object or person after hitting the board, the roll counts; it is not no-dice.

6. If a die comes to rest cocked at an angle on a coin or any irregularity on the playing surface, and there is a difference of opinion as to which number faces skyward, a neutral player, or any player desig-

nated by common consent, or a bystander shall stand at the shooter's position and decide which number counts by stating which top surface of the die appears to be the skyward surface from that position.

7. If, after hitting the backboard, a die rolls out of sight under a bill or any other object on the playing surface, either a neutral player or a player designated by common consent or a bystander shall take extreme care in trying to ascertain the skyward number.

8. The practice of knocking or kicking dice aside on the roll and calling "Gate!" or "No dice!" (known as *gating*) is not permitted.

Betting

1. All bets must be made before the dice are thrown; they cannot be made while they are rolling.

2. **Right bet:** A wager that the dice will pass (win, either by making a natural on the come-out or by throwing a point number on the come-out and then repeating it before throwing a SEVEN). Players making right bets are *right bettors*.

3. **Wrong bet:** A wager that the dice don't pass. Players making wrong bets are *wrong bettors*.

View from above of a modern Las Vegas Bank Craps table during play at the Las Vegas Hilton Hotel Casino in Las Vegas, Nevada.

4. Proposition bets: This term is applied in Private Craps to any bet not a point or off-number bet or flat bet.

5. Center bet: Before the come-out the shooter may (but is not required to) bet that he will pass. Players who cover this wager by betting an equal amount against the shooter *fade* the shooter and are known as *faders*. These wagers, placed in the center of the playing surface, are center bets.

If only a part of the shooter's center bet is covered, the shooter may shoot for that amount or he may call the bet off by saying "No bet."

6. Side bet: Any bet not a center bet is placed at one side of the playing surface and is known as a side bet. The shooter may make any side bet including the flat bet.

7. Flat bet: A side bet that the dice pass, made by a right bettor before the come-out, is a *right flat bet*. A side bet that the dice don't pass made by a wrong bettor before the come-out is a *wrong flat bet*. Flat bets are the same as center bets except that the shooter and fader are not involved.

8. Point bet: After the shooter has thrown a point on the come-out, a side bet made by a right bettor that the shooter makes his point is a *right point bet*. A side bet by a wrong bettor that the shooter misses his point is a *wrong point bet*. The right bettor takes the odds on that point. The wrong bettor lays the odds on the point.

9. Any point or off-number bet may be called off by the bettors concerned before a decision is effected.

10. Come bet: A bet that the dice will pass (win), the next roll to be considered as a come-out roll.

Example: Suppose the shooter's point is FOUR and he bets that he comes. If he throws a SEVEN, he loses any bet he has made on the FOUR but wins the come bet because, on this bet, the roll is considered to be a come-out, and the SEVEN is a natural and wins.

If he throws an ELEVEN, the point bet is still undecided, but he wins the come bet.

If he throws a crap (2, 3 or 12), the point bet is still undecided, and he loses the come bet.

If he throws a FOUR, he wins the original point bet, but must continue throwing and make another FOUR before throwing a SEVEN in order to win the come bet. If he then throws any other number (such as 6), it counts as a second point and he continues throwing in an attempt to make either or both points before throwing a SEVEN.

11. Don't come bet: A bet that the dice don't pass (lose), the next roll to be considered as a come-out.

12. The hardway or gag bet: A bet that a specified even number (which may be either the shooter's point or an off number) will or will not be thrown the hard way with two like numbers; that is, a FOUR with double-two, SIX with double-three, EIGHT with double-four, TEN with double-five. If the number is thrown any other way, or a SEVEN is thrown, the bettor loses the hardway bet.

13. One-roll action or come-out bet: A bet that the shooter does or does not throw

(a) *a certain number any way.* Example: A bet that the shooter will or won't throw SEVEN with any of the combinations 1–6, 2–5, 3–4.

(b) *a certain number a certain way.* Example: A bet that the shooter will or won't throw SEVEN with one specific combination such as 3–4.

(c) *any one of a group of numbers on the next roll.* Example: A bet that the shooter will or won't throw any of the numbers in the group 2, 3 and 12 (craps), the group 4 and 10, the group 11 and 3, etc.

14. One-number bet: A bet that a certain number or group of numbers will or will not be thrown before another number.

15 Off-number bet: A bet made at odds that the shooter will or will not throw a specified number other than his point (any of the numbers 4, 5, 6, 8, 9 or 10) before throwing SEVEN.

PRIVATE CRAPS: HUSTLERS AND CHUMPS

For every Bank Craps game found in gambling establishments there are dozens of private games which take place daily, weekly, monthly or annually in homes, convention sites, factories, office buildings, hotel rooms, saloons, clubs and military installations all over the country, no matter what the law may say.

My gambling survey indicates that the amount of cash which changed hands in 1973 in these thousands of games was about $60 billion, or $10 billion less than the sum wagered at Bank Craps, Money (or Open) Craps, New York Craps or Scarney Craps.

Since the smart wrong bettor in the average Private Craps game enjoys a favorable advantage of about 2% over the sucker right bettor, I estimate that about 900,000 wrong bettors in America took 29,100,000 right or right-and-wrong bettors for about $1,200,000,000 in 1973.

The great majority of right bettors are plain chumps who accept incorrect odds from the strictly wrong bettors, the *Craps hustlers* (players who knowingly hustle a Craps game by offering right bettors wagers at less than the correct odds). A Craps hustler is half gambler and half cheat. He is the guy who won most of the $1,200,000,000 lost by the millions of chumps in the Private Craps games in 1973.

The casino extracts a house percentage by offering the players less than true odds on all Craps bets, in exchange for supplying a place in which to gamble. In the private game the hustler collects the same or an even greater percentage and supplies, at the most, a pair of dice. More often than not, it is the chumps themselves who supply the dice and the place to gamble. It's as screwy as all that.

A Craps hustler may be anyone: your friend, neighbor, co-worker, fellow club member, in fact anyone who knows more about Craps odds than you do. How does the hustler's extra knowledge of Craps pay off such handsome dividends? In the first place, the whole situation is a setup. In most private games there are three kinds of players. About two-thirds, or 66 out of every 100, are right bettors, or chumps. A little less than one-third, about 31, are right-and-wrong bettors, or half-chumps, who usually bet right when they are shooting and try to bet wrong on the other right player's roll. The remaining 3 out of 100 are strictly wrong bettors, hustlers, who always bet the dice to lose and pass the dice when it is their turn to shoot. Now and then—so you won't recognize them as wrong bettors—hustlers make a right bet, but the amount wagered is always small.

Scratch a consistent winner at your friendly private game and it is 97 to 3 that he's not a right bettor.

The consistent right bettor, or chump, must lose in the long run because the odds are stacked against him. Thousands of Craps hustlers in the country work in industrial plants and hustle the Craps games at noon. I knew one hustler who won $20,000 from his fellow workers during one year of lunch-hour Craps shooting.

There are more than 40 million Craps players in America, 5 million of whom are women, and most of them will accept any sucker bet offered them by Craps hustlers. The correct odds at Private Craps given in the following pages should be of particular interest to these people since a knowledge of the odds will enable them to graduate from the chump category.

There are about 900,000 dice hustlers in this country; about 80,000 of these are women, most of whom learned the business from their hustler or gambler husbands or boy friends. Some learned the trade by working as dice girls or shills in casinos. Others learned the hard way —by playing Craps in gambling houses, where their constant losses eventually taught them that anyone who has the odds in his favor must grind out a profit in any game.

I once knew a woman dice hustler who had a working knowledge of odds equal to that of any man. After working as a Craps dealer in Reno she turned to hustling Craps and preyed only on women players. Her particular angle was to rent a suite of rooms in a swanky resort hotel and then give a cocktail party to which she invited women guests staying at the hotel. Once the cocktail party was well under way, she and her shill would start a game, rolling the dice on the thickly carpeted floor. If any of the guests did not know how to play, Nina (as she called herself) gave them a fast lesson. The end result was always the same: She won all the folding money in sight simply by offering her guests sucker odds which were almost always accepted because the chumps knew no better. Nina told me that her Craps hustling for a winter season paid all her hotel expenses, the shill's salary, and netted her about five grand.

The novice Craps player must understand that Craps is primarily a mathematical game of numbers, and the only thing the hustler has which the inexperienced dice player doesn't is a knowledge of the correct odds. He simply offers his victim less than the correct odds.

Suppose you agree to take 9 1/11% the worst of it on every bet you make in a Private Craps game. This is the same as agreeing to accept $1 every time you win and to pay out $1.20 every time you lose. Anyone who bets in such a foolish manner often enough is a rank sucker, deserves exactly what he gets, and goes broke. These are the sort of sucker odds that the Craps hustlers offer and most players accept. Sometimes the chumps accept odds that are even worse. Here is another example of odds cheating in Private Craps. When a player accepts an even-money bet that the shooter will make his point when it is either a SIX or an EIGHT, he is cheating himself just as surely as if he were playing against *six-ace flats* (crooked dice). The proper odds against making SIX or EIGHT are 6 to 5, and yet most Craps shooters are perfectly content to accept even money on such a bet. They accept $1 for $1 instead of demanding the correct payoff price of $1.20 to their $1. Craps shooters who are unfamiliar with the correct odds accept almost any odds offered because it would embarrass them if they admitted out loud that they didn't know the correct odds. The man who claimed that ignorance is bliss was no gambler. In gambling, ignorance is fatal.

The payoff odds used in 999 out of every 1,000 Private Craps games are actually the gambling house payoff odds casinos use at Bank Craps when paying off right bettors; the payoff odds in Private Craps are permanently fixed against the guy who is either shooting or betting the dice to win. This is why "all right bettors die broke."

Players accept winning payoffs at less than the correct odds in a casino because this is the price charged for the use of the casino and its facilities, but any player who accepts such odds from a Craps hustler in a friendly game, which may even take place in his own home, is making a fool of himself. Any Craps player who studies the following text and then still accepts sucker bets in Private Craps games needs the services of a good psychiatrist. Here you will find everything there is to know about Craps odds.

The first step is to find out how many possible combinations of two numbers can be thrown with a pair of dice, what numbers these combinations form, and in how many ways each number can be formed. Elementary arithmetic supplies the answers. There are six numbers on each die. Multiply 6 × 6 and you get 36 possible combinations, or ways, in which the two numbers on a pair of dice can form the 11 numbers 2, 3, 4, 5, 6, 7, 8, 9, 10, 11 and 12. The table below shows these eleven numbers and the number of possible combinations that form each number.

COMBINATIONS OR WAYS

2 can be made in 1 way: 1–1
3 can be made in 2 ways: 1–2 2–1
4 can be made in 3 ways: 1–3 3–1 2–2
5 can be made in 4 ways: 1–4 4–1 2–3 3–2
6 can be made in 5 ways: 1–5 5–1 2–4 4–2 3–3
7 can be made in 6 ways: 1–6 6–1 2–5 5–2 3–4 4–3
8 can be made in 5 ways: 2–6 6–2 3–5 5–3 4–4
9 can be made in 4 ways: 3–6 6–3 4–5 5–4
10 can be made in 3 ways: 4–6 –6–4 5–5
11 can be made in 2 ways: 5–6 6–5
12 can be made in 1 way: 6–6

When we know that there are 36 ways of making these 11 numbers and also how many ways each individual number can be made, we can easily obtain the correct odds on all points and off-numbers. This is done simply by figuring the number of ways the *point* can be made as against the six combinations by which SEVEN can be made. The following chart gives the odds against passing or making the point. The correct odds are also shown in terms of money bets.

ODDS AGAINST PASSING ON THE POINT NUMBERS

The Point Numbers	Correct Odds	Odds in $ and ¢ Bets			
4 can be made in 3 ways, 7 in 6 ways	2 to 1	$.20 to $.10		$2.00 to $1.00	
5 can be made in 4 ways, 7 in 6 ways	3 to 2	.30	.20	1.50	1.00
6 can be made in 5 ways, 7 in 6 ways	6 to 5	.30	.25	1.20	1.00
8 can be made in 5 ways, 7 in 6 ways	6 to 5	.30	.25	1.20	1.00
9 can be made in 4 ways, 7 in 6 ways	3 to 2	.30	.20	1.50	1.00
10 can be made in 3 ways, 7 in 6 ways	2 to 1	.20	.10	2.00	1.00

The trick is to memorize these odds. If you find that they do not tally with those you have been taking, it's a sure sign you have been losing money in your dice playing to dice hustlers or sharpies who have been taking you for a sucker.

Most Craps players think that the shooter and fader have the same chance of winning and that the correct odds on a center or flat bet are 1 to 1, 50–50 or even money. In gambling, one thing you should never do is to take something for granted. Let's analyze this bet and find out the correct odds. We first find out how many of the throws made by the shooter will, in the long run, win, and how many will lose. If there are an equal number of each, it's an even-money bet. And if not— well, let's see.

If we calculate how many rolls out of the 36 possible combinations will win and how many will lose, we will complicate matters with fractions. We can avoid fractions by multiplying 36 rolls × 55 to get a lowest common multiple: 1,980 rolls.

Suppose that Joe Doe, a right bettor, throws the ivories 1,980 times; suppose he considers that each roll of the dice is a new come-out and that it results in a decision; and suppose that each of the 11 numbers is thrown exactly as often as probability predicts it will appear in the long run.

Since SEVEN (natural) can be made in 6 ways out of the total 36, it will be thrown 6/36 of the 1,980 rolls, and Joe will win 330 times. ELEVEN (natural) can be made in 2 ways out of 36 and will be thrown 2/36 of the 1,980 rolls, winning 110 times.

The point FOUR can be made in 3 ways out of 36 and will be thrown 3/36 of the 1,980, or 165 times. But, since SEVEN, which now loses, will be thrown 6 times for every 3 times that FOUR is thrown, Joe will miss the point twice for every time that he makes it. Since he only passes 1 out of 3 times, he will win only ⅓ of the 165 rolls, or 55 rolls.

Since TEN can also be made 3 ways, it will also win 55 rolls.

The point FIVE can be made 4 ways out of 36 and will be thrown 4/36 of 1,980 rolls, or 220 times. Since SEVEN will be thrown 6 times for every 4 times that FIVE is thrown, Joe will win 4/10 of the 220 rolls, or 88 rolls.

Since NINE can also be made 4 ways, it will also win 88 rolls.

SIX can be made 5 ways and will be thrown 5/36 of 1,980 rolls, or 275 rolls. Since SEVEN will be thrown 6 times for every 5 times that SIX is thrown, SIX will win 5/11 of the 275 rolls, or 125 rolls.

Since EIGHT is also made 5 ways, it will also win 125 rolls.

If we put these figures in a column and add up the winning rolls, we get 976, as shown in the table on the following page.

When Joe subtracts his 976 winning rolls from his total of 1,980 rolls he finds that he has lost 1,004 rolls. The fader has an advantage of 1,004 minus 976, or 28 rolls. That is his advantage or edge, and it is Joe's disadvantage.

SHOOTER'S AND FADER'S CHANCES OF WINNING

	Times Thrown	*Winning Rolls*
Natural 7	330	330
Natural 11	110	110
Craps 2, 3, 12	220	—
Point 4	165	55
" 10	165	55
" 5	220	88
" 9	220	88
" 6	275	125
" 8	275	125
Totals	1,980	976

Figure it in percentage by dividing 976 by 1,980, and we find that the shooter, or the right bettor before the come-out, has a 49 29/99% chance of winning. The fader or wrong bettor has a 50 70/99% chance. The shooter's, or right bettor's, disadvantage is the difference of 1 41/99%, which expressed decimally is a percentage of 1.414 plus.

There isn't much that can be done to equalize this bet to make the shooter's and fader's chances exactly 50–50. The fader would have to lay odds of $1.0286 to the shooter's $1. Since this would require 1/100¢ pieces, and since the U.S. Treasury is not likely to go to the trouble of minting such coins just to even up the chances for shooters and faders, it will have to continue being played as an even-money bet. It would just about even things up if everyone would shoot the dice at his turn of play and each player wagered an equal amount when shooting, but this isn't going to happen either.

Whether to shoot money in the center is a decision each player will have to make for himself. If you do shoot money in the center, always insist on the correct odds on all points if you want to stay out of the sucker class. Again, a word of caution. If you don't know the correct odds on all the points by heart and cannot rattle them off as quickly as you can your own telephone number, you should either stay away from Craps and play some game you know something about, or take time out right now and memorize the odds against passing.

Since many one-roll action or come-out bets are often made at Private Craps, and dice hustlers also constantly offer Bank Craps odds on these wagers, you also need to know the correct odds on all the most common one-roll action bets. The odds for each one-roll action bet can easily be calculated by referring to the *Combinations or Ways* table (page 277) and by following the mathematical procedure used in the example below.

Example: Since ELEVEN can be made in 2 ways, its probability is 2 in 36, or 2/36. There are 34 chances that some other number will be thrown, and the odds against throwing ELEVEN in one roll are 34 to 2, or 17 to 1.

Here are all the most common one-roll actions odds with each odds figure also translated into terms of dollars and cents.

ODDS ON ONE-ROLL ACTION OR COME-OUT BETS

Numbers	Correct Odds	Odds in $ and ¢ Bets	
A given pair	35 to 1	$1.75 to .05	$35.00 to $1.00
11	17 to 1	.85 to .05	17.00 to 1.00
Any crap	8 to 1		
5	8 to 1	.40 to .05	8.00 to 1.00
9	8 to 1		
4	11 to 1	.55 to .05	11.00 to 1.00
10	11 to 1		
6	6 1/5 to 1	.31 to .05	6.20 to 1.00
8	6 1/5 to 1		
Any 7	5 to 1	.25 to .05	5.00 to 1.00
1–2 (3)	17 to 1		
3–4 (7)	17 to 1	.85 to .05	17.00 to 1.00
5–2 (7)	17 to 1		
6–1 (7)	17 to 1		

Even more common than one-roll action bets is the wager that one of the even point or off numbers (4, 6, 8, 10) will or will not be made the *hardway* or with the *gag*.

ODDS AGAINST PASSING THE HARDWAY

The Point and Off Numbers	Correct Odds	Odds in $ and ¢ Bets	
4 can be made with 2–2 in 1 way	8 to 1	$.40 to .05	$ 8.00 to $1.00
10 can be made with 5–5 in 1 way	8 to 1	.40 to .05	8.00 to 1.00
6 can be made with 3–3 in 1 way	10 to 1	.50 to .05	10.00 to 1.00
8 can be made with 4–4 in 1 way	10 to 1	.50 to .05	10.00 to 1.00

You are probably all set to give us an argument on this one. Why, since FOUR can be made in only 1 way with 2–2, and since SIX can be made in only 1 way with 3–3, are the odds 8 to 1 on number FOUR and 10 to 1 on number SIX?

Most of the Craps players I have met believe that it is just as easy to make a FOUR the hard way with 2–2 as it is to make SIX the hardway with 3–3. They believe the same when shooting for a TEN or EIGHT the hardway.

The fallacy in the average player's reasoning is that when he makes the statement that it is just as easy to throw double-threes and double-fours as it is to throw double-twos and double-fives, he seems to forget that he is talking about the hardway.

The odds against throwing 3–3, 4–4, 2–2 or 5–5 on the come-out roll are the same—35 to 1. But the odds against making a point or off number with those combinations is something else again.

Suppose your point is Four and you bet that you can make it the hardway, with 2–2. There are, according to our *Combinations and Ways* table, 3 ways to make a Four, with 2–2, 1–3 and 3–1. If either 1–3 or 3–1 is thrown, you have made your point, but, since you didn't make it the hardway, you lose the bet. You have 1 way to win and 2 ways to lose. In addition, you can also lose if you seven out, and since there are 6 ways to make Seven, there are altogether 8 ways you can lose, as against 1 way in which you can win. Consequently the odds are 8 to 1. The same reasoning also applies to making the point Ten with 5–5.

Let's try the same process with the points Six and Eight. Six, according to the *Combinations or Ways* table, can be made in 5 ways. Betting on the Six the hardway means that only 1 of these ways (3–3) wins and the other 4 lose. Add the 6 losing ways that Seven can be made, and you have 10 ways to lose against 1 way to win. The odds, therefore, strange as it may seem to players who don't think logically, are 10 to 1. The same reasoning applies to making Eight with 4–4.

If the Craps player takes the time to memorize the correct Craps odds listed in the foregoing text, and only accepts bets at correct odds, his chances of winning in any private Craps game will be greatly increased and he will no longer be easy prey for the Craps hustler. That is, provided the dice cheat doesn't use phony dice. For information that will help protect you against crooked dice, see page 326.

BANK CRAPS LAS VEGAS STYLE

Bank Craps is the style of Craps played in all Nevada casinos. Money (or Open) Craps is barred by Nevada state law. Bank Craps is the style of Craps favored by the ladies and undoubtedly is responsible for the fact that there are now 5 million women Craps shooters. If you took time out to clock the number of women shooting Craps in the plush casinos on the Las Vegas Strip for a full evening, your clocking would show that about 1 out of every 8 Craps shooters is a woman. You'd get the same clocking results in the plush casinos in the Caribbean islands, at Monte Carlo, and wherever legally operated carpet joints are found.

The maximum betting limits at Bank Craps vary throughout the country. The usual top limits in Nevada casinos are $500 on the pass and don't pass line, and $500 on the place numbers. Some Nevada casinos have a Bank Craps maximum limit as low as $25. The most popular Bank Craps limits in legally and illegally operated casinos in America are $20, $25, $50, $100, $200, $300 or $500, and there are a few illegally operated Bank Craps tables catering to seasoned gamblers and racketeers which have $1,000 and $2,000 maximum limits. Many top Nevada casinos will up their $500 maximum to as high as $2,000 at the request of an outstanding bigtime Craps player.

Betting limits on proposition bets such as the come-out bets and hardways are usually about ⅓ of the table's maximum betting limit. Example: At a $500 limit table the betting limits on the proposition bets (the two aces, two sixes, eleven, all craps, all sevens and the hardway bets) usually range from $50 to $200. At a $300 limit game the proposition bet limits range from $25 to $100. Occasionally a Bank Craps operator will permit a player to bet the usual maximum betting limit on each of the come-out or hardway bets. A player placing a $500 bet on the two sixes coming out and winning would receive a return of $15,000, a figure no casino manager likes to lose on a one-roll bet.

There is little difference between Bank Craps and Private Craps as far as the rules of the game are concerned. The big difference lies in the fact that Bank Craps players cannot bet among themselves; all bets must be placed on the spaces of the Craps layout and made against the bank. Hence the name Bank Craps. Another major difference between Bank Craps and Private Craps is that each bet made at Bank Craps has a percentage in favor of the bank. Bank Craps also has many bets on the layout which are not often made in Private Craps.

Bank Craps is usually played with Craps checks or chips instead of cash, although the Nevada casinos use silver dollars instead of dollar-valued checks. Craps checks in most luxury casinos range in value as follows: $1, $5, $25 and $100 checks. Some sawdust joints deal in dime and quarter chips.

Chips have been used instead of cash in European casinos for centuries. The reasons are obvious: (1) Since each casino gaming table is supplied with thousands of dollars worth of redeemable chips, the casino needs a much smaller bankroll to operate. I know of one casino in the Caribbean which uses $1 million worth of chips nightly, yet its cash bankroll is only about $50,000. (2) Chips in their varied colors make a fine background and make the dealer's job much easier and faster. The possibilities of theft by both dealers and players are minimized because chips are worthless unless they can be cashed.

Bank Craps today is played on a regulation Craps table about the size of a standard pool or billiard table. The first Craps tables actually were billiard tables, and the layout was drawn on the green cloth surface with chalk. A movable wooden rail, about 1 inch thick and 8 inches high, was placed around the outside edges of the table, forming a rectangular enclosure. This served as a backboard and also kept the dice from rolling off the table. The wooden rail was easy to remove, and the Craps table could be quickly converted back to an innocent billiard table in the event of a police raid.

Modern dice tables have grooves on the top edges of the rails in which the players can place their chips during play so that they do not clutter up the playing surface. The inside of the surrounding rail is lined with sponge rubber embossed in various patterns to help ensure that the dice rebound in a random manner. Casino operators, well aware that there are nimble-fingered players who have spent many hours mastering the art of making honest dice roll in a predetermined manner, insist that the shooter throw the cubes so that they strike the rubber-covered backboard before coming to a stop. The rail opposite to the boxmen's seating position is fitted with a 9 inch by 6 foot mirror. This is a protection device to help spot crooked misspotted dice that a cheat may have introduced into the game. The mirror permits the boxmen to see the five sides of each die while it's resting on the table layout. On double-end tables, with two Craps layouts, one at each end, and two dealers working, this is not practical, so a string is stretched across the table's center on the cloth. The shooter must throw the pair of dice out and over the string so that they roll before coming to a stop. In most controlled dice shots the dice must hit the table soon after leaving the shooter's hand, and the string serves as a partial protection against such shots. Some spin-and-slide experts can bounce the dice over the string and still bring up the numbers they want, but smart casino operators insist that dice must roll, not merely slide and spin, after they hit the table surface. In most Nevada casinos the string is not used, but the shooter must throw the dice past the spot where the stickman is standing; and at the slightest sign of a controlled shot, the boxman shouts, "Hit the boards!"

The five men required to run a dice table are three dealers and two boxmen. The boxmen sit between the two dealers at the table's center and are in charge. Their duty is to keep their eyes on everything—dice, money, chips, players and dealers. The dealers who stand by the side of the boxmen, after each dice decision, take in the losses and pay off the winners. The third dealer, who stands opposite the boxmen, is in charge of the dice. He calls out the dice numbers as they are thrown and helps with the proposition bets when placed. He is often referred to as the stickman because he retrieves the dice after each roll with a curved stick and holds them until all previous bets have been settled and new bets are made, whereupon he pushes the dice toward the shooter with the stick.

BANK CRAPS LAYOUTS

The Craps layout, the design printed on the green baize covering the playing surface of the table, is divided into spaces of different shapes and sizes representing different bets. The layouts shown here are common ones, and although you may see others differently shaped, the actual difference is small. Some layouts carry wagers that others don't have; some differ more or less in the odds offered. This last variation depends directly upon the players who patronize the particular game, how much they know about odds, and how much of a house P.C. they will stand to buck. The smarter the patronage, the closer the odds offered approach the correct ones; the less they know, the larger the house percentage.

All Craps layouts are clever exercises in mathematical strategy designed to give the player an exciting run for his money and, at the same time, give the bank a mathematical edge on every bet on the layout.

The present crop of Bank Craps players know little or nothing about the house percentages they are fighting, and, as in Private Craps, this lack of knowledge puts them in the sucker category. The following odds and percentages will show you how you can avoid throwing your money away at the Craps table, especially on sucker bets.

Before we continue with our analysis of Bank Craps odds and percentages, you must remember that if you become a Bank Craps degenerate you will eventually lose, no matter how intelligently you bet your dough on the layout. It makes no difference in the long run whether you make bets having only .832% against you, or whether you place bets on the all sevens, which has a big 16⅔% against you. In the long run the bank's percentage will take both the smart Craps player and the dub, the only difference being that the dub loses his shirt much sooner.

But if you play Bank Craps only occasionally, perhaps during your vacation in Nevada or the Caribbean islands, and want to give yourself the best chance to win, give the following text some study.

The house P.C. against the player at most Bank Craps tables can be as low as .832%, provided the player knows which bets to make and which to avoid. The percentages against the bettor on Bank Craps wagers vary from bet to bet.

The difference between the smart gambler and the dub at Bank Craps is simply a knowledge of percentages. I can easily separate the dubs from the expert Craps players by noting on what layout spaces they place their bets. The player must realize that the smaller the per-

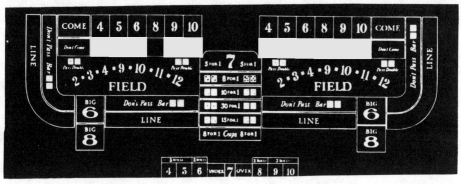

Caribbean Double Side Dealer.

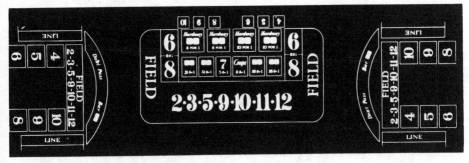

English Double-End Craps Layout.

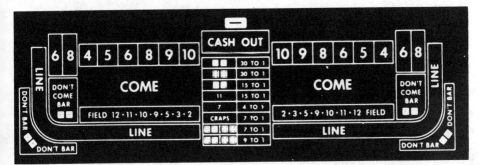

Puerto Rican Side Dealer.

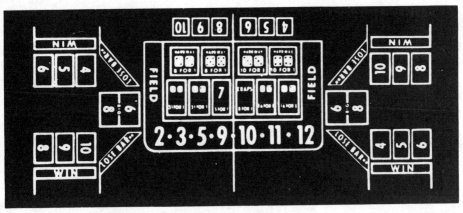

Bahamas style Double-End New York Craps Layout.

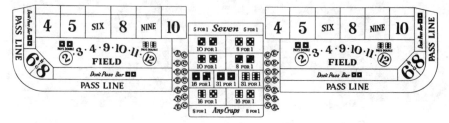

The Scarney Dice Bank Craps layout. The center portion shows the letters C-E which stand for Crap and Eleven. This layout lacks a Come and Don't Come space but pays better odds on most proposition bets.

centage he bucks the better are his chances of winning. Give yourself the best break possible by studying the bets, odds and percentages in the following text.

BANK CRAPS BETS

Since layouts vary somewhat as to the bets permitted, odds offered and percentages against the player, the following analysis will cover all the Common Bank Craps bets without regard to any layout.

Win Line, Do or Pass Line

This is called the *front line* by inveterate gamblers and casino personnel. The players who want to bet the bank that the shooter will win place their chip or chips before the come-out on the long narrow space of the layout marked with any of the following words: WIN LINE, PASS, DO or PASS LINE. The bank pays off at even money (1 to 1) and enjoys the fader's favorable percentage in a private game of 1.414%, or about 7¢ on a $5 wager. This is the most common bet at Bank Craps, and one

The Las Vegas Double Side dealer Bank Craps layout. The center portion shows the letters C-E. They stand for Crap and Eleven.

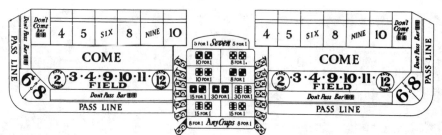

of the best. But most players are attracted by other bets that pay off at bigger odds, and because they don't know percentages they don't know they are bucking larger house percentages.

Lose, Don't or Don't Pass Line

This is commonly called the *back line*. This bet is favored by smart dice players, but few other players take this action. Because this wager has a standoff they think erroneously that it has a high house percentage. To illustrate: The player who wants to bet the shooter to lose before the come-out places his bet on the layout space marked either DON'T PASS, LOSE or DON'T. In a private game this bet would give the player a favorable P.C. of 1.414% over the shooter or right bettor. But no bank could stay in business long taking 1.414% the worst of it. It resorts, therefore, to a simple tactical maneuver; it bars either the two sixes or the two aces on the come-out roll. When the barred combination appears on that roll, it is a standoff; there is no action for the wrong bettor. In a private game the fader or wrong bettor would have won the bet, but at the Bank Craps table it is no decision for the wrong bettor only.

In order to see what this means to the bank, suppose we place a $5 bet on the win line and a $5 bet on the lose line. The shooter can be expected to throw two sixes an average of once out of every 36 come-out throws, and whenever this happens, the bank sweeps the $5 off the win line while the $5 on the lose line must remain there until a new decision is effected. If the bank had not barred the two sixes, it would have broken even. Barring the two sixes has earned it $5. The same, of course, holds true for the bar on the two aces.

How much does this cut down that 1.414% advantage? Reference to the *Shooter's and Fader's Chances of Winning* table (page 279) reminds us that the right bettor can expect to win 976 rolls and lose 1,004 out of a total of 1,980. One thirty-sixth of those 1,004 losing rolls, or 55 rolls, are double-sixes. (The same is true of double-aces.) When the bank counts those 55 rolls as standoff or neutral rolls, it reduces the 1,004 losing rolls by 55 and stands to win 976 rolls and lose only 949.

The bank thus has a 50 54/77% chance of winning as against the wrong player's 49 23/77% chance. Of the 1,925 deciding rolls, there are 27 more rolls that win for the bank than for the wrong player, an advantage of 1 31/77% or a P.C. of *1.402%, which is about 7¢ on a $5 wager.* If you choose to count the 55 ties as trials, the house edge is 27/1980 = .01364 or 1.364%. However, I'll stick with my figure of 1.402%.

The stand-off on the two sixes has not only wiped out the 1.414% advantage which the wrong bettor ordinarily has, but has replaced it with a 1.402% disadvantage! This is so nearly the same that for all practical purposes the bank has just as much edge in its favor, no matter whether the players bet the dice to win or lose.

The Ace-Deuce Standoff

The first Bank Craps games barred ace-deuce insted of double-sixes or double-aces, and some banks still do. Some players think it doesn't make too much difference. And those who do try to figure it out usually decide that since ace-deuce can be made in two ways, and a double-six in one way, ace-deuce must be twice as strong. This may sound good, but the logic is bad and the answer is wrong. The bank won't argue the matter with you, however; it's the customers with the wrong answers who make their business a profitable one.

The correct computation is made as follows: 1,004 losing rolls for the bank which is acting as a right bettor, minus 110 standoff rolls, leaves 894 rolls that lose for the bank as against 976 that win for the bank. The bank's edge is 82 rolls or 4 72/187%. Decimally this is *4.385% or about 22¢ on a $5 wager.*

Consequently, when the bank bars ace-deuce, instead of double-six or double-ace, the P.C. in its favor is not merely doubled, as so many players think; it has more than tripled! And when the ace-deuce is barred, it is a tip-off that the bank is either not patronized by smart-money wrong bettors or doesn't care for that kind of action and is trying to discourage it.

Come and Don't Come Bets

The player who wishes to bet the come or don't come places his bet on the spaces of the layout marked "Come" or "Don't Come." The P.C. on these wagers are the same as on the pass and don't pass bets, which is *1.414% or about 7¢ on a $5 wager made on the come, and 1.402% or about 7¢ on a $5 wager made on the don't come.*

Big Six and Big Eight

The player who places his bet on the spaces of the layout marked "Big Six" or "Big Eight" is wagering that the number will be thrown before a SEVEN. He can put his money on that space at any time. The bank pays even money, and most players labor under the impression that it is an even-money bet. The SIX and EIGHT spaces on most layouts are usually made large and are positioned where the players can reach them easily. Why any player should think the bank would emphasize a bet which gives the house no percentage at all is a mystery.

A famous syndicated sports columnist once offered to bet me that SIXES and EIGHTS are thrown just as often as SEVENS. His argument was the common one that each number can be made in three ways (the SIX with 1–5, 2–4, 3–3, the Eight with 2–6, 3–5, 4–4, and the Seven with 1–6, 2–5, 3–4). He deduced from this that Six and Eight have the same chance of being thrown as does Seven and that the correct odds must therefore be 1 to 1, or even money.

What the columnist persisted in overlooking was that the smart-money players who never bet the big six or the big eight would, if his theory were correct, concentrate entirely on those bets. Eventually other players would follow suit and, in the long run, instead of show-ing a profit, the bank would merely break even on the betting and have nothing in the cashboxes with which to pay operating, maintenance and other costs. Since the bank is a business proposition and the operator is not running it for the thrill of gambling, this just doesn't make sense. The very fact that the Six and Eight spaces are made large and/or convenient to entice bets should be sufficient proof that the Six and Eight can't possibly be even-money bets.

We know from our *Combinations and Ways* and our *Odds* tables (see page 277) that since either Six or Eight can be made five ways and Seven in six ways, the real odds are 6 to 5 and that the bank should pay off at $1.20 to each $1 wagered. The bank's advantage is 9 1/11%, which amounts to about 45¢ on a $5 bet.

The Six and Eight spaces on most layouts have grown large and come to be known as the big six and big eight not because they are the best bets on the layout, but because the bank has such a big edge. They are strictly sucker bets.

Take a quick look, for instance, at what happens to the player who puts $1 on one of these spaces and wins five times, letting his money ride. His $1 grows and becomes $2, $4, $8, $16 and finally $32. He takes this down and is more than pleased with $31 profit. But what has actual happened is that his lack of odds knowledge cost the player about $19.54. Want to prove it? Okay. For a bet on the big six at cor-rect odds of 6 to 5, the bank should have paid off $1.20 on the first $1 wager. Then, when the bettor let the whole $2.20 ride, he would, at odds of 6 to 5, have won $2.64 on the second pass and so on. In table form, what happened to him looks like this:

At the Even Money Odds Offered	If the Bank Had Paid Correct Odds
He bets $ 1 and wins $ 1	He bets $ 1.00 and wins $ 1.20
He bets $ 2 and wins $ 2	He bets $ 2.20 and wins $ 2.64
He bets $ 4 and wins $ 4	He bets $ 4.84 and wins $ 5.808
He bets $ 8 and wins $ 8	He bets $10.648 and wins $12.7776
He bets $16 and wins $16	He bets $23.4256 and wins $28.11072
He takes down $32	He takes down $51.53632
His net profit: $31	His net profit: $50.53632

The player won $31 from the bank, but the bank paid him $19.53632 less than it would have had to pay at correct odds.

If you think that $19.54 is merely a paper saving and has not actually earned the bank anything in hard cash, look at it this way. The correct odds are 6 to 5, and the bank that pays even money will, in the long run, collect 6 units for every 5 units that it pays out. The player who continues to place bets of the same amount on the big six or big eight can, consequently, expect to lose the amount of his bet to the bank every 11 decisions.

With these facts staring him in the face, a consistent player of the big six and big eight should not need a crystal ball to dope out whether he will wind up a winner or loser in the long run. If, on some particular evening, he should as much as break even, he should realize that he has been enjoying an exceptional run of luck—luck that, given half a chance, would have won him real money!

Field Bets

Most of the women Craps players whom I have observed playing Bank Craps are suckers for field bets. The Craps stickman, at the sight of a woman player, begins to sell the field bets by chanting constantly during the game, "Place your bet on the field." "Nine, that's a field number." "Ten, another field number." When she hesitates he adds obligingly that the field has seven winning numbers and only four losing numbers. After this pitch, she usually begins betting the field.

The field usually bears the numbers 2, 3, 4, 9, 10, 11 and 12. When the player puts her bet on the space of the layout marked "Field," she is betting that one of the group of seven numbers listed there will be thrown on the next roll. The bank pays even money. Since the field shows seven numbers, and there are only four (5, 6, 7 and 8) which can make her lose, the non-thinker figures that her chances are excellent. She may even believe that she has the best of it or, at the very least, an even chance. But appearances are nearly always deceptive, especially in casino games.

If we add together all the ways in which the winning and losing numbers can be thrown, we find that the field numbers can be made in only 16 ways as against 20 ways for the losing numbers. The bank, consequently, has an advantage of 4 rolls out of 36, which in percentage is 4/36 of 100 or 11 1/9%—about 56¢ on a $5 bet.

When the bank pays double on the 2 and 12, as many of them do, the bank's advantage is reduced to 5 5/19%. And here one of the strangest percentage problems in Bank Craps pops up. Some smart casino operators will tell you that the bank's advantage is 5 5/19%, and others that the player's disadvantage is 5 5/9%. Some of them argue for hours over their differences of opinion, but the curious thing is that the argument is unnecessary because both of them are right!

The discrepancy is explained by the fact that they are arguing, not about the same problem, but about two slightly different problems, with two different answers. This fact—which, to my knowledge, no dealer or operator ever realized prior to its first publication in 1945 in *Scarne on Dice*—and the analysis of both problems given below, should clear up the matter and settle the arguments at last.

Suppose that the player and bank each cover the 36 possible field combinations with dollar bets. The player's wagers will total $36 but the bank's wagers, because it puts an extra dollar on the 2 and 12 that are circled for a double payoff, will total $38.

If the dice fall exactly according to probabilities, all 36 different combinations being thrown in 36 successive rolls, the bank wins 20 bets for a total of $40 and makes a profit of $2. The player wins 16 bets, 14 of which have $2 riding and the 2 and 12 pay $3 each. The player therefore takes down $34 and is short $2.

Since the bank wagered $38 and made a profit of $2, its favorable percentage is 2 divided by 38 or 5 5/19%.

The player, on the other hand, wagered $36 and lost $2. His percentage of loss, or his disadvantage, is 2 divided by 36 or 5 5/9%.

We have two problems rather than one because the bank and player wager different amounts.

Some banks pay 3 to 1 on double-aces, which supplies the same P.C. as paying double on both 2 and 12. Other layouts are made with a 5 in place of the 4, so that the field bears the numbers 2, 3, 5, 9, 10, 11 and 12. This gives the bank 19 chances against the player's 17, and the bank's edge is 5 5/9%. Some banks also pay double on two aces, others pay 3 to 2 on double-aces and double-sixes. In each case the bank's advantage is 2 26/37% and the player's disadvantage is 2 7/9%.

The lure of Craps is its fast action, but because wagers on the field are either won or lost *every time* the dice are rolled, the action is so fast and furious that most players can't take it. With a 5 5/19% or 5 5/9%, depending which way you prefer to figure it, grinding away and taking 1/18 of every bet the players make, the bank can expect to eat up the amount of the player's wagers in 18 rolls.

To show what this means in dollars and cents, let us assume that you place 180 field bets of $10 each, which you can do in an hour's time at many fast-action Craps tables, and assume that the laws of probability work according to expectation. This hour of field betting would cost you exactly $100.

If, after reading the above, you still insist on making field bets, I would suggest that you get yourself a "sponsor" who has plenty of do-re-mi, because, lady, you'll need it!

Hardway Bets

When the player places a bet on the layout marked "Hardway," he is betting a specified even point or off number (4, 6, 8, or 10) will be thrown with two double numbers (*hardway*) before it is made the *easy way* (any way other than a hardway), and before a SEVEN is made. Stickmen, when learning their trade, are taught to hustle players into betting the hardway. For that reason, stickmen are constantly chanting, "Folks, place your bets on the hardway. Get yourself 9 to 1 on the hard six or the hard eight," or "Get yourself 7 to 1 on the hard 4 or 10." The reason for this constant hustling of the hardway bets by stickmen is that the bank earns a percentage of 9 1/11%, 11 1/9% or, at times, 27 3/11% on such wagers. In spite of this, or because they know no better, most inexperienced Craps shooters go for the hardway bets because the payoff odds of 7 and 9 to 1 are tempting.

Hardway wagers can be found on all layouts, and, once again, most players believe that the odds offered by the bank are fair enough. Some even think they are getting correct odds, a lack of logic that almost classes as not thinking at all!

The layout not only does not offer correct odds on any of these bets, but in many cases offers even less than it appears to. This misdirection, as gamblers call it, is accomplished by wording the proposition so as to mislead players who forget that the two little words *for* and *to* do not mean the same thing. You will see how this deception operates in the following analysis of the hardway wagers.

Four the hardway: There are three ways to make a FOUR and 6 ways to make a SEVEN. But, since the player wins only 1 way (by a throw of 2–2) and loses 8 ways, the correct odds are 8 to 1.

Most banks offer 7 to 1 on this bet. Its probability is 1 over the total number of ways that FOUR can win or lose, in this case, 1/9. This probability times 100 gives the percentage on one way: 1/9 of 100 is 11 1/9%. The bank that pays off at 7 to 1 when the correct odds are 8 to 1 thus gains the percentage on 1 way which is *11 1/9% or 56¢ on a $5 wager.* If it paid off at 6 to 1, it would gain the percentage on 2 ways or 22 2/9%.

Some banks do pay only 6 to 1 on FOUR the hardway, although it doesn't look that way. They simply offer to pay 7 *for* 1, and most players take that to mean 7 to 1 and never give it another thought. The difference is this: when paying off at 7 to 1, the bank gives you $7 *and* the $1 you bet. When paying off at 7 *for* 1, the bank pays you $7 but *keeps* the $1 you bet. It pays $7 for your $1. The bank is actually giving you odds of only 6 to 1 on what is really an 8 to 1 proposition! Other layouts try to create the impression that the bank is paying the correct odds of 8 to 1 by offering 8 for 1.

Ten the hardway: Since there are also 3 ways to make TEN, the bank's P.C. is the same as on the FOUR, for the same reasons.

Six the hardway: A SIX can be made 5 ways. One way only (3–3) wins, the other 4 ways lose, as do the 6 ways SEVEN can be made. Correct odds, therefore, are 10 to 1. Most banks pay off at 9 to 1 and thereby have an advantage of *9 1/11% or 45¢ on a $5 wager.* Other banks, without blinking, pay off 9 *for* 1, with an advantage of *18 2/11% or 91¢ on a $5 wager.*

Eight the hardway: An EIGHT can also be made 5 ways, and the bank's percentage is, therefore, the same as on the SIX, *9 1/11% or 18 2/11%.*

In tabular form, for easy reference:

HARDWAY BETS

Bet	Bank Pays	Correct Odds	Bank's Percentage	Bank's P.C. on $5 Bets
4 with 2–2 10 with 5–5	7 to 1	8 to 1	11 1/9%	$ .56+
6 with 3–3* 8 with 4–4*	9 to 1	10 to 1	9 1/11%	.45+
4 with 2–2 10 with 5–5	7 for 1	8 to 1	22 2/9%	1.11+
6 with 3–3 8 with 4–4	9 for 1	10 to 1	18 2/11%	.91+

* Some banks pay only 7 to 1 on the hardway SIX or EIGHT and have an advantage of 27 3/11%, or $1.36 on a $5 wager.

One-Roll Action or Come-out Bets

If you make a habit of betting on one-roll proposition bets such as those marked "Two Sixes," "Two Aces," "Eleven," "All Sevens" and "All Craps," you won't be able to stand the percentage pressure very long. Strange as it may seem, most so-called smart dice gamblers laugh at the field player for paying a big 5 5/9% for one-roll bets, then turn right around and bet $100 on the two sixes or the 11 on the come-out, taking a beating percentagewise of 13 8/9% or 11 1/9%, as the case may be!

The reason many Craps players are suckers for one-roll come-out bets is, again, the big payoff odds of 15 to 1 on the 11, and 30 to 1 on the two aces or two sixes. To show how foolish these bets are, let's assume that the player places a $1 bet on the two sixes for 360 consecutive come-out rolls, and that the theory of probability works exactly as expected: the two aces appear exactly 10 times out of the 360 rolls. Since the player is paid off at bank odds of 30 to 1, he gets back a total of $310, and he wagered $360—for a loss of $50. Imagine what the bank's earning power on the two sixes adds up to during the evening's play when a dozen or more players are wagering tens, twenties and fifties on this bet at the same time! And many players are not content to make one come-out bet at a time; instead, they make four or five.

Many so-called smart Craps players think they have the best of it when they make two wagers simultaneously in an attempt to insure one or the other. For example, a player places a bet on the win line and tries to protect it against a crap on the first roll by making a come-out bet on all craps. He hopes that if he loses one bet he may win the other, and thus cut down or cancel out his loss. Actually he stands to lose at least one of the bets, and maybe both. Or he may attempt to insure a lose bet after the come-out by taking odds on the point. Since every wager in Bank Craps must be considered as a separate and distinct wager, the only effect of insurance betting is simply to give the bank a P.C. on two bets rather than one. Instead of insuring himself against the loss, the player has merely increased the P.C. against himself!

On any of these one-roll or come-out bets, commonly called proposition bets by casino personnel, the player puts his bet on a specified number or numbers, betting that it will appear on the next roll. He can make the bet before any roll.

Two sixes in one roll: This one can be found on nearly every layout. Since the correct odds are 35 to 1 (see table, page 280), and since the bank pays 30 to 1, the bank has an edge of 5 in 36 or *13 8/9%, about 69¢ on a $5 wager.*

Two aces in one roll: Payoff odds and P.C. are the same as on the double-six (see above).

Other double numbers in one roll: Although it is not always shown on the layout, many banks will allow you to place come-out bets on other pairs of numbers. The payoff odds and P.C. are the same as on the two sixes.

Eleven in one roll: Correct odds are 17 to 1. Bank pays off 15 to 1 and has an edge of *11 1/9%, or about 56¢ on a $5 wager.*

Three in one roll: Odds are 17 to 1, payoff is 15 to 1, and the bank's P.C. is the same as on the 11.

All sevens in one roll: Odds are 5 to 1. Bank pays 4 to 1 and has an edge of *16⅔%, or about 83¢ on a $5 wager.*

Any crap (2, 3, 12) in one roll: Correct odds are 8 to 1, bank pays 7 to 1 and has an edge of *11 1/9%, or about 56¢ on a $5 wager.*

3–4, 5–2, 6–1 in one roll: Here number SEVEN must be thrown with the particular combination of numbers on which you place your money. Correct odds in each instance are 17 to 1. Bank pays off 15 to 1 and has an edge of *11 1/9%, or about 56¢ on a $5 wager.*

Horn, Santurce, Miami or Curaçao one-roll bet: Some casino layouts permit the player to make four one-roll bets (2–3–12–11) at the same time. The layout space that permits these one-roll bets is marked differently in various casinos. At Caribe Hilton casino in Puerto Rico it is marked "Santurce"; in the casinos of Curaçao, it is marked "Miami" or "Curaçao," while in some Nevada casinos it is known as the *horn bet.* For instance, in Puerto Rico, when you wish to place a one-roll Santurce bet, you hand the stickman a $5 chip (or a multiple bet of $5) and call *Santurce*—which means you are betting one unit on 2, one unit on 3, one unit on 12 and two units on 11. The one-roll pay-off odds are the same as one-roll come bets: 15 to 1 or 15 for 1 on the 3 and 11, and 30 to 1 or 30 for 1 on the 2 or 12.

BANK'S PERCENTAGE ON THE STANDARD ONE-ROLL
ACTION OR COME-OUT BETS

Bet	Bank Pays	Correct Odds	Bank's P.C.	Bank's P.C. on $5 Wager
Two sixes (6–6) Two aces (1–1)	30 to 1	35 to 1	13 8/9%	$.69
Eleven (6–5) Three (1–2)	15 to 1	17 to 1	11 1/9%	.56
All sevens (7)	4 to 1	5 to 1	16 2/3%	.83
Any crap (2, 3 or 12)	7 to 1	8 to 1	11 1/9%	.56
7 with 3–4 7 with 2–5 7 with 6–1	15 to 1	17 to 1	11 1/9%	.56

Nevada layouts increase their percentage take by listing their odds payoff with the word "for" instead of "to." Their percentages are as follows:

Bet	Bank Pays	Correct Odds	Bank's P.C.	Bank's P.C. on $5 Wager
Two sixes (6–6) } Two aces (1–1) }	30 for 1	35 to 1	16 2/3%	$.83
Eleven (6–5) } Three (1–2) }	15 for 1	17 to 1	16 2/3%	.83
All sevens (7)	5 for 1	5 to 1	16 2/3%	.83
Any crap (2, 3, 12)	8 for 1	8 to 1	11 1/9%	.56
7 with 3–4 } 7 with 2–5 } 7 with 6–1 }	15 for 1	17 to 1	16 2/3%	.83

The following one-roll action bets are listed because some smaller banks carry proposition bets on their layouts and include all possible one-roll bets:

Bet	Bank Pays	Correct Odds	Bank's P.C.	Bank's P.C. on $5 Wager
4 in one roll } 10 in one roll }	9 to 1	11 to 1	16 2/3%	$.83
6 in one roll } 8 in one roll }	5 to 1	6 1/5 to 1	16 2/3%	.83
5 in one roll } 9 in one roll }	7 to 1	8 to 1	11 1/9%	.56

The actual figures for the bank's P.C. on a $5 bet are fractional and have been computed here to the nearest cent.

Place or box number bets are counterparts of Private Craps bets such as laying and taking the odds on a point or off number. Most high rollers favor this type of betting and often will take or lay the odds on the six place bets (4, 5, 6, 8, 9, 10) and let the winnings ride whenever a bet is won. Many women Craps shooters favor place betting, but during my casino survey, I saw only a few women taking the odds on the six place bets at one time.

Place betting accounts for a great deal of the action on Bank Craps layouts. Since the bank cannot pay off the place bets at correct odds and stay in business, it resorts to a simple tactical gimmick to make place betting profitable. It insists that the right bettor accept less than the correct odds on each right place bet, and that the wrong bettor lay greater odds than the correct odds when placing a bet to lose. Place bets may be removed, if so desired, at any time during play. Here is a detailed description of place betting odds and the bank's favorable percentages.

Place or Box Number Bets to Win

Four or Ten: The correct odds are 10 to 5 (2 to 1). The right player wagers $5 on FOUR or TEN, the bank pays off winning bets at odds of 9 to 5. This gives the bank an advantage of 6⅔% *or 6.666% or about 33¢ on a $5 wager.*

Five or Nine: The true odds are 7½ to 5, the bank pays off winning right bets at odds of 7 to 5 and takes an advantage of *4% which is 20¢ on a $5 wager.*

Six or Eight: The correct odds are 6 to 5. The bank pays off winning right bets at odds of 7 to 6. This means that the bank has an advantage of *1 17/33% or 1.515%, or about 8¢ on a $5 wager.*

Some banks pay off this right wager at 11 to 10. This means the bank has an advantage of *4 6/11% or 4.5454%, or about 23¢ on a $5 wager.*

Other banks pay off this right wager at even money or 5 to 5. This means that the bank has an advantage of *9 1/11% or 9.090% or about 45¢ on a $5 wager.*

These percentages prove that the so-called smart dice player who places a right bet on the FOUR or TEN is a bigger sucker than the average field players whom most so-called smart dice players ridicule as being novices and suckers.

Obviously the best place bet is placing the SIX or EIGHT when the bank pays at odds of 7 to 6.

Place or Box Number Bets to Lose

These wagers are not as popular as win place bets, since eight out of ten dice players are born right bettors and don't like the idea of laying the odds (putting up more money than they can win). Here are the bank's percentages the player must buck when he lays a place bet.

Four or Ten: The correct odds are 10 to 5. The player must lay odds of 11 to 5. This gives the bank an advantage of *3 1/33% or 3.030%, or about 15¢ on a $5 wager.*

Five or Nine: The correct odds are 7½ to 5, the player must lay odds of 8 to 5, which gives the bank an advantage of *2½% or 2.5%, or about 12¢ on a $5 wager.*

Six or Eight: The correct odds are 6 to 5, the player must lay odds of 5 to 4, which gives the bank an advantage of *1 9/11% or 1.818%, or about 9¢ on a $5 wager.*

Some banks compel players to lay odds of 7 to 5, which gives the bank an advantage of *7 8/13% or 7.615%, or about 38¢ on a $5 wager.*

Most Nevada Bank Craps tables, in addition to permitting players to place their bets on the box numbers, also allow players to buy the box numbers. In Bank Craps games that permit players to place their bets or to buy them at a 5% charge, it would be to the player's advantage to buy the FOUR and TEN and place the FIVE, NINE, SIX and EIGHT. See Bank Craps percentage table on page 303.

NEW YORK CRAPS

As previously stated, New York Craps is a version of Bank Craps found in most illegal gambling houses in the eastern part of the United States and legal casinos in the Bahamas, England, Yugoslavia and wherever gamblers from the eastern United States operate dice games. The big differences between Bank Craps and New York Craps are that the New York dice layout *does not possess come and don't come betting spaces* and that *place betting is not permitted.* Players are compelled to buy the box numbers (4, 5, 6, 8, 9, 10). In buying the boxes, the player is paid off at correct odds, as 6 to 5 on SIX or EIGHT, 3 to 2 on FIVE or NINE, and 2 to 1 on FOUR or TEN. However, for such services, the bank levies a direct charge of 5% on the total sum of right money wagered; this amounts to a charge of 25¢ on each $5 bet. Whether you take or lay $10 to $5 on a FOUR, the bank charges 25¢.

New York Craps is played on a specially constructed dice table that is similar to a Las Vegas or Bank Craps table; but it is shaped somewhat differently and the dealers are posted at each end of the table. A stickman stands at the center of the table and the two boxmen sit opposite the stickman. A lookout, known as a ladderman, sits on a stand high above the table.

Each dealer is supplied with a hundred or more quarters (25¢ pieces) which are spread out on the table in front of him. These quarters are used to help the dealer in taking his 5% charge on a player's box number bet or bets. There is one peculiar fact about the 5% vigorish charge: in most games, the bank's favorable percentage is larger than most players think, but the 5% vigorish charge at New York Craps is less than nearly all Craps players and most casino operators suspect. Here are the correct percentages in favor of the bank when the operators levy a 5% vigorish charge:

RIGHT BETTOR PAYS   4.761+%, or about 25¢, when taking $5 worth of odds on any point or box number.

WRONG BETTOR PAYS   2.439+%, or about 12¢, when laying odds of $10 to $5 on point or box number 4 or 10.
3.225+%, or about 15¢, when laying odds of $7.50 to $5 on point or box number 5 or 9.
4.000+%, or about 20¢, when laying odds of $6 to $5 on point or box number 6 or 8.

SCARNEY CRAPS

New York Craps has always appeared to me an undignified way to play Craps. The dealer's constant handling of quarters used to make change seems a cheap way of running a modern dice table. Often, while scouting the casinos of the Bahamas and England, I have observed dice players place a $5 bet on a box number (4, 5, 6, 8, 9, 10). The dealer then shouts, "Twenty-five cents, please." The player's usual answer is "What for?" "The 5% house charge," cries the dealer, to the bewilderment of the players.

Some casino operators prefer New York Craps to Bank Craps because New York Craps has a larger house percentage. A casino that opens only in the evening and caters only to gambling junkets— with little or no walk-in business—cannot run a profitable Bank Craps or Las Vegas style of dice game. Many casino operators in the Caribbean where the action is limited to a few hours a day have tried unsuccessfully to operate by dealing Las Vegas odds. The result: They went broke in the attempt, and either went out of business or had to resort to running a bust-out joint.

Early in 1967, the administrator of the Hilton Hotel casino in Curaçao, informed me that casinos in the area, because of the lack of walk-in business (natives are not permitted to gamble), were going broke. Gambling junkets proved to be unprofitable. Then and there I decided to develop a Craps layout that would give casinos such as these a chance to survive and at the same time give the junket player a run for his money. I also took into consideration the fact that for years everything has been increasing in cost, casino rent, salaries, entertainment, drinks, cigarettes as well as paying for hotel accommodations and plane transportation for junket players. Strangely enough, the only thing that has not gone up is the house percentage at casino tables.

Shortly thereafter, a new Craps layout which I invented appeared for the first time at the Curaçao Hilton Hotel casino. I have taken the creator's liberty of naming it *Scarney Craps*. I simply dignified New York Craps by eliminating the 5% charge and made use of place betting. Scarney Craps, like New York Craps, lacks a come and don't come space, but the proposition bets at Scarney Craps pay a unit more than most Bank Craps tables throughout the world. Scarney Craps, which is played on a standard Bank Craps table, is being played in many Caribbean casinos as well as in Europe, Asia, Africa and South America.

Free Single Odds Bets

Free bet (commonly called *front line odds* and *back line odds*): When the shooter comes out on the point, most banks allow players who have placed bets on the pass and don't pass line or on the come or don't come space to make a second bet, usually equal to the original wager, that the shooter will or will not make the point. However, many tables whose limit is $300 or $500 will allow only $150 or $250 respectively as a free maximum-limit odds bet, even though the front- or back-line bet is greater. In brief, the free-bet limit is usually half of the maximum betting limit; any amount over this limit must be bought.

Although a front-line or back-line bet appears to be a free bet, is this actually so? If a right player places a $20 bet on the pass line and the shooter throws a TEN for his point, the bank will allow the player to take $20 to the bank's $40 that the shooter will make it. This bet is paid off at the correct odds and no charge is made for it. How does this affect the bank's percentage? Let's see.

The bank has the usual percentage in its favor of 1.414 on the pass line and 1.402 on the don't pass line. But the second wager on the point is paid off, for a change, at the correct odds. On this bet, the only one of its kind on the layout, the bank has no favorable percentage at all. But, as you might expect, when both wagers are figured together, the bank still has a slight advantage.

On the right bettor's wager to win, the bank has a favorable P.C. of .848. The bank's P.C. on right bets is calculated as follows. The bank has an edge of 28 rolls in every 1,980 rolls before the come-out. Points will appear ⅔ of the 1,980 rolls, or 1,320. Since the two-way bet is made only when a point appears, and since these 1,320 additional rolls have no advantage for either bank or player, the bank's overall advantage is 28 rolls out of 1,320 plus 1,980 rolls or 3,300 rolls. 28 divided by 3,300 gives a percentage of .848 in favor of the bank.

On the wrong bettor's wager to lose, the bank has a favorable P.C. of .832. Barring 6–6 or (1–1) cuts the bank's advantage down to 27 rolls. Since 6-6 (or 1-1) will be thrown 55 times out of 1,980, there are only 1,980 minus 55, or 1,925 decisive rolls. Add the 1,320 that have no advantage either way and the bank has an edge of 27 rolls out of 3,245 rolls, or a favorable P.C. of .832%.

Although this is the best bet the Bank Craps player can make, it is strange how few gamblers, even those who know percentages, take advantage of it. Craps shooters are just as unpredictable as the dice. During the thrill, action and excitement of the game, most players bet as their emotions dictate rather than their minds; they follow their intuition rather than their knowledge of P.C. And they seldom do the right thing at the right time.

The free odds bets made on the pass line, don't pass line, come or don't come may be taken down (removed) at any time before the bet is decided. One thing should be remembered, however; the lowest-valued chip in a luxury casino is a $1 chip, and for that reason dealers can't pay off on any part of a dollar. Therefore, when you're taking the free odds make sure that your bet doesn't pay off in cents. For example, if your pass line bet was $1 and the point is 5, taking the free odds for $1 would hurt rather than benefit you simply because the dealer would not pay you the $1.50 your bet should bring. You would be paid one dollar chip—that's all. To receive the correct odds of 3 to 2, you should have made a pass line bet of $2.

The only way to take full advantage of the free odds is to make your bet a minimum (or multiple) of ten ($10). Since the average pass line bettor usually bets only a buck or two he cannot take full advantage of the free odds. Here's why: When you make your pass line bet, you don't know what the come-out number will be. If you bet $1, and the come-out is 4 or 10, you're all right. You can get the full 2 to 1 odds. If the come-out is 5 or 6, or 8, or 9, you can't. You'd get $1 to $1 instead of $1.50 to $1 on the 5 or 9. You'd get even money instead of $1.20 to $1 on the 6 or 8. On every bet up to $10, you'd be blocked from getting full odds on some point. But on a $10 bet, you can get 2-1, 3-2 or 6-5, depending on the come-out number. This is true of any multiple of 10, but not of any other number or multiple. You can figure it yourself. This does not mean that you have to bet $10. With a smaller bet you can still find free odds on some numbers, though not all.

If you happen to be in a situation like that described above, and the Craps dealer tries to talk you into increasing the amount of your pass line bet after the come-out by telling you that it is to your best advantage since it will permit you to take full advantage of the free odds offer, *don't.* Acceptance means taking even money instead of odds that the shooter will make his point and the free odds bet is no longer free. Although "betting the line" and taking or laying the free odds as described above is the smartest way of gambling at casino dice tables it is strange how very few gamblers take full advantage of such a play. I have found that many players are just as unpredictable as the dice. During the thrill, action and excitement of the game, they bet as their emotions, rather than their minds, dictate. They follow their intuition rather than their knowledge of the game, and seldom do the right thing at the right time.

Free Double Odds Bets

A small number of banks where the action is highly competitive allow players making free front-line or back-line odds bets to wager double the original amount made to win or lose before the come-out. The bank's percentage in the above instances is .606% on right action and .591% on wrong action. Banks that permit such action would not stay in business long if all the players made only that type of bet, because a casino operation doing fair business requires, on the average, a greater percentage than that on all bets in order to pay its operating expenses before showing a profit.

So that reader can see the bank's favorable percentages on all the Bank Craps bets at a glance, they have been placed together in the table opposite. For hardway bets, see table on page 293; for come-out bets, see page 295.

HOW TO GAMBLE SENSIBLY AT BANK CRAPS

As in any banking game, the house earns a percentage on every bet made at Bank Craps. This is not unreasonable because somebody has to pay for the casino rent, equipment, employees' salaries, etc. But how much you pay for the privilege of shooting Craps in a casino is entirely up to you.

Nobody can tell you how to win at Bank Craps because if you gamble long enough and often enough the house P.C. will take its toll. But if you still insist on taking a fling at the dice tables, here are several rules to follow which can save you money.

1. Whenever you gamble at Bank Craps, set aside in advance the amount of money you are willing to lose. If you lose that amount, quit the game for the evening; do not borrow money, write a check or obtain credit to continue gambling.

2. Also set for yourself a reasonable amount that you might expect to win, and if you succeed in winning that much, quit the game, no matter how lucky you happen to feel. If you follow this rule you will retain your winnings more often, and you will have more winning plays because you are trying to win smaller amounts.

3. If you lost yesterday, do not gamble today with the object of recouping yesterday's losses. That is the most dangerous course any gambler can follow. Trying to get even has sent more players to the poorhouse than anything else. Write off yesterday's losses and forget them.

4. Naturally, I expect that after reading this text on Bank Craps you will place your bets on the layout spaces which have the smallest

THE CASINO'S P.C. ON BANK CRAPS BETS

Bet	P.C. in Bank's Favor	Bank's P.C. on $5 Bet
Win (pass)	1.414%	$.07*
Come	1.414	.07
Lose (don't pass) bar 6–6 or 1–1	1.402	.07
Don't come, bar 6–6 or 1–1	1.402	.07
Lose (don't pass) bar 1–2	4.385	.22
Don't come, bar 1–2	4.385	.22
Place bets to win		
Bank lays 9 to 5 on 4 or 10	6.666	.33
Bank lays 7 to 5 on 5 or 9	4.000	.20
Bank lays 7 to 6 on 6 or 8	1.515	.08
Box number bets to win (5% charge)		
Bank lays 10 to 5 on 4 or 10	4.761	.25
Bank lays 7½ to 5 on 5 or 9	4.761	.25
Bank lays 6 to 5 on 6 or 8	4.761	.25
Place bets to lose		
Bank takes 11 to 5 on 4 or 10	3.030	.15
Bank takes 8 to 5 on 5 or 9	2.500	.12
Bank takes 5 to 4 on 6 or 8	1.818	.09
Box number bets to lose (5% charge)		
Bank takes 10 to 5 on 4 or 10	2.439	.12
Bank takes 7½ to 5 on 5 or 9	3.225	.16
Bank takes 6 to 5 on 6 or 8	4.000	.20
Field bets		
Field (2, 3, 4, 9, 10, 11, 12)	11.111	.56
Field (2, 3, 4, 9, 10, 11, 12 with double payoff on 2 and 12)	5.263	.26
Field (2, 3, 5, 9, 10, 11, 12)	5.555	.27
Big Six	9.090	.45
Big Eight	9.090	.45
Win bet (pass) line plus free single point odds bet to win	.848	.04
Lose (don't pass) plus free single point odds bet to lose	.832	.04
Win bet (pass) line plus free double point odds bet to win	.606	.03
Lose (don't pass) plus free double point odds bet to lose	.591	.03

* The bank's edge on a $5 wager given in cents has, in each case (except for the place win bet on numbers 5 or 9 and in the box numbers 6 or 8 to lose) a plus fraction which we have omitted.

percentage against you. If you follow this rule, your chances of winning are greatly increased.

5. Try to win the amount you hoped to win in the fastest time possible. Making bets back and forth all night merely gives the laws of probability a chance to perform as expected in the long run and helps Old Man Percentage slowly but surely to eat up your chances of winning.

If the Bank Craps player follows the above rules, he will be gambling intelligently; his winnings may be greater, and when he does lose, his losses won't hurt him.

MONEY (OR OPEN) CRAPS

Open Craps, now often called Money Craps, is the most popular illegal casino form of Craps played in this country today. It is the favorite gambling game of the country's high rollers and big-money gamblers, but it is seldom found in the legalized casinos.

Money Craps, as the name implies, is almost always played with cash rather than chips. Some big-money Craps operators, in order to speed up the game, use small-denomination chips ($5 or $10), but all the big bets are made with currency. The two biggest money games I ever saw were at the 115 Club in Miami (which closed in 1947), and at the Barn, which is described on page 228. The bigtime gamblers in both these joints had a cute money gimmick which helped speed up the action; it is now often used. Hundred-dollar bills are made up into packets, each secured by a rubber band. One packet contains one hundred $100 bills ($10,000), another, fifty $100 bills ($5,000), another, twenty-five $100 bills ($2,500) and another, ten $100 bills ($1,000). The original owner pencils his initials on the top bill of each packet so that if the eventual winner should find that it contains less than the stipulated amount, he can be reimbursed by the original owner.

This makes it possible to get big bets down quickly without having to take time to count hundreds of bills. A player laying $20,000 on the point numbers FOUR or TEN simply throws down two $10,000 packets; if laying $7,500 to $5,000 on the points FIVE or NINE, a $5,000 and a $2,500 packet do the trick; and if the player lays $6,000 to $5,000 he simply uses one $5,000 packet and one $1,000 packet. It is not uncommon to see 50 or more such packets being wagered on a single point decision in games presently operated in our big cities. Open (or Money) Craps is now played in most sawdust joints and makeshift casinos, but it is not restricted to gambling houses; big and small games cover the country—in streets, cellars, back lots, factories, hotels, poolrooms and on river wharfs. Nearly every town of any size at all (say, 80,000 population) has at least one game regularly operating, law or no law. It may not always be in the same location, but it's there. Because of its hidden and illegal nature, women are seldom found in the game.

Money Craps in a gambling house uses a dice table similar to a Bank Craps table except that the layout does not have proposition bets such as the field, one-roll come-out bets and the hardway bets. The only betting spaces on the layout are the lose line, the win line, and the box numbers (4, 5, 6, 8, 9 and 10).

The banker at Money (or Open) Craps is known as the *book*. When the book operates in the open (back lot, hotel room or street corner) and does not use a Craps table or layout in order to deal the game, the book visualizes the layout and places the players' bets in the same relative position as though a layout were being used.

The book's maximum betting limit at Money Craps ranges from a low $25 on up to $1,000 and $2,000, with even that limit lifted in special cases. Fortunes are won and lost nightly at Money Craps; winnings and losses of $500,000 or more in one dice session are common. Such heavy gambling occurs very rarely at Private Craps, and it is impossible at Bank Craps unless the usual betting limits are upped considerably.

It is in games operated in New York City, Chicago, Philadelphia, Detroit, etc., that the bigtime gamblers, the horse bookies, the Numbers operators, the thieves and dice and card hustlers of the private game and the underworld big-shots gamble with industry's business tycoons, millionaire playboys, stockbrokers, politicians and various other legitimate businessmen.

These people prefer Money Craps because it offers them their biggest opportunity to win large sums of money. Money Craps permits players to take and lay odds on the point number among themselves, something that is not permitted at Bank Craps. Flat or center bets, one-roll come-out bets and hardway bets must be placed with the book, which pays off these wagers at the same odds the bank does at New York Craps (see pages 293, 295–296).

The big action that the book receives is on the off numbers. Players cannot make an off- or box-number wager with each other, and the book gets this action whenever players cannot get other players to take or lay odds on the point.

Open Craps has undergone many betting changes in the past few years. Back in 1945, the book permitted players to make all types of bets among themselves. As the game is played today, it should really be called Semi-open Craps.

Today, most books, when laying or taking the odds on point or box numbers, pay off at the correct odds and charge the player 5% of the right money wagered. The book's favorable P.C. in such instances is the same as the bank's in New York Craps when the right bettor buys the boxes: *4.761%, or 25¢ on $5 worth of right action.* In the wrong bettor's case, the charge is still figured at 5% of the right money wagered (in this case, the book's wager), but the book does not collect the charge. Instead, the charge rides with the player's bet and is picked up by the book only when the player laying the odds loses.

If, for example, the wrong bettor wishes to lay $200 to the book's $100 on a Four or Ten, he must put down $205. If the player loses, he is out $205; if he wins, he takes down $305. In this instance he has paid no charge for his bet. The wrong bettor only pays the book a 5% charge when he loses. You may wonder, in these circumstances, not only why two-thirds of all bettors are right bettors, but why there are any right bettors at all. The answer is that the average player knows next to nothing about percentages and even when he knows a little, he thinks he stands to win more by taking the odds than laying them. He believes in risking a little to win a lot and forgets, or doesn't know, that one of the basic rules is that in the long run the expectation of winning is in direct proportion to the odds.

If they bet the book big and often enough, both the right and the wrong bettor will eventually go broke, regardless of which player pays the greater percentage to the book. For the benefit of the occasional book player, the following table shows the book's favorable percentage on each of the points, off or box numbers when the book picks up the 5% charge on the right bettor and lets it ride for the wrong bettor.

RIGHT BETTOR PAYS   4.761%, or about 25¢, when taking $5 worth of odds on any point.

WRONG BETTOR PAYS   .813%, or about 4¢, when laying odds of $10 to $5 on point or box number 4 or 10.
1.290%, or about 6¢, when laying odds of $7.50 to $5 on point or box number 5 or 9.
1.818%, or about 9¢, when laying odds of $6 to $5 on point or box number 6 or 8.

Some books do not give the wrong bettor such a good proposition as this; they pick up the 5% charge on both the right and wrong action, the same as in New York Craps when buying the boxes. (See page 303 for percentages.)

Some books, in an effort to balance their right and wrong odds action (which is what every book dreams of), charge only 3% and pick it up on both the right and wrong bettor. The exact percentages in both cases are tabulated below:

RIGHT BETTOR PAYS 2.912%, or about 15¢, when taking $5 worth of odds on any point.

WRONG BETTOR PAYS 1.477%, or about 7¢, when laying odds of $10 on point or box number 4 or 10.
1.960%, or about 10¢, when laying odds of $7½ to $5 on point or box number 5 or 9.
2.439%, or about 12¢, when laying odds of $6 to $5 on point or box number 6 or 8.

To sum up, if you insist on playing Money Craps and want to avoid cheating yourself, and if you dislike donating your pay to the Building Fund for the Craps Bookies' Bank Account, paste these simple rules in your hat:

1. Don't bet the book. Know the correct odds on the point numbers, and bet only with other players.

2. Don't bet if you can't afford to lose.

Then, after making sure that the book and his sidekick Old Man Percentage aren't giving you the business, you should also try to make sure that the dice cheat doesn't clip you with his phony dice. Advice on how to do that follows.

HOW TO DETECT CROOKED DICE

As I have mentioned elsewhere, most gambling houses that cater to the masses are *on the square* and earn their profits by employing Old Man Percentage. The same cannot be said for thousands and thousands of Private Craps games or the hundreds of Money or Open Craps floating games. Nearly every Private Craps game has either its Craps hustler or its dice cheat, two characters who are consistent winners in 90% of all friendly games.

Unsuspecting Craps players are fleeced out of several billion dollars yearly by dice cheats who operate in all styles of Craps games. These cheats have increased in numbers in the past decades as a direct result of the indoctrination of 5 million women Craps players.

There are two kinds of dice cheats: the amateur, a player who thinks he has a chance of making money from his friends or co-workers and doesn't care how he does it; and the professional, the skilled dice *mechanic* (sleight-of-hand artist), known in the trade as a *bust-out man,* an experienced cheat who earns his livelihood by hiring out his services to dice mobs who set up their crooked dice games in hotel rooms, poolrooms, private homes, clubs or crooked casinos.

Expert dice mechanics also prey on unsuspecting players in private or floating games, and sometimes make casino operators their victims. Many rug and carpet joints in Nevada and elsewhere have, at one time or another, been cheated out of vast sums of money by bust-out men.

Recently, a top casino on the Las Vegas Strip was taken for $350,000 in several plays by dice cheats. The management asked me to check it out for them—but when I arrived in Las Vegas, all the casino owners had to show me were the dice—and they were perfect dice. The culprits had long gone. In 1956, three Americans were arrested and jailed in Monaco for switching in crooked dice at Monte Carlo casino; they had won thousands of dollars before being arrested. Prince Rainier later pardoned one of the three culprits because of his poor health. The others served two-year jail terms.

Bust-out men are not particular who their victims are, and honest casino operators must maintain a constant guard against them. Bigtime Money and Bank Craps tables employ laddermen and floormen to protect themselves against such cheats.

An example of the financial possibilities of bust-out men: Working in Miami, Con Baker, the greatest dice mechanic ever to whip in a pair of crooked dice, once fleeced one of America's top oil barons for the tidy sum of $835,000 in a two-hour work day. Con didn't manage to hang on to his money; he died penniless at 37.

I know of a bigtime horse bookie who was recently taken for $3 million in a six-month gaming period by dice cheats. Bust-out men move around and are not particular where they operate. Wherever a dice game is in progress the chances are a bust-out man will appear on the scene sooner or later.

The art of professional Craps cheating has several branches. Some cheats travel alone, playing single-o against the suckers in private games or wherever they find inexperienced Craps players. But because there is safety and strength in numbers, and because the professional bust-out man, concentrating on the task of switching in his crooked dice, needs someone else to make the wagers, cheats more often work in groups known as *dice mobs*.

Single-o cheats and dice mobs, when detected, often get beaten up by a group of angry players or by casino strong-arm men, but that doesn't deter them. It's all in the day's work, one of the dice cheat's occupational hazards. Dice cheats have little or no fear of arrest and conviction on the charge of cheating, since gambling is usually illegal in the first place, and sleight-of-hand cheating is hard to prove.

My recent survey of Private Craps games reveals that there are crooked dice in about 1 out of every 10 games in daily operation in the United States, usually introduced into the game by some amateur dice cheat who has no special cheating skill. It is easy for anyone to become a dice cheat. Anyone who doesn't care how he wins can achieve this aim. All he needs is a circle of suckers and a pair of gimmicked dice, which can be purchased in many novelty stores and from most suppliers of honest dice. Nowadays, with so many novice Craps shooters in sight, both the suckers and the crooked dice are easy to come by. I don't know how many dice cheats there are in the United States; but I do know that there are a hundred dice manufacturers, many of whom see nothing wrong in making crooked dice, since there is no law against it.

Unfortunately, the average Craps player has little chance of detecting crooked dice, even if he plays with them for weeks. A woman friend of mine phoned me not so long ago and asked if I would check a pair of dice which she suspected might be dishonest. I paid her a visit and was told that about ten of her women friends met at her house each Friday night for a Poker game, and that they had gotten into the habit of shooting Craps for an hour or so at the end of the evening. My friend said that she had lost $5,000 during the previous six months and was beginning to suspect that everything was not on the up and up.

It wasn't. The dice turned out to be loaded. "How," I asked, "do you happen to have these loaded babies?"

"About six months ago," she explained, "after one of our Poker sessions, I found them on the floor under the Poker table. I thought someone had dropped them accidentally and, at our next session, I asked if anyone had lost them. No one claimed them, but at the end of the Poker game that night, one of the girls suggested that we shoot Craps for a while."

I did a little investigating and found that one of my friend's Poker-playing pals was formerly a Twenty-Six dice dealer in Chicago. She had planted the loaded cubes where they would be found, knowing that someone, she herself, if necessary, would suggest using them— although I doubt that she expected the loads would stay in use for as long as six months before one of the other players, who were mostly losers, would suspect anything was wrong. If there's a Craps game going on in your home and you aren't sure where the dice came from, it might be a good idea to get a pair that you know are honest.

The former dice-dealing gal, apparently having gotten wind of the fact that somebody had blown the gaff, disappeared, knowing, of course, that my friend couldn't beef to the cops because she would also be subject to arrest for running illegal Poker and Craps games in her home.

There are undoubtedly thousands of pairs of crooked dice in use right now that have been planted on innocent and honest players by dice cheats. There are hundreds upon hundreds of amateur dice cheats, male and female, who win money at Craps by clipping unwary suckers

DICEMAKERS SUPPLIES

No. 213.	Liquid Celluloid Cement	Per Bottle	$ 2.00
No. 214.	Celluloid paint for spots, white, black, red or blue	Per Bottle	2.00
No. 215.	Straight drills for boring a straight hole in dice	Each	2.00
No. 216.	Burr drills for hollowing out	Each	2.00
No. 217.	Quicksilver (Liquid Mercury)	Per Ounce	2.50
No. 218.	Polish soap to restore finish	Per Cake	2.00
No. 219.	Dice Cleaner and Polisher, paste form	Per Jar	2.50
No. 220.	Heel Bark for quick spotting, white, black, red or blue . . .	Per Piece	2.00
No. 221.	Spotting drills for concave spots, any size	Each	2.50
No. 222.	Spotting drills for birdseye spots, any size	Each	2.50
No. 223.	Spotting drills for double ring birdseye spots, any size	Each	3.50
No. 224.	Special dice jigs for spotting perfect, any size	Each	7.50
No. 225.	Celluloid plugging rope for plugging, white	Per Piece	2.00
No. 226.	Copper Amalgam for transparent dice	Per Box	2.50
No. 227.	Slugs for ⅝ size dice	Each	2.50
No. 229.	Dicemaker's vice, handles all sizes of dice	Each	5.50
No. 230.	Dicemaker's hand drill, handles all sizes dice drills	Each	4.50
No. 231.	Dicemaker's guide for hollowing out (3 examples)	Per Set	5.50
No. 232.	Dicemaker's sandpaper, for roughing and finishing, coarse or fine	Per Sheet	2.00
No. 233.	Dicemaker's glass finishing paper	Per Sheet	2.00
No. 234.	All sizes Drill Jig	Each	15.00

Gambling equipment company's listing of the tools and materials used for making crooked dice.

with crooked dice. The most popular forms of *gaffed* (doctored) dice and the methods for detecting them are described below.

Percentage dice: Amateur cheats do not have the skill necessary to switch crooked dice in and out of a game, so they use percentage dice, which can be put into a game and left there. They are gaffed in such a way that some numbers will come up more often than probability predicts. There are two main types: *passers*, which are fixed to favor some of the point numbers and thus favor the right bettors, and *miss-outs*, which are gaffed so that SEVEN will come up oftener than it should, thus favoring the wrong bettors. The dice cheat merely makes his bets according to the bias of the dice and usually shows a profit on every game. To avoid the suspicion that constant winning might create, he occasionally goes broke and then gets back his losses and a share of the winnings from the evening's big winner—a confederate he has planted in the game.

Shapes are the commonest form of percentage dice and can be made either as passers or miss-outs. These are dice whose shape has been altered in one way or another so that they are no longer perfect cubes.

Flats are shapes that have been shaved down on one or more sides so that they are slightly brick-shaped and tend to come to rest more often on their larger surfaces. Shaving off as little as 10/5000 of an inch will change the probabilities and earn the cheat a profit. The less his suckers know about crooked dice the more he will cut them down.

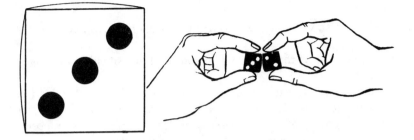

A beveled die and the wobble test for bevels. (Military Service Publishing Company)

A "strong" pair may have as much as 40/1000 of an inch, or even more, taken off, and the cheat gets his profit that much faster.

Six-ace flats are the commonest variety of miss-outs. When the 6–1 sides are shaved down, they thus turn up oftener than they would with square dice, and produce more SEVENS. The cheat bets the point numbers to lose.

Flat passers have had the 6–1 sides cut down on one die and the 3–4 sides on the other, so that the points 4, 5, 9 and 10 appear more often. Or the 2–5 sides are shaved on one die and the 3–4 sides on the other so as to favor the points 5, 6, 8 and 9. The cheat bets the points to win.

Two-way flats (fast sevens or four-way sevens) are shapes that have been shaved down on two non-opposite sides. When a few thousandths of an inch is taken off the six and three sides, for instance, the 6–1 and 3–4 sides are rectangles having a greater area than the 2–5 sides. The numbers 6, 1, 3 and 4 will appear oftener, and when both dice are cut down in the same way, these numbers will combine to form more SEVENS than normally appear. They are, therefore, miss-outs, and cheaters call them *fast sevens* or *four-way sevens*. The 6–1 and 2–5 sides, or the 3–4 and 2–5 sides, when cut down, act the same.

Bevels are shapes having one or more sides sandpapered so that they are slightly rounded rather than flat. Such cubes tend to roll off the rounded sides and come to rest more often on the flat sides. Bevels can also be made as passers or miss-outs, and as weak or strong as desired. Use the "wobble test" to detect beveled shapes. Hold one die in each hand and rub two sides together, trying different sides. When a beveled surface is rubbed against a flat surface or another beveled surface, the dice will wobble, or rock back and forth.

Cut edges are dice whose edges are not all beveled at the customary 45-degree angle. The four edges on some sides are cut at a 60-degree angle. This gives some sides a larger area than others, and the dice tend to settle on the larger surfaces more often. To detect cut edges hold the two dice together and note the width of the separation line between them. If this varies when you try different sides, the edges have been cut.

Loaded dice: The gaff on shapes is called *outside work;* on loaded dice it is *inside work.* Loads may caliper as perfect cubes, but extra weight just below the surface on some sides will make the opposite sides come up oftener than they should. Loads, contrary to what most people think, are not so heavily weighted that the same sides always appear; this behavior in a game would look very odd indeed. Like shapes, loads are percentage dice which throw certain combinations more often than they should.

Most Craps players know so little about crooked dice that they are cheated out of millions of dollars every year because they think that transparent dice cannot be loaded. Dice makers have never found this very difficult; they simply drill the recessed spots on two or three adjacent sides of the dice a little deeper than usual, and insert thin gold, platinum or tungsten amalgam slugs, which are then covered by opaque paint on the spots. In a well-made pair of transparent loads, the other spots are also drilled deeper and filled with paint, so that when you look through the dice all the spots are seen to be recessed to the same depth.

Many players believe that the practice of throwing the cubes against a backboard is protection against crooked dice. This protects you only against controlled shots, not against shapes or loads.

There are a couple of good tests for loaded dice. The best method is to fill a tall glass with water, hold the suspected cube just above the surface and drop it gently into the water; do this several times, holding the die with a different number up each time. Note whether the die settles evenly or whether it turns over as it goes down. If it turns, and if two or three numbers always show up and others never show, the dice are loaded.

If there is no tall glass of water handy, try this: Hold the cube loosely between thumb and forefinger at diagonally opposite corners so that there is as little pressure as possible. Try all four combinations of diagonally opposite corners. If the cube is loaded, when the weighted sides are on top, the die will pivot as the heavier sides swing around to the bottom. The feeling of movement of the die is unmistakable.

Flush spotted dice: The spots are recessed about 1 7/1000 inch into the die's surface. Most casinos use these today because they are much more difficult to load; however, they are perfect for electric dice (see page 321).

There is little point in testing the dice used in most casinos because most Bank Craps and Money Craps games permit both right and wrong action. Perfectly square dice must be used so that the house will receive its favorable percentage no matter which way the players bet. The use of percentage dice by a crooked casino would serve no useful purpose for the house. This two-way betting action has made it necessary for manufacturers to make dice that are true cubes to a tolerance of 1/5000 of an inch or thereabouts.

Tops and bottoms (also **tops, busters, Ts, misspots**): These are the dice used by the professional cheats. They do not use flats, bevels, cut edges or loads because they are usually playing against smart players who would spot these gaffs. Tops are not percentage dice; they do not bring up the same numbers some of the time—they bring up the right numbers all of the time. The cheat's chance of winning is 100%, and the victim's chance of winning is exactly zero.

Since the players can't see more than three sides of a cube at once, they can't see that some numbers are missing and others appear twice. Tops usually bear only three different numbers, each of which is repeated on the cube's opposite side. The players on opposite sides of a Craps circle all see the same three numbers when a top comes to a stop on the playing surface, but since no one individual can be in two places at once, none of them know it. And the misspotting passes unnoticed when they are rolling.

Amateur cheats, however, don't use those sure-fire cubes because, dangerous as they are to the sucker, they are also loaded with danger for the sharp whose sleight-of-hand isn't top-notch. Although the mis-

A die with cut edges (LEFT). *Short arrow points to edge cut at a 60-degree angle, long arrow indicates edge cut at a 45-degree angle. Transparent dice* (CENTER) *are loaded with metallic slugs placed in the countersunk spots. Loads can sometimes be detected because the loaded spots are deeper than the others* (RIGHT), *but careful dicemakers drill all spots to the same depth and fill the others with extra paint. (Military Service Publishing Company)*

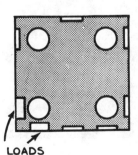
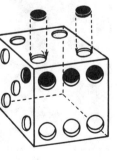

LOADS

spotting passes unnoticed during the action of the roll, if the chump ever gets his mitts on a pair of tops and gives them a once-over lightly, he rumbles the gaff immediately. Consequently, tops must be switched in and out at a split-second's notice, with speed and with smooth, undetectable sleight-of-hand. The switch artist who has mastered that never worries about a personal unemployment problem. The mob he signs up with can throw their P.C. dice out the window and depend on tops to corral all the folding money in sight in practically nothing flat and with 100% efficiency.

If the switch man is good, the chance the sucker has of tagging the cubes for what they are is exceedingly slim. Even the fast-company boys can come a cropper when the Ts start rolling! A dice mob can sense a suspicious player with all the celerity of a lie detector. And when someone grabs for and examines the dice, the chances are a thousand to one that he'll pick up fair dice. The tops go in when the player is confident that the game is on the level and is absorbed in the betting and the excitement of the game. When you look for them, they're not there; when you don't, they are.

Tops come in assorted combinations calculated to meet any Craps situation. Gamblers call them busters because that's exactly what happens to the guy who gets in their way—he's busted. If you should ever find yourself in a *steer joint* (crooked gambling joint) and you hear someone ask, "Where's Buster Brown?" you'll know that somebody's baby is going to get new shoes—but it won't be yours. That query is the

The pivot test for loads. (Military Service Publishing Company)

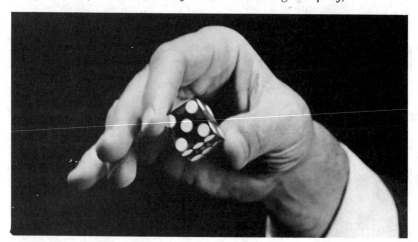

Tops and bottoms as viewed in a mirror.

signal for the *bust-out man* to *bust in* * with tops that will bust your chance of winning and leave it looking like a punctured soap bubble.

The method of using busters varies with the game being played. In Private Craps the mechanic uses a pair of tops so misspotted that they make point after point but no SEVEN. Both dice bear three numbers only, each being duplicated on the die's opposite side. Dice misspotted in this way will throw only 9 of the usual 36 combinations. There are numerous combinations, a pair bearing the numbers 1, 3 and 5 on each die for instance can only make the combinations 1–1, 1–3, 1–5, 3–1, 3–3, 3–5, 5–1, 5–3 and 5–5 forming the points 2, 4, 6, 8 and 10. The shooter consequently can't possibly throw a 7 and must pass. Tops that pass are known as *hits*.†

---

* Don't say that someone busted in with a pair of flats or loads, however. Those are always *switched* in. The terms *bust in* and *bust out* apply only to switching tops.

† The common passing combinations and the numbers they make are:

1–2–3 and 1–2–3 which make 2, 3, 4, 5, 6.

1–3–5 and 1–3–5 which make 2, 4, 6, 8, 10.

2–3–6 and 2–3–6 which make 4, 5, 6, 8, 9, 12.

2–4–6 and 2–4–6 which make 4, 6, 8, 10, 12.

1–4–5 and 1–4–5 which make 2, 5, 6, 8, 9, 10. *(continued on next page)*

If the dice mechanic is working single-o, he busts in with the hits when he is the shooter. But if you suspect tops are being used, the shooter is not the only guy you should keep an eye on. When the mechanic has a partner, he busts in both ways—when he is shooting and from the outside when his pal is shooting. The latter throws the dice toward the bust-out man who picks them up, and busts in with the tops. He repeats the action again later when the shooter wants to have the tops *ripped* (switched) out.

The shooter uses the tops for one or more passes, rakes in the dough, then goes back to fair dice and either continues shooting or passes the dice to the next player. The number of passes he makes before ripping the tops out depends on the action of the players, how well-heeled they are, and the number of passes they'll stand for before scowling suspiciously.

Misses are tops that are made to miss the point. When one die bears only the numbers 1-3-5 and the other only 2-4-6, the only combinations possible are odd numbers. Whenever the shooter is trying for one of the even point numbers (4, 6, 8, 10) with this set of misses, it is impossible for him to throw his point and he must seven out. And when his point is 5 or 9, a set of 1-4-5 2-3-6 misses makes it impossible for him to the throw the point.

Misses are not usually used in private games because the shooter has no legitimate reason to pick the dice up again after he sevens out and thus has no chance to get the tops out of the game. An exception is when the private game has a cutter who may bust them in and out, because, like a house stickman, he has the privilege of picking up the dice and throwing them to the next player.

In house games, the stickman who rakes in the cubes with the dice stick after the roll and tosses them back was originally introduced into the game as a protection against the switching in of phony dice by the players. But in a steer joint the stickman himself is usually the bust-out man who does the dirty work. These boys use several different pairs of tops, both hits and misses, in a manner that gets the money with all the neatness and dispatch of a high-class *cannon* (pickpocket) mob or a *heist* (hold-up) mob.

Bust-out men all have their favorite methods of ripping tops in and out as well as their favorite top combinations. Some dislike to work

---

3-4-5 and 1-5-6 which make 4, 5, 6, 8, 9, 10, 11.
3-5-6 and 3-5-6 which make 6, 8, 9, 10, 11, 12.

Many top cheaters claim that a 2-3-6 pair of tops are the best as passers because they throw all the points except 10, make fewer hardway combinations, and consequently arouse less suspicion. Others favor the 2-4-6 combination because the even point numbers 4, 6, 8 and 10 can easily be broken up with a 1-3-5 2-4-6 set of misses which make only odd numbers.

Palm Switch. (ABOVE) *Crooked dice (numbered 872) are concealed in palm when cheat picks up honest dice.* (BELOW) *He closes hand, lets crooked dice drop to fingers, palms honest ones at the same time, then throws out crooked ones.*

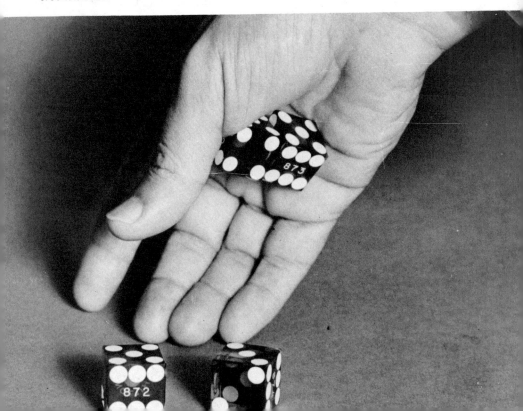

with the stick, claiming that it slows them up, others can't work without the stick and still others prefer to work from the outside, acting as one of the players. Some use four pairs of tops; others, because it is faster, safer and mistakes are less likely to be made, use only two. In Money (or Open) Craps three are most often used—two pairs of hits and a pair of misses.

In the steer joint, the mechanics of the operation of clipping the chump go something like this: The steerer phones in to say he is bringing a sucker—a big oilman. The boys clear the decks for action and the moment the doorbell rings the game suddenly starts rolling full bloom. The book is behind the bankroll, the stickman behind the stick, the shills betting the money with which they have been supplied and the bosses with the big dough, acting as players, are doing the same. A little room is left between two bosses so that the mark walks into that position.

The dice in the game at the start are all levels. But as soon as the mark starts to bet and the bosses discover whether he is a right or wrong bettor, the office is given and the tops go in—misses if the chump makes a right bet, hits if he makes a wrong bet. The mark finds that he can get all the action he wants, and then some. The mob always tries to increase the victim's bets as much as possible, figuring that the larger his bets the faster he gets clipped, the fewer moves the bust-out man has to make and the less chance the mark has of detecting the dirty work. Time is also important; another steerer may be on his way with another monkey.

Suppose the mark is a right bettor and has taken $200 to $100 on the Four which is the shooter's point. The stickman gets the office and pulls the dice in with his stick. As he draws it back, his right hand comes back close to his body and directly over his coat pocket. This pocket has had a specially designed tailoring job, having been built up on the inside so that it is much shallower than usual and divided by partitions so that the pairs of hits and misses are each contained in separate sections. The stickman's fingers dip in and come out with the 1-3-5 2-4-6 misses which do not add up to 4, 6, 8 or 10, any way you look at them.

The chump never glimpses the move because it is covered by the body of the shill who stands close beside the stickman. Sometimes, too, it is the shill's pockets which have been rebuilt and contain the tops, and into which the stickman's fingers dip. The advantage here is that, in case of a blow, the shill walks off and the stickman can stand for a search. An even smarter method, and the one most popular with bust-out men today, not only eliminates the necessity for going into the pocket entirely, but makes the whole move quicker and easier. The stickman's hand goes back between his body and that of the shill and, during the second when the end of the stick is out of sight, the shill simply places the proper pair of tops in the bust-out man's hand.

Once he has the Ts palmed in his right hand, the stickman takes the stick with his left, picks the fair dice up from the table and throws them to the player. Or that is what he seems to do. Actually the tops are thrown out and the fair dice retained, palmed in the right hand, which again takes the stick (see illustrations on page 317).

The dice roll out, the shooter sevens and the chump loses his bet. The stickman pulls the dice in, rips the levels in again, and then moves his hand back for an instant and drops the tops into the hand that the shill at his side holds ready and waiting.

The bust-out man's job is a nerve-wracking one that requires the utmost in timing, speed and smooth precision. His life is no bed of roses. When there are two suckers in the joint, one a right and the other a wrong bettor, he faces a situation he never enjoys. The mark who is a wrong bettor, for instance, has just laid $100 on the FOUR and the stickman has ripped in with a pair of 2–3–6s so that the FOUR must be made. If the other mark wants to take the odds, the bosses pretend they don't hear him. But that stratagem doesn't always work. The right bettor may go to the book and may even take the limit, say $600 to $300.

The moment this happens those hits on the table are a liability. When the shooter passes, the book will lose five hundred bucks more to the right bettor than the boss picks up from the wrong bettor. But that can't happen here—not in a steer joint. The bust-out man may have switched the hits in only a moment ago, but suddenly he gets the office to rip in a pair of misses. He has to have them ready and waiting and must bust in on the next roll without fail. Otherwise he's out of a job.

And, if the tops are still in play, when a player calls for a box-up the stickman must do some more fast, smooth work. He has to pick up the tops, switch them for levels as he throws them into the bowl with the other perfect dice and then spill them all out for a selection. And if he gets the office to put the tops back again on the come-out roll, when the player throws him the good dice the stick man must again make the switch as he throws them back. Good bust-out men die young; it's hard on the nervous system.

And so it goes. Whenever the majority of the money bet by the chumps is right money, the misses go in and the dice lose; when most of the suckers are betting wrong, the hits go in and the dice win. But whether the dice win or lose, the chump gets clipped both ways and the steer-joint boys simply can't lose. With a good bust-out man behind the stick, the fattest mark can be broken in almost no time at all. After a few losses he tends to make bigger bets trying to get his losses back, and he's flat before he knows it. Sometimes the boys break him on one roll.

How do you tell a steer joint from a game that is on the up and up? Well, if smart gamblers frequent the place and if the game has been operating for several months or longer, it's no steer joint; those boys don't stick in one spot that long. If the game is a new one, if a stranger brought you there, if there aren't many players around the table and if most of the action is directed your way—then you're in for it. And don't think you aren't. If you think you spot a move and want to object, don't get noisy about it but call the manager and try quietly to get your money back. If you make a fuss that will tip off any other suckers that may be around, you'll get your ears pinned back pronto. The steer-joint boys don't fool.

How to Detect Tops and Bottoms

The best way to detect tops and bottoms is to take note of the six sides of the two dice when they stop after each roll. Try mentally to form various combinations of the number 7. If the spots showing on the sides of the dice can form these combinations they can be made. If you do this for a number of rolls and can't see any combinations that will form your point or a 7, don't make a big scene about it; just call off your bet and don't make any more. The same holds true if you see the same three numbers on each cube after each roll.

Percentage Tops and Bottoms

Percentage tops and bottoms, also known as One-way tops and bottoms, double-fives or double-deuces, are the newest innovation in misspots. Only one of the six numbers on a die is duplicated on the opposite side, usually the deuce or five. A die with two deuces is called a double-deuce by dice cheaters; a die with two fives is a double-five.

A pair of dice may have both cubes misspotted, or it may be composed of one misspot and one square die. Double-deuces are used together, double-fives together, and either a double-deuce or a double-five may be used with a square die. A pair of double-deuces will not throw an ELEVEN; two double-fives will not throw a THREE. When a square die is used with a double-deuce or a double-five all eleven numbers can be made, a fact which makes the misspot difficult to detect in action. A one-way top was recently switched into a Reno casino and remained in action for several hours before the dice-table personnel got wise.

Here is a comparison of the numbers that can be made and the ways in which they can be made with square dice and with the various one-way tops and bottoms:

Numbers	2	3	4	5	6	7	8	9	10	11	12
Ways to make with											
2 square dice	1	2	3	4	5	6	5	4	3	2	1
1 double-deuce and 1 square die	1	3	4	5	5	6	5	3	2	1	1
2 double-deuces	1	4	6	6	5	4	5	2	2	0	1
1 double-five and 1 square die	1	1	2	3	5	6	5	5	4	3	1
2 double-fives	1	0	2	2	5	4	5	6	6	4	1

Percentage tops and bottoms work both as passers and miss-outs at the same time. Usually, two dice cheats work together; one bets the dice to lose, the other bets the dice to win.

A *double-deuce* paired with a square die gives the right bettor in a private game an advantage of 20% on the point Four and 13 7/11% on the point Five. The wrong bettor lays the odds on the point Nine and enjoys an edge of 16⅔%; when he lays the odds on the point Ten he has an edge of 25%.

A *double-five* paired with a square die gives the right bettor a favorable edge on the point Nine of 13 7/11% and on the point Ten an edge of 20%. The wrong bettor lays the odds on the point Four and has an edge of 25%; laying the odds on the point Five gives him an edge of 16⅔%.

Two double-deuces used together as a pair are much stronger. They are seldom used against smart Craps shooters unless the cheat is a good dice mechanic capable of switching them in and out of the game. A pair of double-deuces give the right bettor in a private game an edge of 80% on the point Four, 50% on the point Five and 22 2/9% on the point Six or Eight. The wrong bettor has an advantage of 16⅔% on the point Nine. The point Ten supplies no advantage either way.

Two double-fives used as a pair give the right bettor an 80% edge on the point Ten, 50% on the point Nine and 22 2/9% on the point Six or Eight. The point Four has no percentage edge either way.

Electric Dice

These cubes contain steel slugs and are used over an electric magnet built into a crap table or counter. The slugs used in transparent dice are made by gluing together 5/1000-inch steel wires to form a grid and punching out circular disks which fit into the countersunk spots. One is inserted in each of the spots on four different sides of the die, leaving the two sides that the operator wants to favor (opposite sides like the 6 and Ace) open.

The magnetic field set up by a concealed electromagnet acts and brings one or the other of the unloaded sides up. Since the load is so light and since it is on four sides, neither pivot nor water test will detect electric dice. Furthermore, their roll is not only natural but even honest some of the time. However, the moment the operator puts on the squeeze by pushing the button that controls the electro-magnet concealed beneath the playing surface, the electric dice act like trained seals. They are not percentage dice; the action is completely positive. The boys who use these don't intend to give anyone a break.

On the steer-joint Craps table the magnetic plate is close to the rail and just beneath the spot where most shooters will throw the dice. The pull of the magnet is less noticeable and operates more efficiently on the cubes as they drop down from the backboard than if they were simply rolled across the magnetic spot. Throwing the dice against the rail is, ordinarily, a protective measure, but in the steer joint the reverse is true. But don't try *not* hitting the rail; you won't like what happens then either!

Electric dice may be either missouts or passers, the latter being most often used. Six-ace missouts have the disadvantages that, because they always bring up one of the numbers 2, 12 or 7, the juice cannot be applied on the first roll when 2 and 12 lose and 7 wins. Once the shooter has come out on a point he will always lose when the juice is on because 2 and 12 are no decision and 7 loses.

Electric passers on the other hand throw a variety of points. A pair of electric dice, one die having the 2-5 sides and the other the 3-4 sides open, will throw the numbers 5, 6, 8 or 9. A pair of six-ace trey-four passers will throw 4, 5, 9 or 10.

These dice are as deadly as a cobra and completely positive in action.

Either the dealer or a shill on the outside controls the juice by pressing a button concealed beneath the green baize table covering or by pressing a screwhead on the side or under the edge of the table or a foot control. The operation is known either as putting *the squeeze* on or putting *the juice* on.

How to Test for Electric Dice: There isn't any safe method. It can be done very simply by applying a magnet, but there's no point in testing for electric dice in a reputable casino, and if you try it in a crooked one, you'll meet the house bouncer but quick and will find yourself sitting in an alley outside, wishing that an ambulance would come along, and still not knowing for sure if the dice were electric or not. If you ever suspect electric dice are being used, your best protection is to take a quick look around for the nearest exit and use it.

The Slick Dice Cup: The average player believes that use of a dice cup protects him against cheats. Nothing could be further from the truth. More cheating at Craps, Backgammon, Poker Dice, Buck Dice, High Dice and other dice games takes place when a dice cup is in use than when the dice are thrown from the hand. Why? Because its easier to cheat and less detectable when crooked dice and dice cup are in use. All a cheat requires to take the unsuspecting player is a slick dice cup and a set of 2, 3, 4 or 5 loaded dice called *first flop dice*, depending on the game being played. The cheat places the loaded dice in the crooked dice cup and the dirty work begins.

The slick dice cup has a smooth slicked inner surface and when the cheat shakes the cup with an up and down and slightly rotary motion of his arm, the loaded dice instead of rattling at random inside the cup spin around the inside surface like wooden horses on a merry-go-round. The centrifugal force lines the dice up within the cup in a horizontal position. The last sideward shake just before they are thrown causes the loaded dice to top over so that their loaded sides are down. When the cheat throws them, he holds the cup parallel with the playing surface, shoves it forward a bit and jerks it back quickly so that the dice all slide out without turning over and the cheat throws a desired number. When the other players throw using the same cup and dice, they shake and throw properly and the loaded dice do them no good. To avoid being cheated with a slick cup, use a "trip cup," which contains obstructions in its inner surface that make the dice tumble as they are thrown and prevents the shark from sliding them out. Some cups have a trip rim; others are lined with ribbed rubber.

If a trip cup is not available, you can insist that the dice be well shaken—and that the cup be turned completely upside down on the throw so that the dice bounce on the playing surface and do not slide out. Don't hesitate to examine the dice.

CHEATING WITH HONEST DICE

There are still a great many Craps players who don't quite believe the stories about cheats who can make fair dice act like performing seals. "Can fair dice be controlled?" is a question I am often asked. The answer is Yes, but only on certain playing surfaces. The dice mechanic has not yet been born who can bounce a pair of honest dice against a hard backboard and bring up two desired numbers when they drop on a hard playing surface. But there are a good many dice cheats who have practiced long and hard and have perfected the ability to make honest dice behave as they want them to under certain conditions.

The spin shot or whip shot, although difficult to perfect, is the commonest dice-control shot. It works best on soft dirt. The dice are held with the desired numbers on top, rattled in the hand but not actually shaken. A quick whiplike snap of the hand sends them spinning through the air like twin helicopters. When the dice land, the spinning motion keeps them from rolling and they settle down, the wanted numbers still on top. This shot can also be done on hard surfaces; some dice cheats sprinkle a few grains of salt on the playing surface, which helps the dice to spin and slide without turning over. It can also be accomplished on the green baize surface of the Bank or Open Craps table, which is why casinos insist that the player hit the backboard or throw the dice over an elastic string stretched across the center of the table.

The *blanket roll* uses the opposite principle. The dice are thrown in such a way that they roll end over end like wheels. The numbers on the outer sides of the dice do not come up, and certain combinations therefore cannot be made. The shot works best on a blanket, a bed cover or a soft carpet, and it is not difficult to learn. Many players have heard of this one, but not many can recognize it when they see it. Watch the shooter, and if he picks the dice up a bit too carefully and seems to be looking for certain numbers, keep your money in your pocket. If the cheat holds the dice so that the sixes, the aces, or an ace and six face each other, these numbers won't show and a crap or 11 cannot be made.

The *backboard control shot* is a modern percentage controlled shot that makes use of blanket, soft rug or carpet plus a three-foot-high vertical backboard lined with foam rubber. As a rule throwing the dice against a backboard is a protective measure against dice cheats, but not with this gaffed setup. Before releasing the dice from the hand, the cheat gives the dice a phony shake, à la spin shot. Then instead of rolling the dice on the soft surface as in the blanket roll, he lets them fly against the backboard in such a way that both dice hit the backboard at the same time causing them to bounce off the backboard onto the soft surface. The momentum causes them to roll back and over end like a pair of cartwheels without turning sideways. If 3–4 is one hub of the wheel and 2–5 the other, the only way the cheat can seven out is with a three and four.

The *three-cushion controlled dice shot* is a highly secretive private dice-game cheating method. This controlled throw requires the use of a three-foot-high vertical backboard and two sideboards, each lined with foam rubber. The table surface must be smooth—usually a piece of linoleum or plastic—so that the dice will slide to a stop. The three-cushion shot is most effective since few gamblers believe it is possible to hit a sideboard, backboard and sideboard, and still control the dice.

The Lock Grip. Dice are held with wanted spots on top and retained as above during the shake. Dice will rattle but cannot turn over. (Conrad Eiger)

To execute this fantastic dice control shot, the cheat shakes the dice, à la spin shot, and throws the dice against the right sideboard where they ricochet off the sideboard onto the backboard and onto the left sideboard. After dropping onto the smooth playing surface, they slide and finally come to rest with the desired numbers uppermost.

The *dice table control shot* is a new casino dice table control shot. It is the most difficult dice throw to perfect because it requires perfect aim and timing that can be gained only by long and arduous practice on a regulation casino dice table. This dice throw has taken many a casino operator for a bundle. Before the publication of this book, it is doubtful that more than a handful of gamblers and casino operators had the slightest idea that such a controlled shot exists. And I firmly believe that once this book hits the stores, dice table manufacturers will make certain that it can't work on their tables.

Most modern dice tables have a sponge rubber embossed zig-zag pattern lining the inside of the four 10-inch upright rails that enclose the table's playing surface. However, a bottom inch of this lining, at the juncture of the table surface and the upright rails, does not possess the embossed zigzag patterns—it is plain sponge rubber. And this is exactly the spot the dice cheat must hit to control this shot.

The pickup of the dice in order to execute this controlled shot is difficult to detect because only one die has to be maneuvered into position. Immediately after the dice have been offered to the cheater-shooter, he picks them up in such a manner that one die has the desired number uppermost. This die is held palm down between the thumb and the first two fingers of the cheat's right hand flat on the table surface. The cheat lets the dice fly out of his palm-down hand from the table surface giving the one die he wants to control a whip-like snap aiming at the juncture of the table surface and the sponge rubber sideboard. When the spinning die hits this spot of the sideboard (the bottom inch), it bounces off at an angle and drops into the center of the table without turning over, with the desired number remaining uppermost. If the cheat holds the die so that a five is always uppermost, a hardway ten becomes an even bet. The same holds true for the point numbers 6, 8 and 9.

The use of sleight of hand with dice or cards is hard to expose because there is no physical evidence to prove it. Even if you can spot a controlled roll, all you can do is insist on the use of a backboard, and if you are voted down on that, stop playing.

PROTECTION AGAINST DICE CHEATS

At this point you're probably wondering if there is any simple sure-fire all-around method of making sure that the dice in the games you play are honest. I'm sorry, but the answer is "No!" Your best protection is to have the information given in this dice chapter in your head. If you are smartened up to all the methods and angles, you will have reduced your chance of being cheated with crooked cubes or a controlled dice throw to a minimum.

The only absolutely certain way of never being cheated at a dice game is not to play. But if this rule proves a little too tough to follow, you should at least take a good look at the cubes and follow these rules:

1. Check that each of the two dice in use total seven on all opposing sides.

2. Check that all sides are level and not concave, rounded or with raised spots.

3. Check that all sides are equally polished.

4. Check that the edges and corners are all straight, square and preferably sharp rather than rounded. If rounded, see that all edges and corners are rounded equally.

5. Check that the spots are all countersunk the same distance and the paint on all spots is the same distance from the cube's surface. Better still, use flush-spot dice.

6. The dice should pass the pivot or water test for loads.

7. Whenever possible, use transparent dice.

8. If the dice cup in use is not a trip dice cup, insist that the dice be well shaken and the cup turned completely upside down on the throw so that the dice drop on the playing platform.

9. Never play dice on a blanket or soft surface and avoid throwing dice against an upright backboard lined with sponge rubber.

If the dice meet the above requirements and you're able to protect yourself against the dice cheat's crooked control throws, your only worry is the dice cheat whose trained fingers can switch a pair of crooked dice for an honest pair as quickly as you can say "Scarne," or if you are playing in a steer joint that is using electric dice.

I have described the most used dice cheating devices and methods, but there are others. For information on such things as the slide shot, the Greek shot, the twist shot, how to switch dice, the dice-cup switch, and (with two dice) the pin gaff, heavy paint work, busters, etc., see *Scarne on Dice.*

CRAPS BETTING SYSTEMS

More betting systems have been created to beat the game of Craps than any other banking game, including race betting, Roulette and Black Jack. The Craps game operator and dice hustler earn money by making Old Man Percentage work for them; the dice cheat earns money by beating the dice chumps with crooked dice. And the average Craps player, nursing a hope of getting rich from the Craps table, usually comes up with a system that he either bought or invented. In most cases he reads, in one of the national men's magazines, of some Craps system that the author states is infallible, or he reads an advertisement in some pulp magazine or gambling-house-supply catalog and invests a few bucks in a booklet that promises to tell him *How to Win at Dice,* or *How to Beat a Bank Craps Game,* simply by following a certain betting method.

The Rothstein System

The Rothstein system uses the general principle on which most dice systems are based. It is our old friend the Martingale, double-up or progressive system in disguise, and it is more commonly employed at the dice table than at any other gambling game. It is advertised this way:

THE ROTHSTEIN SYSTEM

Did you ever try to beat the RACES? It cannot be done. And you cannot beat Craps games any more than you can beat the races. Craps games are MADE TO WIN for the house. Unless you use a SYSTEM.

The Rothstein Craps system is a simple mathematical progressive way of placing bets on the layout. And if the system is adhered to, STICK TO THE SYSTEM, it will win. Figures do not lie and this system is nothing but a simple play of figures.

Anyone that can count 1-2-3-4-5-6 etc., can use the ROTHSTEIN SYSTEM. We sold it to a man in Ohio and he wrote back inside of a week and told us he made $225.00 with the system.

It is guaranteed to win if you FOLLOW THE SYSTEM. The only thing that can keep you from winning is the houseman. He does not like a system player and can, if he wishes, bar anyone. All that is required is that the house fades your bets. Not a crooked move of any kind. . . . $3.00.

It should also be obvious to anyone who "can count 1–2–3–4–5–6" that if a man had a guaranteed winning system, peddling it to all comers at three bucks is the last thing he would do. Actually, this ad does not misrepresent the facts as much as some of them do. After stating that the system is guaranteed to win, it actually tells, in the next-to-last sentence, exactly why the system won't work!

Here's the dope. Your first step is to place 1 chip on the pass line. If you lose, you bet 3 chips, and if you lose that you bet 7 chips. Each time you lose, you double your last bet plus 1. If you win after your first bet, you are ahead 1 chip; after the second bet, 2 chips; after the third bet, 3 chips, etc. And each time you win, you go back and start the progression over again with the 1-chip bet.

"Sometimes," the instructions read, "the dice go clear around the table before they make a pass. This is unusual but it will happen. Nevertheless they *must* pass some time and, while it may take the heart out of players to keep piling chips up, the chips will all come back when a pass is made and there will be surplus chips with them. THIS IS A SYSTEM THAT NO HOUSEMAN LIKES TO SEE USED AGAINST HIS GAME."

That last sentence is strictly off the beam, since stickmen have a habit of crying, "Double up, men! They're bound to change. Double up and beat the bank!" The house likes to see this system used because in trying to win small amounts steadily the player must make many bets; and the more bets he makes, the more the house earns in percentage.

Before I put my finger on the big hitch in the whole scheme, let me first describe another variation of the progressive system known as:

The Watcher or Patience System

The instructions on this one lead off by warning that you must have plenty of patience, and, incidentally, $500 to $1,000 capital. With those two requirements the system is guaranteed to win $10 a day, rain or shine, day in and day out. Don't be greedy, the writer warns, just be satisfied with the ten bucks per day and everything is Jake. "This system has been tried and is recommended by some of the smartest dice players in the country."

This time, instead of betting the dice to win, you are to bet the dice to lose. Much stress is laid on the fact that you must watch the dice and not make any bets until after four successive passes have been made. Then bet $10 that they lose on the fifth. This clever little dodge saves you the loss of four $10 bets! Since a penny saved is a penny earned, you're already making money!

You have a far better chance betting the dice to lose on the fifth pass than on the first because the odds against five successive passes being made are 31 to 1. It's practically a sure thing. You'll lose such a proposition only once in 32 times. Then you take your $10 and leave. Don't be greedy and be tempted to try the system twice in the same night.

And, if you should lose that 31 to 1 shot? You merely bet $20 that the dice will lose on the next pass. The odds against six passes being made are 63 to 1. If, by any strange streak of fate, you lose that one, too, bet $40 that they don't pass. The odds are 127 to 1 against seven successive passes. You can hardly ask for better odds in your favor than that.

I know one player who bought and played this system for four weeks. He came away every night wearing a broad smile and with a $10 profit. Of course, sometimes he had to wait hours before four passes were made in a row so that he could begin betting, but he expected that; instructions told him he needed plenty of patience.

But one night he had a little difficulty. When he walked into the casino, he had won $10 a night for four weeks and was $280 ahead of the game. When the fourth pass was made, he bet $10 on the next. The shooter sevened. He bet $20 and the shooter threw an 11. He bet $40 and the shooter sevened again. He bet $80, and a point was bucked right back. He bet $160 and began sweating. But he had faith in the system; it was guaranteed to win. A miss-out *had* to come sometime, and when it did he'd be $10 ahead once more.

Then the shooter crapped out with two sixes and my friend relaxed, all smiles, but only for a moment. The house made no move to pay off.

"Hey," the player asked, "I had $160 down to lose. Don't I get—"

The stickman gave him a sour look. "Something wrong?" he asked, pointing to the space on the layout which read "Two sixes standoff." "In case you don't know, that means there's no payoff, but you don't lose either."

My friend scowled. He was learning fast now. The system sheet hadn't said anything about a standoff, but he began to see that it gave the house two whacks at his dough. There was nothing he could do, however, but let the $160 ride on the next come-out and hope for any crap except two sixes.

The dice came out—a natural with a 6–5. The house raked in the $160, and my friend, now shy a total of $310, reached shakily for his roll, counted off $320 and threw it on the table.

Then he bumped head-on into another very hard fact that the system had failed to stress.

"Sorry, sir," the boxman said, "but you can bet only three hundred. That's the limit at this table."

Now what? If he bet the $300 and won, he would still be a $10 loser. If he lost he'd be shy $610 altogether. The guaranteed system hadn't said anything about a situation in which he'd lose no matter what happened. He'd forgotten that one little line in the ad which read: "All that is required is that the house fades your bets."

While he was trying to make up his mind the dice came out and the shooter sevened. His hesitation saved him $300. But he was still shy $310, thirty bucks more than the $280 it had taken him four weeks of patient waiting to win.

This is also the flaw in the Rothstein system. In fact, every progressive system eventually runs smack up against the house maximum betting limit and explodes in the player's face. Take a close look at the usual house betting limits and you'll see that the spread between the minimum and maximum betting limits prevents the system player from doubling up more than six or seven times. A 25¢ to $25 top, for instance, allows him to bet 25¢ and then double by betting 50¢, $1, $2, $4, $8 and $16. If he loses each bet he's sunk, because the seventh doubling up will take him above the limit. The same thing holds true of the 50¢ to $50 and the $1 to $75 or $100, the $2 to $200 or $300 and the $5 to $500 limits.

One book on dice systems even introduces the subject by warning the player to find out the rules governing the limit of the stakes before beginning to play. "The best system," it adds, "is worthless unless the house allows adequate margin for raising the stakes." The writer then wades into a complex explanation of the Patience system as applied to all sorts of games and neglects to mention that *all* houses do have a limit that *does not* allow an adequate margin for raising the stakes. This booklet bears a $5 price on its cover and is sold for $2.50 "while they last." It has been in print for years.

There are also a few things wrong with the advice to watch for four passes before betting and then put your money on the fifth pass because the odds against its being made are 31 to 1. Those are the odds that five successive passes won't be made, all right, but you are *not* betting that five passes won't be made. You are betting that the *next* pass won't be made. There's a slight difference. The odds on that are, as always, slightly less than 50–50. (When the two sixes are barred you have a 49 23/77% chance.)

The author of the above-mentioned booklet has a couple of other system secrets that deserve passing mention. "Practice Craps in your home for thousands of shots before you dare enter a gambling house. By doing so you will acquire the necessary intuition for guessing the results of the next shot." Any reader who follows this plan and successfully develops intuition of that kind should set up as a fortune-teller.

And the last word on all the systems in the book is the one in which you are advised to play *against* the player using a progressive system! You always bet the same amount he does and "whenever his guess is wrong you have won as many progressive stakes as he has lost. He has to do the guessing, which is the real trick in every game." This writer not only believes in the maturity of chances (which is what his "watching" tactics imply) but also in the gamblers' superstition that the odds are against the guesser! But even at that, he's a little bit smart; he writes a book on systems instead of playing them.

The Hot and Cold System

This one is a lulu. The gambler who advertises it for sale promises the player that "with this system you will be betting they win *every time* the dice are *hot* (making passes), and betting they lose *every time* the dice are *cold* (not passing)."

You think this sounds impossible? You'd pass it up because there just couldn't be any way to make certain that you would be betting they win during every hot spell and betting they lose during every cold spell? Strangely enough, the method given tells you exactly how to do that, and for only $5.

Before you read further, see if you can dope out a way to do it. I warn you, however, that once you've got the answer it won't make a killing.

Here's the method. Whenever a player makes a pass, you begin betting the dice to win. If he continues through a hot spell of passes, you're on it. And the moment he throws a miss-out you begin, with the next roll, betting the dice to lose. Now you're sure to be on any cold spell. And as soon as another pass appears you switch back again. The moment that someone makes a long series of either passes or miss-outs you are in the big money. Sounds good, doesn't it?

Here's the catch. The instructions forgot to say what would happen when a pass is followed by a miss-out, then a pass, then a miss-out and so on, passes and miss-outs coming alternately. What would happen? Playing the hot-and-cold system, you would lose every single bet during the time the dice acted that way.

And, because this system requires that you bet on every decision, the price you'll pay the house in percentage before you discover for yourself what's wrong will be a darned sight more than the five bucks the system cost you. The house and the guy who sells the system make the money—but you lose.

The Place Betting System

This is one of the favorite Craps systems used by some of the so-called smart bigtime gamblers. When chance is working in its favor, this system, which first made its appearance in 1940, appears so certain to win money that many a player using it has been told by casino bosses in no uncertain terms to scram and take his business elsewhere.

Here's the method of betting. The high roller usually bets the maximum limit, although lesser amounts can be wagered. For example, he puts $300 to win on each of the six place bets: 4, 5, 6, 8, 9 and 10, wagering a total of $1,800. The moment one of these numbers is made, he collects his winning bet and calls off the $1,500 bet on the remaining five place numbers. Place bets can be called down any time in most casinos throughout the country.

Whenever a Four or Ten is made the player wins $540 (at 9 to 5 odds). When a Five or Nine is made he wins $420 (at 7 to 5 odds). If a Six or Eight is made he wins $350 (at 7 to 6 odds). The high roller and also the worried dice game operator figure that he has six numbers, the 4, 5, 6, 8, 9 and 10, going for him, against the bank's lone number, 7. And because he believe he is only paying the bank a percentage on one place bet, he thinks he must eventually beat the bank.

Since those six place numbers can be made in 24 ways and the Seven can only be made in six ways, the odds are 4 to 1 in favor of the system player's winning either $540, $420 or $350. But if the losing Seven appears before one of the six place numbers is thrown, which is 1 in 5, the system player loses $1,800. Even so, it looks like a good bet to the system player because if he makes a couple of Fours or Tens he's beating the game.

To find the fallacy here we must discover whether the player pays the bank a percentage on the bets he calls down, and if so, how much? To do this we must analyze a series of 36 bets.

Let's suppose that the system player in a single dice session makes 36 such $1,800 place bets, and let us assume that the dice fall exactly as probability predicts and each of the 36 combinations on the dice are made. Craps and ELEVENS will be made 6 times out of the 36 rolls, but since they do not affect a decision, we can ignore them and consider only 30 bets of $1,800 for a total of $54,000 wagered.

The numbers FOUR and TEN will each be made three times, or six times altogether, and the player retrieves his $1,800 plus $540 in winnings six times out of 30 for a total of $14,040. The numbers FIVE and NINE will each be made four times, or eight times altogether. The player will retrieve his $1,800 eight times plus $420 in winnings each of the eight times, for a total take-in of $17,760. The numbers SIX and EIGHT will be thrown five times each, a total of ten times, and the player retrieves his $1,800 plus $350 in winnings ten times, for a total of $21,500. These winning totals add to a grand win total of $53,300. Subtracting this win total from the $54,000 wagered, we get a loss of $700, or 1.296%.

This brings up one of the most unusual percentage problems in Craps. Why should this system player pay a smaller overall percentage than the percentage on any single place bet? This is because the system player in this instance is actually laying $1,800 to $540, $1,800 to $420, or $1,800 to $350, instead of taking the odds. However, when the percentage is computed on the actual money turnover ($10,800 lost on the 6 sevens and $10,000 won on the 24 place bets), the house percentage increases to 3.35%.

The Right and Wrong Way System

This two-way betting system has been a conversation piece for many old-time Private Craps game hustlers for years. It recently popped up again in a booklet published by a Chicago gambling-supply house, and the writer assures the reader that he can beat any Bank Craps game simply by betting the dice to lose and win at the same time.

The writer advises the system player to bet heavily right from the start because in a short time the management will realize he has a sure-fire system and will bar him from further playing. The idea is for the system player to win as much as he can before being barred.

Here's the method the system writer describes.

The system player walks up to a Bank Craps table and places a $60 bet on the don't pass or lose line before the come-out. The shooter on the come-out throws a point number, either 4, 5, 6, 8, 9 or 10, and the system player takes $60 worth of place odds on the point. (See page 297 for place bet odds.)

You begin to see what the theory is now? If the shooter fails to make the point, the system player, who has taken $108 to $60 on the point FOUR (or TEN) will lose his place bet, but will win the $60 bet on the don't pass line, thus breaking even. But if the shooter makes the point FOUR, the system player loses the $60 bet on the don't pass line, but wins $108 on the FOUR, for a $48 profit. If the point number is FIVE or NINE, the system player breaks even or wins $24 on either point; on the points SIX or EIGHT, he breaks even or wins $10!

According to the author of this booklet, since the player must either break even or win, he can't lose, barring naturals and craps on the come-out.

This statement leaves us breathless. Since this system is based on betting the don't pass line, it is utterly impossible to bar naturals and craps on the come-out.

But let's forget this little gem and go on to our analysis of what actually happens to the player who bets the system over a long Craps session.

Let's take 360 dice decisions and bet $60 wrong and right. We bet $60 on the don't pass line 360 times for a total of $21,600. Out of the 360 decisions, SEVEN or ELEVEN will appear 80 times on the come-out, losing the system player $4,800. Craps will appear 40 times, but since 10 of these craps will be standoffs, due to the bar on the two sixes or the two aces, the system player will win only 30 times for a total of $1,800. The points FOUR or TEN will appear 60 times, compelling the system player to wager $60 each of the 60 times for a total of $3,600 more. The system player breaks even 40 times when the point is missed and earns $48 each of the 20 times it is made for a profit of $960. The points FIVE or NINE appear 80 times, compelling the system player to bet $60 each of the 80 times for a total of $4,800. He breaks even 48 times when the point is missed, and he wins $24 each of the 32 times it is made for a profit of $768. The points SIX and EIGHT will appear 100 times, and the player is forced to bet $60 each time for an additional total of $6,000. The system player breaks even the 54 6/11 times when the point is missed, and he wins $10 on each of the 45 5/11 times it is made for a profit of $454.55.

If we add the system player's winnings of $1,800 on the craps, $960 on the FOURS and TENS, $768 on FIVES and NINES and the $454.55 on the SIXES and EIGHTS, we get a winning total of $3,982.55. Subtracting this total from the $4,800 our system player lost on the naturals, we find that his net loss is $817.45, and, since the system player risked a total of $36,000 playing the system, his rate of loss is 2.27%.

Scarne's Bank Craps System

This is the Bank Craps betting system I used at the Craps tables I visited in this country during my casino survey.

I used this system not to win money but to cut down my Craps losses during my survey. I selected the Bank Craps bets with the smallest house percentage and systemized them. The bets used were the pass line bet, come bet and free odds bet on the point which carried a house edge of .848%.

Neither the Craps dealers nor the casino bosses like to see this system used at their tables. Not because they are afraid it will break the bank—the dealers don't like it because it makes considerably more work for them than usual; the casino bosses don't like it because each bet made involved in the system gives the house the smallest favorable percentage at Bank Craps.

This system is not guaranteed to beat the bank because, like all other systems, the player is bucking adverse odds. But it will cut the bank's earning power to a rock-bottom minimum and increase your chances of winning as against those of the average Craps player.

Here's the method:

Bet a chip on the Pass line before the come-out. If the shooter throws a natural or crap, again bet a chip on the pass line. If the shooter throws a point number, 4, 5, 6, 8, 9 or 10, you take the odds on the point. You received the correct odds on this bet since the bank levies no charge. (See page 298.)

On the next throw of the dice, you bet 1 chip on the come, and if a 4, 5, 6, 8, 9 or 10 is thrown, you take 1 chip's worth of odds on this number. You again receive the correct odds because of your come bet.

With a rate of loss of .848%, you can expect to pay $84.80 on $10,000 worth of action, and $848 on $100,000 worth of action. So, you see, all systems are worthless, even the best of them.

If you want to shave the bank's percentage down a bit more—to .832%—simply bet the don't pass and don't come space and lay the free odds.

The Craps Hustler's Private Game System

The smart Private Craps game hustlers whom I have seen in action have their own surefire winning system. They manage to get Old Man Percentage to work for them instead of against them. It goes something like this:

Since the hustlers know that the odds in Private Craps favor the wrong bettor, they usually bet wrong. They rarely shoot the dice, but, instead, fade the center or make one or more wrong flat bets because these bets give a favorable edge of 1.414%. When 4, 5, 9 or 10 is the point, they lay the correct odds, but since these wagers give them no percentage they hold them down to a minimum. When the point Six or Eight appears, and they are laying even money, they increase the size of their bets so as to be sure to earn that 9 1/11% edge.

Even with this betting advantage, they still refuse all further action if a player makes two passes. The reason they give for this is that they avoid any chance of going broke while bucking a shooter who might run into a long winning streak. This action, they say, serves as their maximum betting limit and prevents other players from winning too much of their cash in too short a time and then quitting the game. The system works and they earn money with it—against players who don't know the correct odds.

11.
Correct Odds
in Dice Games
Using Two, Three,
Four or Five Dice

Dozens of different private and banking dice games are played today; their names and rules vary in different parts of the country. Some players cannot distinguish between similar games such as Hazard and Chuck-a-Luck.

The great majority of these games make use of from two to five dice, and nearly all the hustler's sucker or proposition bets are made on throws of 2, 3, 4 or 5 dice. They usually involve either the combined total or the appearance of one or one of several possible combinations of hands such as one pair, two pair and three of a kind, etc.

The following tables show the various combinations, the number of ways they can be made and the odds against making them in one trial. These tables will enable the player to analyze most of the dice problems he will meet. Reference to the correct odds shown here will show whether or not a proposition bet is a sucker bet. These odds will also enable the player to figure the house's favorable percentage in a banking game. The tables also give you the answers to odds problems that arise in other dice games. The method for figuring the house percentage is shown in the discussion of Hazard, Chuck-a-Luck, Beat the Shaker and other dice games in Chapter 19.

TABLE OF COMBINATIONS AND WAYS

TWO DICE

Specific Hands and Combinations	Number of Ways		Odds Against, in One Trial
One pair	6		5 to 1
A specific pair		1	35 to 1
No pair	30		1 to 5
A specific no pair		2	17 to 1
Total combinations of all kinds *	36		

* The "total combinations of all hands" figure in the above and following tables do not include the ways of making *specific* combinations. For instance, a specific pair can be made in 1 way and this way is included in the 6 ways that one pair (unspecified) can be made.

THREE DICE

Specific Hands and Combinations	Number of Ways		Odds Against, in One Trial
Three of a kind	6		35.0 to 1
A specific three of a kind		1	215.0 to 1
One pair	90*		1.4 to 1
A specific pair		15	13.4 to 1
No pair	120		4.0 to 5
Total combination of all hands	216		

* Although there are actually only 6 one pairs, from aces to sixes, the figure 90 above gives you the total number of ways of holding a pair plus one of the other 5 numbers on the third die. The same holds true for most of the hands shown in the following tables.

FOUR DICE

Specific Hands and Combinations	Number of Ways		Odds Against, in One Trial
Four of a kind	6		215.0 to 1
A specific four of a kind		1	1295.0 to 1
Three of a kind	120		9.8 to 1
A specific three of a kind		20	63.8 to 1
Two pairs	90		13.4 to 1
A specific two pairs		6	215.0 to 1
One pair	720		4.0 to 5
A specific one pair		120	9.8 to 1
No pairs	360		2.6 to 1
Total combinations of all hands	1,296		

FIVE DICE

Specific Hands and Combinations	Number of Ways		Odds Against, in One Trial
Five of a kind	6		1295.0 to 1
A specific five of a kind		1	7775.0 to 1
Four of a kind	150		50.8 to 1
A specific four of a kind		25	310.0 to 1
Full house	300		24.9 to 1
A specific full house		10	776.6 to 1
Straight	240		31.4 to 1
A specific straight		120	63.8 to 1
Three of a kind	1,200		5.5 to 1
A specific three of a kind		200	37.8 to 1
Two pairs	1,800		3.3 to 1
A specific two pairs		120	63.8 to 1
One pair	3,600		1.2 to 1
A specific one pair		600	11.9 to 1
No pairs *	480		15.2 to 1
Total combinations of all hands	7,776		

* When straights do not count, the number of no pairs increases to 720.

FIVE DICE, ACES WILD

Specific Hands and Combinations	Number of Ways	Odds Against, in One Trial
Five of a kind	156	48.8 to 1
A specific five of a kind (no aces *)	31	249.8 to 1
Five aces	1	7775.0 to 1
Four of a kind	1,300	4.9 to 1
A specific four of a kind (no aces)	260	28.9 to 1
Full house	500	14.5 to 1
A specific full house (no aces)	50	154.5 to 1
Straights	1,320	4.8 to 1
A specific straight (A–2–3–4–5)†	360	20.6 to 1
A specific straight (2–3–4–5–6)	1,320	4.8 to 1
Three of a kind	2,400	2.2 to 1
A specific three of a kind (no aces)	480	15.2 to 1
Two pairs	900	7.6 to 1
A specific two pairs (no aces)	90	85.4 to 1
One pair	1,200	5.5 to 1
A specific pair (no aces)	240	31.4 to 1
Total combinations of all hands	7,776	

* The words in parentheses (no aces) means that you cannot make such a hand. Example: No matter what numbers show on the dice, it is impossible to make a four-ace hand (with aces wild). If you threw four aces and a deuce, you would have five deuces; if you threw two aces and a pair of deuces, you would have four deuces, etc.

† The 360 ways the A–2–3–4–5 straight may be thrown are made up of the following five dice combinations: A–2–3–4–5, A–A–2–3–4, A–A–2–3–5, A–A–2–4–5, and A–A–3–4–5. However, due to the wild ace or aces in each of the 360 ways that make up the A–2–3–4–5 straight, these same 360 combinations may also be called a 2–3–4–5–6 straight, for a total of 1,320 ways.

TABLES OF NUMBERS AND WAYS

TWO DICE

Numbers	Ways	Odds Against, in One Trial
2 (or 12)	1	35.0 to 1
3 (or 11)	2	17.0 to 1
4 (or 10)	3	11.0 to 1
5 (or 9)	4	8.0 to 1
6 (or 8)	5	6.2 to 1
7	6	5.0 to 1
Total	36	

THREE DICE

Numbers	Ways	Odds Against, in One Trial
3 (or 18)	1	215.0 to 1
4 (or 17)	3	71.0 to 1
5 (or 16)	6	35.0 to 1
6 (or 15)	10	20.6 to 1
7 (or 14)	15	13.4 to 1
8 (or 13)	21	9.3 to 1
9 (or 12)	25	7.6 to 1
10 (or 11)	27	7.0 to 1
Total	216	

FOUR DICE

Numbers	Ways	Odds Against, in One Trial
4 (or 24)	1	1295.0 to 1
5 (or 23)	4	323.0 to 1
6 (or 22)	10	128.6 to 1
7 (or 21)	20	63.8 to 1
8 (or 29)	35	36.0 to 1
9 (or 19)	56	22.1 to 1
10 (or 18)	88	13.7 to 1
11 (or 17)	96	12.5 to 1
12 (or 16)	125	9.3 to 1
13 (or 15)	140	8.3 to 1
14	146	7.8 to 1
Total	1,296	

FIVE DICE

Numbers	Ways	Odds Against, in One Trial
5 (or 30)	1	7775.0 to 1
6 (or 29)	5	1554.2 to 1
7 (or 28)	15	517.4 to 1
8 (or 27)	35	221.1 to 1
9 (or 26)	70	110.0 to 1
10 (or 25)	126	60.7 to 1
11 (or 24)	205	36.9 to 1
12 (or 23)	305	24.4 to 1
13 (or 22)	420	17.5 to 1
14 (or 21)	540	13.4 to 1
15 (or 20)	651	10.9 to 1
16 (or 19)	735	9.5 to 1
17 (or 18)	780	8.9 to 1
Total	7,776	

12.
Black Jack,
or Twenty-One:
Casino Style

Black Jack, or Twenty-One, is the most widely played banking card game in the world today. My survey shows that the yearly gross betting handle of private and casino Black Jack was $30 billion. Further, the survey indicates that about half of this, or $15 billion, was wagered at the intriguing and often perplexing form of casino Black Jack. This makes casino-style Black Jack as played in Nevada, Puerto Rico, the Bahamas, England, Turkey, Yugoslavia, Panama, Curaçao, Aruba, St. Maarten and elsewhere second only to Bank and Money Craps in volume of money wagered. This money was bet by better than 24 million players, of whom 8 million were women. Although men still outnumber women Black Jack players 3 to 1, so many more women are playing the game each year that it won't surprise me if the number of women players equals or surpasses that of the men within the next ten years.

Black Jack today is played in every gambling joint in the country, in most private clubs and in about five out of every ten illegally run cardrooms. It is a sure bet that in any bigtime legal gambling spot you will find at least one Black Jack table, two cards in front of each player, and the dealer trying to look as poker-faced as possible, with the players calling "Hit me," "Stand," "That's enough" and "Oh, damn! I busted," or indicating these calls by hand motions.

During the past decade, the popularity of casino-style Black Jack has been growing by leaps and bounds. If it continues to increase at the same rate, another ten years will probably see Black Jack replacing Craps at the foremost casino banking game. This great upsurge in the play of Black Jack playing is due primarily to the first edition of this

342

John Scarne describes the workings of a Black Jack dealing shoe (box) to casino personnel in Puerto Rico. This B-J dealing shoe was developed by the author while acting as gaming advisor to the Havana Hilton Hotel casino in Havana, Cuba, prior to Fidel Castro.

book, because in 1961 for the first time appeared in print the scientific analysis of Black Jack with its optimum strategy. After this book was published the techniques were parroted by hundreds of so-called Black Jack experts and game-book authors.

CASINO BETTING LIMITS

One proof of this vast increase in the popularity of Black Jack is a comparison of the maximum betting limits of a few years ago with those of today. A decade ago, most Nevada casinos had a $50 and $100 maximum, and the top limit at casinos in Puerto Rico was $100. Today most casinos in Nevada, the Bahamas, etc., have a $500 limit, and many casinos will raise this to $1,000 or more for a bigtime gambler or high roller.

Most casinos in the Caribbean advertise a $200 or $300 limit but this isn't adhered to for the big bettors. The majority, except the Puerto Rico casinos which keep to $200 limits, will raise stakes to $1,000, $1,500 or even $2,000, and if you think this isn't bigtime gam-

.bling, think again, brother. Recently, at the Curaçao Hilton Hotel casino in the Netherlands Antilles, I saw a woman delegate to the United Nations who had been given a limit of $1,000 lose $80,000 at Black Jack in a couple of hours. The casino manager then offered her a $5,000 limit on each hand. She refused, apparently feeling that an eighty-grand loss was enough for one evening. Incidentally, the largest single loss on record by a Black Jack player was $500,000 over a period of a week's play at the Paradise Isle Casino in the Bahamas a couple of years ago.

THE $250,000 WIN

Black Jack happens to be a very tricky game, and raising the limit to $2,000 may not be so smart if the players are card hustlers who know much more about the game than the casino operator suspects. This is especially true when deviations from the usual rules, such as accepting *proposition bets* (wagers that are not standard), are allowed.

As an instance, let's take the biggest Black Jack winning play of all time. Three men proved to the Cuban casinos that they knew more about the subtleties of Black Jack than the operators by winning a cool $250,000. Let me start with this excerpt from an article written by my good friend Edward Scott, "Going for Broke at the 23rd Parallel." It appeared in the October 16, 1958, issue of the *Havana Post:*

> There's a lot more to this gambling business than meets the eye, as the losers are perfectly willing to admit after they have dropped a packet. But sometimes a man can devote a lifetime to the profession, as has been done by Lefty Clark, and still, along the way, he can pick up important pieces of new information. Sometimes this additional knowledge costs more than a trifling sum of money.
>
> A few weeks ago, a couple of Americans went to the gambling casino then being well and efficiently operated by Mr. Clark in Marianao (he is no longer associated with that establishment) and entered with him into ye gayme and playe of blackjack. At the request of the patrons, a higher limit than usual was fixed for the wagers.
>
> The players were consistent winners. Mr. Clark knew that they were "on the level," but he could not figure out how they could enjoy such amazing luck. Not for one second (and it was he who told me this) did he imagine that they could keep count of the face cards that had fallen, because the dealer's box contained four packs of cards.
>
> That, however, is precisely what they were doing. Mr. Clark then resorted to the practice of shuffling the cards [all four decks] when only a third of them were left in the dealer's box. Nevertheless, the visitors continued to win and cashed in for a substantial sum of money.
>
> The following night, or several nights later, the Americans went to play at another legal establishment in Old Havana, where they have no

limits on bets. [He means that limits are raised for special players—J.S.] After about two hours of play, they cashed in for $59,700. After the pay-off, there was a misunderstanding, but the Americans were able to prove their bona fides. One is a wealthy, highly respected New York business-man, and the other is an atomic scientist.

During the course of the discussion resulting from the misunderstand-ing, the two Americans offered to play the house for half a million dollars —and the New York businessman established that he had that kind of money, and plenty to spare. At first it looked like a good thing to the house, but wiser counsel prevailed. The Americans went away, but they were back in town on Tuesday and I saw them in operation.

These two Americans are a phenomenal couple, and the first one to admit it is Lefty Clark. They memorize the number of face cards, includ-ing aces, which have fallen, and when they get down to about one third of the pack, they know exactly how many face cards have yet to fall and what the possibilities are of making a good hand by opening a pair of tens, jacks, queens, kings, or aces.

On the night of the $59,700 coup, I saw them split a pair of kings on which they had wagered $1,000. The house permitted them to bet $2,000 on each king, and they won on both hands.

When I first read Mr. Scott's article I knew that the people he had interviewed didn't really know just what had happened. I was in Ha-vana at the time, so I'll add a few firsthand details and observations. The Marianao casino mentioned is the one at the famed Tropicana nightclub. The old Havana establishment is the casino in the Sevilla Biltmore Hotel. No mention is made of a third casino which these boys took for $50,000—the Casino de Capri. I like to think that these men didn't show up to play at the Habana Hilton casino because I was there as gambling overseer for the Hilton Hotel chain.

The wealthy, highly respected New York businessman and the atomic scientist were just that, but they were also smart American card hustlers. Actually, there were three of them. I ran into the trio in the lobby of the Habana Hilton just after they had left the Sevilla Biltmore with $59,700 in winnings. A moment later Señor Analito Batisti rushed in, accompanied by several police officers. Batisti at that time operated the casino in the Sevilla Biltmore and was Cuba's top gambler. He was also a former representative of Dictator Fulgencio Batista's Congress. Batisti hurried over to the three Americans and accused them excitedly, "You cheat me! You cheat me!"

The Americans were promptly hauled off to the hoosegow at gun-point. Batisti's beef was that they had cheated him by marking the cards. He said that after the trio left his casino he checked the deck and found that several cards were *crimped* (bent). This is a typical casino operator's reaction when he loses a bundle; they are nearly all bad losers. Batisti was not only a bad loser but he had to squeal to the cops, too. He used to claim proudly that his casino would deal a high roller the biggest limit in Cuba. After this incident his claim wasn't taken very seriously.

THE $1 MILLION FREEZE-OUT

The hustlers denied the charge that they had marked the cards and insisted they had merely used honest mathematical strategy. They also claimed they could beat any casino bank in the same way and challenged Batisti to a $500,000 "Black Jack freeze-out." They would put up $500,000 to Batisti's $500,000 and and play Black Jack until one or the other went for broke. They said that they would not touch any of the cards, and all their cards could be dealt face up. They insisted, however, that the same casino rules be adhered to as on the night they had won the $59,700. They wanted the $1,000 limit, the right to split a count of 20, and to double down on each split hand.

Batisti accepted the challenge. He and the hustlers each posted with the police captain $30,000 in cash as a forfeit, in the event that either backed out. Batisti then withdrew his complaint, and the three Americans were released. During the ten hours they had been locked up, Batisti had been severely criticized by the other casino operators in Havana for having the big-money winners arrested. It might, they objected, scare off high rollers from gambling in Cuba. Forty-eight hours later, an agent of the hustlers arrived from the United States with half a million in U.S. currency. Batisti stated that he had an equal amount tucked away in the casino safe waiting to be wagered.

The news of this million-dollar freeze-out spread like wildfire. Casino, bar, nightclub, restaurant and barbershop patrons talked about little else. As a sample, my barber asked me this:

"Mr. John, I hear one of the Americanos is a memory expert and can remember all the cards in four decks. Another Americano is a scientist and has the brain of an adding machine, only faster, and the other is one of the greatest card players in the United States. So, I think Batisti will lose his half million dollars."

Others wondered whether it was possible to beat Black Jack honestly, as the three winners maintained. People talked about it as excitedly and as often as they talk about baseball in this country during a World Series.

The excitement grew still greater when another $600,000 was added to the money at stake on the day before the freeze-out. A pool of American casino operators, including those who had lost such large sums, asked Batisti if he would accept this 600 grand as an additional wager that the Americanos would win. (Who says gamblers don't gamble?) Batisti accepted and told them to bring the money with them to the big game.

I arrived at the Sevilla Biltmore an hour before the game was scheduled. The casino was packed with big- and smalltime gamblers. The three Americans and Batisti were in one corner of the room talking in low tones. An excited air of expectancy filled the place. And why not? This would be the biggest single gamble between player and bank in the history of gambling. The total sum involved was $2,200,000.

But the big gamble fizzled. At the hour it was to begin the principals left the casino and an attendant announced that the freeze-out had been called off.

The three Americans were staying at the Habana Hilton and I talked to them later in their suite. They said that ten minutes before zero hour Batisti had chilled and called all bets off. "But," they added, "he did apologize for the humiliation and inconvenience he had caused us by the arrest." Batisti's reign as Cuba's top gambler ended suddenly on New Year's Day, 1959, when Fidel Castro overthrew Batista's government.

The gambling fraternity in the Caribbean and America are still trying to figure out how these three hustlers managed to buck the Black Jack percentage over a period of time and win a quarter of a million dollars. They don't like the idea that some players may be able to beat the bank with advance strategy, and they worry even more over the possibility that there may be some hidden gimmick they know nothing about.

In order to bring the reader up to date on the further activities of these three American card hustlers, let's turn to the week of March 27, 1964, when *Life* magazine ran a nine-page story by Paul O'Neil titled "The Professor Who Breaks the Bank." The story concerned Edward O. Thorp, a New Mexico mathematics professor, a man who by making use of an IBM 704 computer developed an unbeatable system to beat the casino dealer at Black Jack. Thorp claimed he could average $300,000 a month if the casinos would permit him to play his system. Thorp further stated that he and two of his gambling backers, whom he dubs Mr. X and Mr. Y, had beaten the Black Jack tables in Reno and Lake Tahoe for $11,000 in five days' play.

My investigation of the *Life* story revealed that Thorp's Mr. X and Mr. Y were not the two innocent gambling backers that he claimed them to be, but instead were two of the three American Black Jack hustlers who had beaten the Seville Biltmore casino in Havana for $59,700 a few years earlier. To get the real lowdown on this big $11,000 win of Thorp and Co., I looked up Mr. X, who at the time was vacationing at the Caribe Hilton Hotel in Puerto Rico. Mr. X in answer to my question why he and his partner teamed up with Thorp had this to say: "I read several magazine stories about Thorp and his unbeatable Black Jack system, and being that he is a mathematics professor, I though there might be something to these stories, so we called him on the phone and inquired if he would like to team up with me and my partner to beat the Nevada Black Jack tables by making use of his unbeatable system. Thorp agreed and after the first three days of play in Reno, Nevada, we realized that Thorp knew nothing about the science of Black Jack play, and his countdown system never seemed to work. We were getting our brains knocked out. We finally decided to resort to our own method of play and recouped a few bucks. It was then that we decided to give Thorp the air. Thorp later admitted to us that he never really gambled, but took this gambling trip with us for material he might gather for the book he was in the process of writing."

My next question to Mr. X was in reference to Thorp's statement that the trio was cheated on a number of occasions in Reno and Lake Tahoe. Mr. X replied, "Scarne, you know better than that—if there was any cheating taking place, we'd be doing the cheating."

Mr. X and I then discussed his caper with Mr. Y at the Seville Biltmore Casino in Havana. I told him that in my opinion he and Mr. Y had the dealer fixed by having him tip off his hole card to them. He replied, "What else? The B.J. proposition bets were made to throw Batisti off the track that we had his dealer in our pocket."

Several years later Mr. Y was caught red-handed at Caesar's Palace in Las Vegas trying to bribe a Black Jack dealer to tip off the value of his hole card whenever the dealer was dealt an ace or ten as his up-card.

BLACK JACK MECHANICS

I made a thorough survey of gambling establishments near Army camps at the request of the Army's General Staff during World War II in order to find out if the GIs were being fleeced. I found at that time that a number of the smaller joints only hired dealers who were card *mechanics* (a mechanic is the card sharp who does the sleight of hand). The first question asked of an applicant for the job of Black Jack dealer was "Can you deal a good second?" I know this because one of the best ways to find out if a casino is using a dealer who cheats is to apply for the job. In 1944, on one special Army assignment, I went into a casino whose name I won't mention because it is still in operation and is now being run honestly under new management.

I approached the casino boss and asked if he could use a good Black Jack dealer.

He half-smiled. "Who recommended you?"

"No one," I told him. "But I need a job and thought you might be looking for a good number two man." A "number two man" is gambler's slang for a second dealer, who can deal the second card from the top and make it look as though he were dealing the top card.

The half-smile was replaced by an icy look. "So you're a mechanic. Okay, come into the office and give me a gander at what you can do."

There he told me his name was Bucky. I gave him an alias, John Orlando, and said I was from New Jersey.

"Okay, John," he said. "Here's a deck. Let me see you work."

I shuffled the cards and dealt myself the same Black Jack hand three times in a row. Bucky's sales resistance vanished.

"You've got a job starting tonight. I'll give you twenty-five bucks a night and ten percent of the table's winnings over and above our normal day's business." Then, as an explanation of why the casino was cheating, he added, "You know our season here at the Lake is pretty short. We have to get the money in only three months."

"Yeah," I told him, "I understand."

John Orlando, however, did not report for work that night, there or anywhere else, although I had accepted two other dealing jobs in this town that same day. Each time I had to prove my ability at ripping seconds. These casinos were no exception to the general rule. The country was flooded with card mechanics, and they didn't worry about whom they clipped, or where. GIs were fair game, like anybody else.

Today, gambling casinos of established reputation in Nevada and elsewhere fight the crooked casino operators as a menace to business. When the players eventually get wise that casinos are cheating, business drops off. Your best protection against the crooked Black Jack dealer is to know the game and to be informed on cheats and their methods. For the last, see pages 382–388.

BLACK JACK'S HISTORY

Black Jack as a private rather than a casino banking game was the most popular card game, even more popular than Poker, among the doughboys of World War I. The GIs of World War II played the banking version of Black Jack more than any other card game. The biggest sum of money won by a Black Jack banker in the Armed Forces during that war was $137,500, won by an Army corporal in the Pacific theater. P.S. His occupation in Chicago before the war: Black Jack dealer.

There is almost as murky a scholarly dispute over the origin of Black Jack as there is over Poker and Gin Rummy. Italy, France and Spain have claimed it. The French allege a blood relationship with

Vingt-Un and Trente et Quarante. The Spanish say it is an adaption of their One and Thirty. The Italians insist that it is a slightly modified form of either Baccara or Seven and a Half. These last two have the closest similarity to Black Jack.

The basic object of the three games is the same: to reach a count of 21 in Black Jack, 9 in Baccara and 7½ in Seven and a Half. The Seven and a Half deck contains only 40 cards, the eights, nines and tens being absent. Court cards each count ½, the others count their numerical value. The king of diamonds is wild and may have any value. When a player, trying to get as close to a count of 7½ as possible, draws cards totaling 8 or more, he busts, as he does when going over 21 in Black Jack. Since this is the feature that has made casino-style Black Jack so popular and since it first appeared in Seven and a Half, I believe that this game, more than the others, is the direct forerunner of Black Jack.

The basic principle of Black Jack is the simple adding of card values in an attempt to reach a total of 21; there have been many similar games. In Crockford's, the celebrated London carpet joint (1827–44), such elite sporting bloods as the Duke of Wellington, Charles, Marquess of Queensberry, Talleyrand, Prince Esterhazy, Disraeli and Bulwer-Lytton played at Quinze, in which the object was to reach a count of 15. In order to conceal their emotions from the scrutinizing eyes of the dealer they sometimes wore masks.

The earliest known printed reference to the Spanish game of One and Thirty appears in *The Comical History of Rinconete and Cortadillo*, published in 1570.

The *American Hoyle* of 1875 calls Black Jack Vingt-Un, and *Foster's Hoyle*, 30 years later, calls it Vingt-et-Un. The English corrupted this to Van John; the Australians' French pronunciation was even wider of the mark—they called it Pontoon—but the basic principle, a desired count of 21, was the same.

Through most of its history Black Jack, or Twenty-One, its earlier name, was a private game, and it wasn't until 1915 that it began to make its appearance as a banking game in the top casinos of this country. I queried many old-time gambling-house operators and Black Jack dealers in an effort to pin down the exact date of the first Twenty-One banking table. None had seen one prior to those which were introduced in horse rooms in and around Evansville, Indiana, in the early part of 1910.

HOW BLACK JACK GOT ITS NAME

The betting limits at these first Twenty-One tables ranged from a low of 25¢ to a high of $1, but they received little action, and the tables

Johnson style Black Jack layout.

disappeared only a few months later. Then, late in 1912, a new form of Twenty-One appeared in the Evansville horse rooms. Players were paid off at 3 to 2 odds when they made a count of 21 with the first two cards, and if the two-card 21 was made up of the ace of spades and the jack of either spades or clubs, the holder received a $5 bonus for each 50¢ he had wagered. This induced the horse bettors to take a whirl at the game, and it began to receive more action. Before long, the players began to distinguish the two-card count of 21 from a three-or-more-card count of 21 by calling it "Black Jack."

In 1917, printed signs began appearing above the Twenty-One tables reading: "Black Jack pays odds of 3 to 2." Early in 1919 a Chicago manufacturer of gambling equipment began selling tables with this announcement printed in bold black letters on the green baize playing surface. Since then the game itself has been called Black Jack.

At that time, gamblers in the eastern states paid little attention to Black Jack; they devoted their time to Indian and Take-off Craps, which were faster and could be played in back alleys, open lots and cellars, as they required no table. But the game spread, and early in 1920 Black Jack tables began to appear in horse rooms and sawdust joints throughout the country.

From 1920 to 1930 its growth was gradual. Each year various casinos added new rules and dropped old ones. Then, in 1931, Black Jack tables were introduced in most of Nevada's legalized gambling establishments, and visiting players from other parts of the country spread its popularity across the nation. Prior to this it was a man's game because it had been played only in sawdust joints and horse rooms, dives which women did not frequent. Now women began to play Black Jack.

The most popular banking card games at this time were still Banker and Broker, Red Dog, Stuss and Skin, to name a few; but when thousands of servicemen who had learned Black Jack in the Armed Forces during World War II returned home, Black Jack rapidly became America's most popular banking card game. By 1948 it was second only to Craps in the casinos.

Before the publication in 1949 of *Scarne on Cards,* which contained the most comprehensive treatise on Black Jack up to that time, the gambling-house operators and Black Jack dealers had almost no idea of what the bank's favorable percentage at Black Jack was. The game-book writers had even less. (This is especially true of those Bridge experts who stray from their subject and write books and articles on other gambling games. Some state that no one knows what the bank's P.C. is except the casino managers, who aren't telling. In spite of this, they proceed to outline a strategy or system which, they claim, will beat the game. Any system or strategy for winning that is cooked up by someone who admits he doesn't know what odds he is bucking has to be sheer nonsense. Some of these Bridge experts seem to know less about gambling than the average casino sucker, and the editors who buy their "authoritative" articles obviously know even less.)

The first printing of *Scarne on Cards* did not contain an exact mathematical breakdown on the bank's favorable edge, but it did give the first approximate percentage breakdown. It would have been foolish at that time for me to undertake the complex calculations required because the rules governing the dealer's play often varied from casino to casino. In some the dealer's count of 16 was optional; he could either draw or hit. Other casinos specified that the dealer's count of 16 was an automatic hit; others ruled that a dealer's soft 17 had to be hit.

To add to the general confusion, some casinos paid a bonus on a 21 count with two nines and three aces; some paid bonuses on a 21 count with the six, seven and eight of one suit, or a count of 21 with seven cards; others paid a bonus to the holder of the ace and jack of spades. The bonus amounts also varied from a low $5 on the ace and jack of spades to a high $25 on a seven-card count of 21. These bonuses were paid off on any bet larger than the minimum bet permitted.

Since the rules governing the Black Jack dealer's play when staying or drawing are much more standardized today, I decided it was high time someone figured out the exact percentage in the bank's favor. I spent several months on the mathematical calculations this required; you will find, for the first time anywhere, the correct percentage in favor of the bank or Black Jack dealer on pages 361–365. But before we get to that, you should know the present-day casino rules on which my figures are based.

This one-in-a-million photograph, taken by John Scarne with a hidden camera during one of his recent casino investigations, caught two card mechanics cheating at the same Black Jack table. The dealer cheat was caught dealing the second card instead of the top card of the deck; the player cheat was caught with a palmed ace in his left hand prior to his switching it for the dealt ten of hearts. This fantastic photograph amply demonstrates why one should avoid playing Black Jack when cards are dealt from the dealer's hand rather than from a dealing box.

CASINO VARIATIONS

The basic rules of Black Jack as played in legal casinos the world over are the same except for some dealing and "doubling down" variations. Some casinos deal Black Jack with single or double decks from the hand. Others use two, three or four decks dealt out of a miniature Chemin de Fer box called a shoe. Some European and Caribbean casinos, in order to prevent the Black Jack dealer from tipping off (signaling) his hole card to agents (player cheats), do not permit the dealer to look at his face-down card when his up card is an ace or a ten. This rule was devised by me for Cuban casinos back in late 1957. English casinos have gone one step further: they rule that the Black Jack dealer is to be dealt only one card face up: the dealer's second card is dealt face up after all the players have played out their hands. This is known as the "London deal." However, should the dealer hit a natural 21 with his second card, players who have split pairs or doubled down lose all their bets. This ruling is unfair to the player, and anyone who plays against this rule and splits pairs or doubles down when the dealer shows an ace or ten as his first card is, at times, donating half of his bet or bets to the house. Should the dealer hit a natural 21 with his second card, players who have split pairs or doubled down should lose only their original bet. All split and double-down bets should be returned to the players. This dealing method, like that of not permitting the dealer to look at his face-down card at any time, makes for a slow game, but it does help eliminate player and dealer collusion by tipping off the hole card. But it permits a crooked casino dealer to cheat the players by using marked cards and signaling a player confederate, who plays last, to draw or not to draw as the dealer wishes. My advice is not to play Black Jack under such rules.

When the London deal or a like deal is in use, my recommendation to casino owners is as follows: Whenever the dealer's up card is an ace or ten count card, players cannot split pairs or double down. This ruling makes for a faster game and avoids arguments.

Some Nevada casinos deal the player's first two cards face down and permit a double down on any two cards. Some Caribbean and European casinos permit doubling down on counts of 9, 10, 11; others on counts of 10 and 11; and others permit doubling down on 11 only.

As far back as 1949, while acting as gaming consultant to the Puerto Rican government, I developed the two- and four-deck Black Jack dealing box and ruled that all cards be dealt face up except the dealer's hole card and the player's double-down card. In 1963 I devised the ruling that 50 or more bottom cards of the four-deck packet should never come into actual play. This was achieved by having the dealer insert an indicator card 50 or more cards from the bottom of the 208-card packet and end the hand when the indicator card made its appearance. These innovations accomplish the following: (1) The card box eliminates 95% of the cheating methods employed by crooked house dealers. (2) When the player's cards are dealt face up, it helps the dealer to correct any errors that the player may have made when totaling the numbered value of the playing hand. In addition, it prevents any card-cheat player from switching one or both of his face-down cards that he may have secretly palmed, and at the same time, owing to the fact that the dealer (house) does not have any discretionary powers on when to hit or stand, it doesn't matter whether the dealer sees the player's cards or not. (3) The purpose of inserting the indicator card toward the bottom of the 208-card packet is to prevent the cut-off cards from coming into actual play, which in turn prevents "card counters" or "countdown" players from memorizing or clocking the cards as they are being dealt and by so doing learn the identity of the last 30 undealt cards, and thereby gain an advantage over the house.

(4) The only other method of cheating that the house could resort to would be to use marked cards and deal seconds. When the dealer recognized a valuable card by the hidden markings on the back, he would deal a second (the card below the top card of the packet). This method is commonly used by dealer cheats when Black Jack is dealt from the hand. To eliminate this house-cheating possibility, I recommend that the four-deck packet be comprised of two red- and two blue-backed decks—because if a valuable red-backed card is on top the dealer would not dare to deal the card below, because he has no way of knowing if the card below is a red- or a blue-backed card. Imagine six players at a Black Jack table seeing a red-backed card about to be dealt and a blue-backed card turn up.

I have selected for analysis the Black Jack rules I formulated, which are now in use in countless casinos the world over. They have been chosen because they are the best of all casino rules—not only for the player's protection, but for the casino's as well. I predict that, within a few years, Scarne's Black Jack casino rules will be adopted by most casino operators throughout the world.

View from above of casino Black Jack table depicts Scarne's four-deck B-J method of dealing from a card box and each player's two initial cards dealt face up. This Scarne method of dealing insures the best possible protection against both dealer and player card cheats.

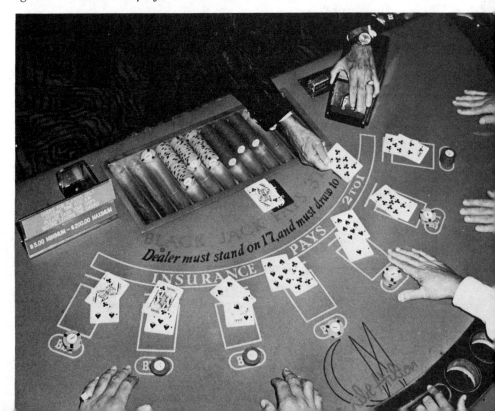

SCARNE'S CASINO BLACK JACK RULES

Requirements

1. A regulation Black Jack table with six or seven betting spaces on its layout.

2. A check rack filled with betting chips and silver dollars.

3. A card-dealing box called a shoe.

4. Four standard decks of 52 cards each (two red-backed decks and two blue-backed decks) shuffled together and used as one, a total of 208 cards dealt as a single packet.

5. Two indicator cards—one is used by players to cut the packet, the other is used to determine the end of the deal.

6. A shill, a house employee (male or female) who poses as a player to stimulate business.

7. A pit boss who is a casino inspector and who stands alongside the dealer, observing every action of play. He sees to it that no mistakes are made by the dealer or players. He is in complete charge; he rules on all disagreements and his decisions are final. All players and the dealer must abide by them, provided they are within the laws set down by the casino and in conformity with the regulations set down by the particular state or country.

Number of Players

1. The houseman who is the steady dealer and the banker. He never surrenders the deal or bank.

2. One to six or seven active players, each of whom may bet on several hands depending on the betting space available.

3. Any number of outsiders, kibitzers, who may wager on each player's hand. They must not advise the player how to play his hand.

Value of Cards

The cards have the following value:

1. Aces count either 1 or 11 at the discretion of the player holder. However, the dealer must value the ace as set down by the casino rules (see the dealer's turn at play, page 359).

2. Kings, queens, and jacks each have a count of 10.

3. All other cards are counted at their face value.

The Object of the Game

A player tries to obtain a higher total card count than the dealer by reaching 21 or as close to 21 as possible without exceeding that count.

If the player's total count exceeds 21, he has *busted* and must turn his cards face up at once. He has lost his bet, and the dealer immediately scoops it up. The player, at his proper turn of play and at his own discretion, may stand or draw one or more cards in an attempt to better his count.

The Betting Limits

The casino sets its own limit, but the minimum and maximum bet must be announced to the players.

The minimum bet limit in the Las Vegas Strip casinos is always one silver dollar. The maximum limit is $100 in some; in others it is $200, $300 or $500. The operators will often raise the maximum to $1000 or more at the sight of a high roller.

If you like your Las Vegas Black Jack action small and can't stand the silver-dollar minimum, you can go to the downtown Las Vegas tables, where the minimum may be as little as 10¢. This also holds true in Reno and other Nevada towns.

The Shuffle and Cut

The cards are shuffled by the dealer, who then hands a player an indicator card and says, "Cut, please." The player inserts the indicator card into the packet to show where he wants the cards cut. The dealer cuts the cards at this position, putting the indicator and all the cards above it on the bottom. The indicator goes to the bottom of the packet. The dealer then inserts the second indicator card fifty cards or thereabouts from the bottom of the deck, and places all the cards into the dealing box face down. The shoe is now ready to be dealt by the dealer. When the indicator card inserted by the dealer makes its appearance and enough cards have been dealt to complete the hand in progress, the deal ends—and the dealer must begin a new shuffle and again repeat the above-described procedure.

Betting

Before the deal begins, each player must place his bet in cash or chips in the betting space—which may be indicated as a circle, rectangle or some other symbol—painted on the playing surface directly before him in full view of the dealer.

Nevada casinos permit players, especially high rollers, to bet as many hands as there are available *holes* (betting spaces). Most Black Jack tables bear six or seven betting spaces. When a player plays more than one hand at a time, he must play the hand farthest to his right to completion before being permitted to look at his next hand or hands.

The dealer may check the amount of the player's bet to see that it is not greater than the maximum limit. If a player desires a higher limit, he may ask the pit boss, who will either grant or refuse it.

The Deal

After all players' bets are down, the dealer removes the first card from the dealing box and places it face down without showing its face value in the discard receiver. This is known as burning a card or a "burnt card." All cards used to make a hand are discarded in the same manner. After the first dealt card has been burnt, starting with the player on his extreme left, the dealer begins dealing clockwise, giving one card face up to each player and one face up to himself. He next deals each player, starting with the player on his extreme left, a second face-up card, and one face down to himself.

The Play

If the dealer's face-up card is a 10 count or an ace, he must look at his *hole* (face-down) card. If he has a natural 21 (a count of 21 with two cards), he must face it and announce "Twenty-one" or "Black Jack."

Any player with a natural 21 also announces it, and the dealer declares this to be a *standoff* or *push*. There is no action on this hand, and no payoff is made.

The dealer wins and collects bets from players not having a natural 21.

When the dealer does not hold a natural 21, the player at his extreme left plays first. If the player holds a natural 21, he announces it and faces his cards so the dealer can verify the count. The dealer pays off the winning natural at 3 to 2 odds. This means that if the player has bet $2 he collects $5—his own $2 plus an additional $3. The dealer then burns the two played-out cards.

If the player's two cards total less than 21 he may elect:

1. To stay. Either he is satisfied with his count or he fears that a third card may make his count go above 21. He says, "Good," "I have enough" or "I stand"; or he signifies that he is staying simply by sliding his cards under the chips he has bet.

2. To draw a card or cards. When the player is not satisfied with his count, he says, "Hit me," or makes a beckoning motion by closing and opening his hand, or a come-on motion with a finger. The dealer then deals another card off the top of the deck face up before the player and next to his original two cards. Although the cards are dealt one at a time, the player may continue to draw as many as he likes. When he believes his count is as good as he can do, he stays. If he draws a card which puts his count above 21, he must announce a bust.

The dealer scoops up the player's bet and cards and burns the cards in the discard pile.

The play moves to the player's left, clockwise around the table until all players have played out their hands.

The Dealer's Turn at Play

If all players have busted, the dealer merely places his own cards in the discard pile and deals a new hand. If any active player or players are left, the dealer plays his hand.

1. He turns up his hole card so that all his cards are exposed.

2. If his count is 17, 18, 19 or 20, the dealer must stay.

3. If his count is 16 or less, he must draw a card and continue to draw until his count reaches 17 or more—at which point he must stay. If the dealer holds a *soft 17*, i.e., a 17 count which includes an ace, he must also stay. This also applies to a soft 18, 19 or 20.

It is important to note here that the Black Jack dealer has no choice of whether to stay or draw. His decisions are predetermined and known to the players. Since all the dealer's cards are exposed at his turn of play, he has no opportunity for any departure from these rules.

The rule requiring the dealer to hit on 16 or less and stay on 17, 18, 19, 20 and 21 is standard today in all major casinos here and abroad.

Additional rule: If a dealer errs and deals a player a card which the player did not call for, and the card is refused by the player, the card is considered a "dead" card and must be burnt and placed in the discard receiver. The B.J. pit boss has the last word in deciding whether the player called or did not call for a card.

Final Settlement

At the end of his play the dealer starts with the first active player on his extreme right and moves around the table counterclockwise, paying off players who have a higher count than his with an amount equal to the bet they placed, and collecting the placed bets from players showing a lesser count. If player and dealer have the same count, it is a *standoff*, or tie, and no one collects or loses. If the dealer busts, he pays off each surviving active player an amount equal to his bet.

Splitting Pairs

Any two cards that are identical except for suit may be treated as a pair. Also, any two cards each having a value of 10 may be treated as pairs, such as a ten and jack, jack and queen or queen and king.

A player who receives two cards forming a pair or considered to be a pair on the initial round may, if he chooses, separate the two cards and treat each card as the first card dealt in two separate hands. This is called *splitting pairs*. When pairs are split, the player's original bet is placed on one of these cards and an equal amount must be bet on the other.

The player is then dealt one face-up card on the face-up card on his right, and he must play this hand out. If, in drawing to the first face-up card, he forms a pair again, he may again split pairs, betting an amount equal to his first card on this third hand. He may continue to split any further pairs.

The first hand on the player's extreme right must be played to completion before the adjacent split hand is dealt a second card. Each split hand must be played out in its proper order from the player's right to his left.

When a player splits a pair of aces, he is only permitted to draw one card to each split ace, giving him two cards in all.

If a *paint* (picture card) or ten or ace is part of a split hand and the player makes a two-card count of 21, it is not a natural and the player is paid off at even money.

The Double Down

A player, after being dealt his first two cards (which may be any two cards), may elect to double his bet and draw one additional card only. This is known as a double down or down for double. A player, before calling "Double down" or "Down for double," must double his original bet. He is then dealt a third and final face-down card on his two face-up cards. Player is not permitted to look at the face-down card until the dealer turns it face up after the deal has been completed. Some Nevada casinos allow a second double down on a count of 9 if the player draws a deuce as his first double-down card. Many Caribbean casinos permit doubling down on an 11 count only. Others permit a double down on counts of 9, 10 and 11.

Insurance Betting

In many casinos, when the dealer's face-up card is an ace, players may make an insurance bet against losing to the banker's possible natural. The dealer, before looking at his down card, inquiries if any player wants insurance. A player who desires insurance places an amount equal to half his present wager on his own hand.

When this bet is made, the dealer looks at his down card. If it is a 10 count, he turns it face up and announces a natural. The insurance bettor is paid off at the rate of 2 to 1 for every unit wagered. If the dealer's down card is not a 10-count card, the player loses his insurance bet.

THE BLACK JACK DEALER'S EXACT PERCENTAGE TAKE

Why do you lose at Black Jack? What is your chance to win? What odds are you bucking? What is the bank's favorable advantage, and where does it exist?

Before I calculated the bank's advantage at 5.90% when the player adheres to the dealer's fixed strategy, no one, including mathematicians, bridge experts, game-book authors, players and casino employees, knew the right answers. Without this information, any mathematical analysis of Black Jack would be meaningless.

Bridge experts Ely Culbertson, Albert Morehead and Geoffrey Mott-Smith admitted they didn't know either. In *Culbertson's Card Games, Complete with Official Rules,* they say: "In no game that has been played for high stakes has there been less analysis of the science of playing than in Black Jack. The only available guide to strategy is empirical; no one has more than his opinion on which to estimate the advantage of the dealer."

Within a few years after this book first hit the stores, more than 500 books and pamphlets were published on the subject "How to beat the game of Black Jack." Each author told how he was barred from playing in Las Vegas because his system was sure to beat the house. Several of these authors, notably Professor Edward O. Thorp and Dr. Allen N. Wilson, told their readers in effect that Scarne's Black Jack strategy was for the birds; that their Black Jack system of play was far superior because it permitted even an amateur to consistently beat the Las Vegas Black Jack tables over the long run. Rubbish! Need I say more? For further information concerning Thorp's Black Jack system, see page 347.

In 1964, in an effort to test Professor Thorp's "winning Black Jack" statements I challenged him to a $100,000 contest to be staged in Las Vegas. Thorp's reply was a big "No." Later I issued the same challenge to Dr. Wilson—I'm still waiting for his reply. It's time we went on to something important.

Before we dive into a mathematical analysis of the game, I should tell you just what part of the game gives the bank an advantage. If you ask a dealer what happens to your bet when he and you tie with the same count, his stock answer is: "All ties are a standoff; no one wins and no one loses." This implies that the dealer doesn't take your bet if you tie. This isn't quite right; in fact it's dead wrong.

True, the dealer doesn't take your bet when you tie on a count of

21 or less, but if his statement that all ties are standoffs is true, then he should keep his hands off your dough when you tie at 22, 23 or anything above 21. Does he? No, that's not the way Black Jack is played. When a player busts, the dealer doesn't wait to see whether he will also bust and tie at a count above 21. He rakes in the bet and closes that transaction. The player has lost, even though his count may later tie the dealer's.

This is the crux of the hidden P.C. in the bank's favor. This is the real reason why casino operators like Black Jack and why most players lose at the game.

The bank has an advantage in the unspoken and largely unnoticed provision that ties stand off, or push, *provided the count is 21 or less*. Want to prove it? That's easy. Just ask your dealer to play his hand out after you have busted and if he also busts and goes over your count to pay you off. You'll get a fast answer telling you exactly where to go and when.

It is, of course, not feasible to figure the exact percentage against individual players because their play differs so much. Some players will stay on 12, 13 and 14; some will draw on 15 and 16; others stay on 15 or more; and there's always the dub who will draw to an ace and nine.

However, since the dealer has no choice whether to stay or draw, because the rules predetermine this, we can calculate the exact percentage working in his favor. It isn't easy, but it can be done. We know first that the banker's hidden advantage lies in the fact that the player must play first, and if dealer and player both bust at a count above 21 the player loses his bet. If it were not for this (and if, when the dealer's face-up card was dealt face down the bank paid off a natural at even-money odds, and a player could not split pairs or double down) the game would be an even-up proposition.

There is also another complication. Unlike the bank's P.C. at Craps and Roulette, which doesn't vary, the bank's P.C. at Black Jack changes considerably during the play. It goes up or down as each card is dealt. The following analysis, therefore must be based on a full-deck composition. We assume, for purposes of analysis, that all 52 cards are present, none having yet been dealt.

Next, we find out how many dealer busts may be expected in the long run. We make use of the standard permutation and combination formulas, plus some straight thinking and simple arithmetic. We calculate how many different ways (using a 52-card deck) the dealer's initial two face-down cards can produce all the possible counts. Like this:

BLACK JACK TABLE I

THE 1326 TWO-CARD COUNTS IN BLACK JACK

Count	Number of Ways It Can Be Made
21	64
20	136
19	80
18	86
17	96
16	86
15	96
14	102
13	112
12	118
11	64
10	54
9	48
8	38
7	32
6	38
5	32
4	22
3	16
2	6
Total Number of Ways	1,326

We find that the dealer's first two cards can produce the counts from 2 through 21 in 1,326 different ways. Note that the player can count an ace as either 1 or 11, but the dealer must count the ace as 11 in all soft hands with a count of 17 or more; the above table is figured on that premise. We won't try to calculate how many hands out of these 1,326 the dealer will bust, because we'll run into too many fractions. We'll discover what we need to know, however, and avoid most of the fractions, if we multiply 1,326 × 169 to get a common multiple of 224,094. Now suppose your favorite dealer dealt this many hands and suppose each combination of two cards appeared exactly as often as probability theory predicts it will in the long run.

Two-card counts of 17, 18, 19, 20 and 21 will show up 462 times out of 1,326, which is 462/1326 × 224,094 = 78,078 times. The Black Jack rules demand that the dealer must stay on all these hands, so he cannot bust on any of them.

Two-card counts of 12, 13, 14, 15 and 16 will be held by the dealer 514 times out of 1,326 or 514/1,326 × 224,094 = 86,866 times. Since the rules demand that the dealer must draw to a count of 16 or less, he will bust 47,456 times and reach 17 to 21 counts 39,410 times out of the initial 86,866 dealt hands.

Two-card counts of 2, 3, 4, 5, 6, 7, 8, 9, 10 and 11 will appear 350 times or $350/1,326 \times 224,094 = 59,150$ times. When the dealer gets any of these counts he must, according to the rules, draw one or more additional cards; he will bust 17,018 times and reach a 17 to 21 count 42,132 times out of the initial 59,150 dealt hands.

Now, adding the busts gives a total of 64,474, and adding the non-bust hands gives a total of 159,620. Divide the 64,474 busts into the total 224,094 hands and we find that the dealer will bust on an average once out of every 3.47 dealt hands, or about 28 out of every 100 dealt hands.

Since the rules of play give the player more freedom in his decisions and since players don't conform to any single strategy (many aren't even consistent, playing one way at one time, another way a few minutes later) how do we arrive at a figure for the number of busts the player may expect? First we must consider a hypothetical player who is consistent in his play and who follows the same rules as does the dealer. He stays on a count of 17 or over, draws to a count of 16 or less, and cannot split pairs or double down. If we assume this, we can calculate an exact percentage by finding out how many times probability theory says that dealer and player will bust on the same round.

Since we calculated above that the dealer can expect to bust 64,474 times out of 224,094, and since our hypothetical player is playing according to the rules governing the dealer, he will bust the same number of times. We multiply their chances, expressed as fractions like this: $64,474/224,094 \times 64,474/224,094$, for an answer of $4,156,896,676/50,218,120,836$. Now divide the top figure by the bottom one, and there's the answer: The bank or dealer has a favorable bust percentage of 8.27%.

Out of this 8.27% that the bank collects in hidden percentage, it has to pay off players holding a natural 21 count on their initial two cards at odds of 3 to 2. This occurs, in the long run, once in 21 deals. The bank, therefore, pays out one additional unit as a bonus once every 42 deals, or 2.37%. (The standoff, which occurs when both dealer and player hold a natural 21, happens once in 441 deals; it affects the P.C. figure so very little that we can forget it.)

When you deduct the 2.37% player's advantage from the 8.27% bank advantage, the final favorable percentage for the bank comes to 5.90%. Make a note of that 5.90%. Better yet, memorize it: you now know something about Black Jack that your dealer doesn't know—at least, not until he reads this.

Any questions? Yes, I can hear someone saying, "Wait a minute, Scarne. If the only advantage the bank has is the one it gains when player and dealer both bust, why can't the player turn this bust factor to his advantage? He merely doesn't draw to a count of 12, 13, 14, 15, 16 or more, thus avoiding all bust hands, while the dealer, who must draw on a count of 16 or less, will still bust once out of every 3.47 hands. Brother, I'm heading right now for the nearest Black Jack table!"

Don't be in such a hurry, Dick. The casino operators won't argue the matter with you, because it's the players with the wrong answers who give them a handsome profit. But take it from me, the answer to your question is a big NO in capital letters.

Why? Remember that the bank's advantage is based on two factors, not one: the double-bust factor and the fact that the player must play his hand out first. If your strategy consists in avoiding bust hands by not drawing on counts of 12, 13, 14, 15, 16 or more, you'll be fighting an even greater percentage than if you followed the dealer's rule of hitting on 16 or less and standing on 17 or more.

You want proof? Okay, here it is. Let's assume the game is two-handed—playing are the dealer (who must abide by the casino rules) and one player whose fixed strategy is never to draw to a possible bust hand. The dealer's 224,094 completed hands will be made up of 64,474 bust hands and 159,620 hands with counts of 17, 18, 19, 20 and 21.

The player is also dealt 224,094 hands, but since he refuses to draw on counts of 12, 13, 14, 15, 16 or more, he doesn't bust a single hand. He will, however, get 106,133 hands with counts of 17, 18, 19, 20 and 21, and 117,961 hands with counts of 12, 13, 14, 15 and 16. Since the dealer's lowest count of a completed hand is 17, the player never wins except when the dealer busts by exceeding 21. The dealer's 64,474 bust hands appear as follows: 33,939 (117,961/224,094 × 64,474) occur when the player holds a count of 12 to 16, and 30,535 (106,133/224,094 × 64,474) occur when the player holds a count of 17 to 21. Subtracting the 33,939 dealer busts from the player's 117,961 12-to-16-count hands, we find that the player will lose 84,022 such hands. Subtracting the 64,474 dealer bust hands from the 84,022 player's losing hands, we note that the player loses 19,548 more hands than the dealer. In percentage that is 19,548 divided by 224,094, or an edge for the bank of 8.72%.

Again we deduct the 2.37% which the bank pays to holders of a natural 21 and get a final favorable percentage for the bank of 6.35%. I am sure you don't want to buck 6.35% instead of the 5.90% we were talking about before you got this bright idea of standing on a 12-to-16-count hand.

13.
Black Jack
Strategy

THE SCIENCE OF BLACK JACK

Shortly after the first edition of this book was published in 1961, thousands of gamblers learned from these pages that the more aces remaining in an undealt portion of a single deck, the greater were their chances of beating the house. So hundreds of Las Vegas players began casing the deck, and it seemed at that time that every other player at a Black Jack table in Nevada was clocking aces. Casino operators became so alarmed that they changed a number of rules. They ruled that players could not double down on a count of 11, and players could not split aces, but to no avail. Thereafter came my four-deck deal with its indicator cut, and Black Jack play was restored to normal.

A player can cut down the bank's edge of 5.90% considerably if he follows the Scarne Black Jack strategy that follows:

1. About 2½% for proper hitting or standing on both "hard" and "soft" hands.

2. About 2½% for proper doubling down when the casino permits a double down on any two cards. About ¼% for proper doubling down when the casino permits a double down on a count of 9, 10, or 11—it holds about the same for proper doubling down when the casino only permits a double down on 11.

3. About ½% for proper splitting of pairs.

These figures apply only when the Scarne strategy is used intelligently. The mathematical analysis that follows is based on the use of a single deck. However, when four decks are used, the bank's favorable advantage increases to 6%. The Scarne strategy applies to both single and multi-deck Black Jack.

To use the Scarne strategy successfully demands an unusual combination of skills on the part of the player in Black Jack.

1. The player must have a vast knowledge of the game's mathematics so that he knows when it is to his advantage to hit or stay, when to double down and when to split pairs.
2. He must be an expert at *casing the deck*, which is the ability to remember all cards previously dealt or exposed. This is far more difficult than it is in Contract Bridge, because in Black Jack there is no set way the cards will fall.
3. He must know money management—when to bet big and when to bet small.

Plenty of vital information (much more than you'll find in any other book) is given and, if properly used, will reward the average Black Jack player with a surefire formula for cutting down his losses. And, if you happen to have a flair for the game, you'll find enough valuable hints here to give the bosses of your favorite casino a headache because of your above-average winnings.

I must begin by re-emphasizing one fact you should not forget: that the only positive advantage in favor of the bank is the edge it gains through double busts and having the players play first. And keep that 5.90% favorable percentage to the bank in mind, remembering also that it is calculated on a full-deck composition of 52 cards before the deal begins, and assumes that the player follows the draw and stand rules that govern the dealer.

There are several situations which, played properly, give the player an opportunity to cut down this house percentage. Most players handle these situations so inexpertly that instead of reducing the percentage they are bucking, they add to it. Here are the playing factors which can be utilized to the player's advantage:

1. The player actually knows a little more than the dealer because one of the dealer's two initial cards is dealt face up; this gives the player important information about his possible card count. The rules governing the dealer's play prevent him from making use of similar information about the player's hand, even if the latter's first two cards were dealt face up.
2. Unlike the dealer, the player can stay or draw on any count provided it does not exceed 21. At one turn of play he may draw to a count of 12 or more and at other times may stand on the same count. In some situations the player can gain an advantage from this.
3. The player can decide to double down or split pairs, a strategy denied to the dealer.

4. The player is paid off at odds of 3 to 2 when he holds a natural, but when the dealer holds a natural he only receives even money.

5. The player may play as many hands as there are available betting spaces; the dealer can only play one hand.

6. The player is the one who decides the amount of the bet and can raise or lower it at will within the prescribed betting limits.

7. The player can case the deck. If he can remember the cards previously dealt or exposed it will greatly improve his chances of winning.

A player who can take full advantage of all seven of these factors can join the select few who are considered experts at Black Jack.

BEATING THE BLACK JACK TABLES

The most valuable natural aptitude a Black Jack player can possess is the fairly rare faculty of remembering most of the previously exposed cards. The player who cannot do this has little or no chance of beating the bank in the long run, no matter how well he plays otherwise. Since the bank's favorable percentage goes up or down with the dealing of each card, the expert player will not use any cut-and-dried strategy. The more dealt cards the player can remember, the greater chance he has of making the correct play on future hands in that deal.

You can't remember all the exposed cards dealt to a full table of players. One reason is that in most casinos the first two cards to each player are dealt face down. Also, the dealer scoops up the completed hands so fast that there is hardly enough time to spot their value, let alone memorize them. The card caser minimizes these factors by playing, whenever possible, at a table that has only a few players, and, better yet, at one where he is the only player. He prefers *third base*, the seat at the dealer's extreme right, as his base of operations because this is the best vantage point for keeping track of the exposed cards. Even under these conditions, an expert job of card casing requires unusual natural ability and considerable practice at the table. Although remembering the cards at Black Jack is much harder than at Contract Bridge, there are a number of Black Jack players whose talent for card casing has won them fortunes. That is before Scarne's Black Jack rules of play came into use.

The player who can case the deck is better able to evaluate his chances of winning after about half the deck has been dealt. Since a full deck has four cards in each of 13 ranks (four aces, four twos, four threes, etc.), the proportion in each rank is 4 in 52, or 1/13. As the cards are dealt, the proportion in the undealt portion of the deck keeps changing. This means that the dealer's favorable percentage (5.90% before the deal starts) also changes, increasing and decreasing. At times the composition of the remaining undealt portion of the deck gives the player a favorable percentage rather than the bank. When the card caser knows the odds are in his favor he increases the size of his bets; if the odds figure is against him, he decreases his bets or even backs away from the table and stops betting.

I have seen card casers who had been betting $2 on each hand suddenly bet the $300 or $500 limit on the next hand and win. Suppose, for example, the expert card caser, playing alone, is aware that the last five undealt cards are three eights and a pair of sevens. He now simply plays one hand, betting the maximum limit on the hand; he cannot lose. Why? Because he and the dealer will be dealt a two-card count of either 15 or 16, and the card caser stands and the dealer busts.

During my many years in gambling, I have known of only six Black Jack players who beat the game by putting the percentage in their favor through "card casing," or as it is more commonly known, "counting down the deck." And three of these players made use of my countdown gimmick. In fact, I was the first person playing alone to beat the game in Las Vegas with a countdown system. I was also the first player barred from playing Black Jack there.

In 1947, I was barred because I told several casino owners in Las Vegas that I could beat their game with a countdown. Several of the casinos challenged me to prove my statement and when I beat every casino that was there at that time, I was barred from the casino Black Jack tables throughout Nevada.

In the first edition of this book, published in 1961, I wrote: "I must admit that there are a few bits of information I am going to have to hold back. This information is good only when everyone doesn't know it. Publication would merely result in destroying its value, not only to the few players who now possess it but also to the readers of this book, because the casino operators—and they are the first to buy my books —would then cancel it all out for their own protection by changing the Black Jack rules." The information I was then referring to was my countdown gimmick involving the use of chips. This is the very gimmick that I used back in 1947 to beat the casinos.

My countdown system is very simple and puts all other so-called "point count systems" to shame. Actually the winning strategy in my system is based on the fact that the composition of the undealt cards changes during play and because of this, the advantage in Black Jack shifts back and forth between player and dealer. Contrary to what most writers on Black Jack suppose, memory plays a very small part in my system. That is, when using my counting or checking gimmick, I bet small until about two-thirds of cards are dealt. Then I consult my count gimmick to know exactly how many 10-count cards and aces remain in the undealt portion of the deck. With this information I can decide if it is wise to draw a card, double down, split a pair, and what the chances are of busting my hand. You must remember that Black Jack is the only banking game where the odds fluctuate and at times the deck favors the dealer and at other times it favors the player. My scheme is to find out if the remaining undealt cards favor the player or the dealer. If they favor the player, I increase my bets and play more hands than before. My hit and stand strategy as detailed in this book was not put to use when the remaining undealt cards were unfavorable to the player.

My Black Jack system involves three basic requirements or considerations:

1. Keep a mental running count of cards as they are dealt.

2. When the remaining undealt cards are rich in low cards (ace, two, three, four, five, six), it indicates that the dealer has the advantage; then hands containing a count of 16, 17 or 18 should be hit, since the dealer's chance of busting with a count of 14, 15 or 16 are less than if the undealt cards were mostly high cards. If undealt cards are rich in high cards (seven though king), the dealer is at a disadvantage in hitting a count of 13, 14, 15 or 16.

3. Play the dealer head to head (alone).

Now for the secret of my Scarne Countdown System. First thing I did when I sat down at an empty Black Jack table was to buy in several stacks of chips. As you know, each stack contains 20 chips. I would place one stack away from the dealer and behind the other stacks, to be used for casing the deck. There are, of course, sixteen 10-count cards (tens, jacks, queens and kings) in the 52-card deck, plus four aces. During the dealing of the first hand, I would remove 4 chips from the 20-chip stack that I reserved for casing the deck, and place them alongside it. The 16-chip stack represented the 10-count cards, the 4-chip stack represented the four aces. The chips used to place my bets before the start of each deal were taken from the non-casing stacks. As each new hand was played I counted the 10-count cards as they were dealt. Let's say that five 10-count cards were dealt, I removed 5 chips from my 16-chip stack. This left 11 chips—the total number of 10-count cards left in the undealt cards. Every time an ace showed, I would remove a chip from the 4-chip stack. I followed this procedure with each deal, and whenever I wished to know exactly how many aces or 10-count cards remained in the undealt cards, I would simply consult my two caser stacks. The number of chips remaining in each of the stacks gave me the answer. It's as simple as ABC. By the way, I also employed this system when two or four decks were in use simply by working several stacks of different-valued chips.

Before writing this edition, I gave the just mentioned system to only four men and three of them won about $250,000 each before they were barred from playing single deck in Nevada. Today, of course, Nevada pit bosses keep a sharp eye out for single deck card casers. If a pit boss suspects a player of casing the deck, he instructs the dealer to reshuffle the complete deck when only half of it has been dealt. Known card casers are either barred from playing or not permitted to play alone. If a card caser is the only player at the table, the management sends in a shill so that casing the deck becomes much more difficult. And the ruling that I devised that 50 or more bottom cards of a four-deck packet should never come into actual play makes it virtually impossible to count down four decks.

Today card casing or counting down the deck is a lost art. However, now and then you spot a Johnny-come-lately trying it on some casino boss. If the boss doesn't know his business, the card caser may get away with it.

The machinations of a modern-day single deck card caser stand out like a bright light in a moonless night. First, he seeks a vacant Black Jack table for himself. Then his stooge, who is a partial card caser, takes a position beside him—sometimes he makes use of two stooges. At the beginning of each deal, his bets are usually the house minimum on each of the six or seven betting spaces. This type of betting continues until near the end of each deal, when a whispered consultation takes place between the card caser and his assistants. If they agree that the remaining undealt cards appear disadvantageous to the house, they increase the size of their bets to the maximum house limit. A smart houseman counters this Black Jack chicanery by reshuffling the entire deck, including the undealt cards. The card caser complains a bit, calls off his bets, exits from the casino and shops around seeking a casino whose boss is stupid enough to stand for such nonsense. That's the life of a professional card caser. Most of those casers haven't got a dime. Therefore my advice is: Don't try to be a card caser.

SCARNE'S FOUR-DECK BLACK JACK SHUFFLE

One of my major complaints about gambling in Nevada, as stated earlier, is that some casinos still insist on dealing a single deck from the hand. If a player isn't an expert on card cheating detection, he doesn't stand a chance in a Black Jack game being dealt from the hand. Too much cheating on the part of the dealer can take place. In addition, there is no advantage for a player in attempting to count a single deck since the entire deck is reshuffled when a player increases the size of his bet. So take my advice: Do *not* play Black Jack at a table where the cards are dealt from the hand.

The Sands Hotel casino in Las Vegas was the first casino in Nevada to deal Black Jack from a shoe (card box) with four decks. The first night the new system went into effect, my friend Carl Cohen, then casino manager of the Sands, now casino manager of M.G.M.'s Grand Hotel, requested me to study each dealer as he shuffled the four decks prior to placing them into the shoe. Later that evening I informed Carl Cohen that the shuffling method employed by his dealers made the Sands a real setup for top-notch card casers.

Basically, the shuffle that dealers were using at the time was as follows: They would divide the 208-card deck in three piles and shuffle each pile individually. The piles were then put back together and then cut several times by both the dealer and the player. The deck was finally placed in the card box ready for dealing.

I explained to Carl that although the cards were being shuffled, few cards left each of the three piles. For example, let's say that 12 aces fell in the bottom 70 cards of the 208-card deck. Should the dealer follow his normal procedure of shuffling, the 12 aces would probably remain in the same 70-card group regardless of the shuffle. Right then and there, the Scarne Four-Deck Shuffle was introduced at the Sands; later it was parroted by casinos throughout Nevada and eventually around the world.

The Scarne Four-Deck Black Jack Shuffle—which you may have seen—is executed as follows: The dealer separates the 208-card deck into two piles. Then he removes about 30 cards from each pile and shuffles them together. He repeats the same procedure for the remaining cards. The complete deck then is given several running cuts by the dealer before it is pushed to a player to be cut.

Before discussing Black Jack strategy I must ask the reader once more to remember that complexities of the game have made it necessary to base the following analysis on a full-deck composition involving a dealer and one player, and the player's initial two-card count and the dealer's face-up card are considered as part of the full-deck composition. However, the recommended strategy is also applicable when two to four decks are used in dealing the game, because in this case the odds run somewhat more true to form after a number of cards have been dealt.

STRATEGY FOR DRAWING AND STANDING

The most important decision the Black Jack player has to make is whether to hit or stand on a count of 12, 13, 14, 15 or 16. The question arises in the long run a little more than once every two hands (to be exact, 698 times in every 1,326 hands). In practice it can occur three or more times during a single hand. Players who do not understand the reasoning that should determine such a vital decision have little or no chance of beating the Black Jack bank in a long session.

The only cut-and-dried procedure of hit-or-stand play that is sound for the player is to hit a count of 11 or less and stand on a count of 17 or more. This will keep most players out of trouble. But the player who doesn't know how to answer the question of whether to hit or stand on a count of 12, 13, 14, 15 or 16 is sure to run into double trouble.

The player who goes against the bank's favorable edge of 6.35% by refusing to draw a card when he has one of these counts for fear of busting his hand is a member in good standing of the Black Jack Chump Society. The lure of Black Jack is its fast action. Wagers are won and lost with the dealing of each new hand, and the pace is so fast and furious that the bank's favorable 6.35% will eat up the amount of the chump player's wager in about 16 dealt hands. Let me illustrate how this works out in dollars and cents. Assume that you are the chump and have played the dealer single-handed and made a $10 bet on each of 300 dealt hands for a total betting handle of $3,000. The bank collects, in hidden percentage, .0635 × $3,000 or $190.50. This is what you pay to sit at Black Jack table for two or three hours of play if you stubbornly refuse to hit a count of 12, 13, 14, 15 or 16.

Suppose you adhere to the dealer's fixed strategy of hitting a count of 16 or less and standing on 17 or more. Here the bank's favorable edge is 5.90%, and on $3,000 worth of your action it would cost you $177.

These figures should make it obvious that both of these hit-or-stand procedures add up to a big percentage charge to the player in the long run.

Since a player's position is weakest when he holds a count of 12 to 16, he should use some strategy that will cut down his losses by helping him to win or draw as many of these hands as possible. He must find a way to cut down the bank's 5.90% edge over the player who adheres to the dealer's fixed strategy. The player can do this by varying his hit-and-stand strategy to fit specific situations. The following three factors, when considered together, will enable him to do that.

1. *The knowledge of the dealer's fixed strategy (hit 16 or less; stand on 17 or more) and its influence on the dealer's completed hand.*

2. *The sight of the dealer's upcard and its mathematical bearing on the dealer's possible two-card count.*

3. *The knowledge of the mathematical possibilities of the player's own count of 12, 13, 14, 15 or 16.*

The hit-or-stand strategy that follows is based on these three factors. Before we suggest any hit-or-stand rules, the player must know what his chances are of busting a count of 12, 13, 14, 15 or 16, or bettering it by reaching a count of 17 to 21. These chances, some exact, others approximate, are shown in the following table:

BLACK JACK TABLE II

Player's Count with Two or More Cards	Total Chances of Bettering the Count by Reaching a Count of 17 to 21	Total Chances of Busting when Trying to Reach a Count of 16 to 21	Chances of Busting with a One-Card Draw
16	20 in 52	32 in 52	32 in 52
15	22 in 52	30 in 52	28 in 52
14	23 in 52	29 in 52	24 in 52
13	25 in 52	27 in 52	20 in 52
12	27 in 52	25 in 52	16 in 52

This table can be very helpful to the player even if he only retains a general idea of his chances of busting on each of these counts. Probability theory says that, in the long run, when the player and dealer are both holding a count of 17 to 21 they are expected to win, lose or draw an equal number of hands. Therefore, the only losses suffered by the player in the long run under similar conditions will be on the bust hands.

The information in the table becomes very important when combined with a knowledge of the strength of the dealer's upcard. We have no sure way (short of cheating) to know the value of the dealer's hole card. But knowing the value of his upcard enables us to calculate how many completed hands he will bust and in how many he will reach a count of 17 to 21 in the long run. Then, by considering these results in relation to the possible results of the player's completed hands when holding a count of 12, 13, 14, 15 or 16, we can decide whether it is more advantageous to hit or stand in certain situations.

I am always amused by the Black Jack strategy recommended by Bridge experts. Since they all seem to copy from one another, they usually end up with the same wrong answers. For instance, they all state that when the dealer's upcard is an ace or ten the player should hit a count of 16 because, they say, the dealer's hand is best when he shows an ace or ten spot. This may seem like good common sense at first glance but what seems like common sense is noted for supplying wrong answers. This is one of them.

Let's analyze it. Assume that the dealer's upcard is an ace and the player's first two dealt cards total 16. Should he draw a card, as the Bridge experts recommend, or should he stand?

Whenever the dealer's upcard is an ace, he must peek at his face-down hole card to see if it is a 10 count. If it is, he turns it up, and there is no problem; the player has lost the bet then and there. If, however, the dealer fails to turn up a natural (21), we know that he doesn't have a 10 count in the hole, and that his highest possible two-card count is 20 and his lowest 12. We can now calculate the exact number of hands the dealer will bust and the exact number of completed 17-to-21-count hands he will hold in the long run.

Since most of our Black Jack calculations are based on a full-deck composition, with the dealer's upcard and the player's considered mathematically in the full-deck composition, we will do the same here. To simplify the mathematics, suppose that dealer and player are each dealt 52 hands, that each of the dealer's 52 upcards is an ace, and each of the player's 52 hands has a 16 count. Also suppose that each of the player's hole cards and all the remaining cards dealt to both dealer and player fall exactly as probability theory predicts.

Out of 52 hands, the dealer will turn up a natural Black Jack 16 times, bust 11 hands, and reach a count of 17 to 21 on the remaining 25 completed hands.

Because the player holding a 16 count immediately loses the bet each of the 16 times (out of 52 hands) that the dealer holds a natural, these 16 hands cannot be considered. Therefore, a player who stands on a 16 count when the dealer's upcard is an ace will collect 11 dealer busts and lose 25 dealer completed hands out of every 36 dealt hands —a net loss to the player of 14 hands.

If the player hits the 16 count in each of his 36 dealt hands, then he will bust 22 hands and reach a count of 17 to 21 in the remaining 14 hands. From this player loss of 22 bust hands we must subtract the dealer's busts.

We calculate the number of dealer busts in the player's and dealer's 14 competing hands by multiplying the dealer's bust probability by 14. In this case $11/36 \times 14 = 4\,5/18$ dealer busts. Since the dealer will hold $1\frac{1}{2}$ twenty-one counts less than the player, he will lose $1\frac{1}{2}$ completed hands out of his remaining 9 13/18 completed hands. We subtract the 4 5/18 dealer-bust hands and this $1\frac{1}{2}$ completed hand loss from the player's 22 bust hands and find that the player hitting a count of 16 when the dealer shows an ace will suffer a net loss of 16 4/18 hands out of each 36 hands. And the player who stands on the 16 count will suffer a loss of only 14 hands.

This proves that, in spite of the advice to the contrary given by the Bridge experts, it is to the player's advantage to stand rather than hit on a count of 16 when the dealer shows an ace as his upcard.

This example should make it clear to the reader why Black Jack experts attach so much importance to the dealer's upcard. It should also indicate why the following table based on the strength of the dealer's upcard is of the utmost importance, especially when it is used in conjunction with Black Jack Table II. Remember that the table is based on 52 hands, each possessing the same-valued upcard, with the hole card and all other dealt cards falling exactly as probability theory predicts they will fall in the long run.

BLACK JACK TABLE III

Dealer's Upcard Count for 52 Hands	Completed Hands with a Count of 17 to 21 in 52 Hands	Number of Dealer's Busts in 52 Hands
11 (ace)	41	11
10	40	12
9	39	13
8	39	13
7	38	14
6	29	23
5	30	22
4	32	20
3	33	19
2	34	18

The table does not take the natural 21-count hands the dealer receives into consideration because if he turns up a natural when his upcard is a 10 or 11 count, there can be no hit or stand action for the player.

Taken together, Black Jack Tables III and II are the most valuable information a Black Jack player can possess.

Note that, since he will bust about 23 hands out of 52 in the long run, the dealer is in his weakest position when his upcard is a six spot.

Since our analysis shows that the player should stand on a 16 count when the dealer's upcard is an ace, common sense would seem to indicate that the player should also stand on a 16 count when the dealer's upcard is a seven spot. Again, common sense isn't to be trusted; this is another wrong answer.

Here's the proof. When a player stands on a 16 count and the dealer shows a seven spot, the dealer will bust 14 hands and complete 38 hands with a count of 17 to 21. Since the player will lose the 38 completed hands and win the 14 dealer busts, he will have a net loss of 24 hands out of 52 hands.

If the player hits his 16 count for each of his 52 hands, he will bust 32 hands and make 20 completed hands equally divided among the counts of 17, 18, 19, 20 and 21. The dealer's 20 opposing hands will be comprised of approximately 5 busts ($14/52 \times 20 = 5\ 5/13$ and about 15 hands comprised of a count of 17 to 21, about 7 of which possess a count of 17. The dealer loses about 4 and a fraction of his 15 completed hands for a total loss of about 10 of the 20 dealer hands. Subtracting the 10 dealer losses from the player's 32 busts, we find that the player who hits a count of 16 against a dealer's seven spot upcard will have a net loss of 22 hands, 2 hands less than the player who stands on 16.

Therefore it is to a player's advantage to hit 16 when the dealer shows a seven spot as his upcard.

Let us analyze another believe-it-or-not factor of Black Jack. The dealer's upcard for 52 hands is a 10 count (ten, jack, queen or king) and the player's count is 16 for the same number of hands. When the dealer's upcard is a 10 count the dealer must peek at his hole card to see if it is an ace. If it is, he immediately turns up his natural and collects the player's bet. Since the dealer's hole card will be an ace 4 hands out of 52, that leaves us with 48 hit or stand hands. If on these 48 hands the player stands on his 16 count, the dealer will bust 11 times and reach a 17, 18, 19, 20 or 21 count 37 times—a net loss of 26 hands to the player. If the player hits his 16 count in each of his 48 dealt hands, he will bust 30 hands and reach a 17-to-21 count 18 times. Of the dealer's 18 opposing hands the dealer will bust about 4 hands. Subtracting the 4 dealer busts from the 30 player busts, the player has a net loss of 26 busts or hands out of 48. In this case it would seem to make little difference if the player hits or stands on the 16 count, since each action shows a loss of 26 player hands.

But it does make a difference because the player's 18 hands are equally divided among the counts 17, 18, 19, 20 or 21, while 7 of the dealer's completed 14 hands carry a high count of 20 and the remaining 7 are divided among counts of 17, 18, 19 and 21. This means that the dealer will win 3 more completed hands than the player. Adding these 3 additional player losses to the 26 losses he suffered previously, we find that the player who hits 16 against the dealer's 10-count upcard will suffer a net loss of 29 hands in 48 hands compared to the 26 lost hands suffered by the player who refuses to hit.

Therefore it is to the player's advantage to stand on 16 when the dealer shows a 10 count as his upcard.

It should now be clear that for each possible upcard the dealer shows, there is a certain player's card count on which the player should stand, and up to which he should continue to draw, in order to cut down the bank's favorable percentage.

The hit-and-stand rules which I recommend below will shave the bank's 5.90% edge down to about 3½% against the player who follows the same hit-and-stand rules as does the dealer.

1. *When the dealer's upcard is a five or six spot, the player should stand on a count of 12 or more.*

2. *When the dealer's upcard is a two, three or four spot, the player should stand on a count of 13 or more.*

3. *When the dealer's upcard is an ace or 10 count the player should stand on a count of 16 or more.*

4. *When the dealer's upcard is a seven, eight or nine spot the player should hit a count of 16 or less.*

I have not given the mathematical proof for all these contingencies, in order to save space. The reader who wants to work it out can do so by using the figures in Black Jack Tables II and III and following the same procedure I used when calculating the strength of the dealer's hand when his upcard is an ace, 7 or 10 count, in relation to the strength of the player's hand.

PLAYER'S SOFT HAND, OR TWO-WAY COUNT

When a player holds a hand that contains an ace, there are sometimes two possible counts neither of which exceeds 21. A hand containing an ace and a six may have a count or value of either 7 or 17 because an ace can be valued as either 1 or 11. This ambiguous type of hand is known to Black Jack dealers as a *soft count* or a *two-way* hand. Playing it correctly requires special strategic considerations, as follows:

1. *When the dealer's upcard is an eight, nine, ten or ace, the player should stand only on a soft 19 or higher.*

2. *When the dealer's upcard is a two, three, four, five, six or seven, the player should stand only on a soft 18 or higher.*

Note that the holder of a soft hand should never stand until his total count is at least 18. He should continue to drawn to his soft count and stand as indicated above. If, when the player draws one or more cards, his soft count exceeds 21 (this occurs often, since a high soft count is being hit), the player should revert to the standard hit-or-stand strategy, because he no longer holds a soft hand.

Example: The dealer's upcard is a six spot, the player hits a soft 14 and draws a nine spot. If he counted the ace as 11, he would have a count of 23. The hand is no longer soft, so the player reverts to his standard strategy and stands on 13.

Soft hands are advantageous to the player because if he uses the right strategy he gets two chances: he first tries for a high count by hitting a soft count, and if that fails he reverts to the standard hit-and-draw strategy.

SPLITTING PAIRS

Splitting pairs of any two 10-count cards allows the player to make two hands out of his initial two cards. If this situation is handled properly the player can cut down the bank's advantage by about ½%. As before, the important factors which tell the smart player whether or not to split are the value of the dealer's upcard and the strength of the player's initial two-card count.

The descision is made this way: Add the values of the two cards of the pair to get the total count and compare this with the total count of each single card. If the single-card count has a better mathematical chance of winning than the two-card count, split them. If the two-card count has the best chance, don't split. The chances are shown in Black Jack Tables II and III on pages 374 and 376.

Here is a specific example showing how the tables are used for this purpose. Suppose the player is dealt a 16 count composed of two eights, and the dealer's upcard is a six. First refer to Table II in which a 16 count shows 20 completed hands and 32 busts. Then turn to Table III which tells you that when the dealer's upcard is a six there are 29 completed hands and 23 busts.

Mentally split the 16 count into two eights. Table III shows that when the dealer's upcard is an eight there are 39 completed hands and only 13 busts. Since this holds true for each of the player's split eights, it is obvious that he should split them.

Another bit of strategy when splitting pairs is one I use which I have named the *overlay*. The rule is that it is to the player's advantage to split when his single card has a greater count value than the dealer's upcard.

If, after splitting a pair and drawing one or more cards, the player finds either or both hands have a count of 12, 13, 14, 15 or 16, he should resort to the original hit-and-draw strategy.

Here are my rules for splitting pairs or two 10-valued cards:

1. *Never split fours, fives, sixes or nines.*

2. *Always split eights unless the dealer's upcard is a nine or ten spot.*

3. *Split sevens when the dealer's card is a five, six or seven.*

4. *Always split aces even when the casino rules permit only a one-card draw to a split ace.*

5. *Always split 10-count cards when the dealer's upcard is a five or six.*

6. *Split twos and threes when the dealer's upcard is a two, three, four, five, six or seven.*

As a matter of fact, I often split 10-valued cards when the dealer's upcard is a 10-count. Under most conditions this gives me an advantage of 7 7/13% on each split hand. I don't, however, recommend such a split for the average player.

Here again, remember that these splitting recommendations are based on a full-deck composition of 52 cards.

DOUBLING DOWN

The technique of doubling down, like the technique of splitting pairs, deserves close study, because when properly handled it can also cut down the bank's advantage about 2%.

As in splitting pairs, there are many times when the initial two-card count indicates that it is to the player's advantage to double his bet.

This is the only single play at Black Jack which permits him to bet an amount that exceeds the casino's maximum limit. The double-down rules give the player a chance to increase his bet to twice the amount of the bank's maximum limit.

Because most Black Jack players know little or nothing about the mathematics of a double down, their lack of any suitable strategy for using it actually increases the bank's favorable percentage instead of cutting it. Most players double down merely because the dealer asks, "Do you want to double down?"

The art of doubling down at the proper time is an integral part of the best Black Jack strategy and a powerful tool in the hands of an expert.

Since the standard Black Jack rules permit a player to draw only one card to double down a hand, the player should have some good reason to back up his decision as to whether or not to double down. In deciding this question we again have to consider the possible strength of our double-down hand and the value of the dealer's upcard. Assume that the player was dealt 52 hands, each of which has a double-down count totaling 11. Then assume that each card dealt to the 11 count falls just as probability predicts. There will be 20 hands with a count of 12 to 16, and 32 hands with a count of 17 to 21. Note that 16 of these 32 hands are made up of a 21 count. If the dealer shows a 10 count as his upcard, turn to Black Jack Table III and note that the predicted value of the dealer's exposed 10 count is 40 hands with a count of 17 to 21, and 12 bust hands.

This shows that the player will gain an advantage of approximately 2 hands in 52 by doubling down on an 11 count when the dealer's upcard shows a 10 count. Since the dealer, showing a 10 count, is in his strongest position, the player will gain a still greater advantage doubling down on an 11 count when the dealer's upcard is an ace, nine, eight, etc.

This is the best strategy for doubling down:

1. *Always double down on a count of 11 no matter what the value of the dealer's upcard is.*
2. *Double down on a count of 10 when the dealer's upcard is anything but a 10 count.*
3. *Double down on a count of 9 when the dealer's upcard is a two, three, four, five or six.*
4. *Double down on a soft 12, 13, 14, 15, 16 or 17 when the dealer's upcard is a six.*

The player is in the most advantageous position for a double down when the dealer's upcard shows weakness, i.e., any card with a count of from 2 through 6. Proof of this weakness is shown in Black Jack Table III.

The strategy rules given above take into consideration all the Black Jack bets permitted in any casino the world over. However, only in Nevada will you find a casino in which you can put into play all strategy rules described above. For example, casinos in Puerto Rico permit a double down on 11 only. Casinos in Curaçao, Aruba and St. Maarten permit a double down on 10 and 11 only. Most casinos in Nevada permit a double down on *any* two cards. And so it goes, from country to country. However, the hit-and-stand strategy rules on both the hard and soft counts are usable in all casinos, and will be of great help in cutting down the house's advantage. So, memorize them first.

INSURANCE BETTING

Whenever the dealer shows an ace as his upcard, players may elect to make a so-called insurance bet against losing to a dealer's Black Jack. Since the insurance bet pays off at 2 to 1 odds, the player should win one-third of the time to get a dead-even proposition. If the dealer's upcard is an ace, and you have no knowledge of any other cards, then the dealer's down card may be considered drawn at random from 51 cards that remain unseen. But under such conditions the 51-card deck contains 16 10-count cards, and the player can win this bet only when the dealer has a 10-count card in the hole. In the long run he will win only 16 of his bets, losing 35. Since insurance bets are paid off at 2 to 1, or 32 to 16 against an expectation of 35 to 16, the player is shorted 3/51, or approximately 6%, or, to be exact, 5 15/17%.

Most players insist on buying insurance whenever they hold Black Jack on the grounds that they want to be sure of a win. The odds are 34 to 15 the dealer doesn't have a natural, and you will not receive the

2 to 1 insurance odds. Your expectation is minus 4/49 for a house edge of about 8%.

The casual card caser (counter) can use the insurance bet advantageously if he has kept track of the 10-count cards dealt in previous hands. For example, suppose half the deck (26 cards) has been dealt and the card caser recalls that only three 10-count cards have been dealt. If an insurance bet could be made on the next deal, it would be wise to take out insurance. For the above reason, insurance bettors are only permitted to bet half of their initial bets.

ADDITIONAL BLACK JACK STRATEGY

Here I would like to submit an additional bit of mathematical proof that the bank percentage at Black Jack not only varies with the dealing of each card, but may, at times, even be in favor of the player.

Since the bank pays off a holder of a natural Black Jack at odds of 3 to 2, the bank's advantage (based on a full-deck composition) is sliced down by 2 8/21%. Because this percentage goes up and down during the deal it can easily be used to the player's advantage.

Suppose, for example, than an experienced Black Jack player has remembered that in the first 26 cards dealt there were no aces, and only half (8) of the 10-count cards were dealt. He now knows that in the remaining 26 undealt cards there are four aces and eight 10-count cards. The partial card casing tells him that the bank's edge has been cut down considerably more than 2 8/21%, and that this is the time to increase the size of his bets.

However, if all the aces have made their appearance in the first 26 dealt cards, the player has no natural percentage in his favor and the bank's advantage cannot be sliced down by the dealing of a natural.

The average Black Jack player who fights the usual house percentage has almost no chance of winning in the long run. I am sure that the reader will feel that the price he paid for this book has been well spent when he realizes that a study of and proper use of the Black Jack strategy recommendations I have given will cut the bank's advantage—which ranges from 5.90% to 6.35% or more. If the player is skilled enough, the house percentage may sometimes even be canceled out entirely or even be replaced with a percentage in the player's favor.

CHEATING AT BLACK JACK

Because most private Black Jack games and illegally operated gambling joints as well as a number of major casinos in Nevada still insist on dealing single- or double-deck Black Jack from the hand, this section is of vital importance. Casinos which insist on dealing Black Jack from the hand reshuffle the entire deck when half or more of the deck has been played out or whenever a player substantially increases the size of his bet or bets. Therefore, all reasons given by the casino management that it's to a player's advantage to deal Black Jack from the hand are pure rubbish.

More cheating takes place at the Black Jack tables when the cards are dealt from the hand than when they are dealt from a card box because Black Jack dealt from the hand offers more opportunities for cheating. Most complaints made to me about cheating in Nevada casinos concern Black Jack dealt from the hand. The latest complaint brought to my attention by a high roller went like this: "I was a $30,000 Black Jack winner at———[name purposely omitted] in Las Vegas where the cards were dealt from a card box. Then around 4:00 A.M. I was informed that the table I was playing at was being closed and I was asked to move over to the open Black Jack section, which I did. At this table, the cards were dealt from the hand. Two hours later, I had not only lost my $30,000 in winnings but $20,000 of my own money besides. Scarne, was I cheated?"

I shrugged my shoulders and said, "I don't know. I didn't see the play, but since it's so easy to cheat at Black Jack when the cards are dealt from the hand, my advice is to seek a table where Black Jack is dealt from a card box."

Sometimes it is the casino operators who complain that they have been cheated by hand-muckers or cross-roaders (card sharps). This occurs when a player's two cards are dealt face down and are switched for two palmed cards, or a cold deck is switched into play.

Nevada casinos are fleeced out of millions of dollars yearly by agents (cheats acting as players) in collusion with crooked Black Jack dealers and pit bosses. This happens in spite of their so-called ironclad security controls, which include the hiring of ex-card cheats as pit bosses and the use of one-way mirrors in casino ceilings. In fact, casinos the world over are fleeced out of untold millions of dollars annually by crooked dealers tipping their hole card when an Ace or ten shows as their upcard, and by dealers overpaying bets or paying off losing bets as winning bets. I doubt that there is a casino anywhere operating Black Jack tables that is not taken for a bundle each year by outside and inside cheats.

Some agents pose as card casers or countdown artists when in fact they are working with a Black Jack dealer who is tipping off his hole card. This gimmick is used to avoid suspicion of collusion. Caesar's Palace on the Las Vegas Strip recently caught one of the country's best-known so-called card casers trying to bribe one of their Black Jack dealers. So much cheating of this type took place in England's casinos that the government passed a ruling that the Black Jack dealer is to receive his hole card after all players have completed playing out their hands. See page 354 for further information.

Most gambling casinos of established reputation fight both the casino and player cheat as a menace to the business, but some of their unscrupulous competitors hire card sharps to deal the game and instruct them to play honestly with the smaller players but *to go for the money* (cheat) when a high roller makes his appearance. Black Jack is the card cheat's paradise, whether it is a casino or private game, because a new hand is dealt every minute or so, because the action is fast, because the players are occupied in studying their own hands rather than the dealer's hand and because only a few cards, all of them crucial, are dealt each hand. These circumstances all combine to make cheating downright easy and steadily profitable.

Many of the methods described in Chapter 26, such as stacking, palming and second dealing, are used at Black Jack. Marked cards and a mastery of their use are for obvious reasons a tremendous advantage in a game in which a knowledge of the next card to be dealt is so important.

There are a few crooked tricks which are peculiarly suited to Black Jack. *Peeking* is an example. The dealer gets a peek at the top card of

Cheating at Black Jack. Scarne demonstrates how a dishonest dealer can, under cover of looking at his hole card, get a peek at the top card of the deck held in his left hand. (Conrad Eiger)

If the top card is one the dealer wants to retain, he deals the second card instead, but you can't stop the action as the photographer did here; the move is undetectable when it is fast and smooth. (Conrad Eiger)

the deck. He usually does this while pretending to examine his hole card, but the fact that the deck is held in the left hand, which is often in motion, gives him many other opportunities to obtain a secret glimpse. He also uses misdirection; he makes a gesture or some other move with his right hand which takes attention away from his left hand. At that precise instant the deck is turned slightly and the left thumb pushes the top card forward against the index finger, causing the card to buckle just enough so that the dealer gets a quick glimpse of the index. Because of the position of the indexes, this sleight is easier for left-handed dealers; instead of having to buckle the card they can merely move the top card so that it projects slightly over the side of the deck, far enough for part of the index to show.

When the top card is known, the second deal comes into play, a feat made easier by the tradition in Black Jack that the cards are usually held in the left hand and dealt with an overhand motion. When the second dealer peeks and sees a card he could use himself, he simply deals seconds until his own turn comes and then goes honest for a split second.

Dealers who cannot deal seconds—it's not an easy move—use an *anchor man*, who sits in the playing position farthest to the dealer's right. Assume the dealer has a 16 and a peek at the top card shows it to be a six spot or more, which would make him bust. The dealer signals the anchor man to ask for cards and continues to deal to him until a card he wants comes to the top. Then he signals the anchor man to stand and deals the useful card to himself.

The most common stacking method, the ancient business of arranging cards as they are picked up, is easy at Black Jack and very effective because certain cards and their sequences are so important. The dealer cheat reaches out with the left hand, which holds the deck, turns the deck over and gathers up some of the face-up discards with this hand. This maneuver places these cards on the top of the deck instead of the bottom where they should go. It is made quickly and smoothly, and most players never see anything wrong with the action. The right hand helps misdirect because it is also in action at the same time, picking up the remaining discards which, when the deck has been turned right side up again, are then slowly burned on the bottom in the usual manner.

Hole Card Switch. Cheat looks at his hole card (BELOW) as right hand approaches with Ace palmed. Ace slides in under King (TOP RIGHT), and is left on table (BOTTOM RIGHT) as right hand goes away with the King palmed. The whole action takes only a second or two. (Conrad Eiger)

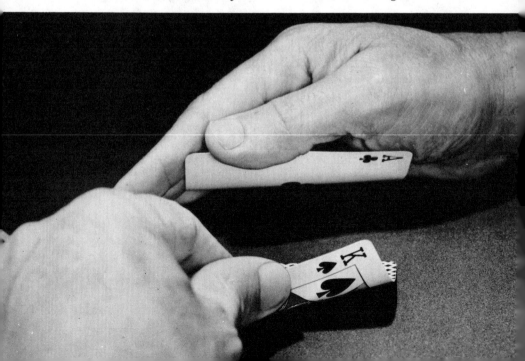

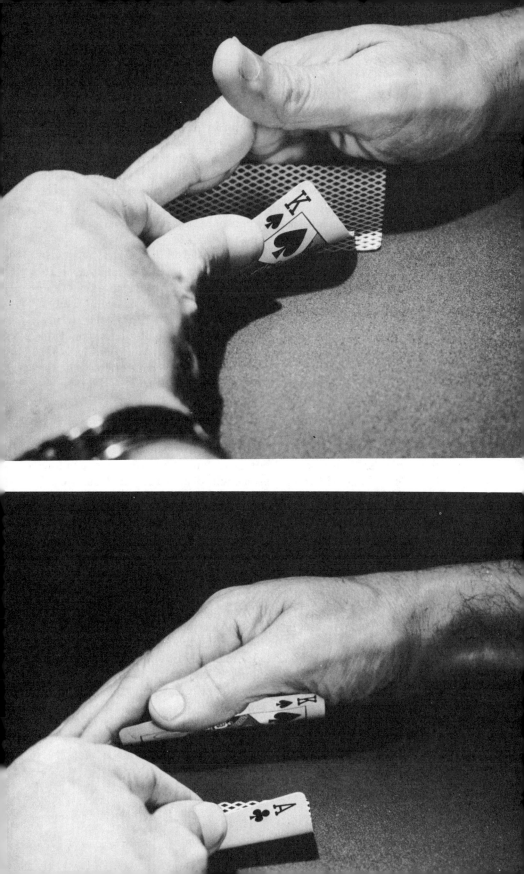

Usually a 20 or a natural is stacked in this fashion. When the dealer sees a 10 count and an ace, and the game is three-handed, he arranges the cards during the pickup in such a way that ace is third and the 10 count sixth. When this sequence is returned to the top rather than the bottom of the deck, the next deal will give the dealer a natural; he'll get the ace as his face-down card and the 10-count as his upcard. Beware of the dealer who constantly keeps turning the deck over while picking up discards. And if you ever see a card dealt which was dealt in a previous hand when only one deck of cards is being used, take your business elsewhere.

The most common cheating method used in crooked casinos when making use of four decks (208 cards) is to remove a number of 10-count cards and to replace them with 5-count cards. Because the dealer must hit a count of 16, the substitution of fives for tens avoids many a normal dealer bust and supplants these with additional dealer twenty-ones. To protect yourself against such cheating subterfuges, count the 5-counts and 10-counts as the hands are played. If you count less than sixty-four 10-count cards or more than sixteen 5-count cards—seek the nearest exit. For your own safety, don't make a scene. A thief caught red-handed is always a dangerous thief.

For information on crooked dealing boxes (shoes), see Cheating at Baccarat and Chemin de Fer, page 474.

The best assurance you can have that the game is honest is to see the cards dealt out of a card box as is done in most casinos. I predict that before long *all* Nevada casinos will deal Black Jack from a card-dealing box rather than from the hand.

SCARNE'S RULES FOR PRIVATE BLACK JACK

The private, or non-professional, game of Black Jack is played throughout the United States. I found that it surpassed Poker as the most popular game in the Armed Forces during World War II.

Most of the strategy I have recommended for use in the casino type of Black Jack can also be used to the player's or dealer's advantage in the private game, even though some of the rules are different. The major difference, of course, is that, unlike the casino dealer who must draw on a count of 16 or less and stand on 17 or more, the dealer in the private game can draw or stand on any count.

The following rules are the best for a private game. They first appeared in print in *Scarne on Cards*.

Requirements

1. Two to seven players constitute the best game, although as many players can play as can fit around a table.

2. Kibitzers may bet on the hand of any player except the dealer.

3. The standard 52-card pack plus the joker is used.

Value of the Cards

1. Any ace counts either 1 or 11 according to the discretion of the possessor.

2. Kings, queens and jacks count 10 each.

3. All other cards count their face value.

4. The joker has no value and does not enter into the play; it is used only as a locater in the deck.

Object of the Game

To get a higher count (total value of cards in hand) than the dealer up to but not over 21. Should the player draw cards forcing his total over 21, he must immediately pay the dealer-banker, and he sacrifices any chance to beat or tie the dealer. The player may demand and draw any number of cards until he reaches or exceeds a count of 21.

Selecting the Dealer

The first dealer shall be selected as follows *and in no other manner:*

1. Any player by mutual consent may shuffle the deck.

2. Any player may cut it.

3. Any player, acting as dealer pro tem, deals one card face up to each of the players.

4. The player dealt the first ace becomes the dealer-banker.

Losing the Deal and Bank

Ordinarily I don't think a game lawmaker should build variations into the basic structure of a game, but Black Jack is an extremely special case. Here are two rules under which the bank may be lost: either is legal. I recommend that the second be adopted for the private sociable game. I must also emphasize that before play starts all players must be acquainted with the rules under which they are playing.

1. Any player dealt a natural (two cards totaling 21) shall become dealer and banker at the completion of that deal. If more than one player is dealt a natural, the player nearest the dealer's left wins the deal. If that player refuses the deal, the player holding a natural nearest to that player's left wins the deal. If all players holding a natural refuse the deal, it remains in possession of the present dealer. Should he refuse to continue dealing, the deal passes to the player to his immediate left. If that player refuses, it passes to his left. If all players refuse it, a new dealer is selected as stated above under *Selecting the Dealer.*

2. The following rule is added to stabilize the situation, too often encountered in Black Jack, in which one player gets the bank for a single deal, then loses it to another player who, through sheer luck, holds it for eight or ten deals.

(a) After the first dealer has been selected by the procedure set forth under *Selecting the Dealer,* he shall deal (bank) five complete deals.

(b) On completion of these five deals, the deal and bank shall pass to the player at the dealer's left and, each five deals thereafter, shall move to the dealer's left, clockwise.

(c) When using this alternate rule, a natural 21 does not win the bank, although the player drawing it is still paid 2 to 1 on his bet.

The Betting Limit

The dealer arbitrarily establishes his own betting limits. For example, he may declare that while he is dealing the bets are 25¢ to $2, meaning that the smallest bet that can be put on a hand by anyone, player or kibitzer, is 25¢, the largest, $2.

If a dealer, after suffering losses, has less money in the bank than the players want to bet, he is privileged to lower his limit. If he has a winning streak he may increase it.

A dealer who decides he no longer wants the bank is privileged to put the bank and deal up for auction and sell to the highest bidder. He may auction the deal at any time, provided there are no uncompleted hands on the board.

If the dealer offers the bank at auction and no player bids, it passes to the player at the dealer's left. If he rejects it, the deal passes clockwise around the table until it is accepted or, if no one accepts, there is a deal for selecting a new dealer.

The Shuffle and Cut

The dealer shuffles the cards and puts them in the center of the table to be cut.

Any player may call for the right to shuffle any time he likes, but the dealer shall have the right to shuffle last.

Any player may cut the cards. If more players than one want to cut, they must be allowed to do so.

After the cut has been completed and the cards are squared, the deck is placed on the upturned joker, which is left resting before the dealer. This face-up card is used as a locater in the deck.

If a joker isn't available, the dealer shall remove the top card of the deck, show it to all other players, then put it on the bottom of the deck, face up.

This is called *burning* a card.

Payoffs

All bets are paid off at even money by both dealer and players, except when a player is dealt a natural, when he is paid 2 to 1.

Betting

Before any cards are dealt, each player must put the sum he proposes to bet (within the limit) in front of him, within full view of the dealer.

The Deal

The dealer gives one card face down to each player beginning with the player on his left and then going clockwise. He deals to himself last; this card is dealt face up. He then deals each player a second card face up, and a second card to himself face down. (I have suggested that the dealer's first card be dealt face up instead of his second because this gives the players more time to study the dealer's upcard and its possibilities and tends to speed the game.)

The Play

The dealer now looks at his two cards. If he has caught a natural— that is, a ten or picture card plus an Ace, with a total count of 21—he immediately faces his cards and announces a natural.

Any other players who have naturals announce them. If anyone does, that sets up a *standoff* or *push*. The dealer collects the bets of all players not holding naturals and the payoff is at even money. In case of standoffs, no bets are paid.

If the dealer hasn't caught a natural, the player to his left plays first. If that player has 21 he calls a natural and turns over his two cards, and the dealer puts them on the bottom of the deck face up. If the player's two cards total less than 21, the player indicates whether he will stay or get hit.

If he is satisfied that his count is closer than the dealer's to a total of 21, the player may stay by declining another card. He signifies this intention by putting his bet on top of his cards and/or saying, "Good" or "I stand" or "I have enough."

If he is not satisfied with his count and elects to draw more cards he says, "Hit me!" and the dealer gives him another card face up. The player may draw one or as many more cards as he likes, as long as his count does not exceed 21. When the player is satisfied with his count, he says, "I stay," and puts his bet on his cards.

When a player draws a card forcing his total count over 21 he must call, "Bust!" and turn up all his cards. The dealer collects the bet and burns that player's cards face up at the bottom of the deck, and the player is out of competition until a new hand starts.

Like the deal, this play always moves around the table to the left, clockwise, a player at a time.

The Dealer's Play

The dealer plays last. He may, like the players, elect to stay or draw. He turns his down card face up and announces, "Stay" or "Draw."

If he draws one or more cards and goes over 21, he must pay all players still in the game.

If, when either staying or drawing, he remains below 21 on completing his play, he collects bets from players who have a lower count than he, and pays all surviving players having a higher count.

When dealer and player have the same count, it's a standoff, and neither wins.

Additional Rules

The above rules will suffice for a quiet private game, but there's nothing sacrosanct about them. Players may, by agreement, incorporate into their private play as many rules as they like from *Scarne's Casino Black Jack Rules* (see page 356).

14.
Roulette

Roulette, the glamour casino game, is the favorite gambling game of 9 million American women and 4 million American men. Visit any casino in Europe, South America, Nevada or the Caribbean islands and you will find that on the average three out of the five players seated at a Roulette table are women. My survey reveals that each year approximately $150 million was lost by Americans at Roulette, of which 50% or $75 million is lost by women.

Roulette is said by some historians to have been invented in 1655 by the French scientist Blaise Pascal, during his monastic retreat, and first played in a makeshift casino in Paris. Other historians say it was invented by a French monk to help break the monotony of monastery life. Still others say it originated in an old Chinese game whose object was to arrange 37 statuettes of animals in a "magic square" of 666, but they fail to describe the method of play. They add that the game was later played in Tibet and eventually by French Dominican monks, one of whom transposed the statuettes into numbers from 0 to 36 and arranged them haphazardly along the rim of a revolving wheel. Since the early French wheels of the 1800s had both the 0 and 00, this theory does not sound plausible.

ROULETTE WHEELS—YESTERDAY AND TODAY

Despite considerable research, I have not found any reliable evidence on the true origin of the game, but I did discover that the modern game historians who say that the first Roulette wheels to appear in French casinos were identical with those used today in French and other European casinos are wrong. The *American Hoyle,* printed

John Scarne observes the play at a roulette table in the Caribe Hilton casino in San Juan.

in the mid-1800s, describes in detail the playing rules and the design of the wheels and layouts used in France and America at that time. Both the French- and American-style Roulette of that day differed considerably in structure and rules of play from the present European and American wheels.

My research shows that from the day Roulette was first introduced into American casinos and up until about 1890 the American wheels were of a special design unlike the European wheels. They had 31 numbers and symbols: the numbers 1 through 28, a single 0, a double 00, and a picture of an American eagle which was the equivalent of a triple 000. When the ball dropped into either the 0, 00 or Eagle, the bank won all bets on the layout except those bet on the winning symbol. These winning single-number bets were paid off at odds of 27 for 1.* All other winning single-number bets also paid off at 27 for 1, and

---

* In odds terms this is 26 to 1. If a player bet $1, the roulette dealer would first collect his $1 winning bet, then pay him $27. The player was really collecting $26 in winnings, and getting back the $1 bet. This misdirective device, which led some players to think they were winning more than they really did, is no longer used at Roulette. The odds are quoted at 26 to 1, the dealer pays $26, and the winning bet is left on the table. This procedure tends to give the casino additional action because the player may make the bet again by leaving his bet on the layout. This former gimmick of using the word *for* in odds quotes is, however, still found on many American Craps layouts.

3 for 1	3 for 1	3 for 1	3 for 1
28	27	14	18
26	25	12	11
24	23	10	9
22	21	8	7
20	19	6	5
18	17	4	8
16	15	2	1
0 0	Eagle.		0

O	Eagle.		O O
1	2	15	16
3	4	17	18
5	6	19	20
7	8	21	22
9	10	23	24
11	12	25	26
13	14	27	28
3 for 1	3 for 1	3 for 1	3 for 1

Nineteenth-century American roulette layout and wheel, which bears only 28 numbers and has a 0, a double 00, and an eagle, the symbol for a triple 000.

the only other bets permitted were bets on red and black, which paid even money, and on the four columns, each comprised of seven numbers, which paid off at 3 to 1. The bank's favorable percentages on this roulette wheel were: single-number bet, 12 28/31%; red or black color bet, 9 21/31%, and seven-number-column bet, 9 21/31%. This high percentage take for the bank is obviously the main reason why Roulette did not become popular in American casinos at that time.

The French Roulette wheel of the middle 1800s was built like the modern American wheel with its single 0 and double 00. Although there were 36 numbers, the bank paid off at odds of only 34 to 1 on a single-number bet. Also, the single 0 was black, the double 00 was red, and when the ball dropped into either the 0 or 00 all bets on the corresponding colors were considered *bars*. This meant that when the ball dropped in the single 0 all bets on black neither won nor lost, and when the ball dropped in the double 00 all bets on red neither won nor lost. We have the same situation today in Bank Craps with its bar on the don't pass line of either two aces, two sixes or the ace-deuce (see page 287). There is no doubt in my mind that the bar used at Bank Craps was taken from French Roulette.

Roulette wheels found today in Monte Carlo, Deauville, San Remo and other European casinos have 36 numbers (1 to 36) and a single zero (0). When zero appears, all bets paid off at even money such as red, black, odd or even are "imprisoned" and their ultimate fate is determined by the next spin of the wheel. They are either lost or are returned to the winning player, who gets back only his original bet. The player loses half of his wager on red, black, odd or even, when the zero appears. The bank's favorable percentage, in this case on red, black, odd or even, is 1 13/37%, and on all other types of bets it is 2 26/37%.

The modern American-style Roulette wheel with its single 0 and double 00 is similar to the wheel discarded by French and European casino operators decades ago. This indicates that the first American Roulette operators of the early colonial days used the early French-style wheel with its 28 numbers and 3 symbols for a total of 31, rather than the 36 numbers and single zero used in European casinos today.

These changes in Roulette wheels and layouts are caused by the fact that players shy away from the game after suffering constant losses and after discovering the percentage they must buck. When this happens, the operators, in an attempt to retrieve their lost business, make changes which give the player a better percentage break. Example: the first Roulette wheels in American casinos had the 0, 00 and Eagle. Present-day wheels have the single 0 and the double 00. I predict in

Roulette wheel in action at the Hilton Flamingo casino in Las Vegas. Black Jack tables and slot machines can be seen in background at left. (Las Vegas News Bureau)

the next decade or two American Roulette wheels will have only the single 0, as do the present European wheels.

Fortunes have been won and lost by women and men at Roulette. The largest sum of money known to have been won on a single spin of the wheel is $67,500. The incident took place at Caesar's Palace, a swank Las Vegas hotel casino. The winner, a Mexican businessman on vacation, asked for and was given a $500 maximum limit on straight, split, corner, street and line bets. The businessman, after making several small bets, placed a $500 straight bet on 4 and backed it with four $500 split bets and four $500 corner bets. The croupier spun the wheel, then the ball, and lo and behold, the little ivory ball dropped and came to rest in the number 4 slot and the Mexican gambler collected $67,500 in winnings.

A California woman, the wife of a retired oil magnate, once confided to me that during the past five years her total losses at Roulette in European and American casinos exceeded the $3 million mark.

The largest sum of money known to have been lost at a single roulette session in the United States was $1,250,000 lost by an American industrialist at a Saratoga casino one evening during the month of August 1946. The special limit put into effect for the industrialist was $25,000 on an even-money bet and $1,000 on a single number, with an additional $1,000 any way he could reach the number, such as a split, corner, or street bet. For example, a $2,000 limit bet on a single winning number paid $72,000 ($70,000 in winnings plus the original $2,000 wager).

P.S. The high limit didn't worry the casino operators because the wheel was gaffed! The industrialist settled his losses for $500,000.

Europeans and Latin Americans play Roulette much more than Americans do, but Roulette tables can now be found in most legal and illegal gambling casinos in this country, especially in the luxury rug joints. More than any other casino game, Roulette has an aura of glamour that makes it especially attractive to women. When a woman enters a casino for the first time, it is almost a sure bet that, after playing the slot machines, the first game she tries will be Roulette.

This is the game which the handsome hero and well-dressed heroine have played for years in countless motion pictures, books and short stories. It has been publicized as the game of millionaire playboys, of kings and princes. It is celebrated in many stories of fortunes won and lost, of mathematical wizards who have spent years developing Roulette systems, and even in a song: "The Man Who Broke the Bank at Monte Carlo." Roulette is the world's oldest banking game still in operation, and through the years it has given rise to many true stories, as well as much that is legend and myth.

A great part of Roulette's fascination also lies in the beauty and color of the game. The surface of the handsome mahogany table is covered with a blazing green cloth which bears the bright gold, red and black of the layout. The chromium separators between the numbered pockets on the wheel's rim glitter and dance in the bright light as the wheel spins. The varied colors of the wheel checks stacked on the table's apron and before the croupier and scattered on the layout's betting spaces, the evening clothes of the women, the formal dress of the men, the courteous croupiers—all add to the enticing picture.

The neophyte soon discovers that although the betting layout looks complicated the game is easy to learn. The women are also attracted by the odds the bank offers, which are higher than most other casino games. One chip on a straight winning number is paid off at 35 to 1 and the player receives a stack of 20 and a stack of 15 chips.

Before entering on a detailed discussion of the game, we need to examine the equipment used. In the description that follows you will find, for the first time in print, a detailed explanation of the construction and inner workings of the Roulette wheel itself.

STANDARD ROULETTE EQUIPMENT

Roulette tables: There are two styles of Roulette tables found in American casinos. One is the standard table, which has one betting layout with the Roulette wheel at one end; the other, called the double-end table, has two layouts with the wheel in the center between them.

Roulette layout: The layout is a multicolored design printed on green baize that covers the players' side of the table and forms the betting section. The main portion of the design is comprised of 36 numbered rectangular spaces arranged in three long columns of 12 spaces each. The spaces at the head of the columns are numbered 1, 2, 3, and are nearest the wheel. The numbering continues in sequence across the columns, ending with 34, 35 and 36 at the foot of the columns farthest from the wheel. Directly below these numbers are three blank spaces. A chip placed on one of these indicates that the player is betting on the 12 numbers on the long column directly above the space on which the chip rests. (On some layouts these squares are marked "2 to 1" and are located on the player's side of the table.)

Along one side of the long columns are three rectangular spaces marked "1st 12," "2nd 12" and "3rd 12." A chip placed on one of these spaces indicates that the player is betting on the first 12 numbers, 1 through 12; on the second 12 numbers, 13 through 24, or on the third 12 numbers, 25 through 36.

Next to these are six more spaces which read from left to right: "1–18," "Even," "Red," "Black," "Odd," "19–36." Above the three long columns are two spaces with pointed tops containing the figures 0 and 00.

Roulette balls: The balls used are made of ivory or synthetic plastic. They vary in size from ½ inch to ¾ inch in diameter.

Wheel checks, or chips: The standard Roulette table employs 5, 6 or 7 sets of wheel checks (usually called chips). Each set is differently colored, each consists of 300 chips, and there is one set for each player. The chips are usually valued at 25¢ each, and the minimum number a player can buy is 20, $5 worth. Some sawdust joints also sell 5¢ and 10¢ chips. The color of the chips indicates the player, not the value of the chips. If a player wishes to buy 50¢ or $1 chips, the croupier places a 50¢ or $1 marker on top of the stack of chips in the table's chip rack whose color corresponds to the chips purchased. Five-dollar and $25 chips, which may be used at any gambling table in the casino, may also be purchased. These, unlike the other chips, do have a color indicating value.

Roulette wheels: There are two styles. The American wheel has 36 numbers and the signs 0 and 00. The French or European wheel, which has 36 numbers and only the single 0, is found mostly in European and South American casinos and is seldom seen in this country.

The American wheels used in the United States and the Caribbean islands are, except for the double 00, similar in construction to the French wheels. They are made up of two separate parts; the table, which is stationary, and the wheel itself, which is movable and manually rotated.

Most of the table's area consists of the betting section and a large wooden, bowl-shaped recess called the *bowl*. This contains the wheel, which is called the *wheel head*. The interior diameter of the bowl is approximately 32 inches. It has a back track made of sturdy wood which contains an inch-wide groove running around the bowl's circumference. It is in this groove that the croupier spins the Roulette ball. When the speed of the ball diminishes it falls on to the bottom track of the bowl. The revolving wheel head and the bottom track are marked off by black lines into eight equal sections. In the center of each section on the bottom track there is a small metal obstacle 2 inches long, ½ inch wide and ½ inch thick. These obstacles are placed alternately vertically and horizontally and the rolling ball, as it strikes them, is given a random and unpredictable motion.

The bowl's bottom underneath the wheel is open, and below it there is a flat wooden base from the center of which rises a steel spindle, ¼ inch in diameter and 4 inches high.

The wheel head, the only moving part, consists of a solid wooden disk or plate, slightly convex in shape. Around its rim are metal partitions known as *separators* or *frets*, and the compartments or pockets between these are called *canoes* by Roulette croupiers. These pockets are metal, painted alternately red and black, except for two pockets which are green. Each of the red and black compartments bears a number from 1 to 36 in gold. The green pockets carry the signs 0 and 00, also in gold.

Most players and croupiers believe that the numbers 1 through 36 are arranged on the rim of the wheel head in a haphazard manner, except that red and black numbers alternate. There is nothing haphazard about the arrangement. An attempt has been made to alternate low, high, odd and even numbers as well as the red and black colors in such a way that each group of numbers and each color is spaced out in a mathematically balanced fashion. A perfect mathematical balance is not possible since the sum of the numbers 1 through 36 is 666, and the 18 odd numbers add to only 324 while the 18 even numbers add to 342. In order to attain the best possible mathematical balance, Roulette manufacturers use the following arrangement:

The signs 0 and 00 are directly opposite each other on the wheel-head rim, separated on each side by 18 numbers. The 0 pocket is between two black-numbered pockets and the colors alternate in both directions around the wheel, ending in two red pockets, one on each

Roulette wheel showing number arrangement. (B. C. Wills & Co.)

side of the 00. Odd numbers alternate with even numbers. In order to get the best possible distribution of high and low numbers, the sum of each two successive numbers of the same color must equal 37. There are two exceptions: the numbers 9 and 28 and the numbers 10 and 27 are not the same color; each pair is made up of a red and a black number.

A shining steel ornament rises about eight inches above the exact center of the disk. Inside it, a four-inch hole runs upward from its bottom. This fits over the steel spindle, crowned with a ball bearing, which rises from the center of the bowl. The wheel, perfectly balanced at its center on this single ball bearing, spins in an almost frictionless, smooth and precise manner.

ROULETTE PERSONNEL AND THEIR DUTIES

A Roulette table with a single layout is usually worked by two croupiers. A double-end table with two layouts is operated by either three or four croupiers. The croupier who spins the wheel and deals the game is called the *wheel roller* by casino employees. To keep our explanation simple we'll call him the *dealer*, and call his assistant a *croupier*. We will describe the operation of a table with a single layout.

The dealer is in charge of the conduct of the game. His main duties are selling chips to players, spinning the wheel, throwing the Roulette ball, announcing winners, collecting losing bets and paying off winning bets. The croupier separates and stacks the losing chips that have been collected or swept from the layout by the dealer. He stacks the chips in piles of 20 of the same color and places them in the chip rack on the table's apron. He helps the dealer pay off winning bets by stacking the correct number of chips in a convenient place to the left of the table's apron.

All large casinos use an additional employee, the *pit boss* or *inspector*. He stands in the pit ring, watches the game and is in charge of its conduct. He makes out cash-out, credit and fill slips, corrects any errors made by the croupiers or players and watches for cheating.

SCARNE'S RULES FOR PLAYING ROULETTE

The players begin making their bets placing chips on the spaces of the layout in any manner permitted by the rules. The dealer starts the wheel spinning in a counterclockwise direction, then flips the ball on to the bowl's back track so that it travels clockwise. Players may continue placing bets while wheel and ball are in motion until the dealer calls: "No more bets!" He does this as the ball slows down and is about to drop off the back track. Bets placed on the layout after this announcement are not valid and must be returned to the player or players.

When the ball falls and comes to rest between any two metal partitions of the wheel, it marks the winning number, a zero or double zero, the winning color, and any other permitted bet that pertains to a winning number or symbol. The dealer immediately announces the winning number and its color, and he points with his index finger to the corresponding number on the layout. Some dealers place a plastic peg (a half inch in diameter and two inches tall) on the winning number for all to see. He collects all losing bets, not disturbing the chips resting on winning spaces, and pays off the winner or winners with the correct amount of chips due each winning bet. The signs 0 and 00 win for the bank all bets except those placed on 0 and 00.

On the first spin the dealer has no fixed point from which to spin the wheel or ball. Thereafter he must spin both from the winning pocket into which the ball dropped. The croupier dealing the wheel is obliged to spin the ball with the hand nearest the wheel.

Some casinos give the player the privilege of asking the inspector or casino operator to substitute another dealer, and this may be done provided one or more of the other players at the table do not object.

No such substitution may take place until after the dealer has thrown the ball five times.

POSSIBLE ROULETTE BETS, ODDS AND PERCENTAGES

Since Roulette layouts do not vary in bets permitted, odds offered and percentages against the player, the following text covers all of the common bets permitted on any layout.

Straight bet or single-number bet: The player places his chips squarely on one number on the layout, making certain that the chips do not touch any of the lines enclosing the number. This indicates that the player is betting that number to win. Since there are 36 numbers on the wheel, plus the signs 0 and 00, making a total of 38, the correct odds are 37 to 1. The bank pays off at 35 to 1 and consequently has the advantage of the 0 and 00. In terms of percentage this is 2/38 of 100, or 5 5/19% (about 26¢ on a $5 bet).

The signs 0 and 00: These can be played the same as any straight or single-number bet. The bank's favorable percentage is the same as on a straight bet: 5 5/19% (about 26¢ on a $5 bet).

Split bet or two-number bet: The player places his chips directly on any line separating any two numbers. If the winning number is one of the two wagered on, the player wins.
Payoff odds: 17 to 1
Correct odds: 18 to 1
Percentage favoring bank: 5 5/19% (about 26¢ on a $5 bet)

Street bet or three-number bet: The player places his chip or chips on the outside line of the layout. This indicates that he is betting the three numbers opposite the chips, going across the layout. If the winning number is one of these three the player wins.
Payoff odds: 11 to 1
Correct odds: 11⅔ to 1
Percentage favoring bank: 5 5/19% (about 26¢ on a $5 bet)

Square bet, quarter bet, corner bet or four-number bet: The player places his chips on the intersection of the lines between any four numbers. If any one of these four numbers wins the player collects.
Payoff odds: 8 to 1
Correct odds: 8½ to 1
Percentage favoring bank: 5 5/19% (about 26¢ on a $5 bet)

Line bet or five-number bet: The player places his chips on the line separating the 1, 2, 3 from the 0 and 00 spaces at a corner inter-

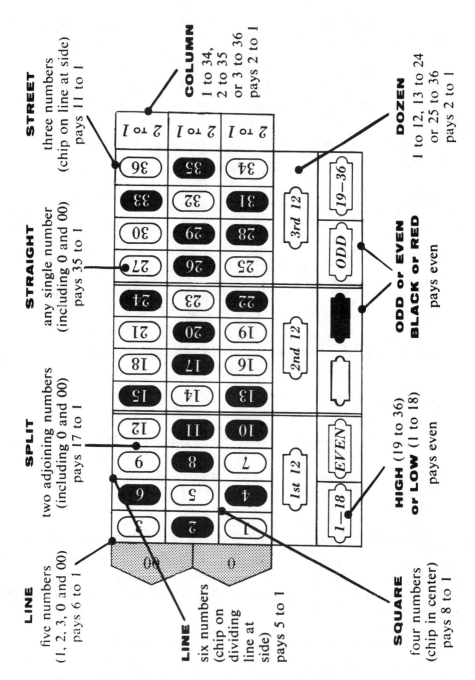

Players indicate the bet or bets they make by the placement of chips on the layout as shown here.

section. This indicates that he is betting that one of the numbers 1, 2, 3, or 0 or 00 will win.

Payoff odds: 6 to 1

Correct odds: 6 ⅗ to 1

Percentage favoring bank: 7 17/19% (about 39¢ on a $5 bet)

Note that the house percentage differs from the 5 5/19% which is the bank's edge on all other Roulette bets. From the player's viewpoint it is therefore a bet to avoid because it has 2 12/19% more against the player.

Line bet or six-number bet: The player places his chips on the intersection of the side line and a line between two "streets." If any of these six numbers wins, the player collects.

Payoff odds: 5 to 1

Correct odds: 5⅓ to 1

Percentage favoring bank: 5 5/19% (about 26¢ on a $5 bet)

Column bet or 12-number bet: The player places his chips on one of the three blank spaces at the bottom of the layout (some layouts have three squares marked "1st," "2nd," "3rd"). This indicates that the player is betting the 12 vertical numbers above the space wagered on.

Payoff odds: 2 to 1

Correct odds: 2⅙ to 1

Percentage favoring bank: 5 5/19% (about 26¢ on a $5 bet)

Dozens or 12-number bet: The player places his chips on one of the spaces of the layout marked "1st 12," "2nd 12" or "3rd 12." The 1st 12 indicates that the player is betting on the numbers 1 to 12 inclusive; the 2nd 12, the numbers 13 to 24 inclusive, and the 3rd 12, the numbers 25 to 36 inclusive.

Payoff odds: 2 to 1

Correct odds: 2⅙ to 1

Percentage favoring bank: 5 5/19% (about 26¢ on a $5 bet)

Low-number bet (1 to 18): The player places his chips on the layout space marked 1 to 18, which indicates that he is betting on the numbers 1 to 18 inclusive.

Payoff odds: Even money

Correct odds: 1 1/9 to 1

Percentage favoring bank: 5 5/19% (about 26¢ on a $5 bet)

High-number bet (19 to 36): The player places his chips on the space of the layout marked 19 to 36, which indicates that he is betting on the numbers 19 to 36 inclusive.

Payoff odds: Even money
Correct odds: 1 1/9 to 1
Percentage favoring bank: 5 5/19% (about 26¢ on a $5 bet)

Black color bet: The player places his chips on a space of the lay-out marked "Black." (Some layouts have a large black diamond-shaped design instead of the word "Black.") The player is betting that the winning color will be black.
Payoff odds: Even money
Correct odds: 1 1/9 to 1
Percentage favoring bank: 5 5/19% (about 26¢ on a $5 bet)

Red color bet: This is the same as a black color bet except that the player places his chips on the space marked "Red," or the red dia-mond, and is betting that the winning color will be red.

Odd-number bet: The player places his chips on the space of the layout marked "Odd." The player is betting that the winning number will be an odd number.
Payoff odds: Even money
Correct odds: 1 1/9 to 1
Percentage favoring bank: 5 5/19% (about 26¢ on a $5 bet)

Even-Number Bet: This is the same as the odd-number bet, except that the player is betting that the winning number will be even.

ROULETTE BETTING LIMITS

The maximum amounts permitted to be wagered on different spaces of the layout vary with each casino. The minimum bet allowed is usually four chips, be they 5¢, 10¢ or 25¢ chips. A player betting 25¢ chips must bet a minimum of four chips on one spin of the wheel, although the four chips can be spread over the spaces on the layout as desired, excluding even-money and 2 to 1 spaces. A minimum of four chips or a bet valued at $1 is required on all even-money or 2 to 1 bets.

The standard maximum betting limits in Nevada are as follows: $100 on a straight, split, street, corner or line bet and $500 on any 2 to 1 or even-money bet. However, major casinos in Nevada will up their maximum betting limits at the sight of a high roller. Casinos in the Bahamas adhere to the same betting rules as Nevada. Puerto Rican casinos, where betting limits are government regulated, and various other casinos in the Caribbean permit the following maximum limits: $10 on a single-number bet and any other way you can reach it (split, street, corner, line); $180 on black, red, odd, even, high and low, and $120 on dozens and columns. Although maximum limits may vary from casino to casino, the following maximum limits on all possible roulette bets are fairly standard in most major casinos throughout the world:

MAXIMUM BETTING LIMITS AND PAYOFF ODDS

Type of Bet	Maximum Limit	Bank's Payoff Odds
Straight	$100	35 to 1
Split	100	17 to 1
Street	100	11 to 1
Quarter or corner	100	8 to 1
Line (1–2–3–0–00)	100	6 to 1
Line (six numbers)	100	5 to 1
Columns	250	2 to 1
1st, 2nd, 3rd dozen	250	2 to 1
Color (red or black)	500	Even
Even	500	Even
Odd	500	Even
1 to 18 (low)	500	Even
19 to 36 (high)	500	Even

A single number may also be played with $100 straight and another $100 placed on split, corner, street, line or other bets. In other words, a $100 maximum can also be bet any way you can reach the number. Many casino operators will increase these limits for bigtime bettors. Some casinos have lower maximum betting limits than those listed above. Usually, when the limit on one bet is smaller, the limits on all others are proportionally smaller. Example: If the maximum straight bet of $100 is reduced to $25, all other bets would also be reduced by about 60%.

THE $400,000 ROULETTE WIN

Roulette happens to be a very tricky game, and raising the standard maximum betting limits may not be too wise if the player is mathematically smart and knows more about betting systems than the casino manager suspects. This is especially true when the deviations from the standard maximum limits are increased from $500 to $7,000. Here's a good instance of this.

While on a recent casino inspection tour at the Curaçao Hilton casino in the Netherlands Antilles, I received several long-distance telephone calls from the casino manager of Harrah's casino in Lake Tahoe, Nevada, asking me to make a hurried trip there to analyze a Roulette betting system being used by a high roller. The first phone call I received informed me that the high roller had won $250,000 in five days of play, an average of $50,000 per day. Since my mission in

Curaçao was not completed, I asked the casino manager to call me back in three days. When I received the phone call three days later, he informed me that the high roller was now a $400,000 winner.

As I could not leave the islands at the time, I asked the excited casino manager to brief me about the details of the player's system. This is what he told me: The high-rolling Roulette player asked for special limits before he began his play. After some back-and-forth bickering, the casino manager agreed to a $7,000 maximum betting limit and a $25 minimum on all 2 to 1 and even-money bets (red, black, odd, even, high, low, dozens and columns). In addition, a $400 maximum limit and a $25 minimum bet was permitted on a straight, split, corner, street and line bet.

After analyzing the data the casino manager had given me, I had the answer to the system. The high roller was making use of a sophisticated progressive system betting on the color black. That is, he used an irregular progressive betting system, sometimes doubling his previous bet, sometimes betting the same amount as his previous bet, and sometimes nearly tripling the size of a previously lost bet. And whenever he was a winner of $100 or more, he began his progressive system all over again.

To best describe this progressive system, let us assume that Mr. High Roller lost ten consecutive bets. His bets would be made as follows: He would start with a $25 bet on black and continue his black progressive system as follows, $50, $50, $75, $100, $100, $500, $1,500, $3,500, $7,000 for a total loss of $12,900. The chance of Mr. High Roller losing ten black bets in a row is about 1 in 970. If Mr. High Roller lost nine consecutive bets and won the tenth bet, his profit would be $1,100 and he would start his progressive system again with $25 for his first bet. If he lost eight consecutive bets and won the ninth bet, his profit still would be $1,100 and he would start his system anew. If he lost seven consecutive bets and won the eighth, he would win $600 and start his progressive system over again. If he lost six consecutive bets and won the seventh, his profit would be $100 and he would start his system anew. The most he could stand to lose on five consecutive losing bets would be $300. The $400 maximum betting limit on the straight, split, corner, street and line bets were also placed on the layout in an irregular fashion, as were bets on the color black.

After explaining to the casino manager the reason for the success of the high roller's betting system, I instructed the manager to increase the minimum betting limit on the black and all other 2 to 1 and even-money bets from $25 to $100. His mistake, I explained, was not in giving Mr. High Roller the $7,000 limit but in giving him a $25 minimum limit. This small limit permitted the high roller to double each previous losing bet nine consecutive times and still show a profit: for example, $25, $50, $100, $200, $400, $800, $1,600, $3,200, $6,400. The spread between the low and the high limit given by the casino manager violated the basic concept of professional gambling limits which, of course, is not to allow more than six or seven consecutive doublings up. For instance, Puerto Rican casinos have a $200 maximum limit and a $5 minimum. Note the double-up sequence: $5, $10, $20, $40, $80, $160, cannot bet $320. This also holds true for a maximum of $300 and a $5 minimum. A $500 maximum limit and a $5 minimum permits only seven consecutive double-up bets. P.S. The introduction of the $100 minimum bet by the casino manager was first refused by Mr. High Roller, but he eventually went along with it. In the end, he lost the $400,000 back to the house.

ROULETTE BETTING SYSTEMS

Undoubtedly more betting systems have been created in an effort to beat the bank at Roulette than at any other casino game. Every now and then one of our national magazines carries an article describing a surefire system for winning at Roulette. The authors of these articles usually swear that the system was successfully used by a friend at Monte Carlo and promise the reader that if he is not greedy he can earn $50 to $100 a week playing the system. I am sure that some of these magazine editors must know better. They apparently print the articles because they know they will sell magazines, and they are not much concerned about the fact that some readers may actually try the system and lose their shirts. I do know that whenever an article touting a system appears in print the casino operators silently thank the author, editor and publisher.

I recently saw a young lady lose $5,000 at a Roulette table in a Las Vegas Strip casino playing a system which had been described in a leading men's magazine. I am sure she would never have lost so much if she had not believed implicitly that the system was workable. When I told her afterward that the only thing the system did was to help her lose her money faster, she replied that she had won several hundred dollars using the same system several months before and wanted to know how I explained that. I said, "That's easy. You won simply because you had a streak of good luck. The system had nothing to do with it."

Whenever a player wins a little money using a system, he is convinced that he has found one that works and immediately envisions himself winning great sums. And if a system player has a winning streak that lasts for a month or so he will spend so much time thinking about the millions that will soon be his that he will never get any sleep. Systems are even bad for a player's health.

The Martingale and Great Martingale Systems

The two oldest and most popular Roulette betting systems in casinos the world over are the Martingale and the Great Martingale. The basic idea of the Martingale system is that whenever a player loses a bet, he doubles or increases his next bet or bets until he makes a win that recoups all his previous losses and leaves him with a one unit profit. Though it was invented for Roulette, the Martingale is used in many games in which the payoff odds are even or about even, like the red, black, odd, even, high or low bets made at Roulette, the banker or player's bets at Baccarat–Chemin de Fer and the pass and don't pass line bets at Bank Craps.

The Great Martingale is based on the player's doubling his previous losing bet and adding one unit: For example, 1, $2 + 1 = 3$, $6 + 1 = 7$, $14 + 1 = 15$, $30 + 1 = 31$, etc. The system player must win so he believes, the logic being that if he keeps betting the same even money bet (red, black, odd, even, high, or low) he must win sooner or later.

Let's analyze this system: The system player bets $5. If he loses, he doubles his bet and adds $5 to it making his second bet $15. If he loses again, he doubles his bet and adds $5 for a total of $35. On paper, five consecutive losses and one win look like this:

Number of Bets	Lose	Win	Total Losses
1	$ 5		$ 5
2	15		20
3	35		55
4	75		130
5	155		285
6		$315	
	Won	$315	
	Lost	−285	
	Profit	$ 30	

If the player wins the sixth bet, he recoups all his losses and makes a $30 profit. If he starts with enough money to cover seven consecutive losing bets ($1,235), it looks like a sure thing he'll catch one winner out of seven spins of the wheel. If he plays the system several times a day, he can spend the rest of his vacation having fun. After all, how often does the same color come up seven times in a row? It sounds wonderful. But, first of all, if he loses six times in a row, that's the end of his Great Martingale system. He will have lost a total of $600. His next bet must be $635 in order to make $35. And he can't make that bet because the maximum bet permitted in Nevada casinos is $500. If he bets $500 instead of $635, his predicament becomes worse: he's placing a bet which may cause him to lose a total of $1,100, and the best thing that can happen to him is that he will lose a total of $100. If he believes it's not possible for an even-choice bet (red, black, odd, even, high or low) to lose seven times in a row, I would like to point out that the odds state that it is expected to happen about once in every 121 spins of the wheel.

D'Alembert System

The most popular roulette system used by players at Monte Carlo and Latin American casinos is the d'Alembert system. It is based on what its proponents call the "law of equilibrium." This is nothing more than the doctrine of the maturity of chances, which mathematicians call the gambler's fallacy (see page 27). The theory is that any two opposite chances, such as red and black, odd and even, must sooner or later win an equal number of times. If red, for instance, dominates for a series of spins, it is only a question of time until black will make up its retard. The d'Alembert system player, therefore, after every losing bet, adds an additional chip or chips to his bet on the next spin, and after every winning bet, reduces his bet by one or more chips. These players misinterpret the theory of probability. They think that opposite chances will even up in a short run, whereas probability theory only gives an approximate statement of what can be expected to happen in a very long run.

The bank's favorable advantage of the 0 and 00 will, in the long run, break all the players.

Cancellation System

Players who have never been in a casino or seen Roulette played are always impressed by the stories they have read or heard about some mathematics professor who, without even having seen the game played, has spent years doping out a Roulette system. I have met several hundred men and women who have never set foot inside a casino who believe they have a winning Roulette system, and most of them, ironically, are intelligent, well-educated people.

One of them once phoned me at my home from Dallas, Texas, with the exciting news that after ten years she had developed the perfect system. Mrs. Blank, as I shall call her, offered to let me in on this marvelous get-rich-quick system if I would deposit $15,000 to her credit in her Dallas bank, and added that if I was able to find a flaw in the system the money would be returned to me. If I failed to find a flaw in it, then she would keep the $15,000 and I could go to Vegas, use the system and win it back in an evening of play.

When I pointed out that this proposition already had one flaw because the Las Vegas operators won't permit me to play at their dice or Roulette tables she suggested that I could easily get some friend to play the system for me. I told her to read the chapter on systems in *Scarne on Dice* which would tell her what I thought of systems in general. "I have," she replied, "but those were dice systems; mine is for Roulette." She thought she had an answer for everything and she ran up quite a phone bill before I could shake her, which I did by saying that I might be playing a convention date in Dallas shortly and that I would look her up when I got there.

I heard no more from her until one day in February 1959 a woman walked up to me in the casino of the Caribe Hilton Hotel in San Juan, Puerto Rico, where I was then and still am gambling consultant. It was Mrs. Blank.

"My husband and I are spending our vacation here," she said.

"How is that perfect system of yours working?" I asked.

She replied, "My husband has been playing it here all week. He's won an average of $100 for each night's play. So, you see, Mr. Scarne, it does work."

"Shouldn't you warn your husband," I asked, "that I'm here? I might learn your system by watching him play."

She shook her head. "We discovered that your casino manager knows it already."

"I saved myself the fifteen grand you wanted for it, didn't I?"

She laughed. "Yes. I guess it isn't worth quite as much as I thought then. But it still works."

Just then a man walked up to her and said, "I just won another $110 at the Roulette table. We're $868 ahead of the game on eight nights' play."

Mrs. Blank introduced me to her husband, who turned out to be a professor of psychology at a Texas college. I had seen him playing at the table, and I knew the system he was using. System gamblers at Monte Carlo have used it for years and it has appeared in several magazines under different names. Gamblers call it the Cancellation system.

It consists in writing down a column of figures in serial order beginning with 1. Suppose we use the sequence 1, 2, 3, 4, 5, 6, 7, 8, 9, 10.

The player begins by betting the total of the top and bottom figures—in this instance, 11 chips. If he wins, he crosses out the top and bottom figures and then bets the total of the new top and bottom figures —in this case, $9 + 2$, or 11. If the player loses, he adds the amount lost at the bottom of the column and then bets the total of the new top and bottom figures. In this instance he would bet $11 + 2$, or 13 chips. This procedure of betting and crossing out and adding numbers continues until all the numbers in the column have been crossed out.

As in the Progressive or Double-Up system (see below), the player must increase the amount of his bet after each loss. In the Cancellation system the player sticks to bets which pay even money, and the theory is that since he crosses out two numbers of his series when he wins and adds only one number when he loses, he must eventually cross out all the numbers. When this happens, he will have won 55 betting units.

On paper it looks good, and I don't blame Mrs. Blank for thinking she and her husband were on to a good thing. But, as she had already found out, there's no fortune in it. Her husband wasn't winning $15,000 in a night's play as she originally thought could be done; he was winning small amounts. What she still didn't know was that if he continued using the system he would lose in the end.

There are several catches. First, of course, is the fact that the player is forgetting that 0 and 00 win for the house. In the long run the player will lose 38 bets for each 36 that he wins. Even with the system, he is still bucking that house advantage of 5 5/19%.

The Cancellation system, like the Progressive or Double-Up system and others, sooner or later is interrupted by the fact that the player goes broke. Since in this system the player increases his bets by small amounts, it takes him longer until his bets increase to the point where he is stopped by the house limit. But when a long losing streak hits the player he may find himself so far in the hole that he has reached the limit of his own bankroll. Or he discovers that the constantly increasing size of his bets has put him in the position of having to risk a large amount of money to win a small amount. At this point, afraid that the losing streak will continue, he quits a loser, saying, "Well, it didn't work that time. I'll try again tomorrow."

Another catch is that if the table is busy the croupier views this process of placing a long series of small bets with distaste. The player is giving him a lot of work and he is very likely to drop a broad hint that he doesn't want your business. "Look, buddy," he'll say, "play your system somewhere else. We're busy now."

It doesn't matter how you place your bets; in the long run you can't beat the 5 5/19% that the Roulette bank has stacked against you.

System Players

Thousands of inveterate Roulette players refuse to believe this. Many of them haunt the casinos day after day, endlessly recording statistics, noting how often certain numbers, colors or combinations have or have not appeared in the last few hours, nights and even weeks. No casino operator is ever worried that these players will come up with a workable system. In fact, on request, they will supply the addict with a chart on which the Roulette numbers are printed so that he can save time, paper and pencil by merely checking off the winning numbers instead of having to write them down.

Some addicts compile all this data for a different reason. They compare their statistics with all sorts of probability calculations, hoping to find some indication that the wheel is biased. A wheel very seldom goes haywire of its own accord, and I can't think of any fault a wheel could develop by itself that would not be spotted by the croupiers in very short order.

Other addicts believe that their figures will indicate when a wheel has been gaffed and allow them to take advantage of it. The only advantage these addicts have is that they spend so much time making notes that they do less betting and hence lose less money.

The Mental Bet

Another type of Roulette watcher is the character who stands for hours by the wheel making mental bets. When he has lost a number of bets in succession he begins to play, believing that the wheel must even things out and that the tide must turn in his favor. He forgets that the little ivory ball can't read his mind, can't see where it is going, and has no memory of what it has been doing. These players are never convinced of this until after they are dead broke.

One of my favorite gambling stories is about mental bets. A few years back in a Houston, Texas, casino an elderly, distinguished-looking gentleman slightly in his cups wavered back and forth behind a group of women players at the Roulette table. Nobody paid any attention to him until he began complaining how unlucky he was.

"What do you mean, unlucky?" the croupier asked.

"Number thirty-two just won, didn't it?" the grumbler said.

"Yes, but you didn't have a bet down. What's unlucky about that?"

"Oh, yes, I did," the drunk groaned. "I made a ten-dollar mind bet on twenty-six and lost!" Then he handed the croupier a $10 bill. "I always pay my losses—even on mind bets."

The croupier tried to return the money, but the old gentleman stub-

John Scarne and casino personnel at the Caribe Hilton casino watch a high roller who is playing a "progressive" system and using one of the record sheets supplied by the management. (Conrad Eiger)

bornly refused to take it. Since this argument was creating a commotion and interrupting the game's action, the croupier finally shrugged, smiled wryly and shoved the bill into the money box.

The drunk, apparently satisfied, disappeared in the direction of the bar, but he was back again before long. He walked up to the table just as the croupier spun the ball. He wobbled unsteadily and watched until the ball dropped; then he came to life, shouting excitedly, "That's me! That's me! I bet ten bucks on number twenty and I won!"

The croupier tried to continue the play, but the drunk, who suddenly seemed much more sober, interrupted loudly, demanding to be paid the $350 he had won on his mind bet. He kept this up until the casino manager was called. After hearing what had happened, he ruled that since the croupier had accepted a $10 losing mental bet, he must pay off on the winning mind bet. You can be quite sure that this was the last mental bet which that croupier or any other in that casino ever accepted.

And don't try this stunt yourself; everybody in the casino business knows about it.

The Scientific System

Another type of Roulette watcher is the Scientific system player who clocks the wheel for hours and hours at a time without making a bet, or if he does bet, it's the minimum the casino will allow. This type of player watches the wheel for days and even weeks until he's detected a pattern, or until he believes he's detected a pattern. Certain numbers or sections of the wheel are turning up more than they should, he feels. The wheel must be off. There must be something wrong with the mechanism. "At last," he says to himself, "I have found a defective roulette wheel. Now, I'll clean up."

The classic story of this type has as its hero an English engineer, Charles Jaggers, who latched on to a biased wheel at Monte Carlo and won a big $100,000 before the casino caught on to the bias and switched wheels on him.

In most major casinos throughout the world, Charles Jaggers, or anyone who wants to emulate him, is wasting his time and any amount of money he might bet on such a wheel. The reason is that every wheel is periodically thoroughly inspected. It is checked with a balance and each fret or partition in the wheel head is examined for the smallest sign of wear and unevenness. And, whenever a wheel shows a loss of some magnitude, the wheel head is replaced with another and thoroughly examined in the casino's workshop. No, the myth that the Scientific system player or those unknowledgeable gambling writers would have you believe, that there are defective wheels in major casinos, is just that, a myth and to put it bluntly, "just bunk."

While on the subject of biased wheels, I once discovered one in a Caribbean hotel casino in my first days' work as a gambling consultant. I arrived in the casino several minutes before closing, but early enough to hear an unfamiliar sound at one of the Roulette tables. The Roulette ball in play failed to echo the familiar sound of tock-tock-tock-tock. I immediately knew that a magnetized Roulette ball was in play and that several of the wheel head's pocket separators or partitions were made of steel since the ball slowed up more abruptly than it normally would when it hit a particular section of the partitions. After the casino closed, I ran a magnet over the partition or pocket separators and found that six partitions separating the adjacent pockets numbered 7, 20, 32, 17, 5 and 22 were made of steel instead of the non-magnetic chromium plated metal used in honest wheels. The gaffed roulette ball had a magnetized steel core in its center which accounted for the strange bouncing sound when it dropped into the bottom of the wheel head. A former casino manager was the perpetrator of this swindle.

The Perfect Roulette System

This Roulette system first appeared in 1959 in *Bohemia,* a Cuban monthly magazine sold throughout Latin America. The writer introduced it with this glowing testimonial:

> This, dear reader, is a sure-fire system to win at any roulette table in the world. Don't say it can't be done. It can. The mathematical calculations prove it. The system to be divulged to you proves it. The many times I have tried it at Monte Carlo proves it. The results you will get will prove it to you.
>
> Everybody knows, of course, that in normal betting at Roulette the odds are against the player, which is caused by the fact that the zero and double zero work for the operator. However, by playing this system I can assure you that not only will you overcome this mathematical disadvantage, but will supplant it with a favorable percentage.

To say simply that this article increased the Roulette action in the Caribbean and other Latin American casinos is the understatement of the year. I saw at least 20 players betting the system within a few weeks. I did *not* hear any of the operators complain about it.

The system works, the *Bohemia* writer explains, because the third column of the layout possesses 8 red numbers and only 4 black numbers, an arrangement that is a mathematical flaw in the layout. Here is the simple betting method and mathematical proof that he says is guaranteed to make any Roulette player rich.

You make two bets on each spin of the wheel. Bet one $1 chip on the color black, which pays even money. And bet one $1 chip on the third column which contains 8 red numbers, 3, 9, 12, 18, 21, 27, 30 and 36, and the black numbers 6, 15, 24 and 33. This bet pays odds of 2 to 1.

There are 36 numbers plus the 0 and 00 on the layout. Suppose you make 38 two-chip bets for a total of $76. In the long run this should happen:

1. The zero or double zero will appear 2 times in 38, and you lose 2 chips each time—a loss of 4 chips.

2. Red will appear 18 times out of 38. Each time one of the 10 red numbers listed in the first and second column appears you lose 2 chips—a loss of 20 chips on those 10 numbers. But when the 8 red numbers in the third column appear you win 2 chips on each for a total win of 16 chips. This gives you a net loss on red of 4 chips.

3. Black will also appear 18 out of 38 times. Each time one of the 14 numbers in the first and second column appears, you lose 1 chip—

a total loss of 14 chips. But since you also bet on the color black, you win 14 times for a gain of 14 chips. This loss and gain cancel out and you break even 14 times. But when the 4 black numbers in the third column (6, 15, 24 and 33) appear, you win 3 chips each time (2 chips on the number and 1 chip on the color) for a profit of 12 chips on black.

Having lost 4 chips on the zero and double zero, and 4 chips on red, and having won 12 chips on black, you come out ahead with a final profit of 4 chips. Divide your total bet of $76 into your profit of $4 and you find that you have not only overcome the house advantage on the zero and double zero of 5 5/19% but have actually supplanted it with an advantage in *your* favor of 5 5/19%.

The system has turned everything upside down and it is the house that is bucking a 5 5/19% disadvantage! But don't withdraw all the money in your savings account and make tracks for the nearest Roulette table. Not yet. Stop long enough to ask yourself: If the *Bohemia* writer won with the system at Monte Carlo, as he says, why is he still in the position of having to earn a living selling articles to magazines? And why does he want to let everyone else in on this marvelous, money-making secret?

The editor who bought the article apparently couldn't spot any flaw in what the writer claims is "mathematical proof that this system in the long run will beat any Roulette game." As in all systems, there is a fallacy here—one little monkey wrench that louses up the system's mathematical machinery. Can you find it before you read the answer below?

The joker is in the statement that "when the 8 red numbers in the third column appear, you win 2 chips on each for a total win of 16 chips." This is incomplete. When those 8 numbers win and pay off 16 chips, *you also lose 8 chips on black,* making the net payoff only 8 chips. Since you lose 20 chips on the red numbers in the first and second columns, your net loss on red is not 4 chips, as stated, but 12 chips. Having lost 12 chips on red, won 12 chips on black, and lost 4 chips on the zero and double zero, you end up losing 4 chips. And that washes that system out completely. The house still has its favorable edge of 5 5/19%, as usual, and the casino operator is the guy who is going to get rich—not you.

The Concentration System

Another recent betting system to make its appearance on the American gambling scene is the Concentration betting system, and it is, for my money, the most ridiculous of them all. It results from the many magazine and newspaper articles describing the experiments of Dr. Joseph

Banks Rhine in his parapsychology laboratory at Duke University in Durham, North Carolina.

Dr. Rhine is a psychic researcher who claims that his PK (psychokinesis) experiments have proved that the mind can influence and control the action of inanimate objects. He says that some people have a mysterious supernormal, possibly psychic, power, which enables them occasionally to make desired numbers come up on dice, just by wishing, much oftener than probability predicts. He even believes that this mental force, for which he admits he has no explanation, can control the position of playing cards during a shuffle.

The fact that he is a college professor and Duke University appears to approve his conclusions has convinced a lot of newspaper and magazine readers that he must have something. Many of them decide that if Dr. Rhine's subjects can emit thought waves that make dice and cards behave as desired, perhaps they can, too. So they hunt up the nearest casino, hoping that these mystic powers will bring them a fortune.

I stopped in at the Casino de Capri in Havana one evening before Castro took it over to say hello to my friend, movie star George Raft, who was casino host there. George said, "I've got something to show you, Scarne. Look over there." He nodded toward a lone player at a nearby Roulette table whom I recognized as a personable young master of ceremonies then appearing on a national TV musical quiz show back in the States. I couldn't figure out what had attracted George's interest, but I got it as soon as our hero made a bet. He pushed a stack of $5 chips on the red number 3 and then, as the croupier spun the wheel and the ball, turned his head up and gazed steadily at the ceiling. He held this position until the last clicking sound of the ball indicated that it had come to rest in one of the pockets.

I turned to Raft. "No," I said.

He nodded. "Yes. He concentrates that way every time the wheel spins and he won't let anyone talk to him while he's projecting thought waves. I expect to see Dr. Rhine walk in here any day now to try it himself."

We watched him concentrate for a while and then, over a cup of coffee, Raft said, "He came in here several nights ago, and Nick, Larry, Joe and some of my other partners watched him concentrate. They were quite amused—at first. But later in the evening he was a five-thousand-dollar winner, and the boys began to look thoughtful. As a matter of fact, three nights later he was still ahead, and Harry, one of the pit bosses, decided he wasn't going to take any chances that Doc Rhine might be right, so he went over to the table and did some anti-concentrating to cancel out our friend's thought-wave advantage."

"How did that work?" I asked.

George grinned. "I guess Harry concentrates better. Our friend started to lose."

The TV actor joined us at our table a bit later. He looked glum. I've had it," he said. "No more Roulette. I'm $17,000 in the hole."

"You've been reading about Dr. Rhine?" I asked.

"Yeah. According to what I read, the laws of probability have been taking quite a licking at Duke University."

"He's been working with dice and cards, not Roulette," I said.

"I know, but I figured a Roulette ball should be even easier to control. Just one little mental nudge from a thought wave ought to have even more effect on a falling Roulette ball than on rolling dice. But when PK experiments cost $17,000, I'll let somebody else experiment. I'm through."

Hundreds of people have also been trying this concentration at dice and cards, and their faith in Dr. Rhine loses these Concentration system players a good many hundreds of thousands of dollars every year. If you want my further comments on his dice-rolling experiments, see *Scarne on Dice*, where I have discussed them at some length.

One final word about Roulette system players: Most of them seem normal enough, except that they all have a greater capacity for self-deception than non-system players.

CHEATING AT ROULETTE

Here is a paragraph taken from a recent book on gambling whose author claims to be an authority:

> An experienced croupier (even with an honest wheel) is able to plunk that little ivory ball into a section almost as accurately as you could make a ringer in horseshoes if you played every day of the year. On more than one occasion I have seen a croupier at an absolutely honest table give some attractive lady a break who had lost too much. He would tell her which numbers to play and when the excessive loss was retrieved somewhat, send her away with a "That's all now." I have seen that happen more than once and am certain that his charity was due merely to the experienced rolling of the ball.

When this statement appeared in print I was bombarded with letters from Roulette players asking whether this was possible. My answer in capital letters was and is a great big NO. The modern wheel, with its obstacles on the bottom track of the bowl, together with the fact that the croupier must spin the wheel and ball in opposite directions and must spin the ball from the last number into which it dropped, makes it an impossible feat even for the greatest of all Roulette croupiers. I once heard a lady friend of mine ask a croupier in a Las Vegas casino if he could drop the ball into any slot he wished. "Lady," he said, "if I could do that I wouldn't be working here. I'd have been worth millions years ago."

In some makeshift casinos throughout the country you may, however, find croupiers who can drop the little white ball into any predetermined group of twelve adjacent numbers on the wheel. Doc Winters, an old-time crooked Roulette dealer, could even drop the ball into any six-numbered section he desired. But this can only be done by spinning wheel and ball in the same direction and using a wheel that has no obstacles. You can guard against this sort of cheating by not placing your bets until after wheel and ball are spinning, just before the croupier announces that no further bets are allowed.

GAFFED ROULETTE WHEELS

Few, if any, of the top casinos resort to cheating at Roulette or any other game; it isn't necessary. But there are crooked wheels operating in many *sneak* (illegal) games throughout the country.

The misinformation in print on crooked Roulette wheels and how they are gaffed is amusing. Each one of the self-styled gambling experts and card detectives who write on the subject believes that one of the others may know more about the subject. They, therefore, copy from each other and are, consequently, wrong. The same situation existed as to dice and cards until the two standard reference works, *Scarne on Dice* and *Scarne on Cards,* were published. Since then, the writers who have done their copying from those books are getting their facts straight. From now on perhaps the writers on Roulette will also be able to get some facts straight.

"The most common method of rigging a Roulette wheel," one of these writers said, was "by the installation of several small electromagnets under several desired numbers. In this case the ball is not solid ivory, as it appears, but contains a steel slug in its center. When the croupier wishes to protect the casino against some heavily-backed number or combinations, he touches a concealed switch activating one or more of the electromagnets, drawing the ball into a numbered slot not covered by the players."

This description gave some law-enforcement agents in New Jersey a headache a few years ago. They had raided a gambling joint in a shore resort town and confiscated a Roulette table. Dry batteries hidden in the money drawer indicated that the wheel was crooked. The prosecutor wanted to introduce the wheel as evidence and needed to find the hidden electromagnets. He read several books on gambling which contained information like that quoted above, and he and the county detectives went to work with hammer and chisel in an effort to get under the numbers. They chiseled and chopped until the wheel was in a hundred pieces without finding a single electromagnet. The crooked gambling charge was finally dropped for lack of evidence.

Neither the writers, the prosecutor nor the detectives stopped to ask themselves how the electric current coming from the batteries could possibly feed into electromagnets concealed inside a spinning wheel. Inaccurate and misleading information supplied by self-styled experts who are merely guessing is worse than useless. It actually aids the cheats when it leads investigators to look for something that isn't there and causes them to conclude that the game must be honest when it is not.

The electromagnets, as the batteries indicated, were there, but they were in the table, not the wheel. This is one of the commonest methods of cheating at Roulette. There are four magnets equally spaced around the track and they are inside the woodwork of the bowl directly behind the back track in which the ball spins. Wires lead from the magnets through the batteries, which are usually hidden in the bowl or in the table's money drawer, and to the concealed switch, usually under the green baize of the table top. The switch is controlled either by a croupier or a cheat acting as a player.

The ball is gaffed with a magnetized steel core in its center. When the ball has slowed and is almost ready to drop, the cheat studies the now slowly rotating wheel. When he judges that the ball and the desired number are properly positioned, he presses the hidden control, putting the juice on for just an instant. The ball hesitates, then drops like a homing pigeon into the desired section of the wheel.

Unsuspecting players are fleeced of tens of thousands of dollars each year with wired Roulette wheels. I can't tell the occasional gambler any sure way of detecting a wired wheel while it is in operation, but I can give him a few tips as to what to watch for. The croupier in a *juice joint* (gambling house which has an electromagnetic wheel) can successfully operate the gaff only when the wheel is spinning very slowly. If he gives the wheel a slow spin and you see him or some other casino employee, hands on the table, watching the revolving wheel and ball with concentrated intensity just as the ball is about to drop, it's quite possible that the wheel is rigged.

The little ball doesn't always land just where the cheat wants it; considerable skill is required to judge the precise moment to apply the juice. The cheat, therefore, usually aims the ball at the 0 or 00. If the big bets are on red, he sends the ball toward the 0, which has a black pocket on either side. If the big money is on black, he aims for the 00, which has a red pocket on its left and right. This gives the croupier three chances to drop the ball into a losing pocket. So, if you see the

Scarne examines gaffed roulette wheel in the collection of a friend, the late Audley Walsh, who is showing the batteries and electromagnets which were hidden in the bowl behind the back track.

ball head for the signs 0 and 00 more often than it should, you'd be wise to take your Roulette business elsewhere.

Some operators don't like the magnetic wheel because they fear that the hidden control button may stick. If this happens when there are big losers in the joint and they see the ball defy gravity by adhering to the wheel's back track instead of dropping into a number, there is bound to be trouble.

Embarrassing situations of this sort can be avoided by the use of the pointed needle gaff, a mechanical non-magnetic gimmick. A cable runs from the back of the money drawer to a tiny hole in the bowl's back track on the side nearest the 0 and 00 on the layout. A long, flexible rod inside the cable has a pin-pointed end which fits into the hole and can be made to project and retract. When the operator presses his body against the money drawer, the long rod moves forward in the cable and its tiny pointed end projects slightly from the small hole in the back track. This knocks the spinning ball off the back track and down toward the desired section of the slowly spinning wheel. As with the magnetic wheel, the operator aims for the 0 and 00. The hole, because of its location, cannot be seen by the seated players, and it is so small that it is difficult to see even when one is looking at it.

Rigged wheels, which, at the time of writing, cost about $1,000 more than an honest wheel, may be purchased from at least a half-dozen manufacturers throughout the country. There are no laws against the sale of rigged wheels or other crooked gambling devices, and such laws would probably be ineffective in any case, since the boys who deal in such equipment pay no attention to anti-gambling laws. Widespread exposure of these devices is the public's best protection because the more the players know about such gimmicks the riskier their use becomes for the crooked operator.

There is another way to protect yourself against a magnetic wheel, but I don't advise you to try it unless you are adept at sleight of hand. In 1935 James J. Braddock, who was heavyweight champ at the time, and I were on vacation and staying at the Dempsey Vanderbilt in Miami Beach. One evening Jim said, "I'd like to play a little Roulette tonight, John. How about you?"

"This isn't the place to do it," I told him. "You won't find an honest wheel in any rug joint in Dade County."

"You're kidding," Jim said.

I shook my head. "No, I'm not."

"I'd still like to play," Jim said, "even if it is a crooked game."

I pulled open a bureau drawer. "Maybe we can, at that," I said. "I've got an idea." I took out and opened a box containing some of the exhibits I used in my gambling lecture demonstrations.

Jim said, "You've got enough dice there to open your own casino, John."

I nodded. "A crooked casino. These dice are all gaffed—loads, shapes, cut edges, tops—I've got them all, but this is what I wanted to show you."

I took out two Roulette balls, placed them on the dresser top close together. When I released them they rolled toward each other and stuck together.

"Magnetized," Jim said. "Where did you get them?"

"I picked this pair up in a casino in Memphis about a year ago. I have quite a few of them and I think we can add another to my collection tonight." I took another ball from the box and handed it to Jim. "This is an honest ball." I held it a few inches above the dresser top and let it fall. It bounced several times, giving out a solid ring before coming to a stop. "Now, you bounce one of the magnetic balls."

Jim did. It only bounced twice and stopped with a thud. "Quite a difference," Jim said. "It has a dead sound, too. What does a crooked ball like this cost?"

"Anywhere from a hundred bucks up. It has a magnetized steel core." I told him about the electromagnets behind the wheel's track and explained how the gaff works.

"I see," Jim said. "If we could get an honest, unmagnetized ball into the game the croupier could switch on the juice all he wanted and nothing would happen."

"That's just what we're going to do," I said. "For one night at least, we'll make an honest man out of the croupier."

I gave him a few instructions and then we drove out to the Drum, a nightclub on the outskirts of Miami. The owner and several of the guests spotted Jim as we entered and came over to get the champ's autograph or shake hands. Inside the casino I whispered to Jim, "Look at the legs on the Roulette table. Notice how much thicker they are than the usual. That's where the batteries are."

We took seats at the table and the croupier said, "Good evening, champ. What will it be, quarter or dollar chips?"

Jim bought fifty $1 chips and I did the same.

Then, as we had planned, Jim asked the croupier, "Okay if I spin the ball on my first play? I feel luckier if I always do that."

"It's okay with me, champ," the croupier said, handing him the ball. Jim placed it on the table to his right, took his handkerchief from his pocket and wiped off his hands. It was a hot, sticky night. Then, just before Jim picked up the house ball I reached over and pushed it closer to him. At least, that is what seemed to happen. Actually, I switched the house ball for an honest one I had palmed.

Jim gave the ball a perfect spin. "You spun that like a pro," the croupier remarked.

"Thanks," Jim grinned and put four chips on number 24. I made a few split bets and put a few chips on straight numbers. I also kept one eye on the croupier. As the ball slowed I saw him press downward slightly on a stack of chips. I knew now where the switch was concealed.

I also saw a brief surprised look on the croupier's face as the ball spun smoothly on past the spot where he had expected it to drop. Later he pressed the control a few more times without any effect on the spinning ball, and he finally gave up, apparently figuring that the batteries were dead or there was a bad wiring connection. Jim and I played for a couple of hours and were lucky enough to win about $300, bucking the house P.C. of 5 5/19%.

And then Jim asked me for the magnetized ball. I slipped it to him, and he approached the casino owner who had just come in. The first croupier, having been relieved, had probably reported that the gaff wasn't working, and the owner had come to take a look for himself.

Then Jim did something I don't advise you to try unless you are the world's heavyweight champ. He held up the crooked ball, and in a loud voice that carried across the casino, he asked the owner, "Hey, boss, how would you like to buy a magnetized Roulette ball?"

The owner, who was walking toward the table, stopped as suddenly as if he had walked into a brick wall and his face went white. He knew now why the gaff wasn't working. His mouth opened and closed a couple of times, but nothing came out. He was still trying to think of something to say as we made a quick exit.

CHEATING WITH AN HONEST WHEEL

There are also a few methods of cheating with an honest wheel. Several years ago I was retained by an American high roller who asked me to find out if the Caribbean casino in which he had lost $200,000 had got it honestly. I won't mention his name, nor that of the casino, which is still operating but under new management and honestly. Under the name of Pietro Orlando, which I sometimes use on such investigations, I registered at the hotel of which the casino is part. I also sported a new mustache, long sideburns and an Italian accent. I played Roulette for several hours the first night and lost about $20 but could see nothing wrong with the operation of the wheel. For the next few nights the action at the wheel was small, and there was no indication that the croupiers were cheating. I did, however, spot a dice mechanic working at one of the Craps tables, and I know that if one game in a casino is crooked they all are.

I hung around for another week and still found no cheating at the Roulette table. But on Saturday night an American tourist began betting $100 on each spin, placing his bets on straight, split and corner bets. After he had made a few such bets I noticed that several casino employees had unobtrusively gathered around the table. A woman shill had taken the seat nearest the table's apron, and another casino employee stood directly at her left close to the wheel and directly opposite the croupier who was dealing. Cheaters always tense up just before they do their dirty work, and I could sense the tenseness around this table.

After a few more spins, the tourist asked for $5,000 worth of black $100 chips. He spread them all over the layout, but put none on the 0 and 00 spaces. I was tense myself now, and I watched the play closely. The croupier spun the wheel and ball in the usual manner, and, just as the ball was about to drop, the woman shill stood up, leaned forward and began putting chips all over the layout. She was still leaning over when the ball dropped into a slot.

Since the woman was between all the other players and the wheel, none of them could see the ball at the moment it dropped into the slot, but when she moved back and sat down again, there it was, resting innocently in the green 0. We had been *screened out*. Just to make absolutely sure this wasn't accidental I stuck around until I had seen the same thing happen several more times. Since I knew the dodge, I also knew, without actually having to see it, what had happened behind her. When she leaned across the table to place her bets (honest players often do the same), she always did it just as the ball had slowed and was almost ready to drop. Under this cover, the casino employee at her side and right next to the wheel simply lifted the ball from the track and dropped it into the green O.

There is always more than one way to skin a cat—or fleece a chump.

HOW TO PROTECT YOURSELF AGAINST SHORT PAYOFFS

It's easy to learn how to play Roulette, and yet surprisingly few players know exactly how many chips they should receive when they win on a combination of several bets, particularly if the wager involves single, double or four-number wagers. When a croupier pushes over several stacks of chips, only about 5 out of 100 hundred players have any idea of whether or not the payoff is correct. I have seen a good many players shorted on chips in many of our top casinos. It is often an honest mistake on the croupier's part, but whether it is or not, if you are going to play Roulette you'd be smart to learn how to calculate your winnings. Why should you pay an extra charge by being short-changed?

Here is a mathematical short cut the reader can use to calculate mentally the number of chips to be paid off on single-number bets on which the odds are 35 to 1. For any even number of chips, simply divide by 2, multiply by 7, and tack a zero onto your answer. Example: You bet 16 chips on a single number and win. Divide 16 by 2, which gives you 8, multiply by 7 which gives you 56, add the zero, which gives you 560—the correct number of chips due you.

If you wager an odd number of chips, you make the same calculation except you subtract 1 before you start and add 35 at the end. Example: You wagered 15 chips. Subtract 1, getting 14, divide by 2, getting 7, multiply by 7, getting 49, add a zero, getting 490, and add 35 for a final answer of 525.

If you want to avoid mental calculation, give the following chart a little study and memorize the payoffs on the more complicated bets. Here are all the correct payoffs on straight, split, street, quarter and line bets when wagering 1 to 20 chips. Simple multiplication will enable you to extend the chart to payoffs on more than 20 chips.

Curiously enough, there are many more methods used by cheats to beat a Roulette game than there are cheating methods to beat the player. Roulette mobs have on several occasions secretly got into Monte Carlo during the night, gaffed the wheels and then won con-

ROULETTE PAY CARD

Straight 35 to 1		Split 17 to 1		Street 11 to 1		Quarter 8 to 1		Line 5 to 1	
1	35	1	17	1	11	1	8	1	5
2	70	2	34	2	22	2	16	2	10
3	105	3	51	3	33	3	24	3	15
4	140	4	68	4	44	4	32	4	20
5	175	5	85	5	55	5	40	5	25
6	210	6	102	6	66	6	48	6	30
7	245	7	119	7	77	7	56	7	35
8	280	8	136	8	88	8	64	8	40
9	315	9	153	9	99	9	72	9	45
10	350	10	170	10	110	10	80	10	50
11	385	11	187	11	121	11	88	11	55
12	420	12	204	12	132	12	96	12	60
13	455	13	221	13	143	13	104	13	65
14	490	14	238	14	154	14	112	14	70
15	525	15	255	15	165	15	120	15	75
16	560	16	272	16	176	16	128	16	80
17	595	17	289	17	187	17	136	17	85
18	630	18	306	18	198	18	144	18	90
19	665	19	323	19	209	19	152	19	95
20	700	20	340	20	220	20	160	20	100

siderable amounts from the house before the casino discovered what had happened. This also happened in a good many other casinos. The methods they use to gaff the wheel are much easier to install than the two I have described, but I won't discuss them here because I'm not trying to smarten up any cheats. Also, this cheating doesn't affect the honest players at the table; only the cheats who know about the gaff gain by it, and it's only the house that loses.

HOW TO GAMBLE SENSIBLY AT ROULETTE

The best way to avoid losing at Roulette is to stop playing the game, but since it is such a favorite with so many millions of people I doubt that very many of them will take this advice. And I can't give a best bet at the game because, unlike all other casino games, all but one of the bets have the same 5 5/19% against the player. The best I can do to save you some money is to suggest that you avoid the five-number combination bets with their 7 17/19% advantage for the bank.

You may be lucky and win at Roulette over a short period, but your chances of beating the wheel if you play continuously through several long sessions are very dubious.

If you intend to play for several sessions, budget yourself. Divide the amount of money you can afford to lose by the number of times you expect to play, and don't exceed that loss limit in any sessions. If you should at any time find yourself ahead of the game by a good sum, pack the game in. Tomorrow is another day. This advice will at least prevent you from becoming a Roulette degenerate.

15.
Slot Machines:
The One-armed
Bandits

Automation came to the gambling industry in 1887, when Charles Fey placed the first nickel-in-the-slot machines in the gambling palaces of San Francisco. Today the slot machine, long known as the "one-armed bandit," is without any doubt gambling's most consistent money-maker. There has never been any other gambling device which has produced such enormous profits with so little effort on the part of the operator.

My survey shows that in 1972 about 15 million Americans, of whom 10 million were women, played the 42,000-odd legal slot machines found in Nevada casinos. These slot machines show a combined yearly gross casino win of about $300 million. My survey also shows a gross game-and-table revenue of about $423 million. That's the total of all winnings by the casinos from all the other casino games such as Craps, Black Jack, Roulette, Baccarat, etc.—everything except slot machines. In other words, slot machines gross about 70% as much money as all other games combined—about 40% of the casino's revenue comes from slot machines. These figures are the gross earnings, not the gross handle.

LEGAL AND ILLEGAL SLOTS

At the present time, five states permit slot machines varying degrees of operation.

Nevada, with an all-out slot machine operation, has about 42,000 in operation, of which about 1,500, the largest number under one roof, are to be found in Harrah's luxury casino in Reno. The state of Maryland allows slot machines in varying degrees of activity. Idaho permits them on a local referendum basis. Montana and Washington allow them in privately run clubs.

The biggest loss suffered by a slot machine degenerate (what else would you call them?) was $250,000 which a California woman lost over a two-year period in the Reno area.

I know at least 20 casinos in Nevada and the Caribbean whose individual yearly slot take is from $2 million to $7.5 million and more. This leaves a very handsome net profit when you consider that a modern machine costs $1,500 to $3,000 or even more, and that such a casino operation may require only about 40 employees—change girls, collectors, mechanics, cashiers and inspectors. Slots are found not only in casinos; they are in hotel lobbies, taverns, clubs, lodges, bowling alleys, bus-stop restaurants, grocery stores and even airline terminals such as McCarran Airport in Las Vegas. Where slots are legal, you'll find them almost anyplace where people congregate—except churches.

It may interest the reader to know that slot machines situated in Las Vegas's downtown casinos account for more than 60% of gross casino revenue. Slots in Reno casinos account for more than 65% of their gross casino revenue. However, in the Las Vegas Strip casinos the table games get the most action.

The slot machine is on the only gambling device with a mechanical banker that collects losing bets, pays off winning bets and makes fewer mistakes than any human dealer in any casino banking game.

My survey estimates that for every legal slot machine in the country, there are four operating illegally. Although some illegal slot ma-

Charles Fey, inventor of the first slot machine, standing in the doorway of his small machine shop at 631 Howard Street, San Francisco, California. (Slim Ewing)

Clipping from San Francisco Chronicle, 1887.

chines have been known to earn $2,000 or more per week, my survey shows that the average national weekly take for such a machine is only $100.

How much money was fed into the slot machines in Nevada and Caribbean casinos to get that $300 million yearly gross revenue? If we figure that on the average 10¢ of each dollar that goes into the innards of a slot machine is retained by the operators as gross winnings, then $3 billion in pennies, nickels, dimes, quarters, half dollars, silver dollars, dollar bills and even $5 bills moves through the 50,000 slot machines each year.

The slot machine is essentially a cabinet housing three or more narrow cylindrical drums, commonly called *reels*, which are marked with symbols. Vertically disposed on a common axis, the reels are caused to revolve freely when a player activates the machine and pulls a leverlike handle affixed in the side of the cabinet. Awards or payoffs, which are generally paid automatically, are usually based on the horizontal alignment of symbols, when the spinning reels come to a position of inertial rest.

The nickel and quarter machines are the most popular, and their action accounts for about 85% of the yearly slot handle. They are followed by the dime, half-dollar and silver-dollar machines, in that order.

There is also a two- to seven-coin, flat-top type of electrically controlled machine known to the industry as a *console*. This is actually two or more one-armed bandits in one. Because they look different and are not called slots, thousands of these consoles can be found in localities where the slot machine is illegal.

The modern super deluxe one-armed single-coin bandit with its shining chromium finish, its array of glowing neon lights and its progressive jackpot sells for as high as $1,700—the retail price of a modern Bally slot machine one-to-eight coin three- or four-wheeler, progressive jackpot ranges from $1,500 to $3,000. The price of a standard single-coin three-wheeler machine ranges from $900 to $1,300, and consoles sell for from $1,600 up.

The latest change in size is the six-feet-tall machine dubbed Big Bertha. This machine accepts half dollars or dollar bills and pays back about 80% of its gross take. At present, no casino has more than one Big Bertha; it is used primarily for propaganda purposes and to make a few bucks at the same time.

The success of Big Bertha is responsible for its enlarged counterpart, Super Big Bertha, a six-by-ten-foot slot machine which is said to have cost $150,000 to design and engineer. It makes use of a five-horsepower electric motor to power the 20-inch-wide chain-driven wheels. The Super Big Bertha possesses eight reels each containing 20 symbols for an overall 25.6 billion different combinations, only one of which will pay out the $1 million promised by its developer, that is, providing you play eight Eisenhower dollars at the same time. Smaller amounts will be paid off when fewer coins are played. Though the probabilities are one in 25.6 billion of hitting the $1 million dollar jackpot, and since you have to play eight coins at one time to do so—our mathematics shows that on the average, the player would have to pump close to 205 billion silver dollars into the machine to win the $1 million jackpot. The biggest jackpot payoff at time of writing was $65,093 won on a one-dollar progressive jackpot slot at Harold's Club in Reno on September 5, 1973.

Except for horse bookmaking and Policy Numbers, the slot machine in the past 50 years has been the cause of more legal indictments, court decisions and police raids than all other forms of gambling combined. In spite of all attempts at restriction, the slot business keeps growing. Perhaps the biggest reason for this is the manner of play. It is doubtful that any other form of gambling has the hypnotic fascination of the slot machine. It is difficult even for a person who believes gambling is morally wrong not to drop at least one coin in the slot and pull the handle, if only to watch the wheels spin.

Slot players seem to get more excited when they hit a jackpot than do players winning much greater sums at Black Jack, Craps, Roulette,

The first slot machine (LEFT), built in 1887 by Charles Fey, and (RIGHT) the first machine to take a silver dollar, which Fey also built, in 1929. These and other early machines are on display in the Liberty Belle Saloon and Restaurant in Reno, which is run by Fey's grandsons. (Marshall and Franklin Fey)

Big Six, Numbers and horse racing. When I was the gambling consultant at the Habana Hilton casino in Cuba, before Castro's time, I was watching a bigtime Roulette game in which winning numbers were paying off as much as $25,000. The game, naturally, was tense. Suddenly everyone's attention was diverted by cheers and howls of delight from a group of women across the room. One woman had just hit a nickel jackpot and collected $7.

CHARLES FEY AND THE FIRST SLOT MACHINES

The slot machine, an American invention, is now found in all parts of the world—Europe, Africa, South America, Asia, the Caribbean and of course the United States.

A 29-year-old mechanic, Charles Fey, made the first slot machine in 1887 in a small machine shop in San Francisco; he began manufacturing them by hand and placed them in the local gambling palaces on a 50% rental basis. He is, therefore, not only the inventor but also the first slot machine operator.

His first machine was not, as some gambling historians say, cruder and bulkier than modern machines, nor did its reels carry the fruit symbols commonly used today. His original one-armed bandit, called the Liberty Bell, was somewhat smaller than present-day slots, although mechanically very similar. It had three wheels carrying bright lithographed pictures of playing-card symbols—hearts, diamonds and spades—and bells, horseshoes and a star. This original machine can be seen today in the collection of old machines at the Liberty Belle Saloon and Restaurant in Reno, which is owned and operated by Charles Fey's grandsons, Marshall and Franklin Fey. Charles Fey also developed many other slots which old-timers may remember: Draw Poker, On the Square, Little Chief, Duo, Little Vender, Silver Cup and Silver Dollar, the first one-armed bandit designed to take that large a coin.

The wheels on the first machine were smaller than those used today; each had only 10 symbols instead of the 20 now used; only the three symbols on the pay line could be seen through the small window. Also, there was no jackpot. Fey's wheels, like the present-day three-wheelers, were vertical. The player inserted a nickel and pulled the lever to spin the wheels. If the three symbols showing when the wheels stopped were a winning combination, the machine paid out the correct number of coins. A colored reward chart on the machine's front listed the payouts for each winning combination, as follows:

Three bells	10 drinks
Flush of hearts	8 drinks
Flush of diamonds	6 drinks
Flush of spades	4 drinks
Two horseshoes and star	2 drinks
Two horseshoes	1 drink

Although the reward chart listed drinks, the machine's payout mechanism paid out nickels. At that time there was a 2¢ Federal revenue tax on a deck of playing cards, and Charles Fey thought it wise to buy the tax stamp and paste one on each of his slot machines because he used playing-card symbols. A shrewdie, I must say.

His machines were an immediate success, and he couldn't manufacture enough of them in his small workshop to supply the demand in and around San Francisco. Gambling equipment manufacturers soon discovered this and tried to buy the manufacturing and distribution rights, but Fey refused all offers. His invention remained an exclusive California phenomenon until 1907, when Herbert Stephen Mills, a Chicago manufacturer of arcade-type machines, began production of a machine whose automatic payout principle was similar to Fey's.

The Mills machine was named the Operators Bell and because its mechanism was encased in iron as the modern slots are, players nick-named it the "Iron Case." It had three wheels, each bearing 20 symbols, and was the first machine to carry the symbols of bars, bells, plums, oranges, cherries and lemons. Nine symbols could be seen through the window. By 1910, slot machines could be found in every city and nearly every hamlet in the country.

The company started by Herbert S. Mills in 1889 still bears his name—Mills and Company. The Jennings Company was founded in 1906. The Pace Company was founded shortly thereafter. Today the Bally Manufacturing Company is the largest company producing slot machines. Mills has factories in Chicago and Reno, Jennings and Bally are in Chicago and Pace is in Maryland. There are several foreign companies manufacturing slot machines, two in Australia and one in Japan.

FEDERAL TAXES AND LAW ENFORCEMENT

The public and many Federal and state legislators believe that the slot machine industry, from the top level on down, is largely controlled by racketeers and hoodlums. This is not quite the case. The majority of slot machine manufacturers are educated men, highly respected in their communities and active in civic and church affairs. But there is a minority who are not exactly beyond reproach; its members sell slots to some real shady characters.

At the distributors' level, in states where slots are banned, the business of selling coin-operated music machines and legitimate vending machines is used as a front for the illegitimate slot machine business.

At the operators' level, the picture changes. This is where we find the racketeers, hoodlums and their *animals* (professional strong-arm

The Iron Case, the first machine made by Mills and Company in 1910. (Bell-O-Matic)

men) working hand in hand with corrupt public officials and law-enforcement agents on all levels.

On the other hand, in states where the machines are legal, most of
the operators are ordinary businessmen, although racketeers can sometimes be found hiding in the background.

As evidence of the size of the slot machine industry I'll cite a yearly
report of the Bureau of Census of the Department of Commerce which
disclosed that in one year 49,271 slot machines (including consoles)
were shipped to distributors and casinos.

In the late thirties and throughout the 1940s, there was a concerted
drive against the slots. The result was to outlaw them in most states. In
1951, Congress made it a Federal offense to transport slot machines or
consoles or even their components across state lines unless the ultimate
destination is a state or foreign country where slot operation is legal.
The Department of Commerce reports since then don't tell the whole
story, since they have no figures on illegal shipments.

The Bureau of Internal Revenue, however, tries to collect an annual
license fee of $250 yearly for each machine in operation, legal or il-
legal. If we add the state and local taxes to the Federal license fee, the
total levy on a legally operated machine averages about $500 a year.
It costs the illegal operator considerably more. My findings indicate
that he pays in *ice* (bribes to officials) from $1,000 to $5,000 per year
on each machine, depending on locality and circumstances.

In spite of the Federal law prohibiting interstate commerce in slot
machines, the operators in states where they are illegal manage to make
out. They open a receiving office in a legal state, then reship the machines secretly by motor vehicles. Federal agents in Pennsylvania
recently confiscated a truck loaded with 67 slot machines. There is,
apparently, little or nothing that Federal agents can do to eliminate or
regulate the 200,000 illegal slot or console machines. They are much
too popular with both operators and players, and too many public
officials like the ice they get.

HOW TO SPOT A CROOKED SLOT MACHINE

Most of the slots in operation prior to 1940 were real one-armed
bandits for sure. Although each of the three wheels bore 20 symbols,
every other one was a dummy that could not appear on the pay line.
Since only ten symbols could appear on the pay line these machines
were known in the trade as "ten-stop machines." The brakes which
slowed the spinning wheels were so set that the wheels, as they
stopped, fitted into a cog that allowed a stop only on alternate symbols.
The dummy symbols were very effective bait because they often formed
winning combinations which could be seen by the player just above or

John Scarne checking the interior of a single-coin slot machine, which preceded the present day multiple-coin machines.

below the pay line. If you played the slots in those days, this explains why you found yourself saying so often, "Boy! I just missed the three bars and the jackpot! See, they're just above the pay line."

This happened with great regularity because the manufacturers placed the symbols on the wheels in such a way that many more fake winning combinations appeared above or below the line than appeared on the pay line itself. A machine, for instance, might have three bars on each wheel. Normally this would mean that the three-bar jackpot combination could be hit in $3 \times 3 \times 3$, or 27 ways. But when two of three bars on each wheel are in positions at which the wheel cannot stop, there is only one way the player can line three bars up on the pay line and there are eight ways the fake bars can show near-hit winning combinations above or below the pay line. Payoff combinations of the other symbols were gimmicked the same way so that the player saw a great many more paying combinations that were near misses. This induced him to continue feeding in nickels as he tried to hit combinations that would never show.

Many slot operators didn't like to give the player even that one chance to hit the jackpot three-bar combination, so they came up with another gimmick—the *bug*. This is a small, flat half-circle of iron about an inch long, which looks something like a bug. It was screwed onto and closed a cog which controlled one of the three bars, usually the one on the third wheel. When the wheels stopped and the bugged bar was about to appear on the pay line, the brake hit the bug and couldn't slip into the opening of the cog. The bar symbol came to rest just above or below the pay line instead. The best you could get on a machine bugged this way was a two-bar combination.

Sister, if a bar symbol on the machine you are playing has a habit of slipping down or jumping up past the pay line after the wheels have come to a stop, it's an even bet that the machine is bugged. It also means that you're playing an old-timer, because modern machines are all 20-stop machines and no longer gaffed in this way.

Slot machines built during the thirties usually had a payback of about 50% when they weren't bugged. When half the money you feed in is retained, it doesn't take long before the machine has it all. And when the bug was used, you lost even faster. It was this type of machine that was first called the one-armed bandit. The story is that a couple of professional bandits in the Midwest were playing a gaffed machine. After losing consistently, one of them remarked, "You sure don't need a gun to hold up anyone, not if you own a couple of machines like this."

"Yeah," the other crook agreed, as he pulled the handle once more, "and this bandit has only one arm."

The use of this phrase hasn't hurt the slot machine business. On the contrary, it seems to help. Several Nevada casinos have slot machines built into a multi-color cast iron figure of a scowling, bearded Western outlaw. The figure is minus a right arm, and his upraised left, the machine's lever, holds a six gun.

In the early twenties one slot company tried to circumvent the anti-gambling laws of certain states by making a slot that pretended to be a candy-vending machine. Candy mint rolls were contained in a tube at the side. Purchase of the candy entitled the buyer to give the three wheels a spin. When he hit a winning combination, he received slugs which could either be played back into the machine or redeemed for cash.

The innovation didn't last long. There were several court decisions which ruled that, mints or no mints, the machine was a gambling device. The operators argued that it was a candy-vending machine because the players always received a roll of mints for each coin deposited. The courts didn't agree; they knew that most players kept putting in money without bothering to take more than a few of the candies and continued to do so even when the candy tube was empty. By the end of the twenties, after hundreds of machines had been confiscated and the seizures upheld by the courts, the mint-vending machines became extinct.

MODERN SLOT MACHINES AND PAYBACKS

The next innovation, and unquestionably a great stimulant to the industry, occurred in the middle twenties. A simple box-shaped enclosure with a glass front was built into the front of the machine and called the *jackpot*, the term coming from Draw Poker. The machine automatically fed coins into the jackpot, building it up, and the operator also filled it when necessary. When the three bars hit the pay line the jackpot opened and added its contents to the customary three-bar payout of 20 coins.

Millions of slot players and even some people in the gambling business who should know better believe that the operator can adjust a slot machine to pay out any percentage desired merely by turning some sort of screw inside the machine. This belief has arisen because a good many authors of game books write about slots without really knowing what the machines are like on the inside. It is simply not true; the mechanism of a slot machine is quite complicated, and the payback

John Scarne studying the interior of a modern multiple-coin slot machine whose vast electrical circuitry permits an endless variety of payouts.

odds cannot be changed unless the reel's symbols are repositioned and the payoff slots adjusted to coincide with the changed combinations on the reel. The one exception is when the machine is bugged.

To change the payoff odds the machine must be partly dismantled. The reels must be changed and the internal disks which correspond to the reels must also be changed. In the new multiple coin machines there are electronic controls, containing a maze of wires and complicated circuitry. This makes a payout change equivalent to a major overhaul. It takes a good mechanic half a day to accomplish the change.

Most major casinos maintain a slot machine workshop where slots are repaired and payout changes can be made. Competition generally determines the percentage payout on most slot machines. In areas where major casinos are next door to each other, the slots in each casino will pay back from 70% to 95% The few slots with a payback of 95% are usually situated in a conspicuous part of the casino. The machines' payout percentages aren't posted on them. Only the casino operator and his slot mechanic know the percentages and the location of each machine.

Nevada and the Caribbean governments set no payout percentage regulations, feeling competition will take care of that. What they do care about is the honesty of the posted payoff winners. Are they correct? When a sign says 21 ways to a jackpot, there must be 21 ways to the jackpot and all other posted payouts must be possible also. State or government inspectors are always on hand to make periodic checkups on all slot machines. Violations are treated severely.

Wherever slot machines are illegal, the payback is usually 50% or less. This also holds true for legal slot machines situated in private clubs, airports, drugstores, supermarkets and shoeshine parlors.

In the middle thirties the first substantial change in the appearance and design of slot machines came about with the introduction of the flat-top, electrically driven console. Since more than one person can play at a time, the makers hoped it would replace the one-armed bandit. It failed to do this because the slot player seems to be happier bucking the machine on his own and pulling the lever himself. There are, however, about 50,000 such machines now in operation in the United States.

Although the symbols on many modern machines are still Charles Fey's and Herbert Stephen Mills's original bars, bells, plums, oranges, cherries and lemons, some machines now use other symbols. Slot machine manufacturers try to distinguish their own make of machine from others by using their own symbols: the words Tic, Tac, Toe; the numeral 7, pictures of watermelons, star symbols, a cowboy on horse-back known as a "buckaroo" and others. Also, many slots pay out double or twin jackpots and giant awards.

Another important slot innovation appeared it the late 1950s. Actually it was just four single coin slot machines bolted together, but the only handle was placed between the two center machines. The player had to insert four coins—one in the slot of each machine. He would "hit" the jackpot when he got "Three Bars in Any Position." That meant that the bars which appeared below and above the pay line were also counted. In other words, one bar on the pay line, one above and one below it would add up to a jackpot; or any such combination on a single machine meant a winner. Since four machines were working in tandem, it was possible for a player to hit up to four jackpots simultaneously.

These machines, which were often called monsters and Frankensteins, never became too popular and eventually disappeared from the slot machine scene. However, the idea of multiple coin play was introduced and finally lead to the development of single-machine multiple coin play.

Many top casinos make use of the jackpot *light up board*. This is a large electric sign which hangs from the ceiling and can be seen by all the players in the room. Each slot machine has its own number and is electrically connected to the light behind a corresponding number on a glass square on the board. If you hit a jackpot on machine 42, the number 42 on the board lights up, a chime rings and one of the lovely jackpot payoff girls appears at your side pronto. She verifies the jackpot and gives you the cash. The slot machine business has certainly taken on a new look in the past 15 years, yes sirree.

Then in the 1950s came the four-reeler, with four reels instead of the usual three. The first of these to appear, the Jennings Buckaroo, can still be found in some of the top casinos in Nevada. When you line up four buckaroo symbols, this machine's special jackpot pays $250 for 5¢, $500 for 10¢, $1,250 for 25¢, $2,500 for 50¢ and $5,000 for $1. This jackpot is in addition to the regular three-wheel jackpots which run from a guaranteed $7 on a nickel machine to $140 on the dollar machine. This type of four-reeler with the special buckaroo award is usually geared to pay back from 80% to 90%.

In the 1960s, the "hold and draw" class of slot machine became quite popular in the downtown casinos in Las Vegas. This style of machine offers a player a "second chance" to win. That is, after a non-win spin, a hold signal is lit. A player may then press hold buttons to hold any desired reel or reels in a locked position, deposit a second coin and spin the reel or reels not held to try again for a win. For example, if a bell appears on the first and third reels and another symbol on the middle reel, a player may hold the bells and spin the middle reel in hope of "drawing" another bell to fill out a triple Bell win.

Also in the sixties we had the introduction of three-line-pay machines. One of these machines may be played with a single coin, which qualifies only the basic central row of symbols as the win-line. Or, at his option, a player may deposit up to three coins before pulling the handle. When the second coin is deposited, both the central row and the visible row above the central row are qualified as win lines. When three coins are deposited, all three visible rows—the central row and the rows above and below the central row—qualify as win lines. Today, in most casinos, we'll find five-line-pay machines which may be played with a single coin—or a player may deposit up to five coins before pulling the handle. The first coin qualifies the basic center line as the win line; and each additional coin qualifies an additional line as a win line. If five coins are played, five lines—three horizontal and two diagonal—are win lines. Wins in this type of machine are not generally multiplied by the number of coins played, but the player can win on any lines qualified as win lines. An inducement to most multiple-coin play is provided by the fact that the fifth line—qualified by the fifth coin—is a special jackpot line.

Actually, the introduction of the multiple-coin machine, of which the "hold and draw" and "three-line pay" types were the forerunners, is probably the most important design change since the invention of the slot machine. Most casinos are replacing their conventional single-coin machines with multiple-coin machines on which a player can wager from one to eight coins at a time with corresponding multiple payoffs. The reason, of course, is to give the player an opportunity to pump more coins into the machine in the hope of hitting the five-, six- or eight-coin super multiple jackpot which amounts to $500 on a five-coin four-reeler 25¢ machine, $1,500 on a 50¢ six-coin four-reeler, etc. Here's the way some five-coin multiple machines work: the super jackpot on a three reeler, which can be three bars, three 7s (or any other three identical symbols) pay off at the basic rate of 200 to 1 multiple if one, two, three or four coins are played. Example: $50 for one quarter, $100 for two quarters, $150 for three quarters, $200 for four quarters. But if the player wagers five quarters, the jackpot is worth not $250 but $500, which is a potential bonus of $250.

Another new type of machine which steps up the slot action is the "progressive type." Actually, this is a machine in which the top jackpot—called the *super jackpot*—continuously increases in a predetermined ratio to the number of coins played into the machine. The jackpot can in some $1 or 50¢ machines reach a high of $9,999, or $999

A progressive five-coin multiple slot machine whose two superjackpots show possible payouts of $382.02 and $779.36, should either appear on the fifth line. However, for the fifth line to be active, five coins must be played at one time. (Bally, Inc.)

in comparable 5¢, 10¢ and 25¢ models. The super jackpots are usually displayed on two separate super jackpot counters, which advance alternately, while red arrows light alternately to indicate the super jackpot which may be won at each moment of play. Thus, when one counter is reduced to the minimum figure by a super jackpot win, the other counter remains an inducement to continued play.

Progressive slot machines are available in single win-line models and multiple line models, as illustrated above. The numbers 38202 on the top line and 77936 on the bottom mean that if the super jackpot is won the payoff, since this is a nickel machine, is either $382.02 or $779.36. Of course, if this was a $1 or 50¢ machine, the payoff would be $3,820.20 or $7,793.60. But note the gimmick in front of the player: to be eligible for the progressive jackpot the player must wager six coins at a time. Otherwise he is only paid off at the conventional 200 to 1 odds.

These machines, fairly rare a few years ago, are now so common that in many casinos in Nevada or the Caribbean Islands a player is hard put to find a single-coin slot machine. The reasons for the sudden influx of multiple-coin slots in casinos throughout the world are: (1) Hourly income per square foot of floor space is notably increased. (2) Players are free to increase or decrease their bets at will. (3) Players like the action of the big jackpot. The payout percentage of these babies is the same as the' single-coin slots—but with an exceptional jackpot win—you'll go broke much faster.

SLOT MACHINE ODDS

Most present-day three-wheel slot machines have 20 symbols on each wheel. The number of combinations that can appear on the center pay line is $20 \times 20 \times 20 = 8,000$. To get the number of possible combinations on a four-wheel machine, you multiply once more by 20, for a total of 160,000.

If the number of possible payouts on a three-reeler total 7,200 coins, you can divide this by the 8,000 possible combinations, getting 90%. That is the percentage of the total handle the machine will pay back in the long run, leaving a profit to the owners of 10%.

If I were a slot player and in a position to play any machine on the market today, I would select the Twenty-One Bell three-wheel nickel machine. This pays a jackpot in 19 ways and permits the bell symbol on the first reel to pay off either as a bell or as a bar. The payback to players is 94 9/20%. The chances of hitting a jackpot are 1 in 421.

I'd be playing it just for fun; I wouldn't expect to beat it in the long run. Bucking even the low favorable percentage to the machine of 5 11/20% is an impossible winning task.

I'll use the Twenty-One Bell three-wheel machine to illustrate how slot machine percentages are calculated. First, here are the payoff combinations:

PAYOFF COMBINATIONS

				Pays 2 Coins
	Cherry	Anything	Anything	Pays 2 Coins
	Cherry	Cherry	Anything	5
	Orange	Orange	Bar	10
	Orange	Orange	Orange	10
	Plum	Plum	Bar	14
	Plum	Plum	Plum	14
	Bell	Bell	Bar	18
	Bell	Bell	Bell	18
Jackpot:	Melon	Melon	Bar	100
Jackpot:	Melon	Melon	Melon	100
Jackpot:	Bar	Bar	Bar	100
Double Jackpot:	7	7	7	200

And here is a list of the 20 symbols on each reel:

Space	1st Reel	2nd Reel	3rd Reel
1	Orange	Cherry	Bell
2	Melon	Plum	Orange
3	Plum	Cherry	Plum
4	Cherry	7 & orange	Bell
5	Plum	Cherry	Orange
6	Orange	Bell	Lemon
7	7	Plum & bar	Bell
8	Bell & bar	Bell	Melon & orange
9	Orange	Cherry	Bell
10	Cherry	Orange	Plum
11	Bar	Bell	Lemon
12	Plum	Melon & orange	Bell
13	Orange	Plum	Plum
14	Plum	Bell	Bell
15	Melon	Cherry	7 and bar
16	Plum	Bar	Lemon
17	Orange	Orange	Bell
18	Plum	Cherry	Melon & orange
19	Bar	Bell	Bell
20	Plum	Melon & orange	Lemon

Note that in some instances two symbols show in a single space, as in space 8 on reel 1 where a bell and a bar are together. When this shows in the window, it counts either way—as a bell or a bar.

We now count the number of times each symbol appears on each reel:

	Reel 1	Reel 2	Reel 3	
Cherries	2	6	0	
Oranges	5	5	5	(including 2 melons, 1 bar)
Plums	7	3	4	(including 1 bar)
Bells	1	5	9	(including 1 bar)
Bars	3	2	1	
Melons	2	2	3	(including 1 bar)
7s	1	1	1	

This gives you the information you need to figure the number of payoff combinations for each symbol that can be expected to occur in the long run in each 8,000 plays.

Single-cherry combinations: The 2 cherries on reel 1 each pay off with all the symbols on reel 2 that are not cherries (14), and all the symbols on reel 3, which has no cherries (20). Then $2 \times 14 \times 20 = 560$ single-cherry combinations. Since each combination pays 2 coins, there are $560 \times 2 = 1,120$ coins paid out.

Two-cherry combinations: The 2 cherries on reel 1 each pay off with the 6 cherries on reel 2 and any of the 20 symbols on reel 3. Multiply $2 \times 6 \times 20 = 240$ combinations, each paying 5 coins for a total of 1200 coins.

Three-symbol combinations: These are all figured alike. Take plums as an example. There are 7 plums on reel 1, 3 plums on reel 2, and 3 plums plus a bar that counts as a plum on reel 3. Multiply $7 \times 3 \times 4 = 84$ combinations. Each pays 14 coins for a total of $84 \times 14 = 1,176$ coins.

The following table shows the calculations for all symbols. Two oranges and bar are lumped in with 3 oranges, etc.

	Symbols				Payoff		Total
	1st Reel	2nd Reel	3rd Reel	Ways	in Coins		Payoff
1 cherry	2 ×	14 ×	20 =	560	×	2	= 1,120
2 cherries	2 ×	6 ×	20 =	240	×	5	= 1,200
3 oranges	5 ×	5 ×	5 =	125	×	10	= 1,250
3 plums	7 ×	3 ×	4 =	84	×	14	= 1,176
3 bells	1 ×	5 ×	9 =	45	×	18	= 810
3 melons (jackpot)	2 ×	2 ×	3 =	12	×	100	= 1,200
3 bars (jackpot)	3 ×	2 ×	1 =	6	×	100	= 600
3 sevens (double jackpot)	1 ×	1 ×	1 =	1	×	200	= 200
				1,073			= 7,556

There are, as you see when you add the last three entries in the ways column, 19 ways to hit a jackpot.

There are 1,073 ways to hit a payoff combination. Divide 1,073 by total number of 8,000 plays and you find the player can expect to get a payback of some sort on an average of 13.4% of his plays. Of 8,000 coins put into the machine the player gets, in the long run, a return of 7,556 coins. Dividing 8,000 into 7,556 gives a coin-return percentage of 94 9/20%. The machine retains, in the long run, 444 of each 8,000 coins played, a favorable percentage for the operator of 5 11/20%.

Most machines in use are still three-reelers, but the popularity of four-, and even five-reelers is on the increase. Most reels in these larger machines have 20 symbols; some casinos, however, use a limited number of slots with 22 symbols on each reel (22 stops or positions at which each spinning reel can stop), and a few 25-symbol, 25-stop machines. The latter type gives the three-reeler thousands of additional combinations so that the jackpot or bonus awards can be made much larger. You can, for example, have a $50 jackpot on a three-reel nickel machine and still retain all the lesser payouts. The number of possible combinations on this machine is $25 \times 25 \times 25$, or 15,625, which is nearly double the 8,000 on the usual three-reeler. The same applies to five-, six- or eight-coin machines, if you remember that an addition single-coin payout comes with the insertion of each additional coin.

CALCULATING THE PAYOUT PERCENTAGE ON OTHER MACHINES

How does a slot player figure the payout percentage of a particular machine or find out which, of a group of machines, has the best payout percentage? If you ask the machine's operator, the chances are he doesn't know. Even if he gives you an answer, how do you know it's right? You probably wouldn't believe him anyway.

The only sure way to get this information is to open the back of the machine, count all the symbols and calculate the percentage as I did on the Twenty-One Bell machine. The catch here is that there is almost no chance that an operator will permit you to do this. So you try to count the number of like symbols through the machine's little glass window, after the spinning reels come to a stop. They spin too fast for you to do this when they are in motion. This isn't any help. You can see only 9 of the 60 symbols, and you don't know whether or not the bell that shows on the first reel is the same bell that appeared on a previous spin or a different one.

Although I can't give you any sure way of obtaining the information that will allow you to figure the correct percentage, I can give you a system by which you will be able to determine which of a num-

ber of machines is the "loosest" and gives the best percentage of return. That will have to do.

It's a system that was first used by an old-time slot player who had
been a slot mechanic working in Reno years before the machines were
legalized in Nevada. He started with $50 worth of nickels—1,000 coins.
He would select a machine and play the 1,000 coins into it—a little
more than an hour's work. He pocketed all the coins the machine paid
out and did not play any of them back into the machine. Jackpot winnings, if any, were kept separate. When the original 1,000 coins were
gone he counted his payback returns, not counting the jackpot money.
Then he repeated the same procedure with other machines and compared the payback returns from each. The machine that returned the
most coins, he figured to have the best payback percentage for the
player. This system of spotting the loosest and tightest machines is not
100% accurate, but it does work about 95% of the time.

SLOT PLAYERS

If you think that playing the slots is nothing more than a pleasant
pastime, watch a few slot addicts at work. I can name a dozen women
players who have lost as much as $20,000 a year to the machines. For
many addicts, putting coins into one machine isn't fast enough, so they
tackle two, three or four machines at the same time. The left hand
puts a coin in, the right pulls the handle down with a practiced rhythmic motion, the player takes a sideward step and repeats with the next
machine, and the next and the next, then back to the first machine—
hour after hour. Many women addicts wear a glove on the right hand
to avoid getting calluses.

Here's an incident that illustrates the fascination the slot machine
holds for men and women in all walks of life. Five friends of mine—
the socially prominent Chicagoan Mrs. Blanche Sundheim, her husband, Harry, and three friends, Ralph Leonardson, Milton Henry and
Victor Goldberg, were walking through the casino at the Habana
Hilton on the afternoon of August 6, 1958. Mr. Goldberg found a lost
nickel on the floor, handed it to Mrs. Sundheim, and suggested she play
it in one of the machines that line the walls. She dropped the coin in
the slot, pulled the lever and found herself a five-coin winner.

Four hours later I came by and found the group glued to the same
machine. Blanche, with a handful of nickels, was playing, and the four
men were rooting for her to hit the jackpot. Mr. Goldberg, seeing me,
said, "Scarne, this is all happening with a found nickel."

I turned to Mrs. Sundheim. "Why don't you play the nickel four-
reel Buckaroo machine? You might hit the four buckaroos and collect
the hundred-and-twenty-five-dollar bonus award."

"Let's go," she said, and a moment later was pulling madly at the Buckaroo machine lever, occasionally switching from right to left hand. After about 15 minutes of average slot-machine payouts, Whammo! Four buckaroos on the pay line. The four friends let out a whoop that could be heard all over the casino, and play stopped momentarily at the dice, Black Jack, Roulette and Baccarat tables. A few minutes later, with the $125 award, Blanche and her rooting section moved to a quarter Buckaroo machine. She played in about $10 and Lady Luck smiled again—a broad grin. She had hit the four buckaroos for the $625 prize award. More cheers rocked the casino.

After five hours of play Blanche and party adjourned for dinner. After dinner they were back at the slots again. And they did little else for the next six days. They put in about 60 hours of slot play, during which Blanche hit about 40 jackpots. After the first 40 hours, that found nickel had grown to $1,700. This would have been a good place to stop.

For the last two days of play they moved over to the silver-dollar machine, whose Buckaroo award is $2,500. An hour before leaving the hotel to catch a plane for home, Blanche lost her last silver dollar. The

Some of the 800-odd modern multiple-coin slot machines located in the swank Las Vegas Hilton Hotel Casino in Las Vegas, Nevada. (Allen Photographers Inc.)

found nickel had gone; both her hands were callused, and black from handling the coins. I told her she had pulled the slot handle approximately 54,000 times.

She smiled and said, "I enjoyed every one of those fifty-four thousand pulls."

BEATING THE ONE-ARMED BANDIT

Today the slot machine manufacturers seem to be winning their long battle with the slickers who are out to cheat the machines. Years ago slot cheats sometimes managed to empty the coin tube and jackpot by drilling a tiny hole with a special tool through the wood of the cabinet directly opposite the payout slides. They would insert a hooked wire, catch the bottom payout slide, pull it and receive a payout after each play, no matter what combination appeared on the pay line. The manufacturers countered that by lining the wooden interior with a drill-proof steel sheet.

Other slickers used *spooning* devices. The spooner pushed the handle of a teaspoon into the coin-return opening, wedged open the little trap door, put a coin into the slot and pulled the lever. The slide now paid off on any combination. Another method was to insert long flexible rods up through the payout hole into the payout chute. A back-and-forth manipulation of the slide brought the coins out on any combination. Slot manufacturers stopped this by putting two sharp angles on the pay chute, thus making it impossible to insert anything up the chute and still keep leverage.

THE RHYTHM SYSTEM

The manufacturers thought they had outwitted the slot cheats. Then, one day some years ago, a mysterious stranger walked into the Golden Nugget on Fremont Street in Las Vegas. He began playing a nickel slot and about ten minutes later had emptied the machine's coin tube and the jackpot. Within an hour he had hit jackpots on a dozen more machines. The slot inspectors and the Golden Nugget owners watched him hit jackpot after jackpot and eventually walk out with $500 in winnings. Some figured he was just a lucky guy. Others suspected that he might be smart and have something on the machine; but they couldn't prove a thing. He hadn't been drilling or using spooning devices.

That same evening the stranger emptied a dozen tubes and jackpots at the Flamingo and then went on to the El Rancho Vegas, where he had equal success. During the next week he had hit jackpots on about 300 machines all over Las Vegas. He caused quite a lot of talk among the gambling fraternity. "Who is he?" "Can anybody be that lucky?"

"Nobody could hit three hundred jackpots in a week; he *must* have something on the machines." "Maybe, he's a scientist using some top-secret radar gimmick."

His phenomenal run of luck continued and he checked out after another week's play with about $30,000 in winnings. Not bad for two weeks' work.

He dropped out of sight for a month. Then the operators in Reno began to notice a player who was emptying slot tubes and jackpots almost as fast as the attendants could fill them. After a week he disappeared again, and the slot owners, who had begun to wonder if something had gone wrong with their machines, were relieved to find that they were again paying out winners in the usual fashion.

As the months passed, slot manufacturers noticed that they were getting more and more complaints from their customers in various parts of the country. Always the same complaint: a stranger was giving the law of averages a terrific beating.

Early in 1948, operators of casinos in Reno and Las Vegas again noticed that their daily receipts were dropping off; but they didn't remember the stranger who had been so lucky a couple of years before.

Several operators returned machines to the manufacturers and asked for replacements because the machines were no longer earning the expected revenue. The makers replaced the machines with new ones which proved to be afflicted with the same trouble. The entire slot handle in Nevada took a nose dive.

I heard about the situation and went to Las Vegas to get a look for myself. I interviewed a dozen casino managers and they all reported a revenue drop. I also discovered that the same mysterious stranger was in town again, only now he had four companions, all of whom were being much too lucky.

One casino manager had this to say:

"A couple of days ago in walks a guy who the day before had emptied tubes and jackpots of fifteen machines. I figured he must have some gaff so I watched him. He hadn't been playing five minutes when I heard *Klump!*—the sound of a falling jackpot. The machine inspectors refilled the jackpot with thirty dollars in quarters. I moved closer, kept watching, and began counting the coins he dropped in. At forty, the old familiar jackpot sound—another *Klump!*

"Not again, I told myself. I walked over and took a good look. Sure enough, the three bars were lined up on the pay line."

"What did you do then?" I asked.

"What could I do? I paid off. Scarne, after this character hit five more jackpots within the next half hour I knew for sure he had something on the machine. I studied the way he dropped his coin into the slot and the way he pulled the handle. I looked for every cheating gimmick ever used to beat a machine. The only thing unusual I could spot was that he didn't have the usual slot-player's swing. Once he pulled the handle immediately after inserting the coin; other times, after dropping the coin, he waited a bit before he pulled the handle. There were many pauses between plays, some much longer than others. But I wasn't sure this meant anything. And there was nothing I could do about it anyway; a slot player can do as he pleases when playing his own dough."

My next stop was the Golden Nugget. When the then owner, Jake Kozloff, spotted me, the first words he said were, "I'll bet you're in town checking on the rhythm players." This was the first time I had heard the expression "rhythm players."

Jake added, "You're lucky, Scarne; a representative of the Mills Company is arriving in town in about an hour."

"What's so unusual about a slot manufacturer's representative showing up in Las Vegas?" I asked.

Jake grinned. "I've got a ten-thousand-dollar wager with him that I'll empty the coin tube of a machine he's bringing with him from Chicago."

"I'll say I'm lucky, Jake, if what you say is true."

He wasn't joking about the $10,000 bet or his ability to do what he said. The next morning, in the basement of the Golden Nugget, I saw Jake Kozloff feed about a dozen quarters into the new slot machine and pull its lever in the usual fashion with the usual results. Then he turned to the Mills Company man and said, "I'm going to put two cherries on the machine's pay line."

Before anyone could reply, he put in another quarter, pulled the handle and sent the three wheels spinning. Sure enough, when the reels stopped there was a cherry on each of the first two reels. Nobody spoke. The only sound was the jingle of several quarters rattling down the payout tubes.

Jake pulled the handle again and got two cherries again. He repeated this four times in a row—always the same two cherries. It was obvious that all he had to do to empty the tube was to keep going. He did. It took him about 20 minutes.

The Mills man said in an unhappy voice, "Jake, I'm sick. Not about losing the ten-thousand-dollar bet, but about the thousands and thousands of dollars that the slot operators are losing. If we don't find an answer to this rhythm gimmick fast, slot machines are doomed."

Before I left the Golden Nugget that morning Jake gave me an hour's lesson in "rhythming" a machine, and I knew that the slot representative had called the turn. Unless a cure for rhythming could be found, the slot industry would fold.

Shortly after I returned home I heard from my friend Clifford Jones, then Lieutenant Governor of Nevada, that a group of players who called themselves the Rhythm Boys had opened a school in Las Vegas and were charging $500 for a complete course in how to beat the slots by the rhythm system. This was apparently a pretty successful school and it graduated a good many students summa cum laude. During 1949 a couple of thousand rhythm players, most of whom were women, were beating the slots all over Nevada and various other sections of the country. Hundreds were barred from the slot rooms, and slander suits (which were later dropped) were filed by some of the barred players.

My findings show that national slot machine revenue took a real nose dive, dropping from the 1948 figure of $700 million to a rock-bottom low of $200 million in 1949. The rhythm players beat the slots during 1949 for half a billion dollars.

How did the original mysterious stranger happen to come up with his bright idea? And who was he? I did some further detective work and discovered that he was an Idaho farmer who, during his spare time, had been helping a slot-mechanic friend repair out-of-order machines. He discovered that the three wheels in certain makes of machine made exactly the same number of revolutions when the handle was pulled. He studied the clock fan which controls the length of time the reels spin and found that on some machines the clock went dead from seven to eight seconds after the reels stopped spinning. He also memorized the position of each symbol on each reel. In actual play, since he knew the relative positions on the reel of all the symbols, he could deduce from the nine visible symbols he could see through the window just where all the others were. Then, by timing himself to pull the machine's level at precisely the right instant and before the clock gear went dead, he found that he could manipulate the desired symbols onto the pay line. Most of the rhythm players who learned the system later could, as a rule, control only the cherry on the first reel, but even that was good enough to empty the payoff coin tube; it just took a little longer.

In 1950, a ten-page pamphlet explaining how to rhythm a slot machine appeared, selling for $5. Here is a quote from it that gives you more details on the system:

> First of all remember the system of the "Rhythm Boys" is based on timing. Each machine has a clock gear which determines the number of

revolutions that each reel will make. As each reel has 20 symbols, the timing must be precise; i.e., if you aim at a cherry, you don't want to hit the orange above or below the cherry. The average clocks become dead in from 7 to 8 seconds. After that time has elapsed there will be nothing that can be done to control the reels.

The average slot machine has a payback of between 80 to 92 percent of the money that is placed into it. Using our timing system the rate of payback is raised to between 110 and 125 percent.

Although the system is based on timing, standing at a machine with a stop watch would, of course, appear too obvious. So we do the next best thing: we have a "watch" in our minds.

As the first lesson, get a watch and time yourself by the second hand; count under your breath from 1 to 20 in exactly five seconds, then learn to count from 11 to 30 in exactly five seconds. Practice this until you become absolutely perfect. When you are positive you can do this without the help of a watch, we will proceed to the next step, which is learning to play the machine and learning how to apply the count.

Place your money in your left hand, taking each coin out with the right hand, insert the coin in the slot and carry the right hand on over to the handle. Pull the handle, starting the mechanism.

The reason for holding the money in the left hand and operating the mechanism with the right is to stall when you have a long count or to be ready immediately when you have a short count. You will have a count varying from five to twenty-five.

Now start your count with the stopping of the last reel. Practice this until you count one at exactly the same time the third wheel stops. When we say exactly, we mean exactly; it has to be, as the whole system is based on precision. After you have learned this you are now ready for the most important part of the operation, which is learning how to memorize the reel strips.

We cannot stress too much the importance of this part of the system because you will have complete control over any one reel. So when the object you are trying to control goes out of sight you will have a count to bring it right back.

Every machine has a "hold" count. To understand this hold count, say we're playing a machine and the hold count is 16. For example, if the last bar is in the window and if we give it an exact count of 16 from the time the third reel stops until we trip the mechanism with the handle, the last bar should come right back in the pay slot or if it fluctuates, should be no further than three emblems away on each side of the pay slot, which is giving you control of the reel. This eliminates from the pay slot all the dead emblems, lemons, etc., which are no good.

Use a short count to bring symbols up, use a long count to bring symbols down, going on a basis of one count to each symbol.

For example, if the hold count is 16, 1 up from center, count 17; 2 up from center, count 18; 3 up from center, count 19, etc. If 1 down from center count 15; 2 down from center, count 14; 3 down from center, count 13. Center means payoff position.

Each machine has a different hold count. To find this hold count get the object in the window which you are trying to hold, count 14, pull off the mechanism and let it stop. If the object goes down 5 from center, for example, subtract 5 from 14 and the approximate hold count would be 9.

Another example: if the object went up 6 from center, add 6 to 14—an approximate hold count of 20 which, as you start to play the machine again, you will be able to jockey the machine to the exact hold count. If the machine jumps too far away from center the machine is erratic. Try another machine.

This was too good a thing to last. By 1951 all the slot manufacturers knew exactly what was happening and had solved the problem. They simply added another gimmick to the machines—a variator. This mechanical device controls the clock mechanism so that the spin starts at different times.

The variator put an end to what was, for a lot of players, the most exciting period in the history of the slot machine.

PINBALL MACHINES

Pinball machines today are primarily amusement devices and are not used for gambling to the extent they once were. Slot machines and pinball games are, however, related in one way: When slots are banned in a territory the slot operators, instead of closing up, switch over to pinball machines. They want to stay in business so they'll be ready if the one-armed bandits come back.

Pinball machines evolved from a very old game known as Bagatelle which, under various names, can still be purchased in toy stores. Several versions of this have been used for gambling by carnival operators since the early 1900s. One of the earliest, the Drop Case, consists of a vertical board studded with brads, under glass. Marbles dropped in through openings at the top roll down through the maze of brads into numbered pockets at the bottom. Reference to a chart tells the player whether he has won or lost. Drop Cases are usually gaffed so that they can be controlled by the operator. They are still to be found in carnivals.

In larger sizes the pinball machine was designed as a glass-covered wood box with an inner inclined playing surface studded with nails or brads. When the player pulled back a plunger at one side and then released it, a ball was propelled to the upper end of the board and rolled back down through the obstructing pattern of nails into winning and losing sections.

Pinball manufacturers later added many electrical gadgets, flashing lights and sound effects.

About 1928 a Chicago manufacturer took the game out of the carnival class and began making it for sale in quantity. By 1931 the first electrically operated pinball machines appeared with their more complicated high scoring systems.

These first machines were intended for use in locations where slots were prohibited. They were advertised as "skill" games, but the purchaser was told that they were perfect gambling devices for closed territories. The gimmick was that high scores paid off a specified number of winning games which were redeemable in cash over the counter. This subterfuge didn't fool the courts for long, and the machines were banned when used for gambling.

The manufacturers discovered that the public liked to play the pinball game even when it didn't pay off in cash, so they discarded the gambling feature and installed a "free play" feature. A winning score gave the player the right to continue playing without inserting more coins.

Even now, there are many storekeepers who will redeem the winning scores for cash; but the great majority of pinball games are amusement devices only.

ADVICE TO SLOT PLAYERS

As a gambling consultant I see a great many gamblers every day. The biggest gambling fool I've ever encountered is the slot machine degenerate who feeds the machines for hours at a time, day in and day out, in the belief that he can make a killing.

The slot machine player has less chance of winning in a long or short run than does the player at any other casino game: Bank Craps, Roulette, Black Jack or even the Big Six. His chance of beating the slots for even a few bucks over a period of time is exactly zero.

This isn't due, as most people believe, to the slot machine's percentage take, but rather to a betting restriction. "Slot machines," you may object, "don't have realistic minimum and maximum betting limits like other casino games."

Sure. You can bet one to eight coins on a modern multiple-coin machine. But what kind of a limit is that? A three-time double-up (2–4–8) and you reach the machine's maximum betting limit. In other casino games, when you feel lucky, you can step up your action.

If you were playing Bank Craps, Black Jack or Roulette and the rules restricted you to betting one to eight dollars per round or hand, you wouldn't stay in the game for long. You'd soon learn that your chance of winning any decent amount of money was very small. Millions of slot machine players never seem to realize this as they keep feeding in one to eight coins at a time.

Of the thousands upon thousands of slot players I have seen here and in other countries I can't recall one who ever quit a small winner over a long period of playing time, slot cheats excluded. But I can recall easily the names of a dozen slot degenerates who lost fortunes vainly trying to beat the slots.

At a Caribbean casino I once overheard a woman slot player making the old, familiar slot player's complaint to the casino host, Allen Kanter.

"Mr. Kanter, I just dropped twenty dollars in that quarter machine and only got four quarters back. Don't these slot machines ever pay off?"

Allen's reply was classic: "Lady, they sure do. They pay the casino's rent, the light bills, all the casino employees' salaries and a cool half million dollars a year in profits. Sure, they pay off."

My last piece of advice to the degenerate slot player who thinks he can beat the one-armed bandit consists of four little words: It can't be done.

16.
Chemin de Fer
and Baccarat

Baccarat and its variations, Punto Banco and Chemin de Fer, are the most popular games in European and Latin-American casinos, and are undoubtedly the most important and get the biggest play of any banking card games. Baccarat, or Baccarat–Chemin de Fer as it is known in Nevada, is played in most major casinos in Las Vegas, Reno and Lake Tahoe. American gamblers here and abroad wager approximately $1.5 billion yearly at these games. Before 1960, Chemin de Fer, usually called Shimmy by American gamblers, was the type of Baccarat most often played in fashionable casinos in the United States. Another variation, found in European casinos, is Baccart-en-Banque. The present-day Baccarat and Chemin de Fer are French variations of the Italian game of Baccara, which was first introduced into France about 1490 during the reign of Charles VIII. It was for years the favorite private gambling game of the French nobility and did not make its public appearance in the European casinos until many years later.

HISTORY

Baccarat, under its earlier name Baccara, first made its appearance in America in 1911, and by 1912 several New York City sawdust joints, including Big Thompson's on Houston Street, featured Baccara tables. It disappeared from the American scene a few years later when the structurally similar Black Jack was introduced into American casinos.

Chemin de Fer was first played in this country in 1920, shortly after World War I, in the homes of wealthy Americans vacationing in Palm Beach, Florida. It had its biggest boom here during the 1940s, when every big rug and sawdust joint had a Chemin de Fer table. The

Star Dust Hotel in Las Vegas introduced a Shimmy table into its casino early in 1958, the first legalized game of Chemin de Fer in the country. Soon after, other Strip casinos also introduced it, but for reasons which I'll explain later it didn't click in the big way the operators hoped it would (see page 470).

Almost two years later, on November 21, 1959, Carl Cohen, then manager of the Sands Hotel casino in Las Vegas, began operating a Baccarat–Chemin der Fer table. Early that year, Aaron Weisberg, a Sands casino executive, came to see me at the Habana Hilton Hotel casino in Cuba where I was consultant. He wanted to know all the necessary information—house's favorable percentage, method of play, etc.—on Punto Banco. After our discussion, he decided that the game was for Las Vegas and borrowed several Cuban dealers from the Habana Hilton casino to accompany him to Nevada to deal and teach the Sands casino employees the game. An interesting fact was that the first hours of play cost the operators $251,000, which was paid to a dozen winners, the biggest a Texas rancher who pocketed $172,000. But Baccarat–Chemin de Fer proved to be a big success at the Sands.

Las Vegas style Baccarat is similar to the Baccarat found at Monte Carlo, Deauville and the municipal casinos in San Remo, Italy, plus a few Cuban trimmings.

The biggest single loss that your author has ever witnessed at a Baccarat session was $1,500,000 lost by a titled English high roller at the Knightsbridge Sporting Club in London. The biggest loss in Nevada to my knowledge at Baccarat–Chemin de Fer took place recently at the Sands Hotel casino when several Japanese high-rolling businessmen lost the gigantic sum of $2 million in a week's play at the game. At about the same time I saw a well-groomed young Chinese woman run a $200 bet into a $250,000 profit in a week's play in a number of Las Vegas Strip casinos.

There is only a slight difference in the playing rules of Shimmy and Baccarat, or Baccara. In Baccarat, as it is played in Monte Carlo and other European casinos, the game is banked by the casino operators or by concessionaires (usually a Greek syndicate) who pay the casino operators 50% of their monthly winnings for the banking privilege. Players who bet the bank to win are charged 5% of their winnings on each bet. Players who bet the bank to lose do not pay a direct charge, but they do pay a hidden percentage.

Chemin de Fer is played exactly the same as Baccarat, with the exception that the casino operators take no risk, since the players bet against each other. The house acts as a *cutter*, the same as the operator of a Poker game. For a standard *cut* (charge) of 5% taken out of the player banker's winning *coup* (bet), the house rents out the Shimmy

November 21, 1959, the Sands Casino saw the opening of the first Baccarat-Chemin-de-Fer game in Nevada. John Scarne (standing CENTER*) with the now M.G.M. Grand Hotel Casino director, Carl Cohen (*LEFT*), and his former Sands assistant, Tommy Ronzoni (*RIGHT*), checking the first day's action at the table. (Las Vegas News Bureau)*

equipment and supplies three croupiers to operate the game. In return for the 5% charge, the croupiers run the game, manage the banker's money, collect winning bets and pay out losing bets.

During the early forties, when Shimmy was the gambling rage in America, the casino's 5% cut on the banker's winnings was not quite as sure a thing as the income of the Internal Revenue Bureau, but " 'twill do, 'twill do." One night, during that period, I clocked the casino take at the Shimmy table at Ben Marden's Riviera casino in Bergen County, New Jersey. It was approximately $30,000. Further detective work revealed that the yearly house cut at this one Shimmy table during World War II was about $3 million. On a capital investment of the price of a gambling okay, this seems a tolerable dividend.

The vocabulary of Chemin de Fer used in the United States is partly French (*banco, la grande, la petite*), partly Black Jack lingo (Hit me!) and partly from Craps (next shooter, the bank's faded). Unlike the Baccara games in French casinos, *checks* (chips) are seldom used in Shimmy games in the United States; the green stuff makes for a more interesting game.

The bets at Shimmy vary from a low $5 to $50,000 or more, depending on the amount of the player-banker's winnings and the amount anted into the bank. The usual Chemin de Fer banker's ante limits run from a low $100 to $10,000 or more. The largest sum ever anted into

Closeup view of dealing shoe used in Chemin de Fer. (Las Vegas News Bureau)

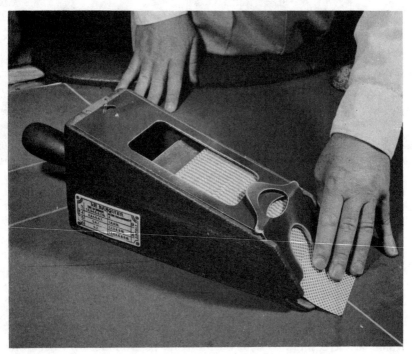

a Shimmy bank in an American casino was the $500,000 bank of an American oil tycoon in a Florida casino one night in the winter season of 1946. The oil tycoon lost $847,000 that evening. Note: He was cheated.

The Chemin de Fer equipment is bulky. The game requires a heavy kidney-shaped table, its surfaces padded and covered with a fancy green baize layout divided into numbered sections for 9 or 12 players. Other requirements are six or eight decks of cards, a mahogany *sabot* or *shoe* (card-dealing box), a *money box* which holds the casino's gambling revenue, and a discard cylinder. The croupier, who handles the dealt cards, sits in the concavity of the kidney-shaped table and uses a wooden *palette* to slide the cards, cash or chips around to the players.

The two croupiers who sit opposite him also have a palette to facilitate handling the bets. A lookout sits on a stand overlooking the Shimmy table. Although Shimmy and Baccarat are as fair percentage-wise as any other banking game, until the first publication of this book in 1961 many American gamblers didn't realize this and rarely sat down to play either game.

SCARNE'S RULES FOR CHEMIN DE FER

Requirements

1. From two to as many players as there are player spaces available on the layout. Some tables have 9, others 12. The banker plays against only one player at a time, but any or all the other players may bet on that one player's hand against the bank, provided the bank possesses enough money to cover the wagers.

2. A regulation Chemin de Fer table with a *discard box* into which the played cards are dropped and *money box* to receive the casino's 5% charge.

3. A card-dealing box called a *sabot* or *shoe*.

4. Eight standard decks of 52 cards, four red-backed decks and four blue-backed decks, plus two advertising cards which are used as indicators. (In some casinos only six decks are used.)

5. Three Chemin de Fer *palettes*, long thin paddles which enable the seated croupiers to transact business at the far reaches of the table.

Object of the Game

To win a *coup* by holding a combination of two or three cards totaling 9 or as close as possible to 9, or to a two-digit number ending in 9. When the total of the cards is a two-digit number, only the latter digit

John Scarne (standing CENTER) with casino executive Larry Snow (RIGHT) checking big-time action at the Baccarat-Chemin de Fer table in the swank Caesar's Palace Casino in Las Vegas, Nevada.

has any value. Examples: A count of 19 has a value of 9; a count of 23 has a value of 3, and so forth.

Value of the Cards

The ace is the lowest ranking card and has a point value of 1 (one). Kings, queens and jacks have a value of 10 each. All other cards have their numerical face value. The suits have no comparative value.

The Shuffle and Cut

At the start of the game, the dealer-croupier spreads the eight decks of cards on the table and all the players and croupiers are permitted to take a group of cards and shuffle them. On later deals when the discard receiver is emptied on to the layout and some cards are face up, some face down, the croupiers and players turn the face-up cards down and shuffle them.

After the players have shuffled groups of cards, the croupier gathers all the cards and shuffles them together, usually shuffling about two decks at a time. Finally, the croupier assembles all eight decks into one

Frank Sinatra, onetime part owner of the Sands, handling the Chemin-de-Fer palette. (Las Vegas News Bureau)

packet and hands a player an indicator card and says, "Cut, please." The player inserts the indicator card into the packet to show where he wants the cards cut. The croupier cuts the cards at this position, putting the indicator and all the cards above it on the bottom. He then inserts the second indicator card seven, eight or ten cards from the bottom of the packet, and places all the cards into the shoe face down. The croupier next deals three cards from the shoe and drops them through a slot in the table into the discard receiver. This is called *burning* the top cards. (Some operators burn five or six cards instead of three.) The shoe is now ready to be dealt by the first banker-player.

Selecting the First Banker

The first player on the croupier's right has the privilege of being first banker. If the first player declines the bank, the privilege passes to the player to his right, and so on, counterclockwise (or the bank may be auctioned to the highest bidder).

The banker-dealer at Chemin de Fer continues to deal until he *misses a pass* (loses a bet). When the active player wins a bet the croupier passes the shoe to the player on the dealer's right. It always moves on counterclockwise. In mid-game, as at the start, the bank may be declined.

When the first advertising card shows, the croupier announces, "One more hand, please." Upon completion of this last hand, a reshuffle takes place which is governed by the rules for the original shuffle and cut.

Preparation for the Play

The croupier slides the shoe to the first designated banker, who places on the table an amount of money within the house betting limits. This amount may be from a low of $100 to a high of $5,000, $10,000 or more, all depending on the banker's gambling spirit. A lucky bank may at times hold several hundred thousand dollars, and a player can bet all or any part of it as he wishes.

The Betting

Before any cards are dealt, the players must make their bets (called *fading*). If a player wants to fade the bank for its total worth, he calls, "Banco." A banco bet has precedence over any other. The player to the right of the dealer has the first privilege of bancoing. If he does not banco, the privilege passes to the next man on the right, and so on around the table. Then, any watcher or former non-player may call banco.

If no one bancos, then partial bets are accepted, with the first man on the right placing his bet, for whatever amount he chooses, on the table before him. Then the player on his right bets, and so on around the table until the bank is partly or completely faded. If the bank is not completely faded, the amount which has not been faded is set aside for the banker.

Anyone who bancos, whatever his position around the table, has the right of *banco suivi* (following banco) if he loses. His right to call banco on the next deal has precedence over all others; if he fails to call banco and more than one other person calls banco, the player nearest the dealer starting from the right has precedence, even though he may call banco after another player has done so. This right is known as *banco prime*.

The player who bancos becomes the active player. If no one has bancoed and there are partial bets, the player who has bet the most money is designated by the croupier as the active player.

Because the rules of Chemin de Fer are so many and so complicated, each player is supplied with a card, as shown, describing the player's and the banker's rules.

CHEMIN DE FER

Game Must Be Played According to Rules

PLAYER

H		
A	0 – 1 – 2 – 3 – 4	Always Draws a Card
V	5	Optional—*Stand or Draw*
I	6 – 7	Never Draws—*Stands*
N		
G	8 – 9	*Turn* Cards Face Up

BANKER

H		Draws If Giving	Does Not Draw in Giving		O
A	3	1, 2, 3, 4, 5, 6, 7, 10	8	9	P
V					T
I	4	2, 3, 4, 5, 6, 7	1, 8, 9, 10		I
N					O
G	5	5, 6, 7	1, 2, 3, 8, 9, 10	4	N A
	6	6, 7	1, 2, 3, 4, 5, 8, 9, 10		L

Banker Always Draws When Having 0, 1, 2
Banker Never Draws When Having 7
Banker Faces 8, 9
If Player Takes No Card, Banker Stands Only On 6, 7

— NO MISTAKES ARE ALLOWED —
IF ANY ARE MADE IT IS COMPULSORY
For The DEALER to Reconstruct The COUP

The Coup, or Play

The banker slides one card out of the shoe and deals it to the active player; then he deals one card for himself, a second card to the player, and finally a second card to himself. All four cards are dealt face down.

The First Turn of Play

The active player now examines his cards. If they total a count of 8 or 9, he turns them face up on the table. If the count is 8, he calls, "*La petite!*" If it is 9, he calls, "*La grande!*" The croupier verifies the count. The banker must now turn his two cards face up.

1. If the active player's count is higher than the banker's, the croupier pays off all the winning players. If the active player's count is lower than the banker's, the banker wins, and the croupier collects all the bets for him.

2. If the active player holds a count of less than 8, he says, "Pass," and the banker now examines his own cards. If they total 8 or 9, he turns them face up, and the croupier collects all the bets for him.

3. If the banker does not hold a count of 8 or 9, play reverts to the active player.

4. If the banker's count is the same as the player's count, it is a *legal tie*, or *standoff*, and neither banker nor player wins or loses.

These four rules apply with equal force to the player's and banker's second turn of play.

Active Player's Second Turn of Play

1. If the active player holds a count of 1, 2, 3, 4 or 0, he must draw a card.

2. If the active player has a count of 5, the draw is optional; he may elect either to *get hit* (draw) or to *stay* (not draw). This is the only discretionary play the active player has at Chemin de Fer.

3. If the active player has a count of 6 or 7, he *must* stay.

Banker's Second Turn of Play

1. If the banker holds a count of 0–1–2 he must draw a card.

2. If the active player stays and the banker holds a count of 4 or 5 he must draw.

3. If the active player stays and the banker holds a count of 6 or 7 he must stay.

Banker Holds a Count of Three

1. If the active player in his turn of play has drawn a card valued at 1, 2, 3, 4, 5, 6, 7 or 10, the banker must draw.

2. If the active player has drawn an 8, the banker must stay.

3. If the active player has drawn a 9, the banker's play is optional; he may draw or stay.

Banker Holds a Count of Four

1. If the active player fails to draw a card, the banker must draw.

2. If the active player draws a card valued 2, 3, 4, 5, 6 or 7, the banker must draw.

3. If the active player draws a card valued 1, 8, 9 or 10, the banker must stay.

Banker Holds a Count of Five

1. If the active player did not draw a card on his turn of play, the banker must draw.

2. If the active player draws a card valued 5, 6 or 7, the banker must draw.

3. If the active player draws a card valued 1, 2, 3, 8, 9 or 10, the banker must stay.

4. If the active player draws a 4, the banker's play is optional; he may either stay or draw.

Banker Holds a Count of Six

1. If the active player fails to draw, the banker must stay.

2. If the active player draws a 6 or 7, the banker must draw.

3. If the active player draws a card valued 1, 2, 3, 4, 5, 8, 9, or 10, the banker must stay.

Banker Holds a Count of Seven

Regardless of the active player's draw, the banker must stay.

Rules Governing the Bank

If the bank loses a coup the deal passes. If the bank wins, the same player holds the bank and all the money in the bank is now at stake—the banker's original bet and his winnings, less the 5% charge (in some casinos the 5% is not collected from the first win by the bank). The banker does not have the privilege of *dragging down* or reducing his bank. It is all or nothing. He may, of course, pass the bank at any time; but if he wants to retain the bank he risks the entire bank, except when the bank exceeds the house limit or the bettors have not faded the full amount of the bank. In either case, the excess is put aside for the banker by the croupier.

When the banker passes, the croupier holds an informal auction of the bank, and gives it to the player who will put up a bank equal to the one that has just been passed. If the high bidder happened to be the player to the right of the banker, that player now gets the bank, in his regular turn.

The bank can pass at any time up to the actual dealing of the cards.

I once saw a friend of mine at a casino in Palm Springs, California, roll up a bank from $500 to about $30,000, never hesitating to continue playing. When it was $30,000 or nothing, he watched the players' bets go down. It happened that only $10,000 was covered, so $20,000 was put aside. My friend dealt the cards out—and lost. But he still received the $20,000. Later he said to me, "John, I must have been crazy to let that thirty thousand ride in the center. I should have passed the bank. I was in a fog and I didn't realize what I was doing." That is how most Shimmy players react when the betting gets big.

BACCARAT LAS VEGAS STYLE

Since many European and South American casinos have 40 or more Baccara tables in action at one time, it is surprising that Nevada gambling operators have waited almost 30 years before giving Baccara, or Baccarat as they call it, a try. At this writing, with Baccarat having recently been introduced in a number of Nevada casinos, I predict that in a few years it will become a standard game in most American casinos, and that operators now operating Chemin de Fer will switch to Baccarat. They will do this when they discover that Baccarat gets more action than Chemin de Fer, and thus earns more money for its operators, for the following reasons:

1. Because the house banks the game of Baccarat, one lone player can play, whereas at Chemin de Fer, players may sit around for hours (as in Poker), waiting for enough players to arrive to get the game started.

2. Baccarat has the advantage that a player can bet two ways: on the bank or on the player's hand. Hence, players often switch their betting from the bank to the player's hand—or vice versa.

3. Baccarat has a bigger draw for the bigtime player than Chemin de Fer: the player knows that if he gets lucky he can win big, because the casino's entire bankroll is at stake. At Chemin de Fer, the amount a player can win is limited by how much the other players are willing to lose.

The betting limits for Baccarat in Nevada casinos run from a low $5 to a maximum of $2,000, with, of course, special betting limits for well-known high rollers, usually the amount of their first bet, $2,500, $5,000, $10,000 or even more.

The Baccarat table and equipment are similar to those for Chemin de Fer, except that the Baccarat layout has two betting spaces at each end of the table, one marked "Bank" and the other marked "Players." There are spaces for 12 players at the table, numbered from 1 to 12. In European and Latin American casinos checks or chips are used to deal the game and run from a low 50¢ to a high of $100. The 50¢ chips are used to facilitate the croupiers taking the 5% house charge from winning players who have bet on the bank. In the Nevada casinos money rather than chips is used.

In most Las Vegas Strip casinos players do not have to keep track of the 5% charge on their winning bets when placed on the bank. The croupier keeps track by placing chips or markers indicating how much each player owes the casino in a small rectangle marked with each player's seat number. The numbered rectangles are marked clearly and are located in a row on the layout directly in front of the croupier. When the 5% charge money owed the house reaches a certain amount, or at the end of a dealt shoe, the player is asked to pay up.

A bet placed on the space of the layout marked "Bank" indicates the player is wagering that the shooter will win or pass; a bet placed on the layout marked "Players" is a lose bet and against the shooter. A count of 0 in Baccarat is known as *baccarat;* a count of 9 is known as a *natural.*

Several shills are used at a Baccarat table to stimulate action.

SCARNE'S RULES FOR PLAYING BACCARAT LAS VEGAS STYLE

The playing rules for Baccarat Las Vegas or Cuban style are the same as for Chemin de Fer, except that the optional plays, such as the banker's optional when holding a count of 3 and dealing the player a 9 and when holding a 5 and dealing the player a 4, are compulsory draws.* The same holds true for the player when holding a count of 5. The abolishment of these optionals at Baccarat make the game mechanical; all a croupier can do is follow the rules. It does, however, eliminate those arguments which arise in Chemin de Fer caused by a player's hitting or staying against the wishes of another player.

The rules of Baccarat, like those of Chemin de Fer, are many and complicated, and each player is given a card like that on page 472, describing rules for players and banker.

PERCENTAGES AGAINST THE PLAYER AT BACCARAT AND CHEMIN DE FER

The rules governing Chemin de Fer and Baccarat seem unnecessarily complicated, but before we blend our voices in with the Shimmy and Baccarat addict's immemorial complaint, "Why don't they simplify the laws?" let's re-examine one of the inner secrets of all banking games.

That secret may be stated as follows: Nothing in gambling is unreasonably complicated. If it's complicated, there's a reason. The reason for the strange and apparently unnatural statutes governing the play at Chemin de Fer or Baccarat is that in their complication lies the hidden percentage against the player.

Before giving a mathematical analysis of the game, I would like to point out to the reader that the source of the banker's advantage is the fact that, as in Black Jack, the player must always play first. Although

---

* In Las Vegas today Baccarat is called "Baccarat–Chemin de Fer" to indicate its similarity to Chemin de Fer.

BACCARAT
— R U L E S —

PLAYER	HAVING	
	1–2–3–4–5–10	Draws a Card
	6–7	Stands
	8–9	Turns Cards Over

BANKER	HAVING	DRAWS WHEN GIVING	DOES NOT DRAW WHEN GIVING
	3	1–2–3–4–5–6–7–9–10	8
	4	2–3–4–5–6–7	1–8–9–10
	5	4–5–6–7	1–2–3–8–9–10
	6	6–7	1–2–3–4–5–8–9–10
	7	STANDS	
	8–9	TURNS CARDS OVER	

PICTURES AND TENS DO NOT COUNT

the Baccarat or Chemin de Fer player cannot bust his hand as in Black Jack, he does expose his possible card count to the banker by his decision of play. From there on, the rules of the game do the rest. They are devised to give the bank or dealer a percentage edge over the player.

Example: It is the player's second turn of play. He draws a card. This indicates that he holds one of these counts: 1, 2, 3, 4, 5 or 10. His drawn card is face up. We see that it is an 8, and we know his total count now must be 9, 10, 11, 12, 13 or 18.

Now the dealer faces his cards. He has a count of 3. Under the rules, he cannot draw a card. He stays, poor devil, and what happens? It is a 3 to 2 bet in his favor that his low count of 3 will beat whatever count is in the player's hand.

Another example? The player stays. The banker-player holding a count of 5 *must draw*. We know, of course, from the player's staying action that he has a count of 5, 6 or 7. If, on his own turn of play, the banker player elected to stay, he couldn't possibly win; so the rules compel him to draw a card and give him a possible chance to beat the player.

These are just two of the countless number of situations I had to analyze to figure the banker's and player's chances of winning. I did not realize when I started this mathematical analysis on Baccarat and Chemin de Fer that it would take so many weeks of laborious computing. I had to fill sheaves and sheaves of paper with numerous and varied computations in order to obtain the following answers which you see here for the first time in print: the chance of winning for the player is 49 33/100% and the chance of winning for the banker-player is 50 67/100%. These percentages apply to the Baccarat rules in use in Nevada casinos or a similar strategy of play used at Chemin de Fer. The player's disadvantage is the difference of 1 34/100%, which expressed decimally is 1.34%.

If the casino did not extract its 5% charge on each of the banker-player's winning bets, the banker-player would naturally have a 1.34% advantage over the other players. Since the banker-player must pay a standard charge of 5% on his winning bets, which occur 50 67/100 times out of every 100 dealt hands in the long run, the 5% casino charge on the banker-player's winnings is actually 2.53%. Subtracting from this the 1.34% advantage the banker-player enjoys over the other players, we find that the banker-player pays the casino 1.19%. The casino enjoys a 1.34% advantage over the player and 1.19% advantage over the banker at either Shimmy or Baccarat, and no matter how you look at it, "If you play, you must pay."

When the casino extracts a 3% charge on the banker-player's winnings, the bank's advantage dwindles to less than ⅕ of 1%: to be exact, .18%. This is the best bet to be found in any casino in the world. I doubt, however, that you'll be able to find this bet in any American casino after the publication of this book.

When the casino extracts a 3% charge from the banker-player before the hand is even dealt (win or lose), the banker-player's disadvantage is 1.66%. When the casino charges the banker-player 2½% (win or lose), his disadvantage is 1.16%. The player's disadvantage always remains the same at 1.34% and is not altered by the percentage charge which the casino extracts from the banker-player.

In addition to the above wagers, Baccarat layouts have bank spaces marked 9 and 8, and below each number the legend: "10 for 1." A bet placed on the 9 means that the player is betting that the dealer on the next turn of play will hold a count of 9 with his first two dealt cards. The casino pays off such winning bets at 10 for 1, actually 9 to 1. And since the correct odds are 9 23/64 to 1, the operators enjoy an advantage of 3.46%.

When a player places a bet on the 8 (same rules apply as on the 9) he is paid off at 9 to 1. But since the correct odds against being dealt a count of 8 in the first two cards are 9 43/62 to 1, the casino enjoys a favorable edge of 6.48%.

Some Baccarat operators permit players to make bets that the dealer will hold either an 8 or 9 count in his first two dealt cards. This bet is paid off at 4 to 1. The correct odds are 4 11/42 to 1, for a favorable casino advantage of 4.98%.

Recently Nevada casino owners have eliminated the bank spaces marked 8 and 9 from their layouts and replaced them with a bet marked "Ties Pay 10 for 1," which means that if a bet is placed on ties, the player is betting that the banker's and the player's hand will have the same count. This change occurred because casino owners became alarmed by several card casers who tried counting down the eights and nines on the old bet. However, if I had been consulted at the time, I would have recommended, rather than changing the layout, that the casino add another 52-card deck to the original eight-deck packet— and before placing the cards into the shoe for dealing, insert a second indicator card about 60 cards from the bottom of the packet to determine the end of the deal. For further information on this kind of anti-card casing device, see page 354.

To make the situation worse, most Nevada casinos pay ties at 9 for 1. This means that any bet placed on such a space is paid off at 8 to 1 odds should the bank and player tie. Since this bet has a house advantage of 9.52%, it is obviously a sucker bet; the bet should either be eliminated from the layout or the winning pay-off odds should be at 10 for 1. Baccarat is too great a game to possess such an outlandish sucker bet.

ADVICE TO BACCARAT AND CHEMIN DE FER PLAYERS

If you still insist on casino gambling after having read this book, and you find yourself in a casino that harbors all the standard casino games including Chemin de Fer and Baccarat, and you would like to give yourself the best possible chance to win, sit yourself down at the Shimmy or Baccarat table. The low house percentage which the player and banker-player must buck in these games makes the 1.34% and 1.19% bets the best available at any casino banking game, with the exception of two bets permitted at Bank Craps: a "front-line or come bet plus the front-line odds" and a "back-line or don't come bet plus the back-line odds."

However, I must again remind the reader that any gambler must lose in the end if he *repeatedly* takes the worst of any game percentagewise, whether his disadvantage is a low 1% or less, or a high 10% or more. The higher the house P.C. the faster the player is sent to the cleaner's.

CHEATING AT BACCARAT AND CHEMIN DE FER

Reputable and long-established casinos do not resort to cheating at their Baccarat or Chemin de Fer tables. When dealing Chemin de Fer, the management is not itself a participant in the game; it is a beneficiary, and there is no economic motive for cheating. Since the casino's edge at Baccarat will eventually get all the money in sight anyway, it would be foolish to spoil the casino's reputation by cheating the game. All it wants is a well-heeled, high-rolling betting crowd with nothing at all (certainly not suspicion) on its mind, and plenty of action. The 1.34% edge which it enjoys over the player and the 1.19% edge it has over the banker-player will eventually earn all the money it needs.

However, because some operators will always cheat and their Baccarat or Chemin de Fer tables are crooked, and because others aren't capable of protecting their players against card-cheat players who have infiltrated the games, much cheating does take place. Chemin de Fer and Baccarat are the international card cheat's paradise because of the high stakes. It requires an exceptionally skilled card cheat to beat these games when they are protected by three croupiers and a lookout, but it does happen regularly. I once proved this to a doubting casino operator.

It happened in 1958 when Mike McLaney, then owner of the Habana Nacional casino, and 19 other operators of American- and Cuban-owned casinos decided to set up a standard code of regulations and a Cuban Gaming Control Board. I was asked to meet with them and they offered me the chairmanship of the board, which, for personal reasons, I had to decline. During the meeting I was asked a great many questions about gambling, and at one point I made this remark: "Every casino which has a Chemin de Fer or Baccarat table—in Cuba, the United States, Monte Carlo or anywhere else—will at one time or another be cheated by international card sharps."

Analito Batisti, then owner of the Sevilla Biltmore casino in downtown Havana, immediately jumped to his feet. "Scarne," he objected, "I think no card thief can steal at my Baccarat game. I got the best croupiers in all Cuba workin' at my casino."

I didn't argue with him about it then. I merely smiled and replied, "The best croupiers in all Cuba should certainly be able to detect any crooked moves at your table." But three weeks later I walked into the Sevilla Biltmore one evening and had a private talk with Batisti. "I'd like to make sure that the best croupiers in all Cuba can spot a Baccarat cheat when he's working. Suppose we test them and find out."

He wasn't sure he liked the idea at first, so I put the proposition to him as a wager.

"I'll bet you $500 I can cheat the game using methods your boys won't detect. I'll play until I either win or lose $10,000, and that money won't be involved in the wager; you'll give me credit for that amount.

If I lose it or am caught in the act of cheating, I'll pay you $500. If I win ten grand by cheating and am not caught, you pay me $500."

Batisti is a gambler, and he figured this was an easy way to pick up five bills. It was early in the evening and the Baccarat table hadn't yet obtained any action. The five players seated at the table were all shills. There were three croupiers and the ladderman.

Bastiti told the croupier that I could have $10,000 worth of credit and took his seat on the ladder stand overlooking the Baccarat table. My first bet was $100 on the player's side, which I lost. I continued making $100 bets on the player's side for about 20 minutes. I took a quick glance at Batisti and saw that he wore a puzzled scowl. I could guess what he was thinking: How does this character expect to win $10,000 by wagering only a hundred dollars on each hand?

I was even when I decided to make my move. I turned to the croupier and said, "Ten thousand dollars on the player's side." The croupier looked up at Batisti who nodded in assent, and placed a $10,000 marker on the Baccarat layout marked "Player." The croupier turned to a shill who had the card-dealing box and said, "Deal the cards, please."

After the player's two cards and the banker's two cards had been dealt, the croupier scooped up the player's two face-down cards with his palette and slid them directly in front of me. My left hand reached for the two cards and I held them face down for a split second, then rapidly turned them face up and called, "Nine," dropping them face up on the layout. As pretty a jack and nine of spades as you'll ever see.

The croupier turned to the shill who still had the banker's two cards in his hand and asked him to turn them over. The croupier saw a 6 count, called, "No cards, player wins." He scooped up the four dealt cards with his hand and dropped them through the slot in the table into the discard cylinder.

As I got up from the table after the croupier had paid the bet, I noticed that Batisti's face was covered with a "What happened?" expression. The croupier and shills acted as if nothing unusual had happened; a $10,000 bet at the Sevilla Biltmore casino Baccarat table was nothing to get excited about. Batisti quickly jumped down from the ladder stand, walked rapidly over to where I was standing and said, "You don't cheat; you lucky!"

"That's what you think," I said. I told Batisti to remove the discard cylinder from under the table and examine the last four cards that were dropped in by the croupier. Batisti found two Tally-Ho cards possessing a different back design from the Bicycle cards that were in use. He turned red in the face. "You change cards?"

"Yeah, I change cards." I reached into my inside coat pocket and brought out the two Bicycle cards I had switched for the two Tally-Ho cards. I collected my $500, and as I was leaving I could hear Batisti and the croupiers buzzing excitedly in Spanish.

Later that same year, casino owner Batisti learned another, more expensive, lesson in the art of gambling. This time it was at Black Jack and at a cost of $59,700 (see The $1 Million Freeze-out, page 346).

Since the average Baccarat or Chemin de Fer player has little if any chance of spotting a slick card cheat in action, the best advice I can offer him is to keep his bets down to a minimum when not playing in a long-established casino.

The most common method Baccarat or Chemin de Fer operators use to cheat players is to insert a previously stacked packet into the card shot. Some operators have been known to switch the entire shoe containing the eight decks for a previously prepared one during play. To avoid being fleeced by such swindles, keep your eyes on the cards as they are being shuffled and placed in the shoe.

CROOKED DEALING SHOES USED TO CHEAT AT BACCARAT AND CHEMIN DE FER

Some crooked casinos here and abroad cheat at Chemin de Fer, Baccarat and Punto Banco by using a crooked dealing shoe. This shoe contains a hidden pocket near the mouth of the dealing box. The secret pocket holds about eight cards which are released singly by the dealer simply by squeezing the box with his left hand near its mouth when dealing with his right. The squeezing pressures opens a slit in the pocket about one-quarter of an inch from the mouth of the dealing shoe, permitting the dealer's right thumb to touch and deal the top card of those hidden in the pocket instead of the card that should be dealt. The eight cards secreted in the pocket of the dealing shoe usually are arranged 9–10–9–10–9–10–9–10. When the big-money hand makes an appearance, the crooked dealer deals his player confederate two cards from the hidden pocket, a crooked 9 and 10 for a natural 9 count. To eliminate crooked dealing shoes, I recommend that the manufacturers of casino dealing boxes make a transparent plastic dealing box which will prevent any cards from being secreted in the shoe's interior.

PRIVATE CHEMIN DE FER, OR SLOGGER

Private Chemin de Fer, or Slogger, is a simplified and demechanized version of Chemin de Fer and was described in print for the first time in *Scarne on Cards*. With Baccarat now being played in Nevada casinos, Slogger could become a serious rival to private Black Jack when played among friends. The special virtue of the game is that the banker and player each have a 50-50 chance to win, which is not true of Black Jack. If you want to play a dead-even banking game at your next private Black Jack session, give Slogger a try; you'll like it.

The game is played exactly like Chemin de Fer, with the following exceptions:

1. One standard 52-card deck is used.

2. Selecting the first banker: Players may sit anywhere they like. By mutual consent, any player may shuffle the cards, any player may cut the cards, and the acting dealer deals each player one card at a time, starting with the player at his left and dealing clockwise until some player is dealt an ace. That player becomes the first banker.

3. The shuffle and cut: The banker shuffles. Any player may ask for the right to shuffle at any time, but the banker has the right to shuffle last. After the shuffle, the banker-dealer puts the cards on the table to be cut. Any player may cut. More than one player may cut. If no other player cuts, the banker must.

4. *Dead cards* (cards which have been played) are *burned* (placed upside down) on the bottom of the pack as in private Black Jack.

5. When the deck is exhausted or it is a new dealer's turn to bank, a new shuffle must be made.

6. There is no restriction in this game—as there is in casino Chemin de Fer—on any player's drawing a card or staying on any count below 8. This includes the banker. Regardless of his count on the first two cards, the banker or the player may draw or stay, at his own discretion.

7. The count of 9 with two cards is called *Big Slogger,* and is immediately turned up by the holder. The same holds true for the count of 8, called *Little Slogger.*

All the cheating methods discussed under Black Jack (page 382) are applicable to private Chemin de Fer, or Slogger.

BACCARAT-EN-BANQUE

Baccarat-en-Banque, also called Baccarat à Deux Tableaux (double table), is an old-time cousin of Chemin de Fer played mostly in France. The game is usually banked by the casino operators or by concessionaires (usually from a Greek syndicate), who pay the casino operators 50% of their monthly winnings for the banking privilege. Unlike Baccarat or Chemin de Fer, there is a permanent bank and three hands are dealt instead of two. There is one hand for the bank and two player hands, one at each side of the table. The table layout is divided at the center by a heavy line.

Players may wager on either player hand, right or left; or they may wager on both by placing their money *à cheval,* that is, across the line. If one side wins and the other loses, a bet placed in this manner is a standoff and no one wins or loses. If both sides lose, the bet is lost; if both sides win, the bet is won.

When all wagers have been placed, the croupier deals one face-down card to the player on his right, one to the player on his left and one to himself. He repeats this procedure and, when each has two cards, the hands are checked. If any of the three has a count of 8 or 9, it must be turned face up and the other two hands are exposed, ending the play. Bets are paid off as in Chemin de Fer. When either player holds an 8 or 9, the player on the dealer's right acts first. He draws or stands, according to the Chemin de Fer rules, and has the option to draw or stand with a 5. Then the player on the left acts and is guided by the same rules.

When the players have completed their hands, it becomes the bank's turn to play. Here is where considerable judgment and skill on the banker's part come into play. In this version of Baccarat-en-Banque, the banker doesn't have any restrictions: he may stand or draw a card as he pleases; he is really the only one who has any opportunity to exercise judgment in the play of his hand. It must be remembered that the banker will mentally total the amount wagered on each side of the table, and will draw or stand to try and beat the side betting the most money. Example: The banker has 5, the player on his left has drawn a 10 and the player on his right did not draw. The banker will stand or draw depending on which side has bet the most money. If the left-hand player is the big bettor, the bank will stand on 5. The reasoning is that the player on the left, having drawn a 10, has a count of 0, 1, 2, 3, 4 or 5. The banker is about a 5 to 1 favorite to win the big bet. If the right side has the big wager, the banker will calculate the difference between bets and then decide whether to draw or stay.

One reason Baccarat-en-Banque has not made any headway in the United States is that it is open to all sorts of cheating—especially player cheats who signal their card count to a banker cheat so that, in a short time, the bank must win all the money in sight. The cheats split the take later, and the honest player hasn't a chance.

17.
Scarney Baccarat

HISTORY OF THE GAME

Scarney Baccarat is the first really new casino banking card game in the past century. This new game, which I invented, combines the principles of the great casino games of Baccarat–Chemin de Fer, Baccarat-en-Banque, Bank Craps and Black Jack, plus several entirely new game principles. Scarney Baccarat was first introduced at the Curaçao Hilton Hotel Casino in Curaçao, Netherlands Antilles, and spread rapidly to Nevada, England, Turkey, France, Italy, Yugoslavia, North Africa and around the world. (Scarney Baccarat is a "proprietary" game —its designs and name are trademarked and its rules of play are copyrighted. No part of this game can be reproduced in any form without written permission from the owner and distributor, John Scarne Games, Inc., 4319 Meadowview Ave., North Bergen, N.J. 07047.)

SCARNE'S RULES OF PLAY FOR SCARNEY BACCARAT

Requirements: The following are required to play Scarney Baccarat:

1. A regulation Scarney Baccarat table with six or seven betting spaces on its layout.

2. A dealer (houseman) who deals the game and functions as the banker, collecting player's losing bets and paying off player's winning bets.

3. One to six or seven players, each of whom may bet on one to three hands, depending on the betting spaces available.

4. A card-dealing box called a shoe.

480

5. Four standard packs of 52 cards each, shuffled together and used as one, a total of 208 cards dealt as a single deck.

6. Two indicator cards. One is used by players to cut the deck and the other indicator card is used to determine the end of the deal.

Value of cards: The ace is the lowest-ranking card and has a point value of 1. Kings, queens and jacks have a value of 10 each. All other cards have their numerical face value. The deuce is counted as 2, the three is counted as 3, the four is counted as 4, etc. The suits have no value.

Object of the game: Each player tries to obtain a higher total card count than the dealer by holding a combination of two or three cards totaling 9 or as close as possible to 9, or to a two-digit number ending in 9. Examples: $1 + 8$ gives point 9; $2 + 5$ gives point 7; $3 + 1$ gives point 4; and so forth. When the total of the cards is a two-digit number, only the last digit has any value. Examples: $10 + 9$ gives point 9; $9 + 3 + 1$ gives point 3; $1 + 3 + 10$ gives point 4; $6 + 7 + 9$ gives point 2; and so forth.

A player, at his proper turn of play and at his own discretion, regardless of the value of his two-card count, may stand or may draw a third card in an attempt to better his card count.

The shuffle and cut: The cards are shuffled by the dealer who then hands a player an indicator card and says, "Cut please." The player inserts the indicator card into the deck to show where he wants the cards cut.

The dealer cuts the cards at this position, putting the indicator and all the cards above it on the bottom. The indicator goes to the bottom of the pocket. The dealer then inserts the second indicator card 60 cards or thereabouts from the bottom of the deck and places all the cards into the dealing box face down. The dealer next deals three cards from the shoe and puts them to one side out of play. The shoe is now ready to be dealt by the dealer. When the indicator card inserted by the dealer makes its appearance, and enough cards from below the indicator card have been dealt to complete the round in progress, the deal ends. The dealer must begin a new shuffle, repeating the above procedure.

Betting: Before the deal begins, each player must place his bet, in chips, in one of the rectangular betting spaces that are painted on the playing surface; all bets are in full view of the dealer. I repeat, players may place bets on one to three betting spaces providing there are available holes (betting spaces). When a player places bets on more than one betting space at a time, he must play the hand farthest to his right to completion before being permitted to play his next hand or hands.

The deal: After all players' bets are down, the dealer, starting with the player on his extreme left, begins dealing clockwise. He gives one card face up to each player and one face up to himself. He next deals each player, starting with the player on his extreme left, a second face-up card and one face-down card to himself.

Player's turn at play: The player to the dealer's extreme left makes the first play of the hand. He may elect to stay or draw.

1. To stay: Either he is satisfied with his two-card count or he fears that a third and final card may reduce his count. He says, "No card," "I have enough," "I stand" or "Good."

2. To draw the third and final card: When a player is not satisfied with his count, he says, "Hit me," "Give me a card," makes a beckoning motion by closing his hand or makes a come-on motion with a finger. The dealer then deals a third and final card from the shoe face up before the player and next to his original two face-up cards. A player isn't permitted to draw more than one card. Each dealt hand remains in front of the player or players.

The play moves to the player's left, clockwise, around the table until all players have played out their hands. At this time it becomes the dealer's turn.

The dealer's turn at play: After all the players have played out their hand or hands, the dealer must play his hand and abide by the following rules:

1. He turns up his hole card so that his two cards are exposed.

2. If his count is 5, 6, 7, 8 or 9, the dealer must stay. He is not permitted to draw a third card.

3. If his count is 0, 1, 2, 3 or 4, he must draw a third and final card, after which he must stay. However, if a dealer's three-card count totals zero (0), and is made up of three 10-count cards, he must continue to draw cards until his total count is anything except zero (0). This is called the *Scarney baccarat* or *baccarat*. With the above exception, every Scarney Baccarat hand is made up of either two or three cards.

Final settlement: At the end of his play, the dealer starts with the first active player on his extreme right and moves around the table to the left; he pays off players who have a higher count than his with an amount equal to the bet they placed, and collects the placed bets from players showing a lesser count. If a player and the dealer have the same count, it is standoff or tie, and no one collects or loses. A total three-card count has the same value as a similar total two-card count. Example: A 9 count made with three cards ties a 9 count made with two cards. (The same holds true for a Scarney Baccarat hand of 3, 4, 5 or more cards.)

Splitting pairs: Any two aces, cards that are identical, regardless of their suits, may be treated as a pair. Also, any two cards each having a count of 10 (totaling zero) may be treated as a pair, such as two tens, two jacks, two queens, two kings, or a combination of any of the two above 10-count cards; such a combination is called baccarat. Each of the above pairs, at the discretion of the player, may be treated as the first card dealt of two separate hands.

A player being dealt two cards forming a pair on the initial round may, if he chooses, separate one from another and treat each card as the first card dealt in two separate hands.

When the pairs are split, the player's original bet is placed on one of these cards and an equal amount must be bet on the other card. The player is then dealt a second and final card face down on the face-up card on his right and then a second and final card face down on the other face-up card. When splitting pairs, at no time is a player permitted to draw a third card on any hand.

Players are not permitted to look at a face-down card until the dealer turns it face up after the deal has been completed.

The double-down bet: A player after being dealt his first two cards (which may be any two cards) may elect to double his original bet before drawing his third card. This is known as a double down or *down for double*. A player at his turn of play, and before calling "Down for double" or "Double down," must place an amount equal to the original bet on the betting space. The player is then dealt a third and final face-down card on the two face-up cards. The player isn't permitted to look at his face-down card until the dealer turns it face up after the deal has been completed.

The Scarney insurance bet: If the dealer's face-up card is a 9 count, players (at the dealer's turn of play) may elect to make an insurance bet against a loss or standoff to the dealer's possible two-card 9 count (9 + 10), called *Scarney*. The dealer, before turning his hole card face up, inquires if any player wants *Scarney insurance*. A player who desires insurance places an amount equal to half his present wager toward the center of the table.

After the dealer faces his hole card, if it is a 10 count, he calls "Scarney" and each insurance bettor is paid off at the rate of 2 to 1 for each unit wagered. If the card is not a 10 count, the dealer collects the player's insurance bet and continues to play out his hand.

The Scarney Baccarat insurance bet: After the dealer faces his hole card (at dealer's turn of play) and his initial two dealt cards are both 10 counts, players may elect to make the Scarney Baccarat insurance bet. The dealer, before drawing his third card, inquires if any player wants Scarney Baccarat insurance. A player who desires the Scarney Baccarat insurance places an amount equal to half his present wager toward the center of the table.

After the dealer draws his third card, if it is a 10 count he calls "Scarney Baccarat" and each insurance bettor is paid off at a rate of 2 to 1 for each unit wagered; the dealer continues to play out his hand. If the card is not a 10 count, the dealer collects the players' insurance bets and that ends the play. If the dealer's third dealt card is a 10 count, a second Scarney Baccarat insurance bet is permitted. Should the dealer's fourth dealt card be a 10 count, a third Scarney Baccarat insurance bet is allowed; and so its goes, insurance bet after insurance bet, until the dealer fails to draw a 10-count card and the hand ends.

The side bets: Scarney Baccarat layouts have betting spaces marked 5–6–7–8–9, and above these numbers appears the phrase "Each Pays 10 for 1." Before a new deal begins, the player places his side bet by betting on a specified number or numbers, betting that on the next round of play the dealer's first two cards will total the count he bet on. The dealer pays off such winning bets at odds of 10 for 1. These wagers are also called *propositions*.

Field bet: The field bears the numbers 5, 6, 7, 8, 9. When a player put his bet on the space of the layout marked "Field," he is betting that on the next round of play the combined count of the dealer's first two dealt cards will be 5, 6, 7, 8 or 9. The dealer pays off winning bets at even money. If the dealer's first two cards total 0, 1, 2, 3 or 4, the players lose their field bets.

A dealer's two-card 9 count comprised of a 9 and 10 is known as "Scarney." A count of zero with two or three cards is known as "baccarat." A dealer's count of zero with three or more 10-count cards is known as "Scarney baccarat."

A player is not permitted to double down on a split pair.

Optional protective deal rule for Scarney Baccarat: To help protect both casino management and players from being cheated by worn, bent, defaced or marked cards by either house employees or player cheats, and to help avoid a conspiracy between both house cheats and player cheats, the following optional deal rule is recommended.

After all players bets are down (field and side bets included) the dealer, starting with the player on his extreme left, begins dealing clockwise dealing one card face up to each player and one face up to himself. He next deals each player starting with the player on his extreme left a second face-up card—but omits dealing himself (the dealer) a second card. After all players have finished playing their hands, the dealer removes (discards) the top card of the card packet and places it in the discard receiver without showing its face value. Next, the dealer deals himself his second face-up card and the standard rules follow. However, if the dealer's first up-card is a nine spot, he must inquire if any player desires a Scarney insurance bet immediately after players have played their hands and prior to discarding the top card of the card packet.

SCARNEY BACCARAT STRATEGY

Before giving a mathematical analysis of the game, I would like to point out that, in Scarney Baccarat, a player can't bust his hand as in Black Jack. A player's cards are always in play until the dealer completes his play and the payoff takes place. In Scarney Baccarat the house advantage is the result of the dealer's special play of the game. If the dealer's three-card total is zero and is made up of three 10 count cards, the dealer continues to draw cards until his final count is different from zero. This is the only time a Scarney Baccarat hand contains more than three cards. It isn't feasible, of course, to figure the exact percentage against individual players because their playing differs so much. Some players will stay on a count of 5 or more; some will draw on 5 and 6; others stay on 4 or more; and there's always the hero who will hit a 7 or an 8. However, the rules allow the dealer no choice of staying or drawing: he must draw to a count of 4 or less and stay on a count of 5 or more. A house P.C. can be calculated for a player who matches dealer's play (and thus does not split pairs or double down).

If the player adheres to the dealer's fixed strategy, and doesn't split pairs or double down, the house percentage in which a hand consists of a play of the game which terminates in a win, loss, or tie is a low 2.44 percent. If a tie isn't counted as a trial, then the house advantage is 2.71 percent. In other words, Scarney Baccarat will appear on the average of about once in 37 deals. I must reemphasize one fact you should not forget: the only positive advantage in favor of the bank is the 2.44 percent that it gains through a Scarney Baccarat.

There are several situations which, played properly, give the player an opportunity to cut down this house percentage. Most players handle these situations so inexpertly that, instead of reducing the percentage they are bucking, they add to it. Here are the playing factors which can be utilized to the player's advantage:

1. The player actually knows a little more than the dealer because one of the dealer's two initial cards is dealt face up—this gives the player important information about his possible card count. The rules

John Scarne playing Scarney Baccarat (his own casino game invention) in the Istanbul Hilton Hotel Casino in Istanbul, Turkey, in 1974. (Turkish News Bureau)

governing the dealer's play prevent him from making use of similar information about the player's hand, even if the latter's first two cards were dealt face up.

2. Unlike the dealer, the player can stay or draw on any count he wants. At one turn of play he may draw to a count of 3, 4, 5, or more; and at other times he may stand on the same count. In some situations this is advantageous to the player.

3. The player can decide whether or not he wants to double down or split pairs, a strategy denied to the dealer.

4. The player may play one to three hands when there are available betting spaces; the dealer can only play one hand.

5. The player is the one who decides the amount of the bet and can raise or lower it at will within the prescribed betting limits.

6. The player may case the deck. If he can remember the cards previously dealt or exposed, this knowledge will greatly improve his chances of winning.

If you adhere to the strategy that I shall outline for you in the following pages, I promise that you can cut down the house 2.44 percent considerably. The strategy utilizes these factors: the dealer must hit a 4 or less and stand on 5 or more; the knowledge of the dealer's face-up (exposed) card; the player's total count; when it is to your advantage to stand, to draw, to split pairs, and to double down.

Playing according to upcoming information will assure you that you are fighting an average house advantage of considerably less than 2 percent. However, my strategy doesn't guarantee that you will win—it simply cuts down the house percentage to its lowest possible level and gives you a much better opportunity to win than any other method of Scarney Baccarat play.

SCARNEY BACCARAT STRATEGY TABLE

Hit-and-Stand Strategy:

1. When the dealer's upcard is anything, stand on a count of 6, 7, 8, or 9.

2. When the dealer's upcard is anything, draw to a count of 0, 1, 2, 3, or 4.

3. When the dealer's upcard is 0, 1, 5, 6, 8, or 9, draw to a count of 5.

Splitting pairs:

1. Split threes when the dealer's upcard is 7, 8, or 9.

2. Split fives when the dealer's upcard is 1, 2, 3, 4, or 5.

3. Split sixes when the dealer's upcard is 0, 1, 2, 3, 4, 5, or 6.

4. Split sevens when the dealer's upcard is 0, 1, 2, 3, 4, 5, 6, or 7.

5. Split eights when the dealer's upcard is 7.

Doubling down: Double down on a count of 4 when the dealer's upcard is 0, 1, 2, 3, or 4.

Double down on a count of 3 when the dealer's upcard is 0, 1, 2, 3, 4, or 5.

Double down on a count of 2 when the dealer's upcard is 0, 1, or 2.

Scarney insurance bet. Whenever the dealer shows a nine as his upcard, he will invite you to place an additional wager (called Scarney insurance) equal to half the amount already bet, which will pay you 2 to 1 if the dealer's down card is a 10-count card, and which you will lose if it is not. In this optional bet, you are thus "insuring" your hand against the possibility of a loss to a dealer Scarney. In order for this bet to be a profitable bet, more than one-third of the undealt cards must be a 10-count cards. This is not very often the case, so let's take a look at the usual odds. If the dealer's upcard is a nine, and you have no knowledge of any other cards, the quadruple deck would contain 64 10-count cards.

Suppose you do not look at your own cards, nor do you see any of the other players' cards prior to taking the insurance. Then the dealer's

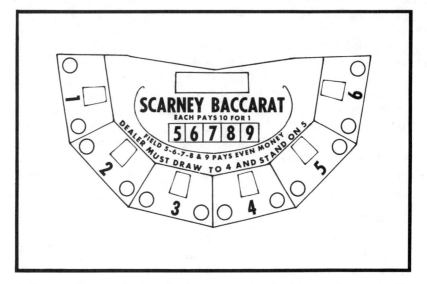

A Scarney Baccarat layout, the first new casino banking card game in the past century.

down card may be considered drawn at random from the 207 cards that remain unseen. Clearly, 64 of these cards are 10-counts and the other 143 are not 10-counts. The odds are 143 to 64 against the dealer having a 10-count in the hole. The payoff is 128 to 64, approximately 7% against the player. As a general rule, I don't recommend insurance betting. However, the casual card caser (counter) can use the insurance bet advantageously if he has been keeping track of 10-count cards in previous hands. *Example:* Suppose half the deck (104 cards) has been dealt and the casual card caser recalls that only 12 10-count cards have been dealt. If an insurance bet could be made on the next deal, it would be wise to take insurance because the player has an edge of more than 33% over the house on this bet.

Scarney Baccarat insurance. The house advantage in Scarney insurance also holds true when placing a Scarney Baccarat insurance bet.

Proposition or side bets. In addition to the preceding wagers, Scarney Baccarat layouts have spaces marked 5, 6, 7, 8, or 9, and above these numbers appears the phrase "Each Pays 10 for 1." A bet placed on a 5 means that the player is betting that the dealer, on the next turn of play, will hold a count of 5 with his first two dealt cards. The dealer pays off such winning bets at 10 for 1 and since the correct odds are 9 23/64 to 1, the house enjoys an advantage of 3.46%. The same house percentage holds true for the numbers 7 and 9.

When a player places a bet on the 6 (same rules apply as on the 9), he is again paid off at 10 for 1. But since the correct odds on being dealt a count of 6 in the first two cards are 9 43/62 to 1, the house enjoys an advantage of 6.48%. The same holds true for number 8.

Field Bet. When a player places a bet on the space of the layout marked "Field" he is betting that the dealer's first two dealt cards on the next round will total a count of 5, 6, 7, 8, or 9. The dealer pays such winning bets at even money. The dealer may be dealt 1,326 different two-card counts, of which 632 comprise the field (5, 6, 7, 8, and 9) and 694 comprise the losing numbers (0, 1, 2, 3, and 4). When we subtract 632 winning two-card counts from the 694 losing two-card counts, we find the field bettor has a disadvantage of 62 two-card counts for a dealer's edge of 4.67%.

18.
Keno:
Nevada's Solitaire
Bingo-Type Game

Racehorse Keno, a variation of old-fashioned Keno, is played in most gambling establishments in Nevada and many illegal gambling joints situated in the western United States. Before the acquisition by big business of the major casinos on the Las Vegas Strip, Keno, by Strip standards, was looked down at as a cheap gambling pastime for tourists. Today, however, Strip casinos such as Caesar's Palace, Dunes, Las Vegas Hilton, Frontier, and Sands have replaced their cocktail lounges (which previously boasted of round-the-clock star-studded entertainment) with Keno parlors. Their electric Keno tally boards are situated throughout the casino and adjacent restaurants, and if you happen to be in the restaurant, a traveling Keno girl will place your bets for you while you're dining.

PLAYING RULES

Racehorse Keno—today generally called just Keno—differs from regular Keno in several ways. The old Keno, like Bingo, required large numbers of players for successful operation; the purchase price of a Keno or Bingo ticket was the same for all players, and games were usually run one night a week, each session lasting only a few hours. Racehorse Keno, on the other hand, can be dealt to one or more players; each player can wager any amount he likes on a single ticket provided it is within the house betting limits, and the Racehorse Keno parlors in Nevada operate 24 hours a day, with a new game dealt every few minutes.

Racehorse Keno parlors seating from 50 to over 300 players are usually located in a prominent part of the casino. They contain several

490

John Scarne in the Horseshoe Club in downtown Las Vegas, directing the operation of a Keno game. (Las Vegas News Bureau)

tables loaded with Keno *outside tickets,* and the players are supplied with ink and brushes or black crayon. Each ticket bears the numbers 1 through 80 and the player marks on his ticket the numbers he wishes to play and the sum he is wagering. He presents his cash and the marked outside ticket at the Keno counter where the dealer makes two duplicates by punching out the numbers on an *inside ticket* which bears the 80 numbers and also the number of the game to be played and the name of the casino. The dealer gives the player one copy and retains the original and the other copy. These are checked after the

(LEFT) *Outside ticket marked by the player and, after the game, stamped and displayed to show that player won $25,000.* (RIGHT) *An inside ticket is a duplicate of player's ticket with punched holes replacing ink marks. (Dick Graves' Nugget)*

game has been played and are paid off if the ticket wins. If seated in a casino restaurant, the player simply marks his ticket with a black crayon and hands the marked ticket and cash to a traveling Keno girl who handles all the details.

A Bingo blower behind the Keno counter contains 80 numbered Ping-Pong balls and 20 of these are drawn. As each ball is drawn, its number is called and flashed on the electrically lighted tally board. When the 20th ball has been drawn, the game ends. A great number of different bets can be made at Racehorse Keno because the players can select various combinations of numbers. A 1-spot ticket is one on which a player has marked, and is betting on, a single number. If that number appears in the 20 drawn numbers, the player wins. If he marks two numbers it is a 2-spot ticket, and he wins if both numbers appear among the 20 which are drawn. He may mark and bet on groups of as many as 15 numbers, but the most popular ticket is the 10 spot.

The player selects ten numbers, marks his ticket, gives it with the amount of his bet to the dealer and receives a punched duplicate. The player wins if 5 or more of his numbers appear in the 20 drawn numbers.

Many different combinations can be bet. On a high-low ticket the player marks 3 groups of 4 connecting numbers. If 1, 2, 3, 4 or none of his 12 selected numbers is drawn, he wins nothing. If he catches 5 spots, the payoff varies according to the location of the numbers. If 2 numbers are in one group, 2 in a second and 1 in the third, he is paid 20¢. A 3–1–1 arrangement of the numbers is paid 25¢; a 3–2 arrangement, 30¢, and a 4–1 arrangement, 35¢. The payoffs for catching 6, 7, 8, 9, 10 and 11 spots are shown on the high-low ticket list below. The high payoff for catching all 12 spots (4–4–4) is $1,296.

The player can also bet groups of 4, 5, 2 and 3 spots as shown under high-low ways, 10 spot, deuce ways and 9 spot. A typical casino's payout chart listing the bets permitted and the payoff odds on each is reproduced on page 494.

Other bets not listed on the chart are used by some casinos, such as the three-way eight ticket in which the player marks three groups of four adjacent numbers. He must catch four numbers in each of two groups to collect the minimum payoff. A four-way 10 spot is four groups of three adjacent numbers plus a single number called a "king." For a minimum win the player must catch five numbers within three groups, plus the king. There are also three-way nine tickets and others.

CALCULATING THE HOUSE PERCENTAGE AT RACEHORSE KENO

First, let us analyze the simple 1-spot ticket on which the player has marked only one of the 80 numbers and which, when his number appears among the 20 drawn numbers, pays him $3.20 for a $1 bet.

To figure the house percentage let's assume that you mark 80 tickets, betting on a different number on each. At $1 per ticket this costs you a total of $80. Since you are betting on every possible number, each of the 20 drawn balls gives you a winner. You collect $3.20 on each for a total of $64. Subtract this from the $80 bet and your loss is $16. Divide $16 by $80 and you find that the house has a favorable edge on a 1-spot ticket of 20%.

On the 2-spot ticket the player has marked 2 of the 80 numbers, and if they appear among the 20 drawn numbers he is paid off at 13 for 1. Here we must find the number of two-digit combinations which are possible with 80 numbers. The calculation is $\frac{80 \times 79}{1 \times 2} = 3160$. Suppose you bet $1 on each of these 3,160 two-number combinations for a total wager of $3,160. After 20 numbers have been called, you will hold $\frac{20 \times 19}{1 \times 2}$, or 190 winning tickets and, at 13 for 1, will collect $13 on each, a total of $2,470. Since you bet $3,160, your loss is $690. Divide your loss by the total amount bet and you find that the house has a favorable edge of 21.8%. The same method can be used to find the house percentage on all the other tickets. —

$25,000.00
LIMIT — EACH GAME
TO AGGREGATE PLAYERS

HIGH-LOW TICKET, 12 SPOTS
3 groups of 4—35c rate pays

5 Spots	2-2-1 pays	$ .20
	3-1-1 pays	.25
	3-2 pays	.30
	4-1 pays	.35
6 Spots	2-2-2 pays	1.50
	3-2-1 pays	1.80
	3-3 pays	2.40
	4-1-1 pays	2.40
	4-2 pays	2.65
7 Spots	3-2-2 pays	11.35
	3-3-1 pays	14.25
	4-2-1 pays	17.15
	4-3 pays	23.00
8 Spots	3-3-2 pays	76.50
	4-2-2 pays	87.70
	4-3-1 pays	98.85
	4-4 pays	132.30
9 Spots	3-3-3 pays	194.40
	4-3-2 pays	198.00
	4-4-1 pays	205.20
10 Spots	4-3-3 pays	432.00
	4-4-2 pays	450.00
11 Spots	4-4-3 pays	756.00
12 Spots	4-4-4 pays	1296.00

HIGH-LOW WAYS
(Groups of 4)

12 Spots,	1 way	Cost $ .35
16 Spots,	4 ways	Cost 1.40
20 Spots,	10 ways	Cost 3.50
24 Spots,	20 ways	Cost 7.00
28 Spots,	35 ways	Cost 12.25
32 Spots,	56 ways	Cost 19.60
36 Spots,	84 ways	Cost 29.40
40 Spots,	120 ways	Cost 42.00

'10 SPOT
5c Per Way Ticket
(Groups of 5)

15 Spots,	3 ways	Cost $ .30
20 Spots,	6 ways	Cost .30
25 Spots,	10 ways	Cost .50
30 Spots,	15 ways	Cost .75
35 Spots,	21 ways	Cost 1.05
40 Spots,	28 ways	Cost 1.40
45 Spots,	36 ways	Cost 1.80
50 Spots,	45 ways	Cost 2.25
55 Spots,	55 ways	Cost 2.75
60 Spots,	66 ways	Cost 3.30
65 Spots,	78 ways	Cost 3.90
70 Spots,	91 ways	Cost 4.55
75 Spots,	105 ways	Cost 5.25
80 Spots,	120 ways	Cost 6.00

DEUCE WAYS
(Groups of 2)

12 Spots,	6 ways	Cost $ .30
14 Spots,	21 ways	Cost 1.05
16 Spots,	56 ways	Cost 2.80
18 Spots,	126 ways	Cost 6.30
20 Spots,	252 ways	Cost 12.60

9 SPOT
(Groups of 3)

9 Spots,	1 way	Cost $ .35
12 Spots,	4 ways	Cost 1.40
15 Spots,	10 ways	Cost 3.50
18 Spots,	20 ways	Cost 7.00
21 Spots,	35 ways	Cost 12.25
24 Spots,	56 ways	Cost 19.60
27 Spots,	84 ways	Cost 29.40
30 Spots,	120 ways	Cost 42.00

1-SPOT ($1.00 Minimum)

Spots	$1.00 Ticket	$2.00 Ticket	$3.00 Ticket
1	$ 3.20	$ 6.40	$ 9.60

2-SPOT (25c Minimum)

Spots	$ .25 Ticket	$ .50 Ticket	$1.00 Ticket
2	$ 3.25	$ 6.50	$ 13.00

3-SPOT (25c Minimum)

Spots	$ .25 Ticket	$ .50 Ticket	$1.00 Ticket
2	$ .25	$ .50	$ 1.00
3	11.75	23.50	47.00

4-SPOT (25c Minimum)

Spots	$ .25 Ticket	$ .50 Ticket	$1.00 Ticket
2	$ .25	$ .50	$ 1.00
3	1.25	2.50	5.00
4	29.50	59.00	118.00

5-SPOT RATE

Spots	50c Ticket	$1.00 Ticket	$5.00 Ticket
3	$ 1.50	$ 3.00	$ 15.00
4	13.00	26.00	130.00
5	166.00	332.00	1,660.00

6-SPOT RATE

Spots	50c Ticket	$1.00 Ticket	$5.00 Ticket
3	$ .50	$ 1.00	$ 5.00
4	2.80	5.60	28.00
5	55.00	110.00	550.00
6	620.00	1,240.00	6,200.00

8-SPOT RATE

Spots	50c Ticket	$1.00 Ticket	$7.00 Ticket
4	$ .80	$ 1.60	$ 11.20
5	7.20	14.40	100.80
6	53.90	107.80	754.60
7	402.50	805.00	5,635.00
8	1,920.00	3,840.00	25,000.00

9-SPOT RATE

Spots	35c Ticket	70c Ticket	$1.05 Ticket	$4.20 Ticket
4	$ .15	$ .30	$ .45	$ 1.80
5	1.80	3.60	5.40	21.60
6	17.80	35.60	53.40	213.60
7	110.70	221.40	332.10	1,328.40
8	1,000.00	2,000.00	3,000.00	12,000.00
9	2,250.00	4,500.00	6,750.00	25,000.00

Spots	50c Ticket	$1.00 Ticket	$2.00 Ticket	$4.00 Ticket
4	$ .20	$ .40	$ .80	$ 1.60
5	2.55	5.10	10.20	20.40
6	25.40	50.80	101.60	203.20
7	158.10	316.20	632.40	1,264.80
8	1,428.55	2,857.10	5,714.20	11,428.40
9	3,214.20	6,428.40	12,856.80	25,000.00

10-SPOT RATE

Spots	25c Ticket	50c Ticket	$1.00 Ticket	$2.50 Ticket
5	$ .50	$ 1.00	$ 2.00	$ 5.00
6	4.50	9.00	18.00	45.00
7	45.00	90.00	180.00	450.00
8	325.00	650.00	1,300.00	3,250.00
9	650.00	1,300.00	2,600.00	6,500.00
10	2,500.00	5,000.00	10,000.00	25,000.00

11-SPOT RATE

Spots	$ .55 Ticket	$1.10 Ticket	$2.75 Ticket
5	$ .60	$ 1.20	$ 3.00
6	5.10	10.20	25.50
7	42.30	84.60	211.50
8	267.00	534.00	1,335.00
9	845.00	1,690.00	4,225.00
10	1,800.00	3,600.00	9,000.00
11	5,500.00	11,000.00	25,000.00

12-SPOT RATE

Spots	$ .40 Ticket	$ .80 Ticket	$2.40 Ticket
5	$ .25	$ .50	$ 1.50
6	2.25	4.50	13.50
7	14.95	29.90	89.70
8	85.20	170.40	511.20
9	299.25	598.50	1,795.50
10	720.25	1,440.50	4,321.50
11	1,533.25	3,066.50	9,199.50
12	4,000.00	8,000.00	24,000.00

13-SPOT RATE

Spots	$ .95 Ticket	$2.85 Ticket	$5.70 Ticket
5	$ .35	$ 1.10	$ 2.20
6	2.85	8.55	17.10
7	17.70	53.10	106.20
8	100.10	300.30	600.60
9	360.10	1,080.30	2,160.60
10	950.30	2,851.00	5,702.00
11	2,035.00	6,105.00	12,210.00
12	4,110.00	12,330.00	24,660.00
13	9,540.00	25,000.00	25,000.00

14-SPOT RATE

Spots	$1.25 Ticket	$5.00 Ticket	$10.00 Ticket
5	$ .30	$ 1.25	$ 2.50
6	2.30	9.25	18.50
7	13.40	53.50	107.00
8	70.65	282.65	565.30
9	253.25	1,013.05	2,026.10
10	694.00	2,775.90	5,551.80
11	1,552.40	6,209.50	12,419.00
12	3,060.00	12,240.00	24,480.00
13	5,900.00	23,600.00	25,000.00
14	13,000.00	25,000.00	25,000.00

15-SPOT RATE

Spots	$1.50 Ticket	$7.50 Ticket	$15.00 Ticket
5	$ .25	$ 1.25	$ 2.50
6	1.80	9.00	18.00
7	9.80	48.85	97.70
8	48.85	244.20	488.40
9	172.35	861.70	1,723.40
10	480.00	2,400.00	4,800.00
11	1,107.45	5,537.30	11,074.60
12	2,225.00	11,125.00	22,250.00
13	4,130.00	20,650.00	25,000.00
14	7,700.00	25,000.00	25,000.00
15	16,000.00	25,000.00	25,000.00

DEALER WILL BE GLAD TO EXPLAIN ANY TICKET TO YOU

THE BREAKDOWN ON THE 10-SPOT TICKET

Of the tens of millions of dollars wagered annually at Racehorse Keno, about 80% is bet on the 10-spot ticket. This one isn't easy to figure. Thousands of Keno players have wondered just what their chances were of hitting the ten numbers on a 10-spot ticket. During the past year, many Nevada Keno operators, hearing that I had worked out the mathematical breakdown of the 10-spot ticket, asked me for it, but I withheld it for this book, where it now appears in print for the first time.

To calculate the probability that a specified 10 numbers will appear among 20 numbers which are drawn from a group of 80, we must first find out how many different combinations of 10 numbers can be formed with 80 numbers. In mathematical language, we are looking for the number of combinations of n things taken r at a first time. The formula is: $\dfrac{n(n-1)\,(n-2)\cdots(n-r+1)}{r!}$. We substitute 80 for n and 10 for r and get the equation that follows.

Punched inside tickets are fed into a machine which counts, sorts and locates the winning tickets at game's end. (Dick Graves' Nugget)

Keno charts which players receive listing the various wagers that may be made. (Dick Graves' Nugget)

$$\frac{80 \times 79 \times 78 \times 77 \times 76 \times 75 \times 74 \times 73 \times 72 \times 71}{10 \times 9 \times 8 \times 7 \times 6 \times 5 \times 4 \times 3 \times 2 \times 1} = 1,646,492,110,120$$

Step number two consists in discovering how many different combinations of 10 numbers can be formed with the 20 drawn numbers:

$$\frac{20 \times 19 \times 18 \times 17 \times 16 \times 15 \times 14 \times 13 \times 12 \times 11}{10 \times 9 \times 8 \times 7 \times 6 \times 5 \times 4 \times 3 \times 2 \times 1} = 184,756$$

Step number three: We find the number of combinations of groups of 9 numbers which can be formed with 20 drawn balls:

$$\frac{20 \times 19 \times 18 \times 17 \times 16 \times 15 \times 14 \times 13 \times 12}{9 \times 8 \times 7 \times 6 \times 5 \times 4 \times 3 \times 2 \times 1} = 167,960$$

We must then calculate the number of ways these winning 9-group combinations can be formed with the 60 remaining numbers in the total of 80 balls: $167,960 \times 60 = 10,077,600$. This is the total possible number of ways 9 numbers plus one other number can be made.

We apply this same method to find the total possible combinations of 8 numbers, 7 numbers, 6 numbers, 5 numbers, 4 numbers, 3 numbers, 2 numbers, 1 number and 0 (zero) numbers.

Groups of 8 numbers:

$$\frac{20 \times 19 \times 18 \times 17 \times 16 \times 15 \times 14 \times 13}{8 \times 7 \times 6 \times 5 \times 4 \times 3 \times 2 \times 1} = 125,970$$

$$\frac{125,970 \times (60 \times 59)}{2 \times 1} = 222,966,900$$

Groups of 7 numbers:

$$\frac{20 \times 19 \times 18 \times 17 \times 16 \times 15 \times 14}{7 \times 6 \times 5 \times 4 \times 3 \times 2 \times 1} = 77,520$$

$$\frac{77,520 \times (60 \times 59 \times 58)}{1 \times 2 \times 3} = 2,652,734,400$$

Groups of 6 numbers:

$$\frac{20 \times 19 \times 18 \times 17 \times 16 \times 15}{6 \times 5 \times 4 \times 3 \times 2 \times 1} = 38,760$$

$$\frac{38,760 \times (60 \times 59 \times 58 \times 57)}{4 \times 3 \times 2 \times 1} = 18,900,732,600$$

Groups of 5 numbers:

$$\frac{20 \times 19 \times 18 \times 17 \times 16}{5 \times 4 \times 3 \times 2 \times 1} = 15,504$$

$$\frac{15,504 \times (60 \times 59 \times 58 \times 57 \times 56)}{5 \times 4 \times 3 \times 2 \times 1} = 84,675,282,048$$

Groups of 4 numbers: (Since no payoffs are made on 4 numbers or fewer of a 10-spot ticket, the double calculation above can be combined into one.)

$$\frac{(20 \times 19 \times 18 \times 17) \times (60 \times 59 \times 58 \times 57 \times 56 \times 55)}{(4 \times 3 \times 2 \times 1) \times (6 \times 5 \times 4 \times 3 \times 2 \times 1)} = 242,559,401,700$$

Groups of 3 numbers:

$$\frac{(20 \times 19 \times 18) \times (60 \times 59 \times 58 \times 57 \times 56 \times 55 \times 54)}{(3 \times 2 \times 1) \times (7 \times 6 \times 5 \times 4 \times 3 \times 2 \times 1)} = 440,275,888,800$$

Groups of 2 numbers:

$$\frac{(20 \times 19) \times (60 \times 59 \times 58 \times 57 \times 56 \times 55 \times 54 \times 53)}{(2 \times 1) \times (8 \times 7 \times 6 \times 5 \times 4 \times 3 \times 2 \times 1)} = 486{,}137{,}960{,}550$$

Groups of 1 number:

$$\frac{(20) \times (60 \times 59 \times 58 \times 57 \times 56 \times 55 \times 54 \times 53 \times 52)}{(1) \times (9 \times 8 \times 7 \times 6 \times 5 \times 4 \times 3 \times 2 \times 1)} = 295{,}662{,}853{,}200$$

Groups of no-hit numbers:

$$\frac{60 \times 59 \times 58 \times 57 \times 56 \times 55 \times 54 \times 53 \times 52 \times 51}{10 \times 9 \times 8 \times 7 \times 6 \times 5 \times 4 \times 3 \times 2 \times 1} = 75{,}394{,}027{,}566$$

Placed in tabular form the total number of possible combinations in a 10-spot ticket are as follows:

	Number of Ways	*Odds Against*
10 numbers	184,756	8,911,710 + to 1
9 numbers	10,077,600	163,380 + to 1
8 numbers	222,966,900	7,383 + to 1
7 numbers	2,652,734,400	619 + to 1
6 numbers	18,900,732,600	86 + to 1
5 numbers	84,675,282,048	18 + to 1
4 numbers	242,559,401,700	5 + to 1
3 numbers	440,275,888,800	2 + to 1
2 numbers	486,137,960,550	2 + to 1
1 number	295,662,853,200	4 + to 1
No numbers	75,394,027,566	20 + to 1
Total number of combinations	1,646,492,110,120	

We then add all the ways that the winning groups of 5 or more numbers can be formed:

10 numbers	184,756
9 numbers	10,077,600
8 numbers	222,966,900
7 numbers	2,652,734,400
6 numbers	18,900,732,600
5 numbers	84,675,282,048
	106,461,978,304

Now we divide the total number of winning ways into the total number of possible ways: $\dfrac{1{,}646{,}492{,}110{,}120}{106{,}461{,}978{,}304}$.

We get an answer of 15+, which means that the odds are 14 to 1. For every fifteen 10-spot tickets you purchase you can expect in the long run to collect on one winning ticket.

THE HOUSE PERCENTAGE ON THE 10-SPOT TICKET

To figure the house percentage on the 10-spot ticket we must refer to the payoff chart below which lists the payoffs on catching 5, 6, 7, 8, 9 and 10 numbers.

5 numbers pay 2 for 1
6 numbers pay 18 for 1
7 numbers pay 180 for 1
8 numbers pay 1,300 for 1
9 numbers pay 2,600 for 1
10 numbers pay 10,000 for 1

Again we suppose that you mark all the possible 10-spot tickets (1,646,492,110,120), which, at $1 each, will cost you $1,646,492,110,120. After the 20 numbers are drawn, you will find you have 106,461,-978,304 winning tickets ranging from 5 to 10 numbers. And here is what you collect:

Winning Numbers	Number of Winning Tickets		Amount Won on Each Ticket		Total Amount Collected on Each Winning Number
10	184,756	×	$10,000	=	$ 1,847,560,000
9	10,077,600	×	2,600	=	26,201,760,000
8	222,966,900	×	1,300	=	289,856,970,000
7	2,652,734,400	×	180	=	477,492,192,000
6	18,900,732,600	×	18	=	340,213,186,800
5	84,675,282,048	×	2	=	169,350,564,096
Total	106,461,978,304		Total money won		$1,304,962,232,896

Our final step is to subtract the total money won from the total amount bet: $1,646,492,110,120 minus $1,304,962,232,896. This gives a loss of $341,529,877,224, a favorable edge to the house of 20.74%.

When the house pays 25,000 for 1 on 10 numbers, 2,800 for 1 on 9 numbers, and 1,400 for 1 on 8 numbers, as some Nevada casinos do, the house edge is 19.10%.

HOUSE PERCENTAGES ON ALL TICKETS

The table opposite shows the percentages in favor of the house on all tickets from the 1 spot through the 15 spot, calculated on the payoff prices shown on page 494.

The 12-spot high-low ticket, 10-spot groups of 5, deuce ways groups of 2, 9-spot groups of 3 and similar tickets average about 25% against the player.

Ticket	House P.C.	Ticket	House P.C.
1 spot	20.0%	9 spot	21.2%
2 spot	21.8%	10 spot	20.7%
3 spot	26.4%	11 spot	25.6%
4 spot	24.7%	12 spot	18.9%
5 spot	21.5%	13 spot	20.1%
6 spot	21.3%	14 spot	23.1%
8 spot	20.2%	15 spot	23.8%

A final bit of advice to Racehorse Keno players. Don't gamble your money away expecting to win $25,000 on the 10-spot ticket, because this is about nine times more difficult than winning the $50,000 top prize in the New Jersey or New York State lottery, in which, by the way, the odds happen to be one in a million to win.

Players at the Mint watch light-up board as balls are drawn from the Keno blower and the numbers announced. (Las Vegas News Bureau)

19.
Casino
Side Games

Since casino operators, legal and illegal, seldom overlook an opportunity to grab an extra buck, any available space not suitable for a major standard casino game like Bank Craps, Black Jack or Roulette is usually occupied by one or more minor banking games known as *side games*. Most of these are games of chance of the carnival variety such as one finds at amusements centers, county and state fairs, American Legion and firemen's carnivals, and church bazaars.

The seven most popular side games, listed in order of their popularity, are: the Big Six, the Money Wheel, the Race Horse Wheel, Chuck-a-Luck, Hazard, Beat the Shaker, and Under and Over Seven.

The American gambling public loses about $500 million annually playing these games, of which $150 million is pocketed by the casino operators of the hundreds of big and small carpet and sawdust joints, and $350 million by the amusement centers, fairs, carnivals, bazaars and fund-raising affairs.

These side games are all clever exercises in mathematical strategy designed to give the operators a big favorable percentage and at the same time make it as difficult as possible for the player to calculate the percentage. Casino operators and carnival hustlers have learned by experience that these games will get the players' dough much faster and more surely than any of the major casino games. The reason is that the house percentage averages three or four times more, running from a minimum 8% to a high of more than 20%. Betting limits vary, ranging from 10¢ to $10 for some games and for others from $1 up to $100 and sometimes $200 or $300.

In casinos today it is the novice gamblers, male and female, who give the side games their big action. Any gambler who knows even a little about house percentages and how they work avoids these games like the plague.

THE BIG SIX

The Big Six, or Jumbo Dice Wheel, is a giant wheel of chance five feet in diameter which, with its pedestal, stands eight feet high. It is the most popular of the casino side games and often earns the house $1,000 or more per day.

There are 54 spaces around the rim of the wheel's surface, each of which shows one side of three dice bearing different combinations of the numbers 1 through 6. There is a layout which also bears the numbers 1 through 6. The players *cover* (put their money on) one or more numbers on the layout and the dealer spins the wheel in a clockwise direction. Projecting *posts* (nails) on the outer edge of the wheel's rim separate the spaces and pass by a leather indicator at the top. When the wheel comes to a stop, the section in which the indicator rests is the winning combination.

This is how one of the "Gaming Guide Souvenir Booklets," which most luxury casinos distribute free to hotel and casino guests, describes the payoff odds.

> It's THE BIG SIX FOR BIG THRILLS. You'll enjoy a thrill a minute at this spell-binding Wheel of Fortune. If you put $1 on 1 and the wheel stops at 1–2–3, you get back $1 plus the $1 you invested since the 1 showed only once. If the wheel stops at 1–1–2 you get back $2 plus the $1 you invested since the $1 shows twice. This holds true for all the numbers, i.e., if you play $1 on 5 and the wheel stops on 4–5–6, you get back $1 and your dollar. If it stops at 5–5–5, you receive $3 and your $1.

If you are still not convinced that this is the game for you, the Big Six dealer will explain further advantages of the game. He tells you that "there are three winners and three losers on each and every spin of the wheel." He illustrates this by putting a silver dollar on each of the six numbers on the layout, then he points to a space on the wheel marked 1–2–3 or a space marked 4–5–6 and tells you that if the wheel stops on either of these spaces the player who wagered $1 on each of the six numbers on the layout can't lose any money. The player would win three $1 bets and lose three $1 bets, thus breaking even. He demonstrates this by collecting the three silver dollars on the losing numbers and uses them to pay off the three winning numbers. "Nothing," he adds, "could be fairer than that."

But what the casino booklet and the dealer fail to point out is that there are only six sections on the wheel that are dead even and contain

A casino Big Six wheel found in many Nevada casinos and elsewhere.

three different numbers. The other 48 sections contain 24 doubles (pairs), and 24 triplets (three of a kind). This arrangement gives the Big Six operator a favorable advantage of 22 2/9%, which is much too large for any player to overcome.

Here, without the help of algebra, trigonometry or differential calculus, using only simple grade-school arithmetic, is the proof that this is the correct percentage.

The wheel bears 54 sections of which 6 have no pairs, 24 have pairs, and 24 have three of a kind. Let's put a $1 bet on each of the six numbers on the layout, spin the wheel 54 times, and assume that the "laws of probability" are strictly enforced and that each of the 54 spaces appears once as a winner. We wager $6 on each of the 54 spins for a total of $324.

In 6 spins of the wheel we get "no pairs," winning $3 and losing $3 each time. We come out even, having bet $36 and taken down $36.

On the 24 spins in which pairs appear, we have wagered a total of $144. We take down $72 on the double numbers at 2 to 1, and $48 on the single numbers at even money, a total of $120. Our loss is $24.

On the 24 spins in which three of a kinds appear, we have wagered a total of $144 and at 3 to 1 take down only $96 for a loss of $48.

Our total loss of $72 divided by the total $324 wagered gives us the percentage in the operator's favor of 22 2/9%, or, in decimals, 22.22+%.

Since your average rate of loss is 22 2/9¢ on each dollar wagered, do you still think the Big Six is as attractive a proposition as the booklet and the dealer tried to make out?

Some Big Six wheels have fewer than 54 sections—48 or 30 or some other number—and the dice arrangements on their winning sections vary as well. The more often triplets appear on the wheel, the greater the operator's percentage.

THE MONEY WHEEL

The mechanical structure and rules of play of the Money Wheel are very much like the Big Six except that it uses a different betting layout and has a different number of sections on the wheel's rim. This changes the payoff odds and the operator's favorable P.C.

The rim of the wheel is divided into 50 sections covered with glass, and in 48 of these are new American greenbacks in denominations of $1, $2, $5, $10 and $20. The remaining two sections bear a picture of the American flag and of a joker. There are seven corresponding betting spaces on the layout showing $1, $2, $5, $10, $20, flag and joker.

The values of the bills indicate the payoff odds to winners. A winning bet on the $1 bill is paid off at even money or 1 to 1 odds. A winning bet on the $2 bill is paid off at 2 to 1 odds, on the $5 at 5 to 1 odds, on the $10 at 10 to 1 odds, on the $20 at 20 to 1 odds. A winning bet on the flag pays off at 40 to 1 odds, and you also receive 40 to 1 for a winning bet on the joker.

Some Money Wheel players think that the big odds offered cut down the operator's edge, and some even believe that the game is almost dead even. This logic, or rather lack of it, is what makes Money Wheel operators rich. The operator's favorite percentage is calculated in the same way as on the Big Six.

Of the 50 sections on the wheel, 22 contain a $1 bill, 14 contain a $2 bill, 7 contain a $5 bill, 3 contain a $10 bill, 2 contain a $20 bill, and there is one flag and one joker. There are 7 betting spaces on the layout corresponding to the betting groups.

If we cover each of the 7 betting spaces with a $1 bet, spin the wheel 50 times and assume that each of the 50 sections wins once, we will wager $7 on each spin for a total of $350.

The wheel stops at the $1 bill 22 times and we take down $44.

It stops at the $2 bill 14 times and we take down $42.

It stops at the $5 bill 7 times and we take down $42.

It stops at the $10 bill 3 times and we take down $33.

Money Wheel in action in a plush Las Vegas Strip casino. (Allen Photographers, Inc.)

It stops at the $20 bill 2 times and we take down $42.

It stops at the flag once and we take down $41.

It stops at the joker once and we take down $41.

Our winnings add up to $285. We subtract this from the total $350 wagered and get a loss of $65. Divide this $65 by the $350 total wagered and we find that the operator has a percentage in his favor of 18 4/7%, or, in decimals, 18.57+%.

There are other types of money wheels. All are basically the same in structure and method of operation, but some give the operator a greater favorable percentage. This runs from a low 18% to a high of 30% or more.

THE RACEHORSE WHEEL

The Racehorse Wheel is very much like the Big Six and the Money Wheel. The number of sections on the wheels varies, with layouts to correspond, and the sections bear pictures of racehorses and numbers specifying payoff odds. Man o' War may pay 40 to 1, Morvich 20 to 1, Teeko 5 to 1, etc.

The operator's favorable edge on most Racehorse Wheels runs from a low 15% to a high of 25%.

CHEATING AT WHEELS OF CHANCE

The Big Six, Money Wheel and Racehorse Wheel in a permanently established casino are almost never rigged for two very good reasons: (1) The house advantage is so great that the wheels will win all the loose money around, and cheating is not only unnecessary but downright foolish. (2) The day-in-and-day-out casino operation of a gaffed wheel would be certain suicide for the owner, because even the rank suckers would sooner or later *rumble* (catch on to) the mechanical gaff.

These reasons are not so valid for some carnival hustlers operating at one-night stands. The best protection against their gaffed wheels is to be able to spot one when you see it. For information on this see Chapter 25 on carnival games.

CHUCK-A-LUCK

Chuck-a-Luck, commonly called the Bird Cage, is the game from which Big Six was derived. Since the introduction of Big Six into the casinos the popularity of the Bird Cage has hit a new low. Smart casino operators prefer Big Six because their take is triple that of the Bird Cage. You'll still see the Cage occasionally in some rug or sawdust joint, and it is still widely used by carnival hustlers working around outings, picnics, carnivals, fair grounds and bazaars.

The Bird Cage equipment and rules of play are simple. Three two-inch dice are tumbled in a wire cage shaped like an hour glass. The

Chuck-a-Luck cage with layout. (H. Baron Corp.)

slim waist of the cage is encircled by a metal band connected to an axle on which the cage turns. The three captive dice tumble from end to end of the cage when it is spun, and they come to rest on one of the drumlike coverings at the ends of the cage.

As in Big Six, the layout bears the numbers 1, 2, 3, 4, 5, 6. Players put their bets on one or more of the layout numbers. After the cage is spun and the dice come to rest, if a player's number appears on one die he gets even money (1 to 1); if his number appears on two dice, he gets paid off at 2 to 1; and if all three bear his number he gets paid off at 3 to 1.

Many casino operators whom I have questioned believe, since the payoff odds at Chuck-a-Luck and the Big Six are the same, that the house advantage must also be the same. Nothing could be further from the truth. The operator's edge of 22 2/9% at the Big Six is considerably more than his edge of 7 47/54% at Chuck-a-Luck.

This big percentage difference arises from the fact that there are only 54 three-dice combinations painted on the Big Six wheel, most of which are pairs and three of a kinds, whereas the three dice used in Chuck-a-Luck possess a total of 216 combinations comprised of 120 no pairs, 90 pairs, and only 6 three of a kinds. I won't repeat the calculations here, but if you follow the same procedure as was used to figure the Big Six house percentage, and don't make a mistake, you'll find that the operator's favorable P.C. is 7 47/54%.

Cheating at Chuck-a-Luck

Some Bird Cage operators who want a stronger P.C., because they believe implicitly in the cheater's adage "Never give a sucker an even break," employ a gaffed Bird Cage outfit when dealing the game. Steel-loaded dice (known as *electric dice*) are used in the cage and an electromagnet is concealed in the table on which the cage rests.

Electric dice are so loaded as to bring up either of two opposite sides. Opaque celluloid dice are loaded with steel slugs. The slugs used to load transparent dice are circular disks punched out of a grid of 5/1000-inch steel wires. These are placed in the countersunk spots. One is inserted in each of the spots on four different sides of the cube, leaving the two opposite sides which the operator wants to control unloaded. All three dice are loaded the same way, and when the juice is on, either a pair or three of a kind must appear. If the unloaded sides are the six and ace, the dice will show three sixes, three aces, a pair of sixes and an ace, or a pair of aces and a six.

The tip-off on the electric cage is the distance between the bottom of the cage and the table top in which the electromagnet is concealed.

If this is so small that the cage just barely clears the table when it turns, it may mean that the cage is gaffed.

HAZARD

Today's most popular dice games, Private, Bank and Money Craps, are descended from the 700-year-old private game of Hazard. The casino banking game of Hazard, originally known as Grand Hazard, using three dice, had an era of great popularity during the early 1900s, both in our western sawdust joints and in our fashionable casinos. I first saw it played in Colonel Bradley's famous Beach Club in Palm Beach, Florida, in 1932. Players placed their bets on the Hazard layout and the dealer, standing behind it, dropped three dice through a device called a *Hazard chute*. A series of inclined planes called steps, inside the chute, tumbled the dice as they went through the chute and out onto the layout surface.

Years later, after Black Jack was introduced into the casinos, Hazard's popularity waned and it became a side game. About the same time, a Chicago manufacturer marketed the first Chuck-a-Luck cage, and since then most operators have discarded the chute and dealt Hazard with a Chuck-a-Luck cage.

In the top casinos today Hazard runs a poor fifth in popularity behind the Big Six, Money Wheel, Racehorse Wheel and Chuck-a-Luck. It is still popular, however, in many western sawdust joints and with carnival hustlers.

Hazard is now played much like Chuck-a-Luck except that the layout permits 25 additional wagers not found in Chuck-a-Luck. Here is the percentage breakdown on the more important bets:

Raffles: The player bets that any specific three of a kind (three aces, three deuces, etc.) will appear. This bet is paid off at odds of 180 for 1; the correct odds are 215 to 1, which gives the bank a favorable edge of 16⅔%.

Any raffle: The player bets that *any* three of a kind will appear. This bet is paid off at odds of 30 for 1 and the correct odds are 35 to 1; the bank's advantage is 16⅔%.

Low bet: a bet that the total count on the dice will be 10 or below.

High bet: a bet that the total count on the dice will be 11 or more.

Odd and even bet: a bet that the total count on the dice will add up to the number selected by the player.

Since the player loses when his selection appears if it is made up of three of a kind, the bank has an edge on each of these wagers (low, high, odd-and-even) of 2 7/9%. This low percentage makes it much the best bet for the player.

Numbers bet: The player bets that he can pick the exact winning number of the total count such as 4, 5, 6, 7 and so on, up to and including 17. The bank's favorable edge runs from a low 9 13/18% on a count of 7 to a high of 30 5/9% on a count of 8.

Chuck numbers: These are the same bets as in Chuck-a-Luck, and they get the most action at Hazard. The player bets on the numbers 1 through 6, and a winning number pays even money if it appears on one die, 2 to 1 if it shows on two dice, and 3 to 1 if it shows on three dice. The bank's edge is the same as in Chuck-a-Luck: 7 47/54%.

Cheating at Hazard

The electric cage is gaffed as in Chuck-a-Luck (see page 506).

BEAT THE SHAKER

In various sections of the country this is also known as *High Dice, Beat the Banker, Beat the Dealer, Beat the Shake* and *Two-Dice Klondike.* This side game is popular in honky-tonk gambling houses, where it is operated as a counter game and usually dealt by dice girls. It is such a simple and deceptive game that the average gambler believes it should be easy to beat. He's wrong.

When operated as a counter game, the dice are thrown from a cup. When dealt in a sawdust joint or by a carnival hustler, the dice are on a high perch, and when the operator pulls a string they drop through a transparent chute out on to the playing surface. Two dice are used, and the banker and the player each get one throw. The banker goes first. To win, the player must get a higher total count on his throw than the banker; the banker wins on all ties.

Layout used in Beat the Dealer (or Shaker).

The game is a dead even proposition except for the ties; they constitute the bank's advantage. To calculate this we simply find out how many ties can be expected in the long run. The banker stands to throw the number 2 (two aces) once out of 36 throws. The player's chances are the same. The chance that they will tie by throwing two Aces each is 1/36 × 1/36, or 1/1,296.

If we multiply the probabilities on each of the numbers 2, 3, 4, 5, 6, 7, 8, 9, 10, 11 and 12 and then add, we find that in the long run ties can be expected 146 times. Dividing the favorable chances of 146 by the total chances of 1,296 gives us a percentage in favor of the bank at Beat the Shaker of 11 43/162%, or, in decimals: 11.26+%.

Some carnival operators who want to speed up the action and take the chump even faster use only one die. The operator's advantage in this case is 16⅔%.

Cheating at Beat the Shaker

The most common method, when the dice are thrown from a cup, is the use of a *slick dice cup* which is gaffed by having its inner surface slicked or polished, and a pair of first-flop dice which are so heavily loaded that, when properly thrown from the slick cup, they will always show fives and sixes (making the combination 10, 11 or 12). On the dealer-cheat's turn, he shakes the cup with an up-and-down and slightly rotary motion of his arm. Instead of tumbling at random inside the cup, the dice spin around the slicked inner surface like horses on a *chump twister* (merry-go-round).

The centrifugal force created by the rotary up-and-down motion of the cup causes the loaded sides of the dice to face the cup's inner surface. When the cheat slides the two dice out and across the playing surface, the desired unloaded sides are up and he gets a high count of 10, 11 or 12. He can win whenever he likes—which is most of the time.

For information on how to spot loaded dice see page 307.

UNDER AND OVER SEVEN

This game, also called *Over and Under,* is an old-time carnival game which is still going strong at outings, picnics, carnivals, fairs or wherever the carnival hustler is found. It is also very popular in many honky-tonk gambling joints. Like Beat the Shaker, it is usually dealt from a chute when played outdoors, and indoors by dice girls from a cup.

A pair of dice, the cup (or chute) and a betting layout with three betting spaces are used. The center is marked with a large 7, the space on the left reads "Under 7," that on the right, "Over 7." The player puts

Layout for Under and Over 7.

his money on any one of the three spaces, and throws. A bet on under 7 wins if he throws a 2, 3, 4, 5 or 6, and the player is paid off at even money; he loses if he throws 7 or more. A bet on over 7 wins if he throws an 8, 9, 10, 11 or 12, and he is paid off at even money; he loses if he throws 7 or less. If he puts his bet on the 7 space and throws 7 (a natural) he wins and is paid off at odds of 4 to 1; any other number loses.

It looks as though the operator is leaning over backward to give his customers a fair chance to win. He's leaning all right, like the leaning tower of Pisa, but in the other direction. Since there are six ways to make 7, the player who bets on that space can expect to win ⅙ of the time. If the operator paid off at 5 to 1 it would be an even-up proposition. He pays 4 to 1 and has an advantage on that bet of a big 16⅔%.

Of the 36 combinations with a pair of dice, 15 will total less than 7; the player has 15 chances out of 36 to win a bet on under 7, making the correct odds 7 to 5 against him. The operator pays off at even money and again has a favorable edge of 16⅔%. The same holds true for the over 7 space.

It doesn't matter on which space you put your money, that stiff 16⅔% P.C. will grind down your bankroll almost as fast as if your pocket was being picked.

Cheating at Under and Over Seven

Since the operator seldom handles the dice and since that take of 16⅔% is plenty big enough, the operator rarely cheats. Player cheats, however, have been known to beat operators by switching crooked dice (see page 307) into the game.

BARBOUTH

A favorite among Greek and Jewish players, Barbouth (also known as Barbudey, Barbooth, Barabout) is now popular in this country and often played for large stakes. It is a dead even game, shooter and fader each having an exactly even chance.

Any number can play, usually as many as can sit around a regulation Poker table. Two peewee dice (small .375-inch dice) and two dice cups are used. Each player rolls one die and the high man becomes the first shooter. The shooter does not specify the amount of his wager the way he does in Craps, but the player on his right, called the *fader*, bets any amount up to the limit that the shooter will not win and places it in the center of the playing surface. The shooter may cover the bet, allow other players to take all or part of the bet, or he may refuse the wager and pass the dice to the player on his right. The fader also has the privilege of refusing to fade and passing his opportunity to fade. The other players make side bets on whether or not the shooter or fader will win.

After his bet has been covered the shooter throws out the dice for one roll. If the number thrown does not effect a decision the dice pass to the fader, who takes one roll. If his roll is also no decision, the shooter throws again; and shooter and fader continue to throw alternately until a decision is effected. If the shooter or a fader throws 3–3, 5–5, 6–6 or 6–5 he wins. If he throws 1–1, 2–2, 4–4 or 1–2 he loses. All other throws are meaningless. If the shooter loses with a throw of 1–1, 2–2, or 4–4, or if the fader wins with a throw of 3–3, 5–5, or 6–6, then the dice pass to the player on the shooter's right who becomes the next shooter, and the player on the right of the new shooter becomes the new fader. But if the shooter loses with a throw of 1–2 or the fader wins with a throw of 6–5, the shooter retains the dice and continues to shoot.

A house employee known as a *cutter* takes the charge of 2½% of each winning bet. A bookmaker or banker is usually available to accept side bets for a charge of 5%, which is divided equally between the bookmaker and house cutter.

Since the small opaque dice used in Barbouth are easy to switch and load, and considering the present method of play in which the shooter and fader each use their own dice and dice cup, a player must be on guard against a slick cup used with first-flop dice, controlled shots with the cup, and switching of tops and bottoms (see page 320).

FOUR FIVE SIX, OR THE THREE-DICE GAME

This game is popular throughout the northwestern United States, including Alaska, and western Canada. Most players believe it is an even-up game with no advantage for the banker.

As many players may play as can crowd around the playing surface. Three dice are used, and are thrown from a cup. Each player puts the amount he desires to wager in front of him and the banker, who covers all bets, plays against each player in turn. After the first round, the player on the banker's left becomes the banker and so on.* The banker shoots first.

When either banker or player throws (1) the combination 4–5–6, (2) any pair and a six or (3) three of a kind, it is a winning decision. If (1) 1–2–3 or (2) any pair and an ace is thrown, it is a losing decision. When any pair is thrown and the third die is a 2, 3, 4 or 5, the number on the third die becomes the shooter's point. If his opponent fails to score a winning or losing decision, and also throws a point, the player whose point is highest wins.

A tie is a standoff. When a player does not get a pair and does not throw either 4–5–6 or 1–2–3, the roll is neutral and he must continue shooting until he wins, loses, throws a point or ties.

Since the banker wins and loses according to the same deciding throws as the player, there would seem to be no advantage in his favor —until we break it down. A glance at the *Combinations Table* (see Chapter 11) shows that there are 216 different combinations possible with three dice of which 120 are no pairs, 90 are pairs and 6 are three of a kind.

Of the 90 pairs ⅙ can be expected to have a 6 as a number on the third die, a total of 15. There are 6 ways to throw three of a kind and 6 ways to throw 4–5–6, a total of 27 winning ways.

The losing throws: Any pair with an ace and 1–2–3 can·be made in 15 ways and 6 ways respectively for a total of 21 losing ways.

Point numbers (any pair with a 2–3–4–5) can be made in 60 ways (the 90 ways pairs can be made minus the 30 ways pairs with aces and sixes can be made).

All these winning and losing and point number ways added together show that just half of the possible 216 ways are of importance or 108 ways. The other 108 rolls are neutral and do not effect any decision.

The banker's advantage lies in the fact that he always throws first. Out of 108 decisive rolls he can expect to win 27 times, lose 21 times and throw a point 60 times. Considering only the first throw, he has an advantage of 6 winning ways in his favor, a P.C. of 6/108 times 100 or 5 5/9%.

If he throws a point, his opponent takes the cup and throws, and the 5 5/9% is now in the opponent's favor. But while the bank always has this P.C. on his throw, the player has it only when the banker throws a point, or 60/108 of the time. (On the other 48 throws, the

---

* Except when the game is operated by the house, in which case the bank does not rotate. The bank usually has a $25 limit.

player never gets a chance to shoot.) 60/108 of 5 5/9% leaves a favorable percentage of 3 7/81% for the player.

Subtracting the player's percentage from the banker's percentage leaves a 2 38/81% advantage in the banker's favor. This is about 12¢ on a $5 bet.

Because they think Four Five Six is an even-up game, many players pass up their opportunity to be the banker when it is their turn. The 2 38/81 P.C. is always working against those players and grinding them down. The game is an even-up proposition only if each player takes his turn at banking so that the P.C. works for as well as against him.

MONTE

This game is also called *Spanish Monte* and *Monte Bank*. Due to its big moneymaking feature and its lack of bulky equipment, which minimizes police raids and arrests, Monte has replaced Bank Craps as the number one banking game in most illegal gambling clubs operating in the big cities of the United States.

Requirements

1. A standard deck of 52 cards from which the eights, nines and tens have been removed, making a 40-card deck.

2. A banker chosen from two or more players. As a rule, the admissible maximum is the number that can crowd around the card table.

3. A houseman, called a *cutter*, whose official duty is to aid the player-banker in his dealing chores, including the payoff, collection of losing and winning bets, and collection of a 25% charge from each player's door or gate winnings. This 25% charge is known as a "cut" and is divided equally between the banker and the house at the end of a player's banking role.

Object of the game: To win a bet that one or more face-up cards on the table layouts will be matched before one or more of the remaining face-up cards on the Monte layout.

Value of the cards: The cards have no special value relative to each other, and neither do the suits.

Selecting the banker: By mutual consent any player shuffles the pack, then puts it in the center of the table. Each player cuts a group of cards off the pack. The player cutting the low card is the first dealer and banker. In case of a tie for low card, the tied players cut until one is low. On completion of the banker's deal, the deck and the deal pass to the player on the dealer's left; thereafter, it rotates to the left, clockwise. At any time, the dealer may pass the bank (i.e., decline to bank the game), if there are no unsettled bets on the table. To announce that he means to pass the bank, the dealer utters the word "Aces!"

Betting limit: The dealer is privileged to place as much money in the bank as he chooses. If a player wagers more money than is in the bank, and the bank loses the bet, the largest wager is paid off first; the second largest is paid off next, etc. Other bets are called off. The banker is only responsible for money in the bank. The wagers are always in cash.

Shuffle and cut: The dealer shuffles the pack. Any player may call for a shuffle before the cut, but the dealer is entitled to shuffle last. After the shuffle, the dealer puts the cards before the player at his right to be cut. That player must cut, although the other players may also call for the right to cut before the player to the dealer's right completes his own cut.

Start of the deal: After the cut the banker, holding the pack face down, deals two cards off the bottom of the deck, facing these two cards and putting them in the center of the table two or three inches apart. This is known as the *top layout*. Then the dealer takes two cards off the top of the deck, and puts them face up two or three inches below the first two cards, about the same distance apart, forming the *bottom layout*. Should the two cards of the bottom layout be of the same rank, there is no play and a new deal is in order. If the two cards of the top layout are of the same rank, the dealer places one card on top of the other and then deals a third card alongside it. Bets placed on a pair indicate that a player is betting against two same-rank cards of the opposite color of the other card in the top layout. Example: If the other card is red, the player is betting against a black card (spades or clubs) of the same rank; or vice versa. Should three cards of the same rank appear in the top layout, they are grouped in threes and a bet on a triple means that the player is betting against the same color and same rank of the other card. The above bets are all paid off at even money.

Types of Monte Bets

Crisscross bet: To bet that a selected one of four face-up cards will be matched before a designated card of the other three cards. (A card is matched whenever one of three remaining cards of the same denomination is dealt from the pack.) Example: Face up on the table are the ace, two, three and four of clubs. The player puts his bet on the ace, placing his cash in such a way that it points to or just touches the deuce. He's now betting that one of the three remaining aces will be dealt from the pack before one of the three remaining deuces.

Doubler or doubler bet: To bet that a card in the top layout will be matched before a card is matched in the bottom layout, or vice versa; or that one of the two cards resting on the dealer's left will be matched before one of the two cards on his right, or vice versa. This bet is paid off at even money.

Circle bet or circling a card: To bet that one card will be matched before any of the three others. This bet is paid off at 3 to 1 odds.

Monte Carlo bet: To make a combination of the three bets at one time. The payoff of such bets is determined by the sum wagered on each. All Monte Carlo wagers are indicated by the placement of the money (bills) as described under the crisscross bet. Bets can be placed any time during a deal.

The Play of Monte

After the bets have been placed, the cutter tells the dealer, "That's all," which formally terminates that phase of the game, and the dealer turns the deck face up in his hand. From then on the cards are dealt face up one at a time. Some gambling joints insist that after each decision the deck be turned face down and future bets placed before the deck is turned face up.

If the top card of the deck matches one of the four layout cards, either the dealer or a player (or players) wins; and the dealer keeps taking cards off the pack until (1) all the cards bet on are matched or (2) the cards the players are betting against are matched. As a card is matched, it is removed from the board. When all bets are won or lost the deal is completed and a new deal starts.

The House Take

When a player places a bet (any time during the game) and the next (first) dealt card matches his winning card, the cutter takes 25% of the player's winnings. This is called the *door* or *gate*. This cut is put aside and divided equally by the banker and house at the end of the player's banking session. Percentagewise, this 25% cut amounts to an overall advantage of about 3%.

TRENTE ET QUARANTE

Also known as *Rouge et Noir* (red and black), Trente et Quarante is a standard European casino banking card game and is most popular in French and Italian casinos, and the world-famous Monte Carlo Casino, where its popularity is only surpassed by Baccarat and Roulette. The name Trente et Quarante ("30 and 40") is derived from the fact that the winning point always lies between these two numbers.

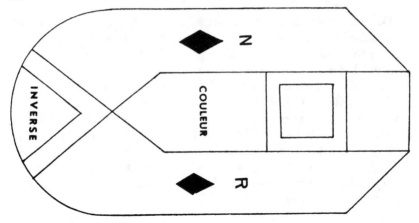

Trente-et-Quarante layout as seen in European casinos including Monte Carlo.

Requirements

1. A regulation Trente et Quarante table with a double layout. See the illustration showing half of the Trente et Quarante layout.

2. Any number of persons can play against the bank, as many as can be accommodated at the gaming table.

3. Five croupiers. Four serve as banker and one as dealer (tailleur) and count caller. A supervisor sits on a stand overlooking the Trente et Quarante table to see that no errors are committed.

4. Six standard packs of 52 cards each, shuffled together and used as one deck of 312 cards.

Value of cards: The ace is the lowest-ranking card and has a point value of 1. Kings, queens and jacks have a value of 10 each. All other cards have their numerical face value. Deuce is counted 2, three is counted 3, etc. Suits have no value. Only colors count: hearts and diamonds are called red; spades and clubs are called black.

Shuffle and cut: At the start of each round of play, the dealer spreads the six packs of cards on the table and all players and croupiers are permitted to take a group of cards and shuffle them. On later deals, when the discard receivers are emptied onto the layout and some cards are face up and some are face down, the croupier and players turn the face-up cards down and shuffle them.

After the players have shuffled groups of cards, the croupier gathers all the cards and shuffles them together, usually shuffling about two packs at a time. Finally, the croupier assembles all six packs together and then hands a player an indicator card, saying, "Cut, please." The player inserts the indicator card into the packet to show where he wants the cards cut. The dealer cuts the cards at this position, putting the indicator and all the cards above it on the bottom.

Object of the game: To bet that a specific color (black or red) will produce a count of 31 or a total nearer to 31 than the opposite color. The player may also place his bet on *rouge* (red), *noir* (black), couleur or inverse.

The Play

All betting is done against the casino or bank. Before the deal begins, the players place their bets. The dealer takes about 50 cards off the top of the pack and deals out the first card face upward onto the noir (black). He then deals a second, a third, etc., which he places in the same row, right and left, announcing the cumulative total of the spots with each card dealt. The dealing stops with the card which causes the total to reach or exceed 31. The second row, rouge (red) is dealt below the noir row in the same manner.

The row with the total nearer to 31 is the winning row. For example, a bet on noir wins if the count of the first or noir row is 34 while the rouge row totals 36. A bet on couleur wins if the very first card dealt is the same color as that designating the winning row. If this card is of the opposite color, a bet on inverse wins. The dealer traditionally announces the result for red and color only, calling "Rouge gagne" (wins) or "Rouge perd" (loses) or "couleur gagne" or "couleur perd." All bets are paid off at even money (1 to 1).

If both rows total the same count (tie), it is called a *refait* and all bets are called off. If there is a refait at 31—refait de trente-et-un—the bank takes half of all bets; however, the player has the option of leaving his bet in *prison*, where it remains for the next game or coup. If he wins on this coup, he withdraws his bet; but if he loses, he loses the whole.

As bets are settled, the cards dealt for that coup are brushed into the discard receiver. When there are insufficient cards for the next coup all the cards are reshuffled.

Refait insurance bet: Before the cards are dealt, players may insure their bets against a possible loss of half their bets when a refait at 31 takes place. The insurance charge is 5% of the amount wagered.

Probabilities: Of the ten numbers from 31 to 40, the number 31 appears more often than any other:

Number	Times
31	13
32	12
33	11
34	10
35	9
36	8
37	7
38	6
39	5
40	4

Our mathematics informs us that a refait (tie) of 31 will happen about once in 41 dealt hands of play, which is about 1½% when the bank takes 50% of each player's bet when a standoff of 31 occurs.

20.
Backgammon

Backgammon, the parent of all track games such as Parcheesi, is perhaps the oldest game with dice still being played today. The French and Germans call it *Tric-Trac*; the Italians, *Tarola reale* ("royal table"); the Romans who played it with three dice knew it as *Duodecim scripta* ("12 lines"). The word "Backgammon" has been ascribed to the Welsh words "back" and "gammon" ("little battle") and also to the Saxon "bac" and "gamen" ("back game").

Backgammon as played today is simply a bigtime fashionable illegally operated gambling game, infested by hundreds and hundreds of dice hustlers and cheats. Untold millions of dollars change hands nightly at the game, most of which eventually winds up in the pockets of Backgammon hustlers. The introduction of the doubling block has made Backgammon the bigtime gambling game that it is. For example, in some close big-money games, the doubling block moves almost as fast as the dice. What may begin as a $100 game can easily double and redouble to $25,600, and since the stakes are tripled when an opponent is backgammoned, a single game can cost the loser $76,800. The biggest Backgammon winning that has come to my attention was a $250,000 three-day score made by three American Backgammon hustlers on the French Riviera.

Anyone can learn the rudiments of the game in a half hour or so, but to become an expert or hustler at the game requires considerable knowledge of dice mathematics plus months and months of practice.

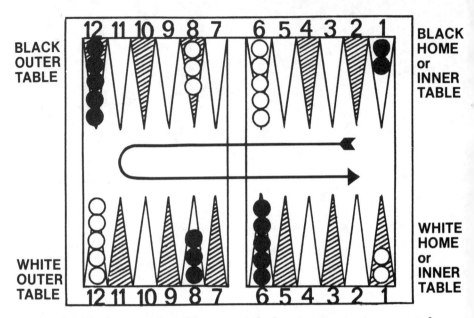

BLACK OUTER TABLE

BLACK HOME or INNER TABLE

WHITE OUTER TABLE

WHITE HOME or INNER TABLE

Modern Backgammon board layout and the location of opposing men at the start of game. The directional arrow is for the Black counters; White moves similarly from his inner table around and back to Black's inner table.

RULES OF PLAY

Requirements

1. Two players; three or more sometimes participate in the stakes (see Chouette, page 528).

2. *The Board.* A rectangular board is divided into two halves by a vertical *bar.* One half is called the *inner* (or home) *table;* the other the *outer table.* (Traditionally the inner table is the one nearest the light.) The players, designated Black and White, face each other. Twelve alternately colored triangles, called *points,* project from each side of the board toward the center. The players sit on opposite sides of the board.

3. *Pieces.* Each player has 15 checkerlike pieces (often called "men" or "stones") of one color; usually one player has black pieces and one has white. Their starting positions are shown in the illustration above. The movement of White's pieces is from Black's inner table clockwise to White's home table. Black's pieces travel in the opposite direction.

4. *Dice.* Each player has a dice cup and two dice.

5. *Doubling Cube.* A large die whose faces are numbered 2, 4, 8, 16, 32, 64.

Notation: Each point is numbered as in the illustration, although

the numbers do not appear on the board. The initials B and W indicate which side of the board the point is on. A move lists the point
moved from and the point moved to. Example: White, B12–W6,
B1–B3 means: White moves one stone from Black's 12 point to White's
6 point, and one stone from Black's 1 point to Black's 3 point. If more
than one stone makes the same move, the number of stones being
moved is added in parentheses: B1–B3(2).

Start of the game: Each player throws one die from his cup and
the player throwing the highest number has the choice of seat and
color of men. If both players throw the same number they throw again.
The player throwing the highest number is the winner and plays first
by using the numbers on his own die and his opponent's die. Thereafter, the turn of play alternates and each player throws both his own
dice.

The Play

The object of the game is for each player to move his 15 men toward
the inner table on his own side of the board, and bear them off the
board. White moves clockwise, Black moves counterclockwise. The
first player to bear all his men off wins the game.

The numbers on the two dice, taken separately, show the number
of points over which the men may be moved. When one man has been
moved the number of points indicated by one die, the other number
may be used either to move the same man farther or to move another
man. When a player throws a doublet (both numbers the same) it
counts double. A 6–6, for instance, counts as four sixes: a total of 24
points, not 12. Since a doublet consists of four numbers, the player may
move as many as four men, or stones.

The player must attempt to use both (or all four) numbers if he
can. If he can use only one number, he must try to use the higher (or
as many as can be used of a doublet). If none of the numbers thrown
are usable, the play passes to his opponent.

The moves: A point is open to a player when it is not occupied by
two or more of his opponent's men. A player who has two or more men
on one point has *made* that point and his opponent's men may not
land on it. A man may pass over a closed point in using the total of
both numbers on the dice provided each number can be played
separately.

A single man on a point is a *blot*. When a man of the opposite color
lands on that point the blot is *hit*, and the man originally there is taken
off and placed on the bar. A man on the bar may enter again when a
number is thrown that will place the man on an unoccupied point of
his opponent's home table. All men on the bar must be re-entered

before any other moves may be made. When a player has two or more men on a point it is said to be *blocked,* and an opponent's man may not come to rest on the point, although it can move past the blocked point. If a player blocks six adjacent points and has one or more of his opponent's men behind it, he has made a *prime.* If he blocks all six points of his home table when his opponent still has one or more men on the bar, he is said to have *shut out.*

Bearing off men: Once a player has advanced all 15 of his stones or men to his own inner table, he may start bearing off, which consists in removing men from the board. The first player to bear off all 15 men wins. A man may be borne off a point whose number shows on either die. Example: If White rolls 4–3, he may remove a stone from W4 and another from W3. Instead of bearing off, he may use the numbers to move inside his inner table.

When a number rolled is higher than the highest point on which a player has any men, he bears off from the highest number. If, after having started to bear off, a man is hit, it goes to the bar and must enter and come around again to the inner table before the player can continue bearing off.

Scoring: The first player to bear off all his men wins the game. If the loser has borne off at least one man, and has no man left in the winner's inner table, he loses a *single* game. If he has not borne off a single man, he loses double (*gammon*). If, in addition, he has a man left in his opponent's inner table or on the bar, he loses triple (*backgammon*).

Doubling: Backgammon is played for an agreed stake which may be increased by doubling during play, or by gammon and backgammon. An automatic double occurs when equal numbers are thrown on the first roll, and both players roll again. (Automatic doubles may be waived by agreement; if not, they are usually limited by agreement to one or two per game.)

Either player has the right to offer the first voluntary double before casting, and this right alternates thereafter. The opponent must agree to play at the double stake, or forfeit the game and the stake. If he accepts the double, the game continues at the increased stake. The player who offered the double may not immediately double again. The privilege of making the next double falls to his opponent and if he doubles, the first player either resigns and pays the double stakes or accepts and the game continues with stakes of four times the original amount. There is no limit to the number of doubles that may be made but the option of offering doubles alternates between players. These doubles are cumulative and in addition to increases from gammon or backgammon.

Additional Rules

The following additional rules cover most irregularities that may occur:

1. After the game has started, if it is seen that some of the men have been set up in the wrong position, the game must be started again.

2. The dice must be thrown from the box onto the player's right-hand table. If the dice are thrown out of the right-hand table, or if they are tilted and don't rest flat on the surface, or if either die is touched by either player during the throw or before the player has called the numbers showing, the throw is faulty and must be thrown again.

3. A player must not throw his dice until his opponent's play has been completed.

4. After a player has moved a man and taken his hand from the piece, he can't change his play.

5. If a player moves incorrectly, his opponent can demand that the error be corrected provided he does so before he has made his own throw.

BACKGAMMON OPENING MOVE STRATEGY

There are really three distinct styles of playing Backgammon:

1. **The running game:** This is usually adopted by a player when he gets several high throws at the outset of the game; he plays full speed ahead with no concern about his opponent's moves.

2. **The block game:** The object of this strategy is to block as many points in a row as possible to impede opponent's progress. This is a defensive game.

3. **The back game:** With this strategy, a player, instead of trying to rush his men forward concentrates upon doing everything possible to delay his own forward progress: he endeavors to have his own men set home and re-entered in his opponent's inner table, making points, so that later they may hit the opponent's blots.

Actually, there are two kinds of Backgammon players, those who depend entirely on the element of chance to win and those who put their trust in the fascinating factor of skill. Skill does play a very important part in winning Backgammon; still, the element of luck is always present. Therefore, of paramount importance to a winning player is an accurate knowledge of the odds of the various dice throws that arise during play. For example, suppose you want to calculate your opponent's chances of a 2 or a 3 compared to the probability of his throwing a 6 or a 7. This can be figured out as follows: The number of combinations that can be made with two dice is 36 (see page 277). Of course, a double can be thrown only one way, but there are two ways to throw any other number, such as 4–2 or 2–4. A single 2 can be made on the dice in 12 different ways. It can be made as a double, it can be a double itself and it can be made with any of the other five numbers on the dice. thus: 1–1, 2–6, 6–2, 2–5, 5–2, 2–4, 4–2, 2–3, 3–2, 2–2, 2–1, and 1–2. Hence the chances of throwing a 2 in one throw of the dice are 24 to 12, or 2 to 1 against.

The player with a special knowledge of two-dice mathematics need only apply it with intelligence to have a decisive advantage over an opponent whose plays are contrary to the mathematical chances. It takes a knowledgeable player to tell whether or not he is facing a worthy opponent on the first few throws of the dice. A player who fails to play his opening moves correctly cannot be expected to play a good game. To aid such a player, the following examples depict all the first throws with two dice and the best way to play each to gain the best advantage. The various parts of the board and the different points mentioned that follow may be readily located by looking at the diagram on page 520, which also shows the setup for the start of the game.

The best doubles plays to make at start of game are as follows:

6–6: Move two men from your opponent's 1 point to his bar point. Move two men from your opponent's 12 point to your bar point (a very strong throw). Another strong play is to move three men to your bar and one man to your opponent's bar point.

5–5: Two men from your opponent's 12 point to your 3 point.

4–4. Move two back men from your opponent's 1 point to his 5 point and two men from your opponent's 12 point to your own 9 point.

3–3: There are two excellent ways of playing this throw: (1) Move two men from your 6 to your 3 point, and two men from your 8 to your 5 point. (2) Move two men from your opponent's 12 point to your 7 or bar point.

2–2: Move two men from your opponent's 1 point to his 5 point.

1–1: The best opening throw of two dice: Move two men from your 8 to your bar point, and two men from your 6 to your 5 point.

The best plays with non-doubles are:

6–5: Move one man from your opponent's 1 to his 12 point.

6–4: Move one man from your opponent's 1 to his bar point, and one man from opponent's 12 to your 9 point. This is a weak throw.

6–3: Move one man from your opponent's 1 point to his bar point and one from opponent's 12 to your 10 point.

6–2: Move two men from your opponent's 1 point to his bar and 3 point.

6–1: Move one man from your opponent's 12 point to your bar point and one man from your 8 to your bar point. A strong throw.

5–4: Move one man from your opponent's 1 point to his 5 and one man from his 12 to your 8 point.

5–3: Move two men from your opponent's 12 point, one to your 10, and one to your 8 point.

5–2: Move two men from your opponent's 12 point, one to your 11, and one to your 8 point.

5–1: Move one man from your opponent's 1 point, one to his bar point. A weak throw.

4–3: Move two men from your opponent's 1 point, one to his 4 point and one to his 5 point.

4–2: Move one man from your 8 and one from your 6 to your 4 point.

4–1: Move two men from opponent's 1 point, one to opponent's 2 point and one to opponent's 5 point.

3–2: Move one man from opponent's 1 to opponent's 4 point and one from opponent's 12 to opponent's 11 point.

3–1: Move two men, one from your 8 and one from your 6, to your 5 point.

2–1: Move one man from opponent's 1 point to opponent's 2 point and one man from opponent's 12 to your 11 point. The weakest throw of the dice.

BACKGAMMON STRATEGY

Now that we have discussed opening-move strategy, we continue with the following abbreviated tips, hints and strategy that are essential to good Backgammon playing.

1. The most important strategy of Backgammon is to start the two men on the opponent's table as soon as possible to prevent their being blocked. These two men are the weakest members of your forces and you should bring them to safety without delay. Once you form this habit you will have improved your game many times.

A good double throw early in the game will prevent these men from being blocked; even a small double will help. Also, if your two farthest men are on your opponent's 5 point, it will slow the progress of his men as they arrive at his home table. If you advance these two men to your opponent's bar point, it is also an advantage, but at the start of the game it is wise to hold them on the 5 point just in case you decide to switch to a back game.

2. Avoid taking unnecessary chances. This is next in importance to advancing your outposts. The beginner usually attempts an overbold game, taking all kinds of chances to make points. This is a bad habit, for reckless play generally ends in a lost game.

3. The primary objective of a strong opening is to obtain advantageous points that will slow up the advance of your opponent's two men in your home table. The most important point to secure first is your 5 point, then your bar point, which furnishes you a powerful blockade on your opponent's two outposts. While some players prefer the bar point before the 5 point, all agree that the bar point and the 5 point are the two strongest points to secure. Next in order comes your opponent's 5 point, which permits the escape of *your* two outposts.

4. Don't crowd your men on your points. Getting a long string of six or more men on a point limits your position and puts a number of your men out of play. Also, avoid playing your men to the low points in your home table, as these men also are out of action, and the position puts you at a disadvantage.

5. Never take up a blot in your home table unless you are certain you can block that point. Remember that the men reaching your home table have theoretically traveled all around the board, and their value is much greater than your opponent's two men in your home table. If your opponent's men are hit in your home table, they're only set back a few points, whereas if your men are hit in your home table, they must retravel 19 points to again reach the point where they were hit.

6. Don't expose a man to being hit unless the risk means a greater risk for your opponent if he takes advantage of it.

7. Learn to shut out your opponent by closing your home table. Basically, this consists of blocking all the points in your home table so that if you hit an opponent's blot on some other part of the board, he'll be unable to restart that man and must remain idle while you continue to play.

8. When forced to leave a blot, always attempt to keep it as far as possible from your opponent's men. A blot 7 points away from your adversary can only be hit with a combination throw, and the chances of doing this are about 5 to 1 at that distance. If you are forced to leave a blot within 6 points of your opponent, leave it as close as possible, 1 point away being safest. Also, when leaving a blot, try to choose a point which is more likely to be covered next throw.

9. When the numbers thrown on the dice are not available to make points, be sure to use them to make preparations for securing points. If your opponent is a safe distance away, spread these builders so that the following throw will permit you to make another point.

10. The expert Backgammon player always knows at all times

exactly how far ahead or behind he is. The best way to determine your comparative strength or weakness is as follows: First, pair any men you and your opponent have on opposite points; then calculate how many points your unpaired men are from the home table. Then by making the same calculation with your adversary's unpaired men and comparing totals you can estimate which player is ahead. Once your position is known, you'll know just when you must change your tactics or resort to a back game.

11. If your adversary is ahead of you when bearing off, never play up from your 4 or 3 points while there are a large number of men on your 6 point. Example: Suppose your 6 point is loaded with six men and you obtain a small throw of a three and a two; it would be wiser to move two men up from your 6 point than to play the men up from the lower points. The two men played forward from the 6 point would leave only four men on that point, and a lucky throw of double-sixes would clear these men from the board and give you a chance of overtaking your opponent. If you had played up the low throw from the 4 or 5 points, the double-sixes would still leave two men on your 6 point, and the chances of hitting two more sixes in the next few throws would be highly improbable.

12. After sending one or two of your opponent's men to the bar and having three or more points blocked in your home table, do not fail to spread your oncoming men so that you can make a new point in your home table or be ready to rehit his men as they re-enter.

13. Guard against decoy blots left by your opponent, especially if he is an experienced player. Make doubly sure that the blots are forced or attempted at a great risk, and before hitting them, make certain that his home table is not closed so that if your men are rehit they will be locked out on the bar.

14. If your adversary has locked your two outposts in his home table on his 1 point and has already brought all his men into his home table and is bearing them off, the only chance of victory you have is to hold your outposts in position in the hopes of forcing him to leave a blot as he bears his men. If he should open another point in the midst of his men, try to split up your two men, leaving two blots which form a greater menace to him, as you still have the opportunity of hitting him with a favorable throw and you are putting him in a position where an unfavorable throw on his part may force him to hit one of your blots which may then re-enter and send his man or men back to start over. If you can establish your two outposts on the 5 point in your opponent's home table, you are quite safe from an effective block of these two men, and your outside men can then be advanced more effectively.

15. When the game nears the end and the contest is tight, the men must be advanced to the home table as fast as possible. One way of doing this is to make plays that will carry a man from one table to another. Example: If you have a man on your opponent's 10 point and a three is thrown, move this man across the table to your 12 point—a play that takes him into your outer table. If you have a man on your 12 point and six is thrown, the play is to move this man into your home table. Playing your men so that they can go from one table to another permits you to gain the maximum amount of speed in bringing them home.

16. In throwing off, when your home table is closed and your opponent has men on the bar, the safest procedure is to move your men up in your home table rather than to take men off for the throws. This opens up the high points in your home table so your adversary can enter on these points, which removes the danger of his hitting you on re-entry.

17. In throwing off, when your opponent still has a man or men in your home table, try and keep an even number of men upon the points nearest the bar, to avoid an unnecessary blot.

18. In throwing off, after your opponent has passed your men, try to bear off with all possible speed. Remove as many men as possible with each throw, and when certain throws compel you to move up, try to cover the vacant points. A home board with all points covered is more quickly cleared in bearing.

CHOUETTE

This variant of Backgammon is played by three or more players, although it is still a two-handed game. The players cast dice for precedence, and the one throwing the highest number becomes the *man in the box;* second highest is *captain* for all the others, and they rank below the captain in accordance with the numbers they throw. Players who tie throw again to determine their rank.

The play is between the man in the box and the captain. Other players may advise the captain, but in case of disagreement he himself has the final decision as to how a move shall be made. If he wishes to double and any of his partners do not want to take the risk, they must resign and forfeit their stakes to him. He continues the game on his own responsibility, assuming all risk. The man in the box then decides whether to accept the double or resign.

If the man in the box doubles, each opponent must accept individually or pay the current stakes and resign. If the opponent of the man in the box resigns, the next highest player in standing who accepts the double takes his place at the board as the new captain.

If the player in the box wins the game, he stays in the box, and the next member of the team in order replaces the losing captain. If the man in the box loses (including loss by refusal of a double), he becomes the lowest-ranking member of the team. His place in the box is taken by the winning captain, and the next player in order moves up to captain. When a game ends, the player in the box collects from or pays to each remaining active member of the team the full value of the stake at that time.

PARTNERSHIP BACKGAMMON

Backgammon can be played, like many other two-player games, in partnership—two players versus two, or three against three. In the two-against-two partnership game, one member of each team plays against a member of the other, their Backgammon boards arranged so that rolls of the dice can be seen by all four players. On each side, one player plays Black, while the other partner plays White. The members of only one team roll the dice; one casts for Black and his throws are used by the Black players on both sides, the other rolls for White and his casts are used by both White players. When any player has borne off all his pieces, his team wins the contest.

CHEATING AT BACKGAMMON

Beware of a slick cup used with loaded or magnetized dice and table board that favor doubles, and switching in and out of one or two *tops* and *bottoms* especially marked to favor throwing doubles. See Cheating at Dice, pages 307–327.

21.
Scarne's Rules
for Private
Betting Games

There are dozens of private gambling games played in thousands and thousands of homes, clubs and bars throughout the United States. My survey reveals that about 50 million Americans, of whom 12 million are women, lose about $1 billion annually playing these games. Half of this amount, or $500 million, goes to sharpers (cheats), game hustlers and more skillful players. These games include such national favorites as Backgammon, Hooligan, Poker Dice, Scarney 3000, Scarney Put and Take, Scarney Duplicate Jackpots, Scarney 21 Up and Down, Money or Liar Poker, the Match Game and General. First let's discuss Hooligan.

HOOLIGAN

This is a popular bar game played for drinks (low man or men paying) or played as a betting game. Any number may play and five dice are used with a cup. Score is kept on a sheet ruled into boxes that bear the numbers 1 through 6 and the letter H for hooligan, which is a straight (a throw of 1–2–3–4–5 or 2–3–4–5–6). Each player throws dice to determine order of play, high man going first, next highest second, and so on.

Each player takes three throws per turn, called a *frame*. After the first throw, he may select any number as his point. He then puts all dice bearing this point number to one side and throws the remaining dice a second time. If one or more point numbers appear on this throw, those dice are also put aside and a third throw is made with any dice that remain. If after the first or second throws the player has thrown five point numbers, on his next throw he uses all five dice

530

again. After the third throw, the point number is multiplied by the number of points thrown to get the score for that frame. If the player has thrown five threes his score is 15, if seven sixes his score is 42, etc.

If in coming out for any number (that is, on the first roll) a hooligan is thrown the player is credited with 20 points for hooligan. If, however, a player has tried for all of the points with the exception of hooligan he must then try for hooligan on the last frame and is allowed three throws.

The player isn't required to select a point after the first throw, but may, if he likes, pick up all five dice and throw again for a point; he may do the same after the second throw.

On each succeeding turn the player must shoot for a different point number than any played previously, so that at the end of seven turns, which constitutes a game, he will have shot for each of the point numbers: 1, 2, 3, 4, 5, 6 and hooligan. The scores for each frame are added and the player having the highest total score wins; or, when played for drinks, the low man or sometimes the two lowest men pay. Example: If the first player throws three deuces and a pair of threes, he may select either the deuce or three as his point, or if he likes he may pick up all five dice and throw again, selecting his point from among the numbers thrown on his second throw, in which case none of the numbers which appeared on the first throw are scored.

When three deuces and a pair of threes are thrown, the logical choice is to select the deuce as the point, place the three dice that show deuce to one side, and throw the remaining two dice for a second throw. If the player throws two deuces for a total of five, he throws all five dice for the third throw. If he should throw three deuces on this last throw he has made a total score of eight deuces or 16 points. If on the second throw one deuce is thrown, that die is placed to one side and the remaining die is thrown for the third and last throw. If a deuce is thrown for a third time, the player scores 10; if not, the player has made 4 deuces altogether for a score of 8 for that frame. On his next turn the deuce is dead and he must shoot for some other point.

Hooligan is also played as a banking game in which the player doesn't shoot against an opponent but tries to reach as high a total as possible. The player usually pays a quarter to play and the operator pays off various amounts (usually in trade rather than cash) for high scores. Sometimes a score between 84 and 89 inclusive will get the player $1, a score between 90 and 93 is paid off at $2, and so on, but the payoff varies with different operators and in different places.

It is impossible to figure an exact house percentage on this game because different operators pay off differently, and because the players

A set of Scarney Dice, invented by the author. Each die of this five-dice set is marked with 1,3,4 and 6 spots, plus the word dead *repeated on two opposite sides.*

have a choice as to the order in which they select their points and the way they play them. A perfect score is 335.

POKER DICE

This game is usually played with five Poker dice whose sides bear playing-card denominations: ace, king, queen, jack, ten and nine. Conventional dice are sometimes used, ace being high and followed by six, five, four, three and two in that order. The ace is also sometimes played wild. Any number can play and each player throws one die to determine the order of play, highest man going first, next highest second and so on.

The object is to throw the highest Poker hand in either one or two throws as desired. After the first throw, the player may stand pat or may draw (as in Draw Poker) by throwing one, two or three dice again. The object is to secure high Poker hands which rank as follows: five of a kind, four of a kind, full house, straight (any five cards or numbers in numerical sequence), three of a kind, two pair, one pair. The extra die or dice not included in one of the above hands do not have any value. If a player throws four jacks, for instance, the fifth die does not help to decide the winner in case of ties. Tying players throw off. In the two-handed game, best three hands out of five wins.

SCARNEY DICE

Several years ago I created Scarney Dice—with which over 40 different exciting dice games can be played. While these Scarney Dice games can be played with two or more standard dice by considering the two and five spots on each die to indicate the word "dead," they are considerably more enjoyable when played with the specially created Scarney Dice. Each of these dice is marked with one, three, four and six spots, plus the word "dead" repeated on two opposite sides.

While there are over 40 different games, due to limited space only the rules for Scarney 3000, Scarney Put-and-Take Dice, Scarney Duplicate Jackpots, Scarney 21 Up and Down and their variants are listed in this chapter. For the other Scarney Dice games, see *Scarney Dice,* an 80-page book that contains complete rules for the more than 40 Scarney Dice games.

SCARNEY 3000®, THE BEST PRIVATE DICE GAME

Scarney 3000 is a most exciting bar, club and home dice game. It is the favorite dice game of the members of the John Scarne Game Club in my hometown of Fairview, New Jersey. A game consists of an undetermined number of rounds of play, and the player who first obtains a score of 3,000 points or more wins the game and receives the difference in points between his total and that of each of the losing players.

Requirements: Any number can play, each playing for himself. Five Scarney Dice, a dice cup and pencil and paper to keep score are used to play the game.

Seating position and turn of play: Each player throws the five dice from the dice cup. The player throwing the highest five-dice total number selects any seat he wants (and throws first), the player throwing the next-highest number sits on his left, and so on. (Dead dice count nothing.)

Point values of the dice: Any throw which contains one or two *dead* dice is a point-scoring throw and each dead die is valued at 50 points. A dice throw containing three, four or five dead dice is a bonus hand (see **Point values of bonus hands**). The only time the point numbers (1, 3, 4 and 6) have any value is in bonus hands. Otherwise they are known as "bust dice" and count nothing, zero points.

To emphasize: A bust hand is a dice throw neither possessing a bonus hand nor one or more dead dice. When a bust hand is thrown, the player loses the dice and scores zero points for that turn of play.

Point values of bonus hands: Any dice throw containing three or more dice of the same number, aces, threes, fours, sixes, is considered a bonus hand when accompanied by one or two dead dice on the same throw, or if one or more *dead* dice appear on the next toss. Throwing a dead die with a bonus hand or on the next roll is known as "confirming the bonus."

Any throw containing three or more dead dice is also a bonus hand but needs no confirmation because dead dice are point-scoring dice.

Bonus hands are valued as follows:

Bonus Hands	Point Values	Bonus Hands	Point Values	Bonus Hands	Point Values
3 dead	200	4 dead	400	5 dead	3,000
3 aces (1's)	100	4 aces (1's)	200	5 aces (1's)	3,000
3 threes (3's)	300	4 threes (3's)	600	5 threes (3's)	3,000
3 fours (4's)	400	4 fours (4's)	800	5 fours (4's)	3,000
3 sixes (6's)	600	4 sixes (6's)	1,200	5 sixes (6's)	3,000

Rules for Bonus Hands

1. If a dice throw contains a bonus hand plus one or two dead dice, the hand is confirmed and all points scored on the hand including 50 points for each dead die count.

2. If a dice throw reveals a potential bonus but does not include a dead die, the bonus hand is not confirmed and the player must put aside the bonus dice and throw the remaining dice or the five put-aside dice as the case may be. If this subsequent throw contains one or more dead dice, the bonus hand is confirmed and all points made on the hand count.

3. If the confirming throw doesn't contain a dead die but does contain another potential bonus, the player throws again in an attempt to confirm all points made on the hand.

4. If the confirming throw doesn't show a dead die the potential bonus hand is busted and all previously made points for the hand plus the potential bonus points are canceled out. The player scores zero points for the hand and passes the dice and cup to the player on his left.

5. A bonus throw made up of dead dice doesn't require confirmation since they are point-scoring dice.

The Play: At each turn of play, unless a player throws a bust hand, he must throw the dice until he scores a minimum of 200 points. Then he can do one of two things: (1) he can "stand" (pass) and enter his score on the score sheet and pass the dice and cup to the player on his left, or (2) he can continue to throw the dice in an attempt to better his score. If, however, he throws a bust hand, his turn immediately ends, he scores nothing, and the turn of play passes to the player on his left.

The Play in Detail

1. The shooter shakes the five dice inside the cup and throws them onto the table. If he fails to throw a dead die or a bonus hand, he calls, "Bust," and passes the dice and cup to the player on his left, his turn of play being ended.

2. If the shooter throws a hand whose point total is less than 200, such as *dead*–3–4–6–6, he counts aloud 50 points for the dead die and puts it aside with the dead side facing upward.

3. He returns the non-scoring (3–4–6–6) dice back into the cup and throws these four dice again. The second throw shows dead–3–6–6, the shooter counts aloud 50 for the dead die, puts it aside with the previously scored dead die, and calls aloud his point total which is now 100.

4. He next places the three non-scoring dice (3–6–6) back into the cup and throws them again. This throw reveals two dead dice and a 6. The shooter adds the 100 points for the two dead dice to his 100 previously scored points and calls 200. He then puts the two dead dice aside with the two previously put-aside dice.

5. Since the shooter has scored the required 200 points for a score to be valid, he may do one of two things: (1) he may call, "Stand," and pass the cup and dice to the player on his left and enter the 200 points to his credit on the score sheet, or (2) he may call, "Hit," and throw the remaining non-scoring die in an attempt to better his 200-point score. If, however, the shooter throws the non-scoring die and it fails to show dead, the hand is busted and the player scores nothing for the hand. But if the throw produces a point-scoring dead die, its 50-point value is added to the previously scored 200 points, and he calls 250. The player then may as before stand or hit, and throw out the five put-aside dice and continue the same procedure of play as described above until he decides to stand or until he busts.

6. If during his turn of play, a player should throw a potential bonus hand, the rules as described under Rules for Bonus Hands apply.

7. The procedure of placing point-scoring dice aside and rethrowing the non-scoring dice continues until one of two things happen: either the player throws a bust hand and loses the dice as well as all points scored for the hand, or the player says, "I stand," and enters his scored points which must be 200 or more for each round of play. The dice and cup are then passed to the player on his left.

8. A player never enters his hand score until he decides to stand and his turn of play is finished.

End of game: The game ends when a player scores 3,000 or more points. By so doing, he wins the game and gets credit for the point difference between his score and that of each opponent. Following is a sample score sheet of a Scarney 3000 game played by four persons. The score for each player's turn of play is written down to the left of the dash and the cumulative score to the right. This makes it known to each player at all times what the total score is and how far below or above the 3000-point game mark each player is. Bust hands are not entered on the score sheet.

A	B	C	D
200–200	200–200	450–450	600–600
450–650	200–400	200–650	800–1,400
200–850	550–950	200–850	1,900–3,300
950–1,800	200–1,150	300–1,150	
1,050–2,850		650–1,800	
2,850	1,150	1,800	3,300

Player D, the winner of the game, with 3,300 points, is well over the 3000-point mark for game. Because the game was played for points, A owes D 450 points, the difference between his final game score of 2,850 and D's 3,300. B owes D 2,150 points and C owes D 1,500 points.

Note: For players who prefer a longer game, a 5,000-point game is recommended.

PARTNERSHIP SCARNEY 3000

This is four-handed Scarney 3000. Two players are teamed against the other two. The rules for Scarney 3000 apply with the following exceptions and additional rules.

1. Each player throws five dice for partners. Holders of the two highest number totals (dead dice count nothing) are teamed against the holders of the two lowest. If three- or four-way ties occur on the throw for partners, one or more extra throws must take place until the ties are broken. Partners seat themselves opposite each other, and the holder of the highest number total starts the game by becoming the first shooter. From then on, each player's turn of play moves to the left, clockwise from player to player.

2. The score sheet heading is marked "They" and "We." Each player enters his hand score under his partnership heading and when a partnership's score totals 3,000 or more points, the game ends and each of the winning partners collects the total point difference between their total and that of the losing partnership.

Note: Team play can be extended to six players, three against three.

SCARNEY PUT-AND-TAKE DICE

Scarney Put-and-Take Dice is without a doubt one of the best Poker-style betting dice games in history. It combines the ante and pot-building flavor of Poker, the double-down psychology of Black Jack and the thrill and chance uncertainty of dice throwing.

Requirements

Scarney Put-and-Take Dice can be played by as many players as can sit around the playing surface. Three Scarney Dice, dice cup and a set of gaming chips are used to play the game. The main objective of the game is to throw "Scarney" (any three of a kind including three dead dice) which wins the game and takes the pot.

Selecting Seating Positions and Turn of Play

For seating position and turn of play, see page 533.

The Ante

Each player before the round (game) gets started antes (puts) an agreed upon equal number of chips into the center of the playing surface known as the pot. Each player must ante in turn starting with the first shooter and rotating clockwise.

The Play

Each player's turn of play is governed by the following rules:

1. The shooter places the three dice in the cup and after a proper shake promptly throws them onto the playing surface.

2. When the thrown dice show two dead dice and a number known as a "put," the shooter must pass the dice to the player on his left and contribute to the pot as many chips as there are spots on the third numbered die. Examples: The shooter throws (1) two dead dice and a four, he must put four chips into the pot; (2) two dead dice and a six, he must put six chips into the pot; and so on.

3. When the thrown dice show a double (two identical numbers) and a single (different number or a dead) known as a "take," the shooter takes from the pot as many chips as there are on the single die and throws again. Example: The shooter throws (1) two threes and a dead die. Since a dead die counts zero, no chips are taken from the pot. This is known as a push or standoff and the shooter throws again; (2) the shooter throws two fours and a six; he removes six chips from the pot; and so on.

4. When the shooter throws three single (three different numbers) or two singles and a dead die such as 1–3–6, 3–4–6, 3–4–dead, and so on, the throw does not count and the shooter throws again. This is known as a split, in-between, neutral or no decision throw.

5. When a shooter throws a three of a kind including three dead dice (1–1–1, 3–3–3, 4–4–4, 6–6–6, or dead–dead–dead) he calls, "Scarney," is declared the winner of the round, and takes the pot.

6. Before any throw of the dice, the shooter may, if he cares to, call "Double down." The double down option gives the shooter an opportunity on a possible hit to take double the number of chips from the pot as the throw indicates. *Example:* The shooter's throw is 4–4–6. He simply doubles the six and takes 12 chips from the pot. If, however, when doubling down, the shooter throws a put, he must put double the number of chips that the put indicates. *Example:* The shooter's put shows dead–dead–4; he simply doubles the four and puts 8 chips in the pot. To emphasize: A player continues to throw the dice until he throws a put and passes the dice to the player on his left and so it goes from player to player until a player throws Scarney and wins the pot.

7. Should the number of chips in the pot be reduced to five or less, each player puts into the pot an amount equal to his original ante. Should a player throw a take on a double down and the number of chips in the pot is less than the take calls for, there is no redress, he simply takes the remaining chips in the pot and a new round gets underway.

SCARNEY DUPLICATE JACKPOTS

Scarney Duplicate Jackpots is without a doubt the most thrilling and fastest-action dice game ever invented. The object of the game is to win the jackpot by throwing the same three-dice number total as did the previous shooter.

Requirements

Any number can play. This is an excellent four-, five-, six- or seven-person game. Three Scarney Dice, a dice cup and a set of gaming chips are used. Dead dice count zero.

Seating Positions and Turn of Play

For seating positions and turn of play, see page 533.

The Jackpot Ante

Each player, before the game, antes (puts) an agreed-upon number of chips in the center of the playing surface, known as the jackpot. All players must ante in turn, starting with the first shooter and rotating clockwise.

The Play

The first shooter places the three Scarney Dice in the dice cup and after a proper shake throws them onto the playing surface. There is no action for the first shooter on his first throw. He merely calls the total of the three thrown dice and passes the dice cup and the three dice with the same numbers face up toward the player to his left, whose turn it is to play.

From then on, the rules governing each shooter's turn of play (one throw with three dice) are as follows:

1. If the shooter throws (matches) the same number total as the previous shooter (player to the shooter's right) he calls, "Scarney," wins the game and takes the jackpot. Example: previous shooter made a total of 13 points (3, 4, and 6). Upon completion of his throw he passed the cup and three dice—with the 13 points face up to the next shooter. If the next shooter throws any 3 dice combination totaling exactly 13 points, he calls, "Scarney," and takes the jackpot.

2. If the shooter throws a lower number total than the previous shooter, he puts one chip in the jackpot for each point below the previous shooter's total. Examples: (1) Previous shooter's total was 15. Next shooter throws 10 and puts 5 chips in the jackpot. (2) Previous shooter's total was 16. Next shooter throws 4 and puts 12 chips in the jackpot. The cup and dice with the same numbers upward are passed to the next player.

3. If the shooter throws a higher number total than the previous shooter, he simply passes the cup and dice with the new total upward to the player on his left.

4. If the shooter throws three dead dice, called "craps," his score is zero points, and each player except the shooter must put five chips in the jackpot. And so it goes, clockwise, until a shooter wins the game and jackpot.

SCARNEY 21 UP AND DOWN

Anyone can learn to play this game in a few minutes, yet it is an unending source of entertainment for children and adults alike. The game is scored the direct opposite of most Scarney Dice games. With the exception of Big Scarney, only dead dice count. That is, the object of the game is to win the pot by bringing the player's combined total of thrown dead dice to exactly 21—and then following with a confirming throw of numbers (no dead dice).

Requirements

1. Any number may play, singly or in partnership. Needed are 5 Scarney Dice, a dice cup and a set of gaming chips. Score is kept by oral count.

2. For seating positions and turn of play, see page 533.

The Ante

Each player, before the game gets started, antes (puts) an agreed-upon equal number of chips into the center of the table, known as the pot. All players must ante in turn, starting with the first shooter and rotating clockwise.

The Play

The first shooter begins by throwing five dice. If one, two, three or four dead dice, or craps, are thrown, they are counted aloud and put aside and the remaining numbers (dice) are thrown again. The shooter continues throwing, each time adding aloud each crap (dead die) thrown to the previous total. The shooter continues to throw the remaining numbers until he fails to throw a dead die—whereupon the dice and cup pass to the player on his left.

If all five dice show dead either on the second throw or after any number of throws, they are added to the score and all five dice are thrown again by the same shooter; any subsequent dead dice thrown are added to the running total. And so it goes until the shooter fails to throw a dead die and his final score is the second shooter's starting number. If the first shooter threw 9 dead dice, the first dead die thrown by the second player is numbered 10, and so on. This continues until one player throws a dead die which brings the total to exactly 21; but the game does not end unless his next throw is comprised of all numbers (no dead dice). This is known as confirming the 21 score.

If a dead die appears on the next throw, the total is 22. If two dead dice appear, the total is 23 and the shooter continues throwing and adding dead dice to the total until no dead die is thrown. Whenever a player's starting number is 22 or more, all subsequent thrown dead dice are subtracted from the total until the shooter fails to throw a dead die. Example: If a player's starting number is 25 and he throws 11 dead dice and then fails to throw a dead die, the total number is now 14. To emphasize, whenever a player's starting total is 20 or less, all subsequent thrown dead dice are always added to his starting total. But when a player's starting total is 22 or more, all subsequent thrown dead dice are subtracted from his starting total. If a player's down total reaches zero, his next thrown dead die is counted as 1, and the second dead die is 2, etc.

Chip Penalties

Whenever a player's dead dice total passes the magic 21 mark, he must put one chip in the pot for each dead die he throws below or above 21.

Examples: (1) Player's starting number is 19. He throws 6 dead dice for a new total of 25. Since he is 4 over 21, he must put four chips in the pot. (2) The player's starting number is 23. He throws 7 dead dice for a new total of 16. Since he is 5 under 21, he must put five chips in the pot.

Note: Some players prefer to pay only a one-chip penalty for passing the magic 21, no matter by how much. For this option to be valid, it must be agreed upon before the start of the game.

The End of the Game

The game ends when a player hits 21 exactly and then throws "numbers" (fails to make a dead die on his next throw). When this occurs, the player calls "game" and is declared the winner and collects the pot —except when Big Scarney (any five of a kind including five dead dice) made on any one (single) throw automatically wins the game and takes the pot regardless of the dead dice total. Upon the winning of the pot, the right to start the next round and throw first goes to the player to the left of the previous winner.

LIAR OR DOUBTING DICE

Any number can play. Five dice are used with a dice cup. Each player throws five dice and the player throwing the highest Poker hand (ace is high, and 6, 5, 4, 3 and 2 represent king, queen, jack, ten and nine, respectively) takes any seat and is the first shooter; the player throwing the second-highest hand sits at his left and shoots second, and so on. Tying players shoot again.

At the beginning of play, each player places three betting units in front of himself. The first shooter shakes the dice, turns the cup upside down and lifts it, shielding the dice from view with his hand. He then announces the value of his hand, but need not state the truth. The player on his left must either accept the statement or call him a liar.

If the first shooter's statement is doubted and if he has at least as good a hand as he called, the doubter puts one betting unit in the pot. If the shooter has lied about his hand, he must pay one unit to the doubter and put one unit in the pot. It is the doubter's turn to throw, and he plays against the player on his left, and so on around the table.

If the first shooter's statement is accepted as true by the player at his left, it becomes the latter's turn to throw. He may use all the dice originally thrown or leave as many of them as he cares to and throw the others. As the first shooter did, he covers the dice he throws and must announce that the five dice have a value that beats the hand the first shooter announced and got accepted. The first shooter either accepts or doubts this statement, and this continues until one of the two players has doubted a hand which the other player has actually thrown or bettered. The doubter then puts one of his units in the pot.

When a player has placed all three betting units in the pot, he drops out of the game and the other players continue until only one player is left. He is declared the winner and takes the pot.

The player on the left of the first shooter begins the next game.

22.
The Match
Game

The Match Game is deceptively simple. Its rules of play are few and easily learned, but it is much more than a game of chance. It contains mathematical and psychological factors which introduce a skill element and make it one of the most fascinating of all guessing games in the world of gambling.

For the past 20 years the Match Game has been played on Friday nights at the Artists and Writers Restaurant on West 40th Street in New York City. This sustained record is unusual for any game. Among the many writing and publishing celebrities who played in these Friday night games was the late John Lardner, to whom this chapter is dedicated.

The loser in an Artists and Writers Restaurant Match Game usually buys a round of drinks for the other players. Some Las Vegas gamblers, however, have wagered as much as $5,000 on the outcome of a single Match Game.

SCARNE'S MATCH GAME RULES

Requirements: A set of three paper or wooden matches for each player. Two, three, four, five, six or more persons can play. The game is best suited to six-handed competition.

Object of the game: Each player tries to guess the sum total of the matches held by all the players. The one who guesses the correct total is declared the winner of the game, or a *hand* or *leg* (one game of a series) and is eliminated. The remaining players continue playing until only one player is left; he is the loser of the game.

Selecting the first player or caller: Before beginning the game, each player hides his three matches from his opponent or opponents (behind his back or under a table). He puts one, two, three or no matches in his right hand, closes his fist tightly and brings it into view.

Any player, by mutual consent, calls out his guess as to the sum total of the matches held by all the players, including himself. Then the player on his immediate left makes the second call, followed by calls from the others in turn, proceeding clockwise.

No player is permitted to call a total which has already been called.

After the last player has called his guess, the first caller opens his hand, showing his matches; then the other players, in turn, do the same. The exposed matches are counted. Since the person who makes the last guess has the best chance to win because he can base his guess on information derived from the other player's calls, the player whose guess is closest to the total gets the advantage of becoming the last player in the game or hand about to be played. The player who makes the next closest call becomes the next-to-last player, and so on. The player whose guess is farthest from the correct total starts the game by making the first call.

With the start of each new hand or game the first call passes to the left so that each player has an opportunity to be last caller and has an equal number of chances to win.

THE TWO-HANDED GAME

The first player tries to guess how many matches his opponent is holding, adds this to the number he himself holds, and calls the total, which may be any number from 0 through 6. His opponent follows suit, but may not call a total that has previously been called.

If neither player guesses the correct total, it is a *no game* or *stand-off*. Neither players wins or loses, and the play continues until one player makes a correct call. Players alternate in making the first call, even after a no game.

The player who first makes two correct calls out of three wins the game.

Two-Handed Strategy: Many people, at first look, think the Match Game is purely one of chance, but any beginner who sits down to play against experts soon discovers that he is losing far too often and that something more than chance is involved. There are two additional factors: a knowledge of the game's mathematics and skill in judging the psychology of the other players. The best two-handed playing strategy is based on the following mathematical analysis of the game.

Each of the two players may hold 0, 1, 2 or 3 matches. In order to win, the first player must add to the number of matches he himself holds a correct guess as to the number his opponent holds. Since his opponent may hold 0, 1, 2 or 3 matches, the first player has 1 chance in 4 of making a correct guess—a 25% chance to win the hand.

In a two-handed game the first player's chance of winning the hand is always the same (1 out of 4, or 25%), but the second player's chances vary, depending on the first call, from 25% to as much as 75%.

The second player has a better chance of winning most of the time because six of the seven possible calls (0, 1, 2, 3, 4, 5, 6) which the first player can make reveal information that enables the second caller to infer, rather than to guess blindly, the number his opponent holds.

A first call of "None" tells the second player that his opponent probably holds no matches and is guessing that the second player also holds none. If the first player calls "Six," his opponent can infer that he holds 3 matches and is guessing that second player holds 3. In the two cases above, the first caller has 1 chance in 4, or a 25% chance to win. But since he will miss 3 times out of 4, or 75% of the time, his opponent will win 3 out of every 4 times—a favorable chance of 75%.

A first call of either 1 or 5 is slightly less informative. A call of 1 indicates that the first player is probably holding none or 1, and a call of 5 indicates that he is probably holding 2 or 3. This gives the second player an even chance of guessing correctly the number of matches the first player is holding and his chance of winning, therefore, is 37½%. The chance that neither player will make a correct guess and the game will be a standoff is also 37½%.

A first call of 2 or 4 reveals still less. A call of 2 indicates that the first player may be holding zero, 1 or 2. A call of 4 indicates that the first player may be holding 1, 2 or 3. The second player has 4 chances in 7 of winning. The odds favor him at 4 to 3, and his chances of winning are 33½%. His chances that it will be no game are 41⅔%.

A call of 3 by the first player reveals nothing because he could be holding zero, 1, 2 or 3 matches. From a mathematical standpoint this call is, therefore, the first player's best strategy. But because of psychological factors the expert seldom sticks to a first call of 3. He studies his opponent's playing characteristics for faults. If he sees that his opponent prefers a hold of 3 more often than 0, or if he often repeats previous holds on the next play, etc., the expert may change his strategy accordingly.

The second call: Having heard the first player's call, the second player uses whatever information this has given him as a basis for his own call. If the first player calls "None," he probably holds no matches and the correct total is the number the second player holds. If the first call is 6, the first caller probably has 3 matches, and the second player simply adds 3 to what he himself holds. In both cases the second player has a 3 to 1 chance against the first player of winning the hand.

ODDS AND CHANCES IN TWO-HANDED MATCH GAME

	CHANCE TO WIN		CHANCE OF NO GAME	
First Call	1st Player	2nd Player		Odds in Favor of 2nd Player
0 or 6	25%	75%		3 to 1
1 or 5	25%	37½%	37½%	3 to 2
2 or 4	25%	33⅓%	41⅔%	4 to 3
3	25%	25%	50%	1 to 1

The miscall: Because the second player has a mathematical advantage, the first player sometimes purposely makes a miscall by guessing a total which can't possibly win for him. His object is to make the first call revert to his opponent. For instance, when the first caller holds 1 match he calls "None." He cannot win the hand; he will either lose or the hand will be a no game. If the second player does hold no matches and supposes that his opponent's call of "None" means that his opponent is holding none, he cannot call "None" because the rules prevent this, so he calls 1 and is surprised to find that this call wins.

Here are all the possible miscalls the first player can make in a two-handed game.

1st Player Holds	His Possible Miscalls
0 matches	4, 5 or 6
1 match	0, 5 or 6
2 matches	0, 1 or 6
3 matches	0, 1 or 2

The miscall, when used wisely, is a valuable asset to Match Game strategy and can be compared to the bluff in Poker.

THREE OR MORE PLAYERS

When there are three or more players in the game, the rules of play are the same as for two players, with one exception. The game is now an elimination contest. As each player wins a hand by guessing the correct total he drops out of the game; he is safe and cannot become the final loser. For example: There are six players—A, B, C, D, E and F. B guesses the first hand correctly, and is eliminated. A, C, D, E and F play the next hand. D wins and is eliminated. This elimination process continues until only two players remain. They continue the play, and the winner of two out of three hands is eliminated. The sole remaining player is declared the loser of the game, and he must pay the amount of the stake originally agreed upon (5¢, 25¢, $1, etc.) to each of the players, or as is the custom at the Artists and Writers Restaurant, he buys a round of drinks.

Three-handed strategy: The last caller again has a mathematical advantage, although it is not quite as strong as in the two-handed game. The first caller knows that the total number of matches his opponents may hold ranges from none to six.

The number of ways each of these totals can be made are as follows:

0 or 6	Each can be made 1 way
1 or 5	Each can be made 2 ways
2 or 4	Each can be made 3 ways
3	Each can be made 4 ways

A combined total of 16 ways

The first player's call, of course, is the sum of what he guesses his opponents hold *plus the number of matches he himself holds.*

The first caller's best chance to win, therefore, is to add 3 to the number of matches he himself holds and call the total. This gives him 1 chance in 4 of winning, or 25%.

The second player reverses the strategy of the first player by subtracting 3 from the first player's call. Example: The first player calls 6; the second player subtracts 3 and infers that the first player holds 3 matches. The second player now has a 25% chance of guessing the number held by the third player. He makes a guess as to the third player's hold, adds the number he calculated the first player may be holding, adds the number he himself holds, and announces the total.

On the occasions when this total has already been called by the first player, the second player's next best bet is to add or subtract 1 to the number already called and to announce this total.

If the second player calls three more or three less than the first call, he gives the third player too much valuable information. Example: The first player calls 6. If the second player calls 9, he is telling the third player that he holds 3; if he calls 3 the third player can assume he holds 0.

Whenever the second player makes a lower call than the first player, the third player can assume the second is holding either 0 or 1. If the second player call 2 or 3 more than the first player, the third can assume that the second holds 3.

To summarize: When three experts are playing, the first caller has a 25% chance of winning the hand, the second has a 25% chance, and the third and last has a 33⅓% chance. The remaining 16⅔% chance is the percentage in favor of a no-game result.

FOUR, FIVE, SIX OR MORE PLAYERS

When there are four or more players, the last caller's advantage is diminished somewhat because the more players there are the greater are the chances that the number the last player wants to call has already been called. Often the next nearest numbers above and below have also been called. All the last player can do in this case is to call the closest number that has not yet been called.

The best strategy in a game with four or more players is to play the averages. Assume the average number held by each player is 1½ matches. Example: In a five-handed game in which you call first, you guess that each of the other four players holds 1½ matches, a total of 6. Add the number you hold to this 6 count, and call the total. If you hold none you call 6; holding one you call 7; holding two you call 8 and holding three you will call 9.

When you have an odd number of opponents and assume that each holds an average of 1½ matches, your total will contain the fraction ½. Here you either add or subtract ½. Example: When there are five opponents you arrive at a total of 7½. Add or subtract ½ for a total of either 7 or 8, then add the number of matches you yourself hold.

In a five-or-more-handed game, if the calls made by the preceding players add to a total considerably above or below the total obtained by allowing them each an average of 1½ matches, the remaining players or player should increase or decrease the 1½-match average to conform to the information he has gathered from the preceding calls.

23.
General

Puerto Rico's most popular dice game, played in bars, clubs and homes throughout the island, is Generala or, in English, General. In bars it is usually played for drinks, low man paying, but I have also seen thousands of dollars change hands at a single General game session. Because it contains an element of strategy which other dice games do not have, it is in my opinion one of the most fascinating of all present-day dice games. Since so many mainland tourists visit Puerto Rico, I suspect General may soon become equally popular here. For that reason I have included the rules.

Any number may play, singly or in partnership. Five dice are used with a dice cup. Score is kept on a sheet ruled into boxes. The players' names are entered across the top, and down the left-hand column are the numbers 1, 2, 3, 4, 5 and 6, followed by the Poker hands: straight, full house, four of a kind, and small general (five of a kind), as shown on page 552. The big general listing is not necessary.

VALUE OF POKER HANDS AND POINT NUMBERS

Five of a kind when made on the first throw is known as the "big general" and automatically wins the game, regardless of the score. Five of a kind made on the second or third throw is known as the "small general" and is valued at 60 points.

Four of a kind made on the first throw is valued at 45 points, on the second or third throw, 40 points.

A *full house* made on the first throw is valued at 35 points, on the second or third throw, 30 points.

A *straight* (1, 2, 3, 4, 5 or 2, 3, 4, 5, 6) made on the first throw is valued at 25 points, on the second or third throw, 20 points. Aces (1) may be used as "wild" in making a straight, but they can only be used to equal a 2 or 6. They cannot be used to equal a 3, 4 or 5 to make a straight. This is the only time during the play of the game that aces may be wild.

The point numbers (1, 2, 3, 4, 5 and 6) are valued at their total spot value. Examples: three sixes are 18 points; two fives are 10 points; four aces are 4 points; and so on.

THE PLAY OF THE GAME

Each player throws the five dice to determine the order of play, holder of lowest-valued hand going first, next lowest second, and so on. In determining partners, the two lowest and two highest hands are partners. The dice and cup pass to the left, clockwise.

Each player may take either one, two or three throws per turn, called a "frame." A complete game consists of ten frames, unless some player throws a big general.

FIRST THROW OF THE DICE

The player shakes the five dice in the cup and throws them onto the bar or table. If he throws a pat Poker hand, such as a four of a kind, full house or straight, he enters his score on the sheet. If, however, he throws any other hand, a pair, two pair and so on, he has the following option:

He may put aside one, two, three or four dice and throw the left-overs, or he may throw all five dice again. Example: If the player has thrown a total of two or three sixes, he may decide to hold the sixes and try to better the hand by throwing the remaining dice. This is similar to holding certain cards and drawing to improve the hand in Draw Poker.

SECOND THROW OF THE DICE

The same rules apply as in the first throw, except that a general becomes a small general and the values of the Poker hands diminish.

THIRD THROW OF THE DICE

After the third throw, if a small general, four of a kind, full house or straight has not been made, the player may select any number for his scoring point number. Example: His hand is made up of three aces, a five and six. Since the best score he can make with the ace (1) is 5 points, it is to his advantage to name the aces as his point and enter 3 points alongside number 1 on the sheet. Or if his hand is a pair of twos, a pair of fours and a five, his best bet is to name the twos as his point number and score $2 + 2 = 4$. He would then enter 4 points on the sheet next to number 2.

However, after a score has been entered on the sheet, the player cannot shoot for that hand or point number again. On each turn of play, the player has one less hand or point number to shoot for, so that, at the end of the game, the player will have shot and entered a score for each of the ten frames.

If the player fails to throw a five-dice Poker hand or he does not wish to enter a low point score, he may value his score as zero and place it next to any Poker hand or point number on the sheet. When a zero (0) is placed on the sheet opposite a Poker hand, double zeros (00) are used. Placement of these zeros is part of the strategy of the game.

When all the players have had their ten turns of play and no big general has been thrown, the game is completed. Each player's score is totaled; in case of team play, partnership scores are totaled. The player or partnership having the highest total score wins. When played for drinks, the low man or sometimes the two lowest men pay. The same holds true for team play.

ADDITIONAL RULES

(1) If a player has four of a kind showing and is trying for a small general, he may, if he likes, take the remaining die, put it in the cup, call, "Opposite," shake and turn the cup mouth down on the table. Example: "Opposite" when holding four threes is a four, four fives is a deuce and so on. When a player calls, "Opposite," the right to lift the cup off the die goes to his opponent.

(2) If a small general has already been scored and the player throws a small general on his second throw, he cannot count it as four of a kind. However, he can pick up the fifth die and throw it for his third throw, hoping to throw one of the other 5 numbers. If he still has a small general after the third throw, he cannot value it at four of a kind. However, he can use the number as a point number, provided the number is open. If not, the five of a kind is valued at zero.

(3) If a player has already filled in a straight and a full house on his score sheet, the dice he puts aside must all have the same value—all aces, deuces, threes, etc.

Following is the score of a game as played by four Puerto Ricans:

	Tito	Juan	Raul	Mario
1	0	0	4	3
2	4	6	6	4
3	9	9	6	6
4	8	8	12	12
5	20	10	15	20
6	12	0	18	18
Straight	25	25	20	25
Full house	35	30	30	30
Four of a kind	40	40	45	40
Small general	00	00	00	60
Total	153	128	156	218

Note: Mario, with a total of 218 points, wins the game. And because the game was played at $1 a point, Raul owes Mario $62 (the difference between his final count of 156 and Mario's 218). Juan owes Mario $90 and Tito owes Mario $65.

24.
Money Poker

Money Poker, also known as Liar Poker or Dollar Poker, is a fascinating guessing game played with one-dollar bills. It is most popular in bars, cafés and clubs where it is usually played for the dollars used to play the game.

Requirements

1. Two to nine players. Five or six make for the best game.
2. Five or more dollar bills for each player, although only one bill is used by each player. A dollar bill, as you probably know, possesses a two-letter eight-digit serial number on its face. Money Poker is based on eight digits and the two letters are disregarded.

Rank of the serial numbers: 0 (high), 9, 8, 7, 6, 5, 4, 3, 2, and 1 (low).

Object of the game: To bid (call aloud) a specific amount of digits that you believe are on the combined dollar bills held by all contestants. If the player who bids highest makes his bid, he is the winner and collects the dollar bills in play for each player. If he fails to make his bid, he must pay each player a dollar.

Start of the game: The first dealer is decided by mutual consent. The dealer collects five one-dollar bills from each player and shuffles (mixes) them up with their serial numbers face down. Then the dealer, starting with the leader (player on his left), deals each player including himself five face-down bills, one at a time, clockwise. Each player studies his five bills and selects any one he wishes. The remaining four bills are put aside for future use. Caution is used by each player not to expose the serial number of the bill in play to the other players. This is usually accomplished by folding the bill in such a way that the serial number is visible only to the owner.

How to score the game: I recommend that the maximum amount of numbers that can be scored from each dollar be three. To illustrate, suppose a player's bill shows five 6s. Only three of these 6s are counted toward the bid. The other two 6s do not count in the scoring. The reason for this three-number maximum count in the scoring is to nullify the advantage gained by a dishonest player when he introduces a bill into the game which shows four, five, six, seven or eight of the same number. However, if you are the trusting kind and want to count all the numbers on each bill, go ahead and do so—but if you get rooked don't say I didn't warn you.

The bidding: The leader has the first privilege of play. After studying the serial number of his bill, he must do one of two things:

1. He may bid any number he wants.

2. He may pass, which indicates he passes his privilege of bidding for the present. However, he may re-enter the bidding at any time it is his turn to play.

After the leader has decided, each player in turn, starting with the player on the leader's left and moving clockwise, must do the same (bid or pass). This procedure is followed until the end of the game. Each successive bid must be higher than the previous one, either in the amount or in the same amount of a higher-ranking number. Example: The leader bids two 5s. The next bidder's lowest progressive bid must be two 6s, 7s, 8s, 9s, 0s; or three 1s, 2s, 3s, 4s, 5s. When a player bids and all the other players pass, he (being the highest bidder) gets the bid. On the showdown, should he fulfill his bid, he is the winner. If he fails to fulfill his bid, he is the loser.

Players at the showdown usually take each other's word about the amount of numbers they hold and do not bother to verify. However, if a player so desires, he may ask each and every player to show his bill to verify the called count.

End of the game: Once the bidding has ceased and the high bid of the last bidder has been established, the bidder calls out the amount of the bid number shown on his dollar. Let's say his bid was nine 8s and his dollar shows three 8s. He calls, "Three," and the player to his left calls, "Two" (indicating that his dollar possesses two 8s). And so it goes, from player to player. Should the sum total of 8s held by all the players total nine or more, the bidder wins and collects one dollar (the dollars in play) from each player. Should the number of 8s total eight or less, the bidder loses and he must pay each player one dollar—and that game is ended.

Start of a new game: Each player selects one of his four remaining bills and the second game begins. If the previous bidder made his bid, the player to his left must bid first. But if the previous bidder failed to make his bid, he must bid first.

The same procedure is followed game by game until each player's five one-dollar bills have been played. Then a new shuffle of five one-dollar bills from each player takes place and a new series of five games is played.

25.
Carnival, Fair, Bazaar, Arcade and Amusement Park Games

If you should make a sample survey of the adults in cities, towns and villages in various parts of the country, as I have done, you would find that most of the people you question would admit that they had, sometime during the year, taken at least a quarter chance on some carnival game. My survey shows that about 70 million Americans (a good many more if you count young people under 18) patronize one or more of the many games which are found at carnivals, bazaars, arcades, picnics, outings, state and county fairs, amusement parks and other amusement centers. About 40 million of these players are women, and the total handle is about $13 billion. Since the carnival game operators' net profit averages about 30% of the handle, the players spend or lose, whichever way you want to look at it, about $4 billion annually.

The owner of a traveling carnival or bazaar usually comes to town under the auspices of some local branch of an organization such as the American Legion, the Knights of Columbus or the Volunteer Fire Department. In most cases the owner needs this sponsorship in order to obtain a license to operate. If he had to depend on the income derived from the Ferris wheels, *chump twisters* (merry-go-rounds), dodge'ems, fun houses, shooting galleries, ten-in-one shows and similar amusement devices, the owner would be lucky to break even after paying expenses and sharing his net proceeds with the sponsor. His profit comes from granting concessions to concessionaires who operate gambling games.

The carnival, fair or bazaar stays in town anywhere from a three-day weekend to two weeks, and the concessionaire pays so much per day plus a percentage of his profits, depending upon the location and type of game being operated. A week's stand at a big church bazaar

John Scarne on an amusement-park midway. (Stanley Einzig)

may cost the operator of a Big Six wheel $1,000 down plus 40% or more of his gross revenue. A small blanket-stand concession may cost $200 or more in advance, and possibly a percentage as well. Since the initial payment is in advance the operator has no weather insurance; if it rains all week and the bazaar is a financial bust, the game operators *blank out* (do not make expenses). They call it playing a *bloomer* (a losing stand).

The operation of carnival games is a seasonal proposition and the *carnies* (carnival employees) try to make enough money during a four- to five-month season, usually late spring and summer, to tide them over the rest of the year. They may also do some business during the off-season at indoor local bazaars and other fund-raising affairs for charity.

The average carnival game operator is not trying to take your shirt. Like the casino operators, many of whom are former carnies, he believes that he is entitled to a favorable percentage edge on his game for operating it, and he has learned by experience that if he gets enough action the business is a profitable one, even though he may have to pay as much as $25,000 or more for a season's choice game concession at some amusement center. He may gross $10,000 or more at such a spot over a Fourth of July, Decoration Day or Labor Day weekend.

THE LANGUAGE OF CARNIVAL GAMES

The carnies, like horse bookies, casino operators and most specialized groups, have a lingo or jargon of their own, and a quick look at some of it is necessary before we discuss the gambling games in detail. Here are the most important terms; others will be explained as we come to them.

ADVANCE MAN OR AGENT: The man who travels ahead of a carnival or traveling bazaar and who arranges for licenses, lots, advertising, publicity and also puts in the fix with local officials.

AGENT OR CONCESSIONAIRE: A carnival game operator.

ALIBI STORE: A carnival game which pretends to be a skill or science game but which gives the player little or no chance to win. Any carnival game in which the player needs as much skill or dexterity as does a champion bowler scoring 270 or better, in order to win a doll or ham, is not a skill game—it's an alibi store, so called because the operator always has an alibi which pretends to explain why the player lost.

BAG MAN, FIXER OR ICEMAN: The local official or anyone acting for him to whom protection money is paid.

(to) BLOW, GO WRONG: To lose money.

(the) BUILD-UP, PITCH OR CON ACT: Act performed by the operator and his shills to arose the player's gambling spirit during a carnival game so that he will bet big.

CARNIVAL WHEEL: There are many carnival wheels which appear to be different, but they are all essentially the same. The wheel is usually made of wood, 1 to 2 inches thick and from 17 to 41 inches in diameter. It rotates about a steel or bronze bearing mounted on a steel axle that is set either horizontally or vertically. A circular area around the wheel's rim is divided into sections, usually painted in flashy colors, or bearing numbers, symbols or a number-color combination. A nail or pin projects from the wheel's surface between each section and these projections brush against a rubber, leather, spring or plastic indicator fixed to a wall or post. When the wheel stops, the indicator is between two nails, and the section at which it points is the winning section.

COP, n: A win; v: To steal or cheat.

COUNT STORE OR ADD-UP JOINT: A flat joint (see below) which requires that the player score a specified number of points to win, something he can't do because the cheating lies in the count or add-up itself.

(*to*) FAIRBANK OR THROW A COP: To make a cheating move in favor of the player to entice him to continue playing or increase the size of his bets.

FIX OR ICE: Protection money paid to the police or to some town, county or state official (usually through a bag man) for permission to operate an illegal gambling enterprise.

FLASHER: A modern carnival game of chance in which electrical circuits and lights have replaced the old wheel. In some localities where P.C. games are barred, the authorities permit flashers and can still pretend they are not allowing carnival wheels to operate.

FLAT JOINT: Any crooked carnival game.

FLATTY, THIEF OR GRIFTER: The operator of a flat, alibi, two-way or G-joint. Any crooked game operator.

FUZZ: Police.

GAFF, G OR GIMMICK: Any secret device or method that accomplishes the cheating. A gaffed or G-joint is a game that can be operated dishonestly.

GRIFTER: One who operates any of the rackets that make up the *grift*, which is characterized by the use of the sharp wit or skilled hand as opposed to the use of or threat of force or violence in the *heavy* rackets. Grifters include all kinds of thieves: professional gamblers, confidence men, pickpockets and many other types. A *carnival grifter* is one who travels with a carnival, a flat-joint operator, a stick (see below), a Three-Card Monte or Three-Shell operator.

GYPSY: An unreliable carnival employee or operator, a drunk.

HANKY-PANKY OR GRIND STORE: Any small-time game which operates on a nickel-and-dime play and requires lots of action in order to grind out a profit, such as weight- and age-guessing, cigarette shooting gallery, and pitches of all kinds: tossing coins into a dish, throwing Ping-Pong balls into small goldfish bowls, throwing darts at balloons. The payoff is usually in cheap merchandise.

ICE: See *Fix*.

INSIDE MAN: See *Outside man*.

LAYDOWN: A diagram of betting spaces, usually on the counter in front of the game, on which the players place their bets.

LIVE ONE: A player with money.

MONEY STORE: Any carnival game which pays off in cash rather than merchandise.

MOOCH, MARK OR CHUMP: Carnie slang for sucker. Anyone who plays a percentage game, hanky-pank, alibi store or flat joint. All of the 70 million Americans who gamble at carnival games each year fall into this category from the carnie's viewpoint.

OUTSIDE MAN: A carnival game employee who pretends to be a player and assists in the buildup. He is usually an elderly man with a good gift of gab. INSIDE MAN: The operator of any carnival game.

PADDLE WHEEL OR RAFFLE WHEEL: A carnival wheel each of whose numbered sections contain one, two or three numbers. Most such wheels have a counter laydown raffle chart on which bets are placed. Some operators sell *paddles* (numbered paper slips) which correspond to the numbered spaces on the wheel.

PATCH OR MENDER: The lawyer who travels with the show.

PEEK STORE: A flat joint in which part of the gaff consists in the operator's peeking at a number and then miscalling it, or resorting to a sleight-of-hand move (usually holding his thumb over part of the number) to clip the player.

PERCENTAGE OR P.C. STORE: Any game which earns its profits by paying off winners at less than the correct odds.

SKILL OR SCIENCE GAME: Any carnival game which requires skill to play; also any carnival game of chance that is called a skill or science game in order to mislead the authorities and get around the laws prohibiting games of chance.

SLUM: Cheap merchandise prizes.

SPINDLE: A metal or wooden arrow mounted on a horizontal base. A paper, celluloid, rubber or leather indicator protrudes from the arrow's point and brushes against the surrounding circle of posts or nails separating the sections. Here the indicator spins while the numbered sections and posts are stationary, just the reverse of the wheels.

STICKS OR SHILLS: Carnival game employees who pretend to be players in order to attract and stimulate business, and who "win" prizes which they secretly return later.

STOCK OR MERCHANDISE JOINTS: Carnival games that pay off in merchandise—dolls, lamps, blankets, groceries, silverware, parakeets, etc.—called, depending on their merchandise, doll joints, lamp joints, parakeet joints, etc.

STORE OR JOINT: Any carnival game, honest or crooked.

TIP: The crowd of players and prospective players who gather around the game.

TWO-WAY JOINT, GAFFED JOINT, G-JOINT, STRONG JOINT, SKIN JOINT, FLAT JOINT: A game that can be operated two ways—honest or crooked. When the big money appears, you can be sure the gaff is on. THREE-WAY AND FOUR-WAY JOINTS: Games that can be played from three and four sides.

(*to be*) WITH IT: "He's with it" means that he is a carnie, i.e., he's with the carnival.

WHY NEW JERSEY LEGALIZED CARNIVAL GAMES

In 1953 the voters of New Jersey made Bingo and raffles legal. A Bingo and Raffles Commission was set up which for several years called itself the Legalized Games of Chance Control Commission and which, by its own ruling, took authority not delegated by law to regulate carnival games as well. They did this by defining carnival games as "non-draw raffles," and they issued licenses permitting charitable organizations to run certain carnival games as indicated by the following excerpt from the commission's rule book:

> It has been determined by this commission that the following games qualify as non-draw raffles and may be licensed under the Raffles Licensing Law: Ring Toss Game, Fish Pond, Penny Pitch, Duck Pond, String Game, Baseball Game, Hoop-la Game, Ball Roll, Bumper Car, Dart Game, Jar-A-Do, Grab Bag, Horse Racing Game, and Wheels of Chance.
>
> Any games that are not listed above and which have not received the express approval of this Commission may not be licensed.
>
> If your organization conducts any other games, you are jeopardizing your rights to conduct raffles and bingo. . . .
>
> Any person playing for money or other valuable things at cards, dice, billiards, pool, tennis, bowling, shuffleboard, etc., is guilty of a misdemeanor.

It is this sort of action on the part of state officials which creates public contempt for and disobedience of gambling laws.

At the same time that the Control Commission took it upon themselves to license carnival games operated by charitable organizations, state law-enforcement agencies clamped down on all other carnival games. The game operators in amusement centers, parks and carnivals were, for a time, put out of business. They promptly set to work to circumvent the law by installing games which they advertised with big display signs as "games of skill and science." All too often the law-enforcement authorities fell for this gimmick and permitted their operation, forgetting that a bet made at a game of skill is gambling just as much as one made at a game of chance.

The game of One-Ball is a sample of what these "skill and science" games are like. One-Ball is usually a homemade affair, and individual operators add their own personal touches, but the basic principle is always the same. The player throws a soft rubber ball from three to six inches in diameter over the game counter and against a wooden backboard from which the ball rebounds down onto the game layout. This is divided into from 60 to 144 three-inch numbered squares with

*The customer starts and stops an electrically powered wheel in a hanky-
pank in New Jersey, where wheels of this type are legal. (Stanley Einzig)*

raised edges. If the ball comes to rest in the numbered square on which
the player bet he wins a ham, doll, or perhaps a stuffed toy rabbit. This
the authorities accept as a game of skill because at the beginning the
player threw the ball. This is the same as saying that Craps is a game
of skill because the shooter threw the dice!

Most of the so-called skill or science games give the players even
less chance to win than the wheels. I talked to a great many women
in New Jersey amusement centers at this time and they all said they
preferred the wheels. One 70-year-old woman playing Ring Toss expressed the general attitude: "I've been coming to this resort on my
vacation for twenty years and I always came over on Saturday nights
and played the wheels. It was only a dime a spin and I nearly always
went home with a basket of groceries. Maybe it cost me a couple of
dollars more than the groceries were worth, but it was fun. Now
there's nothing but these silly 'skill' games and I never win anything.
I'm not very good at tossing hoops. Why do those crazy state officials
bar the games at which I could win once in a while, and insist on
games where I always lose? How do they figure this is protecting the
public?"

This situation, in which charitable organizations were permitted to operate the standard carnival games of chance, while the carnivals and amusement centers got around the law by operating a strange assortment of games of chance which pretended to be games of skill or science, lasted from 1954 until late 1959, when public opinion forced state legislators to place a carnival referendum on the ballot. On November 3, 1959, an overwhelming number of voters voted Yes, and New Jersey became the first state to legalize carnival games.*

For the benefit of other state officials who may be considering the legalization of carnival games, I quote the New Jersey Amusement Games Licensing Law:

> An act authorizing the conducting and playing of certain amusement games, whether of chance, skill, or both, where the prizes or awards to be given shall be merchandise only, or a retail value not in excess of $15.00; and the charge for the privilege of playing shall not exceed $0.25; providing for the licensing, regulation and control by a commissioner of the conducting and operating of such games; providing restrictions as to the places where such games may be conducted and operated; providing that certain playing for money or other valuable things is not authorized; providing for the operation and incorporation of the act in any municipality when so determined by referendum vote therein.

The Amusement Games Control Commissioner appointed to supervise and regulate carnival game operations has a tough problem on his hands. This task is much more complicated than the regulation of such legalized forms of gambling as Bingo and raffles. You'll see why when you read the following text.

THE LOWDOWN ON CARNIVAL GAMES

Forty years ago when I began analyzing carnival games and getting flatties and grifters to talk about their secrets, 50% of the games were gaffed. My recent survey indicates that today only about 10% are run crookedly. This decrease in dishonesty is not due to any change of heart on the part of the flatties; most of the managers and promoters of state fairs, carnivals, bazaars and amusement parks have finally smartened up. They realize that they get more business and more profits in the long run if they do not "burn up the territory" by allowing strong joints to fleece the customers.

The many different games that line the midway are not as different as they may look to the uninitiated. Different names are used for what

---

* The situation that existed in New Jersey before legalization still prevails in a great many of the amusement centers throughout the country.

are essentially the same games. The basic principles employed are few. The most common principle used in the so-called science or skill games is the throwing or tossing of a ball, ring, hoop, dart or coin. In games of chance, it is the spinning of a wheel, spindle or flasher, or the throwing of one or more dice or balls.

These are the most popular carnival games found in amusement centers throughout the United States: Skillo Game, Pin Store, Bucket Store, Bumper Game, Balloon Dart, Parakeet Pitch, Pitch Till You Win, Hoop-la, Watch-la, Fish Pond, Duck Pond, Roll Tables, Bushel Baskets, the Milk Bottles, Penny Pitch, Ringer Coke, Darts, Age and Scales, Basketball, Cat Rack, Ring Toss, Swinger, Spot the Spot, Horserace Game, Mouse Game, Bowling Game, Nail Hammering Game, Six-Ball Roll-Down, Knife Rack, Hand Striker, Three-Pin Game, Cigarette Shooting Gallery, Razzle Dazzle, Dropcases, Three-Marble Tivoli, String Game, Grab Bag, Chuck-a-Luck, Under and Over Seven, Beat the Shaker, Big Six, Racehorse Wheel, Carnival Wheels, Spindles and Flashers.

You can win, probably have won, prizes at carnival games. But, as in any other form of organized gambling, don't expect to come out ahead of the game in the long run. The games are designed to earn money for the operator, pay his expenses and give him a profit. The amount you lose in the long run is the price you pay for the pleasure of playing the game. This is reasonable and fair. But some carnival games are run by grifters who look on their customers as suckers and

Game of skill (tossing Ping-Pong balls into bowls to win a goldfish) at New Jersey's Seaside amusement center. (Stanley Einzig)

who will, if you let yourself fall into that category, clip you for all they can get.

The only way you can be 100% sure that you are not being fleeced is not to play. But since carnival games can be fun, and you don't want to go this extreme, your next best bet is to study the following text which gives you the information you need to avoid being a mooch.

HANKY-PANKS

Hanky-panks include such games as Fish Pond, Balloon Dart, Cigarette Shooting Gallery, String Games, the Parakeet Pitch and pitching coins or Ping-Pong balls into a receptacle of some kind. When the prizes offered are cheap ones they are actually games of skill and can, for this reason, run anywhere. Since most people play these games primarily for fun and have no great interest in the small intrinsic value of the prizes, they are more amusement devices than they are gambling games.

This is true as long as the game is run honestly. But if the prizes are expensive ones, or if the operator offers to bet cash money and tries to get you to increase the size of your bets, that is your cue that the harmless hanky-pank has been converted into a gaffed alibi or flat joint, and your chance of winning has been reduced to zero.

PERCENTAGE GAMES

Percentage games are the biggest and most consistent carnival money-makers. Carnies also refer to them as *group games* because, unlike most of the hanky-panks, which permit only one person to play at a time, as many persons can play a percentage game as there is space at the game counter.

Today's most popular P.C. games are those old favorites, the carnival wheels and spindles and their modern equivalents—the electrically operated flashers, One-Ball group games, the Mouse Game, Chuck-a-Luck, Beat the Shaker, High Dice, Under and Over Seven and many of those chance games which masquerade as skill games.

WHEELS OF FORTUNE

The carnival wheel is one of the oldest and still the most popular of all carnival gambling devices. The players like the wheels because they win more often at them than at any of the homemade games of chance or so-called skill games.

The wheel is usually made of wood and rotates around a steel axle, either in a vertical or horizontal plane. Small nails, called posts, are evenly spaced around the rim of the wheel and they strike against a

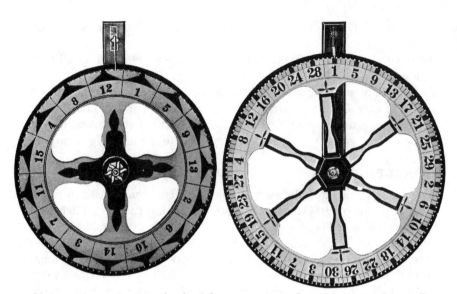

Common type of carnival wheel bearing 15 numbers (LEFT), *and a raffle wheel.*

pliable stationary indicator. The space in which the indicator rests after the wheel has stopped is the winning space.

The wheels are essentially all the same, varying only in details such as size, design, bets permitted and prize awards.

Merchandise is usually used for prizes although cash awards are made if the fix is in. A popular merchandise wheel which can also be played for money bears 30 numbered sections, each divided into 5 smaller colored sections. One section, usually red, pays off at odds of 50 for 1, and the remaining four white sections pay off at 10 for 1.

There are thirty matching numbers on the laydown chart. If you put your dime on number 3 and the wheel stops with the indicator pointing at that section, you win; the color of the section determines the payoff. A red space pays $5 on a time bet, and a white space pays $1—or the equivalent in merchandise.

If we bet 30 dimes, one on each numbered space, five times in succession, for a total of $15, and assume that the wheel stops once on the red and four times on the white, we will win the $5 prize once, and the $1 prize four times for a total of $9. Since we made a total of $15 in bets our total loss is $6. The operator takes in $15, pays out $9, and retains $6, a percentage in his favor of 40%. In the long run you pay him 4¢ of each dime bet, or $4 for each hundred dime bets made.

Merchandise wheel operators in amusement centers, in order to keep their players coming back, give the players tickets valued according to red or white wins. These can be redeemed for such valuable prizes as a television set, radio, clock, camera or silverware. The catch is that it will probably require playing the wheel nightly for the entire season before a player wins the large number of tickets that are required to win a capital prize.

The biggest money-making P.C. wheels are the Big Six, Money Wheel and Racehorse Wheel, which can also be found in casinos (pages 501–505). They appear at bazaars, carnivals and other amusement centers only where the fix is strong, i.e., where the cops have been properly iced.

If you want to play carnival wheels for fun, you would be smart to consider that 25% to 50% of the money you wager on each spin is a donation; when you reach the total amount you wish to donate—stop playing. If you continue to play, or permit the operator to hustle you into making big-money bets, brother, you are a born mooch, and nothing will save you from losing your bankroll.

ONE-BALL GAME

The One-Ball Game is a percentage game found in most amusement centers. It is usually advertised as a skill game wherever the authorities bar games of chance. The player throws a soft rubber ball (3 to 6 inches in diameter) against a wooden backboard from which the ball rebounds and bounces down onto the game layout. The layout is divided into numbered squares, and the one on which the ball stops determines whether or not the player wins or loses.

Since these games are usually homemade jobs, you seldom find two that are exactly alike. Some layouts contain 60 squares, others 100, and I have seen some that contain as many as 144 or more three-inch squares, each of which is separated from its neighbors by several thicknesses of adhesive tape forming a raised edge which serves to hold the ball in place when it comes to a stop.

The most common layout is made of ordinary ashtrays. Inside the booth, four or five feet from the game's counter, is a square wooden platform covered with 64 ashtrays, each about four inches square and arranged in eight rows of eight trays each. Twenty-four of the ashtrays are painted red, 15 blue, 10 green, 5 white, 4 brown, 3 orange, 2 silver and 1 gold. Players may bet any amount from a dime up on any color. The color betting layout on the counter gives the following payoff odds:

Gold	20 to 1
Silver	10 to 1
Orange	8 to 1
Brown	6 to 1
White	5 to 1

Green	3 to 1
Blue	2 to 1
Red	1 to 1, or even money

Although the game is amusing, is such entertainment worth the price you pay? Let's find out what the cost is. Suppose we cover each of the eight color betting spaces on the laydown with a $1 bet, throw the ball 64 times, and assume that it comes to a stop once in each of the 64 ashtrays. We will wager $8 each of the 64 times for a total of $512.

Color	Wins	Player Receives
Gold	1	$ 21
Silver	2	22
Orange	3	27
Brown	4	28
White	5	30
Green	10	40
Blue	15	45
Red	24	48
		$261

We have bet a total of $512, taken in $261, and lost the difference of $251. Our total loss divided by the amount wagered gives a percentage in favor of the operator of *49 3/128% which, expressed decimally, is 49.02%.*

THE MOUSE GAME

The Mouse Game attracts many spectators as well as players because it is probably the most fascinating carnival game to watch. The operator's spiel goes something like this: "Here y'are folks, one dime and you take home a lamp, camera or any valuable prize you see on the shelf. All you gotta do to win is guess what hole the little mouse will jump into. Pick your number! You can keep betting until I lift the tin can and free the mouse."

A large revolving horizontal wheel about four feet in diameter is divided into 60 sections numbered from 1 to 60. At the outer rim of the wheel there is a small hole in each numbered section.

A mouse is placed in the center of the horizontal wheel and covered with a tin can, and the wheel is then spun vigorously. When the wheel stops, the tin can is lifted and the mouse, apparently dizzy from the spinning, hesitates a moment, then moves around the wheel for a moment or so and finally ducks into one of the 60 numbered holes for safety. The number of the hole into which the mouse disappears becomes the winning number.

There are many variations of the Mouse Game: the wheel sections may be colored rather than numbered, the betting limits higher and the carny's spiel more elaborate, but the percentage is usually the same, about 40% to 50% in the operator's favor. Many Mouse Game operators, not content with such a high percentage take, gaff their game, using a mechanical gimmick under the wheel which can close every alternate hole. If the big money is on the hole the mouse heads for, a hidden foot control is pressed, closing that hole. The mouse, discovering this exit blocked, goes to another. An even simpler, non-mechanical gaff: when the mouse is near a hole on which little or no money has been bet, the operator scares him into it by suddenly shouting an order to an assistant.

CARNIVAL DICE GAMES

The most popular percentage dice games at carnivals, bazaars, picnics, outings and charitable fund-raising affairs are the familiar ones usually found in honky-tonk gambling joints: Beat the Dealer, Hazard, Chuck-a-Luck and Under and Over Seven. These games are analyzed in Chapter 19.

There are carnival games such as Penny Pitch, Skillo and Ring Toss that could probably be classified as combination chance-and-skill games. But even when these are run honestly, such great skill is required to win that the average player has almost no chance. If he does win, the prize is seldom worth as much as the money he has wagered. I have conducted experiments in which seasoned carnival game operators tried to win at their own skill games, and I found that they were successful only about 10% of the time.

Since games in which skill is a factor cannot be analyzed mathematically, it isn't possible to compute the operator's favorable percentage, but you can be sure that his percentage is much greater than in any game of chance. The operator determines his favorable edge himself. If his game earns less money per week than he thinks it should, he remedies the situation either by cutting down the number of prizes, substituting cheaper prizes or tightening up the game so that winning becomes more difficult.

PENNY PITCH

This is a big money-maker at amusement parks and county fairs because it looks easy and has a small 1¢ charge per toss.

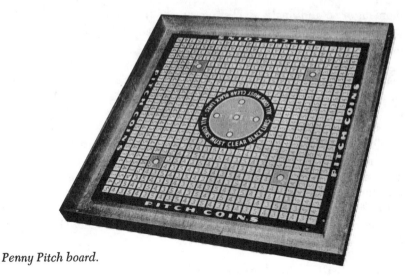

Penny Pitch board.

A low platform inside a railed enclosure bears a highly polished four-foot-square layout which has 500 or more small colored circles, each slightly more than an inch in diameter; the circles are arranged in rows spaced about a half inch apart. Most of the red circles are numbered 2, 3, 4, 5 and 10; six are numbered 25, four are numbered 50 and one, usually centered in the layout, is numbered 100.

The players toss pennies from outside the wooden rail onto the layout. Whenever a penny comes to rest completely inside a circle, the tosser receives the number of pennies indicated by the circle's number. If the tossed penny does not come to rest completely inside the circle, or if it slides off the layout into the surrounding cloth apron, the player loses his penny.

Since a game of this sort cannot be analyzed mathematically, I resorted to gambler's non-mathematical method of calculating probabilities—the clocking system. When I recently clocked the Penny Pitch at Connecticut's Danbury Fair, I found that 1,500 pennies were tossed during a one-hour period, and the total paid out to winners was about $3. This is favorable percentage to the operator of 80%, a payback to the players of only 20% of the money risked. Since most players play back their winnings, the operator usually gets 100% in the end.

Paybacks of honest "skill" games seldom total more than 20%. Some Penny Pitch layouts use about 600 small numbered squares rather than circles. They look larger than the circles because of the extra space in the corners, but a player's chances are only slightly improved when the width of the square and the diameter of the circle are the same.

To sum up, if you dislike being classified as a mooch and if you don't want to donate more than you can afford to help finance a winter Florida vacation for the carnival game hustlers, paste these simple rules in your bonnet:

1. Don't gamble away your bankroll at a carnival game of chance that offers cash awards.
2. Don't play any carnival game if you can't afford to lose.

CROOKED CARNIVAL GAMES

Most present-day carnival-game operators are average Americans, whose major sin against society is that they earn their living by running a gambling device in violation of state anti-gambling statutes.

Among them, however, we find grifters whose cynical attitude enables them to fleece an old man of his life's savings without any twinge of conscience. They state their code of ethics this way: "We do not steal from cripples, paupers or pregnant women."

Most of these thieves are uneducated, some are nearly illiterate, and very few are intelligent, but they all consider themselves much smarter than the tens of thousands of suckers they fleece yearly. The flatty or grifter learns his trade the hard way, usually serving his apprenticeship as an outside man. The skillful operation of a flat store is a cheating art that is passed along from one generation of grifters to another strictly by observation and word of mouth. The art of flatting has several branches. There are grifters who work *single-o* (alone), but since there is safety and strength in numbers and because outside men are a great help in building up a sucker, grifters often work in groups of two, three or four.

The expert flatty is not out to fleece a lot of players of a dollar or two each; he is out to catch that big sucker whom he can cheat to the tune of hundreds and even thousands of dollars. This fact can be attested by the $95,000 loss suffered recently by an American industrialist at one of these flat joints. While he waits for the big-money sucker to come along, the flatty makes do with the small ones.

Old-time flatties usually shy away from operating mechanically gaffed joints. They prefer working the *peek*, or *miscount*, at a so-called "science and skill" game for the sound reason that if their cheating gimmick or angle should be spotted they can usually alibi themselves out of the mess (hence the name "alibi store"). When a mechanical gaff is spotted by an angry group of players, the flatty is caught red-handed and there is nothing he can do but run or stand his ground and take his shellacking. And if his fix is not strong, he may go to a local jail also. This is why there are many more gaffed "skill" games than gaffed games of chance.

There isn't a carnival game in operation today that hasn't been gaffed at one time or another. This is also true of any other gambling game: dice, Poker, Bridge, Backgammon, Gin Rummy, Old Maid, the TV quiz games, etc. Games such as Chess, Checkers and my own games—Scarney and Teeko—are exceptions because they really are games of pure skill. If big amounts of money were bet on these games I suppose the grifters would try to figure out an angle, but about the only possible way would be by bribing or doping the players!

Where the local authorities or officials of county fairs, traveling carnivals and local bazaars do not permit the operation of flat or alibi stores, the flatties usually set up small portable flat joints on the fringes of these amusement centers. A little protection money paid to a local peace officer often permits them to operate without fear of arrest, and if such protection is not forthcoming, the flatties sneak their games and use a lookout to warn them of the arrival of the cops. Flatties who are bent on taking suckers for big money prefer to work the carnival's back lots rather than the bright lights of the midway: they can make a faster and safer getaway after taking a mark for his bankroll.

Flatties working on the sneak seldom stick around long after making a big touch. They have learned by experience that when the sucker who has lost his bankroll tells his friends about it, they usually tell him that he was cheated, and he either beefs to the cops or comes back with his friends and demands his money back. As a rule, when the cops or the sucker and his friends arrive, the grifter is miles away, usually waiting for the carnival to arrive at its next stand, where again he sets up his gaffed game, ready for the next chump.

Crooked carnival games have been exposed in the past, but these exposures are usually either too inaccurate or incomplete to do the carnival game–playing public much good. Mechanical gaffs are described which the grifter has long since discarded. In the following text you'll find out for the first time how present-day flatties build up a mark, together with explanations of the various gimmicks, angles and gaffs that are necessary to operate a peek, count, flat or alibi store successfully.

CROOKED CARNIVAL WHEELS

Thirty years ago about half of all the amusement centers I visited had one or more gaffed wheels. Today only 1 out of 30 amusement centers uses them.

This doesn't mean that today's wheel flatties have had a change of heart. They have switched to gaffed skill games because the fact that no mechanical gaff is employed makes the operation less detectible.

I have seen hundreds of gaffed carnival wheels of chance. Some employ a hidden control or brake on the counter which can stop the wheel at any time; the operator simply leans on or against the counter. Carnies refer to this type of store as a *belly joint*. Others have a hidden control, also operated by pressure, under the boardwalk inside the booth.

The tip-off on most controlled wheels is the indicator. Honest wheels have a sturdy pliable leather, rubber or spring indicator at the top of the wheel which makes a loud *tat-tat-tat* noise as it strikes the *posts* (nails) dividing the numbered sections while the wheel spins. On most gaffed wheels the indicator is a softer, more flexible piece of leather or plastic. This bends more easily and does little to hinder the movement of the wheel, thus making it easier to control.

I do not imply that every wheel which has a soft leather or celluloid indicator is gaffed, but the odds favor it, so why take chances? Here is an advertisement describing a gaffed wheel, in a catalog published by a park and carnival game equipment company. This is the same wheel shown on page 566 except that it comes already gaffed at double the price.

THE WONDER G. WHEEL

This is the leading G. Wheel on the market today and is acknowledged by all operators to be the most practical and satisfactory outfit ever offered. The Wonder G. Wheel needs no introduction to the experienced concessionaire and it is an outfit that must be in every line up for stock protection on rainy days.

The complete outfit consists of one 36 inch wheel in any numbered or colored winning combination, one special 1 × 4 upright and two special 42 inch jacks for 24 inch counter. Instructions for setting up are simple and the action is positive, no fine adjustments to make. The Wonder G. Wheel operates in a 12 foot concession as well as a 24; nothing to see, nothing to detect and operates from any position on the counter—Complete $97.50.

If you spot a portable horizontal wheel—usually it will be operating just outside a carnival or bazaar—that employs an arrow or spindle instead of a wheel, you have run into the number one crooked wheel of all carnivals. This was originally called "the Flat Joint" and the present use of the expression in its broader sense derives from this game because it lies flat rather than being suspended vertically on a post like other carnival wheels. Its indicator projects from the point of

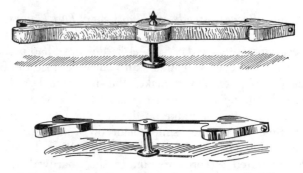

The original flat joint. Metallic and wooden arrows called "creepers," which can be controlled by the operator.

the arrow and is almost always a piece of paper or very flexible celluloid. The arrow or spindle spins very slowly; for this reason carnies now call it a *creeper*.

To illustrate the sucker's buildup by a flatty operating a gaffed spindle, here is an incident which took place many years ago. My lifelong friend Jack Reme and I were playing detective at a carnival in Bergenfield, New Jersey. We spotted a wheel whose spaces were not numbered but merely colored red and black alternately. As a bystander moved over to the creeper, we heard the flatty say, "Mister, you can bet any amount you wish, fifty cents, one, two, three, four or five dollars. The layout has the same number of red and the same number of black spaces. It's a dead even bet. You bet five and win, I pay you back ten. You lose, I take your five. Simple as all that. Make your bet and pick your color."

The man put a dollar on red and the flatty gave the arrow a gentle push. It spun around the layout, then slowed and kept creeping in slow motion until it finally stopped. This slow-moving action supplies suspense and tension and makes it exciting for the players. It also makes the game easy to gaff.

After the man had lost about $5, the flatty turned to him and said, "You seem to be a nice fellow and I'm gonna give you a break to win some real money."

The flatty took out several red and black pieces of cardboard which were made specially to fit in the nail slots of the layout and said, "Pick your color."

The player chose black this time, and the flatty placed black cardboards over several red spaces on the layout, thus giving the player a better than 50–50 chance to win—or so it looked. The player lost again, and he kept increasing his bets as the flatty kept building him up by covering more red spaces with black cardboards. Finally 30 spaces on the layout were black and 10 were red.

The flatty now said, "I hate to see you lose, but a gamble's a gamble, so here's what I'm gonna do for you. You've lost $48 up to now. I don't want your $48, but naturally I just can't give it back to you because I won it. If you'd won forty-eight smackers from me, I know you wouldn't have gave it back to me. But you're a nice guy, and I got a real sporting proposition for you. May I ask you a personal question?"

"Sure, go ahead," the man answered.

"How much money have you got in your pockets?"

"Let's see, I'm not sure." The sucker pulled out his bankroll and counted it. "Seventy-five bucks."

"I thought you had much more than seventy-five," the flatty replied, "but anyway, you've been a good sport and here's what I'm gonna do for you."

The flatty took out six more pieces of black cardboard and covered six of the remaining ten red spaces on the layout. "You now got thirty-six ways of winning against my measly four. But that's not all. Listen closely and hear what I'm gonna say. Here's the forty-eight bucks that I won from you. Now all you gotta do is put your seventy-five up, which makes a total of $123, which is all the money you had when you started to play. Now I'm gonna put up $123 of my own dough. The total bundle is now $246, that is if you put your seventy-five up, and winner takes all! And, look at those odds! You have thirty-six chances to win against my four. And that's not all. Listen to what else I'm gonna do for you. I'll even let you spin the spindle yourself. How about that, is it a bet?"

The player hesitated a bit; the prospect of receiving his losses and winning $123 besides was a deal he couldn't resist. He handed the flatty his $75. "Okay, it's a bet."

"Fine," the flatty said. "Now, to show you how honest this game is, I'll let you come behind the counter where I'm standing so that you can spin the arrow yourself. I'll walk over there to where those three gentlemen are standing."

The three men he referred to were Jack Reme, myself and another man, who had some money in his hand and had made several attempts to play only to be told by the flatty that he would accept no further wagers from anyone else until the first man had stopped playing. "This way," the flatty went on, "you'll know that there's no chance of you being cheated. No doubt you've heard some stories of crooked carnival people, but I'm honest and I'm going to prove it to you."

The player then moved in and took the flatty's station. He gave the spindle a rapid twirl while the flatty walked around in front of the gaffed joint. The spindle finally slowed down and started to creep very slowly; at last it came to a stop on one of the four red spaces. The flatty picked up the $246, telling the player with a touch of regret in his voice, "That's a real bad break, fella."

Just then the man next to Jack and myself pulled out a bankroll and asked, "How about giving me the same break for $246?"

The flatty removed all the black papers covering the red slots. "If you want to bet your $246, you'll only get an even break."

"Okay." The man quickly counted out $246. "Spin the arrow, I'm betting on the red."

Guess what? The spindle stopped on the red. The player scooped up all the money and quickly disappeared in the crowd. The flatty grumbled, "How do you like that for tough luck? Tonight I played a real bloomer. How do you like a creep like that winning and runing?"

The flatty then began to pack his spindle and layout into a carrying case, saying it was time to close up. He said good night to the man who had lost $123, and the latter walked away looking glum.

The creeper has two controls for stopping the spindle, one located on the flatty's side, the other on the player's side. The man who won the $246 was an *outside man,* and when the flatty walked away from the game, the outside man controlled the spindle from where he stood. The last bet, which the flatty permitted the outside man to win, was, of course, returned later. They enacted this little drama to prevent the sucker from realizing that he was fleeced and perhaps cry Cop and have the creeper sloughed and the flatty arrested. The chumps often leave feeling sorry for the poor flatty who lost everything to another player!

Since the arrow or spindle merely balances in its socket and can be removed at any time during play to prove to the player that it has no connections to any hidden control, it seems to be perfectly honest. What the player does not suspect is that the long axle of the arrow which passes down into the stationary socket can be controlled by a brake beneath the oilcloth-covered layout. A long hole runs through the wooden counter top horizontally from the operator's side in to the center, and another enters from the player's side. Each hole contains a movable rod; the head of a false thumbtack, which matches those used to hold down the oilcloth, is soldered to the rod's outer end. The inner end of each rod terminates at the side of the arrow axle, not quite touching it. The flatty or the outside man rests his hand on the counter, his thumb on the fake thumbtack. When the arrow is creeping very slowly, the operator pushes gently on the tack, causing the hidden rod to move inward against the arrow axle. A sudden stop would be obvious if the arrow were moving fast, but when it turns slowly the

A creeper with the twisted-pin gaff.

braking action is imperceptible. It stops, of course, on a number that loses for the player.

Twisted Pin Gaff

The pins around the rim of some carnival wheels are made of twisted metal strips. These twisted chromium-plated pins are apparently designed that way to give the wheel a flashy appearance. Actually this is part of the gaff. The pins are not all aligned so that their inward and outward curves match exactly. When the wheel is honestly run, the plastic arrow indicator hits all the pins. But the operator can press a concealed lever which raises the wheel axle slightly so that the indicator now just misses the narrow inward curving part of the pins which are not lined up with the others. These pins are on that section of the wheel which has a star signifying a grand prize; when the gaff is working, no one ever wins a big prize.

The twisted pin gaff is also used with a spindle. In this case the pins, arranged in a circle around the arrow, are stationary. In its proper position the indicator on the arrow will hit all the pins; when the gaff is on, it will miss the pins which might otherwise stop it at one of the big prizes. Sometimes the plastic indicator projects from under the arrow rather than from its tip and the lever arrangement, concealed within the arrow, raises or lowers the indicator, instead of moving the wheel axle up and down.

THE FLATTY'S "TEN POINTS OR MORE WIN" GIMMICK

The dream of every carnival grifter has always been to have a buildup or angle that will stir up a player's emotions to such a degree that he wants to keep betting and increasing the size of his bets until he goes flat broke.

About 20 years ago, with the introduction of the now popular *Ten Points or More Win* scoring system, this grifter's dream came true, although I doubt that the flatty who first applied the system to his flat store realized at the time that it would be responsible for more big-money swindles than any carnival gaff invented in the past century, or that within a few short years every peek- and count-store operator would employ this scoring gimmick to insure a big killing.

All present-day flatties exhibit a large printed card with the heading: TEN POINTS OR MORE WIN. Below this heading are 30 or 40 or more printed numbers—the numbers being used in the particular game being played. Under about half of these numbers appear some or all of the following: ¼ Point, ½ Point, 1½ Points, 2 Points, 3 Points, 4 Points, 5 Points, 8 Points and 10 Points. Under one number, usually 28 or 29, appears the word *Add*. This means that whenever the player scores this number he must double the amount of his previous bet to stay in the game. The remaining numbers on the card do not carry point values. (See illustration, page 583.)

Operators of various peek and count stores use point values which depend on the numbers used in each particular game. However, the scoring gimmick works the same. The player must score ten or more points with as many plays or chances as required; he receives credit for the combined total number of points scored on each play, paying an additional charge for each subsequent chance he takes. If a player's total points for one, two, three or more chances or plays reach a total of ten points or more, he wins and is paid off at 10 to 1 odds. Remember, I said *if a player's total reaches ten points or more.*

A detailed explanation of how the Ten Points or More Win gimmick works appears on the following pages.

Count Stores

Of all the carnival flat stores ever invented, the most notorious is the count store of the game known as Razzle Dazzle, Razzle, Bolero, Double Up, Ten Points or whatever name its operator prefers to call it.

The game has two distinct variations. One is played with eight or ten marbles and a small wooden roll-down having many small numbered holes for the marbles to settle in. The other variation, more streamlined, makes use of eight or ten dice. Both variations employ the Ten Points or More Win scoring gimmick.

Veteran carnival grifters prefer this kind of flat store to all others, first, because it is safer to operate since there is no mechanical gaff, and second, because it earns more money in a shorter period of time than any other flat joint. Flatties frequently win $1,000, $2,000, $5,000 or more with this kind of count store.

Under the name of Razzle Dazzle, the ten-dice version of this count store received considerable publicity in the American press a few years ago when an American industrialist lost $95,000 playing the game in a night spot on a Caribbean island. He paid $40,000 of his loss but refused to pay the balance after he learned that the operator of the game was a well-known American carnival grifter.

SIX-BALL ROLL-DOWN

Razzle Dazzle is of American origin and is an adaptation of the old carnival game of Six-Ball Roll-Down, or simply Roll-Down, which most flatties discarded years ago. During my recent carnival survey, I did, however, spot a couple of giant Six-Ball Roll-Downs back in action. Because of its historical importance and because you may still find a giant old-fashioned Roll-Down in some amusement center, I record the following incident.

In company with my carnival game fact-finding assistant and friend Walter Scott, I was scouting a carnival playing Nyack, New York, when I spotted a Six-Ball Roll-Down game. The operator, holding three small cork balls in each hand, was waving his arm toward a printed sign hanging above the game and shouting at the top of his voice, "Look! Look! Look! Six balls for twenty-five cents. . . . Win yourself a hundred-dollar radio, an electric toaster, a beautiful lamp or any one of those big prizes you see on the back shelves."

Scotty and I looked at the sign:

Numbers 6 – 7 – 8 – 34 – 35 – 36 win a beautiful $100 Radio
Numbers 9 – 10 – 11 – 31 – 32 – 33 win an electric toaster or lamp
Numbers 12 – 13 – 14 – 28 – 29 – 30 win a consolation prize

As we watched, a man started to play the game, and while Scotty observed his play, I began to study the game board. The playing surface was about two feet wide by six feet long with a raised edge to prevent the balls from rolling off the board. The board was slightly slanted so that the balls, about 2 inches in diameter, would roll down toward the end of the board and settle where 36 pockets were arranged in a two-foot square at the foot of the incline. Each hole bore one of the numbers 1 through 6. There were six holes for each number and no two adjacent holes had the same number.

When the six cork balls settled in the pockets, the operator added their numerical values, and if the total corresponded with one of the numbers on the cardboard sign, the player won a prize—at least that is what was supposed to happen. After playing about 20 games, the player we were watching handed the operator another quarter. He placed the six balls in a little rack near the top of the game board, then tilted the rack, and the six balls rolled down the incline. They settled in 6 of the 36 pockets. I mentally added the values of the pockets the balls were in and got a total of 34, which was a radio winner.

The operator added the numbered values aloud and called out, "Thirty! I believe you gotta big prize winner, sir, let's check and see." He looked at the sign. "Sorry, mister, it's only a consolation prize." He handed the man a 25¢ ballpoint pen, adding, "I certainly thought that beautiful hundred-dollar radio was all yours. Well, better luck this next game."

As Scotty and I walked away from the count store, I said, "Scotty, that man scored thirty-four points, not thirty as the operator announced. He won the radio, but the flatty resorted to a little sleight of hand and cheated him out of it. When the flatty was adding up the values of the six balls, he lifted one of the balls from a number four hole and, as he moved it back a few inches and called, 'Four,' his hand came directly above and concealed the ball in a number six hole. A flip of his fingers secretly rolled the six ball out of its hole and into the number two hole directly behind it."

"What are the player's chances," Scotty asked, "of winning a grand prize when that game is played on the square?"

"A paper and pencil is all we need to find out." My mathematical analysis showed that the total possible number of six-ball combinations of the roll-down game totaled 1,947,792, and the number of possible ways a winning total of 6, 7, 8, 34, 35 and 36 could be made was 596. Dividing 596 into 1,947,792 my result read 3268+.

Scotty studied the figures a moment, then looked at me with an "I don't believe you" expression on his face and said, "Do you mean to say that the man we just saw playing Roll-Down hit a 3267 to 1 shot? Why, the odds on hitting the Numbers game are only 999 to 1 with a $600 payoff if you win. And that character running the game cheated the player out of a cheap twenty-dollar radio which he claims is worth a hundred bucks!"

"That's right, Scotty. A flatty never gives a player a thing, and takes him for all he can get."

"You have to be good at arithmetic to run a game of that type."

I nodded. "All flatties who operate roll-down count stores eventually become rapid calculators at the game. They usually know the exact total as soon as the last ball finds a pocket—or, if not, then they are certain whether or not the total is a big winner."

"How do they know that?" Scotty inquired.

"It's simple enough. If there is a mixture of high and low numbers when the six balls come to rest in the pockets, it's a cinch numbers 6-7-8-34-35-36 can't be the total. At least four balls must settle in

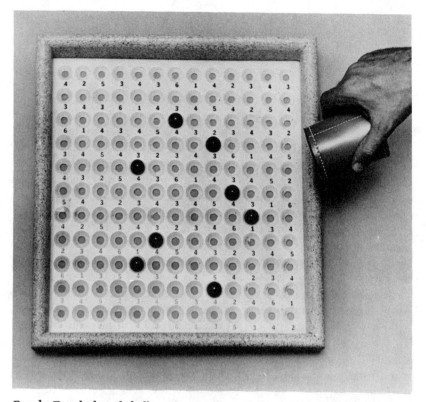

*Razzle Dazzle board, balls and cup. The number arrangement here differs
from the board described in the text. These boards are often homemade and
various number arrangements are employed. (Stanley Einzig)*

holes numbered one to produce a low total of 6, 7 or 8, and at least
four balls must come to rest in holes numbered six to produce a high
total of 34, 35 or 36.

"As a matter of fact, Scotty, most count-store operators don't even
use sleight of hand; they cheat their victims simply by miscounting.
The miscount in this game is difficult for the player to detect because
it is done fast, and he is standing three or four feet away."

"How is the miscount done, John?"

"When the flatty sees that the player has a winner, he doesn't remove the balls from the numbered pockets one by one as he does
when he knows the total is a loser. Instead, he picks up two balls at a
time, one in each hand, and calls the numbers of both as one total.
When this is repeated three times, the expert count store operator can
add or subtract one, two, three or more numbers to or from the correct total, and a winning player almost never realizes that he was
counted out. It's as simple as that."

RAZZLE DAZZLE

The marble-game version of Six-Ball Roll-Down with its six multi-colored marbles and its miniature roll-down with 36 numbered holes fitted into a small suitcase later became known as Razzle Dazzle.

Our police officials are partly responsible for the creation of Razzle Dazzle. The roll-down flatties of years ago, who used to sneak their game into "closed territory" where the authorities strictly enforced the anti-gambling statutes, could not afford to carry elaborate roll-down equipment which might be confiscated. In order to minimize the chances of such seizures they made use of six marbles and a small portable roll-down which was fitted into a small suitcase. This enabled them to make a quick getaway when they saw a police officer coming their way.

At first, this miniature roll-down did not prove popular with carnival game players because it seemed too much like a child's game. After a couple of years it almost disappeared from the carnival scene. Then the ten-point scoring system came along and the roll-down flatties added 36 or more numbered holes to their miniature roll-down and reactivated the Razzle Dazzle.

They discovered that the miscount which was so successful at a distance with the giant-sized rolldown was more difficult at close range; too many players spotted it. But flatties are ingenious people and they soon solved the problem. They added two more marbles making 8 in all; this increased the game's total count and made the miscount harder to detect. With the introduction of the ten-point scoring system, the popularity of the miniature roll-down skyrocketed. The game soon became known to all flatties as Razzle Dazzle or Razzle. This term describes both the game and its gaff perfectly. The player hasn't a chance because he is dazzled by the swiftness of the count, which is usually a miscount.

Most Razzle Dazzle operators make their own game equipment; you seldom see two games that look exactly alike. Many flatties have crudely built wooden games, others have expensive, flashy equipment built inside a suitcase. Carrying the suitcase, the flatty appears to be an ordinary traveler or businessman. When he has found a suitable operating spot, he opens the case, takes out a small folding table, and sets the open suitcase on it. He then removes a plastic cup and eight marbles and is ready to take on all comers. The inside cover of the suitcase displays a large printed chart that reads as follows:

TEN POINTS or more WIN

P O I N T S	18 H. P.	42 1½ PTS.	38 H.P.	15 1½ PTS.	19 H.P.	41 1½ PTS.	37 H.P.	14 1½ PTS.	P O I N T S
N O T	8 10 PTS.	20 5 PTS.	45	36 5 PTS.	13	21	46 8 PTS.	35	G O O D
T R A N S F E R A B L E	22	9 8 PTS.	34 10 PTS.	48	23 5 PTS.	10	33 8 PTS.	47	O N L Y W H I L E
	11 5 PTS.	24	44 5 PTS.	32	12 5 PTS.	25	43 5 PTS.	31	P L A Y I N G
	26 ½ PTS.	40	30 ½ PTS.	17	27 ½ PTS.	39	29 ½ PTS.	16	

28 ADD

NO. 28 DOES NOT ADD POINTS

The abbreviation H. P. under 18, 38, 19 and 37 on the top line of the chart has two meanings: House Prize or Half Point. Early in the game the mark is *fairbanked* (allowed to win) into one of these numbers and awarded a cane or some other cheap prize. Later, when he has been built up to play for money, he is allowed either another house prize or he can count it as a half point.

Some Ten Points or More Win charts list 29 as their odd number.

Some operators list *2 for 1* or *3 for 1* under the same numbers instead of H.P. This is done to let the mark win occasionally so that he will keep playing.

Let's see how a typical player, Joe Mooch, is taken for his bankroll at Razzle Dazzle. The Razzle operator sees Joe passing his flat store and begins his spiel: "Hey, mister, did you ever play this game before?"

Joe shakes his head. "No."

The grifter indicates the printed chart. "All you gotta do is score ten points and you win. When you win, I pay you off at ten to one odds; if you bet a dollar, I pay you ten; fifty cents gets you five dollars. It's as simple as all that." He gives Joe the cup and the eight marbles. "Go ahead, drop them on the inclined board. It's a free roll; it's on me."

Like most people, Joe is a sucker for a free offer, so he rolls the marbles from the cup down the inclined board onto the game's wooden layout and watches them settle in 8 of the 120 holes.

The grifter, wearing a big smile, says, "Okay, let's see what score you rolled. I must warn you I count fast but right. I never could add slow, even when I went to grammar school." The flatty picks the marbles from the numbered holes in groups of one, two or three, rapidly adding their values aloud: "Twelve, twenty-four, thirty, thirty-seven, and the last two marbles come to seven for a grand total of forty-four. Look at the chart and see if forty-four lists a point value."

It takes Joe a moment or two to find 44 on the chart, because the numbers are not in sequence. When he finds it, the grifter points excitedly to the words below the number. "Mister, today's your lucky day! You scored five points. All you need is five points more and you're a winner. And, mister, when you win, I pay off at ten to one odds. You look like a sport, so I'll tell you what I'm gonna do. I'll give you the five points you just scored on that free roll if you bet me a dollar on the next roll. If you score five points the next roll you get ten bucks and your dollar back. Even if you score only five points in ten rolls of the marbles, you break even. How about it, mister, is it a go? Give me a dollar and try your luck."

Joe hands the grifter a dollar, shakes the cup and rolls out the marbles. The grifter picks up one, two or three marbles at a time from the layout, adding their numbers aloud: "One—two—four—six—eight, and the last three marbles add up to seven for a grand total of fifteen points.

"Look at the chart, mister, see how many points you made on fifteen." Joe finds that 15 receives 1½ points. "Too bad, mister," the grifter says. "You are 3½ points short of ten points. You scored 6½ points in two rolls, but it shouldn't be hard to score 3½ more points. A dollar will still get you ten on the next roll."

This looks exceedingly attractive to Joe, so he hands the grifter another buck and tries again. The grifter quickly adds the numbers and gets a total of 28.

"Look at the chart, mister, the top number on the chart is twenty-eight, the word below it reads: *Add.*" Now the flatty explains that this means that if he wants to continue to play, he must add an amount equal to his previous bet on the next bet. Joe thinks that's fair enough, because if he wins he will receive $20 for his two-dollar bet instead of

$10 for a dollar bet. He gives the grifter two dollars and takes another chance. The grifter adds again and calls 41 as the total. The chart shows that 41 has a point value of 1½ points.

"Wow!" exclaims the grifter. "You have a total of eight points; you only need two more points. Close, but not close enough. Why don't you bet ten dollars this time? If you score two more points you win a hundred dollars."

The flatty takes his bankroll from his pocket, begins to count it, and Joe sees that it is mostly hundred-dollar bills. This sight arouses his gambling spirit. He bets $10 on the next roll of the marbles, and the grifter's count totals 14. This chart lists 14 at 1½ points. Joe is starting to perspire now. His total is 9½ points. He only needs a half point to win.

The grifter turns to the chart, quickly counts aloud the 24 printed numbers which show a scoring value and says, "The chart has twenty-four winning numbers and only seventeen losing numbers, so your chances of winning on the next roll are 24 to 17, that's 3 to 2 in your favor; and remember, if you throw any one of these twenty-four numbers, you win and are paid off at ten to one odds."

Joe shakes his head and says, "I don't know, I guess it sounds okay."

The grifter looks at Joe and says, laughing, "You only have half a point to go. I hope you run out of money because if you don't and have any sporting blood in your veins, you'll be betting high and will eventually win my bankroll."

Joe bets $10 again. The grifter makes his quick count and announces a total of 28. Joe knows by now that 28 reads *add* and that he must double the previous $10 bet to stay in the game.

Joe thinks the situation over. Having invested $24, he decides he can't stop playing now—now, when he has come so close to winning with his 9½-point score. He only needs a measly ½ point to win. He takes his money from his pocket and begins to count it, and the grifter who counts along with him says, "It's okay. You got a hundred bucks. Bet the twenty. You will still have eighty left if you lose, and if you roll half a point, you collect two hundred dollars."

Joe can't resist the temptation of those 10 to 1 odds. He bets the $20, and the grifter's count adds up to 25 which, on the chart, has no point value. "Too bad," the grifter tells Joe. "If every number on the chart had a point value, I'd have to be crazy to book this game."

Joe, with $80 left, is just starting to think the whole thing over when a bystander who has been watching the game says, "Mister, I'll give you fifty dollars for your 9½ points. Do you want to sell them?"

The grifter growls at the stranger. "What do you take this man for? He'd be a fool to sell you 9½ points for fifty dollars. Anyway, didn't I tell you a half-dozen times before to stop trying to hustle my customers, and stay away from my game? Look at the chart. Down at the bottom it says in plain English, *Points Not Transferable*. And if you think you are going to wait for this man to lose his money and then meet him somewhere outside the lot, buy his 9½ points and have him come back and play for you, that won't go either. The bottom of the chart also says *Points Good Only While Playing*. See it? When this man quits and leaves the game, his 9½ points are lost. But if he keeps playing and scores the needed half a point, he wins the game." The grifter finishes by telling the stranger to get lost.

The stranger leaves and the grifter asks Joe, "How do you like that for gall? That creep wants to buy your 9½ points so he can bet me fifty dollars or maybe more. He only has to score ½ point and I'm out five hundred bucks. I've been around carnivals too long not to know how to handle a wise guy like that character."

Joe receives the message. He realizes he must continue to play until he scores the much-needed ½ point. If he quits he forfeits his credited 9½ points and loses all the money he has bet. So Joe, like most Razzle Dazzle players, continues playing, eventually winds up broke and walks away dejectedly, wishing he had more money so he could keep playing and eventually score that last ½ point.

The only fortunate thing that happened to Joe is that he didn't have a bigger bankroll with him. No matter how big his bankroll was, he would have lost it, because no one ever scores that small ½ point when the Razzle Dazzle operator is running a flat store—not unless the grifter has a good reason to let the player make it.

Why did Joe succeed in scoring 9½ points so quickly and then find it so hard to get that additional ½ point?

Let's look at the selection of the point-scoring numbers and their arrangements on the *Ten Points or More Win* chart (page 583). Forty-one printed numbers are shown, twenty-four valued at ½ to 10 points each, and the remaining seventeen are valueless or losing numbers.

Joe's chances of scoring that ½ point (or more) needed to win are considerably less than the 24 to 17 odds in his favor quoted by the grifter.

By glancing at the *Ten Points or More Win* chart, you'll also note that the forty-one printed numbers are haphazardly arranged. This is done to keep the mathematically inclined player from noticing that the twelve low and twelve high numbers are point scorers and the seventeen in-between numbers are valueless.

Most flatties make their own Razzle Dazzle layouts, each of which has from 72 to 143 or more holes numbered from 1 to 6. Each grifter arranges these numbers to suit his fancy.

To understand the crooked operation of Razzle Dazzle, a look at a 120-hole layout will do the trick. A Razzle Dazzle layout with 120 numbered holes or pockets usually has 15 vertical rows each with eight numbered holes about ½ inch in diameter and spaced about ¼ inch apart—just enough flat space for a printed number (1, 2, 3, 4, 5, or 6). A peculiar but essential feature of the number arrangement is the fact that each vertical row of eight numbers is made up of four groups of two alternating digits adding up to 7. The chart below shows the number arrangement.

```
3  5  4  1  3  2  4  6  5  3  2  1  3  5  3
4  2  3  6  4  5  3  1  2  4  5  6  4  2  4
3  5  4  1  3  2  4  6  5  3  2  1  3  5  3
4  2  3  6  4  5  3  1  2  4  5  6  4  2  4
3  5  4  1  3  2  4  6  5  3  2  1  3  5  3
4  2  3  6  4  5  3  1  2  4  5  6  4  2  4
3  5  4  1  3  2  4  6  5  3  2  1  3  5  3
4  2  3  6  4  5  3  1  2  4  5  6  4  2  4
```

Notice that any number in the vertical column added to either the number just above it (or the one below) gives a total of 7. This arrangement enables the grifter to add the player's total score very rapidly. Sometimes he even knows the combined total of the eight marbles without having looked at the value of any hole, merely by the positions of the marbles. For instance, if two marbles fell in each of four vertical columns, and there are no intervening holes between each pair, the grifter knows immediately that each pair adds to 7, and he merely multiplies 7 × 4 for a total of 28. He can also use the fact that any two marbles in the same row which are separated by an even number of holes also add to 7.

Since this arrangement enables him to calculate the total before the player can do so, the operator can either change a point-scoring total into a losing total or can fairbank a losing total into a point-scoring total by employing a bold and barefaced miscount. Also notice that the game board contains more threes and fours than other numbers. This is because miscalling a 3 as a 4, or vice versa, is less likely to be detected than miscalling a 1 as a 6 and a 2 as a 5, or vice versa.

The grifter, already knowing the total while the player is still trying to add, picks up some of the marbles rapidly, sometimes using both hands and picking up two at once. The presence of so many numbers so close together makes it almost impossible for the player to be sure that the ball actually was in the hole bearing the number which the grifter calls. The flatty calls the number just above rather than below the hole when it suits his purpose, and once the marble has been taken out the player is in no position to prove otherwise. The marks are seldom suspicious in any case because most of the time the flatty counts slowly and sometimes even lets the player make the count; the fast miscount is used only when needed.

When a player is suspicious he has no recourse, as the grifter is an expert at alibiing himself out of a miscount. The usual line is "Mister, I'm sorry. I can't count slow, but I always count right. I wouldn't cheat you, I'm an honest man. . . ."

Getting back to Joe Mooch, when he accepted his free roll, the grifter fairbanked his losing total into a 5-point score. This was done principally to lure Joe into the game, and also to make him think that scoring ½ point or more on a single roll would be easy.

The flatty continued to fairbank Joe by miscounting his total until his score reached the magic 9½ points.

From then on the grifter can count mostly on the square. There are 12 to 20 times as many losing combinations on the Razzle Dazzle layout as there are winning combinations and if Joe is lucky enough to roll a winning combination and get ½ point or more, the grifter becomes dishonest again and miscounts the total into a losing total.

The stranger who offered to buy Joe's 9½ points for $50 was the grifter's outside man; his little act was another part of the buildup to keep Joe playing.

The illustration (page 581) depicts a Razzle Dazzle layout with 143 numbered holes arranged differently from the layout just described.

RAZZLE DAZZLE VARIATIONS

Some Razzle Dazzle operators use ten marbles instead of eight, and their Ten Points or More Win chart shows 51 printed numbers running from 10 to 60. Such charts have numbers valued at ¼ of a point, 1 point, 2 points, etc.

Other Razzle Dazzle operators use eight or ten dice instead of marbles and a roll-down. The equipment required in the dice version of Razzle Dazzle is a dice cup, eight or ten dice, and a Ten Points or More Win chart. The player throws out the dice and the fast-talking grifter miscounts the totals in the same fashion as his miscounts the totals scored on a marble roll-down, because the spots on each die run from 1 to 6, the same as the numbered pockets of a marble layout. There are many variations of this game. The stakes may be higher or lower, the game may be played with dice or marbles, the numbered totals may have different point values, one grifter may use the 9¾-point build-up, another the 9½.

The spiel may vary, but the result is always the same—Joe Mooch always loses all the money he bets. The edge in favor of the grifter is 100%.

You seldom find two Razzle Dazzle marble layouts with the same number of pockets and the same numbered arrangement. Therefore, it is impossible to calculate Joe Mooch's chance of scoring that much-needed ½ point when the game is played on the square. However, if Joe is playing Razzle Dazzle with eight dice, his chances of scoring that ½ point (or more) needed to win are approximately 128,572 in 1,679,616 or 1 in 13. And the probability of rolling a score of 5 points or more on any given throw of eight dice is 1 in 652. And to disillusion the Razzle Dazzle players further: the chances of scoring 10 points in one throw of eight dice are 1 in 839,808.

Would it surprise you now to learn that number 28 (the double-your-bet number) has a greater chance of being thrown than all 24 point-valued numbers combined? Your chance of throwing 28 is 135,954 in 1,679,616 and the combined probability of the 24 point-scoring numbers is 128,572 in 1,679,616. The reader may rest assured that the odds against the player at the marble version of Razzle Dazzle are considerably greater.

DROP CASES

A drop case is a variation of the old game of Bagatelle built into a carrying case. When opened, the cover lies horizontal and the other half remains upright. The game layout, a diagram of numbered squares, is on the inside of the cover. The other half of the case is covered with glass under which is a game board studded with many small nails. A row of numbers across the bottom of the board are duplicates of those on the laydown. The player is given a marble which he drops into a hole at the top of the board. It drops down, bouncing from nail to nail until it comes to a stop in a pocket above one of the numbers. If this number corresponds to the one on which the player has wagered his money he receives a prize.

There are several styles of drop cases, all of which are gaffed in essentially the same way. The nails on the game board are arranged in such a pattern that the ball will fall into either an odd- or even-numbered pocket, depending on where the marble enters the maze at the top. The downward course of the marble seems to be dictated by chance, but if the player's money is on an odd number the flatty can

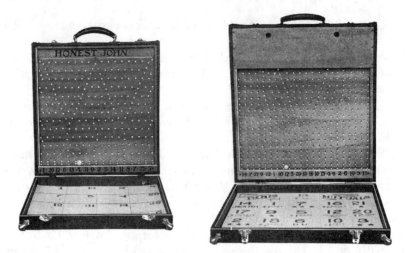

Two varieties of drop cases, descendants of the old game of Bagatelle.

control it so that the marble falls into an even-numbered pocket, and vice versa.

The Honest John drop case has 16 numbered pockets and 16 numbers on the laydown, and the player may drop the marble into any one of three holes at the top of the case. A covered section just below the holes across the top of the case hides the marble for the first few inches of its drop. The gaff is also hidden here. A rod running across the top of the board has projecting guards which block off the spaces between certain nails. A hidden control allows the operator to move the rod back and forth. In one position the marble can only drop into spaces that lead down into even numbers; in the other, it will fall only into odd-number spaces. The guards can also be swung out of the way so that none of the spaces are blocked; then the operation becomes honest.

The Chicago drop case has only two holes into which the marble can be dropped, and 21 numbers. The gaff is the same.

THREE-MARBLE TIVOLI

Here, instead of dropping vertically, the marbles roll down an inclined board studded with nails. Three marbles are placed in a box at the top of the game board, one marble in each of its three compartments. The box has no bottom and is hinged at the rear. When the operator pulls a string, the box lifts and all three marbles roll down simultaneously, finally stopping in numbered pockets at the bottom. The three numbers are added and if the total is even, the player gets a good prize; if odd he gets slum.

The pockets at the bottom of the board are numbered in this order:

6 4 8 2 5 3 1 7 3 5 8 4 6 2

Notice that all the odd numbers are grouped in the center. Because of the pattern in which the nails are arranged, the two outside balls always roll down the left and right sides of the board and fall into even-numbered pockets. The center compartment of the box has a concealed stop inside. If the operator drops the ball in to the left of the stop it will follow a diagonal course down the board and also arrive at an even number, making the total even. If he drops it to the right of the stop it will follow a course down the center of the board, go into an odd-numbered pocket and supply an odd total. The stop, usually a push pin, can easily be removed if the operator wants to demonstrate to the *town clown* (any police officer) that the game is not gaffed.

PIN STORES AND PEEK JOINTS

The skill game (so-called) of tossing small rings at clothespins is known to the public by various names such as *Aunt Lucy's Clothes Line, Pegs and Prizes, Mother's Wash Line* and the *Clothespin Game*. But to carnies and people in the know it is called a *pin store*. This is the most popular *peek joint* on the midways of country fairs, traveling carnivals and bazaars.

From the player's viewpoint, the operation of this peek joint is simplicity itself; any passerby seeing it for the first time understands at once how it is played. But, from the operator's side, when this store is *running strong* (running dishonestly), it is the most difficult flat store to operate successfully. The grifters who operate peek stores are, as a rule, the most skilled of all carnival cheats because the gaffing of the game depends upon the adroitness and dexterity of the flatty as he executes a bold and barefaced swindle. Some state fairs have as many as four flatties working under the same roof, each running his own pin store.

Three-marble Tivoli, a descendant of Bagatelle and forerunner of the modern pinball machine.

Scarne in a pinball parlor. (Stanley Einzig)

The pin store which Walter Scott, my man Friday, and I recently scouted near Huntington, West Virginia, was a one-man store. The operator stood before his booth rattling a dozen or so three-inch wooden rings on a cane. A printed sign hanging over the game read:

Numbers 110 – 111 – 112 – 113
Win a Television Set
Numbers 114 – 115 – 116 – 117
Win a Record Player
Numbers 118 – 119 – 120 – 121
Win a Radio
Numbers 25 – 35 – 45 – 55 – 65 – 75 – 85 – 95
Win a Consolation Prize

The operator was shouting, "Three rings for a quarter! All you have to do is ring a winning clothespin and take home a television set, radio or Victrola."

Inside his small tent, about four feet from the counter, was a large wooden frame about six feet wide and five feet high. Running horizontally across the upper half of the wooden frame were five one-inch wooden *racks* (slats), each firmly secured about six inches above the other. On each of these racks were *strung* (clipped) about 50 spring-clip clothespins.

Seeing Scotty, the operator said, "Look, mister, it's not hard to ring a clothespin." He began tossing rings in the direction of the clothespins, as he explained that each pin had a two- or three-digit number stenciled on the side away from the player. The operator tossed about 20 rings and succeeded in ringing 6 pins. He removed these, took them down and turned them over. One of the pins bore the number 113. The operator pointed to the printed sign. "Mister, if you had rung this pin, you would be the owner of that beautiful twenty-one inch television set resting on that shelf in between that record player and radio."

Another man who had joined us gave the operator a 50¢ piece and received six rings. The flatty moved over to the game rack and replaced the six pins. Then he quickly moved some 20 pins into different positions so that the player could not know the location of the winning pin numbered 113. When the operator had completed the mixing, the player began to toss his rings.

We watched for about an hour as this player and several others tossed about 300 rings toward the pins. They ringed an average of one pin for every seven rings tossed, but each time the operator took down the ringed clothespin and turned it over, the number on the reverse side proved to be a losing number.

As Scotty and I left the midway, he said, "John, I have learned by now that any time you spend an hour or more studying a carnival game it must have a hidden gimmick. But after seeing those players each ring about forty different pins and get nothing but losing numbers and a few consolation prizes, my guess is that the only big prize-winning pin was the one numbered 113. And I'm not so sure that he didn't palm that and go south with it."

"No, Scotty, all the winning numbers on the sign above the game are among the pins. They have to be, in case the fuzz [cops] get a complaint from some loser and want to examine the pins. The pins with the big prize-winning numbers are often ringed by players, but they never know it!"

The flatty who plies his trade in spots where other strong joints are barred is usually a peek-store operator. Because the gaffs on these games are not mechanical, the pin-store flatty has no fear of being caught red-handed using equipment which will convict him. He depends, instead, on several non-mechanical devices, the most important of which is his selection of winning and losing numbers and the manner in which they are marked on the clothespins.

One side of each of the 200 or more pins used in the pin store we

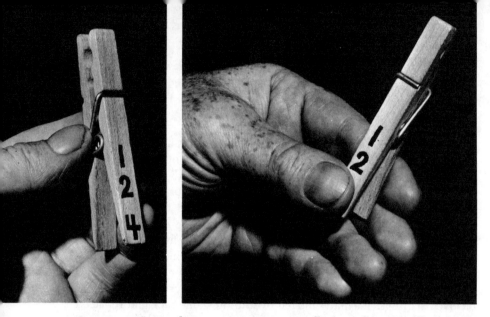

Pin-store gaff. Numbers on pins are not equally spaced (LEFT), *allowing operator to cover one digit of a winning number with his thumb* (RIGHT) *and turn it into a losing number. (Stanley Einzig)*

had scouted bore either a two- or three-digit specially selected number, as in most pin stores. The digits are stenciled one above the other. Since the clothespins are only about a half-inch wide and about 4 inches long, the players do not suspect that this arrangement serves any purpose other than to get the whole number on the pin. Another arrangement players do not notice is that all the top winning numbers are three-digit numbers whose first two digits are 11 or 12. If you ever had a chance to examine these prize numbers closely—which you don't— you might notice that there is more space between the middle and bottom digits than between the top and middle digits. This is part of the gimmick.

When the player rings a clothespin, the operator removes it from the rack and, during this action, peeks at the hidden number (this is why it is called a *peek store*). If the number is a three-digit grand-prize winner, the operator merely places his thumb over the bottom digit as he turns the pin to display its numbered side. It appears to the player to be a two-digit losing number. The four-foot distance between operator and players, the extra space between the bottom and second digit, the speed with which the operator reverses the pin, calls out the phony two-digit number and quickly puts it back in some other position on the game rack make it almost impossible for a player to detect the hocus-pocus. If he should suspect the swindle and beef about it, the operator would claim he had no idea where he had replaced the ringed pin. Every angle is covered; carnies rate high in the angle department.

THE DART GAME

All peek-store flatties who make use of the two- and three-digit hidden-number gimmick operate along the same lines. The Dart Game is an example.

A Dart Game operator working a peek store has a large backboard inside the booth, several feet from the counter. Sixty or more three-inch square paper tags arranged in rows hang from hooks on this board. The hidden side of each tag bears a printed number like those used in the pin stores. The player throws darts at the tags. When he has succeeded in impaling a tag, it is taken down and the number on the reverse side is shown. If the player has hit a winning number, the dart game flatty covers the third digit with his thumb, and the lucky winner loses.

THE DEVIL'S BOWLING ALLEY

At the front of the Devil's Bowling Alley a hundred 2½-inch hardwood balls roll continuously down an inclined trough. They disappear through an opening at the lower end, roll back along another incline beneath the counter and into an electrically driven elevator gadget that raises them back to the top of the first incline and starts them down again (see next page). The sight of this perpetual stream of rolling balls and the noise they make as they knock against each other seldom fail to attract a crowd as soon as the machinery is set in motion—and this two-way joint is open for business.

Inside the booth a sign is displayed which reads:

NUMBERS: 10   11   12   13   14   15   16   17   18   19
WIN TOP PRIZE AWARDS

ALL NUMBERS OVER 100 RECEIVE
CONSOLATION PRIZES

The operator explains that inside each ball is a number which may be as low as 10 or as high as 199. All the player has to do is buy a chance and select one of the rolling balls. If it contains a number from 10 to 19 he'll win the color television or the sterling silver table setting for six. Numbers over 100 pay off a consolation prize such as a cane, toy or some other less expensive item—lots less, because it is all slum.

The operator demonstrates how easy it is by picking three or four balls at random. He shows that a hole running through each ball is filled with a metal plug called a *slide*. He has a metal pin which he uses to push the plug most of the way out of the ball, and he shows a

Automatic Devil's Bowling Alley.

number on the slide. One of the balls he has selected bears a two-digit figure in the series from 10 to 19, a big prize-winner. He pushes the slide in again and replaces the balls on the incline.

The gaff is like that used in the pin store. Ten balls contain three-digit numbers with extra space between the second and third digits. When the operator pushes the slide out using one end of the pin, the slide comes out only two thirds of the way and shows a winning two-digit number. By reversing the pin and using its other end, he can push the slide out still further, so that it shows all three digits. When you are lucky and select the ball containing the number 12, which wins the color TV set, he pushes the slide out so that it reads 129, and you win a cheap cane.

No player, unless he is a shill, ever gets anything but three-digit numbers. When the flatty has a real live mark he plays the joint for cash and resorts to the Ten Points or More Win buildup.

What if some smart chump suspects the three-number slide gimmick or some town clown not *on the pad* (fixed) gets nosy and wants to inspect the game to satisfy himself that it is honest? That's easy. Inside the elevator cabinet directly above the incline there are ten concealed balls which contain the honest two-digit big prize-winning figures 10 through 19. When necessary the flatty releases a secret catch and the ungaffed balls drop onto the incline and roll out among the others.

FISH POND

An example of hanky-panky that can be flatted is the game of Fish Pond. This is an elaborate affair, usually found only in amusement parks and at large fairs. About 100 five-inch wooden fish float on a stream of water flowing down a narrow channel past the game counter. A wire loop projects from the back of each fish, and the player, using a small rod with a two-foot line and a hook, tries to hook one of the fish as they float by. When he succeeds, the operator removes the fish from the line and shows a number on its bottom. When he does not want to pay off, he resorts to the thumb hocus-pocus explained earlier. Less experienced flatties use fish which are gaffed like the Devil's Bowling Alley balls with the numbers in a hidden slide.

Peek-joint operators used to employ a simpler number arrangement in flatting their store. Only two-digit numbers were used, and these were drawn by hand. They were arranged horizontally in the conventional manner. The winning top-award numbers were 9, 16, 18, 61, 66, 89 and 98. The gimmick was that the winning numbers when held upside down, became the losing numbers: 6, 91, 81, 19, 99, 68, and 86.

When a peek-store operator really wants to run strong, he dispenses with the merchandise prizes, reaches under the counter and produces his *Ten Point or More Win* chart (page 583). Example: The pin-store operator described in the foregoing text would list his numbered point values as follows: 110 scores 10 points; 111 scores 5 points; 112 scores 4 points, etc.

HOOP-TOSSING GAMES

Hoop-tossing games—Ring Toss, Ring It, Watch-la, Hoop-la Game, Tossing Game and others can be found at nearly all carnivals, bazaars, fairs and amusement parks.

Circulating fish pond.

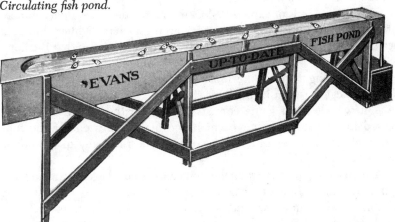

A legal hoop game at a New Jersey park. (Stanley Einzig)

There are slight variations in each of these games, and whether each store will be operated as a hanky-pank, alibi or even a flat joint depends upon the local authorities and the larceny of the operator.

The object of any hoop-toss game is always the same: to throw the hoop in such a way that when it lands it not only encircles a prize but also the small wooden block on which the prize rests. Ring-store operators exhibit all kinds of expensive-looking merchandise: watches, bracelets, cameras, leather wallets, pipes, cigarette holders, lighters, fountain pens, harmonicas, souvenirs, novelties—almost any article that the hoop will fit over.

Hoop-tossing games, like most carnival games, are easy to learn. No complicated rules disturb their simplicity.

A new-style hoop game consists of 16 brightly colored blocks arranged in four rows of four each. If the player rings one of the four center blocks he receives a capital prize; if he rings any of the others he gets a cheap prize.

A metal rod projects from the center of each block and makes the feat much more difficult than it looks because the hoop must drop straight down from above and not touch the rod if it is to encircle the block completely. Since all the hoops come in at an angle, even a well-aimed toss usually fails. The inside edge of the hoop hits the metal rod and either rebounds or spins around the rod as it drops so that it falls off center. The twelve outer blocks are small and can sometimes be ringed by chance, but the four center blocks which pay off the big prizes are only slightly smaller than the inside diameter of the hoop, and the chance of ringing one of these is almost nil. The operator standing inside the counter is close enough that he can drop a hoop straight down over the block, missing the rod.

WATCH-LA GAME

On a recent carnival fact-finding trip through Pennsylvania, my friend Walter Scott and I were scouting the games at a church bazaar in Philadelphia when we heard an operator at a ring-toss joint delivering his pitch. "Step this way, folks, and take home a solid gold, twenty-one-jewel Elgin wrist watch for only fifty cents! All you gotta do to win one of these beautiful watches is to toss one of them hoops over the watch you like. But remember, folks, players can win only one watch apiece. Step right up here, mister, and try your skill. Here you are, sir, three hoops. Fifty cents is correct. Thank you."

"I haven't seen this type of Watch-la game in years," I told Scotty. "It went out of existence with high-button shoes. Just to refresh my memory, I'm going to invest a half dollar and give it the once-over."

Inside the booth, several feet back from the counter, was a series of steps on which were about 30 small wooden blocks known as watch

Hoop-tossing game in which prizes stand on blocks. Hoops are a tight fit and seldom land completely encircling block, which is necessary to win prize. (Baron & Einzig)

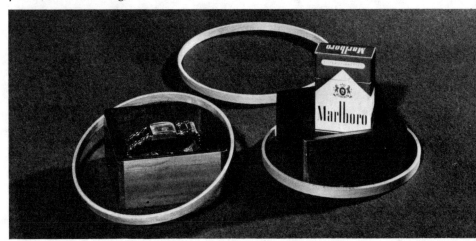

stands. Each stand, square at the base, was about twice as tall as it was wide, and its top surface was cut at an angle slanting down toward the front. Expensive-looking watches were displayed on the tops of the stands. I handed the operator a 50¢ piece and he gave me three wooden embroidery rings.

"The object of the game, mister is to toss the hoops, one at a time, and ring any one of the watch stands." I asked if the hoops were large enough to ring completely all watch stands. He smiled, took one of the three hoops I held, and looped it over a stand with a fast downward movement from the back. He repeated this on several other stands.

"All you need, Mac, is a sharp eye, good aim, and a steady hand to win a watch worth fifty bucks, and all for a measly half a buck."

I said nothing and tossed the three hoops without really trying. I knew already that this two-way store was operating crookedly at the moment.

As we moved away, Scotty said, "It's gaffed. Am I right?"

"It sure is," I replied. "Tonight that Watch-la game is as crooked as a corkscrew. The gaff is in the velvet covering which increases the area that the hoop must encircle.

"When the operator demonstrated that it was possible, he pushed the edge of the hoop behind the stand against the velvet and forced it to give a bit. The operator himself couldn't toss those light hoops over any stand and encircle it completely."

Scotty said, "But if no one ever wins at the game, which has been running all week, don't the church members who are in charge of the bazaar know by now that it's crooked?"

"Tonight is the last night of the bazaar. He probably played the game as an alibi store all week and tonight is the first night he's flatting. He's working strong now because he won't be here tomorrow to listen to any complaints."

"How come the watch stands can be ringed the early part of the week and not tonight? I don't get it."

"It's a two-way store," I replied. "When it's an alibi joint he displays inexpensive prizes and makes use of slightly larger hoops. But he still doesn't have to pay out very often. Even if the velvet covering is removed, a player has almost no chance of ringing a stand, and only if he tosses one of the hoops high in the air, so that it comes squarely over the watch stand without touching the stand. The chance of doing that with a hoop which just barely fits over the stand is anyone's guess."

The flatties later discovered an even more ingenious gaff. They discarded the velvet covering and simply cut the top of the block at a more acute angle (page 602). Measured at the base the block is smaller than the hoop, but the distance from front to back along the slanting surface of the block is greater than the hoop's inner diameter. The operator can demonstrate that the hoop will pass over the block by holding it in his hand, swinging it over the high rear edge of the block first, and then pulling it down so that it encircles the block. But the player, tossing the hoop from the other side of the counter, can't possibly throw it so that it falls in this manner. When the inside edge of the hoop strikes the front of the block, its opposite edge won't clear the block's high rear edge. If the hoop drops over the rear edge first, it can't slide down the slanted top surface because it is stopped by the watch.

Some experienced operators are able to ring the block by tossing it, but only because they have had long practice, because they are much closer to the block and are in a position to make the throw so that the hoop approaches the block from the side and hits one of the high back corners from the side.

Present-day flatties usually use only a few gaffed blocks among others which can be ringed. The honest blocks hold cheap prizes, the gaffed blocks the valuable prize. One manufacturer's catalog copy says: "Our Watch-la Blocks offer the only safe method of using valuable watches on a Hoop-la stand . . . the operator is perfectly safe in using Elgin movements."

When prizes other than watches are used they are displayed on a wooden stand four to six inches square and about three inches high, with a flat top. These are sometimes covered with velvet, the gaff consisting in the fact that covered block is made up of three separate layers of wood. When these layers are lined up flush the flatty can show that the hoop will pass over the block. Then, as he replaces the block on the platform, his fingers push the center layer of wood out of position about a half inch. The velvet covering, loosely draped, conceals this, and the block is now just enough wider on one side so that the most skilled hoop tosser will find it impossible to ring the valuable prize.

On most stands of this shape the velvet covering has also been discarded. The stand most often used today is a plain wood block without any covering. Each block holds a prize of recognized value—a small camera, a vanity case, a harmonica, a safety razor; I've even seen a cornet standing upright on one of these blocks. The store is usually a large, square wooden platform surrounded by a waist-high railing. The player buys three light wooden hoops for 10¢, or nine for a quarter.

The most valuable prizes are the most difficult to win because they are usually placed in the center and are surrounded by cheap, tall, bulky prizes that protect the more valuable ones.

The operator controls the amount of merchandise he desires to give away as prizes. If he wishes to loosen up his store to attract players, he

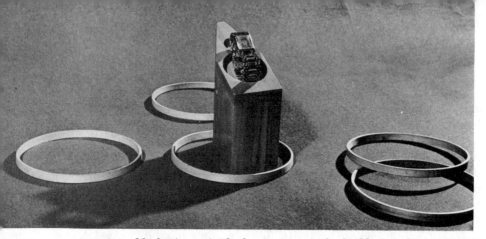

Watch-La blocks. (ABOVE) *The hoop can encircle the block and win a watch but it is next to impossible when thrown from the front. (Baron & Einzig)*

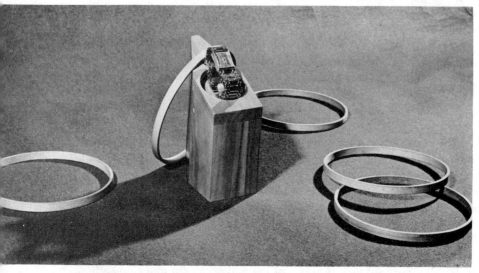

(ABOVE) *If the near edge of the hoop hits the near edge of the block, the hoop cannot pass over the top far edge of the block. (Baron & Einzig)*

(BELOW) *When the far edge of the hoop passes over top rear edge of the block the hoop's near edge cannot quite reach the front of the block and the hoop cannot slide down because of the watch. (Baron & Einzig)*

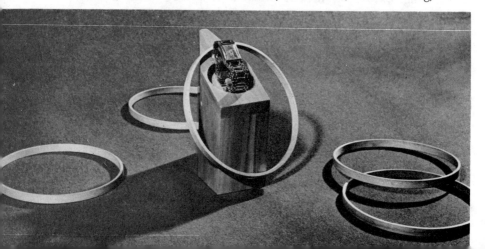

uses larger hoops. When he decides not to give out any prizes he uses hoops that just barely ring the blocks, and the height and bulk of the prizes do the rest. There is something tantalizing about hoop-tossing games; though the players miss time after time, they still continue to play.

Even when a two-way store operates fairly, the player has little chance to win any of the big prizes; when the gaff is used he has no chance. And they call it a skill game!

RING A PEG, OR PITCH TILL YOU WIN

This one is found at almost all carnivals, fairs and amusement centers, and the operator guarantees that you will get a prize. "Step right up, folks," he shouts. "A winner every time, no blanks. Everyone goes home with a prize. Pitch till you win. It may be a big prize worth five dollars or a small consolation prize, but you won't leave without a prize." The chump pays a quarter and gets as many rings as he needs to ring one of the upright wooden pegs on an elevated three-by-four platform about four feet behind the counter.

Each peg fits into a hole in the platform, and bears on its bottom a number which corresponds to one of the numbered merchandise prizes displayed. When a peg is ringed, the operator pulls it from the board and shows its number. Since there are 156 or more pegs and only about 3 whose numbers correspond to the big prizes, the player has 3 chances in 156, or 1 in 52, of winning a capital prize. The rest of the time he gets slum: nickel ashtrays, whistles, cuff links and the like.

Flatting this joint is simplicity itself. The operator has the pegs bearing the big prize numbers marked so that he always knows where they are. If one of these is ringed, he moves in front of the platform, blocking your view for a second, and with one hand lifts off the ring

X-ray showing how blocks are unevenly stacked to prevent hoop from dropping down.

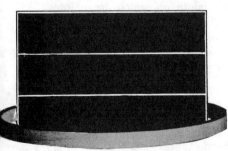 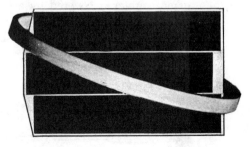

and removes not the peg that was ringed, but one next to it. The pegs are set so close together that this is a simple matter.

CANE RACK

This is a two-way joint in which the players toss small heavy wooden rings toward a display of expensive-looking fancy canes which stand upright in a wire mesh. The gaff is the same as the Watch-la blocks. The heads of the canes are angled. If they point toward the player, it is possible, although not at all easy, to ring them. When the operator is running the joint strong, he simply turns the canes so that the heads slope toward the back, making it impossible to ring them from the player's position. The flatty can always demonstrate the honesty of the game by dropping a ring over a cane from the rear.

KNIFE RACK

This is the same as the cane rack except that imitation knives or household sharpening steels called *pegs* are used. These have staghorn-shaped handles which are angled like the cane heads. If the player manages to ring a knife, he receives it as a prize. Sometimes a wristwatch, clock, knife or other object is tied to the peg, and this is given as the prize. The catalog says, "With these pegs are safe in using the best prizes available." Flat triangular pegs are also used. The ring can be thrown over the peg when its narrow side is toward the player, but not when it presents its broad surface. The catalog says, "With this peg it is possible to flash your stand with watches, guns, knives, etc., with perfect safety. The top of the peg is reversible, making it cop or blow as desired." *Cop or blow*, of course, means win or lose.

COVER THE RED SPOT

Cover the Red Spot, also known as Spot the Spot, is probably the most perplexing and most scientific alibi store in the history of the carnival racket. Any person, young and old, who lays eyes on this joint is immediately impressed by its simplicity and apparent fairness. The game counter is covered by a strip of oilcloth on which are painted several red circular areas, each five inches in diameter. Beside each spot lie five disks of tin, each slightly more than three inches in diameter.

Staghorn-shaped sharpening steels used on a Knife Rack and called "safety pegs" because shape of handle makes them difficult to ring.

The operator, having obtained a willing listener, demonstrates the game by holding the five disks stacked in his right hand, five or six inches above the red circle. "Mister," he says, "all you have to do to take home that big beautiful doll on the shelf, is to drop these five disks from this distance onto the big red circle. If you cover it and no red shows, brother, you got it made." Then he drops the disks rapidly, one at a time, onto the big red circle. They overlap so neatly that the red spot is completely covered. "Try it once," the operator adds. "It's for free, it's not hard to do. Drop the disks from a distance of about six inches above the circle. You can't change their position after they have been dropped. All that is required to cover the spot is skill; a little practice will do it. Here, go ahead and try, it's a free chance, and maybe you'll be lucky and win that big beautiful doll."

Most marks, having nothing to lose and a doll to gain, take the free chance. After the mark has dropped the fifth disk, the operator points to a small red speck that still shows among the placed disks. He moves one of the disks just a little and the red disappears. "See," says the operator, "if you had dropped that one disk just about a sixteenth of an inch to the right, you would be on your way home with a big beautiful doll. Look how close you come to winning on your first try. Try it again, it will only cost you a quarter."

The mark starts to play. Time and again he tries to spot the spot, but never quite covers all the red. Some players attempt a geometric solution, but still the last disk never quite covers the remaining red area. Each time, the operator, with apparent unconcern, moves one or two of the disks a fraction of an inch one way or another and the red spot is completely hidden.

If the operator figures the player is well heeled, he builds him up by saying, "You seem like a nice guy, so I'm going to give you one dollar in cash instead of a doll if you win. Anyway, those dolls I have on the shelf are only worth about half a buck apiece."

Switching from merchandise to cash prizes is the first move in the carnie's buildup attempt to fleece a sucker out of his bankroll. The next step is to get the player to increase his betting from 25¢ to 50¢ to $1 to $5 to $10; he leads the player into doing this by offering increased odds. A 50¢ winning bet collects $2.50; a $1 winning bet receives $5; a $5 winning bet receives $25, and so on.

I recently visited a carnival in Windsor, North Carolina, which was loaded with two-way joints and alibis. Here I saw a mooch lose $100 at Spot the Spot and then go home three times for more money. The mark, after dropping $700, was so sure that he could cover the red spot on the next try that he pleaded unsuccessfully with the operator

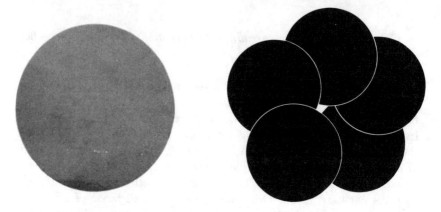

Spot the Spot. The red spot (LEFT) is 5 inches in diameter. The flatty drops the slightly more than 3-inch disks and neatly covers the large spot, but the chump almost always finds that a small part of the spot remains uncovered (RIGHT). (Stanley Einzig)

to accept his automobile as a wager for just one more chance at covering the red spot.

A Spot the Spot game, like all other flats and alibi stores, is not the harmless game it seems to be even though there is no secret contrivance. Nothing can get out of order, and if a nosy sheriff or police officer wants to examine the equipment, it's okay with the operator. The only gaff is a little misdirection used by the operator when he demonstrates that the spot can be covered.

If there ever was a game of skill or science, Spot the Spot is it. But when any skill or science game demands of the average player the skill or dexterity equal to that of a champion golfer shooting six under par, brother, that's not a skill game, that's a Spot the Spot alibi store.

Experiments I have made show that chance and skill both play a role in Spot the Spot. The probability that a skilled player can drop a disk from a six-inch height onto the exact position on the red circle which it must occupy is about 1 in 3, or 2 to 1 against. This means that the probability that a player will make five perfect drops is 1 in $3 \times 3 \times 3 \times 3 \times 3$, or 243. The slightest deviation from a perfect drop with any of the five disks dooms the player to failure. Most players don't realize this until they have played the game for some time; others never do; they continue to play until the give up in exasperation or until they are broke.

The operator is able to succeed in his demonstration because he has practiced a smooth, deceptive move. His hand sweeps quickly over the red spot in a fast back-and-forth and up-and-down movement which is confusing and hides the fact that the disk, at the moment he drops it, is only an inch or so above the layout. When the player drops his disks, the operator insists that it be done from a height of five or six inches.

Some operators also carry a slightly larger set of disks, with which it is easier to cover the red spot, but when these are in use only slum is given away as prizes. When passersby see that nearly everyone is winning, they join the *tip* (group of suckers). But when the big cash betting takes place you can be sure that the smaller disks have come back into use and that the odds are 242 to 1 against the player.

THE NEEDLE BET

The inventor of Spot the Spot may have been some carnie who knew about the needle experiment performed by the eighteenth-century naturalist Count Buffon. This consisted in dropping an inch-long needle onto a flat surface bearing parallel lines ruled one inch apart. He found the probability that the needle would fall across a line rather than between lines to be $2/\pi$ or 2 in 3.1416. Lazzerini, an Italian mathematician, repeated the experiment in 1901; he tossed a needle 3,408 times, and got a result of 2 in 3.1415929. Since π carried to seven places is 3.1415926, Lazzerini's result deviated from theory by only .0000003. *

Some gamblers use this as a sucker bet. They offer even money that the needle will fall across a line rather than between the lines. Since the probability is 2 in 3.1416 the correct odds are 2 to 1.1416 and the gambler who offers to pay even money on the bet has a 31% edge in his favor.

THE SWINGING BALL AND PIN

The Swinging Ball and Pin, commonly called the Swinger, is one of the oldest two-way joints. It is advertised as a game of skill.

A five-inch bowling ball at the end of a three- or four-foot chain hangs above a 15-inch bowling pin which stands on a counter. The player tries to swing the ball past the pin, releasing it before it passes the pin in such a manner that it strikes and knocks the pin down on its return swing. This one looks at though it would be hard to gaff, but don't jump to conclusions. The handsome prize which is at stake never leaves the display shelf, and all the player gets is exercise. It's another *G-joint* (gaffed joint).

The very simple gaff is not in the chain or ball, but in the stationary bowling pin. A projecting nail in the counter serves as a guide to position the pin exactly under the spot from which the ball hangs. It fits into a hole in the bottom of the pin, and the hole is bored slightly off center. If the bulk of the pin is set to the left of the nail, a well-exe-

---

* If d is the distance between lines and n is the length of the needle, the formula $\frac{2n}{d\pi}$ gives the probability for any needle whose length is equal to or less than d.

cuted swing will cause the ball to pass the pin and hit it on the return swing. If the bulk of the pin is to the right the player must start his swing a half inch or so farther to the right to miss the ball on the outgoing swing. The ball describes a greater arc in both directions and can't possibly hit the pin on its return journey no matter how skilled the player.

Sometimes the hole is centered but is larger than necessary. The same result is obtained because this allows the pin to be set in two positions, one fair, the other impossible.

Smart operators today don't bother to use a gaffed pin. They simply cheat on their demonstration swing by pushing the ball past the pin before releasing it, something the player is not allowed to do.

NAIL HAMMERING GAME

This flat store gets plenty of action from members of the local carpenter's union. The object is to hammer the entire length of a 1½-inch nail into a railroad tie with one blow of a hammer. For an experienced carpenter, this is an easy feat. A regulation railroad tie or log rests on two wooden horses, forming a counter in front of a small tent. The operator stands behind this wearing a carpenter's apron and holding a hammer and several nails.

"This," the grifter announces, "is a pure game of skill and strength. All you gotta do to win yourself some dough is to drive a nail all the way into this wooden log with one blow of this hammer. Watch me and see how easy it's done." He starts a nail into the log by tapping it lightly with the hammer. He does this with two more, then, with three nails standing upright, their pointed edges sticking into the log, he adds, "All you gotta do is drive one of these nails all the way into the log. Watch closely and see how it's done." Whammo! Down comes the hammer, and the nail is driven all the way into the log. Two more blows, and two more nails vanish into the log. The flatty brings a handful of nails from his apron pocket and holds them out to a spectator. "Pick a lucky nail out for yourself, buddy."

Joe Mooch selects a nail, the grifter starts it into the log and gives the spectator the hammer. "This try is on me. It's a free chance. Drive the nail into the log. See how easy it is to do."

The player gives it a try, and if he hits the nail squarely on the head it goes all the way into the log. The grifter smiles. "The way you swung that hammer, you are a real carpenter, hey, buddy? You see, this is an honest game of skill and strength." The grifter then reaches out and feels the player's muscle. "Boy, oh boy! Some muscle."

Then he challenges the player. "You did it once because you were relaxed and weren't betting any money, but if you bet me a dollar, I

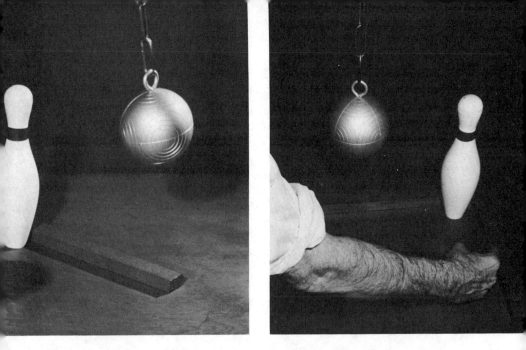

The Swinger. Tenpin in photo at left is positioned directly under point from which the swinging ball hangs, making it impossible to hit. At right the flatty places tenpin slightly to left of center (exaggerated in photo) to demonstrate that pin can be hit. (Stanley Einzig)

don't think you can do it again. You'll get nervous and miss the head. A dollar will get you two dollars. How about it?"

Having succeeded once, Joe figures this is an easy way to pick up two bucks. He puts up his dollar and takes aim. Whammo! The hammer smacks the nail head, but this time the nail remains in full view, bent in the middle.

"You're nervous, buddy," the grifter says. "You didn't hit it square on the head. Money usually makes people nervous. But calm down, take your time, and try again." The player, annoyed, doesn't want to look foolish in front of the bystanders, especially if he happens to have his girl along. So he tries again, and again, and again, at a buck per try, and always gets a bent nail. The grifter occasionally proves again that it's a ridiculously easy feat, sometimes driving two or three nails into the log in rapid succession. Somehow the player can't seem to repeat his first success. Carpenters who try this game really get annoyed and pay out dollar after dollar trying to do something they do hundreds of times every day.

The grifter builds up the player by raising the odds. He offers 2 to 1 if the player will bet $5, then 4 to 1 for a $10 bet, and so on, until the chump finally gives up in disgust or has lost so much of his bankroll that he hardly has enough left to buy his girl a cone of cotton candy. I once saw a flatty in Los Angeles build up a sucker to the point where he was laying him odds of $1,000 to $50.

The gaff here is in the nails. The large pocket in the apron the grifter wears has a secret inside pocket which contains hard nails that can easily be driven into the log with one blow; the large pocket itself contains soft nails that bend easily. Since the nails all seem to come from the same pocket, the player assumes they are all alike. Sometimes the grifter also resorts to some sleight of hand as he switches a hard nail for a soft one, or vice versa, as required. This is easy because he often has both kinds of nails in his hand at the same time. Occasionally he allows the player to select a nail from a handful, but only when all the nails are soft.

Some grifters do not use soft nails; they simply bend the points of some nails slightly so that, when hit, they will bend.

BUCKET STORE AND BUSHEL BASKET GAMES

This is an always popular science-and-skill grind store in which the player buys baseballs at three for a quarter and throws them into one or more wooden buckets or into bushel baskets having reinforced wooden bottoms. The balls must remain in the bucket or basket without bouncing out. If the player can do this successfully with three successive throws, he wins a capital prize; if two out of three balls remain inside the bucket he wins a piece of slum; one or no balls get him nothing. The balls the operator tosses in seldom bounce out, the player's almost always do.

The buckets and baskets are always tipped toward the player at an angle, and the greater the angle the more likely the balls are to bounce out. Ninety tosses out of 100 will hit the upper half of the bottom of the bucket and bounce or roll out. The operator can accomplish the feat easily from his side of the counter because he can throw from the side and hit the side of the bucket. The ball bounces but hits the bucket's opposite side on the rebound, and this tends to keep it inside. Huckley Buck operates on the same principle but uses six to ten buckets or kegs. Most bucket and basket games also use this principle.

When the operator decides not to award any big prizes at all, he gaffs the game. One method is to use a bucket with a hidden movable wooden drumhead that fits either tightly or loosely under the bottom of the bucket. The drumhead is controlled by a lever running from below the bucket under the counter to a foot rest. When the flatty steps on the foot rest, the drumhead is pressed tightly against the bucket bottom and the added thickness of the bottom causes balls from any angle to bounce out.

Sometimes the gaff is the ball itself. The grifter uses a soft baseball,

John Scarne and his survey assistant, Walter Scott, try their luck at a basket game. (Stanley Einzig)

which has less tendency to bounce than a hard ball, when he demonstrates how easy the game is. He may even give the marks a free trial or two to prove that they can also do it. But as soon as the mark pays for his chance, the balls he gets are harder and have a lot more bounce.

THE MILK BOTTLES

Six pint-size milk bottles made of wood or aluminum are set up on a 12-inch-square board in a pyramid; the top bottle balances on two others, and those two on a row of three. They are about 16 feet behind the game counter where the player stands. For a quarter, he receives three baseballs, with which he attempts to knock all six bottles off the board. If he succeeds he gets a prize of some value—perhaps a ham, blanket or silverware set. If he knocks off all but one, he gets slum. Otherwise he gets nothing.

It looks easy, but it's another two-way store. Three of the bottles

Scarne tosses baseballs at a group of six small buckets. The buckets here are not tipped up at an angle, showing that the game (called Huckley-Buck) is honestly run. (Stanley Einzig)

are heavy, three are light. If the three light bottles are on the bottom, the player who can throw a baseball with fair accuracy can knock them all off. When the three heavy bottles are on the bottom and spaced as far apart as possible, even a professional big-league pitcher can't do it. "It can only be accomplished," the catalog promises, "when desired by the operator." And he desires it only when he lets a stick win to impress the customers.

CAT GAME OR CAT RACK

This is another ancient but still very popular carnival game. It appears to be purely a game of skill, but can be gaffed like all the others. Baseballs are thrown at stuffed cloth figures of cats lined up on a shelf. Sometimes one large, heavy *punk* (cat) about two feet tall is used, more often there are four 18-inch cats lined up side by side on a shelf or rack. The player gets three baseballs for 25¢ or 50¢ and throws from a distance of 16 feet. If he succeeds in knocking three cats off the rack he wins a good prize; two cats get him a slum souvenir worth perhaps half what he paid for the chance.

The game usually gets a good play because the cats aren't hard to hit. The catch is that they can be knocked completely off the rack only with a well-placed center hit. They may fall when hit on the side, but will not roll off because they are flat. Most Cat Game operators run an honest store, but there are many who follow the flatty's motto: "Never give a mooch a winner."

The Cat Rack can be gaffed in many ways. The commonest is to use two light and two heavy cats, the latter being weighted at the bottom. When the operator puts on his throwing demonstration, his setup boy places the two heavy cats side by side on either right or left so that the operators knows which they are. He also places all four cats close to the rear edge of the shelf so that even a hit that is not in the direct center will knock the heavy cats off the shelf. An ornamental upright slat of wood on the rack's front edge conceals this slightly changed position. When the player throws, the cats are set close to the front edge of the rack. He may succeed in knocking the two light cats off the shelf, and he may even knock a heavy cat down, but its weighted bottom keeps it from falling off.

The most ingenious Cat Game gaff I have come across is one in which all four cats have a wooden base that projects about two inches at the front. The rear side of the upright slat on the rack's front edge is beveled at the bottom, and when a cat is placed closed to the front of the rack so that its bottom extension fits into the groove made by the bevel, it can be knocked down, but not off the rack. The projecting

The Milk Bottles. A game of "skill and science" which is not easy when it is honest, but nearly impossible when gaffed. (Stanley Einzig)

The author watches a player try to knock the cats off the shelves. (Stanley Einzig)

extension slides upward along the groove as the cat falls and there is enough friction so that the cat's backward movement is slowed. If two of the four cats are in this position it is impossible to knock off three. Since these cats all weigh the same, the operator can bring them forward for inspection.

I know one flatty who gaffed two of his cats with steel plates in their bottoms and had two strong magnets concealed in the rack. When the ungaffed cats were placed above the magnets, any of the cats could be knocked off; when the gaffed cats were placed above the magnets they would fall down but not off the stand.

Still another method is the use of several sharp pointed nails protruding about half an inch above the surface of the rack directly behind the cats. When a cat falls, the projecting nails catch and hold it so that it cannot slide or tumble off the stand.

Operators who work the game without a setup boy often use cats which are fastened to the rack by a hinge, and the player only needs to knock them over. To set up the cats that have been knocked down, the operator pulls a wire at the game counter, raising metal rods behind each cat which push them up into position again. But there is also a hidden control that can be used to keep the rods in an upright position when the operator releases the wire, making it impossible to knock two of the cats over.

A cat has nine lives, and a carnie cat has even more gaffs.

STRING GAME

This is one of the oldest carnival games, and it is still seen in some amusement centers. It is a grind store which is often run by a woman grifter. Merchandise prizes are displayed on a stand behind the counter, and a string tied to each prize runs up over a crossbar above the stand and then down to the operator who holds a collar (a cloth band, wooden ring or wide rubber band) through which all the ends pass.

The flatty demonstrates the fairness of the game by gripping the strings just above the collar and pulling them. This lifts all the prizes on the stand showing that each one is attached to a string and can be won. The player pays a nickel or dime for the privilege of pulling the end of any one string, and he gets a duplicate of the prize at its other end.

The gaff is simple. When setting up the stand, the operator gathers all the strings and places the collar around them a few inches from their ends. Then he traces the strings attached to the more valuable prizes and pulls each one so that its end is drawn back into the collar. The projecting ends available to the player will, therefore, never raise anything but cheap prizes. If any suspicious customer makes a beef the operator can trace the course of any string from the prize directly to the collar.

HAND STRIKER OR BINGER

This is a counter version of the familiar 28- to 36-foot Hi Striker in which the player strikes a pivoted beam with a maul and tries to send a sliding weight up a vertical track to hit a gong at the top. Counter versions are from 22 inches to 42 inches high, and the player strikes a springboard with his fist, sending a weighted indicator sliding up between two posts. A spring ratchet inside the indicator moves past notches on a rod inside one of the posts. When it reaches its highest point the ratchet engages a notch and is prevented from falling down. There is a vertical row of numbers on each post, and the number at which the indicator stops indicates whether the player wins or loses.

The Hand Striker is usually played for cash and the player is charged anywhere from 25¢ to $1 or more for each strike. When the indicator stops at the number on which the player has bet he is paid off at odds as high as 20 to 1. If it stops at a losing number all he gets is exercise. The sucker build-up is similar to that used on the Spindle (page 850), and the player can eventually find himself betting his whole bankroll on one try.

The gaff is mechanical. The concealed rod has three sets of notches. One set is fair, the second set has only notches that will hold the indicator at even numbers, the third set will stop at only odd numbers. The rod can be turned by a hidden control as the operator lowers the indicator so that any one of the three sets of notches comes into use. Since odd and even numbers run alternately, the indicator never drops down more than one notch before it catches and the stopping seems natural. Since the Hand Striker can also be set to operate honestly, it is called a three-way store; it can be set to win, lose or work fair.

THREE-SHELL GAME

You don't see this one much around carnivals at the moment, but the old-time swindles never die; they keep coming back for a new play with each new generation of suckers. The Three-Shell swindle is the oldest of them all. Magicians have long used it for entertainment purposes, and a description of it is to be found in the earliest known conjuring catalog in the English language, printed in London in 1843 for W. H. M. Crambrook. It was then called "Thimbles and Pea." The operator was known as a *thimble-rigger;* his shills were called *bonnets.* The principle of the bent corner used in Three-Card Monte (see page 619) was also employed. An outside man would flick the pea (often a small piece of red brick) off the table when the operator wasn't watching. He would then induce the *pigeon* (sucker) to bet that the pea was not under any of the thimbles.

After the bet was made the pea was found to have mysteriously reappeared, the operator having secretly replaced the missing pea with another.

The origin of thimble-rigging is ancient. There is little doubt that it is a simplification of what is probably the earliest of all conjuring tricks, the Cups and Balls. In this trick three cups are used, and several balls, which jump mysteriously from one cup to another just as the pea once jumped from thimble to thimble and now jumps from shell to shell. A good description of the Cups and Balls trick as it is still done today was written by Alciphron of Athens in the second century A.D.

Since the dice cheat has been with us at least since prehistoric times, it is very likely that the Cups and Balls was used for swindling purposes by Greek sharpers, and probably the Egyptians as well.

Thimble-riggers probably came to this country very soon after the *Mayflower.* Along with Monte, thimble-rigging was one of the sharper's favorite swindles on the riverboats. J. H. Green, in his *Gamblers' Tricks with Cards* (1868), wrote about how he once saw Dr. Bennett, who was known as the Napoleon of the thimble-riggers and who claimed to have

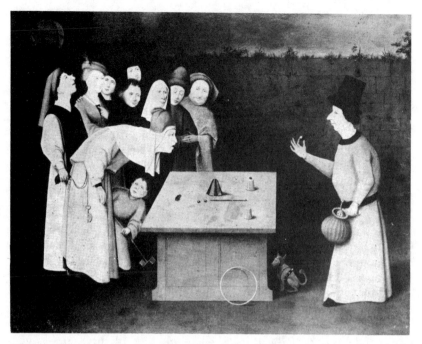

The Cups and Balls, probably the world's oldest conjuring trick and the father of the Three-Shell Game. Painted by Hieronymus Bosch in the late 15th century. Note the pickpocket at work.

invented thimble-rigging, work the swindle one evening on a river boat using three borrowed thimbles and a small ball of rolled-up paper. And we also find that the Doctor used the same stratagem as the bent corner in Three-Card Monte. He let his mark win a few small bets to lead him on—something no modern Monte man ever does; the latter makes the mark lose from the beginning so that he will continue to play in the hope of retrieving his losses. Green writes:

> Now, in the moving of the little paper ball, we thought we had discovered the source of the Doctor's misfortunes, for becoming a little unrolled, a portion of the paper which it was made of, stuck out from under one of the thimbles. This our Connecticut friend [the sucker] plainly saw, and we presumed the Doctor, through old age (now about 70), had his sight so impaired as not to be able to see it, and could not, therefore, play the game with his usual adoitness. But the tale was soon told. Our "Yankee friend" proposed to double the bet "having the thing so dead." The Doctor, impatient of repeated losses, told him to make it hundreds instead of tens. This was done, and our friend bet three hundred dollars against one hundred (just here I thought it was a shame to take advantage of a professional gambler's blindness, for the location of the ball was evident).

When the sucker lifted the thimble, the ball was, of course, no longer there. When the astonished victim declared that "all was not right," the Doctor said, "Never mind, what's a few hundred dollars to a young man with your eyes? The ladies all admire them—I heard them speak of them today—and you won twice out of three times; that's the best two in three anyhow."

Dr. Bennett's claim that he invented thimble-rigging is dubious, but the old boy obviously knew how to play the game.

Thimble-riggers were found in abundance during the early twentieth century around all amusement centers and racetracks, and about 1915 some ingenious grifter began using walnut shells instead of thimbles. Since then it has been known to the public as the Three-Shell Game, the Shell Game or the Pea and Shell Game. Later, perhaps to disguise the game with a new look, another grifter began using pop-bottle caps. The operators have long called the game simply "the Nuts."

No matter whether thimbles, shells or bottle caps are used, it is still the same old flat joint. The game is most often played on a small folding table with a velvet-covered top. The pea, usually made of rubber, is covered by one of the three shells, and then all three are moved about. The player tries to follow the shell containing the pea and then bets the operator that he knows where it is. The operator, as in Three-Card Monte, uses outside men to build up the sucker, although only one is needed here. He doesn't need a shill to *cross* (double-cross) the spectator when the latter guesses right. In Monte the player can pick the winning card by chance; in the Shell Game this is impossible, because, when the grifter accepts the player's bet, the little pea is not under any of the shells.

The pea makes its disappearance almost automatically. In the process of moving the three shells about, the one which covers the pea is pushed forward about two inches. The operator lifts the back of the shell a tiny bit, and the rubber pea, caught between the rear edge of the shell and the nap of the velvet cloth, is squeezed out and arrives between the thumb and first finger, which pinch it and retain it. When the hand leaves the shell, the first finger covers the pea, concealing it.

Bets are accepted, and when the player turns up his selection and finds nothing, the operator immediately moves the other two shells backward a couple of inches, and the pea obediently squeezes back in under one of the shells, which the operator then lifts. "If you had picked this one," he says, "you would have won your bet."

Experienced Shell operators, as well as a good many present-day magicians, can perform this manipulation without the slightest chance of detection. The magician, of course, doesn't accept bets on the game. but the flatty who is out for the money plays for keeps.

Three-Shell operators giving a chump the business in the 1800s, as drawn by A. B. Frost. Today the costumes have changed but the game is still the same old swindle.

THREE-CARD MONTE

Three-Card Monte was the most popular con game of the old West. Countless Monte operators plied their trade on the steamboats of the Ohio and Mississippi and throughout the West in the 1850s. The most notorious Monte operator "Canada Bill" Jones once summed up the whole philosophy of the card cheat in one sentence: "Suckers have no business with money, anyway."

Nearly all the historians state that Three-Card Monte is of Mexican origin and came from there in the early years of the nineteenth century. They assume this because the national game of Mexico and other Spanish-speaking countries at that time was Monte, a banking game played, as the 1863 *American Hoyle* says, "with cards made especially for the game and known as Monte cards." Mexican Monte was a game; Three-Card Monte is a swindle. It acquired the name because the first broad tossers pretended that their three-card swindle was the Mexican game. Some early writer took this claim at its face value and it appeared in print; for years, his successors have copied the error.

Since they are basically the same game, differing only in the objects used, Three-Card Monte may very well be a descendant of thimble-rigging, the earlier form of the Three-Shell Game. I can see some card cheat, impressed with the way the thimble-riggers were clipping the marks, figuring out a way to play the game using three cards instead of three thimbles and a pea.

Three-Card Monte swindlers were numerous for the next hundred years, up until World War II. In 1935, I exposed their methods in a 40-page booklet titled *Why You Can't Win*. After the war, Monte operators had their difficulties with the cops, and many who had been operating on the outskirts of carnivals and fairs turned to the newly developed peek or count stores.

In the last years, however, the Monte mobs have returned, apparently figuring that there is a new generation of mooches with cash in their pockets who don't know that it is a swindle, not a game. I have spotted 15 Monte men working in various parts of the country, and I know of one New York City businessman who was taken for $5,000 on a Long Island train as he returned from the track at Belmont Park. Not too long ago, the now defunct *New York Herald Tribune* carried a front-page story describing a Monte game on 40th Street in midtown Manhattan, along with a photograph showing the game in action.

The operator of this swindle, usually a clever card sharp, shows three cards, slightly bent lengthwise so as to be more easily picked up by the ends—which in turn facilitates the deceptive flipping of the cards. The three cards most commonly used are the two red aces and the queen of spades.

To illustrate the working of a Monte operator and his confederates, let me relate the following. One day my assistant, Walter Scott, and I were in Hartford, Connecticut, giving a carnival the once-over as a part of my survey. As we left I spotted several men gathered around a rusty oil drum whose top was covered with a newspaper. One was throwing three cards out on the paper. We joined the group and listened to the *broad tosser's* (Monte thrower's) spiel, the standard one: "Men, I have here three little cards, two red aces and the black queen

Big-town chumps gathered around a Three Card Monte game in midtown Manhattan. (Terence McCarten from N.Y. Herald-Tribune)

of Spades. The idea is for you to find the queen. If you find it you win; if you turn up an ace you lose. It's as simple as that. And remember, I take no bets from paupers, cripples or pregnant women. I show you all three cards, then throw them down face down—fast, like this. If your eye is faster than my hand and you find the queen, I pay you the same amount you bet. I'll accept bets of five, ten, twenty, fifty or a hundred that you can't find the lady. Remember, men, if you don't speculate you can't accumulate. Money in hand or no bet. Let's go."

The broad tosser showed the three cards and threw them again. One man handed him a $20 bill, turned over the card he thought was the queen and found himself looking at an ace.

On the next toss another bettor put up $50, turned over the queen and won. The betting went on for about 20 minutes when someone said, "Fold." The operator immediately brought the game to an end, and he and most of the players walked off toward the midway.

Scotty said, "Figuring the odds on some of those carnival games we just saw can be complicated, but this one is a cinch. The player has one chance in three of picking the right card and winning."

"You'd be right," I told him, "if it was a game and if it was honest. But it's a swindle and it's never honest. Even if you do happen to pick the queen by chance, you still won't win."

"But some of those guys did win," Scotty objected.

"Anyone you saw win," I told him, "was a member of the *broad mob* [Monte mob]. The operator almost always has three or four *outside men* [confederates, shills, sticks] who win the money to make it look good and who lure the suckers on with this build-up to get them to bet high. One plays the part of a lookout man; when he calls, 'Fold, fold, fold,' he's signaling that the fuzz is coming their way. In two seconds flat the newspaper is folded with the three cards inside and dropped to the ground, and the *inside man* [operator] and his shills scram in different directions. The outside man we heard call, 'Fold,' said it only once and was merely notifying the broad tosser and the rest of the mob that the suckers they were playing were broke, and that this was the time to *blow* and find another spot to do business. The group gathered around a Monte game sometimes contains only one *live one* [mark with money]; the other players are all members of the mob."

"And when a mark does accidentally pick the right card, how come he doesn't collect?" Scotty asked.

"They put on an act for him. Suppose he puts one hand on the queen and shoves fifty bucks at the operator. One or more shills are also trying to place bets, usually bigger ones, because this is part of the buildup. The broad tosser, knowing the chump has picked the winning card, simply pretends not to see him or his fifty dollars. He takes the hundred bucks an outside man has been offering, and the latter slaps his hand down quickly on one of the remaining cards. The operator then notices the sucker and says, 'No two bets allowed on different cards at the same time.'

"The chump objects that he had his hand on the card first, and the outside man begins arguing heatedly and stubbornly that the chump is wrong. The operator shrugs. 'I'm not sure who had his hand down first. I'm sorry, gentlemen, this toss don't count.' At the same time, he picks up the three face-down cards and mixes them quickly before showing their faces so that the victim never knows that this play-acting has just cost him a fifty-buck winning bet. All the angles are neatly covered. It's a 'heads I win, tails you lose' proposition from the word go."

When the mob is ready to blow, they take the rest of the chump's bankroll with a lulu of an angle that is custom-tailored to fit any sucker with even a little larceny in his heart. This is what puts it in the confidence game category. They offer him a wide-open opportunity to cheat the operator; if he goes for it, he finds that it explodes in his face. An outside man starts an argument which takes the operator's attention off the cards. Another outside man nudges the mark, picks up the queen and *crimps* (bends) one corner. He does this openly so that the other chumps in the crowd can also see it.

The Monte man then throws the cards again, pretending not to notice the bent corner. The outside man who put the crimp in makes a $50 or $100 bet on the bent card, turns it up and wins. The shill makes another bet and wins another hundred. All the marks should, by this time, be ready to *spring* (bet). The operator says, "This next toss is going to be my last, gentlemen. And I'm prepared to accept any size bet, fifty, a hundred, five hundred—whatever your bankroll allows. But after I toss the cards, if anyone touches a card before I call, 'No more bets,' all bets are off."

He shows the three cards again and throws them face down on the newspaper. That bent corner sticking out like a sore thumb seems to be money in the bank to the sucker.

"Okay, men, let me have your bets." Naturally the chumps all bet on the same card. When the operator has collected all the folding money in sight, he says, "Okay, turn it up."

One of the outside men usually obliges and the queen with the bent corner turns out to be an ace with a bent corner.

While the chumps' jaws are still hanging at this totally unexpected development, and before they recover sufficiently even to begin trying to figure out what hit them, the outside men start a big argument among themselves as to whose fault it is that they lost all their dough. While this commotion is going on, the broad tosser fades away with the money and later *keeps the meet* (gets together) with the other Monte mob members to *cut up the score* (divide the loot).

The inside man, of course, straightened out the bent corner on the queen and crimped one of the aces while gathering up the three cards and preparing to toss them. And don't think you can spot this sleight-of-hand maneuver, because it takes place completely under cover of the other cards. There is one simple way to avoid being cheated at this game: whenever you see it being played, turn around and walk quickly away.

Three-Card Monte mobs work the big cities during the winter months, pitching their flat stores in alleys, subway stations, doorways, with the lookout half a block away to give them the *office* (signal) when he spots a cop.

A final word of caution. Don't think, now that you know how the Monte swindle is worked, that you can outsmart the operator at his own game. The only time I ever heard of anyone getting away with this was in a story George Devol tells in his *Forty Years a Gambler on the Mississippi.*

We had a great graft before the war, on the Upper Mississippi, between St. Louis and St. Charles. We would go up on a boat and back by rail. One night going up we had done a good business in our line, and were just putting up the shutters, when a man stepped up and said he could turn up the right card. My partner, Posey Jeffers, was doing the honors that night [tossing the cards] and he said, "I will bet from $1 to $10,000 that no man can pick out the winning ticket." The man pulled out a roll nearly as large as a pillow, and put up $5,000; but it was not the winner. "Mix them up again," said the man, and he put up the same sum as before. He turned [the card], and Posey put the second $5,000 in his pocket. The man then walked away as if to lose $10,000 was an everyday thing with him. We then closed up our "banking house," well pleased with ourselves. The next day we were counting our cash, and we found we had on hand $10,000 in nice new bills on the State Bank of Missouri, but it was all counterfeit. We deposited them in the fire, as we had no immediate use for them.

A FINAL WORD TO CARNIVAL GAME PLAYERS

There are many more carnival games, some advertised as skill or science games, some as games of strength and others as games of chance. With the exception of hanky-panks, which are amusement games and pay slum awards, nearly every carnival game is so designed that the operator is sure to retain from 40% to 95% of all the money wagered. Most of the equipment used comes with the gaff built in and can be operated either honestly or crookedly. Such equipment is described in the manufacturers' catalogs as a *two-way store.* One such description even reads, "This game can also be set fair," which implies that the maker knows very well that the G (gaff) will be used most of the time.

When the flatty is *going for the money* (cheating), his percentage of the money wagered is 100%. Anyone who bucks percentages ranging from 40% to 100% deserves the names the grifter knows him by: sucker, chump, mark or mooch.

26.
Private Card Games:
Cheating and
How to Detect It

Our adult gambling population of 90 million wagers $500 billion yearly at all forms of gambling. Half, or $250 billion, of this is wagered at all those forms of private gambling which do not involve a professional gambling operator, bookie or banker. About 60% of this half, or $150 billion, is wagered at private card games. About half of *this* amount, or $75 billion, is wagered at Poker; 15%, or $22½ billion, at Gin Rummy, and the remainder at other games, such as Black Jack, Pinochle, Bridge, Canasta, Cribbage and Euchre.

The remaining $100 billion is wagered at (1) all kinds of private dice games—Craps, Hooligan, Backgammon, Poker Dice, Scarney 3000, etc.; (2) private betting not involving a bookie on sports contests and elections in which the bettors may or may not be participants; (3) various forms of private proposition betting on the outcome of guessing games such as the Match Game and guessing the serial numbers on bills, or betting on the outcome of tossing or matching coins; (4) all other private gambling, such as betting on the time of a ship's arrival in port or the outcome of a pigeon race.

About 10% of the total private gambling handle, or $25 billion, is won by a group of 10 million gamblers out of the 90 million—the skillful and experienced gamblers, the private gambling hustlers and the gambling cheats.

A total of 70 million adult American card players, of whom half are women, purchase some 90 million decks of playing cards each year.

EVOLUTION of GAMES

DIVINING ARROW

GUESSING GAMES

PRIMITIVE DICE USED WITH STICK COUNTERS

GAMES of CHANCE and SKILL

BACKGAMMON
PACHISI (India)
GO (Japan)
CHECKER
CHESS

RAWSON

ASTRAGALUS

FORTUNE TELLING DICE (India)

DIE (Roman)

DIE (Modern)

DOMINO

AFRICAN DOLLASS

INDIAN GAMING BLOCK

KOREAN WOODEN DIE

TEETOTUM (India)

GAMES of CHANCE

PUT AND TAKE TOP

GAMING STICKS (Alaska)

KOREAN PLAYING CARD

CHINESE PLAYING CARD

AMERICAN ROLLING LOG (Gaffed)

RED AND BLACK PENCIL (Gaffed)

MODERN PLAYING CARD

JACKSTRAWS

SACRED DIVINING STICKS (Persia)

SCEPTRE

MAGICIAN'S WAND

Diagram based on researches of Stuart Culin in his "Chess and Playing Cards."

(Military Service Publishing Co.)

Egyptian and Roman dice. (Culin)

THE HISTORY OF PLAYING CARDS

Gambling began in prehistoric times. The primitive witch doctors in many cultures throughout the world, believing that man's fate was controlled by the gods, threw sticks and arrows and the knucklebones of cattle and sheep upon the ground and read the future in the way they fell. The first gamblers used these same devices, and began betting on the way they would fall. The magic rituals became games of chance.

The four-sided knucklebones (*astragali*) evolved into six-sided dice,

Korean playing cards whose shape and back design, both depicting a feather, indicate that they evolved from the throwing sticks and divining arrows used since prehistoric times for fortunetelling. (Culin)

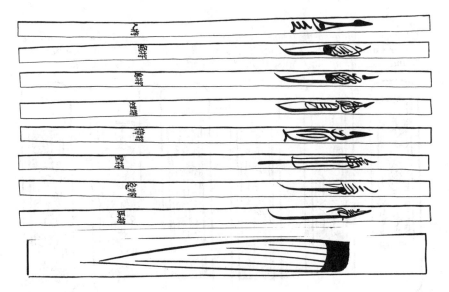

and the sticks and arrows became playing cards. Korean cards, long and narrow in shape and originally made of wood, were once called "fighting tablets." They bear suit marks like the magic symbols used on divining arrows, and have a back design that pictures an arrow feather. Games using these stick cards, which are now oiled paper strips eight inches long by a quarter inch wide, are still played in Korea.

After the Chinese invented paper, sometime between 200 B.C. and 200 A.D., they began to use it for making cards, and they followed the Korean pattern. Their first cards were (and still are) long and narrow, and some use Korean numerals as index marks. The Chinese later developed their own suits, taking them from the designs on the first Chinese paper money of the T'ang dynasty (618–906), which bore pictures of the even earlier metallic money. The suits of coins, strings of coins, myriads of coins and tens of myriads are still used on Chinese cards today.

What is probably the oldest playing card still in existence is one found in Chinese Turkestan that dates from the eleventh century. It is an honor card (the red flower) of the coin suit.

The first cards appeared in Europe in the early fourteenth century, probably in Italy. They spread rapidly into Spain, Germany, France and the Low Countries and were fairly well known throughout Europe by 1375. The earliest written reference to playing cards is in a manuscript written sometime between 1328 and 1341; and the oldest Euro-

Chinese playing cards whose symbols are borrowed from the old Chinese paper money. Cards at left are the 3 and 8 of the suit of Coins; center, the 3 and 8 of Strings of Coins; right, the 3 and 8 of Myriads of Coins.

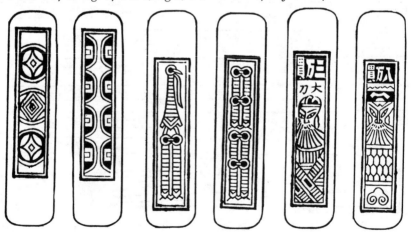

Various styles of money-derived cards of China. Card on the right, the Red Flower of the suit of Coins, was found in Chinese Turkestan, is probably not later than A.D. 11th century, and is the oldest known playing card yet found.

pean cards that have been found to date are a set of 17 believed to be part of a pack painted for Charles VI of France in 1392, and now in the Bibliothèque Nationale in Paris. In the royal account books of that year there is a record of monies paid to one Jacquiem Gringonneur for painting three packs of cards "in gold and diverse colors, ornamented with many devices, for the diversion of our lord, the King." A similar set of 35 cards painted in Italy in the fifteenth century can be seen in the Morgan Library in New York City.

These cards are part of the 22 high cards called atouts, and later triumph or trump cards, of the tarrochi or tarot deck, whose origin no one has ever been able to trace beyond doubt. The atouts are allegorical picture cards representing virtues, vices, natural elements and forces, and originally may have been designed for fortune-telling, for which gypsies still use them today. The symbolism suggests an Eastern origin, the suit designs bear some similarity to those of the Chinese money cards, and one of the suits, coins, is the same—but the connection is tenuous, and the tarot deck may have been almost or entirely an Italian invention. The game of Tarrochi, which uses this deck, is still played in some parts of Italy today, apparently just as it was when the cards first appeared in the Renaissance.

The Hanged Man and the Pope,
two atouts from the pack painted
for Charles VI of France in 1392.

The first printed cards were made from woodblocks. These are the atouts: the Conjurer and the Popess.

The full tarot deck consists of 78 cards—22 atouts and four suits of 14 cards each. In each suit there are ten numbered cards and a king, queen, cavalier or knight, and valet or knave. The four suits represent four major divisions in the society of the Middle Ages. Swords symbolize the nobility; coins, the merchant class; batons or clubs, the peasants; cups or chalices, the church and clergy. These suits are still used in Italy, Spain, Portugal and Mexico.

The earliest cards were hand-painted and much too costly for anyone but the nobility, but by the late fourteenth century they began to be reproduced in quantity from stencils, and they may have been the first articles to be printed by wood blocks in the early fifteenth century.

Sometime in the late fourteenth or early fifteenth century the French dropped the 22 atouts of the 78-card tarot pack. They reduced the number of cards in each suit from 14 to 13 by eliminating the knight, probably to provide an odd number of cards so as to avoid the ties or stalemates that would occur with a 14-card suit. The joker used as a wild card and often pictured as a jester is probably *le fou*, the fool, which was also an extra unnumbered wild card in the atouts.

The earliest known print of persons playing cards, latter half of the 14th century.

Painted playing cards of 15th-century France, after the French had changed the suits from Batons, Cups, Coins and Swords to Clubs, Hearts, Diamonds and Spades.

They also redesigned the old suits and transformed the coins, swords, batons and cups respectively into *trèfles, piques, carreaux* and *coeurs* —the clubs, spades, diamonds and hearts we use today.

For the game of Piquet, which may also date from this time, the two, three, four and five of each suit were omitted, and later, in the eighteenth century, the sixes were also dropped, leaving a 32-card Piquet pack.

The Germans added variations of their own, dropping the queen instead of the knight, retaining the suit of hearts but changing the others to acorns, leaves and bells.

Establishing the date of the first playing cards in the New World is an easier matter than in the Old; they arrived in 1492 with Columbus and were later spread throughout the continent by the early Spanish explorers. The Indians, who had always been inveterate gamblers and used gaming sticks remarkably similar to the Asian ones, first copied the Spanish cards on deerskin or sheepskin. Cards of this kind are occasionally still found among the Indians of the Southwest.

More European cards came with the first settlers, the English in Virginia and the Dutch in New Amsterdam. As early as 1624 the Virginia Assembly enacted a law that "Mynisters shall not give themselfes to excesse in drinking or yette spend their tyme idelie by day or by night, playing at dice, cards or any unlawfull game." In Puritan New England, where cards were called the "Devil's Picture Books," several persons were fined two pounds each for card playing, and in 1656 a Plymouth Colony law fixed a penalty for card playing at 40 shillings for adults, children and servants, "to bee corrected att the discretion of theire parents or masters and for the second offense to bee publickly whipt." In New Amsterdam in the same year a prohibition was put upon playing Tric-Trac during divine services.

As in other countries, playing cards were among the first things off the presses as soon as the first paper mills were started, in the late seventeenth century.

By 1685 imported cards were plentiful enough that the Governor of Canada, Jacques de Meuelles, unable to pay the French troops due to lack of sufficient paper and printing materials, issued paper currency using the backs of playing cards. In 1752 Benjamin Franklin used paper disks cut from playing cards in the construction of his machine for making electrical experiments.

The first American playing-card manufacturer, Jazaniah Ford, born in 1757 in Milton, Massachusetts, founded the Ford Playing-Card Manufactory, which flourished for half a century. The first book on gaming published in this country is said to be a Beaufort edition of *Hoyle's Games* published in Philadelphia in 1796.

Card money used to pay French troops in Canada in 1658.

Court cards of 1567 from Rouen, France (LEFT), *paired with English cards of 1750* (RIGHT), *showing the French origin of the designs still in use today.*

PIER RE . MA RECHAL

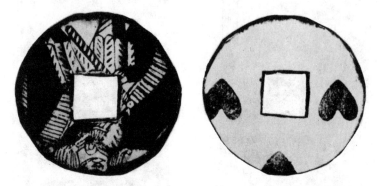

Disks which Benjamin Franklin cut from playing cards and used in the construction of his machine for experimenting with electricity in 1752.

In the early years of the nineteenth century, cards worked their way up the Mississippi and made the long voyage to the gold fields of California, and by 1850 card playing was America's most popular form of gambling.

The Italians use a 40-card deck, the Spanish use one of 48 cards which still bear the old suits of cups, swords, coins and batons. The French today use both the 52- and 32-card pack, and in this country the game of Pinochle uses a deck of 48. When certain cards are removed, the 52-card deck can be made into a Spanish, Italian or French deck and used for the games of those countries. For instance, taking out the eights, nines and tens leaves an Italian 40-card deck.

It is the custom in some European countries to deal, as do the Koreans, from the bottom of the deck and counterclockwise instead of from the top and clockwise. Dealing from the bottom is undoubtedly a holdover from the days when crudely printed cards could be read too easily from the backs, and the dealing was to the right because this is easier when dealing from the bottom.

Like nearly everything else today, some playing cards are now made of plastic, but these are seldom used in professional games. Most cards are still made from two thicknesses of paper glued together with a black paste called *gook*. The two-ply construction gives the cards strength and a tendency to snap back; the gook helps make the cards opaque so that their values cannot be read from the back.

Card manufacturers who claim that "eighty percent of the 150 million decks sold each year are purchased by adults who play cards for fun" always amuse me. They apparently do not want to be thought of as suppliers of equipment for illegal pursuits. My own opinion is that 10% would be a more realistic figure.

CHEATING AT PRIVATE CARD GAMES

My observations over the past 30 years have convinced me that more cheating takes place at private or so-called friendly card games than at all other forms of gambling combined. The main reason, of course, is that cheating in private games is much easier. Ten out of every 100 male and female card players will cheat in private games when they have the opportunity and think they can get away with it. Of the total 90 million card players, 9 million will take a dishonest advantage when they can. Many of these cheaters are highly respected in their communities: businessmen, sportsmen, politicians, civic leaders and just plain housewives. Although most of these people are otherwise honest, they think nothing of trying to steal your last dime in a card game. Private card gambling seems to bring out the worst in many people.

The 1 in 10 ratio varies from game to game and town to town, depending on the ability of the players to detect cheating. A knowledge of cheating methods and the ability to detect them is your only protection against dishonest players in private games. It is for this reason that the most ethical, fastidiously honest card games are those in which the players are top-notch gamblers, gambling operators, gambling-house employees and card sharpers. When they play together the game is nearly always honest. It has to be, because they play in an atmosphere of total and icy distrust, and their exhaustive knowledge of the mechanics of cheating makes using this knowledge much too dangerous. They do not cheat because they dare not.

In a money card game patronized by men and women who know little or nothing about cheating techniques, the odds are 2 to 1 that a card cheater is at work. Even Bridge tournaments, where little or no money is at stake, are infested with Bridge cheats. More than 1,000 Bridge tournaments are played annually in this country and few, if any, are completed without one or more incidents in which a team appeals to the tournament directors for redress from some unfair practice allegedly committed by an opposing team. And much more tournament cheating goes undetected by the players. I know because I have seen it.

Some writers of books on card games contend that explanations of card-cheating methods have no legitimate place in the proper study of card games. They claim that the friendly card game is no place for suspicion and distrust.

Let us say an opponent fails to offer you the deck for the cut and you call his attention to this omission; let us say that in playing Gin Rummy he has a peculiar habit of peeking at the second card of the stack when picking off the first card and you ask him to avoid this eccentricity. He is offended. A beautiful friendship ends. This, these writers say, is to be avoided.

This is rubbish. There is no more excuse for illegal play at any money card game than for dishonest practice in any other human activity. If a player can't abide by the rules of the game, he deserves any embarrassment it causes him. He should obey the rules or get out of the game, and let's not have any false consideration of personal friendship to obscure the issue.

Other writers on card games claim that exposure of cheating methods may teach readers how to do a bit of cheating on their own. This is possible, but the disadvantage is far outweighed by the protection such exposure gives to the many thousands of honest players and by the fact that widespread exposure makes the practice of cheating more difficult for the cheat.

The writers making this claim also have another unstated reason for not discussing cheating methods in detail. They don't do so because they can't—they know so little about the subject; and much of what they think they know is either long out of date or garbled, sometimes both. This becomes obvious whenever they do try to give a few examples of cheating methods. They tell you, for instance, that expert bottom dealers often have the first joint of the second finger of the left hand amputated because the bottom card can be pushed out more easily and more indetectably when this finger is shorter. The amount of protection the reader gets by not playing with strangers whose left second finger is partly missing is exactly zero. This story is useful in only one way: it proves that the writer who peddles such fiction as fact is in the chump class and couldn't possibly spot a good bottom deal if he saw one in slow motion. Expert bottom dealers do not push out the bottom card with fingers of the left hand; they pull it out with the fingers of the right hand.

CARD CHEATS

There are three kinds of card cheats: the amateur, the semiprofessional and the professional. I call the amateur that not because he doesn't win money cheating but because he is a brazen and unskilled cheat. The semipro is one who earns part of his living by cheating but lacks the manipulative skill of the real card sharp, and who, when he is working single-o, has to depend upon marked cards and other gaffed gambling equipment. The professional card sharp is the skilled sleight-of-hand expert who has spent many hours in practice to

Card mobs have been around a long time. Here, three sharps gang up on an unsuspecting mark.

gain the necessary proficiency in crooked card manipulation. He is called a *card mechanic,* and he usually travels a lot, seldom staying in one spot too long.

Cheats working together are known as a *card mob.* The mob is usually made up of a card mechanic, a bankroll man who supplies the necessary money to finance the operation, a couple of shills and several steerers. The latter are often good-looking girls who pick up victims on the pretense of taking them to their hotel rooms, and steer them instead into the crooked game.

The semipro who works with a card sharp helps by misdirecting attention away from the cards at the moment the sharper makes his crooked move, by signaling the value of his hand, by making the right kind of cut when given the deck by the sharper, etc.

The honest player's best protection against these crooks is to learn enough about their methods so that he can spot the most common cheating moves when they occur. The crooked angles, ruses, subterfuges, sleights and mechanical methods are so many and so varied that a detailed description of them all would more than fill this book. The most common methods can, however, be spotted when you know what to look for. Most of them require unnatural moves or actions on the part of the cheat. You may never be able to catch the expert card sharp's bottom or second deal at the split second that it is made, but there is a way of recognizing the expert card mechanic for what he is by the way in which he holds the deck (see Mechanic's Grip, page 644).

I shall try in the succeeding pages to give you the information you need to protect yourself.

THE AMATEUR CHEAT

It is sometimes difficult to distinguish between the amateur cheat and the thoroughgoing, no-holds-barred, but honest player. I used to play Gin Rummy with an elderly lady who had a habit, after the cards had been cut for her deal, of glancing down and noting the bottom card of the deck as she squared it. Harmless? She peeked at a card that would never get into the play of the hand. Harmless? Well . . . her knowledge that the card is dead is useful information in planning her play; it is pertinent information not available to me.

She is a cheat.

And she is the most dangerous kind—the amateur cheat. The amateur is usually a friend whom you don't think of suspecting and who for that reason can get away with murder. The good-natured, trusting American card chumps collectively lose billions of dollars annually to friends and acquaintances whose card-playing tactics are less than honest.

For every dozen crooked moves made by the agate-eyed professional card sharp, the amateur will blandly and brazenly attempt a hundred swindles. At Poker the amateur cheat will connive with a confederate and each will give the other some sort of a signal when he has a good hand and wants a raise. At Gin Rummy, Pinochle or Canasta, the amateur cheat will add an extra five or ten points on the count of the hand. Trapped in a recount—any embarrassment? Not a bit! Aren't we all entitled to a certain percentage of error?

At Black Jack, when the dealer is busy, the amateur cheat will call a phony count on his cards, collect his cash and account the feat an act of skill with not the slightest objection from his conscience.

At Bridge he will deliberately drop a card to the floor and while leaning down to retrieve it try to get a peek at an opponent's hand. He likes to think of this maneuver as Bridge strategy.

What do you do when you suspect a friend or acquaintance of cheating? This is a department of etiquette which Emily Post doesn't mention. It can develop very easily into a sticky situation because it is possible that an honest player may unconsciously do some of the things that cheaters do, and your suspicion may be unjustified. There is no need to raise a hue and cry. Your best bet is to demand quietly and graciously that the rules of the game be strictly followed. This should in most cases remedy what is wrong or looks wrong. If not, then make some polite excuse and leave the game. This will give no offense and do no harm to anyone's sensibilities or reputation or to your pocket-book.

Rules are made to be followed—or broken revealingly—by players. A friend told me once, "John, I play Poker with a good friend. He never offers me the cards for the cut. I'm afraid to insist on the cut because he may think I'm accusing him, and I value our good relation-ship. What shall I do?"

I asked him who was the winner between them, and he said his friend was a few hundred dollars ahead.

"I don't know whether your Poker game is lousy or whether you're being cheated," I told him. "I've never seen you and your friend play, but I know that if the cards were always cut you would not be suspi-cious of your friend—and suspicion is a lot worse than losing a few hundred dollars."

You must decide such things for yourself. As for me, I play by the rules, and I play no more with the old lady who peeks at the bottom card.

PROFESSIONAL CARD CHEATS

The underworld has many names for various types of card cheats. In the western part of the United States, Nevada included, a profes-sional card cheat who travels over the country seeking card games where he can ply his trade is called a *crossroader*. A cheat who special-izes in palming cards is referred to in the trade as a *hand-mucker* or *holdout man;* one who deals from the bottom of the deck is a *base* or *subway dealer*.

The surreptitious manipulation of cards by card mechanics, hand-muckers, holdout men, crossroaders, card sharks, base dealers or other card cheats requires considerable skill and practice, plus the courage of a thief. A top-notch card mechanic must be considerably more adept with a deck of cards than a first-rate magician. The magician is free to use a great deal of conversation and misdirection to fool his audience, but the card cheat is limited by the game's regulations. As a matter of fact, most present-day magicians—including most of those who ad-vertise their act as an exposé of crooked gambling tricks—know little about the operation of the modern card sharper. They themselves are as easily fleeced by a good card mechanic as the average layman. Much of the sleight of hand and nearly all of the mechanical gadgets they expose were discarded by the cheats decades ago.

There is a popular delusion that card cheats and magicians can

Eighteenth-century card sharps signaling and holding out cards.

take a well-mixed deck of cards, riffle and shuffle the pack several times and then deal each player in the game a good hand—in Poker, for example, four jacks to one player, four kings to another and four aces to himself.

The truth of the matter is that no card sharper or magician can take a deck honestly shuffled by someone else, shuffle it two or three times and arrange more than a couple of cards in two different hands without previous sight of or prearrangement of the deck. Whenever you see any sleight-of-hand expert claim to do this and deal out a perfect Bridge hand of 13 cards of one suit, or four or five pat Poker hands, you can be sure that the cards were previously stacked.

Actually the cheat doesn't need to do anything so spectacular. It doesn't matter whether the game is Draw Poker or Gin Rummy in some gin mill or the most recondite Contract Bridge at a Park Avenue club—a cheater can take all the chumps in the game simply by knowing the approximate location of very few cards. If he knows the exact position of only one of the 52 cards he will eventually win all the money in sight.

The Mechanic's Grip. (Conrad Eiger)

Never overestimate a card cheat. Don't expect him to work miracles. Just expect him to win the money. If luck favors him, he may not make a crooked move all night, or he may make only one crooked move in the whole card session. But that one move always comes at just the right time to get the money. In most games the move can even be executed clumsily and get by; the average player almost never spots it because he seldom suspects the people with whom he plays and because, even if he did, he lacks the necessary knowledge to know what to look for and wouldn't recognize it if he did happen to be looking in the right place at the right time.

Believe it or not, most sharpers are poor card players *on the square* (playing honestly). A good card mechanic spends so much of his time practicing cheating moves and concentrating, in play, on watching for the right opportunity to use his skill that he seldom develops a good sense of card strategy.

During one of my recent gambling lectures at a Chicago club a member of the audience asked me, "Isn't the old rule, 'Never play cards with strangers,' about the best protection one can have against cheaters?"

"That rule," I replied, "gives the average player about as much protection as a broken umbrella in a rainstorm." The card cheat has had the answer to it for years. Suppose that Harry the card mechanic discovers there's a big and neighborly Poker game every Friday night in the back room at Joe's cigar store. He also learns, for instance, the name of a doctor who is one of the players. Harry simply puts in a phone call and makes an appointment to have a physical checkup. During the examination Harry steers the conversation around to Poker and manages to get an invite to the game. It's easy; he's done it a good many times before. And when Doc introduces him to the other players as one of his patients, no one thinks of him as a stranger; he's already one of the boys.

I repeat: The best protection against card cheats is a knowledge of how they operate and some ability at recognizing their slick sleight of hand and other crooked ruses. Most cheating moves, fortunately, have one or more giveaway signals, usually an unnatural action, either in preparation for the move or in executing it. If after learning how to spot these clues to trickery you still think you are being cheated at cards, your best bet is to take up some non-card game, preferably a game that can't be cheated. Since I invented it, naturally I hope you'll pick Teeko.

THE MECHANIC'S GRIP

Most card sharpers announce the fact that they are mechanics long before they make a crooked move. They do it as soon as they begin to deal. The giveaway is the peculiar manner in which they hold the deck, known as the *mechanic's grip*.

The cheat holds the deck in either the right or left hand (we will assume from here on that it's the left hand). Three fingers are on the edge of the long side of the deck and the index finger at the outer right corner. Some mechanics keep two fingers on the side of the deck and two at the outer corner.

Many professional dealers in gambling houses also hold the deck in this manner but for a different reason: they do it to prevent players from glimpsing the bottom card. But when you spot a player using the mechanic's grip in a private friendly game, find yourself another game. The odds are that the player who holds the deck this way is doing so because peeking at the top card, second dealing, bottom dealing and other cheating moves require this grip. The index-finger position at the outer corner of the deck acts as a stop when the cheat is second dealing and peeking and also helps conceal a card when it comes from the bottom of the deck. It is possible that an honest, even innocent, player might accidentally hold the deck this way, but it is highly unlikely because it takes practice to hold the cards in this manner while dealing.

The only reason anyone would practice this grip is because he intends to cheat. There's one exception: magicians also use the mechanic's grip, but not many of them play cards for money, for the same reason Howard Thurston always gave: "If I win I am accused of cheating; if I lose they think I am a lousy magician."

THE PICKUP STACK

The pickup stack is the method cheats most often use for stacking cards. Its cleverness lies in its simplicity. It requires no special skill and it rarely fails. Suppose you are a cheater in a five-handed Stud Poker game. The next deal is yours, and two hands were exposed in the hand just completed. In each hand you spot one card you'd like to get for yourself the next time around. Let's say they are two aces.

You simply stack the deck in such a way that you deal the two aces to yourself. You do it in full view, and it's ridiculously easy. As dealer, you pick up the cards, taking them a hand at a time. You pick up the cards lying above the first ace, then use these cards to scoop up the remainder of the hand. Place these cards on top of the deck. This puts the ace fifth from the top. Repeat the action with the remaining hand. That's all there is to it. The deck is stacked, ready for the deal and you will get the fifth and tenth cards—the two aces—back to back. If you have a fair memory and can remember the other cards and their order in the first hand you picked up, you will also know your opponents' hole cards, which can be an equally lucrative advantage.

Yes, you must shuffle before the deal, but that's not difficult either. You only need to riffle and let the top ten or so cards fall last, thus keeping them on top. As for the cut, the cheat has many ways of taking care of that without even resorting to sleight of hand. He may simply deal without offering the cards to be cut, he may cut and then pick up the two packs incorrectly, or he may have a confederate on his right who refuses the cut, saying, "Run them." (Sleight-of-hand methods are described on page 649.) That's darned near all there is to stacking as it is generally practiced by the amateur or semiprofessional cheat. When the cut is omitted, insist that some other player or yourself be allowed to cut. The dealer may feel insulted but he can't object; the rules give you this right.

THE RIFFLE STACK

The riffle stack is the most difficult of card-stacking methods, but the sharper who has perfected it is capable of fleecing the most seasoned players. If, at Poker, Bridge, Black Jack or one of the Rummies, you think you detect an opponent using this cheating method, beware:

you are up against a practiced, unscrupulous and perhaps even dangerous card mechanic.

The sharper, let us say, has three kings on top of the deck. He cuts the deck into two blocks and shuffles them together. It looks like an ordinary standard shuffle, but during the action he puts just the right number of cards between the kings so that in the deal, which will be on the level, his opponents get cards at random and he gets the kings. It may take him four or five riffles to arrange the kings as he wants them, but if the riffle is his specialty, he can and will do it in two or three riffles. He gets the same result as in the pickup stack, but this sleight-of-hand method will take the smart boys who would spot the pickup.

Cleverly executed this stack is almost detection-proof, but there is one way of spotting it, and then, if you can't correct the matter by forcing the cheat out of the game, the only safe thing to do is force yourself out. Most riffle-stack sharpers riffle the first cards fast and slow up perceptibly near the top where they must count the cards as they riffle. They also watch the deck carefully as they count the cards into place. Riffling in this fast-slow tempo and watching the deck too intently during the shuffle are the danger signals. The player may not be a riffle-stack expert, but he's acting like one. Look out!

THE OLD-STYLE OVERHAND SHUFFLE STACK

This is the semiprofessional sharper's best friend. It is used in clipping chumps from New York to California more extensively perhaps than any other stacking method. It involves less skill than the riffle stack and comes in handy oftener than the pickup stack.

The sharper puts the cards to be stacked on the bottom of the deck. During his shuffle he milks the deck, pulling down one card from the bottom and one card from the top at the same time. On these two cards he shuffles off two cards less than the number of players in the game. He repeats this maneuver once for each card he wants to stack. He lets the next card project slightly from the deck, shuffles the remaining cards on top. He is now set for the deal. The wanted cards are spaced out so that they will fall to the dealer, or perhaps to a confederate, during the deal. The cut is then canceled or avoided as explained in the section on the pickup stack.

The giveaway signal here is the unusual sound of the shuffle caused by having to run off so many cards singly. A second clue is the fact that this shuffling sound is interrupted slightly at regular rhythmic intervals each time another bottom card is pulled down. The smart card player keeps his ears open as well as his eyes.

FALSE SHUFFLES

The ability to appear to be shuffling a deck while keeping some or all of the cards in their original positions is an absolutely essential weapon in the arsenal of the accomplished card sharp. The most popular and most deceptive of the false shuffles is the *pull through,* a dazzling and completely crooked shuffle which doesn't alter the position of a single card.

When a hand of cards has been completed the cheat scoops up the tabled cards, taking special care not to disturb certain melds or discards which he wants and which he places on either the top or bottom of the pack. This shuffle is also used when a *cold* (stacked) deck has been switched into the game which must be shuffled without disturbing its prearrangement.

The deck is cut into two blocks and their ends riffled together quite honestly. The move comes during the split second that the cards are pushed together and reassembled into a single pack. The cheat pushes the two blocks of interwoven cards into each other at an angle, an action that is covered by the manner in which he holds his hands. Then, without any hesitation, he gives the cards a fast cut—or that is what seems to happen. Actually, he takes a new grip on the cards, grabs the right-hand block with the left fingers, the left-hand block with the right fingers, pulls the interwoven blocks through each other, slaps the block originally on top back on top, and squares the deck fairly as he should have done but didn't do immediately after the riffle. The pull-through action is done so smoothly and so fast that as far as the average chump is concerned it is quicker than the eye can follow.

Although the cards were fairly riffled and the action had the appearance and sound of a legitimate shuffle not a single card has changed position.

You have only one small clue here—that fast "cut" following so closely on the heels of the shuffle.

NULLIFYING THE CUT

The greatest obstacle the card cheat has to overcome is the cut. If the rules did not ask for a cut, gambling with cards would have long ago become obsolete and playing cards would now be used only for Solitaire. Stacking and false shuffling are moves not too difficult for the average sharper to master, but *shifting the cut* (secretly returning the cut deck to its original order) indetectably under the pressure of the game and under the watchful and observant eyes of experienced card

Deck crimped so that player will unknowingly cut the deck where the cheat wants him to cut. (Conrad Eiger)

players requires the skill of a master cheater. Since most card players are chumps who can't spot crooked card moves even when sloppily executed, average cheaters still manage to get away with it. Other cheats manage to avoid the cut altogether as explained in the section on the pick-up stack.

Ordinarily, when the deck is cut, the dealer pushes it toward you and says, "Cut, Mac?" You take a block of cards off the top, put them on the table, and the dealer completes the cut. He picks up the bottom block and places it on the top block you cut off. This buries the cards the cheater is trying to control; he must undo the cut and return the deck to its pre-cut position. It must be done swiftly and without causing any suspicion.

Crimping is most often used for this purpose because it is much easier than shifting the cut and is almost impossible for the untrained or unsuspecting eye to detect. It has the further advantage that it is the honest chump himself who unknowingly does some of the work.

A *crimp* is a bend placed in one or more cards. When such cards are in the middle of the deck, the crimp causes a small break or opening in the deck's edge which can be felt and cut to. Above, half the deck has been crimped in an exaggerated fashion so that you can see it clearly. Don't look for such an obvious crimp from a pro. His crimp is so slight that the eye can hardly detect it, if at all, but his educated fingers can always feel it. Even when the sucker cuts the deck he is more likely than not to cut at the crimp. Also, the crimp is almost always so placed that the break appears in the edge of the deck nearest the cheater and away from the other players.

A crimp so slight that it can barely be seen is still sufficient to cause the pack to break five times out of ten exactly as the cheater wants, even when the unsuspecting chump does the cutting. The cheat also assists the victim to cut at the proper place by putting the crimp in the middle of the deck, which is where most players naturally cut. The bigger the crimp, of course, the greater the chance that the sucker will cut to it. Some stumblebum cheats even make crimps so big that a tunnel appears in the center of the deck. When the cheater must have an absolutely surefire, foolproof crimp, he simply has a confederate sitting on his right who obligingly cuts to the crimp every time it is needed.

The cheater uses the crimp this way: He stacks his wanted cards as previously explained, has them where he wants them and must keep them there. An honest cut would bury them in the deck, so the sharper simply gives half the deck a fast crimp during another false shuffle or cut, leaves the crimped half on the bottom and offers the pack to be cut. If the unsuspecting player cuts in his usual fashion, the cards break at the crimp. When the dealer completes the cut, the cards he is interested in automatically return to their original position and at least one player is happy.

Shifting the cut: This is a sleight-of-hand maneuver which secretly restores the deck to its original order after the cut. It offers no particular challenge to the magician or exhibition card manipulator, who can employ various types of misdirection to cover it. But it is tough to accomplish indetectably at the card table, where a single slip is disastrous. In fact, there isn't a sharper living who can execute the move successfully without a *cover-up*, i.e., without hiding the move in one way or another.

The crimp and the shift are used together after an honest cut. Before offering the cards to be cut, the sharper crimps the inner half of the deck, usually bending all the cards slightly downward. Because of the deck's thickness the bottom cards are bent somewhat more than those on top, and when the deck has been honestly cut, a small break appears in the middle of the deck at the narrow end nearest the cheat. When he picks up the deck his practiced fingers locate the break, and the cards are shifted back to their original position. There are many cut shifts, the most common of which are described below.

One-handed shift cut: Here the two portions of the deck are shifted back to their original positions with one hand only. It is deceptive because the chumps don't suspect that such a complex maneuver can be done with one hand and do not, therefore, watch closely when the deck

One-hand Shift. The lower half of the deck is being pushed up by the fingers. When it touches the thumb, the top half drops down and the lower half takes its place on top. Done under cover, it cancels the cut. (Conrad Eiger)

is held this way. Since the other hand is away from the deck, some other type of cover must be used. The usual practice is to reach across the body with the free hand to take a cigar or cigarette from an ash tray which has been purposely left at that side. The reaching arm covers the hand holding the deck for a brief moment and the shift takes place unseen.

One-handed table cut shift: After an honest cut, while the two blocks of cards are still on the table, the cheater completes, or rather pretends to complete, the cut. He picks up the cards originally on the bottom and appears to place them on the top block. Actually the bottom block passes above and a bit beyond the top block, comes quickly back and slides in under the top block. This is a very deceptive shift provided that it is done with lightning speed and a single, unhesitating sweep of the hand.

Two-handed cut shift: Magicians, who call this "the pass," have used this shift for many years; it is still used by some sharpers. After the cards have been cut by another player, the cheat replaces the lower block on the upper one, but not squarely; it projects slightly at the inner end leaving what is called a *step*. He scoops up the cards and inserts his little finger into the deck at the step. In the act of apparently squaring the deck and under cover of the hand above the deck,

The Pass. The lower half of the deck moves up to the top as the upper half is pulled out of the way, restoring the original order of the deck. (Conrad Eiger)

The One-hand Hop. Scarne demonstrates this move with the deck face up. When an opponent cuts off the upper half of the deck (topped by the Ace of Spades here) Scarne apparently places the lower half (Five of Diamonds) on it, completing the cut. (Conrad Eiger)

Actually, the fingers of the right hand pull the top half of the deck up into the palm, and when both hands square cards, the original bottom half goes back on the bottom. (Conrad Eiger)

the lower half of the deck is pivoted upward. It pushes against the upper half, which swings aside as though hinged and is deposited again on top, where it was before the cut was made. This is accomplished in a split second.

FALSE CUTS

Like the false shuffle, a false cut, when well executed, appears to transpose the two halves of the deck but actually leaves them just as they were. When the other players are in the habit of letting the dealer do his own cutting, he executes the false cut. Otherwise, a confederate at his right does the dirty work. This last is the most effective method because suspicion is much less likely to fall on the dealer.

In games involving more than two players, particularly Poker, most cheating is done by two cheats who pretend to be strangers to each other. This partnership in crime is more dangerous to your bankroll than any other kind of cheating.

False cuts are employed not only when the cheat is the dealer but also when it is your deal. How? Most players are honest and awkward. When they shuffle, they often fail to mix the bottom cards of the deck thoroughly. The cheater detects something down there he wants, or he may glimpse the bottom card during the shuffle and see that it could be useful. Or, perhaps, after your shuffle, he secretly puts some palmed cards on the deck and false-cuts so that they stay there.

The running false cut: Instead of a single cut, the sharper makes a fast series of single cuts using both hands. He pulls a small block of cards off the bottom, slaps it on top and leaves a step. He repeats the action with the opposite hand, and continues until the block originally on top has gone down through the deck and, on the last cut, comes back once more to the top. It looks good, but nothing was changed; all the cards are in their original order. Many honest players make running cuts like this—but eye anyone closely who does so. Watch for a step in the deck, although the whole action is done so fast your chance of spotting it is slim.

Your best bet is to wait until after the dealer has completed his fancy cut, then ask for the deck, as you have the right to do, reshuffle it and offer it to the dealer to be cut. This will totally upset all his careful preparation and expert card manipulation. He can't very well object because that would be suspicious in itself.

THE PREARRANGED OR COLD DECK

A *cold deck* is any deck that has been stacked (prearranged) either before the game or during the game by a cheat who leaves the room for that purpose. It is switched (exchanged) during the play for the deck in use either on the cheat's or player's deal. If the room temperature is low an experienced player might detect a prearranged deck which has just been switched in because it has not been warmed by the heat of the players' hands—hence the name "cold deck." Cheats sometimes warm the arranged deck before switching it into the game.

The cold deck is useful in any card game. It must, of course, be an exact duplicate of the deck in play. The object of the swindle, in case there are any men from Mars reading this, is to ensure the crook a killing hand and send the chumps home broke.

The cold deck was the favorite cheating device used by the transatlantic card mobs a decade or two ago. In a Poker game the boys would switch in on the chump's deal and let him deal himself a straight flush or four of a kind. The rest of the mob would also get good hands, one of which, perhaps a straight flush, would be just a shade higher than the chump's. Beating a mark for $25,000 on one cold-deck hand used to be a common occurrence on the liners.

Deck switching: The most usual methods of replacing the original deck with a stacked deck are these:

1. The cheat leaves the shuffled deck on the edge of the table just as the waiter arrives with a previously ordered tray of sandwiches or drinks. The waiter holds the cold deck beneath the tray which he rests on the table for a moment above the square deck. When he leaves, the cold deck remains behind and the shuffled deck goes with him. Or the tray may simply cover the shuffled deck for a moment as the cheat makes the switch under it.

2. A special mechanical deck-switching machine strapped to the cheater's body may be used, although its proper handling requires some skill. Not many present-day crooks use this gadget because, if discovered, its possession is prima facie evidence of guilt. A player using a mechanic's grip or a two-handed false cut may possibly be innocent; if not, he can at least try to talk himself out of trouble, since there is no tangible evidence of his guilt. A man caught with a holdout machine can, at best, try to get out of town in one piece.

3. The commonest and cleanest cold-deck switch consists of pure sleight of hand. The sharper surreptitiously spreads his handkerchief on his lap, slips the cold deck from his pocket and holds it in his left hand below the table. When he takes the deck after the cut he pulls it back toward himself and appears to catch it with his left hand just as it clears the edge of the table. Actually the deck drops neatly into his lap and his left hand comes up at the same time with the cold deck. A spot of misdirection by another member of the mob (a paroxysm of sneezing, a spilled drink, or the punch line of a joke) may be used to

take attention away from the action. After the deal, the discarded deck is gathered up in the handkerchief and replaced in the pocket.

4. The best results are obtained by switching the cold deck in on the chump's deal. One method is this: When the sucker has shuffled and offers the deck to be cut by the player (a cheat) on his right, another cheat at his left asks the victim to change a large bill. While he is busy being helpful and making change, the cheat who should be cutting the deck is switching it. He takes his handkerchief out, blows into it and lets it cover the shuffled deck momentarily on the way back to his pocket. As the shuffled deck leaves the table under the handkerchief, the cheat's left hand replaces it with the cold deck. And when the mark turns back to take the deck for the deal the cheat executes a false cut to put him at his ease. The mark is now ready to deal himself to the cleaner's.

SECOND DEALING

One of the most common cheating moves used by both the top-notch card mechanic and the would-be card sharp is the *second deal*.

This consists, as the name implies, of dealing the second card from the top rather than the first one. Any good second dealer will clip the best of players in any card game. He is known to ordinary gamblers and to magicians as a *second dealer;* the underworld knows him as a *number two man.*

Dealing seconds is the move most often used when the cheats have had no opportunity to stack the cards. This time the cheating is done during the deal rather than earlier. The time-honored mechanic's grip is again used. When the left hand holds the pack, the thumb pushes the top card over the side of the deck in the usual fashion so that it can be taken by the right hand. But when the right hand comes up to take it the right thumb strikes against the exposed corner of the second card and pulls it out enough so that it can be gripped and taken by the right thumb and forefinger. As the second card leaves the pack, the right thumb pulls the top card back to its starting position, the curled index finger of the mechanic's grip acting as a stop for the swinging top card. When expertly done, the sleight is a split-second, beautifully coordinated move that is exceedingly difficult to detect even by the most observant players, and it will deceive the average player if done merely competently.

When playing Black Jack or Stud Poker some cheats deal with one hand only, turning the deck over as the card is dealt so that it comes out face up. Don't let this one-hand action convince you that everything must be on the up and up; a good mechanic can and does deal seconds with one hand just as neatly as with two.

Second dealing isn't worth a plugged nickel unless the cheat knows what the top card is and wants to save it for himself or a confederate, or, in Black Jack, give it to the player who doesn't want it. It is, for this reason, mostly employed with marked cards, although it is also used with the peek, which is explained below.

If you suspect a second dealer is at work, look for the mechanic's grip; they nearly all use it.

THE PEEK

Peeking is the art of secretly glimpsing the top card of the deck. This is one of the most useful and valuable dodges in the cheat's repertoire. When the peek is used in conjunction with the second deal, a good peeker is poison in any card game. It is especially useful in Black Jack and Stud Poker.

The move, a simple one, consists in exerting pressure on the top card with the thumb and pushing it against the fingers on the opposite outer corner of the deck. This causes the card to buckle or bend upward near the index corner just enough so that the cheat can look into the opening thus formed and glimpse the index. He gives it a careless glance at the right moment, releases the pressure of his thumb, and the top card flattens out again.

Some cheats peek while dealing one-handed. Others pretend to look at the face-down card in their Black Jack or Stud Poker hand and peek the top card at the same time.

Eye with suspicion the player who uses the mechanic's grip and looks too often at his face-down card.

Peeking on the draw: Both the bungler and the expert cheat use this one, particularly in Gin and other Rummy games, and in Two-handed Pinochle when drawing from the stock. The cheat reaches out to take the top card of the stock and his thumb lifts up two cards at the inner edge. He spots the second card, lets it down again onto the deck and takes off the top one.

The giveaway is that he isn't casual enough; he hesitates briefly as he makes the peek.

THE BOTTOM DEAL

Ordinary gamblers call the cheat who deals cards from the bottom of the deck a *bottom dealer;* the inner circle—the boys in the know—refer to him as a *base dealer* or *subway dealer.*

The bottom dealer, like the second dealer, uses the mechanic's grip. His left thumb pushes the top card over as the right hand comes up to take it, but the right hand has other instructions. Instead, its forefinger moves in under the deck at the outer right corner and pulls out the bottom card while the left thumb is engaged in pulling back the top card. The index finger of the left hand in the mechanic's grip position covers much of the front edge of the deck, making it difficult for an observer to see whether the card comes from top or bottom. The movement, naturally, must be fast and smooth and must follow the same rhythm as when the top card is taken legitimately.

The subway dealer saves time because he doesn't have to fuss around stacking cards. He or his confederate usually picks up the cards after the previous hand and places the previous deal's winning hand or some useful discards on the bottom of the deck. He retains them there during a phony shuffle and deals them off the bottom as needed.

This is easier said than done—much easier. It takes years of practice to become a good bottom dealer, and the chances that you will find yourself in a game with a cheater who can bottom-deal cards from a full deck noiselessly and indetectably are roughly about 100,000 to 1. There is another character, however, whom you might meet oftener. Since it is easier to deal a respectable bottom from half a deck of cards, there are mechanics who have the nerve to pick up the bottom half of the deck after the cut, skip putting them on the top half, and begin dealing. When this happens, ask that the cut be completed in the usual manner; then keep your ears open. If he attempts a bottom deal with a full deck you may hear it—when badly executed, it is noisy.

There's a foolproof defense against the bottom dealer—the Scarne Cut. This is guaranteed to lose the cheat's carefully iced cards in the deck and make him an honest man.

THE SCARNE CUT

This is a cut I invented during World War II as a defensive weapon for the men in the armed forces. It will protect you against all the moves above except the peek and second-deal combination and a cold deck which is switched in after the cut. Top Army brass have told me that it saved GI Joe millions of dollars.

1. Pull a block of cards from the center of the pack.
2. Place them on top of the pack and square it up.
3. Pull a block of cards from the bottom of the pack, place them on top.
4. Repeat steps 1, 2 and 3 again, several times if you like.
5. Finally, square up the pack and cut it in the regular manner.

The drawings on page 657 picture the Scarne Cut in action. Use it and you won't need to worry about nearly all bottom deals, stacked decks, crimps, false shuffles and false cuts. At the very least, it will give

1   Pull a block of cards from the center of the pack.

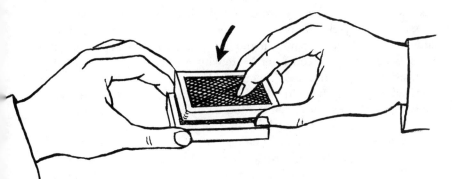

2   Place them on top of the pack and square it up.

3   Pull a block of cards from the bottom of the pack, place them on top.

4   Repeat steps 1, 2 and 3 again, several times if you like.

5   Finally, square up the pack and cut it in the regular manner.

any cheat enough headaches to cut his cheating down close to the
vanishing point. It may frighten him out of the game entirely or even
into playing honestly.

PALMING

Holding out cards by palming them is probably the cheating
method most commonly used and also the one most commonly suspected and detected. Like sex, it can be learned by almost anyone, but
doing it well enough to get by, even with half-smart card players,
requires some native talent and assiduous practice.

A good many hand-muckers, however, have perfected the art to
such an extent that they can palm and switch a Black Jack hand successfully under the sharp eyes of a Nevada casino pit boss and dealer.
I once watched a holdout artist in a Lake Tahoe casino switch six
successive Black Jack hands without either the dealer or pit boss
catching wise. I once used the method to prove to a casino operator
that his Baccarat game could be beaten by an expert holdout artist
(see Cheating at Baccarat and Chemin de Fer, page 474).

Desired cards may be held out while the deck is being shuffled and
cut and then returned to either the top or bottom of the deck or, on
some other player's deal, switched for the hand dealt to the cheat.
When the cheat has cards palmed he may place his hand on his arm in
a natural curved position or rest it, fingers close together, flat on the
table. Often he reaches into his shirt pocket for a match and leaves
the cards under his armpit, or hitches up his chair and puts them
under his knee, later retrieving them. Or he may simply leave them in
his jacket pocket.

In Black Jack the cheat may hold out a 21 count, perhaps an ace
and a ten spot. When he receives his two cards, he covers them for a
second with the hand holding the palmed cards as he takes a quick
look at what he has received. When his hand moves away, the dealt
cards go south with it and the palmed cards are left in their place.
He then turns up his 21 count and leaves the palmed cards under armpit or knee, later getting rid of them by re-palming them and returning
them to the deck or the discards. This is done in any game involving a
dealt hand.

Be suspicious of the player who goes to his pockets for matches too
often, keeps hitching up his chair, or places his hand flat on the table,
fingers close together, too frequently. A player who has all these habits
and is a constant winner is very likely to be a hand-mucker.

The really top-notch mechanic, whom you aren't likely to meet
unless you are in a bigtime game, avoids these giveaways. He palms
cards in a "rear palm," which leaves the fingers free and open, and he

seldom keeps them palmed long enough for anyone to rumble it. The only giveaway here is his use of the mechanic's grip.

BELLY STRIPPERS

Decks in which the cards have been trimmed so that they are not quite rectangular are known as *strippers* because the wider cards can be stripped out. The most highly prized form of strippers, those that get the money fast for the semiprofessional cheat, are known as *high and low belly strippers* (also called *humps*). A deck of this type is so gaffed that the cheat can cut to a high or low card at will.

The crooked gambling supply house dealer makes such a deck by removing the 28 high cards, eights and above. Using special card shears he trims about 1/32 inch off both long sides of each high card, then rounds the corners again. The long sides of the low cards, seven and below, are trimmed in a curve so that they are slightly wider than the high cards at the center and slightly narrower at the ends.

After the deck is shuffled, the cheat merely has to grasp the cards at the center when he cuts and the bottom card of the cut-off portion will always be a low card. If he grips the deck near the ends he always cuts to a high card. What could be simpler?

In any game that involves cutting to a high or low card, such as Banker and Broker, belly strippers are lethal. They are also useful in

Belly Strippers. High-valued cards (LEFT) *are trimmed narrow, low cards* (RIGHT) *are wide at the middle.*

Pinochle or Gin Rummy; the sucker is cheated on his own deal and it is all done with a simple cut.

In Gin Rummy the deck is usually trimmed to favor a four- or three-card meld—let's say four kings and three queens. These 7 cards are shaved like the low cards above; the remaining 45 cards are shaved like the high cards. When the cheat cuts the shuffled deck for his opponent's deal he simply grips the deck at the end with his left hand and holds it at the center with his right. The two hands pull in opposite directions and the four kings and three queens are stripped neatly out of the deck and slapped on top. Done quickly, this appears to be nothing more than an ordinary cut.

When the chump deals, the cheat gets four of these cards, the victim gets the other three, and, since the cheat knows what they are, the mark's chance of winning is zero.

The catalogs list these decks at a low $5 apiece or a dozen for $55.50. "We furnish," they say, "special strippers made to strip any card or combinations of cards you desire. When ordering state what cards you want to strip." At $6 per deck they will also make up a deck of *combination strippers* which will strip one combination from the side and a different one from the end.

MARKED CARDS

About one out of every hundred, or 1,500,000 of the 150 million decks of playing cards sold annually in this country, are doctored at some time or other so that some or all of the 52 cards may be read from the back. Gamblers call marked cards *readers*, cheats refer to them as *paper*, and to the average player's bankroll they are poison. They are the most widely used mechanical cheating device and are used by amateurs, semiprofessionals and top-notch pros because they require no manipulative skill, are surefire money winners and are almost never detected by the average easygoing, unsuspicious card player.

My survey results show that not more than 2 average card players out of 100 know how or where to look for the markings. Not long ago I invited six card-playing couples to my home and tried an experiment. I gave them a dozen decks of cards still sealed in their original wrappers. "You have all been playing cards for the past twenty years," I said. "Some of you have lost considerable sums of money at cards on your winter vacations in Florida. These packs—four Bridge, four Poker and four Pinochle—were made by twelve different manufacturers, and each has a different back design. One deck is marked and can be read from the back. I'll bet that in an hour's examination none of you can find it."

This was a challenge they couldn't resist and they went to work to prove that they could spot marked cards when they saw them. They even examined the card cases before opening the decks, looking for signs of tampering with the government seal. After taking the decks from the cases they did the same with the glassine paper in which the decks were wrapped. They found nothing. Then they began examining the backs of the cards. It was an arduous task but they stuck to it for the full hour; none of them wanted to admit that they couldn't spot a marked deck, even after having been told the marks were there.

"Okay," one of them said finally. "We give up. Which one is it?"

"I have a confession to make," I said then. "I lied when I told you that one deck is marked."

One man, deck in hand, nearly threw it at me. "That," he growled, "is a dirty trick if I ever saw one. We spend an hour looking for something that isn't there. Is this supposed to be funny or something?"

"Well," I said, "it proves something. As a matter of fact, all twelve decks are marked."

Since I had lied once, they wanted proof of this statement. I spent the next half hour reading the backs of cards from all twelve decks before my friends were completely convinced. They all agreed then that they would be smart to stay out of any big-money card games until they had learned how to spot marked cards.

Like millions and millions of players who play regularly and who often lose more than they can afford, all my friends had heard of marked cards but hadn't the slightest notion of what to look for or how to examine a deck properly.

Marked cards are commonplace because they are easy to obtain. Anyone can send a quarter to one of the gambling supply houses whose ads run regularly in certain national men's magazines and receive by return mail an 80 page catalog of crooked gambling devices. One catalog contains 16 pages listing many varieties of marked cards priced at from $5 to $8 per deck. For $20 they sell a do-it-yourself card-marking kit consisting of "two bottles, French type card ink, one Red, one Blue, two brushes, two glass palettes, 24 cellophane wrappers cut to fit, 24 red tear-off strips, one bottle of special cement for cellophane, and full instructions." Marked decks can also be obtained cheaper (about $4 per deck) at many trick and novelty stores whose proprietors sell them "for magic purposes only."

There are a great many anti-gambling laws in the United States but there are none that prohibit the manufacture or sale of marked cards, crooked dice or other cheating gimmicks. Thousands of decks of marked cards are sold each week, and the only penalty is that the user may occasionally get his ears pinned back or his nose pushed in when a knowledgeable player rumbles the gaff.

It's even possible that you might buy a marked deck without knowing it from a retailer whom you know and trust because some cheat has slipped him a few bucks. On one occasion, some years ago, during the racing season at Saratoga, it was difficult to buy anything else. A card mob had jimmied its way into a warehouse and substituted a whole case of marked cards for a case which had been shipped in by a legitimate distributor. As soon as the cards were jobbed and retailed the mob went to work. Nearly every game in town had a marked deck in it, and the chumps were cheated with cards they had purchased themselves. The mob, naturally, made a tidy profit on this wholesale switching operation.

The average player has several misconceptions about marked cards. He believes, for instance, that the markings show both rank and suit. This is true only of Bridge and Pinochle decks, where the suit is important. Usually only the numerical value is indicated; but that is all the cheat needs. If he can identify the value of each card as it comes off the top of the deck or always know what the value of his opponents' hole cards are in Stud Poker, the chumps might just well be playing with their cards face up. That isn't a card game; it's a swindle.

The ordinary player also thinks the cards are marked when they are printed. They aren't; reputable card manufacturers are not on the side of the cheats. But their cards do get marked later. The gambling supply house or the cheat himself buys honest decks of standard brands. They heat and soften the adhesive and remove both the revenue stamp and glassine wrapping. Then the cards are marked by hand with special matching inks. One marked-card supplier employs a crew of 50 girls to mark cards. Finally, the glassine wrapper is replaced and neatly repasted, the deck reinserted in its case, and the revenue stamp glued on again.

Markings may be *light work* or *strong work*, i.e., marked with fine lines or with easier-to-see heavier lines. Light work is used by professional cheats against smart or alert opponents; against the chumps the strong work goes in because it is easier to read during play. Amateur cheats use strong work which can often be read from across the table, five or six feet away. Cards are marked near both ends, so that they can be read no matter which end is exposed in the hand.

Although individual marking systems vary, all card markings fall into eight kinds of work:

Edge work: On cards having white margins on the backs, the line between the margin and back design is thickened slightly at certain points. A mark high up indicates an ace; a little lower down, a king, etc.

Line work: Additional small spots, curlicues or lines are added to the back design.

Cutout: A chemical preparation bleaches out or a sharp knife scrapes off a minute area of ink from the design, thus adding white areas that weren't there originally.

Blockout: Parts of the design are blocked out with white ink, or some configuration in the design is exaggerated slightly. This is especially useful on cards whose back designs are claimed to be markproof —those with overall designs and no white border. An example of this is the Bee card, whose back design is a simple overall pattern of diamond shapes. Certain diamonds are made smaller or larger by blocking out.

Shading: White areas of the card are delicately shaded with a dilute solution of the marking ink. A good marked-card man can read it from across the table.

Trims: A marking method used on cards whose back designs have white margins. The shark removes the cards he wants to be able to recognize (say the high cards) and trims a thin 1/32-inch slice off *one* side edge of the card so that the white margin is narrower than on the opposite edge. So that the remaining cards in the deck will be the same size and the margins will remain equal, he then trims 1/64-inch off *both* side edges. The net effect is that the back design on some cards seems to have been misprinted slightly off center. This can also be done on some cards which have overall back designs. Again the pattern is off center and does not run off the edge of the card in the same way on both sides. The simplest detection method is to place a suspected card on an honest card from another deck. The trimmed card will be smaller.

Pictures: A good rule to paste in your hat is never to play for money with *one-way* cards, i.e., cards whose backs bear pictures or designs that are not symmetrical from top to bottom. During play, a cheat can arrange such a deck so that high cards are right side up, low cards upside down. I know it sounds obvious, but card cheats know from experience that the obvious device is sometimes the one least likely to be suspected. Most players dismiss this idea, if it does occur to them, as too obvious and primitive a device to be used. Therefore the cheat, well aware of this, sometimes uses it; and a quick shuffle, after turning half the pack end for end, will destroy the arrangement and the evidence if anyone shows any sign of suspicion.

Luminous readers: I put this one in mainly because it shows how little trust you or anyone should put in gambling supply house catalog copy. Some of the gimmicks they list, which the amateur cheat buys

The Scarne Marked Card Riffle Test. Riffle the cards as above and watch for the "moving pictures" on the backs. (Conrad Eiger)

because he knows no better, are strictly sucker items. When the would-be cheat orders a deck of luminous readers at $12.50 to $18 per deck, he receives by express (these boys avoid using the mails) a red-backed deck of cards whose backs bear large numerals lightly marked in with green pencil. You also get a cheap pair of glasses with red-tinted lenses or a red-tinted, transparent eyeshade. When the card is viewed in red light the red back design fades out and the green markings turn dark and become visible for you alone. If you suspect this gimmick, simply ask to borrow the glasses or eyeshade for a moment. The cheater, if that is what he is, will probably be out the door and halfway down the stairs before you finish asking, because one look at the cards will convict him. Professional cheaters wouldn't be caught dead with such junk because they know that if they were caught with it they might end up dead.

The latest wrinkle in this department is a pair of tinted contact lenses made to your prescription. There is a nice profit on this sucker item; the charge is $160 per pair and up.

There are many items listed in the catalog which no smart cheat has used in years and for which many amateur cheats have paid good money only to get the horselaugh or a beating in the first halfway smart game they sit in on. The punch line here is that I know of one crooked gambling equipment manufacturer who retired wealthy after years of selling crooked devices (much of it junk) to cheaters and would-be cheaters. Then, with nothing to do and money in the bank, he began gambling, became an addict and went broke. And some of his bankroll went to the professional cheats who used something you can't order from any catalog—sleight-of-hand moves.

How to Detect Marked Cards

There is one detection method that can be used on all marked cards—the Scarne Riffle test. Remember the animated cartoon books you used as a kid in which the pictures moved as the pages were riffled? Hold the deck face down, riffle the cards and watch the backs. Do it several times, watching different parts of the back. An honest design will stand still, but with marked cards the back pattern will move in the area where the marking has been done.

Marking Cards During Play

When the skilled cheat has no good opportunity to switch a marked deck into play, he uses a type of mark which can be applied during the game. The markings are more easily detected by a smart player and the cheat takes more risk, but it is a mighty common practice in high-stakes games where knowing the value of one or two cards is highly important.

Nailing: The cheat digs his thumbnail into the side edge of the card and leaves a small identifying indentation which, like all expert markings, can be seen at some distance when you know what to look for. The mark is placed on both side edges so that it can be spotted no matter which way the card is held, and turning the card end for end does not change the mark's location in relation to the end of the card.

In Stud Poker, for example, only high cards are marked, the others being less important. A nail mark near the upper end of the card indicates an ace, a quarter of the way down it signals a king, halfway down it means queen, and so on. In Black Jack the cheat marks the low cards, since they are more important.

Waving: Essentially the same gaff, except that the cheat places one finger on one side of the card at the edge, two underneath, and applies pressure. This puts a bend or wave in the card's edge and the location (top, middle or bottom) supplies the needed information.

Detection: Square the pack and examine edges. Nail marks and waving will stand out like a well-stacked blonde.

Daubing: A gaff similar to shading, except that the mark can be applied during play. The cheat carries a small flat container of a waxy paste called daub. Pressing the tip of a finger on this and then on the card leaves a light smudge, usually a yellowish brown, which can be mistaken for a nicotine stain. Its location on the card back supplies the information.

Pegging: A very old marking method which is sometimes still used. Here the cheater uses the principle of braille and is able to feel rather than see the marks. When he pegs, the sharper shows up at the game with a Band-Aid on his thumb or finger. This hides a sharpened thumbtack whose point penetrates the bandage and with which the cheat pricks the cards, usually only aces and kings, in the right places. A prick applied to the face of a card raises a small bump on the card's back. When the cheat deals, the thumb of the hand holding the deck feels the bump and he second deals, retaining the high card for himself or a confederate. Your tactile sense is just as sensitive; run a finger over the card backs now and then to satisfy yourself that the cards aren't pegged; when any player has a bandaged finger be sure to do it.

Sanding: Another method of edge marking, also requiring a bandage. There is a slit in the bandage and beneath it a piece of fine sandpaper. The cheat pulls the card's edge along the slit. Card edges become grayed with use, and the sandpaper cleans the dirt off, supplying a white edge that stands out clearly.

HOW TO SPOT A MARKED CARD CHEAT

Suspect the player who concentrates too much on the backs of the cards in your hand, the back of the hole card in Stud, the top card of the deck in Black Jack, the top card of the stock in Gin or the important card in any game. There's nothing wrong with a natural, healthy interest in the cards, but an undue interest in their back designs may be your tip to take a scholarly interest in the deck yourself.

As a general rule be leery of the player who wins continuously against all the probabilities. Any player who wins and wins and keeps on winning has something more than luck working for him.

After you have convinced yourself that you have been victimized by marked cards—then what? That's hard to answer. It depends on whether or not you outweigh and can outpunch the cheat. If you believe you can handle him you can try asking for your money back—

but be careful. Any cheat caught red-handed is dangerous. Move with caution.

I have described the most used card-cheating devices, but there are still a good many others. For information on such things as Dealing from the Middle, Slick Ace Cards, Sorts, Check Cop, Shiners, Locators and Hold-Out Machines, see *Scarne on Cards*.

HOW TO SHUFFLE CARDS

At least 50% of amateur card fanciers make this mistake after a shuffle: They take the pack up into their hands to square it before offering it for the cut. Why, after taking such fastidious pains to conceal that bottom card, must they expose it thus to a hawk-eyed opponent? Because, make no mistake about it, the opponent will take advantage of that card. He'll know where it is after the cut. He can cut the pack in such a way as to force it into the deal (placing it high in the pack) or keep it out. In either case, a significant percentage swings in his favor. Square the cards flat against the table.

It must be a matter of record that I'm a card manipulator by trade, I know how to shuffle, and I'm going to take the liberty of assuming you'd like to be taught by a professional. Nothing fancy about it; it won't take much time; and, while I don't guarantee to transform you into a magician, I think that the next five minutes we spend together will insure you against ever being embarrassed by shuffling badly.

First, hold the pack as I show you in the illustration, (A). Pull about half the cards off the top of the pack with your right hand, leaving the other half in your left, then putting both halves end to end.

Second, keep your hold on the cards as in (B), and riffle the halves together by running your thumbs up the sides of the cards. Hold the blocks firm by setting the fingers on the opposite edge of the cards.

Third, after the cards have riffled together, loosen your hold, and slide them into a single block as in (C). Never take the cards off the table, either for the riffle or in the act of squaring the pack.

Fourth, get into the habit of cutting cards just for insurance at least once during the shuffle by pulling out the bottom half and slapping it onto the top between riffles—good protection against locaters.

The GIs used to call this the Scarne shuffle. It's foolproof, crookproof and tidy as a con man's tuxedo . . . and it'll save you money if you never play anything but Solitaire. It just saves wear and tear on a pack of playing cards. But a couple of last warnings against your most insidious enemy: You're not playing for paid admissions, so you don't have to expose yourself to kibitzers. If you can do so without awkwardness, try to sit with your back to a wall so as to cut down your

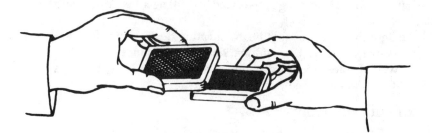

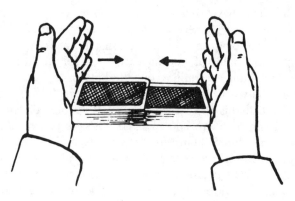

The steps in the Scarne shuffle.

audience. Many a hand is betrayed to an opponent by a spectator's sigh or chuckle or sharp inhalation of breath or such a fool crack as: "What a lucky pick!"

Before each game—whether Stud, Draw, Gin, Pitch, Skarney, Pinochle or any other game—do yourself the justice of counting the cards, just to be sure the whole pack's there and nothing is missing by any accident. And don't play when you're disturbed. Most of us are convinced we play a pretty in-and-out game; we tend to be champs one day and chumps the next; and we attribute it all to the run of the cards.

When you play cards, give the game all you've got, or get out: not only is that the one way on earth to win at cards, it's the only way you and the rest of the players can get any fun out of what ought to be fun. You can't play a good hand well if your mind's on that redhead down the street or the horses or your boss's ulcers or your wife's operation. When you don't remember the last upcard your opponent picked and you throw him the like-ranked card which gives him Gin, it's time to push back your chair and say, "Boys, I just remembered I have a previous engagement."

Do as the professionals do. When they make a few bad plays in a row, they just mutter, "That's all for today, gents"; and they mean it. They mean today is, for certain reasons, written off; they mean they'll be back tomorrow, which is another day. By all means, when you're in this kind of losing streak, don't let yourself get panicky. The more reckless you feel, the more desperate is the necessity that you get away from that table at once. An excited player, a player plunging to recoup losses, is a player at his worst. Learn to recognize him. That player has been and will again be—unless you learn how to deal with him—your own worst enemy. And one more thing. The player who resorts to systems is just adding method to his madness—he is systematically ensuring his losses. There is no such animal as an unbeatable system. Only the chump believes in one.

27.
Poker:
America's Favorite
Card Game

Poker is by far the most popular card game played in America today, both in the amount of money that changes hands every year at this game and in the number of players.

My survey of private card game playing reveals that the annual gambling handle for all kinds of card games totals $150 billion and that about 50%, or $75 billion, is wagered at some form of Poker.

I also found that of the 90 million adults who play cards about 18 million men and 20 million women prefer Poker to any other card game. Of the remaining 52 million card players, 12 million men and 13 million women play Poker occasionally. Altogether a total of 30 million men and 33 million women play Poker either regularly or occasionally —a sum total of 63 million. Poker is as characteristically American as baseball and hot dogs.

Only two states, Nevada and California, permit commercialized Poker playing. Nevada's Casino Licensing law permits all-out Poker playing. The California law considers Closed, or Draw, Poker to be a game of skill and Stud Poker a game of chance. Towns may, by local option, issue licenses for Draw Poker to Poker clubs which rent tables at an hourly rate and supervise the honesty of play. Low Ball is one of the most popular forms of Poker played in these clubs. Gardena, the most famous of these California towns, has seven big Poker palaces, all but one of which has the legal maximum of 35 Poker tables. When Gardena's anti-gambling crusaders tried to have Poker playing outlawed in 1958 they were defeated by a 3 to 1 vote.

I agree with the California law that Draw Poker is a game of skill and am glad that at least one state recognizes it officially as such; all 50

The card room in the Rainbow Club, one of the seven poker palaces in Gardena, California, can accommodate 285 players at 35 tables, the maximum allowed by city ordinance. (Las Vegas News Bureau)

states should do so. I must, however, disagree with those who believe that Stud Poker is a game of chance. Actually, it is far more a game of skill than Draw Poker.

That America's favorite card game can be played commercially in only two states, and that private Poker is not permitted by law in any state, is another example of how unrealistic and outdated our gambling laws are.

Illegal though it may be, 63 million Americans do play Poker in private clubs and homes in every city and hamlet from the Atlantic to the Pacific and from Maine to Florida.

At least a hundred variations of Poker are being played today, but they can all be placed in two large classes: Closed (or Draw) Poker in which each player's cards are hidden from the other players until the showdown or the completion of the hand; and Open, (or Stud) Poker, in which some cards in each player's hand are exposed to all the players as the betting progresses, all the active players' cards being exposed at the showdown.

To most Americans, Draw Poker means the game of Five-Card Draw—Jacks or Better, and its popular variations: Low Ball, Draw Poker—Blind Openers, High-low Poker, etc. Stud Poker usually means

Five-Card Stud and its variations: Canadian Stud, Seven-Card Stud, Six-Card Stud, Low-Hand Stud, High-low Stud Poker, etc. These variations and many others are played in various combinations: Table Stakes, Freeze-out, Deuces Wild, Joker Wild, Dealer's Choice, Jackpots, etc.

In all these variations two factors remain constant:

1. The value or rank of each Poker hand.

2. At the showdown the hand cannot consist of more than five cards, even though more cards are used in many Poker variations.

Poker has achieved its outstanding popularity for the following reasons:

1. It can be played by rich and poor alike. The stakes may vary from no limit to penny ante, just as long as the minimum and maximum betting limits are agreed upon before the game begins.

2. It is easy to learn.

3. It may be played in a great many different ways.

4. Any number of players from two to eight may play, although two to six make the best game.

5. It is strictly a gambling card game, whether it be Draw Poker penny-ante style or Five-Card Stud table stakes. Without the gambling factor it would be one of America's least played games.

6. Each player, on his own, battles all the others. There is no partnership play.

7. It combines both chance and skill and is the only game in which a player can win only one hand all evening and still come out a winner, or win many more than the average number of hands and still lose to the game's action.

If there is any more engrossing card game for a group of reasonably congenial friends of fairly equal playing ability than Poker, I have yet to learn about it. The longest Poker session always seems too short.

WOMEN POKER PLAYERS

Until about forty years ago, Poker was almost exclusively a man's game. Today more women than men play the game. Every day millions of women now gamble with each other in thousands of women's Poker clubs, and more millions gamble with men every day in tens of thousands of mixed Poker games. Mixing of the sexes at cards isn't always amicable; in many Poker rooms man and wife are not permitted to play at the same table!

Are women as good Poker players as men? My observations over the past 40 years have convinced me that it is essentially still a man's game. Most women, even the best players, sometimes call a critical Poker bet against all reason. This may be because women as a group have less interest in mathematical analysis than men do, and consequently are less accustomed to it. To them, Poker is more a game of chance than of skill.

Except for the bigtime male gamblers, women gamble for about the same stakes as men, both high and low. Contract Bridge is not the American woman's favorite card game as many people believe. Poker, with its 33 million women players, is today in the top spot.

ORIGIN OF POKER

It is impossible to say that any specific earlier card game is the direct ancestor of Poker; it seems to have borrowed elements from many games. The basic principle of Poker is such an obvious one that its use must be very old. I once gave my three-year-old son "Teeko" 20 shuffled cards, all the aces, kings, queens, jacks and tens, and without any prompting on my part he separated them into those five groups. The first Poker in this country was played with just such a deck, and one could say that Teeko had discovered its basic principle.

The first reference in print to Poker which I have found is one by Jonathan H. Green published in 1834. He gives the rules for what he calls a "cheating game" which was then being played on the Mississippi riverboats. He stated that this was the first time the rules had been published, he noted that the *American Hoyle* then current did not mention the game, and he called it Poker. The game he described was played with 20 cards—aces, kings, queens, jacks and tens. Two, three or four players could play, and each was dealt five cards.

By the time Green wrote this, Poker had become the number one cheating game on the Mississippi boats. It received even more action than Three-Card Monte. After losing heavily at Monte only the dumbest chumps would later fail to realize that they had been swindled; but 20-card Poker seemed to be a legitimate game, and they would come back for more. In my opinion Poker, like Three-Card Monte, was developed by the card sharps.

Most dictionaries and game historians say that the word "Poker" comes from an early eighteenth-century French game, Poque. Others say it is derived from an old German game, Pochspiel, in which the element of bluffing played a part and the players indicated whether they would pass or open by rapping the table and saying, *"Ich poche!"* Someone has tried to trace the word to *poche*, the French word for pocket, and I have even heard it argued that Poker derives from the Hindu *pukka*.

I doubt all these theories, and I have my own. I believe it was originally underworld slang and came from the pickpocket's term for pocketbook or wallet: *poke*.

The card sharps who evolved the 20-card game as a cheating device to relieve the sucker of his poke may even have called it that among themselves, disguising it slightly by adding the *r* to make it "Poker" when using the term in front of their victims, some of whom might have been hep to underworld slang.

To go even further back, the word "poke" probably came from the hocus-pocus of the magician. In the Middle Ages, before pockets came into fashion money was carried in a bag which hung from the belt, and the first pickpockets were called cutpurses because they lifted the purse by cutting it free. Many of the fifteenth-century paintings and engravings of magicians performing show cutpurses busily at work in the crowd; some of these cutpurses may have paid the conjurer a percentage for working in his audience just as pickpockets once did in this country when they traveled with circuses. Like the magician, they also used misdirection and sleight of hand and were, in their own way, hocus-pocus men.

The Mississippi River sharpers who first called the game Poker may have got their original inspiration in New Orleans from sailors who played a very old Persian game called Âs-Nâs, whose basic structure is the same. Twenty cards are used, five are dealt to each player, pairs and such combinations and sequences as form the melds at Rummy are winning combinations, and bluffing is an important factor.

Âs-Nâs may also have been the father of the Italian game of Primero and the French Gilet which, during the reign of Charles IX (1560–74), became Brelan and later fathered its variants Bouillotte and Ambigu. In *le Poker Américain* as the French play it today *brelan-carré* means four of a kind. The early published Poker rules in this country also hint at French antecedents: the 32-card Piquet pack was used, it was cut to the left, the cards were dealt from the bottom of the deck, and certain combinations of cards bore French names. The draw feature of Poker is found in Ambigu, and the blind, straddles, raise, table stakes and freeze-out in the pre-Revolutionary Bouillotte. Bluffing and the use of wild cards were important features in the English game of Brag. In all these European games, however, a hand consisted of only three cards. The credit for the use of a five-card hand and also the bluff must go to the Persian Âs-Nâs, from which our word "ace" may also have come.

In 1845 an early American edition of Hoyle included Twenty-Card Poker and also "Poker or Bluff." Twenty years later *The American Hoyle* added the game, calling it simply "Bluff." Perhaps a few players

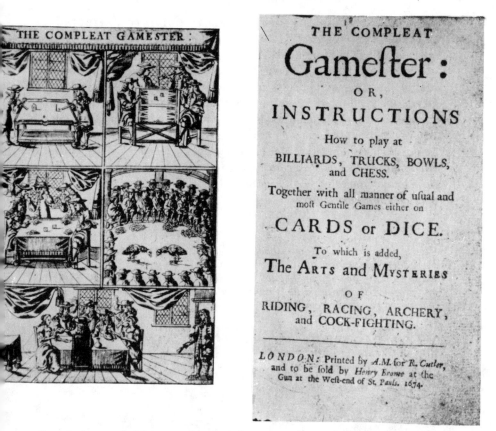

Frontispiece and title page of one of the very earliest rule books, The Complete Gamester, *published in 1674.*

who may have confused it with the English Brag also called it that, but most players have always called it Poker. Game-book editors who do their research in previous game books sometimes still call it "Poker (Bluff)" although no player has used the latter term for nearly a century.

POKER NOT ACCORDING TO HOYLE

Question a sample cross section of the population in various parts of the country as I have done and you will find that 95 out of 100 adults will admit to having gambled at some form of Poker at some time. Ask them what rules they use and they nearly always reply that they play "according to Hoyle." If you take this literally it is about as wrong as anything can be. Edmond Hoyle never played Poker, never wrote a single Poker rule and never even heard of the game. Hoyle, an English barrister, died in 1769, a good many years before Poker evolved. His first game book, *A Short Treatise on the Game of Whist*, was published in 1743. About 14 editions were published during his lifetime; he later added rules for Quadrille, Piquet, Backgammon and Chess. Quadrille and Piquet are now museum pieces and Whist was dropped from the rulebooks in this country some years ago. Since nothing he wrote on card games remains in current editions, the prac- tice of giving them titles such as *The Revised Hoyle, The Up-to-Date Hoyle* and even *Poker According to Hoyle* seems to me comparable to titling an engineering book *Fulton on Diesel Engines,* or one on atomic energy *The Revised Aristotle.*

The first of Edmond Hoyle's books on games was published in 1743, and there were ten editions in the next seven years. Two pages from one of these early editions are shown below. Hoyle and his printer, Thomas Osborne autographed the early editions as protection against the pirated ones which had already begun to circulate.

ADVERTISEMENT.

THIS Book having been entered at Stationers- Hall, according to Act of Parliament, who- ever shall presume to Print or Vend a Pirate Edi- tion, shall be Prosecuted according to Law.

The Proprietor has already obtained an Injunc- tion against Nine Persons for pirating or selling pirated Editions.

No Copies of this Book are genuine, but what are signed by

EDMOND HOYLE
and
THOMAS OSBORNE.

To the READER.

THE Proprietor of the following Treatise has thought proper to give the Public Notice, that he has reduced the Price of it, that it may not be worth any Person's while to purchase the pirated Editions, which have been already obtruded on the World; as likewise all those Piratical Editions are extremely incorrect ; and that the Author will not undertake to explain any Case but in such Copies as have been set forth by himself, or that are Au- thorized as Revised and Corrected under his own Hand.

A SHORT

TREATISE

On the GAME of

WHIST.

THE Author of this Treatise did promise, if it met with Approbation, to make an Addition to it by way of APPENDIX, which he has done accordingly.

It is necessary to premise, that those, who intend to read this Treatise, are desired to peruse the following Calculations; and they need only charge their Memories with those that are marked with a *N. B.* upon which the whole Reasoning of this Treatise de- pends.

B   Ca.

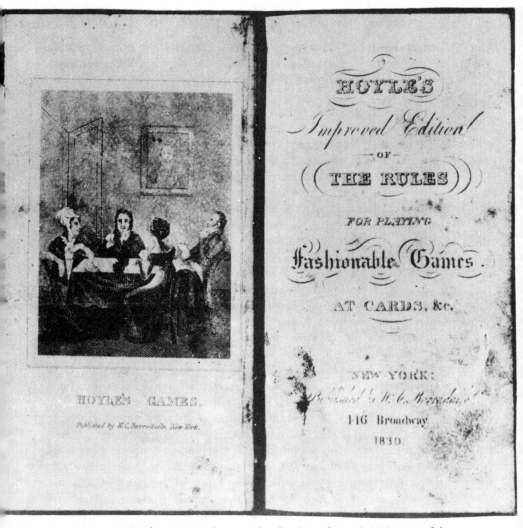

Frontispiece and title page of what may be the first edition (1830) of Hoyle's Games to be printed in this country.

Confronted by the many different "Hoyles" in print, whose rules vary and are often out of date and confused, most Poker players play according to their own regional or house rules.

POKER HAS MORE SCIENCE THAN BRIDGE

A great many players believe that Poker is primarily a game of chance and that most consistent winners at Poker are simply lucky. Actually, Poker contains a greater skill element than any other card game, including Contract Bridge, Pinochle and Gin Rummy. Despite the fact that Poker has so many variations and that the proper winning strategy differs slightly in each one, the better player will nearly always win money and the poorer player nearly always lose money in a long Poker session.

The devotees of Poker and those of Bridge have long argued about the relative merits of these games. In such a debate, naturally, the individual's own preference may color his judgment. Former British champion Maurice Ellinger states, and several present-day Bridge experts agree with him, that Poker demands considerably more skill than Bridge. Other experts take the opposite view, but they seldom give detailed reasons to support their opinions.

I believe that there are more science and skill in Poker than in Bridge for the reasons that follow.

My observations of Poker games over the past 40 years have convinced me that if a Poker expert played three average players for 52 sessions, each lasting six hours, the expert player would emerge the winner 51 times. The odds against any such result at Contract Bridge under similar conditions are high.

Contract Bridge is a partnership game, and, as in all such games, one partner is usually more skilled than the other. Their combined ability is therefore less than that of the better player. In Poker, with each player on his own, a skilled player is not handicapped by a less able partner; his skill potential is not reduced.

Contract Bridge is basically a game of strategy plus partnership signals (bidding). Poker is a game of strategy, deception, mathematics and psychology, with a considerable amount of courage thrown in. Judgment of one's opponent's psychological traits or habits plays little part in Bridge strategy, whereas a top Poker player must be a master of Poker psychology in order to analyze properly and simultaneously the playing traits of as many as seven opponents. Deception is much more used in Poker than Bridge, and a knowledge of the game's mathematics is much more important in Poker than in Bridge. Money management is important in Poker and not in Bridge.

The probability is that in any card game each player will in the long run receive an equal number of good, bad and indifferent hands, and most Bridge experts agree that a skilled partnership will, in the long run, score more points than a less skilled partnership. This means that skill rather than chance is the deciding factor in Bridge. But Bridge partners, no matter how skilled, must always play a series of bad hands out to a finish and take their beating. This is not true of Poker.

In most forms of Poker the game is pure chance only until the player looks at the cards dealt him. From then on, unlike in Bridge and most other card games, chance plays a lesser role, because the players need not play bad hands out to a finish. The player can throw a bad hand in and take a small loss, or perhaps none, or he can continue to play a bad hand and sometimes win by bluffing. In Stud and its variants this decision can be made by the player each time another card is dealt until the showdown.

The skilled Poker player will play fewer bad hands than the unskilled player and thus increase his winning chances in a way that an equally skilled Bridge player cannot do.

HOW TO WIN AT POKER

The remainder of this chapter contains all the advice you need to become a winning player rather than a contributor to some Poker hustler's bank account. If you study the strategy given here and still find that you lose consistently, you may be playing out of your class against opponents who are too skilled. The cure for this is to find a game that is more your speed. If you do that and still lose regularly, then Poker just isn't your game and perhaps you should switch to some other game. There are some people who do not have, and will never develop, a good Poker sense.

Everyone can't be a winning player, but I know that a poor player who studies the information I am about to present, even if he only partly absorbs it, can become, at the very least, an average player. And the average-or-better player will find hints and tips here that will greatly improve his game.

Space does not permit reprinting the up-to-date rules of Poker contained in *Scarne on Cards;* for a thorough study of these you should obtain a copy.* If you don't know the proper rules for the game you are playing you won't be able to take advantage of the finer points of Poker.

Since Poker has so many variations and the strategy varies with the form of Poker played because of the differences in the rules, the stakes involved, the number of players and other conditions, it is difficult to formulate strategy that will be applicable to every situation. But there is still a large body of general strategy that applies to all forms of Poker and is essential to playing winning Poker. I shall first explain some facts that many players don't know and should, and then give the correct odds and probabilities, general Poker advice and some special strategic tips, hints, and psychological maneuvers that apply to each of the most popular forms of the game.

---

* *Scarne on Cards* ($9.95), Crown Publishers, Inc., 419 Park Ave. S., New York, N.Y. 10016.

WHAT EVERY POKER PLAYER SHOULD KNOW

If you play cards in any professional Poker game, whether in a swank home on Park Avenue that caters to women only or with the boys in the dingy back room of Joe's barbershop, you must pay for your Poker seat. Running a professional game is a business and a charge is always made. How much you pay depends upon the game, and the kind of game you pick is entirely up to you.

In the licensed Poker clubs of California and Nevada the operators charge a fee for playing on an hourly basis, usually running from a low 60¢ per person at a 25¢-limit game to a high of $5 in a really big-limit game. This is reasonable enough, and it pays the operator's overhead, salaries, taxes, etc., and earns him a profit. Since Poker gets a lot of play it is sometimes quite a lot of profit: one of the larger Gardena Poker palaces grosses about $15,000 a week or nearly $800,000 a year, which is not peanuts.

But if you are one of the millions of Poker players who patronize games in which the operator takes 5% of the money in each pot for himself, you are paying a lot more than you may think.

For every licensed Poker game in America there are thousands and thousands of illegal games. Many are friendly weekly games which rotate from one player's home to another. Others are house games run as a business. In most house games the operator's *take* (his charge for furnishing the gaming facilities) is a 5% *cut* taken from each pot.

If this doesn't sound like much of a charge, would it surprise you to learn that even the world's best Poker player, playing against rank suckers, would eventually go broke bucking that small 5% cut? The operator calls it 5%, but it is actually much greater, often as much as 10%. In most games the operators get a percentage or cut of the players' winnings, but Poker is one of the few games in which a charge is also taken from the winning player's bet.

An example: Four Stud players play an entire hand to the showdown, the pot totals $20, and the house takes a 5% cut, or $1, out of the pot. The winner of the pot has paid a cut not only on his winnings but also on the $5 he put into the pot. The house is really taking a cut of 6⅔% on that player's $15 winnings.

Or suppose two players play a hand to the showdown. The pot totals $20. The 5% cut gets the operator $1, as in the four-handed game, but from the winning player's standpoint this is 10% of the $10 he won.

I recently clocked 20 different Stud games for a period of two months. The maximum betting limits ranged from a low $2 to a high of $600.* When I averaged my figures I found that:

1. It takes about 1½ minutes to play an average hand.

2. In a fast Stud game approximately 40 hands are dealt per hour.

3. The average pot in an eight-handed $4-limit game contains about $30 on the showdown.

Now let's see how strong the 5% cut can be in this average game. Forty $30 pots per hour means that the operator's 5% cut gets him $60 per hour. In a session lasting six hours the operator takes a total of $360.

Let's assume that each player began with $100 and that he received the number of good, bad and indifferent hands that probability says he can expect in the long run. The total money the players had at the game's start was $800. The total cut is $360, leaving only $440 in the game. Each player has paid the operator $45 of his original hundred. That small 5% cut has accumulated to 55%.

Suppose the game continues and lasts for ten hours, as many Stud games do. If, by that time, six players have gone broke, leaving only two, these two will have only $200 between them. The operator has taken a charge of $600 out of the original $800. That deceptively small 5% cut has taken out 75% of the total amount the players brought into the game!

Never having stopped to dope this out, there are millions of Stud players who try to win under these conditions. Many of them play two or three nights a week without the slightest realization of the enormous price they are paying for the privilege of letting the operator get most of the money.

And, believe it or not, many operators aren't satisfied with the way that 5% cut earns them money. They often steal extra amounts from the pot. This is usually done when making change or taking out the cut. The player who wins the pot is so pleased at winning that he seldom notices that the cut has been taken, let alone spotting the theft.

It is difficult to understand the logic, if any, of Poker-game operators. If they charged a reasonable hourly rate, as is done in the legalized games of Nevada and California, they would have a Poker game

---

* The $600 limit game was the Canadian Stud Poker game played by some Caribbean islands casino operators which took place weekly a few years back. The average pot held about $2,000, and the largest I saw contained $24,600. It was won by my friend Philip Schaffer, undoubtedly one of America's great Poker players. (Canadian Stud is played the same as Five-Card Stud except that a four-card straight or flush beats a pair, and a four-card flush beats a four-card straight. Skill is even more important here than in Five-Card Stud. Try it at your next Poker session.)

most of the time. As it is, they break most of the players in a few weeks and then wonder why they no longer have a game.

The operator's alibi, if you object that the 5% charge is too high, is that the ice he must pay for protection is high. It is. He has to pay quite a bit even to run a $1 limit Poker game, but it isn't so high that he has to take all the players to the cleaner's.

Many Poker players who have gone broke stay away for a while as they try to figure out why. Most lay it to bad luck. Some think they were cheated, which is possible. But more often it's the 5% cut that did the trick. Not knowing the real reason, these losers eventually come back and try again to buck the impossible.

If you play in such a game after reading this analysis of the 5% cut and still think you can hope to come out ahead, don't read any further. Any advice I can give you won't do you any good.

Some operators charge a 2% or 3% cut, which eats up your bank-roll just as the 5% charge does, except that it takes about twice as long before you go broke.

Another thing the player should learn is how to protect his money from cheaters. Otherwise, he should stop playing the game for fair or big stakes right now. The best Poker skill in the world means nothing against a cold deck. Study carefully the information and detection methods explained in Chapter 26, because all the moves and gimmicks described there are used by the cheat in Poker. A sharper at work in a fair- or big-limit Poker game can break you for that session and plenty of others.

Keep your eye on the discards; an unskilled cheater will often reach for a valuable card for use in his hand. When you spot him, he is kidding; when you don't, he takes your money.

If the game is honest and the cut or playing charge is small or non-existent and you still lose consistently, what is the cure? It's a simple one, and I've already mentioned it, but it bears repeating. Here's the way I put it in one of my World War II lectures at Fort Benning when a soldier said, "I have been a consistent loser at Poker since the first day I arrived in camp. Is there any advice you can give me to help me win at my next Poker session?"

"Yes," I told him. "There is one big secret, a Poker policy which, if put to use, will not only make you a winner at your next session but at most of them. It's a policy that is practiced religiously by the country's best Poker hustlers. It is the only surefire rule that wins the money.

"It's a simple rule: *Don't sit in a Poker game with superior players.* If you have been losing consistently in the camp's pay-day Poker games, it's a cinch the boys you've been playing with are better players. Find another game. Find one in which the players are *softies* (poor players). Poker is the world's greatest skill game and an inexperienced player who knows too little about it hasn't the ghost of a chance against seasoned players or hustlers."

I gave him that advice 17 years ago. It is just as true today. You may object that Poker is not as much fun when playing against poor players. I agree. An even better policy is to study the game and improve your Poker skill so that you can win even among good players. In short, don't just read and forget the Poker strategy that follows here: study it, remember it and put it into practice.

TWENTY GENERAL RULES EVERY WINNING POKER PLAYER MUST KNOW

1. The prime rule of Poker is: Don't try to beat the other players; let them try to beat you. This isn't just an introductory sentence; it is probably more important than all the tips and hints that follow. Do yourself a favor by memorizing it.

2. Be sure you know the rules of the game. The player who knows the rules has a decided advantage in any game against players who are vague about them.

3. Study the Poker probability tables that follow this section. A player who knows the Poker probabilities of drawing and improving hands has a decided edge over the player who thinks he knows. But don't become a slave to Poker probabilities. They are probabilities, not laws; and they do not supply a surefire recipe for winning.

4. Observe your opponents; learn their Poker mannerisms. Are they loose or tight players? And avoid giveaway mannerisms of your own.

5. Play as often as possible; experience is the best teacher.

6. Always remember that in a Poker game the average hand becomes less valuable the more players there are.

7. Treat every round of betting as if it were the first. Forget the previous betting rounds and the money you have contributed to the pot.

8. When you hold a cinch hand, wait till the last round to raise.

9. Fold a doubtful hand at the start rather than in the middle or at the end.

10. Call your opponent or opponents when you believe your hand is good enough to win, not merely because you suspect a bluff.

11. As a general rule, don't try to steal a pot by trying to bluff a poor player, a heavy winner or a heavy loser.

12. When you're in a losing streak, don't let yourself get panicky.

The more reckless you feel, the wiser it is to get away from the table at once. An excited player or a player plunging to recoup losses is a player at his worst.

13. You must expect to lose the pot unless you believe you have the best hand going in.

14. Most Draw Poker players would win instead of lose if they never tried to outdraw the opener.

15. Bet your big hands to the hilt and make every active player pay to see your hand.

16. Vary your playing strategy. The player whose game is always the same becomes an easy mark for smart Poker players.

17. Try to keep a poker face. Don't complain when losing or show elation when winning. The emotional aftermath will prohibit clear thinking and proper evaluation of succeeding hands.

18. Try to sit with your back to the wall and try to avoid kibitzers who watch your hand. Many good hands are tipped off by onlookers who don't keep poker faces.

19. Trust no one at Poker; it is a game for blood. If you want to play a good game you must forget friendship and bet your hand for what it's worth. Top-money winners do.

20. When you play Poker, give the game all you've got, or get out. That is not only the best way to win at Poker; it's the only way you and the rest of the players can get any fun out of what ought to be fun.

POKER ODDS AND PROBABILITIES

The relative values of Poker hands were not just conjured up by some rulemaker or arbitrarily assigned by the first Poker players. They were discovered by finding out, through the use of permutation and combination formulas, the exact number of possible five-card Poker hands in a 52-card deck, a total of 2,598,960.

These hands were divided into groups or ranks, no pair, pair, three of a kind, straight, flush, full house, four of a kind, straight flush and royal flush. The ranks were then arranged in relative value according to the frequency of their occurrence. The hands which can be expected to appear most often have the lowest rank; those which appear least often the highest rank.

A good poker player must have a fair idea of Poker odds and probabilities. Without such knowledge he has no good way of deciding on his course of action in the various situations which arise, no way of making any mathematical analysis on which to base a decision. This information is given in the Poker tables that follow.

These same tables can also be used to prove the relative value of Poker hands and to settle disputes that arise regarding the chances of drawing certain valuable hands in Five-Card Draw Poker or in the first five cards dealt in any other form of Poker.

It would be simple if all one had to do to become a winning player was to memorize the following Poker tables. But knowing the exact strength of your hand or the exact chances of bettering your hand on the draw will not always help you, because the playing habits of your opponents will often throw a monkey wrench into your best-laid mathematical plans. Example: A big raise from a habitually tight player means quite a different thing from the same big raise from a drunk who has already been caught trying to *steal* (bluff) the last half-dozen pots.

Although Poker is a game of skill, the judgments and decisions to be made by even the average Poker player involve a general knowledge of the game's probabilities.

The chances of being dealt any certain pat hand are the same, regardless of the number of players in the game. The same holds true in drawing cards to try to improve a hand. There are 2,598,960 different possible poker hands in a 52-card deck.

The following table lists the names of each different possible hand in order of their rank starting from the top, the possible number of ways each can be made, and the chance of being dealt such a hand in the first five cards dealt, such as the original five cards dealt in Five-Card Draw Poker before you draw.

Rank of Hands	Number of Possible Ways Hand Can Be Made	Chance of Being Dealt in Original 5 Cards
Royal flush	4	1 in 649,740.00
Straight flush	36	1 in 72,193.33
Four of a kind	624	1 in 4,165.00
Full house	3,744	1 in 694.16
Flush	5,108	1 in 508.80
Straight	10,200	1 in 254.80
Three of a kind	54,912	1 in 47.32
Two pairs	123,552	1 in 21.03
One pair	1,098,240	1 in 2.36
No pair hand	1,302,540	1 in 1.99
Total	2,598,960	

In the *Chance* column above, fractional figures have been carried out to only two decimal places, since further extension would mean little.

The probability of being dealt a pair or better in the first five cards dealt is almost even—to be exact, .499—and the probability of being dealt a no-pair hand is practically the same—.501. So it's almost a 3 to 1 chance, when playing against two opponents, that one of them will hold a pair or better in the first five dealt cards. The probabilities vary slightly depending upon what you hold.

The 1,302,540 possibe five-card no-pair hands are divided as follows:

POSSIBLE POKER HANDS OF LESS VALUE THAN ONE PAIR

Ace Counting High	King Counting High Ace Low	Number of Possible No-Pair Hands
Ace high	King high	502,860
King high,	Queen high	335,580
Queen high	Jack high	213,180
Jack high	Ten high	127,500
Ten high	Nine high	70,380
Nine high	Eight high	34,680
Eight high	Seven high	14,280
Seven high	Six high	4,080
		1,302,540

The lowest-ranking regular five-card Poker hand is comprised of 7, 5, 4, 3, 2 in mixed suits. The above table is particularly helpful to players who play high-low variants of Poker. In the short run each additional active player in the game increases the odds against you on any particular hand. But in the long run, since all players have to put an equal sum into the pot, thus increasing the size of the pot in direct ratio to the increased odds, it doesn't make much difference, as far as odds are concerned, if you are bucking one or seven players. In High-Low Poker, where aces count both high and low, the perfect low hand is 6, 4, 3, 2 and ace.

To simplify matters, the figures in the following two tables have been rounded out when necessary to the nearest ½ or whole number.

Note that your chances of making four of a kind are three times as great when drawing to a pair minus a kicker than when holding a kicker.

ODDS AGAINST IMPROVING THE HAND IN DRAW POKER WHEN DRAWING THREE CARDS TO ONE PAIR

Odds against any improvement	2½ to 1
Odds against making two pairs	5 to 1
Odds against making three of a kind	8 to 1
Odds against making a full house	97 to 1
Odds against making four of a kind	359 to 1

ODDS AGAINST IMPROVING THE HAND IN DRAW POKER WHEN DRAWING TWO CARDS TO A PAIR AND A KICKER

Odds against any improvement	3 to 1
Odds against making two pairs	5 to 1
Odds against making three of a kind	12 to 1
Odds against making a full house	119 to 1
Odds against making four of a kind	1,080 to 1

In fact, you have a better chance of improving your hand when drawing three cards to a pair than when drawing two cards to a pair plus a kicker. The tables above give ample proof of that. However, good Poker playing demands that a player occasionally hold a kicker with a pair so as to keep your opponents in doubt as to your playing habits.

The odds against making a full house by drawing one card to two pairs are about 11 to 1.

ODDS AGAINST CHANCES OF IMPROVING THE HAND IN DRAW POKER WHEN DRAWING TWO CARDS TO THREE OF A KIND

Odds against any improvement	8½ to 1
Odds against making a full house	15½ to 1
Odds against making four of a kind	22½ to 1

CHANCES OF IMPROVING THE HAND IN DRAW POKER WHEN DRAWING ONE CARD TO THREE OF A KIND PLUS A KICKER

Odds against any improvement	11 to 1
Odds against making a full house	15 to 1
Odds against making four of a kind	46 to 1

These two tables above show that the best chance for improvement with three of a kind is to draw two cards and not hold a kicker. Holding a kicker increases the odds against the player for any improvement.

CHANCES OF ODDS AGAINST FILLING IN A FOUR-CARD STRAIGHT IN DRAW POKER

When drawing one card to a four-card straight in Draw Poker, which may be open in the middle, at one end or both ends.

Odds against making a straight open at one end	11 to 1
Odds against making a straight open in the middle	11 to 1
Odds against making a straight open at both ends	5 to 1

ODDS AGAINST FILLING A FOUR-CARD FLUSH IN DRAW POKER

The odds against making a flush by drawing one card of the same suit are about 4½ to 1. If you insist on drawing to a three-card flush, the odds against your catching two cards of the same suit are approximately 23 to 1.

ODDS AGAINST MAKING A STRAIGHT FLUSH IN DRAW POKER

When drawing one card to a four-card straight flush, which may be open in the middle, at one end, or both ends.

Odds against making a straight flush open at one end	46 to 1
Odds against making a straight flush open in the middle	46 to 1
Odds against making a straight flush open on both ends	22 to 1

The odds against making a royal flush are the same as a straight flush for similar conditions.

CHANCES OF HOLDING VARIOUS POKER HANDS IN THE FIRST FIVE CARDS DEALT WHEN THE JOKER IS WILD MAKING A 53-CARD PACK

Rank of Hand	Number of Each	Chance
Five of a kind	13	1 in 220,745.0
Royal flush	24	1 in 119,570.2
Straight flush	216	1 in 13,285.5
Four of a kind	3,120	1 in 919.7
Full house	6,552	1 in 437.9
Flush	7,768	1 in 369.3
Straight	20,532	1 in 139.7
Three of a kind	137,280	1 in 20.9
Two pairs	123,552	1 in 23.2
One pair	1,268,088	1 in 2.26
No-pair hand	1,302,540	1 in 2.20
Total	2,869,685	

A very unusual mathematical situation arises in Joker Wild regarding the relative value of three of a kind and two pairs. As you see above, the chances of drawing three of a kind are one in 20.9 and the chances of drawing two pairs are one in 23.2. Since there is a better chance of drawing three of a kind than two pairs, the latter should be of a higher rank and beat three of a kind.

This peculiar situation is caused by the fact that there are 82,368 possible five-card Poker hands that contain a pair plus the joker. When a player holds one of these 82,368 hands he values his hand at three of a kind, making the joker count the same denomination as the pair he is holding. But if we should permit the two pairs to rank as a higher hand than three of a kind, we would accomplish nothing; the player holding one of the 82,368 possible Poker hands containing a pair plus the joker would use the joker to form another pair with the highest-ranking odd card and would value his hand at two pairs. This would bring the total number of two pairs in a pack of 53 cards to 205,920 and the possible number of three of a kinds to 54,912. Under these conditions, considering the relative value of both hands, three of a kind must remain of higher value than two pairs.

There are two solutions to this. I give them here in case there are a few players who may want to play a completely sound mathematical game. If the following two rules are used they will mathematically permit three of a kind to retain its higher value in relation to two pairs. I did not incorporate either rule in my laws for Joker Wild in *Scarne on Cards* because I have learned that you cannot change playing habits that easily.

1. If a player has a hand containing a pair plus the joker, the joker cannot be considered wild, and therefore carries no value whatever; and the joker must be considered an odd card; or,

2. If a player has paired aces, kings, queens, jacks, tens, nines or eights plus the joker, he is permitted to rank his hand as three of a kind. If he has a pair ranking lower than eights plus the joker, he cannot value his hand at more than two pairs.

The probabilities of Stud Poker and other variations will be discussed later. Bear in mind, as I said earlier, that a knowledge of Poker odds and probabilities will not make a good Poker player, but total disregard of them will certainly make a poor one.

GENERAL STRATEGY AT POKER

The most important thing to remember if you want to win at Poker is to *be alert*. Every little movement has a meaning all its own. Every draw and every card shown has a vital bearing on the strategy you employ. You must watch every player in the game to see that you are not being cheated or chiseled; you must watch every active player so that you can gauge the strength of his hand and judge his reactions to a raise or re-raise, to a draw of two cards or three cards, etc. In Stud, especially, you must observe each card dealt carefully to see (1) how it affects your own chances of improving your hand; (2) whether it improves the chances of each other player, including the player who received the card. Finally, you have to watch yourself so as not to betray your hand or give clues to your opponents. Yes, you have to be alert.

You *can't* be alert if you are overtired or mentally disturbed by something either in or outside the game. And you can't be alert if your alcohol content is too high. Don't play Poker for sizable stakes if you've had a tough day at the office, if you're worried about business or about Junior's behavior or if you've had a few too many martinis. And don't drink liquor while playing—not if you want to win.

You must always be keen about sizing up situations. If you are, you have a good chance of winning even if you are just an average player. For there will always be one or more players who because of fatigue, irritation, recklessness or fuzziness will play badly and give you the edge.

Whether the game be Stud or Draw Poker, Seven-Card or Five-Card, Deuces Wild or Nothing Wild, there are three very important rules of play. If you remember these rules, it is almost impossible for you to lose in an evening of Poker unless you are playing with a group of experts who also know them. If you play Poker regularly with the same group of players and find that there are a few who win consistently while the rest of you lose—leaving the possibility of dishonesty aside—it is because these players are aware of these rules and play accordingly.

The first rule is: *When you have nothing, get out.* More money is lost by Stud Poker players who go in with two indifferent cards and drop out later, or by Draw Poker players who stay with a low pair and fold after the draw, than is ever lost by having three kings beaten by three aces. The player who has the patience to stay out of pot after pot, for hours if necessary, is the player who, in the long run, will win.

The second rule is: *When you're beaten, get out.* You may have a pair of queens back to back in a Stud game—a high hand good enough to win 99 pots out of 100. But if, on the next card, one of your opponents should show a pair of kings or aces, in most cases the smart play is to *drop out at once.* You may improve your hand, but the odds are against it. Even if you should improve, your opponent may improve also—and his pair was better than yours to begin with. Except for going in on nothing, trying to beat a big pair with a small one loses more money than anything else in Poker.

The third rule is: *When you have the best hand, make your opponents pay.* If *you* have the pair of aces back to back, make it as expensive as possible for the man with the pair of queens to play. It is true that every once in a while he will outdraw you, but you will beat him much more often, and you can afford his occasional victory.

There are many fine points to the game of Poker; but if you get nothing out of this section of the book but these three rules, you will be a consistent money winner against most players.

The following tips, hints, bits of strategy and warnings added to the above, if studied seriously and applied faithfully, should make you a winner at Poker.

I have selected for discussion those traits possessed by gamblers who make their living or a part of it from Poker, i.e., Poker hustlers. Some of the warnings to the reader were inserted after watching numerous Poker games in which cheaters operated.

If the reader believes that a few of the tips given are too severe—such as "Never give a Poker player a break even if he is your best friend"—then he can simply declare his attitude at the start of the game by saying, "Boys, if you get them, bet them up, because that is what I am going to do." If you fail to bet a cinch hand for all it's worth when you hold one, you will rarely, if ever, be a good Poker player. The best gamblers have a slogan: "You must pay to look."

Poker is a money game, not just a pleasant way to spend an evening. If you want to play cards simply for recreation, there are many games more interesting than Poker. Remove the gambling spirit from Poker and it is a bore.

DO'S AND DON'TS

Insist that all players put the proper amount in the pot at all times. Many card hustlers obtain a decided edge by playing shy and forgetting to make good. Nickels and dimes stolen in this fashion amount to dollars at the end of a Poker session. Don't be a sucker for a card hustler: make him put up.

Learn the correct rules of the game so that in an argument you can protect your money. A bad decision against a player can break him for the evening. If you know the rules, no smart aleck will be able to cheat you of a pot by a bad decision.

If you are a neophyte Poker player, don't get into a game in which the boys are old hands. Experience is a big factor in Poker and very hard to overcome with mere talent. If you are lucky in a game with such players, you win little; if unlucky, you lose heavily. Find a game where the players are in your class.

Before joining a Poker game, ascertain the minimum and maximum limits, find out if the game is being played with any special house rules and whether the number of raises is limited or unrestricted. You need this information to determine whether you have enough money on your person to sit in the game. There is no law at Poker that says a player can't sit in a $5 limit game with a $10 bankroll, but you must realize that you will probably lose your $10 on the first pot and get plenty of criticism from the other players. Only very rarely will you be lucky from the start and win many times the $10 invested.

The smart Poker player has a couple of hundred dollars as a cushion in a $5 limit game, and the same ratio applies for smaller or larger limits. For example, a player should figure his cushion at $40 for a $1 limit; at least $20 for a 50¢ limit, etc. The smart Poker player reasons that his skill will win for him over several hours of play but if he lacks sufficient money to overcome a streak of bad luck, which may occur in the first few hands, he has, for that evening, lost any opportunity of putting his skill to work.

Before you sit down to a Poker game with strangers it is suggested that you observe the game for at least an hour, studying the players' characteristics. See who plays the cards loose and who plays tight. When you do join in, play a conservative game at first, just in case it might be a *steer* game (crooked game). If you are dealt an exceptionally good hand in a strange game, don't bet everything you have with you. Be satisfied with small winnings on the hand; if it is a steer game your losses will be small, and perhaps the cheaters will decide you are too hep to be taken in.

Don't lend money to another player in a Poker game. The money you lend will often help break you. Also, it is an even bet you won't get it back. Gambling debts aren't paid back as often as legitimate debts.

If you desire to improve your game, play as often as you can, because skill develops with experience. But don't play in a big-limit game during the learning period.

Poker skill consists of five elements:

1. Knowledge of the game's mathematics.
2. Money management.
3. Psychological deception.
4. Card memory and analysis.
5. Betting courage.

The extent to which a player can use these elements will determine his Poker ability.

It is almost impossible to teach anyone to become a good Poker player by setting a standard pattern because all players have different traits. Some are nervous and crave to be in every pot; others like to raise just for the thrill of the game; others are very conservative; others have no courage (afraid to bet up their cards at the proper time).

I do not believe that giving sample problems and their solutions can lead to better Poker playing. Even if you memorized their solutions, you would grow old waiting for one of these sample hands to occur in an actual game. And even if such a sample hand did turn up, it would be most unlikely that the other players would have the same

Poker characteristics and the same amounts of money as the illustration specified.

There are certain fundamental rules a player must follow if he hopes to play well.

Know the mathematics of the game: It's not difficult. You simply use some common arithmetic plus a little patience to guide your playing. You should remember, for instance, that in Poker the average hand becomes less valuable with the addition of more players.

For example: A pair of jacks is worth holding in a two-handed game, but in a seven-handed game it is very weak. A Poker player will better his game immediately if he remembers this.

Next, a player must have some knowledge of the chances of bettering certain hands. Study the Poker tables in this book. Don't try to memorize them; merely absorb the general implications. Some of the best Poker players just play a tight game, knowing little of specific probabilities but applying the general principles.

Keep a poker face: Don't complain when losing or show elation when winning. Emotional displays prohibit clear thinking and the proper evaluation of your hand. Don't indulge in unnecessary conversation. Keeping a poker face means keeping the same disposition at all times. Such restraints are very difficult to acquire overnight, but they are essential requirements of a good Poker player. When you achieve them, not only will you play your best game, but your opponents will not be able to figure your hand so easily.

Forget friendship: Upon entering a Poker game leave friendship behind. If you hold a "cinch hand" at Stud and you allow a friend to see your hole card without putting in the last bet to call your hand, I can assure you that you won't be a winner. If you want to play a good game, you must bet your hand for what it is worth. Top money winners do. Poker is a game for blood.

Know poker psychology: A good Poker player must be a good psychologist. During a big money game, every type of human emotion comes into play. I used to play Stud with a player who, whenever he was dealer and had a pair back to back, would almost always fail to deal himself an upcard until his attention was called to it. He was concentrating so much on his pair that he forgot he could better the pair by drawing.

Another player at Draw Poker would always ask, "Whose play is it?" When he asked this question, I knew that he probably had openers or a four-card flush—at least he was going to play. When he had a poor hand he would keep quiet and put his cards down before him. These are little mannerisms, if noted by the smart Poker player, that will help him win because they help him to know what to do at the proper time.

STUDY YOUR OPPONENTS' STYLE OF PLAY

Most players follow a pattern of play without realizing it. Some are loose players, some play tight or close to the vest. I know a player who has never tried to steal or bluff a pot in 20 years of Poker playing, and I know another who tries to steal almost every other pot he is in. This knowledge has directed my play with both. In every group you will find players with similar idiosyncrasies. Study your opponents' play. It will pay off. Whenever you get an opportunity to watch the mannerisms of players in a game before you sit down, do so. You can learn much more about technique by watching than by playing.

Study particularly the playing mannerisms and techniques of winning players. They must have something on the ball (if they aren't cheaters) to win most of the time.

When you hold a good hand, don't be too anxious to put your money into the pot until it is your proper turn; don't even have your bet ready. Untoward eagerness will inform an opponent, before he need know, that you intend to play. Most beginners or poor Poker players are very anxious to bet on a good hand and conversely, when holding a weak hand, they turn down their cards before their turn of play.

Don't try to win a small pot with a big bet. Example: A player makes a 25¢ bet at Stud Poker, holding the high card; another player raises the bet $2 for a total of $2.25 in the pot. The first player drops out; the player who raised wins the 25¢ with a lower hand than the player who dropped out hand. That is not considered a bluff. This sort of play may win a few quarters, but it will eventually lose much more on one hand whenever the opponent has that high pair backed up. Winning small amounts with big bets doesn't pay off in the long run.

Don't attempt to bluff a pot when four or five players are still in the game. Don't keep raising before you have your full hand because you intend to bluff. The legends of money won by bluffing at Poker are greatly exaggerated. Good Poker players seldom attempt a bluff simply because when they have a weak hand they are not usually still in the pot at the showdown. The best time to bluff is when one or two players are in the pot—and if they are heavy losers. If they are heavy winners, forget it; it's 99 to 1 you'll be called. Don't try a bluff on a beginner; he almost always calls. Really good Poker players can be bluffed more easily than the beginners.

The only time the bluff is an important factor is when playing table stakes. Here a player may bet $100 on a bluff hand to win a $10 pot.

But when a pot contains $50 and the limit is $2, and you were not the opener or high hand, you will be called at least 24 times to 1.

Never attempt a bluff at Stud unless you have a little something in your hand. In Draw Poker you must start the bluff by raising before the draw in order to sell the other players on the idea that you have a strong hand.

If you get caught bluffing twice, it's about time to stop for that evening. It is too costly to continue bluffing after being burned once or twice. But don't stop trying to bluff entirely. This would mean a considerable loss of call money on the showdown as soon as you become known as a player who never bluffs. The other players would hesitate to call you when you do bet.

It is good practice not to show a hand after a successful bluff, unless you do not intend to bluff for the remainder of the session. And if a player does not call on the showdown, bluff or no bluff, don't show your hand. This merely gives the other players more information about your playing methods. Conversely, a player should sometimes call a hand even if he knows he is going to lose, just to gather information concerning his opponents' methods.

Good memory is a valuable asset in Poker. If you play Draw or any of its variations, practice remembering the number of cards each player draws; that information is vital. Memory also serves in Stud. Several players may, for instance, turn down their hands after the third-card draw, and those cards may include three kings. If you draw a king for your fourth card in a no-pair hand, and the king is your high card and another player has queens, you might—if you don't remember that three kings were dead—gamble on drawing a king because the pot is big. You gamble on an impossibility. Observation plus memory will save you money.

STRATEGY AT DRAW POKER

When to Play or Drop Out

The pot has been opened, and you would like to have some nucleus of fact to guide your play. Common arithmetic plus a little patience will do the trick. If you fail to hold a pair or better, or a four-card flush or straight, the answer is, drop out without hesitation; your chances of drawing a better hand than the opener and the other players is remote. To draw to improve a hand, you must have something to draw to. Drawing to a three-card flush or straight is throwing money away. The chances of making a flush by drawing two cards are approximately 1 in 24. The chances of filling a straight when holding ace, deuce and three are approximately 1 in 68. Sure, you also have a chance of two pair or three of a kind, but you must bear in mind that the other players (especially the *opener*) may have one of those hands or better already, plus the chance of improvement.

You may draw to any pair above a ten, provided the opening bet is reasonable, because the chances of improvement are approximately 1 in 3½. The improvement may be to any one of the following: two pairs, three of a kind, full house or four of a kind, and one of these hands may win the pot.

When to Open

A player should always open the pot when he has an opportunity to do so, regardless of the value of his hand. If the player holds jacks and is *under the gun* (immediately to the dealer's left), he should hold a kicker and make his opening bet rather stiff. This play is made in an attempt to drive out any hand of a higher value.

Some players won't open the pot with a pair of jacks, and then they play with the jacks after another player opens the pot. This is bad logic and poor Poker. At other times a cautious opener will not hesitate to play with a small pair. After watching hundreds of Poker games, my opinion is that it is *unsound* to draw to a low pair if the opening bet is higher than the minimum bet.

Players have often asked me if it pays to hold a kicker with one pair? The answer is, Yes and no. True, holding a kicker lessens your chances of improving the hand. The exact chances of improving a pair with a kicker are 1 in 3.86, whereas the chances of improving a pair without a kicker are 1 in 3.48. But if you hold a kicker you have added a certain deceptive value to your hand. You must judge which seems best at the time, and your decision must be made after analyzing both the players' characteristic methods and the number of cards each player has drawn before your turn to draw.

Here is a hint on whether to stay in with a four-card flush which I have found sound both in theory and in actual play. Calculate the amount of money in the pot and recall the chances of drawing the fifth card to make the flush. The odds against drawing one card to make a flush are about 4½ to 1. Therefore the pot should contain at least five times the amount it will cost you to draw a card; if the opening bet was $1, there must be at least $5 in the pot before it is worth your risk in paying $1 to draw a card in an attempt to make a flush.

"But," you ask, "if I make the flush, it may not win; therefore shouldn't the pot make me better odds?" The answer is No. As a rule there isn't too much money in the pot before the draw; a flush will win many more times for a player than it will lose.

Whether to raise and bluff in Draw Poker is determined by the situation. A player must consider the temperament of the players with whom he is competing, the amount of money in the pot, the number of cards drawn and the relative value of the player's own hand. Years of Poker playing may be necessary to evaluate these factors correctly, but it is necessary to do all these things perfectly to win money at Poker. All you must do is to play a better game than your opponents.

The Poker tables on pages 685–688 are intended as an aid to better Draw Poker playing. A player who has a fair idea of the chances of improving his hand in Draw has a great advantage over the player who hasn't the vaguest idea. Try especially to memorize the exact chances of bettering certain hands, such as a pair, four-card straight and four-card flush.

STRATEGY AT STUD POKER

The better Poker players prefer Five-Card Stud to any other game in the Poker family. They shun such games as Draw Poker, Spit in the Ocean, Twin Beds or any of the variations in which wild cards are used. Stud Poker permits a player to use much more strategy. When wild cards are added, the element of skill is greatly diminished and the element of chance greatly increased.

The best game of Stud, looking at it from a smart gambler's viewpoint, is without an *ante* or *dealer's edge;* but if the dealer does edge, the amount must be comparatively small (for example, in a $2 limit game, the dealer edges 25¢). The reason is that the gambler likes to have some information to guide himself before betting. Gamblers don't like to put money into the pot without seeing at least part of their hand; therefore the first two cards dealt in Stud (the hole card and the first upcard) are the cards that are valued by the gambler and determine the betting.

Let us assume you have been dealt a hole card and your first upcard. This is the most important phase of any Stud game. You must decide the value of those two cards, and you do it by considering the value of both your cards and the value of every other player's upcard. No general rule will cover this situation, so I'll discuss what one of the smartest gamblers in the business does under all conditions.

First, if his hole card is lower than a ten spot, he folds (provided he does not hold a pair back to back), regardless of the value of his upcard. If it is an ace or a high card and he is compelled to make the opening bet, he bets the minimum amount permitted.

Bear in mind that the chances of being dealt a pair or better in five cards are approximately 1 in 2. Therefore, if three or four players remain until the showdown, the winning hand will almost invariably hold a pair or better. With this in mind, the smart gambler, failing to hold a pair, always has to have a higher-ranking card in the hole than any other player's upcard. He figures that if he holds two cards lower than the upcard of one or more players and he has the possibility of pairing one of his low cards, each of his opponents also has the same possibility. And, if he or one of his opponents each pair a card, his hand is valueless, because his opponent paired a higher card. This gambler uses sound judgment.

So much for the first two cards. Now the first betting round has ended, each player has received his second upcard.

This gambler, if he sees any other player's two upcards paired, and if he fails to hold a pair, will at his turn of play fold up. His theory, a sound one, is *"Never play a hand at the start which you know is lower than your opponents'."* In other words, don't chase a pair or a higher hand when the pot is small; because if you did play for the third up-card, you might be tempted to chase the money which you have in the pot. That is not good Poker playing.

It boils down to this: Play them tight, at least until you receive your third upcard.

Let us go back to the hole card and the first upcard. When your hole card has a ranking value of jack or better and your upcard is a ten or lower, it is worth a reasonable bet. That is, provided a jack is not showing as one of your opponent's upcards. If this is the case, fold up at your turn, because your chances of pairing that jack have been reduced 33⅓%.

Always bear in mind that an upcard paired has much less value than a hole card paired. The smart player will consider playing the hand in an attempt to pair his hole card rather than an open card or upcard.

The chances of pairing a hole card with a second upcard (provided no player holds a card of the same denomination as his upcard) are deduced by checking the number of upcards. Example: The game is seven-handed; a player sees seven upcards, none of which can pair up his hole card. The player's chances of being dealt a card to pair his hole card are 3 in 44 or 13⅔ to 1 against. And the chances of pairing either his hole card or his upcard, provided the upcards showing are not of the same denomination, are 6 to 1 against. So if the pot holds seven or more times the amount it will cost you to put in and draw that second upcard, it is worth the gamble. If the pot has much less, it is not worth the risk.

Don't be afraid to fold up. Sure, you like action; that is why you play Stud. But I still have to find the Stud player who enjoys losing money. If you are afraid to fold up and crave action when your hand doesn't merit your playing, you must eventually lose.

If you fold up your first two or three cards, you lose little or nothing, because the big betting is seldom under way at this point. Usually, a player holding a big pair back to back won't raise at that time for fear that this will cause the other players to fold up. And a player holding a weak hand doesn't raise, because he is trying to better his hand with the second upcard.

If a player raises before drawing his second upcard, you must analyze the player who made the raise as well as the upcard he is holding. Is he a winner up to this time? If he is, the chances are better than even that he is bluffing; a big-winning player frequently seems to go on a betting spree. Or is he a heavy loser? If he is, he may be trying to steal the pot or to change his streak of bad luck. If you hold a good hand at this time, play for the second upcard.

Whenever you have your hole card paired with one of your two upcards and another player has an open pair showing of a lower rank, it is worth a raise for two reasons: (1) to attempt to drive out the other players and possibly the holder of the pair; (2) to force the holder of the lower hand to intimate the value of his hand by either dropping or raising. The main reason, of course, is to get the most money possible into the pot with the fewest players remaining in.

One of the stupidest plays in Stud is to play for a flush when holding only three cards of the flush. The chances of making it by drawing two cards depends on the number of cards of the same suit in the upcards. For example: in a five-handed game, with three cards of the same suit showing in the other players' upcards, the odds against making the flush are approximately 24 to 1.

When you are in a pot and have drawn your third upcard with one more to go, and an opponent has you beaten with his upcards and the pot is not especially big, fold up. But if the pot is extra big and only a reasonable amount is required to bet to receive that last card, and if you believe your chances of winning that hand are good if you draw a certain card (and the card is still alive), then by all means play.

If you do not hold a cinch hand and are in doubt about your holding the winning hand, a check is the proper play. You must think about trying to save money on an uncertain hand. By checking you won't play into a trap and give your opponent a chance to raise if *he* holds a cinch hand.

After you have received your last card at Stud, odds should no longer be considered. By this time you know whether you have a cinch hand or not. If you have it, bet the limit; don't check in the hope that your opponent will bet and you can raise him. If he has a raise in mind, the chances are that he will raise anyway when you bet. If not, he probably will also check, and you are out money.

Never give an opponent an opportunity to see your hole card free when holding a cinch hand.

STRATEGY AT SEVEN-CARD STUD

Most of the tips given in the section "How to Win at Poker" and many of the tips under "Five-Card Stud" also apply to Seven-Card Stud, in addition to the following:

This concerns the betting by a player after he receives his first three cards (two down cards plus an upcard). It is more important to have three good cards at the start in Seven-Card Stud than it is in Five-Card Stud. Oddly, most Stud players, even good ones, believe that they should enter the betting round with a lower-ranking hand than in Five-Card Stud.

The Stud player's course of action should be simple. He can see three-sevenths of a complete hand before he bets a cent. If he fails to hold a three-card straight, a three-card flush, three of a kind, a pair or, at the least, two high cards such as ace and king, he should fold without putting a bet into the pot.

STRATEGY AT HIGH-LOW SEVEN-CARD STUD

By far the soundest method of play at High-low Seven-Card Stud is to play for low with the first three cards dealt. If you start with low cards, you have a chance to wind up with a straight or possibly a flush or a straight flush which will win high for you, and at the same time your low cards may give you low hand and you may win the entire pot.

Playing for high at the start, you may win high, but it is practically certain that you will never win low also.

You may ask, "If most players play for low, isn't it a good idea for me to play for high?" If you are playing for low and a high card hits your hand, automatically eliminating your chances for a possible straight or flush, drop out. But when you're playing for high and hold a fairly high pair, you usually play right through.

In short, a player who insists on starting out with a high hand must lose in the long run.

STRATEGY AT LOW BALL

The player should realize that when playing Low Ball, a pair, particularly a high pair (from nine up), is almost worthless.

Never play a hand after an opening bet on the strength of having three low cards with the hope of getting two low cards on the draw.

This is one of the most foolish draws at Low Ball. The probability of drawing two low cards is almost as remote as the probability of filling a three-card straight at Draw Poker. If you draw two low cards, you have the possibility of pairing your other three low cards; and you now hold a pair or probably two pairs.

The best hand at Low Ball is a good pat hand but, since you don't always get good pat hands, I suggest that you draw only one card to a four-card no pair.

Hands such as six high are equal to a straight flush in Draw Poker, and a seven high is equal to four of a kind. These hands usually win the pot.

STRATEGY AT LOW POKER

Most of the tips covered under "How to Win at Poker" apply to Low Poker, plus most of the tips covered under Draw and Stud. But, a specific bit of information on Low Poker:

When playing a Draw variant, play your hand pat. Seldom, if ever, indulge in more than a one-card draw. To warrant drawing two cards in Low Poker the pot must be extra large, and the amount of money required to draw those two cards must be reasonable.

In Low Poker Stud variations, the player should play a tight game. The hole and upcard cannot be higher than seven. Play the game tight and you will be a winner in the long run.

STRATEGY AT WILD GAMES

Most of the tips covered under "How To Win at Poker" and under the "Stud" and "Draw" sections go out the window when more than one card is wild in the game.

If only the joker is wild, the rules are followed except in valuing a player's hand. The player must use caution by attributing a little higher value than usual to his opponent's hand.

Wild-card games with more than one joker, or variations that are not standard—such as Spit in the Ocean and Twin Beds—are not discussed in terms of strategy, because chance is so much more a determining factor.

A final word on Poker ethics: Don't be a poor loser or a gloating winner.

28.
The Wide
World of
Bridge

Bridge is the third most popular card game played in the United States, surpassed only by Poker and Rummy in the millions of its followers. The principle of Bridge goes back more than 400 years in England. Whist, the basic game, developed into Bridge (1896), then Auction Bridge (1904) and finally Contract Bridge (1925). Whist and Auction Bridge still have many followers, but since about 1930 Contract Bridge has been most popular.

Contract Bridge is first in the affections of the ultrafashionable circles that frequent Palm Beach, Newport and other famous resorts; and it is equally the property of all walks of life, all sections of the United States and all types of card players, from those who play seriously in clubs and tournaments to those who play casually in their homes.

Contract Bridge is also played for high stakes and Bridge hustlers and cheats are abundant in the innocent world of Bridge. As a matter of fact, due to its partnership aspect, more cheating takes place at Bridge than at any other card game.

Due to space limitations, the rules of Contract Bridge are omitted from the following pages, but the bidding skill and science, the mathematics of the game and the various methods employed by bridge cheats will be thoroughly discussed.

CONTRACT BRIDGE STRATEGY

The main object in Bridge is to score as many points as possible. This can be done in one or two ways: by securing the contract for your side and fulfilling it successfully, scoring points for tricks, overtricks and premiums; or by keeping your opponents from fulfilling their contract and so scoring penalty points for your side. Often more points can be scored by catching opponents in overbids and doubling them than by taking the bid yourself. Bear in mind that the winner of the rubber is the side that scores the most points and that may not necessarily be the side that plays the most contracts.

In life the fellow who always knows the score holds a definite advantage. The same is true in Bridge. Become thoroughly familiar with the tables of scoring values. Develop the habit of checking your side's score after every hand. Bids and play are affected by the score.

EVALUATING THE HAND

To get some idea of the strength of a hand, the following table of quick tricks may be used in making an estimate. A quick trick is a card or combination of cards which will usually win a trick, regardless of what suit is eventually trump and regardless of who wins the contract. Learn this table by heart if you can. (x refers to a low card, usually lower than jack.)

QUICK TRICKS

	Quick Tricks
Ace and king of the same suit	2
Ace and queen of the same suit	1½
Any ace	1
King and queen of the same suit	1
Any king and x of the same suit	½

Queen, jack, and x of the same suit, or queen and x of one suit plus jack and x of another suit are considered by many to have ½-quick-trick value. Others consider these simply as plus values but give them no definite numerical weight. Any jack added to any of the values in the table is also a plus value. *Note:* Don't count any one suit for more than two quick tricks. Thus, ace, king and queen or ace, king, queen and jack are only counted as two quick tricks each—the values of their ace—kings.

The point count: In recent years there has been a popular revival of the point-count method of evaluating hands for bidding. The point count goes back to Milton Work, who is credited with having originated it some decades ago.

The most useful application of the point count in its modern form seems to be in no-trump bidding, where it has proven itself a precise and scientific instrument. Most good players use both the quick-trick and point-count methods in evaluating the strength of a hand, as circumstances warrant, and rely on neither exclusively. This should be borne in mind when reading the following summary of the highlights of the point count as it is used today.

The point-count table: Any ace, four; king, three; queen, two; jack, one. A combined count of approximately 26 points in the two hands of a partnership normally will produce game in no-trump or a major, 29 points in a minor. A total of approximately 33 points will produce a small slam and 37 a grand slam.

In opening bids of one in a suit the count of the hand is arrived at by combining the point value of high cards and the following: 3 points for a void, 2 for a singleton, 1 for a doubleton. A hand of 14 points should usually be opened, but hands with lesser count may be opened as convenient.

One no-trump and responses: Only high cards are valued when bidding no-trump and no points are assigned for distribution. To open with one no-trump the hand must be of no-trump pattern with at least three suits stopped. The count should be between 16 and 19—some prefer 16 to 18. It is not a forcing bid and may be passed. If the responding hand is of no-trump type, raise to two no-trump with 8 or 9 points or 7 points and a five-card minor. Raise to three no-trump; with 10 to 14, or four no-trump with 15 to 16, to six no-trump with 17 or 18, to seven no-trump with 21.

A response of two in a minor indicates a long suit but less than 7 points; two in a major shows a five-card suit with perhaps as many as 8 or 9 points in the hand and an unbalanced distribution. A response of three in a suit shows an unbalanced hand and 10 or more points. A response of four in a major shows a fairly long suit, an unbalanced hand and less than 10 points in high cards.

The Stayman Convention: In a modification known as the Stayman convention a response of two clubs to one no-trump is artificial. It suggests the responder has one or two major suits of four cards or more and 8 or 9 points. It asks the original no-trumper to name, if he can, a major suit of four cards headed by at least a queen. It looks toward a safer contract in a major. If original no-trumper has no four-card major, he makes the artificial rebid of two diamonds with a hand of minimum point count. This permits responder to rebid two or three no-trump according to the strength of his hand. If responder bids a major suit over declarer's two diamonds, he is guaranteeing five cards in the suit. If responder rebids his clubs a second time, he indicates he wants to play the hand in clubs only, since his holding is insufficient to have the hand play in no-trump.

Two and three no-trump and responses: Open two no-trump with 22 to 24 and all suits stopped; three no-trump with 25 to 27. An opening two no-trump isn't a demand bid and may be passed; an opening three no-trump is not a shutout.

In responding to two no-trump: Raise to three with 4 to 8 points and to four no-trump with 9. With 10 points go to three of a suit and then rebid four no-trump. Jump to six no-trump with 11 or 12 points. Bid three of a suit and then rebid six no-trump with 13 or 14. Jump to seven no-trump with 15. Show any six-card major regardless of how low the point count.

In responding to three no-trump: Raise to four no-trump with 7 points; to six no-trump with 8 or 9. Bid four diamonds and rebid six no-trump with 10 or 11 points; raise to seven no-trump with 12. Show a five-card suit with 5 points in the hand.

Responding to a suit bid of one: Holding 5 to 9 points, a suit may be shown at the level of one; otherwise the response is one no-trump. A suit may be shown at the level of two with 10 points or with fewer points if the suit is fairly long. With no-trump distribution jump to two no-trump holding 13 to 15 points; to three no-trump with 16 to 18. Jump to three in partner's suit with 13 to 15; to three of another suit with 13 to 16.

Bidding inferences: The player should think of the bidding as a kind of special language in which he tries to convey to his partner, or receive from him, information that will help both partners to gauge correctly the possibilities in their combined holdings and so enable them to reach the best contract. He should also pay attention to the bidding of opponents. He can learn things from their bidding that may prove useful in playing a contract or defending against it.

Biddable suits: Generally a suit should have four or more cards to be originally biddable. For safety's sake a four-card suit should have at least ace, king or queen, and ten—though this isn't a must—and a five-card suit, queen or jack, and ten. A six-card suit or longer needs no honor card.

More than one biddable suit: With two biddable suits, bid them as follows: If the suits are equal in length and touch in rank—for example, spades and hearts, hearts and diamonds—bid the higher-ranking one first regardless of which suit has the higher cards. Later the lower-ranking suit is bid. Example: If a player holds two four-card biddable suits in spades and hearts, he should bid spades first, then bid the heart suit when his next turn to bid comes.

If both suits are of five-card length, bid the higher-ranking suit first, even if it is weaker than the other suit; then bid the lower-ranking suit. If the two biddable suits are of unequal length, bid the longer suit first, even if the other has higher cards.

Rebiddable suits: A suit is considered rebiddable—it may be bid again—if it is at least of five-card length. Generally, a five-card suit should have at least a king and a lower honor card or be headed by queen-jack-nine to qualify as a rebiddable suit. Any suit of six cards is rebiddable, regardless of whether it has any honor cards. If there are two five-card rebiddable suits, the lower-ranking one is rebid, not the higher-ranking one. This indicates to the partner that the player holds two five-card suits.

MINIMUM BIDDABLE SUITS
FOR AN OPENING BID

Four-card suits must contain four high-card points (example: K-J-x-x, A-x-x-x)
Five-card suits: any five-card suit (x-x-x-x-x)

FOR A RESPONSE OR REBID

Four-card suits must contain four high-card points (example: K-J-x-x, A-x-x-x)
Q-10-x-x or better (example: Q-10-x-x, K-x-x-x, A-x-x-x)
Any five-card suit (x-x-x-x-x)

REBIDDABLE SUITS

Four-card suits	No four-card suit is rebiddable
Five-card suits	Must be Q-J-9-x-x or better
Six-card suits	Any six-card is rebiddable (x-x-x-x-x-x)

Opening Bids: An opening bid is the first bid made in the deal, and here are basic requirements of such a bid:

One of a suit
  (a) 14-point hands must be opened.
  (b) 13-point hands may be opened if a good rebid is available (a rebiddable suit or a second rebiddable suit).
  (c) All openings must contain two quick tricks.
  (d) A third-position opening is permitted with 11 points if hand contains a good suit.

Two of a suit (*forcing to game*)
  (a) 25 points with a good five-card suit (1 point less with a second good five-card suit).
  (b) 23 points with a good six-card suit.
  (c) 21 points with a good seven-card suit.

Three, four, or five of a suit (*Preemptive bids*)
  Preemptive bids show less than 10 points in high cards and the ability to win within two tricks of the contract vulnerable and within three tricks not vulnerable. They should usually be based on a good seven-card or longer suit.

One no-trump
> 16 to 18 points (in no-trump bidding only high-card points are counted) and 4-3-3-3, 4-4-3-2, or 5-3-3-2 distribution with Q-x or better in any doubleton.

Two no-trump
> 22 to 24 points and all suits stopped (J-x-x-x; Q-x-x; K-x; or better).

Three no-trump
> 25 to 27 points and all suits stopped.

Choice of suits
> Generally speaking, bid your longest suit first.

With two five-card suits bid the higher-ranking first. With two or more four-card suits, bid the suit immediately lower in rank to your short suit (doubleton, singleton, or void).

General principles: Any bid of a new suit by the responding hand is forcing on the opening bidder for one round. Thus, each time the responder bids a new suit, the opener must bid again. If responder should jump, his bid is forcing to game.

With less than 10 points, responder should prefer to raise partner if partner has opened in a major suit, and to bid a new suit himself at the one level in preference to raising a minor-suit opening bid. With 11 or 12 points, responder can make two bids but should not force game. With 13 points or more he should see that the bidding is not dropped before a game contract is reached. With 19 points he should make a strong effort to reach a slam.

Responses to suit bids of one. Raise: To raise partner's suit responder must have adequate trump support. This consists of J-x-x, Q-x-x, x-x-x-x, or better for a non-rebid suit; and Q-x, K-x, A-x or x-x-x for a rebid suit.

Raise partner's suit to two with 7 to 10 points and adequate trump support.

Raise to three with 13 to 16 points and at least four trumps.

Raise to four with no more than nine high-card points plus at least five trumps and a short suit (singleton or void).

Bid a new suit: At one level requires 6 points or more. This response may be made on anything ranging from a weak hand, where responder is just trying to keep the bidding open, to a very powerful one, when he is not sure where the hand should be played.

At two level requires 10 points or more.

Jump in a new suit requires 19 points or more. (The jump shift is reserved for hands where a slam is very likely. Responder should hold either a strong suit or strong support for opener's suit.)

No-trump responses (made on balanced hands): One no-trump requires 6 to 9 points in high cards. (This bid is often made on an unbalanced hand if responder's suit is lower in rank than the opening bidder's and responder lacks the 10 points required to take the bidding into the two level.)

Two no-trump requires 13 to 15 points in high cards, all unbid suits stopped, and a balanced hand.

Three no-trump requires 16 to 18 points in high cards, all unbid suits stopped, and 4–3–3–3 distribution.

Responses to suit bids of two: An opening bid of two in a suit is unconditionally forcing to game and responder may not pass until game is reached. With 6 points or less he bids two no-trump regardless of his distribution. With 7 points and one quick trick, he may show a new suit or raise the opener's suit. With eight or nine high-card points and a balanced hand, responder bids three no-trump.

Responses to preemptive bids: Since the opener has overbid his hand by two or three tricks, aces, kings and potential ruffing (trumping) values are the key factors to be considered when responder is contemplating a raise. One or two trumps constitute sufficient support.

Responses to a one no-trump bid: balanced hands: Raise to two no-trump with 8 or 9 points, or with 7 points and a good five-card suit. Raise to three no-trump with 10 to 14 points. Raise to four no-trump with 15 or 16 points. Raise to six no-trump with 17 or 18 points. Raise to seven no-trump with 21 points.

Unbalanced hands: With less than 8 points plus a five-card suit, bid two diamonds, two hearts, or two spades. (Don't bid two clubs on a five-card club suit.) With 8 points or more and a four-card major suit, bid two clubs. (This is an artificial bid asking opener to show a four-card major if he has one. See section on rebids by opening one no-trump bidder.) With 10 points and a good suit, bid three of that suit. With a six-card major suit and less than 10 points in high cards, jump to game in the suit.

Responses to a two no-trump opening: balanced hands: Raise to three no-trump with 4 to 8 points. Raise to four no-trump with 9 to 10 points. Raise to six no-trump with 11 or 12 points. Raise to seven no-trump with 15 points.

Unbalanced hands: With a five-card major suit headed by an honor plus 4 points, bid the suit at the three level. Show any six-card major suit.

Responses to a three no-trump opening: Show any five-card suit if the hand contains 5 points in high cards. Raise to four no-trump with 7 points. Raise to six no-trump with 8 or 9 points. Raise to seven no-trump with 12 points.

REBID

Rebids by Opening Bidder

The opener's rebid is frequently the most important call of the auction, as he now has the opportunity to reveal the exact strength of his opening bid and therefore whether game or slam is in contemplation. His opening is valued according to the following:

13 to 16 points	Minimum hand
16 to 19 points	Good hand
19 to 21 points	Very good hand

13 to 16 points. **Minimum hand:** If partner has made a limit response (one no-trump or a single raise), opener should pass, as game is impossible. If partner bids a new suit at the one level, opener may make a single raise with good trump support, rebid one no-trump with a balanced hand, or, with an unbalanced hand, rebid his own suit or a new suit (if he does not go past the level of two in the suit of his original bid).

16 to 19 points. **Good hand:** If partner has made a limit response (one no-trump or a single raise), opener should bid again, as game is possible if responder has maximum values. If responder has bid a new suit, opener may make a jump raise with four trumps, or jump in his own suit if he has a 6-card suit, or bid a new suit.

19 to 21 points. **Very good hand:** If partner has made a limit response (one no-trump or a single raise), opener may jump to game in either denomination, according to his distribution. If responder has bid a new suit, opener may make a jump raise to game with four trumps, or jump to game in his own suit if it is solid. With a balanced hand and 19 or 20 points, opener should jump to two no-trump. With 21 points he should jump to three no-trump. With 22 points and up he should jump in a new suit (forcing to game and suggesting a slam).

Rebids by opening no-trump bidder: *Two-club convention.* When the responder bids two clubs, the opening bidder must show a four-card biddable major suit if he has one: with four spades, he bids two spades; with four hearts, he bids two hearts; with four cards in each major, he bids two spades; with no four-card major suit, he bids two diamonds.

Opening no-trump bidder must pass: When responder raises to two no-trump and opener has a minimum (16 points); when responder bids two diamonds, two hearts, or two spades, and opener has only 16 or 17 points and no good fit for responder's suit; when responder bids three no-trump, four spades or four hearts.

DEFENSIVE BIDDING

Overcalls: An overcall is a defensive bid (made after the other side has opened the bidding). Prospects for game are not as good as they are for the opening bidder, in view of the announced adverse strength, and safety becomes a prime consideration. Overcalls are therefore based not on a specified number of points but rather on a good suit. Generally speaking the overcaller should employ the same standards as a preemptor; he should be able to win in his own hand within two tricks of his bid if vulnerable and within three tricks not vulnerable.

One no-trump overcall: An overcall of one no-trump is similar to a one no-trump opening bid and shows 16 to 18 points with a balanced hand and the opening bidder's suit well stopped.

Jump overcall: Any jump overcall, whether it is a single, double or triple jump, is preemptive in nature and shows a hand weak in high cards but with a good suit that will produce within three tricks of the bid if not vulnerable and within two tricks if vulnerable.

Takeout doubles: (also called negative or informatory doubles): When a defender doubles and all the following conditions are present: (a) his partner has made no bid; (b) the double was made at the doubler's first opportunity; (c) the double is of one, two or three of a suit —it is intended for a takeout and asks partner to bid his best (longest) suit. The defensive bid is employed on either of two types of hand; (1) a hand of opening-bid strength where the doubler has no good or long suit of his own but has good support for any of the unbid suits; and (2) where the doubler has a good suit and so much high-card strength that he fears a mere overcall might be passed out and a possible game missed.

Overcall in opponent's suit (cue bid): The immediate cue bid (example: opponent opens one heart; defender bids two hearts) is the strongest of all defensive bids. It is unconditionally forcing to game and shows approximately the equivalent of an opening forcing bid. It normally announces first-round control of the opening bid suit and is usually based on a void with very fine support in all unbid suits.

Action by partner of overcaller: The overcaller's bid is based on a good suit; therefore less than normal trump support is required to raise (Q-x or x-x-x). A raise should be preferred by the partner to bidding a suit of his own, particularly if the overcaller has bid a major. The partner of the overcaller should not bid for the sole purpose of keeping the bidding open. A single raise of a one no-trump response should be made only in an effort to reach game. If appropriate values are held, a leap to game is in order, since a jump raise is not forcing.

Action by partner of takeout doubler: In this situation, the weaker the hand the more important it is to bid. The only holding that would justify a pass would be one that contained four defensive tricks, three in the trump suit. The response should be made in the longest suit, though preference is normally given to a major over a minor. The doubler's partner should value his hand as follows: 6 points, fair hand; 9 points, good hand; 11 points, probable game. Doubler's partner should indicate a probable game by jumping in his best suit, even if it is only four cards in length. Since the partner of a double may be responding on nothing, it is a good policy for the doubler subsequently to underbid, while doubler's partner should overbid.

Action by partner of opening bidder (when the opening bid has been overcalled or doubled): When the opener's bid has been overcalled, the responder is no longer under obligation to keep the bidding open; so a bid of one no-trump or a raise should be based on a hand of at least average strength. Over a takeout double, the responder has only one way to show a good hand—a redouble. This bid does not promise support for opener's suit but merely announces a better-than-average holding. Any other bid, while not indicative of weakness, shows only mediocre high-card strength.

SLAM BIDDING

When the two partners have been able to determine that they have the assets for a slam (33 points between the combined hands plus an adequate trump suit), the only thing that remains is to make certain that the opponents are unable to cash two quick tricks. Various control-asking and control-showing bids have been employed through the years, but only three have stood the test of time—Blackwood, Gerber and cue bids (individual ace showing).

Blackwood Convention (invented by Easley Blackwood): After a trump suit has been agreed upon, a bid of four no-trump asks partner to show his total number of aces. A response of five clubs shows either no aces or all four aces; five diamonds shows one ace; five hearts shows two aces; five spades shows three aces. After aces have been shown, the four no-trump bidder may ask for kings by now bidding five no-trump. The responder to the five no-trump bid now shows kings: by bidding six clubs if he has no king, six diamonds if he has one king, etc., but six no-trump if he has all four kings.

Gerber Convention (invented by John Gerber): This convention is similar to Blackwood in that it asks for the number of aces. Its advantage lies in the fact that it initiates the response at a lower level. A sudden bid of four clubs where it could not possibly have a natural meaning (example: opener, one no-trump; responder, four clubs) is

Gerber and asks partner to show the number of his aces. If he bids four diamonds, he shows no aces; four hearts, one ace, etc. If the asking hand desires information about kings he bids the next-higher suit over his partner's ace-showing response. Thus, if the responding hand has bid four hearts over four clubs to show one ace, a bid of four spades would now ask him for kings and he would now reply four no-trump to show no king, five clubs to show one king etc.

Cue bidding (individual ace showing): The Blackwood and Gerber conventions are designed to cover only a small number of potential slam hands. Many slams depend on possession of a specific ace, rather than a wholesale number of aces. Cue bids are employed in such cases. Example: Opener bids two spades, responder bids three spades, opener now bids four clubs; the four-club bid shows the ace of clubs and invites responder to show an ace if he has one. The responder "signs off" by bidding the agreed trump suit.

OTHER CONTRACT BRIDGE CONVENTIONS

Club Convention: This method of bidding was devised by Harold S. Vanderbilt, who invented the modern game of Contract Bridge, and for that reason it is often called "the Vanderbilt Club." It is very popular in Europe. An opening bid of one club is artificial—it does not necessarily show a club suit but it shows a strong hand with 3½ or more quick tricks. The opener's partner must respond one diamond if he has less than 2 quick tricks. Any other response shows at least 2 quick tricks. After the opening bid and response the partners show their suits naturally.

Two-club Convention: This convention, used by many expert players, is usually combined with "weak two-bids." An opening bid of two clubs is artificial, not necessarily showing a club suit but showing a very powerful hand. It is forcing to game. The opener's partner must respond two diamonds if he has a weak hand. Any other response shows strength, usually at least 1½ quick tricks. An opening bid of two diamonds, two hearts, or two spades is a preemptive bid, made on a fairly weak hand that includes a good five- or six-card suit but does not have 13 or more points. After a two-club opening bid, the opener will show his powerful suit on his next chance to bid.

Unusual no-trump: If a player bids two no-trump after the opposing side has opened the bidding, and when his partner has not bid, the two no-trump bid is a convention showing a two-suited hand (usually with five or more cards in each of the two minor suits). The partner of the two no-trump bidder is required to respond in his best minor suit, even if it is a three-card or shorter suit.

DEFENDER'S PLAY

Opening Lead

In leading against a contract, a defender should consider carefully which card to play. The fate of the contract often hinges on the very first card led. Proficiency in the technique of choosing the proper lead comes only with experience, but below are some suggestions that are helpful as generalizations.

CONVENTIONAL LEADS

Holding in Suit	Lead at Suit Bids	Lead at No-Trump
A-K-Q alone or with others	K, then Q	K, then Q
A-K-J-x-x-x-x	K, then A	A,* then K
A-K-J-x-x or A-K-x-x(-x)	K, then A	Fourth best
A-Q-J-x-x	A †	Q
A-Q-10-9	A †	10 ‡
A-Q-x-x(-x)	A	Fourth best
A-J-10-x	A †	J
A-10-9-x	A	10
A-x-x-x(-x)	A	Fourth best
A-K-x	K	K
A-K alone	A	K †
K-Q-J alone or with others	K, then J	K, then Q
K-Q-10 alone or with others	K	K
K-Q-x-x(-x-x)	K	Fourth best
K-Q alone	K	K
K-J-10 alone or with others	J	J
K-10-9-x	10	10
Q-J-10 or Q-J-9 alone or with others	Q	Q
Q-J-x or Q-J	Q	Q
Q-J-8-x (four or more)	Q	Fourth best
Q-10-9 alone or with others	10	10
J-10-9 or J-10-8 alone or with others	J	J
J-10-x or J-10	J	J
J-10-x-x or more	J	Fourth best

* The lead of the ace of an unbid suit at a no-trump contract requests partner to play his highest card of the suit led, even the king, or queen, unless dummy reveals that such a play might risk losing a trick.
† Usually not a good lead at this contract.
‡ When dummy seems likely to have the king, the queen is a better lead.

CONVENTIONAL LEADS (Cont'd.)

Holding in Suit	Lead at Suit Bids	Lead at No-Trump
10-9-8 or 10-9-7 alone or with others	10	10
10-9-x-x(-x)	10	Fourth best
K-J-x-x(-x-x)	Fourth best	Fourth best
Any other four-card or longer suit not listed above	Fourth best	Fourth best

LEADS IN PARTNER'S BID SUIT

Holding in Suit	Lead at Suit Bids	Lead at No-Trump
A-x, K-x, Q-x, J-x, 10-x or any other doubleton	High card	High card
J-10-x or x-x-x	Highest	Highest
A-J-x or A-x-x	Ace	Lowest
K-J-x, K-x-x, Q-10-x, Q-x-x, J-x-x	Lowest	Lowest
Q-J-x(-x)	Q	Q
A-x-x-x or better	A	Fourth best
A-K-x(-x) or K-Q-x(-x)	K	K
Any other four or more cards	Fourth best	Fourth best

More Information on Making Leads: As a general guide to making leads, the following principles should be observed by the defenders. They are especially helpful when a defender has no good suit of his own to play and there is no indication from partner what his best suit is.

1. Lead through dummy's strong suit other than trump. "Leading through" means that dummy is the second hand to play to the trick and declarer last. This suit is often indicated by declarer's and dummy's bidding. After the dummy goes down, this kind of lead should not be made if it helps declarer establish a long suit that will give him the contract before the setting tricks have been taken.

2. Lead up to the weak suit in dummy. This lead is made by the defender at dummy's left, and it means that dummy is the last hand to play to the trick and declarer is the second hand.

3. Do not lead up to a tenace; this is, do not make a lead that will permit the dummy or declarer's hand to play last to a trick when they hold a tenace in the led suit (see The Finesse, page 717, for description of tenaces).

The Play After the Opening Lead

1. The rule of eleven: When a defender makes an opening lead which is probably his fourth highest card in that suit, his partner can get useful information by applying the "rule of eleven." Here is the way it works: Subtract the denomination of the led card from 11. The resulting number will tell how many cards higher in denomination than the lead are outside of the leader's hand. Since the cards in dummy and in his own hand can be counted, leader's partner knows how many higher cards remain in declarer's hand.

2. Third-hand high: A defender is generally required to play his highest card on the lead of a low card by partner. This is known as "third-hand high," as the player is the third hand to play to the trick. The principle is that a still higher card must be player from declarer's hand, or dummy's as the case may be. This play helps establish cards in partner's hand, since it is assumed he led from his best suit. However, if leader's partner holds a sequence of high cards, he plays the lowest card of the sequence on the lead of his partner's low card. *Example:* If a player holds king-queen-jack or queen-jack-ten or jack-ten-nine, he plays the lowest card of the three. This gives partner valuable information, as declarer in order to take the trick must play a card higher than the top card of the sequence.

Another exception to third-hand high would be as in the following example: Defender A leads a six. Dummy shows queen–ten–nine of that suit. Defender B holds king–jack–x. If dummy plays the nine or ten, B should play the jack, not the king, since the jack in this case is as good as the king and it will take an ace to beat it.

3. Second-hand low: When a low card is led from dummy or declarer's hand and defender is the second one to play to the trick, he should not, as a rule, play his highest card. He plays a low card, because declarer generally intends playing a high card anyway, since he has led the suit. There are, of course, exceptions, such as when a defender as second hand holds a winning card which will set the contract; or when he wants to have the lead for some reason and the playing of a winning card will obtain it for him right away.

4. Come-on signal: When a defender wishes to encourage his partner to continue a suit, he plays high then low, that is, a lower card to the second trick in that suit than he played to the first trick. This is known as a "come-on," "high-low," or "echo." In general, the play of a seven or better on partner's lead of a card which promises to take a trick is a signal that the suit should be continued. The high-low may also be used in leading to indicate a doubleton.

5. Discouraging signal: When a player wishes to discourage his partner continuing a suit, he should play the lowest card he has. This is a signal that partner should consider shifting to another suit unless he has very good reason to continue in the suit led.

6. Returning a lead: When a player's partner has led a suit, the player should try to lead that suit again at his earliest opportunity, returning his highest card in it, unless there is a very clear indication that partner was leading from a weak suit.

DECLARER'S PLAY

Planning the play: Declarer's first step after the opening lead has been made and the dummy hand laid down is to take stock of the two hands. He should figure out a basic line of attack which promises to give him the needed tricks for his contract. Any bids that the opponents have made may provide clues to the location of key defensive cards or the distribution of adverse strength. As the game progresses, he may be forced to modify his plan, but it is better to give some thought to the matter at the beginning than to play along haphazardly, hoping that enough tricks will be made somehow. Experienced players usually plan alternate lines of play that they can switch to if the basic one does not prove feasible.

Playing at a trump declaration: In playing a contract where there is a trump suit, it is generally best to draw opponent's trumps at the first opportunity. This should be done even though the opponents will take a trick or tricks in trump in the process. Trumps are drawn to protect declarer's good no-trump suits and prevent them from being trumped—ruffed—by opponents.

These are occasions, however, when the drawing of opponent's trumps should be postponed or avoided entirely. This is usually the case when declarer is short-suited in no-trump suits in one hand or the other, or in both, and wishes to make some or all pieces of trump individually.

Playing at a no-trump declaration: In playing a no-trump contract, declarer should first work out a simple problem in arithmetic. He should count the tricks he definitely is sure of, then subtract them from the number he needs for the contract. He should then plan now how he can make the needed tricks. These are usually to be made in the suits in which his hand and the dummy's are longest. This generally involves surrendering a trick or two in that suit to the opponents. But it doesn't matter, since the declarer can usually afford to lose a certain number of tricks in the hand and still make his contract. Giving up a trick or tricks in a suit so that the remainder of the cards will be winners is known as "establishing a suit."

Experienced players when holding no high card but the ace of a strong suit led by opponents will often refuse to take the trick until the suit is led a second or third time. This is done in the hope of breaking the connection between the opponent's hands in that suit so that one player will have none of the suit to play when he is next in the lead. This type of play is known as "a holdup."

The finesse: The finesse is an attempt to establish a card as a winner while some higher card held by the opponents in that suit has not yet been played. The combination of cards where an extra trick or tricks may be won by means of a finesse is known as a *tenace*. Thus, ace–queen is a tenace, and other illustrations will be found in the following examples. In each of the following examples, the finesse described is the one generally used. A good way of fixing these finesses in mind is actually to make the plays indicated with cards.

Following are six examples:

Example (1) North holds A-Q-X, South holds X-X; (2) North holds Q-X-X, South holds X-X; (3) North holds A-X, South holds Q-J; (4) North holds A-J-X, South holds Q-X; (5) North holds X-X-X, South holds A-J-10; (6) North holds A-10-9, South holds J-X-X.

1. Lead a small card from South and, assuming that West plays a low card, his normal play, put on the queen from North. If West has the king of the suit, the queen will win to provide another trick besides the ace.

2. Lead the ace from South for the first trick. For the second trick, lead a small card from South toward North. If West has the king, the queen will be established as a trick to be taken later. Do not lead the queen from North for the first trick, since that play will produce only one trick out of the two honors regardless of which opponent holds the king.

3. Lead the queen from South. If West doesn't play the king, put on the small card from North. This is known as letting the queen ride. The lead of the queen in this situation offers a chance to win two tricks if West had the king.

4. The same principle as in 3 applies.

5. Lead a small card from North and play the jack from South to the first trick. The next time, lead a small card from North again and play the ten for a second finesse. If West and East each have one of the two missing honors, or if East has both of them, this line of play is sure to win two tricks.

6. The same principle as in 5 applies. Lead the jack to the first trick and later finesse again by playing a small card from South and putting on the ten from North. These plays in E and F are known as double finesses.

Unblocking: When a suit is longer in one hand than in the other, care should be taken to play the cards in such a way that the player does not prevent himself from continuing to lead that suit without interruption.

The end play: This is a stratagem by which declarer gives opponents a trick, which they must win in any case, at a time when it will be to declarer's advantage to have the opponents in the lead.

The squeeze: This is a stratagem by which declarer squeezes an opponent out of an apparent winner by giving him a choice of plays.

OTHER NOTES ON GENERAL PLAY

Splitting honors: When holding two touching honors, such as king–queen or queen–jack, it is generally wise to play one of them on the lead of a low card by opponent. This is known as splitting honors. It forces opponent to play a higher honor, thus promoting the other honor in the hand to a winner or near winner.

Covering an honor with an honor: When an opponent leads an honor; it is generally wise for a player to put a higher honor on it if he has one. This is known as covering an honor with an honor. It forces declarer to play a still higher honor if he wishes to win the trick, that is, two honors for one. This play may also promote a lesser honor or an intermediate card in partner's hand.

Trump and discard: When a player knows that both opponents are void of the same suit and that both have trump cards, he should not lead that suit, since it provides an opportunity for discarding a losing card in one hand and trumping in the other. This is also known as a *sluff and ruff*.

CORRECT BRIDGE ODDS

The reason Bridge surpasses most other card games in strategy is due to the fact that in dealing out Bridge hands, unlike most other card games, all 52 cards are first dealt out, 13 to each of four players to start the game. Therefore, the number of different card combinations that face each player is virtually infinite: to be specific, the astronomical figure is 635,013,599,600. Because of this factor there is no such thing as 100% accuracy in bidding. Two partners of expert ability are doing well if they bid and get a contract which appears makeable when the dummy hand is exposed. But the contract in question may stand up or fall on the way the opponents' 26 cards (half the deck) are divided. Let's take a simple example: Players A and B are partners, and they bid four hearts on cards they hold. The dummy is exposed and it seems certain that the contract will be made if one particular opponent holds the jack of trump; but A and B will be set one trick if the other opponent holds that jack of hearts. The above is true of most hands with the exception of a laydown hand. No one can predict with certainty how many tricks he can win because the declarer cannot know the exact distribution of cards held by the opposing team. All that is expected of any good Bridge player is to make the bid which has the highest expectation. Following are several tables that will help improve your Bridge playing.

Possible point counts: Almost all Bridge experts agree that the point-count bidding method (see page 703) has improved the bidding accuracy of the average Bridge player. The total number of high-card points in a 13 hand is 37 (out of a possible 40). The following table gives the chance of being dealt any exact number of points from 0 to 37. The chances are expressed in terms of percentages—in other words, the number of times in 100 dealt hands you can expect to hold a specific number of points.

CHANCES OF HOLDING VARIOUS POINT COUNTS

Total Number of Point Counts	Expected Appearance in 100 Deals	Total Number of Point Counts	Expected Appearance in 100 Deals
0	0.364	19	1.036
1	0.788	20	0.643
2	1.356	21	0.378
3	2.462	22	0.210
4	3.846	23	0.112
5	5.186	24	0.056
6	6.554	25	0.026
7	8.028	26	0.012
8	8.892	27	0.005
9	9.356	28	0.002
10	9.405	29	0.0007
11	8.945	30	0.0002
12	8.027	31	0.0001
13	6.914	32	0.000017
14	5.693	33	0.0000035
15	4.424	34	0.00000077
16	3.311	35	0.000000099
17	2.362	36	0.0000000023
18	1.605	37	0.00000000015

Possible suit splits held by opponents: The table depicts the percentage probability of finding all possible splits of cards held by the opponents. The number in the left-hand column is the combined total of cards held by both opponents in the suit in question. The numbers in the center column depict all possible split hands held by the opponents. The percentage figures shown in the right-hand column is the chance possibility of each suit split. These values are shown in terms of percentages; in other words, the number of times in 100 dealt hands you can expect your opponents to hold the suit split in question.

CHANCES OF VARIOUS SUIT SPLITS HELD BY OPPONENTS

Cards Held by Opponents	Split of Suit in Opponents' Hands	Percentage Chance
1	1–0	100.000
2	1–1	52.000
	2–0	48.000
3	2–1	78.000
	3–0	22.000
4	1–3	49.739
	2–2	40.696
	4–0	9.565
5	1–4	28.261
	2–3	67.826
	5–0	3.913
6	2–4	48.447
	3–3	35.528
	5–1	14.534
	6–0	1.491
7	3–4	62.174
	5–2	30.522
	6–1	6.783
	7–0	0.522
8	3–5	47.121
	4–4	32.723
	6–2	17.135
	7–1	2.856
	8–0	0.165
9	3–6	31.414
	5–4	58.902
	7–2	8.568
	8–1	1.071
	9–0	0.046

Cards Held by Opponents	Split of Suit in Opponents' Hands	Percentage Chance
10	5–5	31.414
	6–4	46.197
	7–3	18.479
	8–2	3.780
	9–1	0.350
	10–0	0.011
11	6–5	57.169
	7–4	31.760
	8–3	9.528
	9–2	1.444
	10–1	0.096
	11–0	0.002
12	6–6	30.490
	7–5	45.735
	8–4	19.056
	9–3	4.235
	10–2	0.462
	11–1	0.021
	12–0	0.0003
13	7–6	56.6250
	8–5	31.8510
	9–4	9.8310
	10–3	1.5730
	11–2	0.1770
	12–1	0.0030
	13–0	0.0001

The general percentages on suit splits listed above apply mostly when the opposing side has not bid. Usually when a player bids a specific suit, he shows strength in that particular suit and indicates a shortness in other suits.

Finesses: The table of finesses coupled with the table of suit splits become very useful when a player has a choice of plays. To illustrate, let's suppose that you can make your contract if you win a finesse in spades or if the hearts split favorably. You try for the heart split first, and if the heart suit fails to split favorably, you play the spade finesse later on. If your hand forces you to make one of the two possible plays, you then compare the odds (for the heart split with the 1 to 1 odds or a successful spade finesse) and then you make the best odds play in your favor.

The following table depicts the chance of winning one or more finesses from a given number of attempts. The chance is given in terms of percentages; in other words, the number of times in 100 dealt hands you can expect to win one or more finesses in a given situation. The percentage figures on finesses are as follows:

To attempt 1 finesse and win 1	50.00%
To attempt 2 finesses and win 2	25.00%
To attempt 3 finesses and win 3	12.50%
To attempt 2 finesses and win exactly 1	50.00%
To attempt 2 finesses and win 1 or 2	75.00%
To attempt 3 finesses and win exactly 1	37.50%
To attempt 3 finesses and win exactly 2	37.50%
To attempt 3 finesses and win 2 or 3	50.00%
To attempt 3 finesses and win 1, 2, or 3	87.50%

Possible long suits in player's hand: Every now and then some practical joker gets the bright idea to switch a "cooler" (stacked deck) into a Bridge game so that his buddy Joe Blow gets thirteen spades. If the ruse is executed skillfully, Joe gives the hand the silent treatment for a few seconds, then in a fit of excitement spreads his hand face up on the table and gleefully shouts, "Boys, look at them, thirteen beautiful spades from ace to king, how about that?" Within a few minutes Joe calls the local newspapers and by that time it's too late for the joker to admit it was a gag. It would infuriate Joe to learn he was the victim of such a prank.

Since the chances of holding any thirteen-card suit with an honest shuffle and deal is one in 158,753,389,899 deals, you should look with suspicion upon the honesty of the deal if you pick up a complete suit hand.

If you play Bridge regularly, you probably remember getting a seven-card suit now and then, but an eight-card suit is rather a rare animal. This experience conforms to the expected probabilities. About 4 hands in every 100 dealt hands has a seven-card suit but only 1 in about 200 hands has an eight-card suit. A nine or longer suit appears about once in a minimum of every 2,500 dealt hands. Although I play Bridge occasionally, I don't remember ever holding an honestly dealt eight-card or longer suit in my lifetime. For those who are interested in long suits, the following table gives the chance of being dealt exactly, at most or at least a specified number of cards in a specified suit.

THE CHANCES OF BEING DEALT VARIOUS LONG SUITS

Longest Suit in Your Hand	Odds Against Holding Such a Suit
Any four (4) card suit	About 1 to 1
Any five (5) card suit	About 2 to 1
Any six (6) card suit	About 5 to 1
Any seven (7) card suit	About 27 to 1
Any eight (8) card suit	About 213 to 1
Any nine (9) card suit or longer	About 2,580 to 1
Any ten (10) card suit or longer	About 59,448 to 1
Any eleven (11) card suit or longer	About 2,722,719 to 1
Any twelve (12) card suit or longer	About 312,506,671 to 1
Any thirteen (13) card suit	Exactly 158,753,389,898 to 1

Possible hand distribution: Very often a hand that doesn't contain a long suit is exciting because it contains an unusual four-suit distribution. Hands with two long suits usually have great playing potential and are fun to play out. The table that follows lists the chances of holding each possible suit distribution made up of 13 cards.

CHANCES OF HOLDING VARIOUS SUIT DISTRIBUTIONS

Distribution in Your Hand	Odds Against Being Dealt	Distribution in Your Hand	Odds Against Being Dealt
4-4-3-2	3.7 to 1	7-3-3-0	376.1 to 1
4-3-3-3	8.3 to 1	7-5-1-0	920.7 to 1
4-4-4-1	32.4 to 1	7-6-0-0	17,970.2 to 1
5-3-3-2	5.3 to 1	8-2-2-1	519.0 to 1
5-4-3-1	6.7 to 1	8-3-1-1	850.2 to 1
5-4-2-2	8.4 to 1	8-3-2-0	920.6 to 1
5-4-4-0	79.2 to 1	8-4-1-0	2,211.6 to 1
5-5-2-1	31.5 to 1	8-5-0-0	31,947.0 to 1
5-5-3-0	110.7 to 1	9-2-1-1	5,612.6 to 1
6-3-2-2	16.7 to 1	9-2-2-0	12,164.8 to 1
6-4-2-1	20.2 to 1	9-3-1-0	9,952.1 to 1
6-3-3-1	28.1 to 1	9-4-0-0	103,510.9 to 1
6-4-3-0	74.4 to 1	10-1-1-1	252,653.4 to 1
6-5-1-1	140.8 to 1	10-2-1-0	91,235.3 to 1
6-5-2-0	150.4 to 1	10-3-0-0	647,957.4 to 1
6-6-1-0	1,381.4 to 1	11-1-1-0	4,014,397.1 to 1
7-3-2-1	52.2 to 1	11-2-0-0	8,697,861.7 to 1
7-2-2-2	195.2 to 1	12-1-0-0	313,123,055.9 to 1
7-4-1-1	254.2 to 1	13-0-0-0	158,753,389,898 to 1
7-4-2-0	275.5 to 1		

CHEATING AT BRIDGE

Of all card games, Bridge has probably been responsible for the most crookedness. The game, because of its partnership play, offers more opportunities for the amateur and skilled card cheat than any other card game. The most common cheating method at the game is signaling. A pair of cheats, merely by sorting and holding their hands in a certain way that shows length and strength of the suits they are holding, can get away with murder.

The biggest single loss in any Bridge investigation that I have conducted was $150,000. This amount was lost by a California husband-and-wife Bridge team over a three-week period. Their opponents, a former pair of Bridge masters, turned out to be a pair of signaling cheats. The stakes started at 10¢ a point and eventually were increased to $5 a point. A gain of 5,000 points at $5 a point is $25,000.

Most Bridge players believe that cheating is impossible when three players are known to be honest even if the fourth player is a card cheat. The fact is that one skilled card cheat can lone-wolf any Bridge table very profitably. All the crooked card moves described under Cheating at Private Card Games (Chapter 26) including marked cards, second dealing stacking and others are used to cheat at Bridge.

It was mentioned earlier that of the more than 1,000 Bridge tournaments played annually in this country, few if any are completed without one or more incidents in which a team appeals to the tournament directors for redress from some unfair practice committed by an opposing team. And much more tournament cheating takes place but goes undetected by the players. I know because I have seen it.

Bridge is the game where the woman card cheat has come into her own. The beauty of signaling by a woman is that she can get away with countless unnecessary gestures such as fooling with her hair, getting her makeup out of her handbag and settling her dress, and under cover of these apparently normal feminine movements keep signaling her partner.

Following is a sample series of finger signals used by many top male and female Bridge cheats:

1. When sorting his cards, at his last sort the cheat holds the fifth card from the right between his thumb and index fingers with just the index finger showing over the back of the card prior to pushing it down among the other cards to indicate to the cheat's partner that he is holding five clubs.

2. Two fingers showing holding the sixth card from the right means the cheat is holding six diamonds.

3. Three fingers showing holding the seventh card from the right indicates seven hearts.

4. Four fingers showing holding the fifth card from the right shows the cheat holds four spades.

5. The sixth card from the right protruding slightly above the others but not held by the fingers indicates the cheat holds six no-trump.

During the play of the hand, when the cheat wants his partner cheat to lead a specific suit, he employs the same finger movements as described above when playing to the trick with the exception of no-trump which he indicates by a slight hesitation before laying the card on the table.

In August 1961, as gambling advisor to the United States Senate Permanent Subcommittee on investigating gambling and crime in the United States, I watched as an electronic device used to cheat at Bridge, called a radio cue prompter, was demonstrated to the committee. Read into the *Congressional Record* at the time was an ad from a crooked gambling supply house which described this prompter as follows: "Not to be confused with many inferior units now on the market. This item is the ultimate in precision electronics and enables two people to cue each other, such as actors on a stage, mental reading, etc. Using these two miniature units and a dot-dash system, you can carry on a conversation with your partner in any card game. No wires, all self-contained, card-pack size. Full instructions with every order. Guaranteed the best. Longer distance than many." Senate testimony further revealed that the electronic company in question had sold several hundred of these gadgets in 1960. Since that time, it's anybody's guess how many thousands have been sold and how many are in use today.

In August 1949 I was hired by one of Hollywood's biggest movie moguls to check out a swank West Coast Bridge club where he said he had lost a quarter of a million dollars playing Bridge in a one-year period. My investigation revealed that the Bridge club was as crooked as an electronic corkscrew, and its yearly take from Hollywood celebrities ran into the millions. The club was owned and operated by several Las Vegas gamblers who employed a former movie actor as host. The Bridge club harbored ten tables and no matter at which table the Bridge player sat, he was sure to be clipped with a radio cue prompter.

The swindle was accomplished as follows: Two player card cheats were aided by a third, unseen confederate who operated a radio cue prompter from the room above the club. The Bridge club was rigged up as follows: Ten small camouflaged holes had been drilled from the floor above and through the club's ceiling; each hole was situated directly above a Bridge table. Each hole, known as a "peek joint," contained the eye of a stationary telescope that when looked through by the confederate above revealed each player's hand. In addition, a secret listening device made it possible for the crook above to hear the bidding of the players below. The additional equipment involved a radio cue prompter comprised of three miniature electronic units: one transmitter and two receivers. Each player cheat had a receiver strapped to his bare leg, hidden by his trousers. The cheat confederate above scanned the players' hands through the telescope and directed the cheat's play below by making use of the transmitter, which sent the desired information by transmitting a small electric shock to the leg of each player cheat. I had not completed my investigation when a three-page picture story showing five pictures of me appeared in *Life* magazine describing various cheating methods at Bridge, Poker and Gin Rummy. It was apparent that the operators of the Bridge club read the article and recognized me by my pictures in *Life* because when I arrived at the club several days later, the only cheating evidence that remained was the holes in the ceiling. The crooks had left in a hurry.

In the late 1960s the American team entry in the World's Duplicate Bridge Championship Tournament held in Buenos Aires, Argentina, accused the British team of cheating by making use of a series of hand signals. Do you know what? The signals mentioned were identical to the hand signals I exposed in the August 9, 1949, issue of *Life* magazine.

The late Nick "the Greek" Dandolos, the most famous gambler of the past 30 years, was once cheated of $500,000 with the same above-described device, the radio cue prompter, at a two-week session of Gin Rummy. The game took place at the poolside of the famous Flamingo Hotel casino on the Las Vegas Strip. Nick and the Gin Rummy cheat who fleeced him were attired in bathing suits and the cheat's accomplice with telescope and radio cue prompter operated from a hotel room overlooking the pool. The player cheat's radio receiver was hidden under his bathing suit. Incidentally, the table and chairs were fastened to the pool's concrete floor to prevent Nick the Greek from moving his Gin Rummy hand out of range of the telescope.

The most publicized radio cue prompter cheating incident of all time came to light in the middle 1960s when the court testimony of several Hollywood celebrities described how they were fleeced of hundreds of thousands of dollars playing Bridge and Gin Rummy at a famous club in Los Angeles. This cheating episode made newspaper headlines across the country for weeks. The hole in the ceiling incident and the radio cue prompter explained earlier were again put to work by a number of Las Vegas gamblers. Several perpetrators of this swindle were later convicted and received long jail sentences.

Bridge and Gin Rummy cheats who operate in hotel rooms build their "peek joints" by cutting out a small square from the top of a door of a closet or adjoining room and replacing the missing square with a two-way mirror which to the unsuspecting victim appears as a hanging glass painting. The player cheat's confederate hides in a closet or room, sees through the two-way-glass peek joint and transmits the cheating information by a radio cue prompter to his accomplice who is wearing a hidden receiver. When a peek joint is not available, Bridge cheats armed with radio cue prompter receivers receive signals describing their opponents' hands from a confederate cheat in the room armed with a transmitter. This confederate usually acts the part of a non-player waiting for a seat.

Just to illustrate that a top notch sleight-of-hand card cheat can do just about as he pleases in a Bridge game, I'll repeat a story from my autobiography *The Odds Against Me*, where I discuss a performance of mine attended by two hundred persons including President Franklin D. Roosevelt, Governor A. Harry Moore of New Jersey and Mayor Frank Hague of Jersey City.

I ended my performance that evening by playing two Bridge hands against Governor Moore and Mayor Hague—while President Roosevelt and the assembled guests watched in silence. Two regulation 52-card Bridge decks were produced by Mayor Hague. I shuffled the blue-backed deck and the governor shuffled the red-backed deck. After several shuffles I offered the blue-backed deck to Mayor Hague to cut, which he did. I then instructed the governor to deal out four Bridge hands, first hand to me, second to the mayor, third to my dummy and the fourth and last hand to himself. When I exposed my hand it was found to contain 13 Spades—a cinch grand slam.

For the second Bridge hand the Mayor handed me the red-backed deck to deal. The deck had previously been shuffled by the governor and cut by the mayor. While I was dealing out the four Bridge hands I bid seven no-trump. The hand was played to a finish and I made my bid—another grand slam.

29.
Gin Rummy

My private card game survey reveals that Rummy with its 46 million adherents is the second most popular card game in America. There are a hundred or more games in the Rummy family, some of which are Gin Rummy, Canasta, Six- and Seven-Card Knock Rummy, Skarney, 500 Rummy, Fortune and Continental. The most popular of all rummy games is Gin.

My survey also shows that of the 90 million adult card players, 20 million men and 8 million women prefer Gin Rummy to any other card game, and 7 million men and 4 million women of the remaining 62 million admit to playing Gin Rummy occasionally. This total of 39 million (27 million men and 12 million women) regular and occasional Gin Rummy players makes Gin the most popular *head-to-head* (two-handed) card game in the world.

My survey further reveals that about 20%, or $30 billion, of the $150 billion private card game gambling handle is wagered at Gin Rummy each year.

The reasons for the popularity of Gin Rummy are: (1) it is easy to learn and simple to play; (2) it is one of the finest head-to-head games; (3) it is fast moving and has plenty of surprising and unexpected results; (4) it has such great competitive and sustained action that it will hold one's interest without a penny at stake; (5) all players think they are good at the game—when they lose they attribute it to bad luck, when they win it's skill; (6) although Gin is basically a two-handed game, it is also an excellent game for three, four, six or eight players.

Gin requires far less skill than two-handed Pinochle or Klob (Kalabrias) and is favored by the less skilled players because they can win against a skilled opponent more often than they would at Pinochle or Klob. Even the poor Gin player becomes convinced that he plays well; in no other card game do you find so many self-styled local champions.

Although Gin Rummy gambling is illegal in all states, Nevada permits the annual running of the Las Vegas Gin Rummy Tournament because part of the proceeds go to local charities. This tournament was originated by a group of Las Vegas hotel and casino owners who realized that most Gin players, unlike Bridge players, are by nature gamblers who crave action and therefore also play Black Jack, Craps or the one-armed bandits.

The Las Vegas hotel casinos underwrote the expenses of the first tournament in 1957, which was first advertised as the National Gin Rummy Tournament. This event, as expected, helped the local charities and brought additional business into the Strip hotels and casinos. Since then it has been an annual event, with the Las Vegas hotel casino group underwriting the overhead. It is now called the International Gin Rummy Tournament.

Generally speaking, the tournament is a knock-down drag-out elimination contest; in the opening rounds of the first two days each contestant plays a 250-point game with each of 16 different opponents. The winners of 13 or more games go on to more advanced rounds. With such a setup, luck is much more important than skill, which is what the tournament sponsors intended.

In Las Vegas there is also an annual "Cardcutta Sweepstakes," where you can "buy a player," similar to a Calcutta in golf (see page 137).

But the Las Vegas hotel casinos select the slow season for this event and they care little or nothing who is crowned the World's Gin Rummy Champion. All they are interested in is that the tournament has proven a great boon to casino business in general. Several Gin Rummy contestants recently lost $250,000 at the Craps tables during their time off from tournament play. The annual Gin Rummy Tournament has proven itself so profitable to Las Vegas casinos that they have branched out and have added to their schedule an annual World Series Poker Tournament (which of all things involves the playing of Klondike or Hold-'em, (variants of Spit in the Ocean), a North American Backgammon Championship and a World Bridge Tournament to help increase their table action during the slow season.

HISTORY OF GIN RUMMY

When Gin Rummy suddenly surged to the front in 1938, most dictionaries and almost all Bridge writers jumped to the conclusion that the game was an entirely new form of Rummy. Most present-day Bridge writers and game authors erroneously credit a New York Bridge expert with the invention of Gin Rummy in 1909.

The truth is that game-rule books published in the early 1900s describe a game called Gin Poker which is almost identical to the present Gin Rummy. As for the origin of Gin Poker, in some other country there may be obscure records of some very early game resembling our Rummy games but failing that, my opinion is that the origin of the Rummy games was Whiskey Poker; a peculiarly American variant of Poker. (Poker, as stated in Chapter 27, is probably an adaptation of the ancient Persian game Âs, or Âs-Nâs.)

The tenth (1864) edition of *The American Hoyle* gives these rules for Whiskey Poker:

> Five cards are dealt to each player, one at a time, and an extra hand is dealt on the table, called the "widow."
>
> The eldest hand then examines his cards and decides he has a strong hand; he passes. If not, he may take the widow. Each player in rotation has a chance to take the widow.
>
> When a player takes the widow, he must place his discarded hand face up on the table.

And then comes the crucial detail of the play that is responsible for all Rummy games. The discarded hand is face up in the center of the table, and . . .

> The next player to the left [i.e., from the player who took the widow] selects from it [i.e., the discarded hand] that card which suits him best in making up his hand, and so on around the board, each player discarding a card and picking up another one until someone is satisfied, which he signifies by knocking on the table. If any player knocks before the widow is taken, the widow is turned face up, and each, from him who knocks, has but one draw.

That is the origin of our Rummy games.

Why was it called Whiskey Poker? The 1880 *American Hoyle* says: "The game is often played for refreshments." Most card playing and gambling circa 1864 took place in saloons, and it was natural that this variety of Poker, in which the drinks were the prize, should bear their name. Hundreds of variations followed and slowly Gin Rummy began to evolve. Here, for example, are the rules for Rum Poker:

Each player was dealt ten cards, and each player drew cards until he had 15 points or less in his hand. He could then lay down his entire hand, showing the combinations he could meld and counting the pips of the cards that didn't connect with anything. Thus a player might hold three kings and a run of four cards in sequence, his odd cards being a six, three and deuce of sundry suits. The *deadwood* (unmatched cards) counted 11. All other players laid down their hands now, and the winner collected the difference between his deadwood total and theirs. Sometimes, of course, another player's deadwood was a point or so below the claimant's. The other player got paid.

That's coming pretty close to Rummy. And then, in the early 1900s, along came a third variety of Poker, Gin Poker. Look at these rules:

A standard pack of 52 cards was used. The game was for two players. Game was 100 points. Each player was dealt ten cards, one to each alternately. The 21st card was turned face up. Each player could pick off the top card of the discard pile or take a card off the top of the stock, then discard a card. The object of the game was to get sequences of three or more in a suit or three or four of a kind. As soon as deadwood totaled 10 or less the player could call for a showdown, and had to announce the amount of his deadwood and show his hand, laying the combination aside. If an opponent had less deadwood than the caller (the present game's "knocker") he and not the caller got paid. Not only that—he got a 10-point penalty from the caller.

Why was the name of that game, Gin Poker (obviously the game of Rummy), eventually changed to Rummy? By the time it developed, in the first years of this century, the Poker family had more variations than any other family of games. Here are just a few, a very few, of the games that bore the name "Poker" at that period: Draw Poker, Stud Poker, Freeze-out, Gin Poker, Rum Poker, Jackpot, Whiskey Poker, Tigers, Table Stakes, Deuces Wild, Blazer, Bluff, Double Up, Mistigris and Patience Poker. That's what I said: Patience Poker. You've played it often, probably within the past week, and always with yourself. It's called Solitaire too, as you'll see if you'll examine its basic structure and principles. More than 100 games of the Patience family are played today. (*See Scarne's Encyclopedia of Games.*)

Card games are tribes that break off from the main body and drift away into a separate existence of their own, evolving their own laws, bearing new generations, hammering out their own morals and language and atmosphere. Rum Poker, in the course of its pilgrimage up through the strata of society, must first have dropped its tawdry family name; and then, I suppose, people fell to calling it by the diminutive "Rummy" so as to make it clear that they weren't talking about—or playing for—vulgar booze. But none has prospered like the variation called Gin Rummy. The essential difference between Gin Poker and Gin Rummy is in the scoring. Gin Poker was played the same as present-day Gin Rummy except that it did not possess game bonus, box bonuses or the shutout or schneider bonus.

WHAT EVERY PLAYER SHOULD KNOW ABOUT GIN RUMMY

Much of the Gin Rummy strategy and card lore which follows was first published in *Scarne on Cards*. In the past twenty years, this information has converted more run-of-the-mill Gin players into winning players than anything else. That's why I also include it here. (See *Scarne on Cards* for the rules of how to play Gin Rummy. If you don't know the rules, you're not prepared to delve into the finer points of Gin!)

Before I discuss the strategy of the game, let me dispel at once the popular misconception that "Gin is a game of pure chance." Nothing could be further from the truth.

In any two-handed card game which combines chance and skill, the more skillful player will emerge winner in the long run. As proof, I cite the fact that in the past few years, advanced Gin players have increased the original 100 points required to win to 150 points in order to better their chance of winning. So if you believe your opponent plays a better game of Gin than you do, you can even things up somewhat by insisting on the rule that 100 points wins the game.

Don't misunderstand me. I'm not saying that Gin Rummy is one of the really great card games of skill. It is not. But there is a considerable element of skill involved, and if you are losing consistently you are not as unlucky as you may think. You're being outplayed.

Or perhaps you're being cheated? The first thing a Gin player should learn is to protect himself against Gin Rummy crooks. Take time to study the text that follows.

When 150 points is considered as completing the game, gin, underknock and box bonuses are 25 points each; game bonus and shutout bonus are 150 points each.

CHEATING AT GIN RUMMY

Gin Rummy is the card cheat's paradise. Because Gin is mostly a head-to-head game, it is more susceptible to chicanery than card games involving more than two players. Any player who becomes known as a "high-rolling Gin player" eventually attracts the card cheats as honey does the bees. The structure of Gin makes it easier to cheat than most other card games. And because the cheat usually clips his victim in privacy you seldom read or hear about a crooked Gin game.

I know of dozens of big-money Gin games in which a player lost $50,000 or more in the privacy of his own home or office. I know a New York City garment manufacturer who lost over a million dollars at Gin in a couple of years. Just how much of this was lost to cheats I don't know. But I do know that a nationally known (among gamblers) card cheat fleeced him out of $100,000 in a month's play in his private office. P.S. The manufacturer even served this invited guest refreshments.

The best Gin player in the country doesn't stand a winning chance against even the average gin cheat. So if you want to play winning Gin you must first learn to protect yourself from the sharks.

I do not recommend that you regard all Gin players as crooks or potential crooks. The overwhelming majority of Gin players are, or mean to be, honest. Most citizens are honest too, but we still need police forces and an FBI. And I think that a card player's equipment, especially if he plays for cash, should include a working knowledge of how to protect himself against the crook who believes that all honest players are chumps asking to be fleeced. I've already covered the basic card-cheating methods in Chapter 26; but certain larcenous techniques peculiar to Gin Rummy follow.

Bottom Stack

After a hand has been played and it is the cheater's turn to deal, he scoops up the cards and leaves an entire meld, usually four of a kind, on the bottom of the pack. Then he gives the pack a riffle shuffle that does not disturb the bottom four cards.

He cuts about one third of the pack off the top, puts it on the bottom, and offers the pack to be cut. Most players cut at about the center. This puts the wanted meld near the top and each player in the deal receives two of the four of a kind!

The cheat knows two of the cards in your hand, and you don't know that he has two of the same value. Later in the play you will, usually, discard one of those cards, giving him his meld. Or he will throw you one, proceeding to underknock your knock by laying off that fourth card on your meld.

This is one of the most common of all cheating devices in Gin, and one of the most effective, because it is impossible to accuse anyone of resorting to it. An honest player might even shuffle and cut the cards the same way without intending anything crooked.

You can protect yourself against the bottom stack by shuffling the cards before the dealer shuffles. If you use the Gin Rummy rules in *Scarne on Cards,* which permit this, neither you nor your opponent can be embarrassed if you ask for a shuffle whenever you please.

51-Card Deck

This may seem amateurish, but it is one of the most common and least hazardous cheating devices. When detected it can be made to look like an honest error.

When he removes the new deck from the case, the cheat leaves one card behind. He knows what card that is.

The advantage appears trivial. Is it? Let's see. Suppose the card left unnoticed in the box is the eight of diamonds. What can it do for him?

First, he will rarely try to make a meld of eights, because he knows that the chances are only 25% of normal. Second, he knows—and you don't—that the chance of getting a diamond meld in a sequence involving the eight of diamonds is zero. There are three such melds: the 6–7–8, the 7–8–9 and the 8–9–10. With the three melds of eights in which the diamond would figure, this makes 6 dead melds out of a total of 96 melds in the game. This is a terrific advantage.

There is also a psychological throw-off. If, during the play, you find the missing card in the box, the cheat promptly blames you. "Why," he asks, if he knows his business, "didn't you take them all out when we started?" The chances are that, having forgotten by this time who did remove the deck, you will mumble your apologies.

You can protect yourself against this ruse by counting the cards before you start to play. More candid yet, look in the box.

No Cut

Some cheats will keep a certain group of cards at the top of the pack, shuffle some cards over them and then deal without offering the deck for the cut. The effect on the game is the same as in the bottom stack.

If you ask for a cut they blandly murmur, "Sorry." If you don't, you're a dead duck.

When the cards have been cut into two blocks, but the cut has not yet been completed, some sharpers will lean back, light a cigarette, then simply pick up the cards and put them back as they were before. The lapse of time and the intervening stage business may make you forget which block should go on which. If caught at it, they apologize for the error. Don't take your eye off your game.

Dealing from Half the Deck

When the cheat knows what the top cards are, he shuffles, you cut, and instead of completing the cut he picks up the lower portion of the deck and deals from it. Then he completes the cut by putting the remaining cards of the lower pile on the top.

It is a casual little informality, but the cheat now knows precisely what cards are going to appear, and when, in the stock.

Don't allow anyone to deal from half the pack. Insist on the completion of the cut before the deal begins.

Of course, some cheats have an answer for that, too. When they carry the bottom half over onto the top half in completing the cut, they do not quite square the deck. A tiny step is left, showing them where to find the cards they want. Insist that the pack be squared before the deal.

Signaling

He may look like an authentic kibitzer. But when you're playing for money, watch him. Satisfy yourself that no onlooker with access to your hand is signaling. Signaling is often done, both amateurishly and expertly. It is easy and deadly effective at Gin Rummy because all that your opponent needs to find out is whether you have a high or low count in unmatched cards.

A well conceived signal system is hard to detect. If you entertain the merest suspicion that signals are being passed, play your next few hands too close to your vest for the kibitzer to see. If your luck improves—Q.E.D.

Peeking at Two Cards

This is one of the most flagrant violations in the game. Reaching for his draw from the stock, the cheat affects to fumble and lifts two cards instead of his one. At a critical stage of the play that glance at your next card is all he needs to know.

To protect players against this violation, whether by design or by accident, I suggest that you spread the stock fanwise. This may not completely eradicate the danger, but it will minimize it. And if the violation does occur, the rules of Gin Rummy provide that the player who has committed it must show the card he just picked to his opponent.

By thus canceling his advantage, this will temporarily make an honest man of the cheat.

Recognizable Cards

Some amateur cheats will bend the corner of certain cards so as to be able to spot them in play. This is not a marked card in the professional sense of the term, it is a cheating device of, by and for the cheat and against the decent player. Don't play with an old or defaced pack of playing cards.

Cheating on the Count

The practitioners of this crude larceny will keep a fair score sheet—until the count gets too close for comfort. Then, knowing that 1 point is often the difference between winning and losing a game with its big-money bonuses, they will miscall their points in unmatched cards and, holding them in their hands, fan them casually before you. They will then toss them back onto the deck. To prevent this, insist on the rule that unmatched cards be placed face up on the table, separate from the melds—and count them yourself.

Also, check the addition of points, not only at the end of the game but also when each hand's score is entered; 87 plus 26 might be entered as 103 instead of 113. And it's easy to be an even 100 points out of the way when adding up a long score. Added wrong? Oops, sorry!

Shuffling Cards Face Up

Many amateur cheats, and some honest bunglers, make it a habit to shuffle the cards face up or to shuffle them edgewise to the table in such a way that the faces can be seen. Maybe it's just a carry-over from Solitaire or some other game in which the shuffle is immaterial. But maybe it's cold-blooded robbery. Demand of any such player that he shuffle the cards properly.

Hiding a Card

This is about as old, and fully as sandlot, as baseball's hidden-ball trick. Like the hidden-ball trick, it has a way of working entirely too often. After your opponent has knocked, he lays down his melds, face up, just as the rules provide. His unmatched cards he likewise lays down, face up, right there in front of you.

But under his meld he has concealed an unmatched high card.

It works, unless you glance again at his cards and detect the shortage. Always count your opponent's cards to certify that he has exposed ten of them face up.

The Counterfeit Meld

Do you examine your opponent's melds closely? If not, you tempt him to slip in the queen of clubs between the king, jack and ten of spades. He'll put them down close together and with a little hocus-pocus about his other cards and "How many did I get you for?" distract your attention and get away with it. How many times have you made a similar error yourself when first glancing at your cards? Watch it.

Protection Against a Crooked Gin Deal

Whenever you play Gin Rummy make it a habit to reshuffle the deck when it is offered to you for a cut. And when it comes to cutting, you not only always cut the cards, but use the Scarne Cut (page 656). However, it must be understood, of course, that the dealer is entitled to the last shuffle if he so desires.

Such extra precautionary measures on your part may be construed as a mistrustful gesture by some players, but it pays off in the long run by preventing a great deal of manipulative skulduggery.

How to Beat a Gin Rummy Hustler

Now let's look at the Gin hustler, the character who only plays with opponents who know less about the game than he does. He wins because he possesses a superior knowledge of Gin and knows it. Much of the time he is the guy who starts the game with some chump, usually a friend. He can afford to neglect his work because his winnings make Gin Rummy his real vocation.

A hustler who gambles with friends who know little or nothing about the finer points of the game cannot really be called an honest player, even though he does not resort to cheating. He gets the same end result as the cheat: his opponent always loses.

There are two ways to beat a Gin hustler: stop playing with him or improve your skill to equal or surpass his. If you choose the latter alternative, you can find all the required information on how to beat a Gin Rummy hustler at his own game in the section below.

HOW TO PLAY WINNING GIN RUMMY

At the very outset, I make this promise: No matter how good a Gin player you are, this section will improve your game. It is a collection of tips and hints that I've gathered over the years from the country's crack players. This advice will center on Gin Rummy, but most of it can be put to profitable use in any game of the Rummy family.

Let me say this right now: these games are not played for fun only. They are played for money. Card games that lack the gambling element, the profit motive, don't attain mass popularity. You may not construe it as gambling when you play for small beers, and your wife or mother might be horrified if it were suggested that when she plays for the patchwork quilt at the Tuesday Afternoon she's gambling. But the gambling and gambling incentive are there.

Why do some players win more games than other players do? Why do some players lose constantly to certain opponents, yet win constantly from others? Why are some normally intelligent persons very very bad Rummy players? Is it true that good players don't play the same kind of game? That each one has a little special knowledge—his own system—of the play of the cards?

Watching thousands of Rummy players and tens of thousands of Gin games in the last 20 years, I've made it my business to observe the small mannerisms of winning and losing competitors, to cross-examine hundreds of experts, to measure the difference imposed on the play by the stakes of the game; I have observed not only that sober citizens do indeed bet $10,000 on a single game, but *how* they bet it.

Every player who is a consistent winner has little tricks of his own. There are, in the mass, scores of such tricks, developed by trial and error into a very substantial body of learning. No one player has mastered all of them. Perhaps no one player can. But I'm going to tell you about them.

First, what is this card sense? Its components are simply stated. Card sense is knowing what to do and when. At Gin Rummy, should you go down now or on the next pick? Should you take your chance and go for Gin or wait and see if you can't *underknock* your opponent when he goes down? Should you break up this pair and try for that sequence? Should you throw away this card, or will it help your opponent? To be a good card player, to have good card sense, you must have good reasons for making any of these decisions—and reasoning is the application of intelligence.

Card sense requires an understanding that card games are based on mathematics. The players who really appreciate this are the players who win. Card games are based on the fact that the pack contains 52 cards running in sequences of 13 from ace to king in four suits: clubs, hearts, diamonds and spades. All card players know this, but only a small minority really understand its importance. In the games of Rummy there are 96 three-card melds. There are 52 melds of three-of-a-kind, i.e., cards of the same rank: three aces, three deuces and so on. There are 44 melds of three cards of the same suit in sequence, i.e., 3–4–5 of hearts, 9–10–jack of spades and the like.

After you have formed a three-card meld it is twice as hard to extend three of a kind to four of a kind as it is to extend a sequence. For a sequence meld can be extended at either end (except ace–2–3 and jack–queen–king), whereas three of a kind can be bettered only one way. Besides, a sequence meld of four cards can be extended into five, and one of five into one of six; but four cards of equal rank have no further possibilities. They're dead.

Let's look further into the mathematics of the game. Take the four aces in your hand. These can be formed into four three-card melds:

1. Aces of spades, hearts, diamonds.
2. Aces of spades, hearts, clubs.
3. Aces of spades, clubs, diamonds.
4. Aces of hearts, clubs, diamonds.

But if one of those aces is dead—discarded or held by an opponent in his hand—the chance of making up a meld of three aces is only 25% of the probability if all four were alive.

Not many players carry it to this extent, but even the beginner practices to a degree what I've been preaching. When he holds a pair of tens and knows that there are two more tens in his opponent's hand or in the stock, he says that his two tens are alive—and he is applying mathematics, whether he realizes it or not.

The Gin Rummy player *must* be able to visualize and memorize all the possible melds in a hand the instant he picks it up. He must be able to calculate at sight the probabilities for his two of a kind, his two-card sequences; and he must not overlook any melds he may hold. There is a way—a method devised by a famous Gin Rummy player who has won thousands at the game—of cultivating this knack of forming mental pictures and avoiding fatal plays in the early stages of the game.

It is a way of picking up cards which have just been dealt.

This splendid, ice-cold gambler never picks up his ten cards all at one time. It is impossible, he says, to impress them on the mind when they confront the eye in all their natural confusion. So he picks them up one at a time, sorting them as he goes, impressing them on his mind and marshaling them for his first play. Moving thus deliberately, he can appraise the odds on every possible combination of his cards; and, at the very least, he has them in orderly array when the time comes for him to make his first draw.

This is his secret. More players make their bad play at the start of the hand than at any other time. Never forget it—pick up your hand slowly and arrange it carefully. Think—first about your own resources and strategy, then about your opponent's.

THE SKILL

Gin is a game of deduction and counterdeduction. You must try to figure out what is in your opponent's hand so that (1) you won't give him any useful cards, and (2) you won't be holding cards for an impossible or unlikely meld.

Each upcard your opponent takes and each discard he makes is a clue to what is in his hand and what is not. The cards that are not discarded are clues also. As the play of the hand progresses, you know more and more about the cards he holds, and you get this information by what he has shown you in taking certain cards, in discarding certain cards, and in *not* taking or in *not* discarding certain other cards. This is the simple, obvious part of the game. You don't need me to tell you that the discard of a ten is dangerous if no tens have shown well along in the play of the hand; or that the discard of the ten of clubs is safe if the nine and the jack of clubs and two other tens have been discarded, or that the discard of the ten of clubs is dangerous if your opponent has taken the nine of clubs after the two other nines have been discarded. These are simple deductions.

But let's examine the case of the ten of clubs when your opponent has taken the nine of clubs and no other nines have shown, nor has the eight or seven of clubs. Was that nine for nines or for a club run? The inexpert player will say to himself, Can't tell yet so I'll hold on to it.

This increases his holding of unmatched cards and forces the discard of some other possibly dangerous or useful card. The expert player approaches the matter in a different way. He says to himself, This is a high card, quite useless to me. Can I be reasonably safe in discarding it? Could it form a meld of tens? No, two tens have been discarded. Will this add to opponent's club run, or was that nine of clubs for a meld of nines? Well, let's see what has happened with the eights. Opponent took the eight of diamonds and discarded the seven of diamonds. Therefore the eight of diamonds was taken for eights, including probably the eight of clubs. So, I'll discard the ten of clubs. True, the opponent may have four eights with a club run cutting through, but the greater probability by far is that he has eights and nines.

In other words, the expert player uses not only direct *positive* evidence but also indirect *probable* evidence, and all the previous play goes into the appraisal of the probability in each case. In this case, the seven of diamonds discard indicated that the ten of clubs was a reasonably safe play. That was not the only evidence, of course, but taken together with the other evidence it was the determining factor.

The expert player, then makes deductions not only from the cards he himself holds, but also from *every* card his opponent has taken or discarded.

However, *counterdeduction* is just as important as deduction. Bear in mind that while you are trying to find out what your opponent holds in his hand, he is trying to figure out what you hold. You can't help giving him some clues, but you must try to give him as few as possible. Also, in every possible way, you should try to deceive or confuse him by giving him false clues which lead him to make incorrect deductions, always remembering that, if he knows the game, he is also engaged in this counterdeduction and deception. If he isn't, you'll have a cinch.

Counterdeduction in Gin is an art. Its two major elements are *propaganda* and *false picking* (sometimes called *spitballing*). Conversation is the lesser part of propaganda, and many experts frown on it. Actually it is more effective for amusement and for the relief of the player's own nervous tension than for deception of the other player. But anyone who is good at it will affect his opponent's play occasion-

ally by complaining about his hand, by expressing dismay at some difficult discard, by exclaiming with surprise, "That one!" when the
opponent takes a discard, by an exclamation of satisfaction when picking a card off the stock. Theoretically such conversation will influence
the opponent to be either overoptimistic or unduly scared and thus
cause him to act unwisely. Feeling safe because he thinks you have a
poor hand, he may knock with 7 and be trapped into an underknock.
Or, being scared, he may break up the two kings he has been holding
and thus either give you the card you want or ruin his own chances
for high-card melds that are just about due to come in.

The handling of the hand, however, is the better part of propaganda. What you do with the card you take off the stock is carefully
noted by your opponent. If you discard it immediately your opponent
knows you haven't improved your hand. I don't say you should never
do this. Rather, when you want your opponent to be cautious, when
you want him to believe you are in good shape, it's important to do it a
few times. Then, when you take a card and put it carefully between
two other cards in your hand, he may decide that you have completed
a meld. Conversely, when you want him to be overconfident, be careful, when picking a good card, to avoid making this evident to your
opponent. An occasional shifting of your cards will lead him to think
that you have improved your hand; don't shift if you don't want him to
know of an improvement.

Every element of your behavior during the play of the hand is a
clue to a clever opponent. If you show that you are worried and unhappy about your cards, or, on the other hand, cheerful and confident,
your opponent will, consciously or subconsciously, act accordingly. So
remember that he is playing against *you* as well as your cards. Avoid
giving him any good clues. Either give him false clues or, if you think
you can do it, play it "dead-pan." That's difficult. You must be sure, as
you place each and every card you pick in your hand, to deliberate
just about the same amount of time for each card and then discard,
showing no change of expression throughout the play.

You, on the other hand, may get clues from the way your opponent
handles his cards, provided he hasn't read this book. Observe his placement of cards. Is he aware of the necessity of concealing the development of his hand?

Let's say he doesn't seem to be. He doesn't shift his cards around,
he discards picks immediately, and in general is playing a straightfor-
ward game, unaware of the fact that you are on the *qui vive* for hints
and information. Let's act on that. He picks a card, puts it on the left
end of his hand and discards the second card from the right end, the
king of hearts. It's a fair assumption that the end card on the right is

another king or the queen of hearts. Okay. You knock with 9, confident that he has at least a useless king or queen. Were you right? Yes. Continue to act on this weakness. Were you wrong? Study his technique a little more and see if you can find a dependable hole in his play. Feel him out like a quarterback observing and testing an opposing line.

Now let's get back to the start of the game. When arranging cards in your hand, put together:

1. Your melds.

2. Your unmatched cards according to suits.

3. Your possible melds; that is, two cards of the same rank or suit sequence.

Group your two-way combinations in some logical way, so that they can be recognized easily. If you have the six of diamonds, six of spades and seven of spades, put them together in that order so that if another six or an end card of the spade sequence turns up it will fit tidily into your holding. But—

4. Avoid having a regular high-to-low order for your ten cards. Don't put your high combinations on one end and your low ones on the other. Keep combinations together, but mix high and low combinations.

After having arranged your cards so as to impress them on your memory, mix them up during play (as all expert Bridge players do). Don't keep your melds or possible melds together; this may give your opponent the same kind of information that you are attempting to gather from the way he arranges his cards.

TAKING OR PASSING THE FIRST CARD

Let's say the upcard (assuming you're playing Turn-up Gin) is the three of hearts. It does not give you a meld. Does that mean that you should pass it without question? Not at all. It may be worth taking if it helps your hand, even though it does not give you a meld. If you can reduce your hand by getting rid of a useless high card or if taking that three of hearts gives you a likely combination—say you have the four of hearts and the three of clubs—it may be well worth while because you have the extra advantage of deceiving or puzzling your opponent. Are you losing a turn, giving up a chance to pick a really helpful card by taking a slightly helpful one? No. You have your choice of passing and not helping your hand at all or helping it a little, confusing your opponent a little, and perhaps also depriving him of a chance to improve his hand.

Remember, however, that when your opponent is first, he may also be taking the first card to deceive you.

WHEN TO GO DOWN

There can be no definite instruction at this point without ifs, ands and buts. All things being equal, it is best to go down as soon as you can. Don't let the extra reward in points, thrill and personal satisfaction trap you into waiting for Gin when your knocking hand is an almost certain winner.

The major factor on this point that could influence your decision is the score. Remember that the big reward is the game bonus of 150 points, and the box bonuses of 25 points each are only slightly less important. (Box bonuses often add up to more than the game bonus.) Always keep the score in mind and consider the possibilities and probabilities in the light of the score. This is doubly important in the case of Partnership Gin. If your partner has won 25 points and you can knock even with as much as 10, the thing to do is knock. You can't lose the box even if underknocked (with 10 or 15 points for underknock) and you'll probably win some points. But if you keep playing and are ginned, you can lose 30 points *and* the box (if the gin bonus is 25). The same principle applies with other variations of the scoring system.

Get the box. That's worth 25 points. If waiting for Gin puts the box in jeopardy, the odds are almost sure to be against you when you figure that you are staking that 25 points against the possible extra winnings to be gained by going gin.

On the other hand, if your partner has lost 30 points and you have good possibilities for getting gin, it is probably worth trying for gin instead of knocking because then you get the extra reward of the 25 points for the box as well as the gin points to outweigh the possibility of losing the hand or being ginned. However, if your partner's loss puts the game in danger (your opponent being close to or over 200), then discretion is the better part of valor. Get a few points if you can and save the game.

It may seem elementary to pay attention to the score, but it is amazing how often failure to do so makes the difference between a big winner and a big loser.

This principle applies in even greater degree in Hollywood Gin and in Extra Bonus or Kisses Gin.

You wouldn't give 2 to 1 that a tossed coin will come up heads. Then don't give similar wrong odds by holding a knock hand for gin. Even if your chances of getting gin are very good, count the stakes first: What is there to gain? What is there to lose? If you stand to lose more than you can gain, you may be giving 2 to 1 on heads. If you stand to gain more than you can lose, you may be getting 2 to 1 on heads.

In Extra Bonus Partnership Gin, don't try to get gin (and thereby risk being ginned) when it is hopeless to recoup your partner's loss. If you can't win the boxes for gin, don't risk losing more boxes. There's no percentage in that.

THE KNOCK RESERVE

Keep a few low cards and try to get three or four that total 10 or less. Then if you get two three-card runs or a three-card and a four-card run, you will be able to knock. If the knock point is 2 and you get a deuce or an ace, don't discard it. Save it so that if you fill your other runs you will be able to go down and avoid being frustrated by picking a series of high cards while your opponent is steadily improving his hand.

HOLDING HIGH CARDS OR LOW CARDS

The only thing I can say about this is: Don't have a set policy on this point. Don't become known either as player who always holds high cards or one who always discards high cards. Play your hand for what it's worth. In general, the advantages of high cards (they are most likely to be discarded by your opponent) are matched by their disadvantages: they cost more and they delay your reaching a knock point.

But if you are holding high cards bear in mind—

KEEPING UNDER

When your opponent's point total is close to game you must be extra careful about the unmatched-card point total in your hand. You must try to *keep under*. That means that you must reduce your point total so that, if possible, even if your opponent goes gin you will still be under. Short of that, try to get your total low enough so that a knock will not win the game for your opponent. I agree that there are times when it is a better bet for reduction to hold those two tens with the probability of getting the third one than to discard them in favor of a five and a six. But, in most cases, if you are aware of the necessity for reduction, you will be able to discard high cards as safely as low cards. Also, there are times when your chances of getting low-card melds are just as good as your chances of high-card melds.

Just being aware of the necessity of keeping under will improve your winning chances by 25 to 33⅓%. Except in expert play, my observation is that every third or fourth final hand of a game is lost because of the avoidable failure to keep under.

TIPS ON DISCARDS

Your first discard is, or ought to be, the most difficult to decide. You have no idea what your opponent is holding and looking for. Since the principle is to discard that card least likely to form a meld, you base your judgment on the upcard and the cards you hold.

You are undecided whether to discard this lone king of spades or this lone ten of spades? It's advisable to throw the king. Why? Because there are two ways less to form a meld in a spade sequence using the king than there are when using the ten. The only cards with which the king is useful are the jack and the queen. But the ten will make a meld with 8–9, 9–jack or jack-queen. That's the principle. It holds for every successive play in the game.

To the player with a developed card sense, the first few plays at Gin will always seem the most dangerous. After a few plays it is fairly easy for a good Gin player to recognize a live card—one that can be used by his opponent to form a meld—or a dead card. He deduces this by remembering the discards and whatever upcards the opponent has picked and by watching the shifting array of cards in his opponent's hand.

The more discards you can remember during the play of a box, the better are your chances of winning. This kind of memory must be developed and trained; but one thing the player *must* remember from the very start; the discards which the opponent has picked up. If he can't do that, he can't play Gin; he's playing a game of pure chance, a sort of complicated, bothersome game of showdown.

Throw an opponent two cards in succession that form part of one meld only when you have reason to believe that you can underknock his ensuing knock.

TAKING AN UPCARD THAT DOES NOT HELP

As for speculation in upcards, that's up to you. Some experts strongly advise against picking up a discard unless it will round out an immediate meld. But I've seen excellent gin players snatch up a discard for no purpose except to keep an opponent from knocking—psychological warfare, the war of nerves. I've seen many a speculation end in disaster.

I don't think that any man is master of the game unless he knows how and when to speculate. It's part of bluffing. It's part of the great game of Gin.

One gambler of my acquaintance invariably picks up any upcard valued at 3 or less. His rationalization is:

1. If he should happen to get caught, his points in unmatched cards would be so low that they would profit his opponent little.

2. When he knocks with 10 or less—with the aid of his opponent's low discards—he will tend to catch the opponent with higher unmatched cards. A hand deliberately reduced will average lower than a run-of-the-mill hand with its normal quota of sevens, nines and tens.

I've watched him play hundreds of games over a period of years, and I've just about come to agree with him that there's an advantage in picking up any card valued at 3 or less, except when it involves being compelled to discard a live card that may put your opponent gin.

Since we're speculating about speculation, you'd better hear the other side of the argument. This is the policy of another high-stakes gambler, a consistent winner.

"When I have a hand in which my unmatched cards total eleven or a little more," he told me, "and when I don't think my opponents can knock yet, I'll pick up a live picture-card discard."

That's called a false speculation—*false spec* is the professional idiom. The arguments in its favor are worth your closest attention.

Suppose you're holding a total of 11 points in unmatched cards: five of clubs, three of diamonds, two of spades and ace of hearts. You can't knock. You have to deduce from your opponent's behavior that he can't knock. To knock, you must get a card lower than a five.

Your opponent throws the live king of diamonds. You pick it up. What do you lose? One pick off the stock.

What do you gain? Well, you have probably convinced your opponent that you have just made a meld in kings or completed a sequence in diamonds. And now, if his hand contained two kings and he broke them up, he will suspect you of having a diamond run, and if he is holding the diamond sequence he will be confident that you are playing the kings. In any event, he will, from that point on, hold back his high diamonds or his kings. The chance that he will be throwing low cards—lower than the five—is greatly increased. And you are meanwhile taking your usual picks from the stock, minus the one you invested in the bluff.

When you do draw your knock card, or your opponent throws it to you, you discard the phony king and you catch him with a handful of high cards that otherwise he would have long since thrown away. And if your ruse fails, you lose only 5 points more than you would have lost otherwise.

But it works 9 out of 10 times. And it is still working when you take a picture card off the discard pile to form a genuine meld. For now your baffled opponent, remembering your false spec, will breezily proceed to throw gin-going picture cards at you.

Speculate high or speculate low? It's up to you.

DISCARDING

It is advisable, when possible, to discard a card of rank equal to one which your opponent has previously discarded. There are only four possible ways in which an equal-rank card can be used against you. Any other card can be used six ways in a meld—that is, unless you're holding *stoppers:* cards which will prevent a discard from being used in a meld by your opponent.

But when you throw a discard of rank equal to one previously discarded by your opponent, bear in mind that this may be precisely what he wanted you to do. He may have thrown the first of what is called a *salesman.* He may want your card of equal rank but in a different suit. All players use salesmen from time to time; it is the job of card sense to detect the little fellow and resist his blandishments.

When you decide to break up a pair and the other two cards of the same rank are alive and perhaps in your opponent's hand, don't talk about it. What he doesn't know can't hurt you. And maybe he won't know unless you tell him that all four cards are alive.

FATTENING

Sometimes it is wiser to discard a card that you know will add to your opponent's meld than any other card in your hand. If you know he has a four-card run, say 6–7–8–9, a fifth card probably won't help him much and it is extremely unlikely for him to go gin with two five-card runs. Even if you believe it is only a three-card run, it may be better to *fatten* him with a fourth card rather than give him an alternate card which may give him a new three-card run.

If he has picked the eight of clubs and you have the jack or even the ten, don't hold on to it indefinitely without considering the various possibilities. Did he take it for eights instead of a club run? If it is a club run, how far up does it go? Is it possible that another run has cut it off? He may have the 6–7–8–9 of clubs *and* two other nines. He wouldn't take the ten of clubs if you threw it, and you wouldn't be able to lay it off if he knocked.

Furthermore, when you are aiming for an underknock, fattening can be very useful. You can trap your opponent into going down by giving him that extra card that enables him to get under 10.

Conversely, be careful when you are being fattened. Will the extra card force you to discard a dangerous one and break up a good meld possibility? Is your opponent trying to trap you into knocking? When he gives you that ten of clubs, does he have the jack ready to lay off? What was his purpose? Think it over—it's important.

LOOKING AT DISCARDS, OR THE MAGIC EYE

Although it is my ruling, and the standard practice of the game, that discards cannot be spread and examined, experts nevertheless glean a lot of information from the discard pile.

The discard pile is seldom so perfectly squared up that a player cannot see a few cards whenever he really wants to, and such aid to your memory may be crucial to the development of your hand.

Before discarding, if you are the least bit doubtful about the play, go ahead and take a candid peek at the discard pile. Everyone else in the house is doing it. Don't be a chump.

A crackerjack player put it to me this way: "Don't try to study the discards. Just try to form them into sequences in your mind. If you see a 10–jack-king of spades in the discard pile, you start thinking in terms of queens. All right; look again. You're looking now for any other queen. And if you don't see her in the discards, rest assured that the queens are alive and kicking."

LAYING DOWN HAND WHEN KNOCKING

When laying down low melds—ace-deuce–3–4 and the like—there are abundant chances for error. Whenever a meld can be formed in more than one way, add up the total points of the possible ways and then lay down the meld adding to the highest total.

You have a 2–3–4 of spades and the two of hearts and two of diamonds. The spade sequence totals 9, the three deuces total 6; so lay down the sequence.

Caution! If from the play of the hands up to this time you have reason to believe that your opponent can meld a five of spades on your sequence, it becomes imperative to break up the sequence and lay off the three deuces. The shifting mathematics of the game must dictate your decision.

One canon of melding is inflexible. Should you have a four-card sequence and simultaneously three cards of equal rank matching either of the end cards of the sequence, always lay down the four of a kind as your meld. Your opponent can't lay off cards on four of a kind; he can lay off at either end of a sequence.

SLICING A LAYOFF

When knocking, it is sometimes worth while to discard the top or bottom card of a four- or five-card sequence. Suppose you have picked the ten of spades after two tens have been discarded. The king and queen of spades and two other jacks also have been discarded. But you haven't seen the jack of spades. Your opponent is probably holding it for a layoff. You have just picked a third five, so that discarding a two you can go down with a deuce and two aces for 4. Instead, you discard the ten of spades from the 7–8–9–10 sequence and go down with 6, catching your opponent with a useless jack, perhaps the only unmatched card in his hand. This is a very useful play at times, but it must be used with judgment.

Finally, I advise you to study the mathematics of the game, which follows. Bear it in mind during the course of play and you'll be sure to come ahead of the player who doesn't know his percentages.

THE MATHEMATICS OF GIN

It is, I take it, the author's privilege to point out—and the player's privilege to ignore—the fact that there are 15,820,024,220 possible ten-card hands in Gin Rummy. In every game there occurs a certain incidence of useless statistics. I don't expect you to remember how often in how many billion hands your present holding will occur. I shouldn't be surprised if you fail to remember that the chances of the dealer's being dealt a meld in his first ten cards are about 2 out of 5—although, if you do, it will improve your game. I won't insist that you remember that the chances of the non-dealer's being dealt a meld in the first 11 cards he sees are about 1 out of 2, although noting the subtle difference in those odds will make you a better player. I'm not schoolmarm enough to insist that you learn by rote everything I know about every game I know. When you need the mathematics, they'll be here for you.

But I think I should ask you to pay close attention to what happens when you play certain cards from your hand at Gin.

When you are the non-dealer and have been dealt 11 cards, the chances that your opponent can use the first card you discard from your hand in a meld are:

If the discard is a	The odds are approximately
King or ace	1 in 6
Queen or deuce	1 in 5
Any other card	1 in 4.7

(This calculation is based on your opponent's using the card forthwith in a meld, not on his considering the card as an improvement of his hand or as reducing his total of unmatched cards. Nor is the value of the cards in your own hand taken into consideration. This is a mathematical problem, not a strategic one.)

It is important in your play of the cards that you know and make your play conform to the above odds. It is also important to remember that when you hold a split sequence, such as the three and five of spades, you have only one chance of forming a three-card meld—by drawing the four of spades. Remember also that if the king of hearts is dead and you hold the king of spades, you now have only one way of forming a three-king meld and only one way of making the king-queen-jack of spades. And don't forget that if the ten of spades too is dead, there's no way on earth of your making a four-card meld with the spade king.

Knowledge of the number of ways a card can be used to form a three-, four- or five-card meld must be a part of every competent Gin player's equipment.

In Gin, the seven is the most valuable card in the deck as far as forming melds is concerned, just as the seven is the crucial number at Dice because it occurs oftenest. The seven can be used to extend melds more than any other card. The seven can be used in seven different seven-card-sequence melds, whereas the most valuable of the 12 other ranks can be used only to form six-card sequences.

I don't want to overload you with mathematics. It would confuse rather than enlighten you if I were to detail the number of ways any card can be used to form sequence melds of six or more cards. I have chosen to restrict the following table—which should be memorized by every Gin player—to three-, four- and five-card melds.

NUMBER OF WAYS CARDS CAN BE USED IN MELDS

Card	Three-Card Meld	Four-Card Meld	Five-Card Meld
King or ace	4	2	1
Queen or deuce	5	3	2
Jack or 3	6	4	3
10 or 4	6	5	4
9 or 5	6	5	5
8 or 6	6	5	5
7	6	5	5

The above table is useful mainly when the player is in the throes of deciding which card to discard. Note that the five, six, seven, eight and nine are likely to be most useful to your adversary; the king and ace the least useful. (And observe, too, that the number of ways in which a card can be useful is directly affected by the number of pertinent dead cards known.) The disadvantages of the ace, deuce and 3 are somewhat balanced by the fact that they are low-count cards, useful in knocking.

There are two ways of completing a three-card meld out of a two-card matched combination, whether the meld is to be a sequence or a combination of cards having the same numerical rank. The only exception to this two-way principle is when forming a sequence meld involving the ace or the king. Naturally, the number of ways to complete the meld is reduced by each known dead card. And the split sequence is always the exception. Holding the open-ended sequence of 2–3 of spades, you can fill either end and you can fill two ways. But if you hold the deuce and four of spades, you can form a three-card meld only one way—by drawing the three of spades. The point may seem rudimentary. But watch how often thoughtless players will nurse along relatively hopeless split sequences in the delusion that they are handling their cards with uncanny subtlety.

Let's reduce it to a table again.

WAYS OF FORMING A FOUR-CARD MELD FROM A THREE-CARD MELD *

	Sequences	Equal Rank
Without the king or ace in the three-card meld	2	1
With the king or ace in the three-card meld	1	1

* Be sure to deduct chances that are killed by dead cards.

CHANCE FOR GIN WITH THREE-CARD MELDS

You have nine ways to go gin when you hold three three-card sequences which can be switched about to form three three-card melds of the same rank. This holding constitutes your maximum chance of a killing. (Again we except melds involving dead-end aces and kings.)

Example: You hold the 7–8–9 of clubs, 7–8–9 of diamonds and 7–8–9 of spades. These can be construed and used as three sevens, three eights and three nines. And the player has nine chances of drawing a card to go gin (three sixes, three tens, one each of 7, 8, 9).

Your minimum chance of going gin even with three melds in your hand occurs when you're holding three unrelated groups of cards of equal rank or three unrelated sequences, each involving an ace or king.

You're considering whether or not to try for gin. Let's compute your chances. We will assume that you have the dream maximum set forth above, and also that none of the nines has been discarded. Here's how to compute your chances of going gin:

1. Subtract the 10 cards you hold from the total in the deck, 52.

2. Subtract the number of discards from this remainder, 42.

3. Divide the remaining total by 9. Your chances of going gin are 1 out of the final number computed.

4. To determine the average number of picks a player will need to go gin with a hand composed of 3 three-card melds, divide by 2.

Example: Let's go back to the dream hand described above. Six cards have been discarded.

Subtract from the 52 cards in the deck the 10 cards in your hand plus the 6 discarded cards. This leaves 36.

Divide that by the 9 ways you can go gin. The answer is 4.

In this special circumstance, which is rather special indeed, the player will go gin, on the average, with two picks (half of 4), because he has his choice of the upcard (opponent's discard) or the top card of the stock.

The above method of computation is even more valuable on the minimum chance hands in which the loss of even one chance for gin becomes a dominant factor in the development of the play.

WHEN TO KNOCK

Any attempt to tell the player when to knock or try for gin when he holds an hand that requires only one card for gin seems to me unsound without knowing (1) the cards still alive and (2) the cards his opponent has taken from the discard pile. On this play you must use your own judgment—as, in fact, you must learn to do in any hand at Gin Rummy.

SAUCE FOR THE GOOSE

Card distribution tends to run in patterns in any game. When you draw a good hand on the deal—a hand in which most of the cards are matched or near-matched—the probability is that your opponent holds at least one meld.

Remember also that freak distribution in one hand means a freak all the way around the table. When you get a specially promising hand, don't neglect the possibility that your adversary is at least as well off as you are. This is simply a characteristic of cards. It is of no vital importance, once you've absorbed it. Nor need it be of vital importance that the highest count any player can possibly be caught with on one hand is 98 points. That is, you can trap or be trapped with two kings, two queen, two jacks, two tens and two nines not in sequence. Note that I mean the 98 is made up of actual card indexes and does not include gin or box bonuses.

To go back to the beginning, there are 15,820,024,220 possible hands at Gin Rummy. To discuss any one of them to the exclusion of the rest would be to discuss something that a million chances to one will never occur in your experience. But there are certain valid general principles which I've tried to cover. If you remember nothing else about this chapter, remember this: *If the next opponent you encounter knows the mathematics of the game better than you do, he'll beat you in the long run.* It's as simple as that.

OBSERVATION

One player in the West Coast money crowd likes to arrange to stand behind any potential opponent and size up his style of play. He wants to know whether the man is methodical, whether he speculates rashly or well, whether he tries for a knock hand instead of gin, whether he gets nervous under the baleful glare of a fistful of high cards, how he talks when the cards are running with him and when they're against him. Card players, like everyone else, tend to be creatures of habit. They react, often unconsciously, to their circumstances.

Many players will clam up when they have a bad hand and talk it up when they catch a good one.

The vast majority of players are methodical, no matter how they try to mix up their styles. And method can be observed and learned.

The most dangerous player is the man who has mastered the mathematics of his game, the man who plays what I call the two-way hand—one that enables him to go gin with a pick of one or two cards or to knock with a pick of one or two others.

Each hand at Rummy is a new hand. I can't tell you what cards to hold. I can't tell you in ABC fashion how to play them all. Anything can happen, and you must be prepared to make the best of things as they are. That's the game.

TEN GENERAL RULES EVERY WINNING GIN RUMMY PLAYER MUST KNOW

1. Be sure you know the rules of Gin Rummy. The player who knows the rules has a decided advantage against a player who is vague about them.

2. Try to avoid mechanical errors by arranging your hand in an orderly fashion.

3. Try to get on the score sheet as quickly as possible.

4. Expect your opponent's first two discards to be bait.

5. Observe your opponents. Learn their Gin Rummy mannerisms. Are they speculators? Do they play for gin rather than knock hand? Avoid Gin giveaway mannerisms of your own.

6. Rather than discard a live card, chance adding it to your opponent's discard.

7. When you're in a losing streak, don't let yourself get panicky. An excited Gin player is a player at his worst.

8. Try to sit with your back to the wall and try to avoid kibitzers

who watch your hand. Many good Gin hands are tipped off by actions of onlookers.

9. When tempted to speculate, do so with a poor hand, don't with a good hand.

10. Toward the end of the game, play the score or try to keep under and prevent your opponent from winning the game that hand.

30.
Skarney®:
The World's Best
Rummy-Type Game

Skarney, the first really new card game concept of this century, can be played in more than 30 different ways. However, due to limited space the rules of play for only Skarney Partnership, Skarney Singles and Skarney Gin appear in this chapter. Skarney Partnership is one of the most bizarre, exciting, and charmingly exasperating partnership card games in history. It has bluff as in Poker, scores big like Canasta, and is played like no other game. It has the flavor of Pinochle, the partnership understanding of Contract Bridge, and the suspense of Gin Rummy. And withal, it has an inner world and logic of its own, taxing the capacity of the most inveterate card player. I am especially proud of Skarney because the games are my own invention, which I've taken the creator's liberty of naming Skarney. The complete Skarney set can be purchased at most gift and game stores.

SKARNEY PARTNERSHIP

Requirements

1. Four players, two against two as partners.
2. Two standard 52-card decks, with four added jokers shuffled together and used as one, a total of 108 cards.

The Game

A game consists of seven deals or hands and terminates at the end of the seventh deal, in which a final score is attained by each partnership.

The partnership with the higher score wins the game. The winners of the game score the difference between their total game and that of the losers. Should both partnerships have identical scores, the game is a tie. The four jokers and the eight deuces are wild and can be used to represent any card of any denomination or any card of any denomination and suit their holders dictate.

Melds: The whole game of Skarney pivots around the combinations of three or more cards of the same rank and three or more cards of the same suit in consecutive order, which players singly or in partnership seek to form in order to score points and special bonuses for their side. The four jokers and the eight deuces (twos) are wild and can be used to represent any card the holder dictates. For instance, three or more cards of the same denomination (such as three queens or two queens and a wild card) or three or more cards of the same suit in consecutive order (such as three of hearts, four of hearts, and five of hearts, or the three of hearts, wild card, and five of hearts) when legally placed face up in front of a player are called a *meld*. That is, cards are melded as soon as they are placed face up on the table with the evident intent to meld. If the exact location of a melded card is in doubt, any player may ask that the meld be clarified.

There are two basic kinds of Skarney melds: a *group* and a *sequence*. Each basic meld is subdivided as follows:

1. A *natural group meld* is a combination of three or more cards of the same rank.

2. A *mixed group meld* is a combination of only one wild card (deuce or joker) with two or more cards of the same rank. But only one wild card can be used in a mixed group meld.

3. An *independent deuce group meld* is a combination of three or more deuces. An independent deuce group meld of three or more deuces is commonly referred to as a *deuce spread*, or a *silver spread*.

4. An *independent joker group meld* is a group of three or four jokers. An independent joker group meld is commonly referred to as a *joker spread*, or *gold spread*.

5. A *natural sequence meld* is a combination of three or more cards of the same suit in consecutive order. An ace can be used only to form a high sequence meld such as ace, king, queen of the same suit. It cannot be used to form a low sequence meld such as ace, deuce, three of the same suit.

6. A *mixed sequence meld* is a combination of only one wild card (deuce or joker) with two or more natural cards of the same suit in consecutive order. When a mixed sequence meld is placed on the table, the exact position of the wild card indicates the natural card it is meant to represent. It should be noted that a joker or a deuce can

be used as a king of any suit in a sequence meld such as ace, wild card, queen. It cannot be used to form a low sequence such as ace, deuce, three of the same suit.

It is possible to meld 13 cards of the same suit in a natural or mixed sequence (two, three, four, five, six, seven, eight, nine, ten, jack, queen, king, and ace) with or without one wild card. To emphasize, at no time can more than one wild card be part of a Skarney meld—except when deuces or jokers are melded separately to form an independent deuce group meld or an independent joker group meld.

Laying Off Cards. As in Rummy the addition of one or two cards to a meld already placed on the table is known as a *layoff* and the act of adding one or two matching cards to a meld already placed on the table is known as *laying off*.

After the partnership has fulfilled its initial meld contract, a player at each turn of play, in addition to placing legal melds on the table, may extend his or his partner's previous meld or melds by laying off (adding) one or two matching cards or a matching card and a wild card to a specific melded group or sequence. Players are not permitted to lay off on melds of the opposing partnership. Detailed rules governing natural and wild card layoffs are as follows:

1. A *natural group meld* comprised of the king of spades, king of diamonds, and king of clubs is lying on the table. The melder of this group or his partner holds three or more kings. At his turn, he is permitted to lay off only one or two of these kings on the king group meld. However, the three kings he holds can be melded as a separate group meld and must be placed in front of the melder. They cannot be placed in front of his partner.

2. A *mixed group meld* comprised of the king of spades, king of diamonds, and a wild card (deuce or joker) is lying on the table. The melder of this group or his partner holds two kings. At his turn, he is permitted to lay off one or both of the kings on the mixed group meld.

3. A *natural sequence meld* comprised of the five of hearts, six of hearts, and the seven of hearts is lying on the table. The melder of this sequence or his partner holds the four of hearts, eight of hearts, and the nine of hearts. At his turn of play, he is permitted to lay off only one or two of these cards. He can extend the sequence meld on one or both ends by laying off a single card, such as the four of hearts or the eight of hearts or both—or he can lay off the eight of hearts and the nine of hearts—but never is he permitted to lay off more than two cards on any one meld at any one turn of play.

4. A *mixed sequence meld* comprised of the five of hearts, wild card (deuce or joker), and the seven of hearts is lying on the table. The melder of this sequence or his partner holds the four of hearts,

eight of hearts, and the nine of hearts. At his turn of play, he is permitted to lay off only one or two of these cards. He can extend the sequence meld on one or both ends by laying off a single card such as the four of hearts or the eight of hearts or both—or he can lay off the eight of hearts and the nine of hearts—but never is he permitted to lay off more than two cards on any one meld at any one turn of play.

Wild card layoff: A player at his turn is permitted to lay off a wild card (deuce or joker) on either a natural group or natural sequence meld belonging to his partner providing the wild card is accompanied by a natural matching card that will extend the meld, and the meld does not already contain a wild card such as a mixed group or mixed sequence meld. In addition, a player is permitted to lay off one or two deuces on an independent deuce group meld, and one joker on an independent joker group meld.

Swapping a wild card: One of the many fascinating features of Skarney is the often present possibility of the holder of a natural card exchanging it for a wild card (deuce or joker) that is part of a mixed meld belonging to his opponents. A player under no conditions is permitted to exchange or swap a wild card for a natural card from either his own or his partner's meld. Rules governing the swapping of a wild card for a natural card are as follows:

1. If a partnership has a mixed group of three or more cards resting on the table which includes a wild card, an opponent at his turn may swap the wild card for a same rank card of a missing suit.

2. If a partnership has a mixed sequence meld of three or more cards resting on the table which includes a wild card, an opponent at his turn may swap the wild card for a natural card that the wild card is meant to represent.

3. A player is permitted to swap a wild card in an opponent's meld or melds at any time during the play of the hand but only at his proper turn of play. Failure of the partnership to fulfill its initial contract meld does not alter this ruling.

4. To reiterate, a player under no condition is permitted to swap or exchange a wild card for a natural card from either his or his partner's melds.

5. A player at his turn of play and before melding or laying off can swap from as many mixed melds as possible and from one or both of his opponents at the same turn of play.

Note: Whenever a wild card is swapped from a mixed group or a mixed sequence meld, that meld becomes a natural meld. Whenever a wild card and a matching natural card are laid off on a natural group or sequence meld, that meld becomes a mixed meld. It is not unusual to see the same meld change from a mixed meld to a natural meld or vice versa several times during a hand.

Contract melds: The first meld by each partnership in each of the seven deals must meet the exact initial meld requirement as described by contract. Only one player of each partnership is required to fulfill the initial meld contract.

To simplify matters we shall call an initial basic group meld (natural group meld, mixed group meld, deuce spread, and joker spread) made up of only three cards a "group." We shall call an initial basic sequence meld (natural sequence meld and a mixed sequence meld) made up of only three cards a "sequence." To reiterate, no part of a contract meld can have more than three cards when first placed on the table. Nor can the contract melds be made up of a combination of *groups* and *sequences*. They must be either all groups or all sequences.

CONTRACT REQUIREMENTS FOR FIRST MELD

1st Deal:	3 Three card groups or	3 Three card sequences
2nd Deal:	3 Three card groups or	3 Three card sequences
3rd Deal:	3 Three card groups or	3 Three card sequences
4th Deal:	4 Three card groups or	4 Three card sequences
5th Deal:	4 Three card groups or	4 Three card sequences
6th Deal:	4 Three card groups or	4 Three card sequences
7th Deal:	4 Three card groups or	4 Three card sequences

Skarney or hand bonuses: When a player melds or lays off his last card or cards in his hand, he calls "Skarney," ending the hand. This is also known as Rummy, or Going Out. The partnership going Skarney receives the following designated Skarney bonus for each of the seven hands or deals that follow:

BONUSES FOR GOING SKARNEY

First hand	100 points
Second hand	100 points
Third hand	100 points
Fourth hand	200 points
Fifth hand	300 points
Sixth hand	400 points
Seventh hand	500 points

When a player draws the last card of the stock and does not go Skarney, the hand ends without that player offering a potential discard, and the partnership scoring the higher number of points wins the hand and receives a *hand bonus* equal in point value to the Skarney bonus designated for the specific hand. In case each partnership scores the same number of points, the hand does not count and the same dealer deals again.

Skarney shutout bonuses: Should a player go Skarney (on the fourth, fifth, sixth, or seventh hand) when putting down his partnership's contract meld (four three-card melds) and the opposing partnership has not put down their contract meld, his partnership receives a Skarney *shutout bonus* (also referred to as a Skarney blitz, or a skunked bonus) of 200 points in addition to the Skarney bonus for the specific hand. When a player is trying for a shutout bonus, it is said that "he's blitzing."

Point count of each Skarney card: At the end of each hand, cards melded on table are credited as follows: tens, jacks, queens, and kings are referred to as high cards and each counts 10 points. Threes, fours, fives, sixes, sevens, eights, and nines are referred to as low cards and each counts 5 points. Aces known as stop cards count 15 points each. Deuces and jokers known as wild cards count as follows:

An independent joker group meld of three or four jokers also known as a joker spread or gold spread counts 100 points for each joker. When a single joker known as a lone joker is part of a mixed group or a mixed sequence meld, it counts 50 points. Each unmelded joker caught in a player's hand is referred to as a penalty card or disaster card and counts 100 points against the holder. An independent deuce group meld of three or more deuces also known as a deuce spread or silver spread counts 50 points for each deuce. When a single deuce known as a lone deuce is part of a mixed group or mixed sequence meld, it counts 25 points. Each unmelded deuce caught in a player's hand is referred to as a penalty card or calamity card, and counts 50 points against the holder. All other unmelded cards (threes to aces) caught in a player's hand, even though they may form melds, are also referred to as penalty cards and are deducted at amounts equivalent to their melding values. So that the reader can see the card counts at a glance, they have been placed in tabular form.

POINT SCORING FOR MELDED CARDS
Cards Melded on Table at the End of a Hand

Joker (part of a mixed group meld or a mixed sequence meld	50 points
Jokers (3 or 4 forming an independent joker group meld)	each 100 points
Deuce (part of a mixed group meld or a mixed sequence meld	25 points
Deuces (3 or more forming an independent deuce group meld)	each 50 points
Ace	15 points
10, jack, queen, and king	each 10 points
3, 4, 5, 6, 7, 8, and 9	each 5 points

POINT SCORING FOR PENALTY CARDS
Cards Left in Player's Hand at the End of a Hand

Joker	minus 100 points
Deuce	minus 50 points
Ace	minus 15 points
10, jack, queen, and king	each minus 10 points
3, 4, 5, 6, 7, 8, and 9	each minus 5 points

Selecting partners and seating positions:

1. The four players seat themselves at any four places around the table; where they sit is for the moment irrelevant.

2. Any player may shuffle the pack and offer the pack to any other player for a cut.

3. For the purpose of cutting for partners and seating positions, the cards rank Ace (high) K-Q-J-10-9-8-7-6-5-4-3-2 (low).

4. Each player cuts a group of cards from the pack, immediately exposing to the others the bottom card of his group. Players cutting the two low cards become partners. So do the players cutting the two high cards.

5. If players cut three or four cards of the same rank, one or more new cuts must take place until two high and two low cards are accounted for.

6. To avoid controversy as to seats, one player for each side cuts the pack and exposes the bottom card of his cut. The player who cuts high card has the privilege of taking whichever seats his partnership wishes. In case of a tie, cut until the tie is broken.

The shuffle and cut:

1. The player who cut low card in the cut for partner positions starts the game by dealing the first hand. From then on the deal moves to the dealer's left, clockwise.

2. Dealer shuffles the cards. Any player may call for and shuffle the pack any time before the cut, although the dealer has the privilege of shuffling the pack last.

3. Dealer puts the pack of cards face down on the table to his right. His opponent to his right has first privilege of cutting the cards. If that player refuses to cut, any other player may cut. If all the other players refuse to cut, the dealer must cut the cards. He cannot refuse! At least twenty-five cards must be in one portion of the cut deck.

The deal: Dealer gives each player including himself 11 face-down cards, starting with the player on his left, one at a time in clockwise fashion. The remainder of the undealt cards are placed face down in the center of the table, forming the stock.

The actual play of the hand: Each player, at his turn, starting with the player on the dealer's left and continuing clockwise around the table, does as follows:

1. He draws the top card of the stock.

2. He may, if he chooses, exchange a natural card for a wild card from each of his opponent's melds.

3. After his partnership has fulfilled its initial meld requirement, he may, if he chooses, place on the table before him any possible melds and lay off, either two or one cards, on each of his and his partner's previous melds.

4. He removes a potential discard from the cards he is holding, turns it face up, and offers it to the player on his left by extending it toward him and asking "Do you want this card?" The player may do either of two things, accept or refuse the potential discard. If he refuses it, he replies, "I don't want it," and the potential discard is then offered to the next player, and so it goes from player to player in a clockwise fashion. Should one of the players accept the potential discard, he must say "I'll take it." This action ends the turn of play for the player who offered the card. Or, if each player in turn refuses the potential discard, the player who offered it must keep the card and return it to his hand, and his turn of play is ended. If however, a player's potential discard is either a wild card or an ace, it may be offered only to the player's opponent on his immediate left—and if the opponent accepts it, he loses his turn to pick the top card of the stock. If he refuses it, the player who offered it must keep it. He is not permitted to offer it to the other players. An ace or wild card offered as a potential discard is referred to as a *stop card*.

A player cannot offer his last accepted potential discard (nor an identical card) immediately but must wait until his next turn of play. *Example:* If his last accepted potential discard was the six of hearts, he cannot offer it until he has offered one other card first. Moreover, if he has another six of hearts in his hand, the same restriction applies.

If a player has one card left in his hand after either melding or laying off or doing both, he is not permitted to offer it as a potential discard. He simply says, "Last card," and retains it in his hand. And so it goes, from player to player until the end of the hand.

Giving and receiving information: A player during his turn and at no other time may:

1. Ask any other player how many cards he holds. The question must be answered correctly. However, a player must announce when he has only one card in his hand.

2. Ask the scorekeeper what hand is being played or to announce the cumulative score. He may also ask the point value of the Skarney bonus for the hand being played.

3. Call attention to the correct contract meld requirement if his partner is in the act of making an initial meld.

4. Before melding or indicating by word or action that he holds a Skarney hand ask, "Partner, may I go to Skarney?" It is strongly recommended that only this phrase be used. Partner must reply "Yes," or "No" (nothing more), and the answer is binding. However, a player may go Skarney without asking permission of his partner. For further information, see Irregularities in Asking Permission to Go Skarney, page 770.

End of hand: When a player melds or lays off the last card or cards in his hand, he calls "Skarney," ending the hand. This is also known as rummy, or going out. The partnership going Skarney receives the designated Skarney bonuses for each of the seven hands as shown on page 759. Should the cards in the stock be exhausted before any player has gone Skarney, the hand ends and the partnership scoring the higher number of points wins the hand and receives a hand bonus equal in point value to the Skarney bonus designated for the specific hand. In case each partnership scores the same number of points, the hand does not count and the same dealer deals again.

When the number of cards in the stock is low (ten or less cards), any player is permitted to count the number of cards remaining so as to know the number of rounds left.

How to score a hand: The following steps are used to determine the score. The partnership is credited with the total value of all cards melded. These points are added, and from this sum is subtracted the total penalty point values of the cards remaining in the partner's hands. The net balance is the partnership's score at the end of the hand and this may occasionally be a minus score. Note that all cards left in the hand count against the player regardless of whether or not they could have been melded. Should a player commit a rule violation during the hand and a penalty has been assessed, then penalty points for such offense are charged to the offender and deducted from the partnership's total hand score.

The partnership that went Skarney or won the hand with a higher number of scored points is credited with either a Skarney bonus or a hand bonus for the designated hand as stipulated under Skarney or Hand Bonuses (page 759) and this figure is entered on the score sheet. The scores for each hand are then added to (or subtracted from, as the case may be) each previous cumulative score, if any. In this manner, players can not only check the score and Skarney bonus for each hand but also have a cumulative total at the end of each hand.

To speed up the arithmetic in scoring, first group together your partnership's penalty cards. Second, remove enough cards, if possible, from yours and your partner's melds whose point values equal those of the penalty cards. These and the penalty cards are put aside as they no longer enter into the scoring. Third, add up the point values of yours and your partner's melded cards still left on the table, and from this amount deduct any penalties assessed for irregularities. The balance is the partnership's hand score. The counting process will be further speeded up if the melds are stacked in separate piles of 100 points whenever possible.

End of game: The game ends upon completion of the seventh hand and the partnership with the higher total score wins the game and gets credit for the point difference between both scores. See the sample scoring game that follows:

Score Sheet	They	We
First hand scores	130	65
Skarney bonus	100	
Total scores 1 hand	230	65
Second hand scores	195	50
Skarney bonus	100	
Total scores 2 hands	525	115
Third hand scores	295	345
Skarney bonus		100
Total scores 3 hands	820	560
Fourth hand scores	180	230
Skarney bonus		200
Total scores 4 hands	1,000	990
Fifth hand scores	160	375
Skarney bonus		300
Total scores 5 hands	1,160	1,665
Sixth hand scores	265	15
Skarney bonus	400	
Total scores 6 hands	1,825	1,680
Seventh hand scores	195	−280
Skarney bonus	500	
Total game scores	They 2,520	We 1,400
	−1,400 We's score	
They wins by	1,120 Points	

First Hand: They go Skarney, scoring 130 points + 100 points Skarney bonus. We score 65 points. The score at the end of the first hand is 230 to 65 in favor of They.

Second Hand: They go Skarney, scoring 195 points + 100 points Skarney bonus. We score 50 points. These scores are added to the score of the first hand, showing They leading We at the end of the second hand by 525 to 115.

Third Hand: We go Skarney, scoring 345 points + 100 points Skarney bonus. They score 295 points. These scores added to the previous cumulative scores show They with 820 points and We with 560.

Fourth Hand: We go Skarney, scoring 230 points + 200 points Skarney bonus. They score 180 points. The scores at the end of the fourth hand are 1,000 to 990 in favor of They.

Fifth Hand: We go Skarney, scoring 375 + 300 points Skarney bonus. They score 160 points. At the end of the fifth hand We is leading They 1,665 to 1,160.

Sixth Hand: They go Skarney, scoring 265 points + 400 points Skarney bonus. We score 15 points. The score at the end of the sixth hand is They 1,825, We 1,680.

Seventh Hand: They go Skarney, scoring 195 points + 500 points Skarney bonus. We score minus 280 points. They's game total is 2,520 points. We's game total is 1,400 points. So, They's winnings for the game are the difference in scores or 1,120 points. At one-tenth of a cent a point, partnership They collects $1.12 from partnership We.

Alternate Skarney

This is a most fascinating variation of Skarney and my favorite. It is highly recommended to the experienced Skarney player who wants his Skarney game to have greater scope leading to more possibilities for skilled card maneuvers and more opportunities for error. This is all due to the fact that Alternate Skarney possesses two sensational progressive game features, such as (1) Each of the seven initial (contract) meld requirements becomes a bit more difficult to attain with each succeeding deal. (2) The point value of each of the seven succeeding Skarney or Hand Bonuses increases by 100 points in direct relation to the attainment of the contract meld—thereby making for a more balanced scoring game. The rules governing Skarney apply in full for Alternate Skarney, except as follows:

CONTRACT REQUIREMENTS FOR FIRST MELD PLUS POINT SCORE FOR EACH SKARNEY AND HAND BONUSES

Deals		Bonuses for Winning the Hand
1st Deal	Any 3 three card melds comprised of 3 groups, 3 sequences or a combination of both	100 points
2nd Deal	3 three card groups	200 points
3rd Deal	3 three card sequences	300 points
4th Deal	Any 4 three card melds comprised of 4 groups, 4 sequences or a combination of both	400 points
5th Deal	2 three card groups and 2 three card sequences	500 points
6th Deal	4 three card groups	600 points
7th Deal	4 three card sequences	700 points

SAMPLE SCORING OF AN ALTERNATE SKARNEY PARTNERSHIP GAME

Score Sheet	They	We
First hand scores	130	65
Skarney bonus	100	
Total scores 1 hand	230	65
Second hand scores	195	50
Skarney bonus	200	
Total scores 2 hands	625	115
Third hand scores	295	345
Skarney bonus		300
Total scores 3 hands	920	760
Fourth hand scores	180	230
Skarney bonus		400
Total scores 4 hands	1,100	1,390
Fifth hand scores	160	375
Skarney bonus		500
Total scores 5 hands	1,260	2,265
Sixth hand scores	265	15
Skarney bonus	600	
Total scores 6 hands	2,125	2,280
Seventh hand scores	195	−280
Skarney bonus	700	
Total game scores	They 3,020	We 2,000
	−2,000 We's score	
They wins by	1,020 Points	

First Hand: They go Skarney scoring 130 points + a 100 point Skarney Bonus. We score 65 points. The score at the end of the first hand is 230 to 65 in favor of They.

Second Hand: They go Skarney scoring 195 points + 200 points bonus for Skarney. We score 50 points. These scores are added to the score of the first hand showing They leading We at the end of the second hand by 625 to 115.

Third Hand: We go Skarney scoring 345 points + 300 points Skarney Bonus. They score 295 points. These scores added to the previous cumulative scores show They with 920 points and We with 760.

Fourth Hand: We go Skarney scoring 230 points + a 400 point Skarney Bonus. They score 180 points. The scores at the end of the fourth hand are 1,390 to 1,100 in favor of We.

Fourth Hand: We go Skarney scoring 230 points + a 400 point Skarney Bonus. They score 180 points. The scores at the end of the fourth hand are 1,390 to 1,100 in favor of We.

Fifth Hand: We go Skarney scoring 375 points + a 500 point Skarney Bonus. They score 160 points. At the end of the fifth hand We is leading They 2,265 to 1,260.

Sixth Hand: They go Skarney scoring 265 points + a 600 point Skarney Bonus. We score 15 points. The score at the end of the sixth hand is We 2,280, They 2,125.

Seventh Hand: They go Skarney scoring 195 points + a Skarney Bonus of 700 points. We score minus 280 points. They's game total is 3,020 points. We's game total is 2,000. So, They's winnings for the game are the difference in scores or 1,020 points. At one-tenth of a cent a point, partnership, They collect $1.02 from partnership We.

Additional Rules

The rules that govern irregularities are designed to define the offense and provide adequate remedy in all cases where a player accidentally, carelessly, or inadvertently violates a rule of the game and gains an unintentional but nevertheless unfair advantage. An offending player should be ready to pay a prescribed penalty graciously. The general rules governing irregularities follow:

1. When an irregularity has been committed, a player may draw attention to it and give or obtain information as to the penalty applicable to it. The fact that a player draws attention to an irregularity committed by his partnership does not affect the rights of the opposing partnership.

2. After attention has been drawn to an irregularity, play shall stop and not be resumed until all questions in regard to rectification and to the assessment of a penalty have been determined. Either player of the offended partnership has the right to impose a penalty without consulting his partner.

3. A penalty may not be imposed until the nature of the offense has been clearly stated; however, a penalty once paid, or any decision agreed and acted upon by the players stands, even though it may later be adjudged wrong.

4. The right to penalize an offense or irregularity is forfeited if a player of the offended partnership (a) waives the penalty, (b) consults with his partner as to the imposition of a penalty before a penalty has been imposed, (c) calls attention to an opponent's irregularity after he or his partner has drawn a card from the stock.

5. Rectification or validation proceeds as provided in the following irregularities applicable to the specific offense. When these irregularities are appreciated and the penalties invoked, arguments are avoided and the pleasure and enjoyment which the game offers are materially enhanced.

Dealing out of turn: Should a deal out of turn be discovered before the first play, the deal stands and the first play is made by the player whose turn it would have been if no irregularity had occurred. In this case, the deal passes as though the cards had been dealt by the correct player. But should a deal out of turn be discovered after the beginning of the first play, the deal stands and play continues from that point. In this case, the deal passes as though the irregular deal had been correct.

Misdeals: There must be a new deal if:

1. It is discovered during the deal that the cut was omitted.

2. During the deal the dealer exposes any card other than his own.

3. Before each player has made his first play, it is discovered that any player was dealt an incorrect number of cards. If such discovery is made after each player has made his first play, the play continues without correction.

4. Before each player has made his first play, a card is found faced up in the stock, or a foreign card is found in the pack or in a player's hand, or it is discovered that a card is missing from the pack.

Irregularities in the draw from the stock: The following rules cover irregularities in the draw:

1. If a player draws the top card of the stock and sees or exposes another card or cards of the stock in the process, he must show the card or cards so seen or exposed to all the players and replace them. In addition, he must show his drawn card to all the players before placing it with the cards in his hand. The player whose turn it is to play next may either take the top card of the stock or shuffle the stock and cut before drawing from the stock.

2. If a player draws two or more cards from the stock and puts them in his hand, he must forgo his draw for as many turns as the

number of extra cards he has drawn. He must offer a potential discard at each turn and may not meld, lay off, or swap wild cards until after his next legal draw.

3. If a player draws from the stock before the preceding player has offered a potential discard, the draw stands, and the player loses his turn to accept the potential discard and the offender is not permitted to meld or lay off until his next turn of play.

4. If a player draws from the stock when it is not his turn, he must show the card erroneously drawn to all players and replace it on the stock. The player whose turn it was to play may either take it as his draw or shuffle the stock and cut before drawing.

Irregular deck during play: An irregular deck during play is one in which:

1. A card is found face up in the stock. It must be turned and shuffled with the rest of the stock and cut.

2. A foreign card is found in the pack. It must be removed. If it is in a player's hand, it is removed and replaced immediately by the top card of the stock.

3. One or more missing cards are found and no player admits to their ownership. They should be shown to all players, then put into the pack, which is shuffled and cut.

Stop-card irregularity: If a player's potential discard is a stop card (joker, deuce, or ace) it may be offered only to the player on his immediate left, and if that player accepts the stop card, he loses his turn to pick the top card of the stock. If he refuses the stop card, the player who offered it must keep it. He is not permitted to offer the stop card to the other players. If, however, the player accepts the stop card and draws from the stock inadvertently, he must show the card erroneously drawn to all the players and replace it on the stock. The next player may, if he chooses, take the card as his draw or shuffle the stock and cut before drawing. There is no penalty for this infraction.

Last-card irregularity: When a player holds only one card in his hand, he cannot offer it as a potential discard. When holding only one card, a player must announce "Last card," in a voice that all can hear. Second, he must hold the card so that its value is hidden from the other players' views. If, however, a player inadvertently exposes the value of his last card, there is no penalty, but the player may be reprimanded. If the player repeats the infraction, his partnership is penalized 50 points for each new offense.

Potential discard irregularities: The following covers potential discard irregularities:

1. If a player offers a potential discard without drawing, he must draw the top card of the stock if attention is called to the irregularity

before the next player has drawn. If the next player draws before attention is called, the offending player must take the next top card of the stock and play reverts to the other player.

2. If a player at his turn has refused the potential discard either by word or action, the decision stands. He cannot accept the refused potential discard under any conditions.

3. If a player at his turn has accepted a potential discard either by word or action, the decision stands. He cannot refuse the potential discard under any conditions.

Illegal contract melds: If it is discovered during a player's turn to play that he has:

1. Placed on the table as a contract meld an insufficient or illegal meld, (a) he may correct the irregularity by putting down sufficient melds from his hand, in which case he may rearrange the cards put down in error providing he makes use of all melded cards; or (b) he may return to his hand one or more cards put down in error and rearrange all his melds from melded cards and cards in his hand, in which case his partnership is penalized 100 points.

2. Placed on the table an illegal or insufficient contract meld and cannot remedy the situation, he is permitted to return the cards to his hand and the penalty to his partnership is 100 points.

Irregularities in melding and laying off: After a partnership's contract meld has been fulfilled and a player has laid down a meld or melds, he cannot pick them up and replace them in his hand. Nor is he permitted to rearrange them in any other kind of meld. Cards once melded and laid down on the table remain as legal melds. The same ruling holds true for a one- or two-card layoff on either partner's melds. If a player lays down an illegal meld or layoff and attention is brought to it, he is permitted to correct the irregularity or replace the cards in his hand and the penalty for the infraction is 50 points. If, after an illegal meld or layoff, the next player draws a card from the stock before attention is called to the error, the illegal meld or layoff stands as a legal play.

Irregularities in asking permission to go Skarney: The following cover irregularities in asking to go Skarney:

1. At his proper turn of play and before melding or laying off cards, or indicating he has the necessary melds to go Skarney, a player may ask, "Partner, may I go Skarney?" It is strongly recommended that only this phrase be used. Partner must reply either "Yes," or "No" (nothing more), and the answer is binding. If the player fails to abide by the answer, his side is penalized 100 points.

2. If a player calls "Skarney" without asking his partner's permission and finds he cannot go Skarney, his partnership is penalized 100

points and the cards (if any) that the player may have exposed in attempting to go Skarney are returned to his hand.

3. If the player after asking the question, but before receiving a reply, melds or lays off, indicates a meld or layoff, withdraws the question, or gives any other information; or if the partner, in giving a negative answer, transmits information, either opponent may demand that the player go Skarney (if he possibly can) or not go Skarney.

4. If after asking his partner's permission to go Skarney and receiving an affirmative answer to the question, a player states he cannot go out, his partnership is penalized 100 points and the cards (if any) that the player may have exposed in attempting to go Skarney are returned to his hand.

5. If a player who receives a negative answer to the question "Partner, may I go out?" proceeds to attempt to meld all of his cards, he must rearrange these melds so that at least two cards will remain unmelded. The two cards or more remaining unmelded are returned to his hand and offender must offer a potential discard and the partnership is penalized 100 points.

Score corrections: Here are the important points of rules of scoring:

1. When a score is agreed upon and written down, it may not later be set aside. Proven mistakes in addition or subtraction on the score sheet may be corrected at any time prior to the start of a new game. If the error is proven after the first draw of any hand, the hand must be completed before the error can be corrected.

2. Once a partnership has counted its cards and announced its total score and the score is entered on the score sheet and a new hand has started, the partners cannot call for rectification of some previous mistake they have made. Players are not required to inform their opposition that they have committed an error or failed to lay off a card or failed to meld to their best advantage, nor are they required to notify the opposition that they are calling an incorrect count to their disadvantage.

3. A player who inadvertently mixes his melds with the rest of the cards before counting them forfeits their count.

4. A player who inadvertently mixes an opponent's melds with the rest of the cards before they are counted may not dispute that opponent's claim to their point value.

SKARNEY SINGLES

Double-Deck Skarney Singles is just like Skarney Four-Handed Partnership except that everyone plays for himself. You can use all your knowledge in Skarney Four-Handed Partnership to good advantage except that the partnership factor is missing. Yet it is different enough to create novel and exciting situations that could never raise in partnership play. The official rules for Skarney Four-Handed Partnership apply with the following exceptions and additional rules:

1. Two, three, or four players, each playing for himself.

2. Each player is required to fulfill his initial contract meld.

3. A player at each turn of play may swap (if possible) a wild card (deuce or joker) from one or more melds of each and every opponent.

4. A player is only permitted to lay off cards on his own melds. To emphasize, a player is not permitted to lay off cards on opponent's melds.

5. When a singles player goes Skarney by putting down his contract meld, he receives the Skarney shutout bonus only if each and every opponent has failed to put down a contract meld.

Skarney Strategy

The following are the 20 basic points of Skarney strategy:

1. Learn the rules of the game so that you can recall them at a moment's notice.

2. Pick up your 11 dealt cards one at a time.

3. Take time out to arrange your hand in ranks and suits.

4. Don't give the strength of your hand away by saying you have a weak hand, or no wild cards, or a strong hand and many wild cards.

5. When putting down a contract meld, do not expend vulnerable wild cards in mixed melds too freely when no great urgency presses.

6. Think twice before offering a stop card (ace, deuce, or joker) to your left-hand opponent—especially when he holds only a few cards.

7. When holding a weak hand, accept all matching potential discards. When holding a strong hand, think twice before accepting a nonmatching potential discard.

8. Before melding and laying off, study your opponent's mixed melds for possible wild-card swaps.

9. Study your natural and mixed melds and your partner's for possible layoffs and lock-ups.

10. When melding and laying off, try to keep one wild card in your hand to help a possible Skarney hand.

11. The safest potential discard to offer your opponents is a card of the same rank they have previously refused.

12. Remember the potential discards taken by your partner and try to feed him the like—or hold same for possible layoffs on partner's melds.

13. Try not to leave yourself with just one wild card as your last card.

14. Wild cards without natural pairs near the end of a hand are expendable—too many may be a handicap.

15. Try to put down your mixed meld so that the wild card will be as safe as possible.

16. It's mathematically best to meld groups rather than sequences, better for laying off cards.

17. Think twice before saying "No" to the question, "May I go Skarney?"

18. You should play for Skarney whenever it appears that the prolongation of the hand will benefit your opponents more than yourselves.

19. Don't discuss or criticize your partner's play during the play of the hand.

20. Study the score at the end of each hand.

Probabilities in a Skarney hand: In Skarney, as in all card games of skill, there is a mathematical basis for many correct plays. But mathematics plays only a minor part of Skarney strategy. You do not have to be a mathematician to play well, nor do you have to memorize mathematical rules laid down by anyone. There are, of course, some probability factors in Skarney, which are apparent even to the beginner. It should be obvious that you have a better chance of making a 3-card natural group meld than a 3-card natural sequence meld when you hold a pair of kings than if you hold a king and queen of spades. In fact the odds are 3 to 2 in favor of the natural group. The reason, there are six kings to draw from and there are only four cards (two aces of spades and two jacks of spades) to draw from to make a 3-card natural sequence.

The number of ways that 11 cards can be dealt to a player out of a total of 108 cards is a figure with 15 digits—approximately 344,985,-000,000,000. But this does not represent the number of different Skarney hands because a ten of hearts, for instance, in a group meld is not different from a ten of diamonds or a wild card. The number of significantly different hands that can be dealt in Skarney is very much smaller—approximately 3,500,000.

On the average, you will be dealt one or more wild cards per hand (11 cards) and you are better than a 3 to 1 favorite to be dealt at least one wild card. Your whole hand, on the average, in approximate figures will be:

Wild cards	1 (plus)
Aces	1 (minus)
High cards	3 (plus)
Low cards	6 (minus)
Total	11 cards

Your hand will have two natural pairs (or longer sets) and will for example be: deuce, ace, 3–3, queen-queen, jack, 9, 8, 6 and 5. The most disconnected hand in Skarney is one containing no matched cards and no wild cards, but you will be dealt a hand of this type about once in 3,000 deals.

Techniques in playing for Skarney: The principle of mobility is a general principle common to most card games of skill. In Skarney to keep your hand fluid and to be prepared for most contingencies is of utmost importance. In playing for Skarney, the desired flexibility can be maintained by forming as many two-way melds incorporating the same cards in both groups and sequences as you possibly can. For instance, among your cards you hold three three-card sequences, the seven, eight, nine of diamonds; seven, eight, nine of spades; and the seven, eight, nine of clubs. These same three-card sequence melds can be switched to three three-card groups, such as 3 sevens, 3 eights, and 3 nines. It becomes quite a problem to some players when holding twenty or more cards to segregate the melds in their proper manner. I have seen many players holding a Skarney hand but unaware of it and never going Skarney simply because the hand was not arranged properly. This is especially true when a few wild cards are among the large number of cards a player is holding. The best advice that can be given is to take your time when sorting out melds in your hand, because who knows, a simple rearrangement of melds may spell Skarney for you.

Tactics when you need a contract meld: A contract meld of three three-card groups or three three-card sequences is fairly easy to obtain. Possession of one or two wild cards, for instance, practically assures it. But don't rush to put down mixed melds (melds possessing a wild card) unless they are fairly safe from being stolen (swapped for a natural card) by your opponents. Otherwise it is best to wait even several rounds in order to put down natural melds or closed mixed melds. That is, providing your opponents have not as yet put down their contract meld.

If your opponents have fulfilled their contract meld and your side has not, by all means get down on the board (if possible). It is best to gamble a stolen wild card (deuce or joker) than to be caught with a 50- or 100-point penalty card in your hand. As play progresses, the urgency for putting down a contract meld increases to the point where its desirability can no longer be weighed too delicately.

A contract meld of either four three-card groups or four three-card sequences is difficult to get unless you happen to be dealt two or three wild cards. With no wild cards, it is really tough. The general principles as to when you should put down your four three-card contract melds are simple. You should almost always go down as soon as you can. Only very seldom may you indulge in the luxury of waiting for a more desirable contract meld. Always remember Skarney Four-Handed Partnership is a partnership game and partners must cooperate in putting down a contract meld. Some players holding a contract meld wait for their partners to meld, hoping to go Skarney after their partners fulfill the contract meld. Skarney Partnership, like Contract Bridge, is a partnership game and to win at Skarney, as at Bridge, partnership cooperation is required. So when you have an opportunity to fulfill a four three-card contract meld in the early part of a hand, do so and try for a big scoring hand. The 200, 300, 400, 500, 600, or 700 points for Skarney bonus is big—but so are the penalty cards your opponents may be caught with.

Getting your contract meld down has obvious advantages. It is your race toward going Skarney. It gives your partner a chance to meld groups and sequences, plus laying off on your melds, and vice versa. It also relieves your partner of the pressure of trying to attain the contract meld. Last but not least, it puts the pressure on your opponents, and at times causes them to put down mixed melds with vulnerable wild cards. But as you may already have discovered, it may be to your disadvantage to put down either a natural or mixed contract meld during the early stages of the hand. It makes it easier for your opponents to choose safe potential discards and reduces the flexibility of your own hand. Therefore, you will have to weigh the advantages against the disadvantages such as being left with four or five disconnected cards in your hand, after fulfilling your contract meld.

The necessity for making such decisions arises frequently in Skarney, and the player who consistently uses good judgment will win many more games than his opponents.

To succeed in blitzing, some luck and considerable psychological bluffing on your part and your partner's are required. You both must keep poker faces and play it cool so as not to alert your opponents to the fact that you are attempting a blitz. And, always remember: When you have a good reason to fear that your opponents may go Skarney quickly—it is wise for you, if possible, to unload—put down all your melds and layoffs be they natural or mixed melds.

The subtle art of potential discarding: Skarney is a game of deduction and counter deduction. (1) You must try to figure out what cards each opponent is holding in his hand so that (*a*) you won't give them any useful cards and (*b*) you won't be holding cards for an impossible or unlikely meld. (2) You must try to figure out what cards your partner is holding in his hand so that (*a*) you'll be holding cards you can lay off on his possible melds and (*b*) you'll be offering potential discards that are useful to your partner. Therefore, good potential discarding is both offensive and defensive. Offensively, you want to build up or maintain a hand that will give you a contract meld and a fair chance to go Skarney. Defensively, you want to make the attainment of these objectives as difficult as possible for your opponents.

At the very beginning of the hand the question of what is and what is not a safe potential discard is not too important. On the first few rounds any potential discard is usually accepted by one of your opponents or partner. You should not worry at this point because more often than not some one will take almost every card coming his way, if he needs it or not. Such a player is referred to as a "garbage picker." What you should do at the beginning of the hand is to concentrate on building your own hand and keeping your opponents in the dark regarding the strength of your hand. However, during the middle of the hand, prior to your opponents' fulfillment of their contract meld, you cannot do better than to match your opponents' previous potential discard with a similar rank card. If one of your opponents offers a five, you should retaliate and offer a five if you have one and can spare it. The presumption is that he does not have a pair left in a rank that he has offered so early. Sometimes you will be wrong, but more often you will be right.

If you hold a lone ace (stop card) it is usually wise to offer it to your left-hand opponent. Again the presumption is that he will not accept it for fear of losing a pick from the top of the stock. Think twice, however, before offering an ace or a wild card in the later phase of the hand.

The foregoing advice on potential discards is intended to apply in any situation where the two partnerships are on equal or near-equal terms. The partnership trailing by several hundred points is bound to accept nearly every potential discard that might come its way hoping to net hundreds of points more than you could make by going Skarney quickly.

Once your opponents have put down their contract meld, each of your potential discard plays must be thoroughly analyzed, more so if one of your opponents holds his last card. You must be ultrasafe in offering a potential discard. Study your opponents' and your own melds (if any) very carefully and then think twice before making the play. Owing to the luck (chance) aspect of Skarney, the most skillful potential discarding cannot guarantee success every time.

Acceptance and refusal of potential discards: Prior to either side having fulfilled its contract meld, there is no need to consider taking a potential discard when it matches a card in your hand or gives you a meld: just take it with a feeling of gratitude to the giver. But, when the offered card does not give you a match or a meld, the problem of taking it poses a dilemma. It frequently happens that an opponent tries to pass his partner a card of the same rank as previously taken. When such a condition prevails, it may be good tactics to take it even though it doesn't help your hand. You can always offer it back later on if you must.

An important question that often arises at the beginning of a hand is whether to try for a big score and take almost every card that comes your way or to accept fewer valuable cards and try for Skarney. However, not every hand is suitable for a big score. Often a player is dealt 11 cards which are better adapted for a fast contract meld and a quick Skarney—providing the player gets an assist from his partner. Such a decision depends on the score. If your partnership is far ahead, you should play for Skarney, only accepting a potential discard that gives you a meld or extends a meld. If your partnership is far behind—and all other things being even—try for the big score. The necessity for making such decisions arises frequently in Skarney and the player who consistently uses good judgment will be the winner. Should you be offered an ace (stop card) in the early stages on the game and you are bent on trying for a big score—accept it when first offered. It very often is part of the opponent's meld or matched aces and he is offering it as bluff card so as not to break up any of his other matched sets or melds. If you have what you consider a possible Skarney hand, don't take it, because a disconnected ace is a difficult card to get rid of when your opponents have put down their contract meld.

When both partnerships are down with melds, you should be extra cautious in accepting an opponent's potential discard. Take a careful look before accepting or offering a potential discard. Observe all melds on the table. At this stage, it is fairly easy to tell what card is good or bad for your side or your opponents'.

Most beginners at this stage of the game are tempted to accept an opponent's potential discard merely to extend one of their own melds. By all means, do not accept an opponent's potential discard that he cannot get rid of by laying it off on one of his own melds.

Should you have no quick chance of going Skarney, and your partner holds very few cards in his hand, accept all potential discards from your partner, thereby giving him the opportunity to go Skarney. And last but not least, think twice before offering or accepting an ace or wild card when both partnerships are down to their last few cards.

Defense against opponents who have many cards: Going Skarney? Should the opponents be the ones who are holding big hands of 20 or more cards by taking every potential discard that comes their way, your best defense is, of course, to go Skarney and catch them with a boodle of penalty cards. Partners should cooperate in this situation. For instance, it may easily be that both partners would be in good position to go Skarney if their side puts down its contract meld. In this situation, one of the two partners may have to injure his own Skarney hand by using a couple of wild cards to fulfill his partnership's contract meld. The question arises, which partner should it be? Obviously the one who can best spare the wild cards—but how can one tell? One good indication that the partner has an excellent chance to go Skarney and is merely waiting for his partner to put down the initial meld is that he is not trying to further build up his hand and is refusing most potential discards, and usually offering the drawn card as his potential discard. Consequently, this player's partner should be the one to make the sacrifice and put down the contract meld.

Protecting your jokers and deuces: One of the most important factors in skillful Skarney playing is the use of a wild card. Do you hold it in your hand and wait until you can deploy it in a safe (locked) mixed meld but by so doing take a chance of getting caught with it in your hand? Or do you meld it in an open mixed meld and hope your opponents don't steal it? I can't help you on this one because there are billions of possible hands in Skarney and each requires a different strategy, so you'll have to use your best judgment on how to deploy the wild card. But, whenever you are faced with a decision on whether to use a joker or a deuce in a locked (safe) mixed meld, consider the fact that the joker counts 50 points and the deuce 25. The penalty against you if you are caught with a joker in your hand is 100 points, a deuce 50 points. Hence, there are times when you should use a joker in an open mixed meld, other times a deuce. It all depends on whether your opponents are trying for a contract meld or going for Skarney. Also to be taken into consideration are the opponents' chances of stealing (swapping) the wild card. At times, too many wild cards pose a question. For instance, you hold three jokers. If melded as a joker spread they count 300 points. You wonder if the 300 points are better than a try at the Skarney bonus by using the jokers in mixed melds where they are worth only 150 points, plus the chance of being caught with them in your hand for a disaster penalty of 300 points. Such decisions can only be appraised at the time of happening. There is not cut and dried rule that fits wild cards.

Asking permission to go Skarney: When you are ready to go Skarney, you may, according to the rules, ask permission of your partner. But, remember you are not obliged to ask that question. Ask it only if there is a reason for you to do so.

You should not ask permission whenever your hand clearly indicates what to do. *Example:* If you are able to go Skarney on the seventh hand and win the game at the same time, you should not ask the question. Your partner does not know your hand and it is conceivable that he may give a negative reply. Neither should you ask permission if you are sure that you shouldn't go Skarney because you don't want to risk the possibility of an affirmative reply.

You should ask permission of your partner any time you are really interested in his opinion. For instance, you suspect that the handful of cards your partner is holding contains a number of wild cards whose penalty point values could possibly reduce your hand score to a minus score, but of course you cannot be sure about it. By putting the question to him, you are giving him the opportunity to say "No," if he actually has the hand you suspect. In that case, he will put down all possible melds at his next turn and you may or may not go Skarney on the next round. But, if his is not the type of hand you expected, he will say "Yes."

Expert Skarney players will also sometimes ask permission with the definite expectation of getting a negative reply. For instance, if a partner has just stolen a joker or two from his opponent's melds and has a great many cards in his hand and has not melded any cards as yet, it is obvious that he does not want the hand to end at this stage. By asking him, you simply advise him of the strength of your own hand. He will surely answer "No," and will have acquired the knowledge that as soon as he puts down his melds you will try to go Skarney. If he judges, however, that prolongation of the hand would be more profitable, or by chance he cannot meld as he would wish, he will still not meld, and at your next turn, you should ask again, etc.

For more detailed information and strategy of winning play for all 30 Skarney variants, read *Skarney*, a 145-page book which I wrote several years ago.

SKARNEY GIN®

"What card players the world over need is a great two-handed card game." I have said this for many years, and now it seems Skarney Gin fills the bill. It is truly the most fascinating and exciting two-handed card game in history. Regular Gin Rummy, unlike Skarney Gin, is basically a gambling game. Leave the stakes out of Gin Rummy and it falls flat on its face as a nongambling game. Skarney Gin, however, is a great family pastime. For the millions of married couples Skarney Gin is the ideal two-handed game.

Skarney Gin is the game that I honestly believe will soon displace regular Gin Rummy as America's favorite two-handed card game. It outclasses regular Gin Rummy not only in fun and excitement but in strategic planning. The reasons for the above statements are: (1) Skarney Gin makes use of three melds, groups, sequences, and poker straights—whereas regular Gin Rummy employs only groups and sequences. This factor alone gives Skarney Gin greater scope and flexibility, causing the player to commit more errors than he would in regular Gin Rummy. (2) The ten-card initially dealt hand in regular Gin Rummy always remains the same during play. In Skarney Gin the ten dealt cards held by a player fluctuate. They may increase to twenty or more cards, decrease to one, increase to ten or more, remain the same, or dwindle to zero when a player goes Skarney or gin. This unusual and fascinating scientific aspect of Skarney Gin makes the game much more interesting and requires greater player concentration than regular Gin Rummy. (3) Although Skarney Gin is a scientific game, poor players win occasionally, so that everyone becomes convinced that he plays well. In no other card game do you find so many self-proclaimed local champs.

Ten Things Every Winning Skarney Gin Player Must Know

1. Learn the rules so thoroughly you can recall them instantly and correctly.

2. Minimize mechanical errors by picking up your dealt cards singly.

3. Don't break up a possible meld at the start of the hand to withhold a doubtful card from your opponent.

4. Study your contract meld before putting it down. However, it usually pays to put down poker straights rather than groups or sequences.

5. Risk adding to opponent's meld rather than offer a live potential discard.

6. Late in the hand, think twice before offering an ace (stop card) as your potential discard.

7. It usually doesn't pay to accept a potential discard only for its layoff value.

8. When purposely holding back your contract meld, make sure to study the score.

9. When putting down poker straights, it is best to meld them in sets of threes rather than sets of fours, fives, or sixes—the reason is, there are more opportunities for layoffs.

10. Don't play hunches—play the odds.

Standard Rules for Skarney Gin

Requirements

1. Two players—although the game may involve three or four players, only two of these may be in play against each other simultaneously.

2. A standard 52-card deck. It is recommended that two packs of cards with backs of different colors be used in the play. While the dealer is shuffling for the deal, the non-dealer is giving the other pack a preliminary shuffle, after which it is set to one side. It is shuffled again by the loser of this hand before he deals the next hand.

Point scoring for penalty cards: Melded cards resting on the table at the end of a hand count zero. Only the cards left in a player's hand at the end of a hand are scored. Even though they form melds they are counted as penalty cards against the holder. The ace is the highest-ranking penalty card, having a value of 15 points. The king, queen, and jack are valued at 10 points each. All other cards have their numerical face value, such as deuce 2 points, three 3 points, four 4 points, etc. The suits have no value.

So that the reader can see the penalty card counts at a glance, they have been placed in tabular form.

POINT SCORING FOR PENALTY
CARDS LEFT IN HAND AT
END OF HAND

Cards	Points
Aces	Minus 15 each
Kings	Minus 10 each
Queens	Minus 10 each
Jacks	Minus 10 each
Tens	Minus 10 each
Nines	Minus 9 each
Eights	Minus 8 each
Sevens	Minus 7 each
Sixes	Minus 6 each
Fives	Minus 5 each
Fours	Minus 4 each
Threes	Minus 3 each
Twos	Minus 2 each

Melds: The following three types of melds are permitted in Skarney Gin.

1. *Group Melds.* Three or four cards of the same rank such as three or four eights, three or four kings, etc.

2. *Sequence Melds.* Three or more cards of the same suit in consecutive order. *Examples:* three, four, five of hearts; or eight, nine, ten, and jack of spades. Aces, however, may be used in both low and high card sequences. *Examples:* ace, deuce, three of spades; queen, king, ace of clubs. Aces, however, cannot be used in a round-the-corner sequence such as king, ace, deuce of diamonds.

3. *Poker-Straight Melds.* Three or more cards of various suits in consecutive order. *Examples:* poker straights such as the three of clubs, four of diamonds, five of spades; or ten of diamonds, jack of hearts, queen of clubs, and king of diamonds, etc. Aces, as in sequence melds, may be used in both a low or high card run or straight. *Examples:* ace of hearts, deuce of diamonds, three of clubs; or queen of spades, king of hearts, ace of clubs, etc. Aces cannot be used in a round-the-corner straight such as king, ace, deuce.

Contract melds: The first meld made by each player in each and every deal (hand) until the completion of the game must meet the exact initial contract meld requirement of three three-card melds, a total of nine cards. The three three-card melds may be comprised of any of the following: (*a*) three three-card group melds; (*b*) three three-card sequence melds; (*c*) three three-card poker-straight melds; (*d*) any three three-card meld combinations made up of groups, sequences, and poker straights. *Examples:* (1) one three-card group, one three-card sequence, and one three-card poker straight; (2) one three-card group and two three-card sequences; (3) one three-card group and two three-card poker straights, etc. To emphasize, no part of a contract meld can have more than three cards when first placed on the table, nor can the contract meld be comprised of more or less than three three-card melds.

Selecting dealer and starting position: By mutual consent either player may shuffle the deck of cards. Each player cuts a group of cards from the deck. Player cutting the low-faced card deals first. In case of a tie, players cut again. The loser of a hand deals the next hand.

If players want to cut for seat position, the player cutting low takes his choice of seat.

The shuffle and cut: Dealer shuffles the deck. Opponent may call for a shuffle at any time he likes prior to the cut, though the dealer retains the privilege of shuffling last. Dealer must offer the deck to opponent for cut. If opponent refuses to cut, the dealer must cut his own cards before starting the deal. When cutting, at least ten cards must be in each cut portion of the deck.

The deal: Dealer deals the opponent ten cards and himself ten cards, the opponent being dealt the first card off the top of the deck and so on alternately, until the dealer gets the last, twentieth card. The remainder of the deck, called the stock, is placed face down on the table between both players. It is advisable to spread the stock out fan-shaped on the table to minimize the chances of inadvertently drawing and seeing any cards other than the one to which the player is entitled.

The actual play of the hand: Each of the two players in turn, starting with the non-dealer, does as follows:

First, he takes (draws) the top card of the stock (the remainder of the undealt cards which are face down on the table).

Second, once a player has fulfilled his contract meld, he may, if he chooses, place on the table before him any possible melds and any possible one- or two-card layoffs on each of his previous melds. A player at each turn of play is not permitted to lay off more than two cards on each previous meld. Nor is a player permitted to lay off cards on his opponent's melds.

Third, he removes a potential discard (remember, I said "potential discard") from the cards he is holding, turns it face up in his hand and offers it to his opponent by extending it toward him, asking, "Do you want this card?" The opponent may either accept or refuse the potential discard. If he accepts it, he replies, "I'll take it." This action ends the turn of play for the player who offered the card. If the opponent refuses the potential discard, the player who offered it must keep the card and return it to his hand, and his turn of play is ended. A player cannot offer the same potential discard he just accepted from his opponent at his subsequent turn of play. *Example:* A player accepts his opponent's potential discard, which is the six of spades. He cannot offer the six of spades to his opponent until he has offered another card first.

Fourth, if a player's potential discard is an ace, and the opponent accepts it, the opponent loses his turn to pick the top card of the stock.

Fifth and last, should a player hold one card in his hand, he is not permitted to offer it as a potential discard. He merely says, "Last card" and keeps it.

A player during his turn and at no other time may ask his opponent how many cards he holds. The question must be answered correctly. And, so it goes from player to player until the hand ends by a player getting rid of all the cards in his hand by going Skarney—or two cards remain in the stock. When a player draws the fiftieth card from the stock and puts down his melds and layoffs, if any, the hand ends then and there without the player offering a potential discard.

To re-emphasize, a player at each turn of play after having put down his contract meld may meld and lay off one or two cards on each previous meld as he wishes. A player is not permitted to lay off cards on his opponent's melds.

Note: In Skarney Gin, to minimize the chances of not picking from the stock at a player's turn of play, the following rule should be enforced. Once a player has refused a potential discard, he must immediately pick a card from the top of the stock. The strict observance of this rule will avoid many arguments between players as to whether a player at his turn of play has or has not taken a card from the stock.

How to Score a Hand

1. When a player, after having laid down his contract meld gets rid of every card in his hand, he calls "Skarney," ending the hand. This is also known as *gin,* or *going out.* The player who goes Skarney receives a 20-point Skarney bonus plus a total point count of all the cards that his opponent holds in his hand at the end of the hand even though they form melds. *Example:* A player goes Skarney. His opponent holds seven cards comprised of four tens, two fives, and one ace. The player who Skarneyed scores 65 points. The penalty value of his opponent's seven unmelded cards, plus 20 points for going Skarney, makes a total of 85 points. His opponent does not score.

2. When a player goes Skarney or gin, and his opponent has failed to put down his contract meld, the 20-point Skarney bonus for the hand is doubled to 40 points and is known as *double Skarney,* or *double gin.*

3. When a player has drawn the fiftieth card (the last card, leaving two in the stock), the hand ends without that player offering a potential discard—and the player holding the lower penalty point total in unmelded cards in his hand wins the hand and gets credit for the point difference between both totals. *Example:* The hand ends and player A is caught with 15 points in unmelded cards in his hand. Player B has 36 points in unmelded cards in his hand. Player A is the winner of the hand and scores 21 points, the difference between both totals. Should both players tie, a no-hand is declared and the same dealer deals again.

End of game: A game terminates at the end of any hand in which a total of 200 or more points is scored by either player.

How to Score a Game

1. Winner of the game scores the difference between both totals.

2. Winner of the game gets a *game bonus* of 200 points for winning.

3. An extra 25 points known as a *box bonus* is added to each player's score for each hand won.

4. Should a player score 200 points or more before his opponent scores any points at all, winner gets a 200-point game bonus plus a 200-point shutout bonus—plus all other credits. Following is a sample scoring of a Skarney Gin game, using my new game scoring method. The hand score for each player is written down at the left, then a dash followed by the cumulative game score to the right. This makes it known to each player at all times how far ahead or behind he is.

SAMPLE SCORING OF A SKARNEY GIN GAME

	You	Opponent
	44-44	
		64-64
	36-80	
	40-120	
	27-147	
		70-134
	120-267	
Game scores	267	134
Box bonuses	125	50
Game bonuses	200	
Total scores	592	184
Minus loser's score	−184	
Your net winnings	408 points	

First Hand: You go Skarney. Your opponent is caught with 24 points in unmelded cards (penalty cards). You score 24 points plus a 20-point Skarney bonus—a total of 44 points.

Second Hand: Your opponent goes Skarney. You are caught with 44 penalty points. Opponent scores 44 points plus a 20-point Skarney bonus. A total of 64 points. At the end of the second hand your opponent leads by 64 to 44.

Third Hand: Two cards are left in the stock. No one goes Skarney. You hold 9 penalty points, your opponent 45. You score the difference, 36 points. At the end of the third hand, you lead 80 to 64.

Fourth Hand: You go Skarney. Your opponent is caught with 20 points in unmelded cards (penalty points). You score 20 plus a 20-point Skarney bonus for a total fourth-hand score of 40 points. The cumulative game score at the end of the fourth hand is 120 to 64 in your favor.

Fifth Hand: You go Skarney. Your opponent holds 7 penalty points.

You score 7 plus a 20-point Skarney bonus for a fifth-hand total of 27 points. The score at the end of the fifth hand is 147 to 64 in your favor.

Sixth Hand: Your opponent goes Skarney. You are caught with 50 penalty points. Your opponent scores 50 plus a 20-point Skarney bonus, or 70 points in all. At the end of the sixth hand the score reads 147 to 134 with you in the lead.

Seventh Hand: You go double Skarney. Your opponent holds 80 points in unmelded cards (penalty points). You score 80 plus a 40-point double-Skarney bonus for a total seventh-hand score of 120 points. The 120 points puts you well over the 200 mark with a total of 267 and gives you game. You have five boxes, a total of 125 points at 25 points each, your opponent has two boxes worth 50 points; these are added to the scores. You add a game bonus of 200 points for winning the game. Your grand total is 592. Your opponent's is 184. So your point winnings for the game are the difference in scores, or 408 points net. At one-tenth of a cent a point, you collect 41 cents from your opponent.

Additional Rules for Skarney Gin

If a player accidentally, inadvertently, or purposely violates a rule of the game he must pay a prescribed penalty. The right to penalize an offense or irregularity is forfeited if the offended player (*a*) waives the penalty, or (*b*) calls attention to an opponent's irregularity after he has drawn a card from the stock.

Misdeals: A misdeal is declared, and the dealer of the hand immediately starts a new deal, whenever any of the following improprieties are discovered (there are no penalties for the dealer or the responsible player):

1. If a card is turned over any time during the deal.

2. If either player or both players have been dealt an incorrect number of cards.

3. If a player deals out of turn and the error is discovered before a play has been completed.

4. If a player looks at an opponent's card or cards during the deal.

5. If a card is found face up during the deal.

6. If, however, a card is found face up in the stock, it must be properly turned, the stock shuffled and cut, and play continues.

Irregularities in the draw: Here are problems that may arise when drawing:

1. If a player inadvertently picks off the stock two cards instead of one or inadvertently sees the face of the card below the one he has just taken, or his opponent has reason to believe that he has seen it,

then his opponent at his turn of play, may, if he likes, look at the face of the top card of the stock and take it or shuffle the stock and cut before drawing from the stock.

2. If a player draws from the stock before his opponent has offered a potential discard, he loses his turn to accept the potential discard. Furthermore, he cannot meld or lay off until his next turn of play and the penalty to the offender is 25 points.

Imperfect deck during the play: The following are the rules when a faulty deck is discovered:

1. There must be a new deal by the same dealer:

   (*a*) If it is discovered that the deck has one or more duplicate cards.

   (*b*) If a foreign card (not from either deck) is found in the deck during the deal or in the stock at any time before a player goes Skarney.

   (*c*) If it is discovered while the hand is still in play that the deck has fewer or more than the standard 52 cards.

2. If, however, a card of the other deck, when two decks are being used, is found in the stock, it shall be eliminated and play continues.

3. If it is discovered after a player goes Skarney or the hand is over that the deck has fewer or more cards, it has no bearing on that or previous hands.

Irregularities in the potential discard: Here are rules covering discards.

1. If a player offers a potential discard without drawing, he must draw the top card of the stock if attention is called to the irregularity before his opponent has drawn. If the opponent draws before attention is called, the offending player must take the next top card of the stock and the play refers back to the opponent, and the offender on his next turn to play may not meld or lay off until his subsequent turn to play.

2. If during the play a player should refuse a potential discard either by word or action, he cannot then decide to take it. His refusal to accept it is his final decision on that card.

3. If a player at his turn has accepted his opponent's potential discard either by word or action, the decision stands. He cannot refuse the potential discard under any condition.

4. A potential discard once offered cannot be returned to the player's hand and another potential discard substituted; the play stands.

Illegal contract melds: If it is discovered during a player's turn to play that he has placed on the table as a contract meld an insufficient or illegal meld, the following can be done:

1. He may correct the irregularity by putting down sufficient melds

from his hand, in which case he may rearrange the cards put down in error providing he makes use of all melded cards. The offender is penalized 25 points.

2. He may return to his hand one or more cards put down in error and rearrange all his melds from melded cards and cards in his hand, in which case he is penalized 25 points.

3. If a player errs by placing on the table an illegal or insufficient contract meld and he cannot remedy the situation, he is permitted to return the cards to his hand and he is penalized 25 points.

4. If a player errs by placing on the table more than nine cards (3 three-card melds) as his contract meld, he may correct the irregularity by returning the extra cards to his hand. There is no penalty for the infraction providing no cards from the hand are used to help achieve the contract meld.

Irregularities in melding and laying off: The following details rule melding and laying-off irregularities:

1. After a player's contract meld has been fulfilled, and he puts down an additional meld or melds, he cannot pick them up and replace them in his hand. Nor is he permitted to rearrange them in any other kind of meld. Cards once melded and laid down on the table remain as legal melds. The same ruling holds true for a one- to two-card layoff.

2. If a player lays down an illegal meld or layoff and attention is brought to it, he is permitted to correct the irregularity and replace the card or cards in his hand. The penalty for this infraction of the rules is 25 points.

3. If after an illegal meld or layoff, the opponent draws a card from the stock before attention is called to the error, the illegal meld or layoff stands as a legal play.

4. If a player melds or lays off cards before drawing a card from the stock, and attention is called to the error, the player must draw a card from the stock and return the illegal melds and layoffs to his hand, and he cannot meld or lay off until his next turn of play.

Stop-card irregularity: If a player's potential discard is an ace, commonly known as a *stop card,* and if the opponent accepts the ace, he loses his turn to pick the top card of the stock. If the opponent refuses the ace, the player who offered it must keep it. If, however, the opponent accepts the stop card and draws from the stock inadvertently, he must show the card erroneously drawn to his opponent and replace it on the stock. The opponent may, if he chooses, take the card as his draw or shuffle the stock and cut before drawing. There is no penalty for this infraction.

A last-card irregularity: When a player holds only one card in his hand, he cannot offer it as a potential discard. When holding only one card, a player must announce "Last card," in a voice that his opponent can hear. If, however, a player inadvertently does offer his last card, there is no penalty, but the player may be reprimanded. If the player repeats the infraction, he is penalized 25 points for each new offense.

Score correction: If a scoring error is made, the following rules prevail:

1. When a score is agreed upon and written down, it may not later be set aside. Proven mistakes in addition or subtraction on the score sheet may be corrected at any time prior to the start of a new game. If the error is proven after the first draw of any hand, the hand must be completed before the error can be corrected.

2. Once the winner of the hand has verified his point count for the hand and entered it on the score sheet and a new hand has started, players cannot call for rectification of some previous mistake they all have made. A player is not required to inform his opponent that he has committed an error or failed to lay off a card or failed to meld to his best advantage, nor is he required to notify his opponent that he is calling an incorrect count to his disadvantage.

3. A player who at the completion of a hand inadvertently mixes his or his opponent's penalty cards with the rest of the cards before they are counted may not dispute that opponent's claim to their point value.

Skarney Gin Doubles

This exciting and scientific variation of Skarney Gin is recommended to the Skarney Gin players who want their game to have greater scope plus a reward for skillful preplay card analysis and psychological bluff. The addition of these two scientific maneuvers leads to a more strategic and greater point scoring game. This feat is accomplished by simply adding a pass, double, and redouble bidding system to Skarney Gin. This bidding system corresponds roughly to the passing, doubling, and redoubling elements of Contract Bridge.

Skarney Gin Doubles is played and scored the same as you play Skarney Gin with the following exceptions and additional rules.

1. A game terminates at the end of any hand in which a total of 300 or more points is scored by either player.

2. *How and when to bid.* The bidding begins when each player has been dealt his initial ten-card hand and before either player has drawn a card from the stock. The nondealer makes the first bid, his opponent the second, the nondealer the third if necessary. Following is a description of each of the five possible bids that can be made in Skarney Gin Doubles.

(*a*) The nondealer calls "Pass," and the dealer calls "Pass." The winner of the hand scores the actual penalty point count.

(*b*) The nondealer calls "Pass," the dealer "Double," the nondealer "Pass." The winner of the hand scores double the penalty point count.

(*c*) The nondealer calls "Pass," the dealer "Double," the nondealer "Redouble." The winner of the hand scores quadruple the penalty point count.

(*d*) The nondealer calls "Double," the dealer "Pass." The winner of the hand scores double the penalty point count.

(*e*) The nondealer calls "Double," the dealer "Redouble." The winner of the hand scores quadruple the penalty point count.

3. *How to score a bid hand.* In Skarney Gin Doubles the penalty point score of a pass bid hand remains the same as in regular Skarney Gin, the penalty point score of a double-bid hand is multiplied by two, and the penalty point score of a redouble-bid hand is multiplied by four. *Examples:* (*a*) The winner of a pass hand goes Skarney and catches his opponent with 16 penalty points in his hand. The winner is credited with 16 points plus the 20-point Skarney bonus for a final hand score of 36 points, the same scoring as if he were playing regular Skarney Gin. (*b*) The winner of a double hand goes Skarney and catches his opponent with 16 penalty points in his hand. The winner is credited with 16 twice, or 32 points, plus the 20-point Skarney bonus for a final hand score of 52 points. (*c*) The winner of a redouble hand goes Skarney and catches his opponent with 16 penalty points in his hand. The winner is credited with 16 four times, or 64 points, plus the 20-point Skarney bonus for a final hand score of 84 points.

The above-described method of calculating the penalty point score of the loser also holds true when a player goes double Skarney. Should a player win the hand with a lesser number of penalty points, only the winning difference in points is doubled, redoubled, or remains the same. The pass, double, or redouble bid affects only the specific hand. It does not have anything at all to do with the score of other hands.

Note: Skarney Gin Doubles may be played in all the multiple game and partnership variants described in the following pages.

Round-the-Corner Skarney Gin

This fascinating variation of Skarney Gin is recommended to the non-serious players who like variety and prefer their game to possess more luck and a quicker ending. All the rules governing Skarney Gin apply with the following additional rule:

An ace, in addition to being used in high and low sequences, or poker straights, such as ace–two–three, or ace–king–queen, can also be used to go round the corner, such as king–ace–two; or two–ace–king. These round-the-corner sequence and poker-straight melds may be extended of course. *Examples:* (*a*) king–ace–two–three; (*b*) queen–king–ace–two–three; (*c*) two–ace–king–queen–jack; (*d*) three–two–ace–king–queen–jack–ten, and so on.

Skarney Gin Triples

This variation is played exactly like Skarney Gin except that the scoring system used in regular Hollywood Gin Rummy (see page 743) is employed.

Skarney Gin for Three Players

Skarney Gin, though primarily for two players, makes an enjoyable game for three players. Although three players take part, only two are in play against each other simultaneously, as in captain play (below).

To determine which two shall start, any player, by consent of the others, shuffles, and the three cut cards. Low man—that man whose exposed card is of lowest rank—sits out the first hand. The other two play a game of Skarney Gin.

The score of the first hand is credited to the winner, and the loser drops out. The winner proceeds to play the next hand against the third man. (Generally the nonplayer keeps the score.) So it goes, loser giving way to nonplayer hand by hand, until one of the three scores 200 points or more.

The winner is paid off in the amount of his credit over each opponent. The player with the second highest score collects from low man. A player scoring a shutout can collect his shutout bonus only from the player who scored zero. For example, A scores 205 points; B, 90; and C, none. A gets credit for a shutout over C but not over B. Value of credits and bonuses is the same as in two-handed Skarney Gin. In three-handed Skarney Gin a player may collect from two players, lose to two players, or win from one and lose to one.

Skarney Gin Captains

This is a variation of Skarney Gin for three players, borrowed from Backgammon where it is called chouette or "in the box." A plays the first game as captain against B and C; B playing the first hand and continuing to play as long as he wins. But when he loses, C takes his place and continues to play until he loses, when B comes back again, and so on until the game ends. The captain keeps playing to the end of the game, regardless of whether he wins or loses. A single score is kept and totaled at the end of the game. The captain wins or loses the net total from or to each of the opponents. Then B becomes the captain playing against A and C, and so on.

Skarney Partnership Gin

This is four-handed Skarney Gin. Two players are teamed against the other two. Two games of two-handed Skarney Gin are played simultaneously and the partners enter their score as one. The players cut for partners, holders of the two highest exposed cards being teamed against the holders of the two lowest. All the rules of Skarney Gin apply to this variation. The only variation is in the scoring.

Team scores, not players' scores, are entered. *Example:* (a) A and B are partners playing against C and D. A, playing the first hand against his opponent C, wins by 68 points. D, playing against B, wins by 20 points. Team A-B wins the box by 48 points. That is the only score entered on the score sheet. (b) As before, A and B are partners against C and D. At the end of the first hand A switches seats with B and plays against D, while B plays against C. At the end of the second hand, A and B shift back to the original positions. This alternation continues with each hand until the game ends.

Note: Due to the great number of cards melded, it is suggested that two tables be used, one for each two contestants. Game is 300 points. Game bonus remains at 200, shutout bonus 200, and all other scoring is as in two-handed Skarney Gin.

Skarney Gin Strategy

Skarney Gin becomes a considerably more scientific game than regular Gin Rummy, owing to the lack of a discard pile. However, like regular Gin, it is a game of deduction and counterdeduction: (1) You must try to figure out what cards your opponent is holding so that you won't offer him vital cards; (2) you must try to build up your hand for a possible contract meld.

In Skarney Gin, as in most card games of skill and chance, there is a mathematical basis for many correct plays. There are, of course, some probability factors in Skarney Gin which are apparent even to the beginner. It should be obvious that you have a better chance of making a three-card poker straight than a three-card group when you hold a five and six (any suits) than if you hold a pair of sixes. In fact, the odds are 4 to 1 in favor of the poker straight. The reason is there are eight cards (four fours and four sevens) to draw from to make a poker straight and only two sixes to draw from to make a group meld.

At the very beginning of the hand, what is and what is not a safe potential discard is not too important. On the first few rounds any discard with the possible exception of an ace (stop card) is usually accepted. You should not worry at this point because more often than not, your opponent will take it. Therefore, what you should do at the beginning of the hand is to offer potential discards that you wish to get rid of and at the same time concentrate on building up your hand.

While concentrating on building your own hand you should try to keep your opponent in the dark regarding the strength of your hand. An initial meld of three three-card melds is fairly easy to obtain toward the middle of the hand. Even possession of three three-card melds at the beginning of the hand occurs quite frequently in Skarney Gin. But, what to do with such a hand requires some analytical reasoning. Sure, you can go down with your contract meld and put the pressure on your opponent. Great, but what about the one or more cards that will remain in your hand—are they unmatched cards? How about the next potential discard of yours? Is it a part of a matched set or a possible layoff card? Or, is it a useless card to your hand? Do you believe your opponent will take it? All the above factors are vital in playing a good game of Skarney Gin. And such deductions must be studied carefully.

I've seen many a player put down his initial meld after his first pick off the stock—and see his hand grow from two cards to eight or more cards, and his opponent goes Skarney and catches him with a hundred or more points. This upward movement of the number of cards held by a player is caused by his opponent's refusal to accept said player's potential discard, something the player has no control over.

Study your contract meld before putting it down—study it from one angle—then switch your melds around and study it from another angle. You'll be surprised what you'll see that passed unobserved a moment ago. As mentioned earlier, there are more opportunities to lay off on poker straights than group melds. However, don't rule out group melds—they play a vital part in preventing your opponent from getting such cards. The principle of mobility is a general principle in Skarney Gin. To keep you hand fluid at all times and be prepared for most contingencies is of the utmost importance. There can be no definite instruction at this point without ifs, ands, and buts.

In preparing to fulfill your initial meld or in playing for Skarney, try to form as many two-way melds incorporating the same cards in groups and poker straights. For instance, you hold three sixes, three sevens, and three eights. These same three-card groups can and should be switched to three three-card poker straights. It becomes quite a problem to some players when holding 15 or more cards to segregate the melds to their best advantage. The best advice that can be given to achieve this aim is to take your time when sorting out melds in your hand because a simple rearrangement of melds may spell an eventual

Skarney for you. In fact, more games are lost by an early improper arrangement of cards in the hand than by all other erroneous plays.

As a rule, it is best to wait several rounds before putting down your contract meld. That is, providing your opponent has not as yet put down his contract meld. If your opponent has fulfilled his contract meld and you have not, by all means get down on the board (if possible) with any kinds of melds you can muster together.

Once your opponent has put down his contract meld, each of your potential discard plays must be thoroughly analyzed. You must be ultra-safe in offering a potential discard. Think twice before offering an ace (stop card) in the later phase of the hand. Study your opponent's and your own melds (if any) very carefully and think twice before playing.

When your opponent's point total is close to game, you must be extra careful about the point total (of melds or unmatched cards or both) in your hand. You must try to "keep under." That means that you must reduce your point total so that, if possible, even if your opponent goes Skarney, you will still be under going out. Just being aware of the necessity of keeping under will improve your chances of winning the game by 25 to 33⅓ percent. Except for expert play, my observation is that every third or fourth final hand of a game is lost because of the avoidable failure to keep under.

It is, I take it, the author's privilege to point out—and the player's privilege to ignore—the fact that there are 15,820,024,220 possible ten-card hands in Skarney Gin. In every game there occurs a certain incidence of useless statistics. I don't expect you to remember how often in how many billion hands your present holding will occur. I shouldn't be surprised if you fail to remember that the odds of the dealer's being dealt one or more three-card melds in his first ten cards is about 15 to 1 in your favor—although remembering that will improve your game. To attempt to tell the player whether to hold possible layoffs in his hand or lay them off seems to me unsound without knowledge of (a) the cards he holds, (b) the melds he sees (if any), (c) the cards still alive, and (d) the potential discards taken by one's opponent. As to this play, you must use your own judgment—as, in fact, you must learn to do in any hand at Skarney Gin.

31.
Punchboards,
Chain Letters
and Pyramid Clubs

Although punchboards (sometimes called sales boards) and push cards are not as popular as they once were, about 1½ million Americans, of whom ½ million are women, wager $40 million annually on them. The colorful punchboard is frequently seen behind the counters of candy stores, bars and restaurants, with fancy displays of merchandise prizes ranging from a cheap quarter prize to a valuable prize worth $100 or more—the more costly prizes usually include watches, fishing rods, table silverware and women's handbags. However, the most popular types of punchboards are those whose prize awards are paid out in cash.

THE FIRST AMERICAN PUNCHBOARDS

Handmade raffle gameboards, the forerunners of the modern punchboard and push card, were in use in saloons in this country as early as 1795. The first was probably invented by some ingenious saloon-keeper who saw that such a board would enable him to run a raffle for the individual customer. These early raffle boards were eight-inch-square wooden boards, half an inch thick, with 100 or so quarter-inch holes drilled through the board, each of which contained a rolled-up, numbered slip of paper. The player paid a nickel, dime or quarter for a chance, then used a nail to push out one of the numbered slips. If his number corresponded to a predetermined winning number, he received a bottle of liquor or a cash award.

The raffle gameboard disappeared about 1815 because too many saloonkeepers were holding out the top winning numbers for themselves. They reappeared about 1870 in a slightly different form. Still

Punchboards.

handmade, they were of cardboard instead of wood and were called punchboards because the players pushed out the numbered slips by punching a hole through a paper covering glued to the front and back surfaces of the board.

It wasn't until the invention of the automatic punchboard-manufacturing machine in 1910 that punchboards flooded the country. Five years later one of the largest punchboard manufacturers estimated that 30 million punchboards and push cards had been sold during the period 1910 to 1915.

The popularity of the punchboard reached its peak in 1939, when 50 million were sold in that one year. Since the average punchboard contains 200 holes (chances) and the average price per chance is 7¢, this means that 10 billion chances were sold that year for a gross revenue of $700 million.

As evidence that the manufacture of punchboards was a lucrative business, take the case of one of the many punchboard manufacturers, George D. Sax. He left the business some years ago, used his profits to buy into a Chicago bank and became chairman of the board. Later he retired to Florida, where he built the fabulous Saxony Hotel at Miami Beach for a reputed $5 million.

Since 1950 the popularity of punchboards has declined steadily. They are now outlawed in many states, and many players seem to have caught on to the fact that punchboards are very often crooked and that their chances of winning, even when the board is honest, are practically nil. A crooked punchboard is one which the manufacturer sells with a secret key giving the location of most of the winning holes. This enables the purchaser of the board to punch out these holes before the board goes on display.

Punchboards come in a variety of sizes ranging from the small pocket-sized board with 30 or more holes up to the giant 10,000-hole board whose top prize award may be as much as $500. The player pays from 5¢ to $1 for the privilege of trying to punch out a numbered slip that corresponds to one of the prize numbers printed on the board's display section.

PUSH CARDS

A push card is simply a different version of a punchboard. Two pieces of cardboard are glued together and the outer surface bears partially perforated circles instead of holes. The small rod used to punch out a chance on a punchboard has been eliminated. The player merely needs to push his finger against one of the circles, dislodging two small pieces of card, one of which bears a printed chance number on its previously hidden surface.

The most popular push cards are the folding-board type slightly larger than a man's wallet. A girl's name (Ruth, May, Irene, etc.) is printed on the visible surface of each circle, and the players usually push out the names of their wives, daughters, mothers, girl friends, etc. The manufacturer who thought up this psychological sales gimmick knew what he was doing.

As each chance is taken, the player's name is written opposite the name he selected on a space on the board provided for that purpose. When all the chances have been sold, a perforated seal on the board is broken to reveal the winning name. The crooked manufacturer sells

Push card.

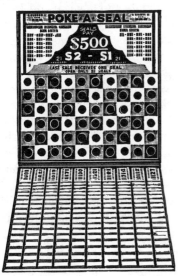

No. 6472—Poke-A-Seal Ticket Deal. A new last selling pad style deal. Colorfully designed with glossy finish. Made with 1,000 consecutive numeral tickets at 5 for 25c with a payout of 50 winners, ranging from 50c to $5.00. 60 seal card but only 21 are taken.

Takes in $50.00
Average payout 23.75
Average profit $26.25

Each **$2.75**
Each
(in lots of 12).... **$2.50**

his crooked customers the winning name so that it can be punched out in advance.

Self-styled charitable organizations often mail push cards out by the thousands. An accompanying letter tells the recipient that if he will sell the chances and return the receipts to the organization, two expensive and beautiful prizes (camera, radio, etc.) will be forwarded, one for the winner and one for the chance seller. When the sucker who falls for this receives the prizes the chances that both he and the winner will be disappointed are 100%. Most punchboards and push cards pay out less than 50% when the prizes are cash awards. When the prizes are merchandise the players get even less, because the merchandise is seldom worth even a third of its advertised price.

THE OPERATOR'S PERCENTAGE

A 10,000-hole giant punchboard whose chances are 10¢ each will take in $1,000 when completely sold. The prize awards paid to winners seldom total more than $400, giving the seller a profit of $600, or 60%. Slot machine or punchboard syndicates install their own boards in bars, clubs, restaurants and other desirable locations when these are under their control. The seller keeps about 30% of the take and the remaining 70% goes to the syndicate which pays the cost of the merchandise prize awards and makes a contribution to the grafting City Fathers who allow them to run this organized racket. The ice is usually about 25% of the syndicate's net profit. The presence of a considerable number of punchboards in your locality, like the presence of any other form of organized gambling, means that one or more of your local politicians and/or police officials are taking graft.

Any player can easily calculate the seller's percentage of profit on any honest punchboard by counting the number of chances on each board, then multiplying the total by the cost of each chance. The result is the board's overall take. Deduct from this the total of the amounts paid out in cash awards and you have the seller's profit. Divide seller's profit by board's take to get the percentage in favor of the seller. Example: A board's total take is $600, the seller's profit $360. Divide $360 by $600 for an answer of 60%. Do I hear anyone disagree with the statement that all punchboard players are strictly chumps?

Add to this the fact that a great many store- and innkeepers who aren't satisfied with a 50% or 60% profit increase it simply by removing the punchboard whenever the board has had a good play and the big prize numbers are still in the board.

About 1930, in order to entice players to lose their money faster, punchboard manufacturers added the slot machine jackpot principle.

They placed a window cutout covered with cellophane at the top of the board.

Before putting the board on display, the seller inserts several coins into this jackpot recess through a slot at the top. Then he builds the jackpot by adding every third or fourth coin gambled by the players. A player who punches out the numbered slip that corresponds with the jackpot number wins the jackpot coins plus a stipulated additional cash prize. Since the players lose three times as many coins as go into the jackpot, it is obvious that in the long run they wind up behind the eight ball. And if the board is crooked and the jackpot number has been punched out in advance, the players all lose in the short run, too.

PUNCHBOARD CHEATS AND THEIR METHODS

Keyed punchboards are commonplace because they are easy to get. Suppliers of crooked gambling apparatus issue catalogs in two colors advertising keyed boards in all sizes from the small 200-hole board to the large 10,000-hole board, at prices ranging from $3.50 to $20. Crooked boards usually cost about four times the price of honest boards of the same size.

The player doesn't have a chance against a keyed punchboard in which all the larger prizes have been punched out before the board is displayed. But it isn't always the storekeeper who profits by this cheating gimmick. Sometimes he is the victim. I first discovered this dodge when, as a teen-ager, I had a job running errands for a dicemaker named Ame who then owned the Lane Novelty Company, a small gambling supply house in Hoboken, New Jersey.

I was behind the counter talking to Ame one day when two tough-looking Chinese came in. "Hello, Punchboard," Ame said to one of them. "Haven't seen you for a while and I've got something you'll be interested in—a new shipment of punchboards. You can have first pick."

"Good," one of the Chinese men replied. "Let's see them."

Ame produced a colored brochure from under the counter and handed it to the customer. The folder depicted ten punchboards of different sizes with a heading above each picture in boldface type that read:

OUR KEYED PUNCHBOARDS WILL WIN THE MONEY FOR YOU

The Chinese man looked it over carefully and then asked, "Do you have all of these in stock?"

Ame replied, "That's right, in just about any amount you want."

"Good," the Chinese man said. "I'll take ten each of these three."

He pointed to three boards priced at $10 apiece. Ame put up the order and then wrapped the boards in plain brown wrapping paper. The Chinese gave Ame $300, thanked him and left.

I looked at Ame and asked, "Why did you call him Punchboard? Is that his name?"

"You never seem to get tired with those questions, Johnny." Ame smiled. "That guy thinks of himself as the Chinese Punchboard King, and he loves it when anyone calls him Punchboard."

"Are the Chinese very big gamblers?" I asked.

"They'd rather gamble than anything else, but mostly among themselves."

"Then he'll probably put those boards to good use."

"I'll say he will, Johnny. He's got the sweetest racket going. He'll spend all day tomorrow selling those boards to Chinese merchants around Mott Street in New York for a dollar fifty each and then—"

I interrupted. "A dollar fifty each! When he just paid you ten dollars apiece?"

"Sure. Later his pal, the guy who was with him, will visit the stores who bought the boards, act like a customer and buy something, then notice the punchboard and start playing it. After a few losing punches —whammo! He'll punch out the top prize of a hundred dollars. Those two guys can afford to sell ten-dollar boards at a buck and a half apiece because they'll get back a hundred bucks apiece, three thousand bucks on a three-hundred-buck investment."

"That's quite a racket," I said. "But why are the manufacturers permitted to make keyed boards if this is what happens?"

"I don't know, Johnny," Ame said. "All I know is that it's big business."

"Are there many sold in the course of a year, Ame?" I asked.

"I dunno what the other guys sell, but I dump about three hundred a week, and I'm only one of hundreds of dealers throughout the United States. There's one merchant here in Hoboken who takes about half a dozen a week for himself."

"What's he do with them?" I asked, rather puzzled. "That seems like a lot for one store."

"Well, he just punches out the big winners before he puts the board on display, and when the board is half sold he sticks up a new one and throws the other one away. And when his regular customers inquire as to who won the big prize on the old punchboard, he tells them a couple of strangers came in, punched out all the rest of the board and won the big prizes."

"That settles that," I said. "I'll never play another punchboard."

"You're smart not to, Johnny," Ame replied.

And since the punchboard racket hasn't changed a bit since then, Ame's advice is still good: "You're smart not to."

JAR GAMES, TIP BOOKS, TIP BOARDS AND MATCH PAKS

These games are all punchboards in disguise. They are examples of the way gamblers and gambling-game manufacturers circumvent the law by giving a prohibited game a new look. Whenever a law is passed making one type of gambling game illegal, the boys merely change its name and appearance. In these versions, instead of numbers punched from a board, numbered slips are drawn from a jar or selected from a group of slips on a display board, in a book or match pack. When the authorities get around to passing laws against the new variation the manufacturers figure out another disguise to hide the same old lottery principle.

Jar games merely consist of a group of 50 to 12,000 or more paper tickets in a glass jar, on the outside of which is a label listing the prize awards. Each ticket is folded at one end and sealed with a pasted strip of paper. The player pays from 5¢ to 25¢ for a chance, reaches into the jar, removes a ticket and tears it open, Inside he finds a number, and the label on the jar tells him whether or not it wins a prize.

This is how a manufacturer's catalog describes a typical jar game:

PICK-WIN. Red, White, and Blue Tab Tickets, the most popular selling tab style ticket ever made. Consists of 2,170 tickets. There are 90 winners ranging from 50¢ to $3.00 Takes in $108.50 at 5¢ per sale. Definite Payout is $54.50. Definite profit is $54.00. Supplied with either 5¢, 10¢ or 25¢ jar label. State which denomination is desired. Glass jar not included. Per deal of 2,170 tickets: $2.75. Per Deal (in lots of 12): $2.60.

Jar game.

In most jar games the operator retains from 40% to 60% of the take.

Tip boards differ only in that the tickets are displayed on counter display boards and tip books are portable folding boards that can be carried in the pocket. Another variation, even more disguised, is the Match Pak. The folded and sealed tickets are stapled inside what looks like a match folder. The manufacturer is quite frank in his catalog about his reasons for giving the old punchboard this disguise:

> The most ingenious and cleverest idea ever developed for use in all territories. Ten to fifteen packs can be carried in each pocket or they can be dispensed right from the box. The payout is printed on the inside cover of each individual pack so there is nothing else to display or carry. Match Pak resembles an ordinary book of paper matches, therefore it can be *Sold Anywhere, Any Time* without attracting attention, since the courtesy of passing anyone a book of matches is a common, everyday occurrence. Another advantage of Match Pak is the many simple ways in which the empty cover may be disposed of or destroyed, leaving no evidence.

Match Pak.

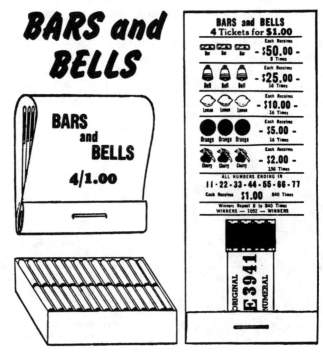

THE CHAIN-LETTER RACKET

The chain-letter scheme is one of the few gambling rackets on a national scale which is not operated by professional gambling operators and from which they derive no profit. The chain-letter scheme and the Pyramid Club racket, which is basically the same, are simply other forms of lotteries. These rackets, as this is written, do not enjoy the national popularity which they did some years ago, but they keep reappearing, and if another variation of these get-rich-quick schemes sweeps the country again tomorrow morning I won't be the least bit surprised.

The chain-letter idea is not new; it began sometime in the Middle Ages when an uneducated population formed "good luck" chains, and it still retains this superstitious feature. The letters always promise that good luck will come to those who participate and bad luck will befall anyone who breaks the chain. It may be that women are more superstitious than men; the ratio of women to men participants in chain-letter schemes is 5 to 1.

Some chain letters are started by honest people who believe that this is a method of getting something for nothing, but a great many of them are started by cheap crooks who have an angle. The principle of the chain letter and the crooked angle are both illustrated by the following incident. In November 1943 I had just returned to my home town of Fairview, New Jersey, after a tour of lecturing to GIs on gambling in a number of southern Army camps. I was having breakfast one morning in the Partview Diner with my friend Walter Scott, who has given me much assistance in my gambling surveys. An attractive blonde approached us, introduced herself and began to give us the chain-letter pitch. I'll call her Alice Blank; the name she gave us was equally phony.

She handed me a letter which I could have read back to her with my eyes closed; it was the standard form. I pretended to study it and then said, "Miss Blank, the letter tells you to contact five close friends. Why are you giving two strangers such a wonderful opportunity to make some easy money?"

"I'm a stranger in Fairview," she replied. "I don't know many people here and I thought you gentlemen would help me continue the chain because it is bad luck to break it." One line in the letter read: "Good luck will come to those who continue the chain; ill luck will befall those who break it." As in all chain letters, a list of five names and addresses was given at the bottom of the letter and the recipient was instructed to send $1 to the person at the top of the list. Then he was to remove that name, add his own name and address at the foot of the list, make four additional copies of the letter and mail them to five friends.

The letter also explained that if no one breaks the chain, each person who adds his name to the list will eventually receive 3,125 letters; each containing $1, a total of $3,125, which is a nice, healthy return on an initial investment of one buck plus five 10-cent stamps.

Miss Blank had already typed up one original and four carbon copies of the letter with her name and address at the bottom of the list. Before she left the diner Walter and I and three other patrons had each accepted one.

As she went out, I said, "I'll bet five bucks she goes into the next diner or bar she comes to, and passes out five more letters."

"And I'll bet you," Walter grinned, "that she's carrying enough letters in that big purse of hers to last all morning."

We both won. We went outside, kept an eye on her and saw her go into a restaurant two blocks down the street. We hit the same restaurant a little later, talked to the cashier and found that Miss Blank had signed up five more customers.

"If she signs up fifty suckers today," Walter said, "she has started fifty chains, and if everybody follows through, Miss Blank will get fifty times 625 letters, each containing a dollar bill, or $31,250."

"If everybody follows through," I said, "Miss Blank will do better than that. The other names on this letter she gave us are all phonies and the addresses are those of rooms she rented so she'll also get the dough sent to them." I listed it for Scotty on the back of an envelope:

Arthur Anderson	$50
Bertha Brown	$250
Catherine Carter	$1,250
Donald Davis	$6,250
	$7,800

"Add that to the $31,250 she gets as Alice Blank and her grand total is $39,050."

"Not bad for a day's work," Scotty said. "If it works."

I did some figuring. "It's too bad she met us. Because we aren't sending Mr. Anderson a buck each, and if we don't write five letters apiece, it means Alice will be out $1,562 for the two chains we didn't start, and if thirty more of the fifty people she propositioned don't follow through on the swindle she is out another $23,430. And all along the line more people will drop out and break the chains. A lot more will write the five letters they are supposed to, but they will forget to send the name at the top of the list the one buck. Instead of trying to get thousands for an investment of one dollar, they will try to get it for nothing. Even Arthur Anderson won't get his full fifty dollars. And out of the fifty chains I doubt if any will go the full first two steps. If that happened and we did write our letters, we wouldn't get back a thin dime because we are in step five. We would be out a buck apiece. Alice Blank will pick up some of the Anderson money, a little of Bertha Brown's money, and still less of Catherine Carter's, and that's about it."

Walter and I did a little detective work and discovered that Alice and her husband spent half their time typing letters and the rest of it convincing honest participants to go along, moving from town to town. Like hundreds of other such swindlers, they made a living at it because they started so many chains and because, under phony names, they always began at the top of the lists. The honest participants who start at the bottom almost never reach the top, never get those 3,125 letters containing a buck each, and realize, too late, that though honest they are also chumps.

A chain in which only a dime is sent instead of a dollar has more chance of partly completing all five steps, but even here, so many people drop out or forget to send dimes that you would be lucky to get more than two or three dollars.

Of the people I questioned in my survey who said they had entered chain-letter schemes, only 1 in 100 got back as much money as he had originally invested. The only people who do any better than that are the swindlers who start the chains. And if the postal authorities catch up with them, they may get a bonus of a jail sentence because the chain-letter racket is a violation of the Postal Lottery and Fraud statutes.

Many of the people who receive chain letters asking them to send five more letters are as greedy as the crooks who started the chain, and they write to dozens of friends, with the result that, although very few chains ever go through five complete steps and very few people receive any money, hundreds of thousands of letters flood the mails, giving the Post Office an additional headache. Actually the Post Office is lucky that scheme doesn't work in practice the way it does in theory—because if everyone who got a letter sent out five more, the twelfth mailing a single series of chain letters would put 244,140,625 letters into the mails.

And at that point nearly everybody you know would, somewhere along the line, have put your name on a list; you would have to write and mail five times as many letters as the number of Christmas cards you get each year. This would happen to everyone in the country old enough to read or write a letter. And since you already would have run out of friends to write letters to, you would have to take names and addresses from the phone book and write to strangers. After a few more weeks, you wouldn't have time to do anything but write letters 24 hours a day. And then both you and the Post Office would collapse; the bad luck the letters predict if you break the chain would arrive because you didn't break it.

In order to circumvent the postal laws, some of the swindlers who start chain letters tried circulating the letters by hand and mailing only the money. The Post Office, learning about this, issued a bulletin pointing out that "depositing any matter, including money, through the mails in furtherance of a chain letter scheme is a violation of the Postal Lottery and Fraud statutes." Some of the crooks who tried this angle were arrested and convicted.

PYRAMID CLUBS

The Pyramid Clubs which flourished a few years ago were another attempt to use the chain-letter principle, avoiding any use of the mails. Mr. A forms a club by phoning two friends, B and C, and invites them to a party at his home. B and C each invite two more guests, D, E, F and G, and these four each invite two more. The guest list looks like this:

A

B C

D E F G

H I J K L M N O

The eight new club members on the last line each pay Mr. A $1 for the privilege of joining the club. Mr. A also has a list of eight names which he has arbitrarily selected if he is the originator of the scheme, or eight names of persons who are previous participants. He sends the $8 he has collected to the name at the top of the list, and then adds his own name at the bottom.

Then B and C each hold parties the next night, and each collects $8 from new members. Everyone on the original pyramids moves up to the line above and, four days later, there are eight such pyramids. As each new member reaches the top of the pyramid and holds a party and collects $8, he turns this over to the name at the top of the list, and adds his own name at the bottom. Each person who reaches the top of the list should receive $8 from 256 other clubs, a total of $2,048 profit on an initial investment of $1.

It sounds fine, but, like the chain letters, it never works, because too many people drop out and many others pocket the $8 they have collected instead of sending it along to the person now at the top of the list. And there's an even bigger flaw in the scheme—a real big one. Let's suppose that no one drops out and that everything works beautifully. There are 15 participants at the first party plus the person at the head of the list. The number of new members doubles each day thereafter until, at the end of two weeks, 262,143 persons are involved; at the end of three weeks there are 33,554,431 participants, and three days after that every man, woman and child in this country, Canada and some Latin-American countries, and about 12 million more besides, are involved—a total of 268,435,455 Pyramid Club members. It is obvious that the whole scheme must collapse with a dull thud long before that point is reached.

Pyramid Club originators and members also forget that although they aren't violating any postal laws, the individual states have anti-lottery laws. Arrest and conviction of a number of such promoters and an announcement by the Bureau of Internal Revenue that it would prosecute anyone who did not report money received from such a scheme put a crimp in the Pyramid Club operations.

Variations of the idea, however, continue to pop up with regularity. A few years ago a couple of shrewd promoters with big ideas took in $50,000 with a Pyramid variation in which each participant was to purchase a $50 government bond and forward it to the name at the top of the list. A five-step chain, if unbroken, was supposed to bring each participant $31,250 in bonds, and the promoters told the suckers that the postal authorities wouldn't mind because the scheme would sell so many bonds. A great many salespeople attending merchandise conventions in Chicago were victimized by this one. And the authorities did mind; it was still a lottery, and a crooked one to boot.

Another very good reason for not participating in get-rich-quick chain-letter and Pyramid Club schemes or any variation thereof is that besides getting swindled yourself you are helping to swindle your friends.

32.
Private Betting
Propositions:
Hustlers and Cheats

A proposition or angle bet is one which appears to give the taker an even chance and at times the best of it, but does just the opposite. There are, among America's 90 million gamblers, about 100,000 proposition hustlers, cheats and confederates who take their victims for $250 million annually with private betting propositions of this sort. The biggest loss on a *percentage proposition* in recent years was the $49,000 lost by Fat the Butch on Chevalier de Méré's historic double-six proposition discussed on page 15. The next largest was the $10,000 freeze-out proposition at Poker Dice (page 825).

A *private betting proposition* is a wager between two or more persons on the outcome of coin tossing, dice throwing, guessing games, feats of skill or, for that matter, any betting situation on which there is a difference of opinion.

A *freeze-out proposition* is a wager, usually between a hustler and a gambler, in which the sum total to be wagered and the betting conditions are mutually agreed upon before the action begins. Example: The bettors agree to wager $10,000 on a series of events. The betting limit for each single event is $500, and the action must continue until one bettor has lost his $10,000. I know of one coin-tossing freeze-out proposition that lasted 72 hours. Some such propositions have continued for weeks, with the participants taking time out only to sleep and eat.

Hustlers prefer freeze-out bets for two reasons. A series of bets gives Old Man Percentage plenty of time to work and can make an almost sure thing of a percentage deal. And even if the sucker begins to rumble that he is bucking terrific adverse odds he can't stop because of the freeze-out condition that if he quits he loses the total sum agreed on.

A *proposition hustler* is a bettor who offers betting propositions of his own choosing in which, when carefully examined, the advantage is found to be greatly in his favor.

A *proposition cheat* is a crook whose policy is never to give a sucker a break. He gaffs or angles his propositions so that they are surefire and he has a 100% edge.

Like con men, proposition hustlers and cheats pretend to be pleasant, friendly, easygoing, good fellows who would never think of double-crossing anyone. They also usually pretend that their prepared proposition bets are something they just happened to think up on the spot. Some of the routine proposition bets are too well known to take any but the dumbest chumps, so the hustlers spend a great deal of time cooking up new angles and studying probability theory hoping to find some mathematical curiosity which they can turn into a sucker bet. They also resort to practicing sleight of hand. This homework pays off in winnings.

They take great pleasure in beating seasoned gamblers. "The Brain," who is probably America's top proposition hustler, plies his trade in Nevada and wherever bigtime gamblers are found. He has won hundreds of thousands of dollars from casino operators and smart gamblers; I have seen him in action many times in the Caribbean and Nevada. "I get my biggest kicks," he once told me, "taking casino owners with proposition bets."

Not everyone who offers you a proposition bet is a professional hustler. He may be a friend or acquaintance who has read an exposé of the wager and is trying it out. Or he may have been victimized by the proposition and, having found out how it works, is trying to retrieve his loss. Since he is out to take you with it, he is no better than the professional.

Often a sure-thing gambler will propose a bet he can't possibly win. This maneuver is aimed at finding out how the prospective victim will react. If the sure-thing proposition is refused, the cheat decides his sucker is a jerk, broke or a non-gambler, and leaves it at that. If the prospect takes the bait, the cheat grins and says, "What do you want to do—rob me?" Then he brings out another surefire proposition that appears to favor the chump but is actually rigged in the cheat's favor. When a bet is made between two strangers, the money must usually be put up before it's officially a bet, and the only time the cheat covers the sucker's dough is when the sure-thing proposition favors the cheat.

Once in a while it's the chump who backs down on a surefire proposition. Take for instance the story the Chicago gamblers tell about the Poker player who missed out on the greatest sure-thing bet in history. He lost a big bundle to an old-timer who really knew how Poker should be played. The game was square all the way, but the chump lost so much so fast that he didn't see how it could have happened honestly, and he accused the old-timer of cheating.

"Look, my friend," the latter said, "I'll tell you why I beat you. You don't know the first thing about gambling. Would you bet me $500 right now that I can't take my right eye out and lay it down on the table?"

The chump blinked. He had just seen a sample of the old boy's play and knew he was a first-rate bluffer. He thought this was more of the same and also figured it was a chance to recoup part of his losses. Without stopping to think further, he said, "Sure." He reached excitedly for his wallet, and threw five $100 bills on the table.

The old-timer covered the bet, took out his glass eye, placed it on the table and scooped up the money. "And now," he said, "will you bet me $1,000 that I can't take the other one out?"

But the chump had had enough, and he didn't have the iron control over his nervous system that a sure-thing gambler must have. Rattled, he decided that this was another fast one, shook his head dazedly and refused the bet. When he came out of his fog later and realized the oldtimer couldn't have played poker with two glass eyes he knew that what he didn't know about betting propositions would fill a library.

The rule in unfamiliar betting proposition is: Look before you leap. It's a 10 to 1 shot that there's a hidden angle. If you can't dope it out, either refuse the bet or, if you want to find out more about the proposition so you can analyze it, keep your bet small. And don't be too confident about figuring the angle; some of the smartest gamblers have fallen victim to the same proposition time after time.

In fast company, of course, nobody dares try any of the standard sure-thing dodges. But smart gamblers all know that in the company of top-notch gamblers they must always be on guard against a new one that may be clever enough to get it by. That's where some of the fascination lies. Among big-money bettors, anything may happen. Back in the early twenties "Titanic" Thompson bet some Broadway wise guys he could drive a golf ball 300 yards. He did it all right—off a hill where the drop was nearly 300 yards.

And he once bet a couple of Washington, D.C., sports writers that he could throw a walnut farther than Walter Johnson, the American League's star pitcher. He won that bet, too. He switched his square nut for one with a lead slug in it.

Titanic is also the guy who clipped a crowd of bigtime horse bettors, including Arnold Rothstein and George McManus, with this custom-tailored dodge. The boys would bet on the number of white horses they could spot from the train on their way from Pennsylvania Station in New York to the Jamaica track. One day Titanic played a hunch. "It looks like a good day for white horses," he said, and put his money down on a number that was eight higher than the next highest guess. He won that one in a walk because he had made a deal with a livery stable and had arranged to have eight white horses planted at a crossroads which the train would pass. Not everybody will go to that much trouble to win, but it pays to keep the possibility in mind.

THE FLY AND SUGAR PROPOSITION

The best proposition bets from the sure-thing gambler's viewpoint are those which look impossible to gaff. Like the two five-grand bets in 1947 between two racket boys, Willie Moretti and Benjamin (Bugsy) Siegel. My wife, Steffi, and I were having dinner in an Italian restaurant in my neck of the woods one night when Willie Moretti came over to our table and said he had a story to tell me about Benny.

"I'm staying at Benny's Flamingo," he said, "and one morning I go up to his apartment to say goodbye before I check out. He's just getting up and asks if I'll join him for breakfast. I say okay and start to go to the phone to call room service when Benny says, 'Let me do it. The phone service here stinks.' He picks up a mike that connects with the P.A. system and makes like Clem McCarthy announcing the winner of the daily double: 'Hey, Chef, this is Benny. Willie's here and we're in a hurry for some breakfast. Get busy. Eggs, toast, coffee—the works, for two. And also a dozen live flies.'"

"The Flamingo," Steffi asked, "has live flies on the breakfast menu?"

"No, this was a special order. And he got it, too. When the waiter brings up the tray he's also got a small box with some holes in the lid and a buzzing sound inside. 'What are the flies for?' I asks Benny, and he says, 'You'll see.' He tells the waiter to make sure all the windows are closed and to turn off the air conditioning. By the time we finish breakfast that hot Nevada air is making things uncomfortable but it doesn't seem to bother Benny. He grins like he is up to something. 'Willie, my boy,' he says finally, 'I know you're a real betting man and will bet on anything. I've come across a little game that beats Craps, Poker or you name it. Would you like to try it once for a five-grand bet?'

" 'Do those flies have something to do with it?' I asked.

" 'You hit the nail on the head, Willie. It's a Spanish game called La Mosca. And the flies do all the work.'

" 'Never mind the buildup. Let's see what it is.'

"Benny picks two lumps of sugar off the breakfast tray, unwraps them and puts them down on the coffee table about six inches apart. The idea of the game, Willie, is for you to guess which lump of sugar you think the first fly will land on after I open the box. I'll bet on the other. For five grand.' This sounded like an even-up bet so I pointed to one lump and gave him the nod to spring the flies.

" 'Now be quiet,' he says. 'No blowing or waving the arms.' Then he flips off the lid, and the flies take off.

"I get to thinking about trained fleas and ask him if he's got the flies trained. He acts insulted and says, 'You just heard me order them fresh from the kitchen.'

"Well, after a couple of minutes the flies spot the sugar and begin buzzing around it, swishing in and out like dive bombers. I was sure once I had the five grand when three of them come down in formation making a low approach toward my lump, but they zoom right past and circle toward the ceiling. I'm watching these three babies when all of a sudden one dives, gives my sugar a miss and lands on Benny's.

"Benny is real sorry for me. 'That was tough luck, Willie, but if you'd like to get even we can go for another five thousand.'

"I figured now there must be a gaff to it, so I say, 'Okay, only this time I'll take your lump and you take mine.'

"Much to my surprise he agrees and says, 'Let's spread the sugar a little further apart this time.' I nod and he moves the cubes and we sit waiting, and then . . . Whammo! A fly makes a three-point landing— on Benny's lump, the sugar I just lost on. 'Well,' I says, 'this must be your lucky day, Benny. I'll send you the ten Gs; I gotta be going.' "

Then Willie added, "I still think he had a gaff, but how do you gaff a fly?"

"I wouldn't know," I told him. "But I've got a confession to make. Benny asked me once for a gimmick to fool the smart boys with—and I showed him how to gaff the sugar."

"You showed him—" Willie burst out laughing. "Since it already cost me ten grand, maybe I can get in on it too?"

"DDT," I said. "A drop on one side of each sugar lump. Benny had both gaffed sides on top to start. Then, after you made your choice, he moved the lumps a bit and turned his over."

Willie was still shaking his head when we said good night. And probably planning to lay in a supply of DDT.

THE ODD MAN COIN PROPOSITION

I know a couple of card cheats who work the tourist suckers at the swank Miami Beach hotels and not only clip them at the card table but make the victims pay their dinner and nightclub checks as well. They invite a mark and his wife to join them and their wives at a dinner show, and when the check arrives one of the cheats digs down into his pocket and produces three quarters. He gives the mark one; he and his confederate take the others, and he explains that it is an old Miami Beach custom to toss for the check.

The mark usually goes along with this; he'd feel embarrassed not to. And, of course, he figures the odds are 2 to 1 in his favor. Actually, he has no chance at all. These same boys once tried the dodge on me in Jimmy Grippo's "21 Club" in Miami Beach with a view to getting me to buy them a round of drinks. I agreed to the toss, but, being suspicious by nature, I noticed that when the coins came out both of those held by the cheats were tails up. If this was the old dodge and they had gaffed coins with tails on both sides, I'd be odd man and lose as soon as I threw a head.

The first cheat tossed his coin, caught it and slapped it down on the bar. His pal did the same. It was a little late to back out now and it would be embarrassing if I tried to do so and the coins turned out to be honest, so I followed suit. When the coins were exposed they were all tails.

We tossed again: same result. The odds against three men throwing tails on the same toss are 7 to 1. On the second toss it is 63 to 1. After the sixth toss and no sign of a head, I said, "It might interest you boys to know that the odds against three coins landing tails six times in a row are 262,143 to 1. Looks like we're going to break a record."

That ended it. One cheat picked up his coin, turned it over, showing tails on both sides. His pal did the same. "Okay, Scarne," he said. "We didn't figure you had a gaffed coin and we didn't spot your switch."

I turned over my quarter and showed a head on the other side. Maybe I should have asked them if they would bet that it had no head; that's what they would have done in the same spot.

I had used sleight of hand, but not a switch. With some know-how and some practice it is possible to feel a coin with your thumb after you catch it and know at once without looking at it which side is heads and which is tails. Then, if it is going to land wrong side up, a sleight of hand move turns it over as it is slapped down on the bar. I'm a bit vague here on purpose; I want to put you wise as to what to watch for but not give lessons in how to do it.

The sleight-of-hand method I used to protect myself is also used by skilled coin tossers to clip the marks. It makes the gaffed coins unnecessary.

THE SPINNING COIN PROPOSITION

Don't ever bet some stranger that he can't guess whether a coin you spin on a bar behind his back falls heads or tails. He can—every time. The coin he gives you has a nick on the edge on one side. As the spinning coin slows down, it runs slower, if spun on the nicked side, and the hustler can hear the difference. You can cross him on this one if, after his back is turned, you put his coin in your pocket and use your own.

Another gaff of this same kind is a coin whose edge is beveled on one side so that the coin, when spun, always falls on that side. Some coins are prepared by beveling half the circumference of the coin to the head side, the other half to the tail side. Spin the coin with the beveled head side down and tails come up, and vice versa.

THE TOSSING COIN PROPOSITION

The most ingenious coin-tossing swindle of them all was one which "the Hiker," a card cheat and con man, used in the twenties. He spent a lot of time in the original Lindy's Restaurant in New York, and it was here I once saw him use it on a bigtime gambler.

"Let's toss for the check and fifty bucks to boot," the Hiker suggested. The gambler nodded. The Hiker tossed a nickel and said, "You call it while it's in the air." The gambler called, "Tails," and it came down heads.

The Hiker often tossed for a thousand dollars and got a good many takers who figured that there was no way to control the coin while it was up there spinning; that since it was allowed to fall to the floor untouched, no sleight of hand could be involved; and that, since the taker called it, a double-head or double-tailed coin would be of no use.

What they didn't know was that the Hiker's proposition didn't always win—but it never lost. And he did use a double-headed (or double-tailed) coin. With a double-headed, if the victim called, "Tails," the Hiker let it fall and he won. And if the victim called, "Heads"? This is the cute part. The Hiker simply caught the coin as it fell and dropped it into his pocket, saying, "No bet, I just wanted to see if you had any sporting blood in your veins." He won half the time and never lost, which is a sure thing any way you look at it.

THE SPELLING PROPOSITION

Gamblers have a saying: "If you bet on a sure thing, be sure to save enough money for carfare home." They say this because even the most carefully planned proposition bet can sometimes have a nasty way of boomeranging. The Hiker once had trouble of this sort. It began when he met Lefty Welch boarding a train in Frisco en route to Miami. Lefty was a Miami rackets boss back before World War II. When it came to figuring odds at a dice table he was a whiz, and this talent earned him a sizable fortune. But he quit school before he learned to read or write and he signed his name with an X. The smart-money boys all knew this and the Hiker knew they knew it, so he dreamed up a proposition that made use of it.

He began by giving Lefty a selling talk on culture, pointing out that if he ever wanted to mingle with the upper social circles he would have to acquire some class. "To get that," the Hiker pointed out, "you have to have a good gift of gab. And first you need to know how to spell."

Lefty wasn't impressed. "I haven't done so bad without this high-class stuff."

The Hiker saw that he'd have to do what he planned the hard way, so he propositioned Lefty. "If you can learn to spell two words by the time we get to Miami, I'll pay your fare. I'll bet you can't do it."

"Two words?" Lefty said. "It's a bet. What are they?"

" 'Hippopotamus,' " the Hiker said, "and 'rhinoceros.' "

"You don't have to make it that tough," Lefty objected. "Give me two easier ones."

The Hiker shook his head. "Two C-notes just to learn to spell two words is a hell of a lot more than the minimum wage. I don't think you can do it."

Nobody like to be thought that dumb, so Lefty rolled up his sleeves and went to work. He studied those two words and practiced all the way across the county. By the time they pulled into Miami he had them down cold. All the Hiker had to do was call out, "Hippopotamus," and Lefty would proudly rattle off the spelling of both hippopotamus and rhinoceros.

The Hiker congratulated Lefty, gave him the two hundred and went off to look up a courtly, well-dressed gentleman whose monicker was Silver Tongue and who had worked with the Hiker on more than one con game.

"Silver Tongue," he said, "when I go into this restaurant where Lefty eats you stick around outside, and when I give you the office, come in. And later, when I ask you to write five words of ten letters or more each, write 'hippopotamus' and 'rhinoceros' and any three Italian dishes on the menu."

A few days later, with some of the smartest money gamblers in Miami at the Hiker's table, Lefty eating across the room and Silver

Tongue staked outside, the Hiker noticed Lefty and remarked casually, "Lefty is the most educated gambler I ever met."

Several eyebrows went up, and one of the boys howled, "Educated! Why that mug signs his checks with an X."

"I don't know how you got an idea like that," the Hiker said. "I know Lefty well. I'll lay you a bet that he can spell any word with ten letters or more in the dictionary." He took out a pencil and asked that someone write down a word of ten letters or more. He got no takers on that one; nobody in the crowd knew any words that long.

At this point Silver Tongue came in on cue, walked past the table, and was stopped by the Hiker. "Pardon me, sir, we want to settle a little wager and would appreciate your help. May I ask what business you're in?"

"I'm a lawyer," Silver Tongue replied.

"Perfect," the Hiker said. "You're our man. Would you be so kind as to write five words of ten letters or more on this menu?"

Silver Tongue scanned the menu, jotted down mozzarella, prosciutto, scallopini, then thought a moment and added hippopotamus and rhinoceros.

"Thank you," the Hiker said. "Now I've got a thousand bucks that says that Lefty can spell any one of those words."

The gamblers figured that if they couldn't spell the words themselves, it was a sure thing Lefty couldn't.

"I'll take part of it," one of the boys said, "provided you cross out those Italian dishes. Maybe he *can* read Italian."

Then somebody also crossed out hippopotamus. Everybody agreed that everything was on the up and up and the bet was covered. The Hiker called Lefty over to the table.

"Lefty," he explained, "the boys and I have a little bet and we need your help." He pointed to Silver Tongue. "This gentleman will read a word which is written on this menu. When he calls it out, I want you to spell it."

"Sure," Lefty said enthusiastically.

"Very well," Silver Tongue said. "Spell rhinoceros."

Lefty grinned. "That's a cinch. H-I-P-P-O-P-O-T-A-M-U-S."

The Hiker's comment after he recovered was: "All that rehearsing from Frisco to Miami, and I never thought to have him spell the words the other way around!"

This story leaves a question: Was Lefty really that dumb or did he double-cross the Hiker? The Hiker thinks he did, but Lefty isn't talking. And all I know is that if you are foolish enough to bet any big money on any similar proposition, I'll give you odds that you lose.

THE LOLLAPALOOZA HAND

You may not run into this dodge today but it's one of the best of all Poker stories, and it so nicely illustrates the old adage that nothing is certain except death and taxes that I can't resist telling it here. It has been around a long time. John F. B. Lillard told it in his book *Poker Stories* back in 1896.

A card sharper entered a Butte, Montana, saloon one night and found four hard-bitten prospectors playing Draw Poker. "Is this an open game?" the sharp asked. One of the prospectors nodded and said, "Sit down, stranger."

The game was table stakes with a minimum limit of three hundred as the "buy in." After playing for an hour or so, the sharp stacked the cards and dealt himself four aces. He made a fair-sized bet and everybody dropped out except one old boy with gray whiskers and a deadpan poker face. At the draw, both stood pat. The sharper counted the prospector's cash by eye and bet an equal amount. The old boy didn't blink; he merely shoved all his chips into the pot and called.

The sharp spread his four aces and reached for the pot. "Not so fast, sonny," his opponent said, laying down three clubs and two diamonds.

"What do you mean, not so fast?" the sharper said. "I've got four aces."

"Sure you do," was the reply, "but in this town a Lollapalooza beats any other Poker hand. And that's what I've got—three clubs and two diamonds."

The other prospectors all nodded solemnly. "That's right, stranger," one of them agreed. "Nothing beats a Lollapalooza."

The sharp knew he had been cheated but he figured he had an answer. On his next deal he stacked the cards again using the pickup stack, dealt himself a Lollapalooza and gave four aces to the prospector who had won the earlier pot. Again he made a fair-sized bet and again the old boy stayed, the others dropping out. Once more both men stood pat on the draw. The sharper pushed all his chips to the center. The prospector called again.

"Well," the sharp said, grinning, "This time I can't lose. I've got the Lollapalooza."

But the old prospector was already raking in the pot. "Sorry, pardner," he said. "You should ask about the rules before you deal yourself in. The Lollapalooza hand can only be played once a night."

Gaffed Put-and-Take top. Arrow indicates edge that has been rounded.

PUT-AND-TAKE TOP PROPOSITION

The sure-thing boys cleaned up big on the put-and-take craze of 30 years ago, and since fads of this sort have a habit of coming back you might file the following information for future use. There are various kinds of tops: high-and-low-numbered tops, tops bearing the names of racehorses and—the most popular of all—put-and-take tops. Crooked gambling-supply houses still do a good business selling fair put-and-take tops at two bucks each and gaffed tops to match at $14. Controlled racehorse tops run as high as $70.

The put-and-take top is eight-sided with the sides marked P-1, T-1, P-3, T-3, P-4, T-4, P-ALL, and either T-ALL or the letter T and a star. Any number can play. At the start of the game each player puts an equal stake in the pot and each player in turn spins the top. When the top stops and a P-4 appears on its uppermost side, the player puts four units into the pot, and so on; if T-ALL appears, he takes all the money in the pot; if P-ALL appears, he must put in an amount equal to that in the pot.

The top swindle is most often worked by two cheats who start playing the game with a fair top, usually in a bar or restaurant. Other people gather to watch, and it is seldom long before one or more of them join the game. When the action really gets going, one cheat switches a crooked top in and out of the game as required. When they want the suckers to put money into the pot, they switch in a top that will only throw P-1, P-3, P-4 and P-ALL. When the pot is big enough and it is one of the cheats' turn to spin, he switches in a top that is gaffed to come up T-ALL.

The gaff is on the edges of the tops, which are rounded on some sides and sharp on others. When the spinning top has lost its momentum and is coming to a stop it will roll off the sides with the rounded edges and stop on the sides whose edges are sharp. Cheats who lack the sleight-of-hand skill required for switching tops in and out of a game resort to the following kinds of crooked tops:

Some tops have alternate edges beveled so that when the player spins the top clockwise with his right hand (the normal manner), it always lands put. The cheat spins the top with his left hand counterclockwise and the top always lands take.

Some gaffed put-and-take tops have a central spindle which projects farther from one end of the top than the other. It is so beveled that take numbers always come up when the cheat is spinning. When he passes the top to the next player, he pushes the spindle down through the top so that the end that projected farthest becomes the short end and what was the upper side of the top becomes the bottom. This end-for-end reversal is the same as reversing the direction of the spin, and the player will throw more puts than takes.

A put-and-take top can be tested by changing the direction to see if that has any any effect on the result. But since most of the sure-thing boys keep switching their gaffed tops in and out of a game, you'll probably find yourself examining a square put-and-take top. The best advice is not to play with strangers, and that includes anyone you haven't known since you were knee high to a pup.

THE MATCH PILE PROPOSITION

This proposition has been kicking around for years, and sometimes I wonder how anybody can still be taken by it. When Barnum said, "There's a sucker born every minute," he meant every word of it. Here's how the proposition works.

From a pile containing an unknown number of matches two players take turns removing matches. Each player may remove any number from one through six at each turn, and the one who takes the last match is the winner. Many *puzzlers* (puzzle fans) know the winning system behind this one: it has been printed and reprinted in the puzzle books for years. When the pile becomes small enough, the player who knows the secret counts the number remaining. He often uses a pencil to push aside the matches he wants to remove, thus slowing the game down a little so he has time to make the count. (The hustlers call him a *pencil pusher.*)

He divides his result by 7. When it does not divide evenly he removes whatever number of matches are left over. As long as he leaves his opponent with a multiple of 7 each time, he will eventually win.

Left with a multiple of 7 himself he takes only one match. This gives him 5 chances out of 6 that an opponent who doesn't know the system won't reply by taking six matches, and he can take enough on the next turn to hit the next winning position. Once he hits one winning position he can hit all the others by noting the number his opponent takes and taking enough more to make a total of 7.

When only seven matches remain and it is the opponent's turn he can't win because he cannot remove more than six and the last match is captured by the puzzler. You have almost no chance of winning if you don't know the system when playing against someone who does.

In this swindle it's not the chump who *doesn't* know the system that the hustler goes to work on; the guy who *does* know it is the one who makes the best victim. Take the time Doc Peters, a carnie from way back, spotted a puzzler using the pencil in a saloon in Montana. The Doc let his mark win 20 clams at his sure-thing game to make him feel confident, then said he had to get back to the show but had time for one more game, provided the stakes were worthwhile. "Make it a hundred," the puzzler said, sure that he wasn't giving Doc anything but the very smallest chance. "Make it five hundred," Doc answered, and the chump agreed.

They broke open a new box of matches, discarded half at random to make sure neither player could know the starting number. Both Doc and the puzzler played quickly at first. Then, as the pile became smaller, the puzzler began to use his pencil to slow it down. And Doc, of course, counted the matches too. The count was 38. The puzzler took away three, and each time thereafter took away as many as Doc did plus enough to add to 7. Then, at the end, the pencil pusher's confident grin suddenly vanished. He found that on his last turn there were seven matches left and that it was Doc who held the final winning position.

Doc collected the five C-notes, said a cheerful good night and took it on the lam. The cute psychological bit here is that the puzzler never rumbles the gaff; he always decides he must have miscounted. What the mark did not suspect was that Doc used a pinch of sleight of hand. Once he saw that the mark had gotten a count, on his turn he reached toward the pile with one match palmed and pretended to take it away, but actually removed nothing. From then on it was Doc who hit the winning positions, and the wise guy with the sure thing was riding for a fall.

THE BIRTHDAY PERCENTAGE PROPOSITION

Not long ago I started to tell this one in a lecture I gave before a group of lawyers. I said that I would ask each person in the room the month and day of his birth and predicted that among the 34 lawyers present at least 2 would have the same birth date. One member of the audience apparently did some quick thinking, arrived at the conclusion that I had gone out on a limb this time and thought he saw an opportunity to make a few buck at the speaker's expense. He stood up and said, "I'll bet you one hundred dollars that you won't find two men here with the same birth date."

Challenged so directly in public, I had to take the bet. Two identical dates turned up with the 23rd lawyer polled and my challenger gave me a check, which I donated to the Bar Association's Christmas charity fund.

Like thousands of other people who have accepted the hustler's birthday proposition, he believed that he had much the best of it. He reasoned that 34 dates out of 365 made the odds more than 10 to 1 in his favor. The catch is that this isn't the way to solve the problem. The odds were actually 4 to 1 in my favor. In a group of 23 persons I would have a 1¼% edge in my favor, and beyond that point the larger the group the higher my favorable odds would be. With 40 persons present, I'd have 8 to 1 odds going for me.

Here is the math. When the second lawyer was polled, the chance that his birthday was not the same as the first lawyers's was $\frac{364}{365}$. Multiply this by $\frac{363}{365}$ for the third lawyer, and then by $\frac{362}{365}$ for the next, and so on for each person polled, the numerator of the fraction decreasing by one each time.

The odds are even when the result reaches ½. This happens between the 22nd and 23rd multiplication. With 11 extra lawyers present I had a big 60% advantage.

At this point a warning is necessary. With 34 people present don't ever word it this way: "I'll bet that another person in this room has the same birth date that I do." Or, if someone wants to bet that no one in the room has the same birthday you do, don't take it. This may sound like the same problem but it isn't. The odds would be 7 to 1 against you, and there would have to be 253 people present for you to have a slight edge.

Why? Well, this time the bet is not that *any* two persons will have the same birthday; one birthday is specified. You must multiply 364/365 by itself until the result is as close to ½ as you can get. This requires 253 such multiplications. More simply, multiply the first number of the 364 to 1 odds figure by .693 (the co-log of the hyperbolic log of 2). This gives an answer of 252.252 persons to make the chances equal. These birthday propositions are typical examples of the ingenuity of many percentage propositions.

AUTO LICENSE PLATE PERCENTAGE PROPOSITIONS

Some hustlers use the birthday proposition in a different form. Waiting with a chump for a green light at a street corner, he'll make some casual remark about the heavy traffic, grin, and add, "I feel lucky today. I would like to make an even-money bet that in the next twenty cars that pass there will be two or more whose license plates have the same last two digits."

You use the same method of calculation to analyze this one: $\frac{100}{100} \times \frac{99}{100} \times \frac{98}{100} \times \frac{97}{100} \times \frac{96}{100} \times \frac{95}{100}$ and so on until the fraction reduces to ½.

The hustler has a slightly better than an even chance when the 13th car has passed. An additional 7 cars give him a 7 to 1 edge.

If you don't go for that proposition, the hustler may offer this one.

"Call any two-digit number," he may say, "and I will bet that they won't match the last two numbers on the license plate of any of the first fifty cars that go past." You say to yourself, "Since there are a hundred combinations of two digits and I have fifty cars going for me, it's an even-up proposition." Chalk up another wrong answer. The odds are 7 to 5 in the hustler's favor. You need 69 cars to have a slightly better than an even chance.

The difference between this bet and the previous one is that a *called number* must be matched rather than a match for *any* of the previously passed cars. The calculation is 99/100 multiplied by itself until the series of multiplications reaches ½ or as close as you can get. It occurs here between the 68th and 69th steps. Or multiply the top figure of the probability fraction by 0.693, as in the birthday proposition, for an answer of 68.607 automobiles.

PERCENTAGE PROPOSITIONS WITH CARDS

Anybody who gambles at cards will sooner or later be invited to bet on some card proposition. More proposition bets have been cooked up with 52 playing cards than with any other gambling device. The biggest bundle lost on a card proposition was the $25,000 lost by a midwestern banker client of mine who suspected he had been cheated out of his $25,000 and hired me to investigate.

The banker had attended a party given by a friend in a New York City hotel suite. Near the end of the evening, a doctor, loaded with a handful of $100 bills and apparently as many drinks, began cutting a deck of cards into three packets and shouting, "I'll bet anybody a hundred bucks at even money that there is no ace, deuce or jack on the bottom of any these packets." He turned the packets face up. If anyone had taken the bet, the doctor would have won: none of the named cards showed. The watchers began to work out the odds mentally. They figured that 12 cards out of 52 gave the drunk a 3 to 1 edge, and it was my banker client who made the mistake of believing he had it figured right. "What do you take us for?" he asked. "A bunch of idiots? You should be offering three to one on that bet."

The doctor wobbed drunkenly. "Okay, you're so smart, you take the cards and cut three piles and *I'll* bet that an ace, deuce or jack *does* show on the bottom." The banker eyed the handful of $100 bills and decided to teach this character a lesson. He accepted the offer.

This was the start of a 12-hour session. At noon the following day the banker quit, a $25,000 loser.

The doctor, who was much soberer than he appeared, never bet less than a hundred or more than three hundred on any single decision. The reason for this was that he wanted to give the 10 10/17% edge—which is what he actually had—a chance to grind away. Figuring the percentage on this isn't quite as simple as it seems, a fact the doctor had counted on. You must first find the total number of possible three-card combinations in a 52-card deck, like this: $\frac{52 \times 51 \times 50}{3 \times 2 \times 1} = 22{,}100$; then the total number of possible combinations that are "misses" (combinations which do not include an ace, deuce or jack), like this: $\frac{40 \times 39 \times 38}{3 \times 2 \times 1} = 9{,}880.$

Subtract the 9,880 misses from the 22,100 total of three-card combinations for an answer of 12,220 hits. Then subtract the 9,880 misses from the 12,220 hits and you find that there are 2,340 more hits than misses, an advantage of 10 10/17% in the doctor's favor, which is quite a lot different from the 3 to 1 odds the banker thought he had going for him.

THE MATCHING CARD PROPOSITION

Nearly everyone seems to enjoy beating someone with a card proposition. My magician friend and pupil Howard Wurst has fun with this one. He shuffles two decks separately, puts them face down on the table, then using both hands begins turning up the top card of each deck simultaneously. He offers to bet that at some point two identical cards will turn up together. He adds that it is obviously a 50–50 proposition because the chance of matching two cards is 1 in 52 and you get 52 chances.

If two decks aren't available he does it with one, this time turning up one card at a time and offering even money that two red or two black cards of equal value, such as an ace of diamonds and an ace of hearts, or a queen of clubs and a queen of spades will appear immediately following each other.

In both the above instances the edge in favor of a hit is about the same: approximately 26%. The proposition hustler sometimes specifies that he is to collect an extra betting unit for each hit over one, and here the P.C. in his favor goes so high that you might as well give him your money at once and save wear and tear on the cards.

THE DECK CUTTING PROPOSITION

Card hustlers also like to offer the chumps even money that they can't cut to a specified card in a complete deck in 26 tries. Suppose you name the queen of spades. Your instructions are to shuffle the deck, put it face down on the table, cut and note the bottom card of the cut-off packet. If it is not the queen of spades (correct odds at this point are 51 to 1), you continue to cut in this fashion until you either cut to the called card or until you have exhausted your 26 chances.

Since 26 is half of 52, it sounds to most people like an even-money bet, but actually you need 35.342 trials to even things up. The hustler would have a slight edge on 35 trials; you would have a shade the better of it on 36.

New England Poker hustlers like to lay odds of 15 to 1 that a single player won't be dealt a four-card flush in his first five cards, and they get plenty of action. The marks have no idea that the correct odds are 22 to 1, which gives the hustler a big 30 10/23% advantage.

Correct odds on other similar card propositions can be found in Chapter 27.

DICE PROPOSITIONS

This proposition is a favorite of the bigtime dice hustler and is usually offered in a gambling house. The last time I saw it worked, a Reno casino owner and his manager went for five grand on the proposition.

It happened on the graveyard shift. The only player in the joint was a tall man who stood by a Craps table talking to the boss and dealers. He pointed a finger at the place numbers (4-5-6-8-9-10) on the Craps layout and asked the boss, "What are the odds of making all six of those numbers before throwing a seven?"

The boss rubbed his chin for a minute or more, and then said, "Well, the four and ten are two to one shots; the six and eight are six to five shots, and the five and nine are three to two shots. If each of the six numbers were 2 to 1 shots, the odds would be two times itself six times. Let's see, that would be two, four, eight, sixteen, thirty-two, sixty-four. The odds on that are 63 to 1. But since the five and nine are three to two shots and the six and eight are six to five, I'll deduct eight points and say roughly the odds are 55 to 1."

The Tall Man said, "I'd like to take a little of those 55 to 1 odds."

"If you take 50 to 1 it's a deal," replied the boss.

"I'll try it for ten dollars a turn."

The stickman sprang into action as the Tall Man began rolling the dice. The casino boss won nearly all the bets—but when he won he only collected $10, and when the Tall Man won he raked in $500. After several hours of play the boss called it quits; he had lost $5,000. He probably figured the sucker was real lucky to win that kind of money bucking such adverse odds, but when he reads this he will discover that the Tall Man knew just what he was doing.

The odds against making all the place numbers (4–5–6–8–9–10) before a seven are 13⅔ to 1 rather than the 55 to 1 the casino boss figured. Here is the mathematical proof of this unexpected fact. Multiply $\frac{24}{30} \times \frac{20}{26} \times \frac{16}{22} \times \frac{12}{18} \times \frac{8}{14} \times \frac{4}{10}$. Then turn the fraction upside down, cancel out and multiply, getting this:

$$\frac{5}{4} \times \frac{13}{10} \times \frac{11}{8} \times \frac{3}{2} \times \frac{7}{4} \times \frac{5}{2} = \frac{75,075}{5120}$$

$$75,075 - 5120 = 69,955 \div 5120 = 13.66 \text{ to } 1$$

A similar but more complex dice proposition, often hustled in gambling casinos, is the one that has to do with all the two-dice numbers (2–3–4–5–6–8–9–10–11–12) being thrown before a seven.

The figures are:

$$\frac{30}{36} \times \frac{27}{33} \times \frac{24}{30} \times \frac{21}{27} \times \frac{18}{24} \times \frac{15}{21} \times \frac{12}{18} \times \frac{9}{15} \times \frac{6}{12} \times \frac{3}{9}$$

By turning the fraction upside down, canceling out and multiplying we get:

$$\frac{36 \times 33}{6 \times 3} = \frac{1188}{18}$$

$$1188 - 18 = 1170 \div 18 = 65 \text{ to } 1 \text{ odds against}$$

A POKER DICE PROPOSITION

Another complex and little known five-dice proposition once cost a part owner of a Detroit floating Craps game ten grand. Mike and Joe ran the game, and every Monday night they would gamble among themselves at Poker Dice (Aces Wild).

One night after a really big losing weekend when they had taken a $100,000 beating from a Chicago gambler, Joe threw the five dice out of the cup and said, "Mike, if you hadn't raised our $200 limit to $1,000 for that Chicago creep, we wouldn't have gone for the hundred big ones."

"That's the gambling business, so stop crying, Joe. It's all part of the game."

But Joe didn't stop crying; he kept complaining all evening while playing Poker Dice. Finally Mike became irritated and said, "Look, Joe, you're chicken. You're afraid to gamble big. You're small time. I'd make a bet that if a guy walked in this room this moment and offered to bet ten grand that in a hundred rolls of these five dice he would throw more three of a kinds than single pairs, you'd back down."

"Why don't you offer me the bet, Mike, and see if I'll back down?"

Before Joe finished the sentence, Mike said, "I'll take you up for ten grand."

"It's a bet," Joe replied.

It took about an hour to shake the dice and throw them out 100 times. The final decisive count was 65 three of a kinds and 35 one pairs, and crying Joe was out ten grand.

Joe thought he had a sure thing, but Mike had set a trap and Joe fell, hook, line and sinker.

If you turn to page 339 and look at the Five Dice, Aces Wild table, you'll find that a three of a kind is considerably easier to throw than a single pair. The odds against throwing a three of a kind are 2.2 to 1, and those against a single pair are 5.5 to 1, more than twice as much.

CRAPS PROPOSITIONS: BARRING THE FIRST ROLL

I repeat that Craps hustlers are ingenious characters who spend a lot of their time trying to dope out new angles when their usual propositions begin to wear thin and don't get the usual action. One of the trickiest propositions they have dreamed up is a simple rule that allows a hustler in a private or friendly Craps game to take right and wrong action on all the point numbers (4, 5, 6, 8, 9 and 10) and actually retain a bigger percentage in his favor than any Nevada casino operator would have the nerve to charge.

The hustler's dodge on this is a lulu. He simply *bars the first roll*, which means that a decision on that roll in the hustler's favor wins for the hustler, but a decision in his opponent's favor is a standoff (no action) and the bet remains to be decided by a later roll (like the two-ace bar at Bank Craps).

When the hustler *lays* the correct odds on the points and bars the first roll, he has the same advantage on each of the points (4, 5, 6, 8, 9 and 10)—a nice big edge of 16⅔%.

Ordinarily, the hustler doesn't bar the roll on sixes and eights in a Private Craps game where the chumps bet even money on these numbers, because he already has 9 1/11% of the best of it, but he'll do it if he discovers that anyone is fool enough to take it. On such a proposition bet the hustler has a 22 79/99% edge!

The hustler will also *take* even money on the sixes and eights for an advantage of 7 19/33%.

When a chump goes for the bar-the-first-roll gimmick, he might as well hand over all his dough to the hustler without bothering to roll the dice.

TWO-ROLL CRAPS PROPOSITIONS

Another Craps proposition is to bet even money that the thrower will or will not roll two called numbers in two rolls. Example: six or eight, five or nine, six or seven, and so on. Like most ingenious propositions, figuring the correct odds and percentages on two-roll bets is tough—unless you know how. That's why hustlers offer them. They also know that guys who try to dope the odds seldom come up with anything but wrong answers and a headache. Ninety-nine hustlers out of a thousand can't even figure the correct odds themselves; they only know that other hustlers have offered them and made money. So they do the same.

Anytime anyone offers you a two-roll proposition bet at even money, it's a 20 to 1 shot that he's a hustler. These bets are sucker bets from the word go. Most two-roll bets are made against the shooter. The percentages against or in favor of the shooter are given on the hustlers' most popular two-roll bets.

A standard hustler's dodge, usually made in Private Craps games, is to offer to bet even money that he will throw a six and an eight before throwing two sevens. The person who accepts this proposition usually figures he has the better of the deal, especially if he knows that the odds against throwing a six before a seven are 6 to 5, and the same odds hold for the eight.

This reasoning would be okay only if the hustler proposed throwing a six first and then an eight, or vice versa. In that case, the odds would be against the hustler the same as if he had bet even money that he would throw six against a single seven.

But the hustler bets that he will throw a six and eight before two sevens. He can throw either number first and thus has 50 chances against 36. Subtract losing from winning throws and we find that the hustler has 14 more chances of winning than losing for an edge of 14/86, or 16.28%.

A proposition usually offered in places where dice playing is permitted is for the hustler to offer even money that he will throw an ace or deuce in one roll using two dice. The hustler sometimes explains to

Hustlers' Two-Roll Bets	In Favor of Dice Thrower	Against Dice Thrower
5 or 7		4.320%
7 or 9		4.320%
6 or 8		4.320%
6 or 9		12.500%
8 or 9		12.500%
5 or 6		12.500%
5 or 8		12.500%
4 or 7		12.500%
7 or 10		12.500%
6 or 7	3.549%	
7 or 8	3.549%	

the prospective mark that the chance of rolling either an ace or deuce with one die is 2 to 1 against, and two rolls with one die makes it a 50–50 proposition because there is no difference in rolling one die twice or two dice once.

Before reading further, can you figure out the correct answer to this problem and what the hustler's favorable percentage is?

If you run into trouble or don't like puzzles or feel the price you paid for this book entitles you to the answer without wear and tear on the brain cells, here's the answer. The correct odds are 5 to 4 in favor of a hit, for a favorable edge for the hustler of 11 1/9%.

Nearly all the hustler's propositions made in private dice games that make use of two, three, four or five dice involve either the total of the numbers thrown or a specific combination or hand. For example, you may be offered 20 to 1 that you can't throw exactly 16 on a single roll of three dice (the correct odds are 35 to 1). Or you may be offered 50 to 1 you don't throw three fives exactly with a single roll of four dice (the correct odds are 63.8 to 1). Or you may be offered 5 to 1 you don't throw a pair of sixes exactly on a single roll of five dice (the correct odds are 11.9 to 1).

For the answers to other dice propositions, see Chapter 11.

Glossary

The glossary that follows includes not only the gambling argot and technical idioms that appear in the preceding pages but also a great many other argot terms in common use among the gambling fraternity.

Above The earnings of a gambling enterprise that are listed in their bookkeeping ledgers.

Accommodation Arrest An arrest of a game operator or employee which has previously been arranged between the police and gamblers to make it appear to the public that the police are doing a good job. Also called *Stand-In Arrest.*

Ace (1) The 1-spot on a die. (2) One dollar. (3) A swell guy. (4) The highest-ranking playing card in Poker and most other card games.

Aces Up *Poker:* A hand of 2 pairs including a pair of aces.

Across the Board Race bettor's term for placing a win, place and show bet. "Six dollars across the board on Teeko in the second at Belmont."

Action The betting. "The action is good."

Ada from Decatur; Eighter from Decatur *Craps:* The point 8.

Add-Up Joint See *Count Store.*

Advance Man or Agent Man who travels ahead of a carnival, bazaar or circus to arrange business details.

Advertise *Gin Rummy:* To discard a card in order to try to lead an opponent into discarding another of same rank or near rank or same suit.

Agent (1) Person who solicits lottery bets. (2) Player cheat who frequents casinos and works in collusion with casino dealers and employees. (3) Person who, for a profit, lures a player to a crooked gambling game to be fleeced. (4) A carnival-game operator, also known as a concessionaire. Also see *Advance Man.*

Ahead To be winning. "I'm ahead fifty dollars."

Alibi Store A carnival "skill" game which gives the player little or no chance to win.

All-Night Board *Bingo:* The card given to a player when he pays his admission, which is good for all games played during that session.

All Out Pushing the limit to win.

Allowance Race A race in which the weights to be carried by each horse are determined by the condition-book rules. See under *Conditions.*

Also-Ran A horse which has finished out of the money.

Anchor Man *Black Jack:* A player who sits to the dealer's extreme right and is the last player to play his hand.

Angle (1) An idea. (2) A cheating method.

Animals Professional strong-arm men on a gambling-syndicate payroll. They keep the syndicate's employees in line and collect overdue gambling losses.

Ante *Poker:* Chips or cash put into the pot before the deal.

Any Raffle A bet that three of a kind will appear at the game of Hazard.

Auction Pool An auction in which bids for contestants are sold to the highest bidders.

Ax (The) When a game operator extracts a cut (charge) from a player's bet, a player may say, "There goes the ax."

Back to Back *Stud Poker:* Two cards of the same denomination consisting of the hole card and the first upcard. Same as *Wired.* "He's got them back to back." "He's wired."

Back Game *Backgammon:* The strategy of not advancing runners early, but of using them to catch adverse blots when opponent is well advanced.

Back-Line Odds (To lay) A Craps player having a bet on the don't pass line lays the odds on the point number. (Some casinos pay this bet off at correct odds.)

Backer Someone behind the scenes who supplies gamblers with their bankrolls.

Backgammon *Backgammon:* When a player wins the game by bearing off all his men from the board, before his opponent has taken off any men and still has one or more men on the bar of the adverse home table. Also called a "triple game" since the winner's score is tripled.

Baggage (1) An observer of the game who does not play. (2) Anyone who does not earn enough to pay his own way.

Bagged Caught. Said of a cheat or crook who has been caught in the act of cheating or stealing.

Bagman See *Iceman.*

Bang Up To close up a gambling house or game voluntarily.

Bangtails Horses.

Bank (1) A gambling scheme's financer. (2) The bankroll. (3) Money used to operate a banking game or gambling establishment.

Bank Craps A form of Craps played on a layout in which players are not permitted to bet among themselves, all bets being made against the house or bank.

Banker (1) An operator of a banking game. (2) A player who accepts bets from other players in a private banking game. (3) An employee of a gambling scheme who pays off winning players.

Banking Game Any betting scheme that gives the operator or a player a percentage or odds advantage over his opponents: lotteries, casino games, Numbers game, race and sports books, etc.

Bankroll Man The man who finances a gambling scheme.

Bar Point *Backgammon:* Either seven point.

Barring the First Roll A Private Craps hustler's bet in which a winning first roll for his opponent does not count but is a no-decision or standoff.

Bearing Off *Backgammon:* To remove men from the board after all of your men are in your inner table.

Beef (1) A complaint. (2) To complain.

Beefer A constant complainer.

Belly Joint A crooked carnival wheel whose control is worked by pressure against a mechanism when the operator leans against the counter.

Belly Strippers See under *Strippers.*

Below Unreported earnings or winnings. Also called *Under the Table.*

Best Bet (1) A handicapper's selection to win a race. (2) A wager at a banking game with the least amount of P.C. against the player.

Best of It (To have the) (1) To have odds or percentage advantage. (2) To wager on a better player or team.

Bet Any wager on the outcome of an event.

Bet Against the House (1) To bet right at Bank Craps. (2) To buck a banking game.

Bet the Limit To bet the maximum amount permitted by the house or game rules.

Betting Commissioner British terminology for race bookie. Another British term is *Turf Accountant.*

Betting Ring A syndicate of big-money race bettors who place large bets on a horse or race when they have inside (often crooked) information.

Bevels or Beveled Shapes Crooked dice having one or more sides slightly rounded rather than flat so that the dice tend to roll off the rounded surface more often than the flat.

Biddable Suit *Bridge:* A player's holding at least a four-card suit that has enough strength in honors for an opening bid.

Big Dick *Craps:* The point ten.

Big Drop A Numbers-game headquarters to which the top runners and controllers bring their day's action, or business.

Big Eight A space (usually large) on a Bank Craps layout. A bet placed there indicates that the player is betting an eight will be thrown before a seven.

Big Nickel Race and sports bookies' and bigtime bettors' term for $500.

Big Order A sports bet. "He's a bigtime bookie; he'll take a big order up to $50,000."

Big Six *Bank Craps:* Same as a big eight bet, except that a player is betting that a six will be thrown before a seven.

Bit A jail term. "He did a year bit." Also *Rap.*

Bite (1) A request for a loan. "I put the bite on him for a fin." (2) To bet. "He's not a live one; he won't bite." See also *Spring.*

Black Jack (1) A banking card game. (2) The highest ranking hand in Black Jack is an ace and a 10-count card.

Blackout *Bingo:* A winning setup in which a player must cover all 24 numbers on his card.

Blackwood Convention *Contract Bridge:* A system of ace-revealing bids to reach slams, invented by Easley Blackwood.

Blank-Out, Bloomer Carnival term for (1) Playing a bad stand. (2) Very little money in circulation. (3) Very little action at the games. (4) A losing proposition.

Blanket Roll *Craps:* A controlled two-dice roll made on a soft surface, usually a blanket.

Blind Bet *Poker:* A bet made before the player looks at his cards.

Blitz *Gin Rummy:* When a player wins a game and his opponent has failed to score any points.

Block Game *Backgammon:* A defensive game, in which you try to place points in your opponent's path to hinder the movement of his men.

Block-out Work A method of marking cards in which parts of the design are blocked out with white ink, or some configuration in the design is slightly exaggerated.

Blood Money Money that is hard to get, that one has worked hard to earn.

Blot *Backgammon:* A single man on a point.

Blow (1) To lose. "He blew fifty dollars." (2) To leave. "The cops are looking for me; I'll have to blow town."

Blow the Whistle (To) (1) To complain to the police. (2) To inform a sucker that he was fleeced.

Bluff *Poker:* To bet an inferior hand in such a way that the opponents will think it is a strong hand and retire from the pot.

Board *Backgammon:* The complete backgammon board or table.

Boards The raised edge around a Craps table against which the dice must be thrown in some Craps games. Also, the *Rail.*

Boat Race A crooked horse race.

Bolt A horse that refuses to run, or that runs off course during a race, is said to bolt.

Book, Bookie, Bookmaker (1) Person who takes race and sports bets. (2) Banker at Money (or Open) Craps. *To Book:* To supply the bankroll; bank the game; take racing and sports bets; finance a gambling scheme.

Bottom Dealer A card cheat who deals from the bottom of the deck while pretending to deal off the top. Also known as a *Base Dealer, Subway Dealer.*

Bottom Figure (1) Money owed to bookie by player (or vice versa) involving previous betting transactions. (2) The bottom figure in a bookkeeping transaction.

Bowl Wooden bowl-shaped recess which holds the Roulette wheel.

Box (1) A method of betting all possible combinations of three numbers in the Numbers game. (2) A square drawn around the number indicating that the player is betting on all combinations of the chosen three numbers.

Box Man A casino employee who is in charge of a Bank Craps table.

Box Numbers A betting space on a Money (Open) Craps layout (nearest to the dealer) where each of the possible point numbers (4, 5, 6, 8, 9 and 10) appear within a square or box. Players may bet each or all of these numbers at any time. The same as *Place Bets* in Bank Craps, or *Off Numbers* in Private Craps.

Box Up or Box Them Up *Craps:* To mix up a set of five or six dice so that a player may select a pair from the group.

Boys (The) (1) Inveterate gamblers. (2) Racketeers.

Break (1) The start of a race. (2) To win a player's bankroll.

Breaks (The) Good or bad luck, depending on the circumstances.

Breaks or Breakage to a Nickel or Dime The rounding out or dropping of the last cent digit or fraction thereof to a 5 or 0 on each $2 mutuel race ticket. "The racetracks in New York State break to a dime."

Brick A crooked die that has been cut so that it is not a true cube.

Broad-Tosser A member of a Monte mob who throws or flips the three playing cards used in Three-Card Monte. Also called *Monte Thrower.*

Broad-Tossing Mob A team of three or four confidence men who work the Three-Card Monte swindle. Also called *Three-Card Monte Mob, Monte Mob.*

Buck (1) A marker placed on a Craps betting space to show what point the shooter is trying for. (2) To go against.

Buckaroo The first slot machine manufactured having four reels and paying giant jackpot awards running as high as $5,000.

Bucking the Tiger Playing against the Faro bank.

Bug (1) A steel gimmick placed in the mechanism of a slot machine which prevents certain combinations from hitting. (2) A clip which can be attached to the underside of a card table to hold cards secretly removed from the deck. *To Bug:* To gimmick as above. "The jackpot is bugged."

Buildup The act put on by the operator of a gambling scheme and/or his employees to arouse the player's gambling spirit. Also called *Pitch* or *Con Act.*

Bum Move (1) A suspicious move. (2) A clumsy or obvious cheating move by a gambling crook.

Bum Rap A false accusation of wrongdoing or crime.

Bum Steer Wrong information.

Bump or Raise *Poker:* To bet an amount greater than that put into the pot by the last preceding bettor.

Bundle A large bankroll.

Burn a Card To take a card out of play. *Black Jack:* After the cards have been shuffled and cut, the top card of the deck is burned by showing it and placing it face up on the bottom of the deck.

Business Double *Bridge:* A double made for the purpose of exacting increased penalties.

Bust *Black Jack:* A player busts when his total card count exceeds 21. "I lost the last five hands by busting."

Busters *Craps:* A pair of *tops* (misspotted dice). Tops are made in various combinations which make only certain numbers and are called busters because one combination will bust up another combination. "He robbed them by shooting in busters."

Bust-out Man A dice mechanic whose specialty is switching crooked dice (usually *busters*) in and out of the game.

By a Nose The horse winning a very close race is said to win by a nose.

Cackle the Dice To pretend to shake the dice by making them rattle when actually they are held by a special finger grip that prevents them from turning freely in the hand.

Calculators Mathematicians, or odds men, who work in the calculation rooms at racetracks and do the work that cannot be done by the track's totalisator.

Call *Poker:* To put into the pot an amount equal to the last preceding bet.

Call Bet To make a bet without putting up the money.

Caller *Bingo:* An employee who calls each bingo number as it is drawn. Also *Tallyman.*

Canoe *Roulette:* A numbered or winning section of a Roulette wheel in which the ball finally comes to rest after the spin.

Captains A variation of Gin Rummy for three players.

Card Mechanic A person who manipulates cards for cheating purposes.

Card Mob Two or more card cheats working as a team.

Card Sense Said of a card player who has natural card-playing ability.

Carny A carnival employee.

Carpet Joint Plush luxury gambling casino. Also *Rug Joint.*

Case Card (1) The one remaining card in the deck which will improve a player's hand. "He caught the case king." (2) The last card of a suit or denomination still in the deck. (3) The last one of anything, as *case note,* one's last dollar.

Case the Deck Ability to remember many of the played and exposed cards during the play of a game. "That Black Jack player has been casing the deck and knows that there are two live aces left."

Cases *Faro:* When three cards of a kind have received action, the remaining card of that group still in the card box and yet to be played is referred to as "cases."

Casino Manager Person in charge of the casino operation—Craps, Roulette, Black Jack and other gambling games. His word is final in all disputes arising between house employees and players.

Center Bet *Private Craps:* A wager between the shooter and fader or faders which is placed in the center of the playing surface.

Chalk Player A race bettor who bets only on favorites.

Chase *Stud Poker:* To play against a better hand which is exposed. "You have to go broke if you keep chasing."

Check Cop An adhesive paste which a cheat places on his palm. When he puts his hand on a stack of checks (chips) or coins, the top one adheres to his palm, and he cops (steals) it.

Checker A casino or Craps game employee who checks *luggers* to see how many players they bring to the casino or game.

Chill To lose interest.

Chip, Check (1) A token used for betting purposes in place of money. (2) To place chips on a betting layout or to put chips in the pot.

Chippy (1) A sucker. (2) An inexpert player.

Chips (In the) Said of a gambler who has a lot of money.

Chiseler (1) A gambler who tries to pick up another player's bet in a banking game. (2) A gambler who borrows money in a private game and doesn't repay it. (3) A person who would like to be a gambler but lacks the money and class.

Chump An inexperienced gambler. A sucker. Also *Mark, Mooch, Monkey, Pheasant, Bird, Greenie, Rabbit.*

Chump Twister Carnival term for merry-go-round.

Cinch Hand *Poker:* A hand which is sure to win the pot.

Claiming Race A race in which each horse is entered at a certain claiming price and any horseman may claim (buy) the horse.

Clean (1) Said of a person who does not have a police record. (2) To win all the money from one or more opponents in a game. The unlucky

Clean (Contd)
one is "cleaned" or "taken to the cleaners."

Clear (In the) (1) Free of debt. (2) Innocent of any wrongdoing.

Clock To count. "I clocked the money bet for the evening."

Clocker (1) One who times a horse during trial runs. (2) One who clocks a banking game.

Close to the Belly or Vest Cautiously. A Stud Poker player who bets only on a wired pair or when he has the best hand showing is playing close to the belly.

Cold Deck Deck of cards which has secretly been arranged by a card cheat in a certain order for the purpose of switching later for the deck in play. Also called *Cooler*.

Cold Player Player on a losing streak. "He's cold as ice."

Colors The riding insignia and colors of a racing stable or owner.

Colt Male horse under five years of age.

Column Bet *Roulette:* A bet on 12 vertical numbers of the layout; a winning unit is paid off at 2 to 1 odds.

Combination Underworld or gambling term for a syndicate.

Combination Strippers See *Strippers*.

Combination Ticket A pari-mutuel win, place and show ticket purchased at a racetrack.

Come-Back Money Money bet away from the track with bookies which they then re-bet at the track to try to change the odds on a certain horse.

Come Bet *Bank Craps:* A bet that the dice will pass (win), the next roll to be considered as a come-out roll.

Come-out, Come-out Roll *Craps:* The first throw of the dice or the first throw after a shooter's decision.

Come-out Bet *Craps:* A bet made on a specific number or on a group of numbers that the number or one of the group will be thrown on the next roll of the dice.

Complimentary Play A gambling session indulged in by a casino manager in a rival casino or by a big-time gambler or racketeer as a gesture of friendship toward the casino bosses.

Conditions Rules set down for a race.

Console A flat-top, electrically powered slot machine which can be played by one or several players simultaneously.

Contract *Bridge:* The obligation to win a certain number of tricks or points.

Controller A head runner or branch or area manager in the Numbers game who has other runners working under him and who receives their daily collections. So called because he has to keep the runners in line—not always an easy job.

Cooler See *Cold Deck*.

Cop (1) To steal or cheat. (2) A win.

Corker A gambler who is unusual, either good or bad.

Corner Bet See *Square Bet*.

Count Room Room or office in which casino receipts are counted at the end of each gambling session.

Count Store A crooked carnival game that requires a player to score a specified number of points to win—something the operator can prevent by miscounting on the add-up. Also called *Add-up Joint*.

Coup French word for "bet," used in the United States by Baccarat and Chemin de Fer players.

Cover (1) To accept a wager. (2) To place a bet on a gambling layout. (3) *Bingo:* To cover a drawn or called number on a card by placing a marker over the number.

Cover-All *Bingo:* A winning position on a card in which all 24 numbers have been called and covered.

Covered Square *Bingo:* The center square in the N column of a Bingo card. It has no number and is considered a free play.

Cowboy A reckless and fast gambler.

Crap *Craps:* A losing throw by the shooter on his first come-out roll of the dice.

Crap Out *Craps:* To roll a 2, 3 or 12 on the first roll.

Craps The most popular and biggest-betting private and banking dice game in the world.

Craps Dealer A Craps table employee who collects and pays off winning and losing bets for the house.

Craps Hustler A player who gets the best of it by placing Craps bets at less than correct odds.

Credit Manager The casino employee who gauges your bankroll as you gamble. He may extend credit up to $50,000 or more—or refuse to give you any credit at all.

Creeper A crooked carnival wheel whose spindle or arrow spins very slowly, thus making it easier to control.

Crimp (1) To bend one or more cards in the deck in such a way that the cheat or his confederate can cut the deck at a certain place, or so that a player will unknowingly cut at the place desired by the cheat. (2) The bend itself.

Crossroader A card cheat who travels over the country seeking card games in which he can ply his trade.

Croupier A casino employee who deals the game and collects and pays off winning and losing bets at Roulette, Baccarat, Chemin de Fer and other games with French antecedents.

Crumb Bun A gambling chiseler.

Cup A leather receptacle used for shaking dice.

Cushion (1) Money in the bank. (2) Reserve bankroll.

Cut (1) To divide the pack into two or more packets and then reassemble them in a different order. (2) A house charge, taken by the dealer, croupier or houseman, such as 2% or 5% of the money wagered by players at Poker or Baccarat.

Cut-Edge Dice Crooked dice with some edges cut at a 60-degree angle and others at a 45-degree angle. They tend to fall in the direction of the 60-degree cut more often than the 45-degree cut.

Cut-out Card Markings To make these, a minute area of ink on the back design is chemically bleached or scraped with a knife, adding a white area that wasn't there originally.

Cutter (1) *Poker:* A house employee who takes a money charge out of the pot for supplying the gambling facilities. (2) *Baccarat:* The dealer who takes the 5% cut from the banker's winning bet.

Cut Up Big Wins (To) To reminisce; to talk over old times.

Cut Up the Score To divide the loot. To share the winnings.

Daily Double A selection of a horse either in the 1st or 2nd races or the 5th and 6th races. The bettor wins if both his selections come in first.

Daub A paste or fluid used in marking cards during play.

Dead Card A card which has already been played or one that cannot be used in play.

Deadwood See *Wood*.

Dealer (1) A houseman who deals a banking game. (2) A player in a private card game whose turn it is to deal the hand. (3) The operator of any game.

Dean (The) A smart gambler who can calculate odds and percentages. Also called *The Professor*.

Declarer *Bridge:* The player who plays both his hand and the dummy. The partner who first bid the trump suit or notrump.

Defender *Contract Bridge:* An opponent of *declarer*.

Desperado A gambler who bets big with bookmakers and cannot pay off when he loses.

Deuce (1) A die with two spots. (2) Any two-spot card. (3) Two dollars.

Dice are Off (The) Said of dice that are not true.

Dice Degenerate Compulsive Craps player who can't control his urge to gamble.

Dice Mob A group of dice cheats who operate crooked dice games.

Dog A quitter.

Dog It (1) To back down in an argument. (2) To be afraid to bet big when luck is running in the player's favor.

Don't Come Bet *Bank Craps:* A bet that the dice don't pass (lose), the next roll to be considered as a come-out.

Don't Pass Line A betting space on the Bank Craps layout. Money placed there is a bet that the dice will lose.

Door *Monte, Spanish Monte, Monte Bank:* See *Gate*.

Double *Backgammon:* To increase the stakes to twice their previous size.

Double *Bridge:* A call which has the effect of increasing the trick values and penalties in case the preceding bid becomes the contract.

Double-Cross To pretend to go along with an honest or dishonest proposition, then do just the opposite.

Double Deuce or Deuces A doctored die having two deuces, the extra deuce taking the place of a five.

Double Down *Black Jack:* A player may double the amount of his original wager on his first two cards; however, if he doubles down he can draw only one card.

Double-Five or Fives A doctored die having two fives, the extra five spot taking the place of the two spot.

Double Sawbuck or **Double Saw** Twenty dollars.

Doublets *Backgammon:* The roll of the same number on both dice.

Doubling Cube *Backgammon:* A large die whose faces are numbered 2, 4, 8, 16, 32 and 64, used to double and redouble the stakes.

Doubling Up To double the size of a previous bet on the next wager. Many betting systems are based on this principle.

Drag Down To reduce the size of a wager on the next bet.

Drivers Seat (To be in the) *Stud Poker:* (1) To have the best hand showing. (2) To have won most of the money in a game.

Drop (1) *Numbers:* The place from which a Numbers controller operates and to which his runners bring their day's action. (2) Money used to purchase chips in a casino game. (3) *To Drop:* To withdraw from betting in a card game.

Drop Box A removable, locked cashbox located under a Roulette, Craps or Black Jack table or casino side game. The money paid by players for chips is dropped into the box through a slot in the table top.

Drowned Said of a heavy loser. "I'm drowned."

Dry Broke.

Duggie's Sobriquet for Douglas Stuart Ltd., Great Britain's largest betting commission house for sweepstakes tickets.

Dummy *Bridge:* Declarer's partner; the hand laid down by him and played by declarer.

Dutch Book A race bookmaker's or pricemaker's odds line which totals less than 100%.

Ear A bent corner put on a playing card to identify or locate it. "He put the ear on the aces."

Ear Bender A talkative person.

Early Bird Ticket Ticket to a Bingo game sold at a special discount to induce players to come early.

Easy Money Guy Anyone who gambles and spends money freely.

Easy Way *Craps:* To make a point number (4, 6, 8 or 10) any way but the hardway.

Edge An advantage.

Edge Work or Edge Markings A deck of cards marked with a slight bevel or "belly" drawn on certain points of each card between the design and the edge of the card. A bevel mark high up indicates an ace, lower down a king, etc.

Eighter from Decatur *Craps:* The point eight.

Electric Dice Crooked dice loaded with steel slugs and used over an electric magnet hidden in or under a counter or dice table.

End A share. "What's my end?"

English The simultaneous sliding and spinning action of the dice that is characteristic of most controlled shots.

Enter *Backgammon:* Move a man after it has been hit from the bar to the adverse home table.

Entry Two or more horses entered in a race from one or more stables and having the same trainer.

Even Roll See *Blanket Roll.*

Even-up, Even-up Proposition (1) A bet or proposition that gives each player an equal chance to win. (2) A bet at correct odds. (3) A 50–50 bet.

Exacta *Horse Racing:* A wager in which bettor must pick the horses that will finish first and second in the same race.

Exit To get out of the game.

Extension The maximum sum of money a bookie will accept or hold on each event. He lays off bets in excess of this sum to other bookmakers.

Face Card A king, queen or jack in a deck of cards.

Fade *Craps:* To cover part or all of the shooter's center bet.

Fader *Craps:* A bettor who has made a fading bet.

Fairbank (1) To make a cheating move in favor of the player to entice him to continuing playing or increase the size of his bet. (2) To let the player win a prize or bet. Also called *Throw a Cop.*

False Cut A cut which leaves the deck or part of the deck in its original position.

False-Picking, False Spec *Gin Rummy:* To pick up an opponent's discard that does not help the player. This is part of Gin Rummy strategy and is done as a bluff or to mislead the opponent.

Fast Company Seasoned or smart gamblers.

Fast Count (1) Rapid counting for the purpose of concealing miscount of one or more numbers. (2) Short-changing a person.

Fat Said of a person with plenty of money. "He's fat." Same as *Loaded.*

Fatten *Gin Rummy:* To discard a card that is useful to the opponent.

Fever The gambling habit. "She has the fever, she can't stay away from that Roulette table."

Field (1) Several horses grouped as one contestant in a race. (2) *Bank Craps:* A space on the layout containing a group of numbers, either 2, 3, 4, 9, 10, 11 and 12 or 2, 3, 5, 9, 10, 11 and 12.

Field Bet *Bank Craps:* A bet that one of the group of seven numbers on the *Field* will appear on the next roll.

Fill Slip A slip of paper signed by a casino pit boss and given to the casino cashier stating that a certain number of additional chips are required at a Craps, Roulette or Black Jack table.

Filly Female horse under five years of age.

Finesse *Bridge:* An attempt to make a card serve as an equal to a higher-ranking card held by an opponent.

Finger or Put the Finger on To squeal to the police or point out a cheat or crook.

Finger Man (1) One who points out a gambler to a holdup mob. (2) One who points out an illegal gambling game to the police.

Fink A stool pigeon or police informer.

First Flop Dice Heavily loaded dice used with a slick cup. So called because the loads are so heavy that a skilled dice cheat can throw five of a kind. Also called *Dead Number* dice.

Fish (1) A gambling sucker with money. (2) A dollar bill.

Five-Cent or Nickel Line A bookie's baseball or sports price line that has a differential of ¼ point between his lay and take odds. The bookie quotes odds of 5⅛ to 5 Pick 'em.

5–6 Sweepstakes Pool A Puerto Rican track and off-track race bet in which a player collects if the six horses he selects, one in each race, all finish first.

Fix To bribe.

Fix Is In (The) The fix has been paid and protection is being received.

Fix Money Money paid to the police or the politicians to buy protection. See also *Ice.*

Fixer A person with political connections through which he can secure the protection necessary for an illegal gambling enterprise.

Flasher A modern carnival game of chance in which electrical circuits and lights have replaced the hand-spun wheel.

Flat Bet *Craps:* A side bet made among players in a private game that the shooter will or will not win. Similar to center bets made between shooter and faders.

Flat Joint, Flat Store Any crooked gambling game.

Flat Passers   Crooked dice which have the 6–1 sides cut down on one die and the 3–4 sides cut down on the other so that 4, 5, 9 and 10 appear more often.

Flats   Crooked dice which have been shaved so that they are slightly brick-shaped. Also called *Bricks*.

Flatty   The operator of a flat, alibi, two-way or G-joint; any crooked carnival game operator. Also *Thief, grifter*.

Floating Game   An illegal gambling game which is shifted from place to place in order to avoid police raids.

Floorman   (1) The floorwalker in a gambling house whose duties are to spot and correct irregularities. (2) *Bingo:* An employee (usually a woman) who verifies the player's card aloud to the caller.

Flush   *Poker:* A hand containing five cards of the same suit.

Flush-Spotted Dice   Dice whose spots are flush with the surface rather than countersunk as with most dice.

Fold or Drop   To retire from a Poker hand or gambling game.

Folding Money   Bills. Also *Old Green Stuff, Scratch, Loot, Dough.* "He's got plenty of loot." "He's in the dough." See also *Hay*.

Form Player   A race bettor who before placing a bet on a horse takes into consideration the past performance of each horse entered.

Forty-Cent Line   A bookie's baseball or sports price line that has a differential of two points between his lay and take odds. The bookie quotes odds of 6 to 5 Pick 'em.

Fouled Up   Said of someone who is not thinking clearly.

Four-Way Joint   Carnival game that can be played from four sides.

Four-Way Play   *Bingo:* A game in which there are four winning positions. Also called *Round Robin*.

Frame   A hand, a deal, part of a game; same as in bowling.

Frankenstein   Four slot machines geared (bolted) together and having only one handle. When the player feeds one coin into one machine and pulls the handle, the reels spin on only one machine; when he feeds a coin into each of two machines, two machines operate, etc.

Free Bet   *Bank Craps:* A bet which permits a player who has made a previous bet on the pass or don't pass line to lay or take the correct point odds equal to the amount he has riding on the line.

Free Double-Odds Bet   Same as *Free Bet*, except that right or wrong bettors with line bets can take or lay double the amount riding on the line. Found in most legalized casinos.

Free Play   See *Covered Square*.

Free Ride   Playing part of a *Poker* hand without betting.

Freeze Out (To)   To force a player out of a game.

Freeze-Out Proposition   Wager, usually a long series of bets between a hustler and a gambler, in which the total sum to be wagered and the betting conditions are mutually agreed upon before the action begins.

Frets   The metal partitions that separate each of the 38 numbered sections of a Roulette wheel.

Frisk   To search a person.

Frisk Room   An anteroom where players are searched immediately before entering the actual gambling room in order to minimize the chances of a holdup.

Front Line   Same as *Pass Line*.

Front Line Odds   Taking the odds on the point number. Some casinos permit a player free action on this bet. See *Free Bet*.

Front Man   A person, usually without a police record, who is the apparent owner of a gambling operation. "He's fronting for the Cleveland boys."

Front Money   (1) Money that has been won. (2) Money used to make an impression on possible suckers.

Front Runner   A horse which quickly takes the lead and sets the pace for the others.

Full Table   A crowded table. *Black Jack, Dice:* Table at which no seat is available or there is no more room.

Furlong   *Horse Racing:* A distance of ⅛ of a mile (220 yards).

Fuzz   A policeman or peace officer. Also *Brass Buttons, Flatfoot, Bull*.

G-Note $1000 bill.

Gaff, G or Gimmick Any secret device or method that accomplishes or aids in cheating.

Gaffed Dice Doctored or crooked dice.

Gag Bet See *Hardway Bet.*

Gammon *Backgammon:* Loss of a game for failure to bear off any men. The winner collects twice the stakes.

Gate (1) To stop the dice before they have finished rolling, usually when a roll appears suspicious. Superstitious gamblers also sometimes do it to change the shooter's luck. Only done in private games. (2) A movable race-starting structure in use on major tracks.

Gate Monte *Spanish Monte, Monte Bank:* The banker's payoff card at Monte in which the banker takes a 25% charge from each player's gate winnings.

Gee Gee A horse.

Get Behind It To back up a crooked gambling move.

Get Out To regain one's losses.

Get To To bribe a police officer or politician to avoid gambling raids or to obtain a release from arrest. "You can get to that cop."

Get Your Feet Wet An invitation to a spectator to get into the game.

Gin (1) A ten-card hand completely formed in melds with no unmatched cards. (2) Short for Gin Rummy.

Go for It To be taken in by a crooked gambling scheme.

Go for the Money To cheat.

Go South With It (1) To put money in one's pocket either legitimately or illegitimately. (2) To remove a card or cards from the deck secretly. "He went south with a couple of aces."

Going Away A horse increasing his lead over other horses while running a race is "going away."

Good Man (1) A player with a large amount of money. (2) A skilled cheater. (3) A good gambling-scheme operator or employee.

Good Thing A good bet.

Gorilla A strong-arm or muscle man.

Grand or G $1,000.

Graveyard Shift The early-morning shift of a gambling establishment.

Grifter See *Flatty.*

Grind (1) A low-limit banking game which requires a good many players and good action in order to make a profit. (Also *Joint* or *Store* in this sense.) (2) A slow and hard way of making money. "The hustler's life is a grind."

Group Game A carnival game which allows more than one person to play simultaneously as opposed to games in which only one player plays against the house.

Gyp (1) A crook or cheat. (2) A small-time horseman.

Gypsy An unreliable carnival employee or operator; a drunk.

Half a Yard $50.

Halter Man A horseman who claims another owner's horse in a claiming race.

Hand (1) One game of a series. (2) One deal in a card game, or the cards held by a player. (3) A unit of height (four inches) used for measuring horses.

Hand-Mucker or Holdout Man A card cheat who specializes in palming cards.

Handbook A street bookie who takes horse bets.

Handicap Race A race in which the weights to be carried by each horse are assigned by the track's racing secretary.

Handicapper (1) Track official employee who assigns weights to certain horses in a race. (2) A writer working for a newspaper or racing sheet who tries to select probable race winners.

Handle The total amount of money that repeatedly changes hands in a betting scheme before it is actually won or lost. "The daily betting handle at the Big A runs into the millions."

Hanky-Pank or Grind Store Any small-time carnival game which operates on nickel-and-dime play and requires a lot of action in order to grind out a profit.

Hard Rock (1) *Poker:* A tight player. (2) A gambler who refuses to lend money. (3) A player who is hard to beat.

Hardway Bet *Craps:* The numbers 4, 6, 8 or 10 thrown with two duplicate numbers such as two deuces, two threes, etc. Also called *Gag Bet.*

Harness Race Race featuring standardbred horses pulling drivers seated on two-wheeled sulkies in a trotting or pulling race.

Has a Sign on His Back Said of a gambling cheat who is widely known as a crook.

Hay Money, chips, dough, sugar, cabbage, lettuce.

Head or Straight-Number Bet *Numbers Game:* A three-digit-number bet. The odds against hitting a straight number are 999 to 1.

Head-to-Head Betting (1) Betting of two players gambling against each other. (2) Two-handed game. "Gin is a head-to-head game."

Heart Courage. "He has plenty of heart; he bets them up."

Heat Is On (The) The officials have ordered a gambling clean-up and the police are on the alert. "The fix curdled and the heat was on."

Heavy A bigtime racketeer.

Heel (1) A cheap gambler. (2) Anyone who is no good.

Heist To hold up or rob someone.

High Belly Strippers A deck of cards doctored so that cards with high numerical values can be controlled.

High Roller Bigtime bettor.

Hip, Hep Knowledgeable. "He's hip to the racket." "He's no chump, he's hep."

Hipster One who knows what is going on, knows the angles, has a good knowledge of odds and percentages or of cheating and cheating devices. Also *Hip Gee.*

Hit (1) *Black Jack:* To draw another card. (2) *Numbers Game:* To have a winning number. (3) To win money.

Hit It (1) *Black Jack:* To ask the dealer for another card. (2) *Craps:* To make the point or any desired number. (3) *Stud Poker:* To call for a desired card.

Hit the Boards *Craps:* Term used by the stickman when he requests the shooter to throw the dice against the dice-table rail.

Hits *Craps:* A pair of crooked mis-

spotted dice that will not throw seven and will always make or hit certain point numbers.

Hold Check A postdated check.

Hold Count A mental countdown once used by slot machine rhythm players to beat the slot machines before the variator was developed.

Hold-out Artist A gambler or cheat who, when calculating the score or dividing the amount of winnings with his partner or partners, says that his winnings are less than they are and pockets the difference.

Hold-out Man A card cheat who specializes in palming, holding out of play and re-introducing valuable cards into a game by means of palming.

Hole The post position of a horse at the starting gate. Also *Slot.*

Hole Card *Stud Poker:* The first and face-down card dealt to a player.

Honor Tricks See *Quick Tricks.*

Honors *Bridge:* The five highest trumps in Bridge, or if there is no trump, the four aces.

Hook Up To team up. "They hooked up with the combination."

Hooked (1) To be on a losing streak. (2) To lose money. "I'm hooked."

Hop A secret sleight-of-hand move made after the cut which replaces the cards in their original position. Also called *Shift.*

Hopped Up Said of a person under the influences of dope; also of a horse which has been doped or otherwise stimulated.

Horse Mob A group of confidence men, some of whom pose as regular race bettors in order to cheat race bookies by past-posting.

Horse Office Bookmaking syndicate made up of three or four or more bookies who are grouped together so that they can handle the bigtime bettor's horse action.

Horse Room A race-betting room with all the necessary betting equipment and latest racing information.

Hot Said of a player on a winning streak. "The dice are making passes; they're hot."

Hot Horse (1) A horse that is being heavily bet on. (2) A horse rumored through inside information to have an excellent chance to win the race. (3) A horse selected by a tout.

Hot Number A policy number that rumor says has a better chance of being hit than any other.

Hot Player Player on a winning streak. "He's hot."

House (The) The operators of a gambling game or games.

Humps See *Strippers*.

Hunch Players Players who know little or nothing about the game on which they are wagering and who bet on impulse.

Hush Money A bribe paid to keep someone from talking.

Ice The money paid to police and other officials for permitting an illegal gambling scheme to operate in their locality. So called because it takes the heat off. Also called *Fix Money*.

Iceman A front man for either a gambling combine or the politicians and police, who collects the protection money from the gamblers and pays off the police and politicians. Same as *Bagman*.

"If" Money Bet A wager made with a race bookie in which a fixed amount is bet on a horse with the stipulation that if this horse wins, another fixed amount will be wagered on another horse or horses.

In the Bag Said of a sporting event or bet that is crooked. "The fight's in the bag for the underdog."

Information Horse A hot horse supposedly being bet on by a bigtime betting ring.

Informatory Double *Bridge:* A double made primarily to give information to a partner.

Inner Table *Backgammon:* The half of the board toward which the men enter and from which they bear off.

Inside Man (1) An employee in any gambling scheme who handles the bookkeeping or gambling finances. (2) Operator of a carnival game. "He's working on the inside."

Inside Ticket A duplicate of a punched-out Racehorse Keno ticket given to a player as his receipt.

Inside Track The rail of a racetrack.

Inside Work Any gaff—*Loads*, for example—placed inside a die or pair of dice.

Insurance Bet (1) *Craps:* Two or more wagers made at a Craps table in an attempt to insure one or the other. (2) *Black Jack:* A bet that a dealer does not hold a natural when he has an ace or ten spot showing.

Intermission Ticket *Bingo:* A ticket sold at a special discount to induce players to continue playing during intermission.

Jackpot (1) *Poker:* A form of betting in which each player antes a chip into the pot before the deal. (2) *Bingo:* The big-money prize. (3) *Slots:* The top-money payback of a machine.

Jackpot Light-up Board A large electric sign that hangs in a slot machine parlor or gambling establishment and is connected to the slot machines. It lights up and a chime rings whenever a jackpot is hit.

Jar Game A form of punchboard in which numbered paper tickets, individually folded and sealed, are drawn from a jar.

Jerk See *Lob*.

John Scarne Games, Inc. Holders of copyright on Scarney Baccarat, Scarney Dice, Scarney 3000 and many other popular games.

Joint See *Store*.

Joker (1) An extra card furnished with each 52-card deck, occasionally used as a wild card to represent any card desired.

Jonah (1) A superstitious player or gambling operator who tries to control his luck with phrases or gestures. (2) One whose presence is thought to bring bad luck.

Jug Jail. (In other underworld usage, it also means bank, but rarely among gamblers.)

Juice Electricity.

Juice Joint A crooked dice or Roulette game in which the cheating is done by concealed electromagnets in the table, and the Roulette ball or the dice are gaffed with a steel slug.

Junior Jackpot Ticket *Bingo:* Tickets which pay off a smaller jackpot.

Kangaroo A pimp.

Keep Under *Gin Rummy:* To reduce your point of unmatched cards under the legal knocking-point number.

Kentucky Derby The Super Bowl, the World Series, the Stanley Cup of horse racing.

Keyed Punchboards Punchboards sold with a secret key (list) that gives the cheat the location of the big prize awards.

Kibitzer A spectator at any game who gives the players advice that is seldom wanted.

Kick Pocket. "He put the bankroll in his kick."

Kids Gunmen.

Kitty (1) An amount taken out of the stakes of a private game to pay expenses. (2) A pool to which special bets are paid and from which royalties or special bonuses are collected.

Knock (1) To make disparaging remarks. (2) *Gin Rummy:* To go down with a count of 10 or less.

Knocked Off (1) Raided by the police; arrested. (2) Murdered.

Ladder Man A casino employee who sits on an elevated stand overlooking a Bank Craps, Money Craps, Baccarat or Chemin de Fer table and whose duty it is to correct dealer's errors and to spot dice cheats. He occasionally alternates with the boxman at the Craps table.

Lam See *Runout Powder.*

Lame (To come up) To be unable to pay off lost wagers with a bookmaker. "Jake came up lame and took a powder."

Last Turn The last three undealt cards in Faro or Faro Bank.

Late Line See *Revised Line.*

Lay or Lay It To bet a greater amount against a lesser amount. "I'll lay two to one the Yankees beat the Indians."

Lay Off (1) *Gin Rummy:* To get rid of one or more cards on an opponent's melds. (2) Not to bet.

Lay the Odds *Craps:* To bet that a point, box or place number (4, 5, 6, 8, 9, 10) will not be thrown before a seven. The right bettor who bets that a point, box or place number *will* be thrown before a seven is *Taking the Odds.*

Laydown (1) A diagram of betting spaces in carnival games, usually on the counter in front of the game, on which the players place their bets. (2) A wager. "The Big Six didn't get a laydown."

Layout A diagram with spaces designated for different bets. The players place their money on the spaces to signify what bets they are making.

Leg One game of a series in many private gambling games. "I'm a leg up on you." See also *Hand* and *Frame.*

Legal Tie, Standoff or No Contest (1) *Black Jack:* When a dealer's count is the same as the player's count. (2) *Poker:* When two players have the same ranking hand.

Legit Game An honest game.

Legit Guy A person who has no underworld connections. This does not necessarily imply that he is an honest man.

Let It Ride To leave the original bet and the winnings of the previous bet on the gaming table and wager them again.

Liberty Bell The first slot machine, invented in San Francisco in 1895 by Charles Fey, a 29-year-old mechanic and the first slot machine operator in America.

Light (1) In an insufficient amount. "He's light in the Poker pot." (2) Weak. "The P.C. is light."

Light Work Doctored cards marked with very fine lines. "I had to put light work in that Stud Poker game because the players were smart."

Limit (1) The maximum amount a player may wager on a specific bet or event. (2) The maximum amount a player may increase a previous bet (at Poker, etc.).

Line See *Price Line.*

Line Bet *Roulette:* A bet on six numbers in two rows of three numbers each running across the layout. The payoff is at 5 to 1 odds.

Line Work On doctored cards, additional small spots, curlicues or lines added to the back design of playing cards so that they can be read from the back by the cheat.

Little Joe or Little Joe from Kokomo *Craps:* The point four.

Live Card A hidden card in an opponent's hand or in the remaining part of the undealt or unplayed part of the deck. A card that is not dead because it has not yet been played.

Live Horse A horse that is in good shape to run his best.

Live One A player with money.

Load A weight placed within a die.

Loads Loaded dice. See also *Inside Work*.

Lob A hanger-on around gambling joints who runs errands for players. Also called a *Jerk*.

Long Shot A horse that is given very little chance to win.

Looking for Action Said of a gambler who is trying to find a game.

Lookout A gambling-house employee who sees that everything runs smoothly and is on the constant alert for crookedness by both player and casino personnel.

Low Belly Strippers A crooked deck of cards in which the edges of the high cards are concave rather than straight, making it possible for the cheat to cut to a low or high card at will.

Lugger A person who transports players to the game. Not to be confused with a *Steerer*.

Lumber (1) Spectators in a gambling joint. (2) Broke players. "There's more lumber around here than players."

Luminous Readers Marked cards that can be read only through tinted glasses.

Maiden A horse which has never won a race.

Maiden Race A race run by horses which have never won a race.

Main *Craps:* An old term for point number from the English game of Two-Dice Hazard.

Map A check. "Don't take that guy's map; he's a paperhanger."

Mare A female horse over five years of age.

Mark Sucker.

Marker (1) An IOU. (2) A numbered chip used at casino games to keep track of money owed the bank by the player during a game. "He's on the Roulette rim for a thousand." (3) A buck or coin placed on a numbered space of a layout to indicate the player's bet.

Martingale system *Roulette:* A progressive system long used in Monte Carlo and other European casinos; now used in many other games.

Match Pak Same as *Tip Book*.

Match Race Race between two outstanding thoroughbreds, winner takes all.

Mechanic A skilled gambling cheat who resorts to sleight of hand to accomplish his crooked work.

Mechanical Games Banking games which lack the element of skill: Craps, Roulette, Hazard, Big Six, etc.

Mechanic's Grip A method of holding a deck of cards (in either the left or right hand) with three fingers curled around the long edge of the deck and the index finger at the narrow upper edge away from the body.

Meld *Gin Rummy:* A set of three or four cards of the same rank or three or more cards of the same suit in sequence.

Memphis Dominoes Dice.

Mender See *Patch*.

Merchandise Joint See *Stock Joint*.

Mexican Standoff Act of quitting a gambling game when one is a very small winner or loser. "I played a Mexican standoff."

Michigan Bankroll A large bankroll consisting mostly of dollar bills with a bill of large denomination on the outside.

Miss (1) *Craps:* A miss-out. (2) To miss or miss it; to make a miss-out.

Miss a Pass *Craps:* To fail to make a point number. "The shooter missed his pass."

Miss-Out *Craps:* A losing Craps decision for the shooter (and the other players who are betting with the shooter) obtained on the come-out when a crap is thrown and after the come-out when a seven is thrown

Miss-Out (Contd)
instead of the shooter's point number.
Misses (1) Crooked dice that are gaffed to make more sevens than point numbers. (2) Crooked dice that are gaffed to make more miss-outs than passes.
Mitt A hand of cards.
Money (In the) (1) Horses that finish 1st, 2nd and 3rd finish in the money. (2) Said of a person who has struck it rich.
Money Poker A guessing game played with dollar bills; also known as *Liar Poker*.
Money Store A carnival game which pays off in cash rather than merchandise.
Monicker Underworld nickname.
Monkey A sucker.
Monte Mob See *Broad-Tossing Mob*.
Monte Thrower See *Broad-Tosser*.
Mooch Carnival slang for sucker. Also *Mark, Chump*.
Mora A guessing game of Italian origin, also known as *Fingers*.
Morning Line A handicapper's or price-maker's morning guess as to the probable odds on horses that are to run in the afternoon races.
Mount A racehorse.
Mouse (1) A squealer; one who complains to the police. (2) A timid person.
Mouthpiece A lawyer.
Move Sleight of hand. "That's when he made the move."
Mudder A horse that runs well on a muddy track.
Mug (1) A low character. (2) A sucker or chump.
Multiple Slot Machines: Modern slot machines which accept from one to eight coins and pay off winners in multiple fashion.
Murder Hard to beat. "That game's murder."
Murdered (To be) To lose heavily. "They all bet on the winning long shot so we got murdered."
Muscle Man A tough guy or bouncer who keeps order in a gambling joint.

Nailed (1) Caught cheating. "He was nailed red-handed switching the deck." (2) Arrested.

Natural (1) *Black Jack:* A high combination of two cards such as a ten-spot card and an ace. (2) *Poker:* A ranking hand without a wild card. (3) *Craps:* A winning decision (7 or 11) on the first roll.
New York Craps A form of *Bank Craps* played mostly in the eastern states in which the player must pay a 5% charge for betting the box or off numbers.
Ninety Days *Craps:* The point nine.
No Dice A dice roll that does not count.
Nonvulnerable *Bridge:* Not having scored a game.
Number Two Man See *Second Dealer*.
Numbers Game Service A service which supplies Numbers bankers with the official winning numbers as they appear with the running of the races.
Nut A gambler's or gambling enterprise's overhead expenses. "The nut's too high."
Nutman A gambling hustler.

Odd Trick *Bridge:* Any trick won by declarer in excess of six.
Odds Correct odds are the ratio of the unfavorable chances to the favorable chances. See also *Payoff Odds*.
Odds-on Favorite A horse which is such a big favorite that the quoted odds are less than even money. "The odds-on favorite is priced at one to four."
Off-Number Bet *Craps:* A bet made at odds that the shooter will or will not throw a specified number other than his point (any of the numbers 4, 5, 6, 8, 9 and 10) before throwing seven.
Off Numbers *Private Craps:* All the numbers 4, 5, 6, 8, 9 and 10 except the point number the shooter is trying to make.
Off the Board A sports bookie's term for refusing to accept bets on a particular sports event.
Office See *Signal*.
Okay Protection furnished by politicians and police enabling illegal gambling schemes to operate. "We got the okay."

Old Bill A word or hand signal (open palm) which means, "Is there another card cheat in the game?"

On the Cuff Bet A free bet for the player.

One-Armed Bandit Slot machine.

One Big One Gambler's term for $1,000.

One-Number Bet *Craps:* A bet that a certain number or group of numbers will or will not be thrown before another number.

One-Roll Action or Come-Out Bet *Craps:* A bet that the shooter does or does not throw (1) a certain number any way; (2) a certain number a certain way; or (3) any one of a group of numbers on the next roll.

One-Roll Bet *Craps:* A bet which is decided on the next roll of the dice.

One-Way Cards Cards whose backs bear pictures or designs that are not symmetrical top to bottom.

One-Way Tops and Bottoms See *Percentage Tops and Bottoms.*

Open Craps A banking dice game in which side bets among the players are permitted only on the point number. Also called *Money Craps.*

Open Up (1) To start a game. (2) To give information. "He's a rat; he opened up to the law."

Operators Bell Slot machine manufactured by Herbert Stephen Mills in 1907. Nicknamed "the Iron Case."

Optional Claiming Race A claiming race in which the owner does not file a claim form, thus preventing other horsemen from claiming his horse.

OTB New York City corporation which operates more than 100 off-track race betting shops.

Out in Front (1) To be ahead money. (2) A leading horse in a race.

Outer Table *Backgammon:* That other half of the board comprising a player's bar, 7 through 12 points.

Outfit See *Combination.*

Outrider Rider of lead horse who accompanies the racehorses to the starting gate.

Outside Man (1) A carnival-game employee who pretends to be a player and assists in the buildup. (2) Any employee of a gambling casino whose duties are not actually in the casino. "The doorman and one lugger are the only outside men that showed up for work today."

Outside Work Anything done to gaff dice on their surfaces.

Overboard (To go) To be unable to make good on gambling debts. "He went overboard betting Mac the sports bookie."

Overlay To make an odds to 1 bet which is greater than the event warrants. "He overlayed the Yankees by two points."

Pad Payroll. "Everybody's on the pad, including the cop on the beat."

Paddle A numbered paper slip which corresponds to a numbered space on a carnival wheel.

Paddle Wheel A carnival wheel each of whose numbered sections contains one, two or three numbers. Also called *Raffle Wheel.*

Paint (1) A picture card. (2) *Black Jack:* A king, queen, jack or ten spot. "There are six paints left in the deck."

Palette A wooden palette with a long thin handle, used by Baccarat and Chemin de Fer dealers to move the cash and chips around.

Paper (1) Marked cards. "I laid down paper in the Poker game." (2) A check or other negotiable document.

Paperhanger A passer of bad checks. See *Map.*

Pari-Mutuel System of betting in which winners receive all money wagered on a race after track's and state's shares and breakage have been deducted.

Part Score *Bridge:* A trick-score total of less than game. Same as *Partial.*

Pass (1) *Craps:* A winning decision for the Craps shooter obtained on the come-out by throwing a 7 or 11 or repeating the point before throwing a 7. (2) *Poker:* A declaration that the player does not wish to make a bet.

Pass Line *Craps:* A space on the Craps layout. Money placed in this space is a bet that the shooter will pass.

Passers Crooked dice which are so gaffed that they tend to make more passes than fair dice.

Past Performance The race record of a horse.

Past-Post To place a bet with a bookie on a winning horse after the race has been run. "He's the best past-poster in the business."

Pat Hand *Draw Poker:* A hand which a player does not try to improve by drawing cards.

Patch A carnival front man who squares complaints with players and the police. Also *Mender.*

Pay Line The center line in the window of a slot machine on which the payoff symbols appear.

Payoff (1) The collection of a bet. (2) Any final event.

Payoff Odds The odds at which a bet is paid off. Usually less than the correct odds, except for honest proposition bets.

Peanuts or Pretzels Small money. "That character pays his help off in pretzels."

Peek To glimpse the top card of a deck secretly.

Peek Store A carnival flat joint in which part of the gaff consists in the operator's peeking at a number and then either miscalling it or changing it by sleight of hand to clip the players.

Peg (1) To place a person in a certain category. "We pegged him right." (2) To place a buck or marker to indicate the dealer in a card game or the point at craps. (3) To mark cards with the sharp point of a pin or thumbtack concealed in a bandage on a finger or thumb.

Penalty Card *Contract Bridge:* An exposed card that must be played at first legal opportunity.

Pencil (The) The privilege of signing checks which the casino pays. "He has the power of the pencil."

Percentage (P.C.) An advantage obtained by offering less than the true odds or by the use of crooked dice or controlled shots. Also *Edge.*

Percentage Dice Crooked dice which over a period of time supply a percentage in the cheater's favor.

Percentage or P.C. Game A banking game in which a favorable advantage is obtained through offering less than correct odds.

Percentage or P.C. Store Any carnival game which earns its profits by paying off winners at less than the correct odds, thus retaining a percentage of the money wagered.

Percentage Tops and Bottoms A pair of gaffed dice, one of which is misspotted. One number, usually the deuce or five, appears on the die twice.

Perfecta A form of horse-race betting similar to the Exacta.

Perfects Dice that are true cubes to a tolerance of 1/5,000 of an inch.

Philadelphia Layout The first Bank Craps layout to give the players an opportunity to bet the dice to win *and* lose.

Philistines Loan sharks.

Phony (1) A person who pretends he is something he isn't. (2) A crooked die.

Photo Finish A race finish so close that the photo of the finish determines which horses are in the money.

Piece See under *Point.*

Pigeon Sucker.

Pinch An arrest. *To take a pinch* is to submit to an arrest arranged beforehand between the police and the gamblers.

Pink A racetrack detective. Short for Pinkerton, the detective agency that supplies many racetrack detectives.

Pit Boss or Inspector *Roulette and Black Jack:* A casino employee who supervises a gaming table. He stands in the pit ring, watches the game, writes cash-out and fill slips, corrects errors made by croupiers or players and watches for cheating.

Place Bet *Bank Craps:* A right or wrong point bet.

Plater A poor horse.

Play The betting. Same as *Action.*

Point (1) Any number or total in a gambling game on which a wager can be placed. (2) *Craps:* The numbers 4, 5, 6, 8, 9 and 10 are possible point numbers. (3) Also called *Piece* in this sense: A share or percentage of a gambling enterprise or play. "He's got five points in the casino." "I've got a piece of his action."

Point Bet *Craps:* A bet at odds that

the shooter's point will or will not be made.

Point Count *Bridge:* A method of evaluating one's hand.

Poke A wallet.

Policy King A boss or big shot in the policy game.

Polly A politician.

Post *Horse Racing:* Starting gate.

Post Position *Horse Racing:* Numbered position of horses at starting gate before the start of a race.

Pot (1) The aggregate of chips or money at stake in a betting scheme usually consisting of bets contributed by each contestant. (2) *Poker:* The total cash or chips bet on any single hand.

Pound $5.

Price Line or Line A sports bookie's lay and take odds on a sports event. "I'll lay seven to five that Navy beats Army or take eight to five that Army beats Navy": This is his price line.

Pricemaker See *Handicapper.*

Pricemakers' Percentage Table A table which transposes the "odds to 1" into percentages.

Prime *Backgammon:* The making of six consecutive points.

Private Game Any game which has no houseman or banker and in which no charge is extracted for the privilege of playing.

Professor See *Dean.*

Progressive Slot Machine A slot machine in which the top jackpot increases in a predetermined ratio to the number of coins played into the machine.

Proposition Bet (1) Any bet made at Black Jack or any other game that is not covered by the rules. (2) A bet to settle any difference of opinion between two or more persons.

Proposition Cheat A crooked gambler whose policy is never to give his opponent a break. He gaffs or angles his proposition bets so that they are surefire and give him a 100% edge, or as close to that as possible.

Proposition Hustler A bettor who offers betting propositions which appear, at first glance, to be fair or to favor his opponent, but which actually give the hustler a big advantage.

Psychic Bid *Bridge:* One made without cards to support it, for the purpose of misleading the opponents.

Pull Down To take down or pocket all or part of a wager just won.

Pull Through A sleight-of-hand move which appears to be a cut made just after a shuffle. It separates the two halves of the deck and replaces them as they were before the shuffle.

Pulled It (He) Said of a jockey who kept his mount from finishing in the money.

Punk (1) A small-time character or chiseler. (2) A young man, a novice. (3) A toy cat used in a carnival game.

Punter *Baccarat or Chemin de Fer:* The player or shooter.

Push Same as *Standoff.*

Push Card A punchboard which is made of two pieces of cardboard glued together. The front surface bears partly perforated circles which can be pushed out with the finger.

Put the Horns On To try to influence one's luck by changing position at a table, carrying a rabbit's foot or using any other superstitious device.

Put the Pressure On To coerce someone by force or strong persuasion.

Puzzler A puzzle fan.

Quarter Bet See *Square Bet.*

Quick Tricks *Bridge:* A count of tricks that can be expected to be won on offense or defense. Same as *Honor Tricks.*

Quiniela A form of betting similar to the daily double except that players try to pick horses which will run first and second in the same race.

Quinze An old Spanish game, a forerunner of Black Jack.

Rabbit (1) A timid person. (2) A sucker or inexperienced gambler. "If I had another rabbit like him I'd never work again."

Rack A box to hold chips or checks.

Raffle Wheel See *Paddle Wheel.*

Rail See *Boards.*

Rail Bird One who watches the races from a rail position.

Raise *Poker:* To put more chips in a pot than any previous player.

Rap (To take the) (1) To take the blame. (2) To take an arrest or prison term.

Rat An informer.

Readers Marked cards.

Ready Up To get ready to make a crooked move.

Red (In the) Owing money. (2) Unprofitable. "The carnival played a series of bloomers and it's in the red."

Red One In a carnival, a show date that lost money.

Redouble *Backgammon:* To double the stakes of a game after a previous double.

Refait *Trente et Quarante:* A tie in totals of cards dealt in two rows in which the bank takes both bets.

Renege To refuse to honor a lost wager or debt; to welsh.

Result Player A gambler who tells you how you should have made your bet or play after a decision has been rendered.

Reverse and Back to Back A race bet made with a bookie which involves more than one "if" bet.

Revised Line A racing sheet which prints the latest revised odds. Also called *Late Line.*

Rhythm System A means of beating the slot machines without using mechanical gimmicks.

Rig To gaff or make crooked. "The game is rigged."

Right Bettor, Right Player, Rightie *Craps:* A player who bets the dice to win.

Ring In (1) To introduce crooked gaming equipment into a game. (2) To force someone into another's plans. (3) To muscle in.

Ring in One's Nose (To have a) To be losing heavily and betting high, hoping to get even.

Ringer A horse run in a race under another horse's name.

Rip In *Craps:* To switch dice into a game.

Rock (1) A player who won't lend any money. (2) *Stud Poker:* A back-to-back player.

Rocks (1) Diamonds. (2) Money.

Roll (1) To roll dice or a Roulette ball.

(2) To rob a person while he is drunk or asleep.

Rope (1) To cheat or swindle. (2) To lure a sucker into a crooked game.

Roscoe A revolver or pistol.

Rough It Up To bet heavily, thus enlivening the tempo of the game.

Round Robin A race or sports bet placed with an off-track bookie which involves the playing of all possible two- or three-race or sports parlays on three or more teams or horses.

Rug Joint A lavishly decorated casino having top-grade gaming equipment. See *Carpet Joint* and *Sawdust Joint.*

Rumble To catch on to a gaffed mechanism or a sleight-of-hand move.

Run *Gin Rummy:* A sequence of three or more cards of the same suit.

Run Strong To operate a game or casino crookedly. "We couldn't pay the nut so we had to run strong."

Rundown A sports bookie's price line on the day's betting events.

Runner (1) One who picks up daily numbers business from several agents. So called because he is always on the go, trying to avoid arrest. (2) A casino employee who carries cash-outs, fill slips and money between the cashier's cage and the pit bosses.

Running Wide Said of a horse running outside the pack.

Runout Powder A gambler who leaves town without paying off his bets is said to take a *Runout Powder* or to *Take the Fence* or to be on the *Lam.*

Saliva Test A check made after the race to determine whether or not a horse has been doped.

Sand To edge-mark cards with sandpaper.

Sandbag *Poker:* A betting technique in which two players have a third sandwiched between them and keep raising without any consideration for the middle player. Same as *Whipsaw.*

Sawdust Joint Unpretentious gambling casino.

Scalpers Players who make bets on two opposing teams with different bookies in such a way that they gain an edge in the betting.

Scarney Baccarat A casino banking card game invention of the author which combines the principles of Baccarat, Chemin de Fer and Black Jack.

Scarney Dice A special set of five dice invented by the author. Each die is marked with 1, 3, 4 and 6 spots, plus the word "dead" repeated on two opposite sides.

Score (1) To win at gambling. (2) To succeed in any enterprise. (3) To win by cheating. (4) The money won by cheating.

Score a Big Touch To fleece a player or players for a large amount of money.

Scratch (1) Money. (2) To remove a horse from a race.

Scratch Sheet A racing pamphlet which lists entries and scratches in races at the major tracks throughout the country.

Screen Out To cover up or misdirect attention away from a crooked gambling move.

Second Dealer A cheat who deals the second card from the deck when he appears to be dealing the top card.

Send It In To make big bets, or many bets, usually against the bank. "When he's on a winning streak, he sends it in." See also *Zing It In*.

Shading A method of marking cards. The backs of cards are delicately shaded with a dilute solution of marking ink which is the same color as the ink already printed on the backs.

Shapes Dice whose shapes have been altered in some way so that they are no longer perfect cubes.

Shark, Sharp A cheater. See also *Mechanic*.

Shift See *Hop*.

Shift the Cut To return secretly the halves of a cut deck to their original position.

Shill See *Stick*.

Shimmy Chemin de Fer.

Shimmy Table Table at which Chemin de Fer is played.

Shiner A small mirror which reflects the face of the top card of the deck as it is dealt. Usually concealed in rings, matchboxes, pipes, coins, etc.

Shoe or Sabot A card-dealing box used to deal Chemin de Fer and Baccarat.

Shooter In any dice game, the player who throws the dice.

Shortcake (The) Short change. "I wound up with the shortcake."

Shortstop A player who can afford to lose only a small amount. "This joint's loaded with shortstops."

Shy See *Light*.

Side Game A minor banking game in a large casino.

Signal, Sign Any secret signal between two or more gamblers. Also *Office*.

Silks A jockey's uniform.

Silver Tongue A high-class member of a mob. A good talker, often a lawyer.

Single-Action Bet *Numbers:* A bet on one digit.

Single-o To work alone.

Singleton *Bridge:* Original holding of one card in a suit.

Sit To run a sports or race book from an office by telephone.

Six-Ace Flats Crooked dice which give a favorable percentage to a wrong bettor.

Skill or Science Game (1) Any carnival game that requires skill to play. (2) Any carnival game of chance called a skill or science game in order to mislead the authorities and get around the laws prohibiting games of chance.

Skimming Secretly taking money from the gross handle of a casino or other gambling operation to avoid taxes.

Slamming (It's) (1) Fast, having plenty of action. (2) Cheating methods are being used.

Sleeper (1) Money or a bet left on the table or gambling layout which belongs to a player who has forgotten about it. (2) A horse which suddenly wakes up and runs a surprisingly strong race.

Slick Dice Cup A cup which is gaffed with a polished inner surface.

Slicker A gambler who cannot be trusted.

Slot (1) A slot machine. (2) Post position of a horse at the starting gate.

Slough or **Slough Up** To close up. "We sloughed the game." "The police sloughed the town."

Slum Cheap merchandise used as prizes in carny games. Also sold on the midway at carnivals and circuses.

Small Nickel $50.

Small One $100.

Smart Bettor Seasoned gambler who knows odds and percentages.

Snake Eyes *Craps:* A one spot showing on both dice.

Sneak (1) To operate a gambling scheme without the knowledge of the police. (2) To run a game without paying protection money. "We ran a sneak game."

Soft Player (1) An inexperienced gambler. (2) A player who can't stand to win big money.

Soft 17 *Black Jack:* A count of 17 which includes an ace.

Softy A poor player.

Solid Bet or Person (1) A good bet. (2) Anyone with money.

Spell A series of winning or losing decisions. "The dice had a hot spell."

Spill An accident involving one or more horses and jockeys.

Spindle A metal or wooden arrow mounted on a horizontal base; a variation of a carnival wheel.

Spit A small amount of money.

Spitballing Same as *False-Picking.*

Split Bet *Roulette:* A bet on two adjacent numbers. Each winning unit is paid off at 17 to 1 odds.

Splitting Pairs *Black Jack:* To separate two cards of the same numerical value and consider each card as the first card of a new hand.

Spooning A method of cheating a slot machine by inserting a spoon-shaped device through the payout opening into the payout mechanism.

Spot (1) To give a person or team a handicap. (2) To detect an irregularity.

Spot Card Any card ranked from ace to ten.

Spot Controller A controller who operates without runners. He takes big action from a select clientele of big-time numbers bettors, usually soliciting his business in bars and clubs.

Spring (1) To bet big. "He's ready to spring." (2) To treat.

Square, On the Square Honest. "He's a square guy." "The joint is on the square." (2) *To square:* To satisfy a complaint. "We squared the beef by paying him off."

Square Bet *Roulette:* A bet on four spaces of the layout. Each winning unit is paid off at 8 to 1 odds. Also called *Corner Bet, Quarter Bet.*

Squawker (1) A poor loser. (2) A chronic complainer.

Squeeze (1) The control that operates an electrically operated cheating device. (2) Pressure or force. "We put the squeeze on him and he opened up."

Stacked Deck A deck which has been secretly prearranged.

Stand *Black Jack:* To refuse to draw another card.

Stand-in Arrest See *Accommodation Arrest.*

Stand-up Guy A person who won't squeal under any circumstances or implicate another person in any wrong doing. "He's a stand-up guy. The cops can't get anything out of him."

Standoff (1) No decision, a tie, cancellation of a bet. (2) *Black Jack:* So called when player and dealer have the same count of 21 or less. (3) *Craps:* A two-ace standoff means that the wrong bettor does not win when two aces appear on the first roll.

Stay *Poker:* To remain in the pot without raising. To call or see.

Steeplechase A race of two to four miles with ten to twenty hurdles (jumps).

Steer Game Crooked game into which the marks are steered.

Steer Joint A crooked gambling house.

Steerer An individual who secretly works for a crooked gambling establishment and persuades customers to patronize it.

Stick (1) A Craps stick used by the stickman to push the dice around the table. (2) An employee of the house who bets house money and pretends to be a player in order to attract business or stimulate the action. (3) A carnival-game employee who does the same and also assists in the buildup and wins prizes which are later secretly returned. (In sense (2) and (3) also known as a *Shill.*)

Stickman Craps dealer who pushes the dice from player to player and calls out the numbers thrown.

Stiff (1) An unlucky player. (2) A non-player.

Stock Joint A carnival game that pays off in merchandise. Also called *Merchandise Joint.*

Stooper One who makes a practice of hunting for discarded winning tickets at the racetrack.

Stopper *Gin Rummy:* A card which will prevent a discard from being used in a meld by an opponent.

Store Any carnival game, honest or crooked. Also *Joint.*

Storm An apparent upset in the law of averages.

Straight *Poker:* A hand of five cards in sequence, not all of the same suit.

Straight Bet *Roulette:* A bet on one number. Each winning unit is paid off at 35 to 1 odds.

Streak A run of good or bad luck.

Street Bet *Roulette:* A bet on three numbers running across the layout. Each winning unit is paid off at 11 to 1 odds.

Stretch or Home Stretch A racetrack straightaway beginning from a certain position to the finish line.

Stretch Runner A horse known to start slowly but to finish strong.

String A group of horses.

Strippers A deck of cards whose edges have been trimmed, making some cards either narrower or shorter than others. *Combination Strippers:* A deck so trimmed that certain desired combinations (such as a Gin hand) can be stripped out of the shuffled deck and brought to the top. *Belly Strippers* or *Humps:* A deck in which cards are trimmed narrow, others cut so that they are narrower at the ends only, leaving a belly in the middle. When the low cards belly out it is a deck of *Low Belly Strippers,* and the chump who, in cutting, grasps the deck at the mid-

dle of the long sides will always cut to a low card. *High Belly Strippers* are trimmed in the opposite manner. Belly strippers are primarily for use in the game of Banker and Broker.

Strong Arm (1) A muscle man. (2) *To strong-arm:* To use force.

Strong Work Crooked cards marked with heavy lines.

Stuck Lost. "I'm stuck fifty dollars." Also *Out.*

Stud Form of Poker in which three or more cards are dealt face up.

Sucker Bet A bet that supplies the operator or hustler with a high percentage.

Superfecta *Horse Racing:* A form of betting in which the bettor must pick four horses that finish first, second, third and fourth in the exact order in the same race.

Switch To secretly exchange one object for another. "When the paper was switched into the Poker game, the mechanic's confederate had the mark changing a hundred-dollar bill."

Table Stakes *Poker:* A method of placing a maximum betting limit on wagers.

Tail To follow someone.

Take (1) The receipts of a banking game or gambling scheme. (2) To accept a bribe. (3) To cheat. "We took him for all he had."

Take a Bath To lose heavily or to go broke.

Take a Pinch See *Accommodation Arrest.*

Take the Odds To accept the larger figure in an odds to 1 figure. "I'll take 2 to 1 on the underdog." See also under *Lay the Odds.*

Tallyman See *Caller.*

Tanked or Tank Job Crooked, as in a prizefight. "The bookies say the fight is tanked."

Tap Out To bet one's last bit of money.

Tear-up (the) A method of blowing off a suspicious mark. The cheat pretends not to accept the mark's gambling loss and tears up his check. Actually he switches in a

Tear-up (the) (Contd) dummy check, destroys it and then cashes the original before the sucker stops payment.

Telegraph To give away unconsciously the fact that a cheating move is about to be made, usually by some clumsy preparatory action or by a change in attitude.

Telephone Numbers Big money.

Ten-Cent or Dime Line A bookie's baseball or sports price line that has a differential of ½ point between his lay and take odds. The bookie quotes odds of 5¼ to 5 Pick 'em.

Ten-Stop Machine A gaffed slot machine that has 20 symbols on each of its reels but is gaffed so that only 10 of them can appear on its payline.

There's Work Down Crooked cards or dice or some gimmick is being used to cheat.

Thimble-Rigger The operator of the forerunner of the Three-Shell Game which used three thimbles.

Thoroughbred A horse bred from the best blood through a long line. Any horse eligible to registry in an American studbook.

Three-Card Monte Mob See *Broad-Tossing Mob.*

Three-Way or Four-Way Joint A carnival game that can be played from three or four sides. "The Penny Pitch is usually a four-way joint."

Throw a Cop See *Fairbank.*

Ticket Picker See *Stooper.*

Tip The crowd of players and prospective players who gather around a carnival game.

Tip Book A variation of the punch board made to resemble a paper match folder and containing sealed and numbered paper tickets.

Tipster See *Tout.*

Top (1) The gross handle of a game or gambling scheme. "Take the expenses off the top." (2) The officials who supply protection. "The okay came right down from the top."

Top Horse (1) Horse in the number 1 post position. (2) The favorite.

Tops and Bottoms Gaffed dice which bear only three different numbers on each die. Also called *Tops, Busters, Ts* and *Misspots.*

Tote Board The infield board which flashes the totals bet and the approximate odds on the horses while the betting windows are open and, after the race is run, shows the pay-off prices on the first three horses, and names the fourth horse.

Touch (1) A loan. (2) To borrow money. (3) A score.

Tout One who makes a living trying to convince anyone who will listen that he knows which horse will win a race.

Town Clown *Carnival:* Police officer.

Trap (1) A banking game. Term used by operators. (2) A bet that is not what it appears to be.

Treasury Ticket A form of lottery in which the winning numbers are obtained from the last five digits of the daily United States Treasury balance.

Trifecta See Triple.

Trim To fleece, gyp, clip, beat, etc.

Trims Crooked cards gaffed by trimming some cards one way and the others another way.

Triple *Horse Racing:* A form of betting in which the bettor must pick the horses that finish first, second and third in the exact order in the same race. Also called *Trifecta.*

Triple Game *Backgammon:* A *backgammon* in which the winner collects triple the stakes.

Turf Accountant See *Betting Commissioner.*

Twenty-Cent Line A bookie's baseball or sports price line that has a differential of 1 point between his lay and take odds. The bookie quotes odds of 5½ to 5 Pick 'em.

Twenty-One (1) The game of Black Jack. (2) The highest hand at Black Jack when made with two cards.

Twin Double *Horse Racing:* A form of betting in which the bettor must pick the winners of the first and second races—then exchange his winning ticket and pick the winners of the fifth and sixth races. The bettor must pick the winners of each of four races to collect.

Two-Horse Parlay A wager placed on two horses, each in a different race. The player wins if both horses finish as stipulated by his bet.

Two-Number Bet *Craps:* A bet that one of two specified numbers will or will not be thrown before a seven.

Two-Roll Bet *Craps:* A bet which is decided within the next two rolls.

Two-Way Joint (also *Gaffed Joint, G-Joint, Strong Joint, Skin Joint, Flat Joint*). A carnival game that can be operated two ways—honest or crooked.

Under the Gun *Draw or Stud Poker:* A situation in which a player must pass, bet or check before other players do so.

Under Wraps Said of a horse who is restrained from running his best.

Underdog A contestant or team which the bookies or experts rate as having less than an even chance (50%) to win. "Army is a two to one underdog in today's game."

Underknock *Gin Rummy:* To show a hand that has the same or fewer points in unmatched cards than the player who has knocked.

Unpaid Shill Casino operator's term for describing a consistent small-money bettor.

Upcard (1) *Gin Rummy:* The first card turned up after each player has been dealt his ten cards. (2) The uppermost card of the discard pile.

Velvet Money that has been won.

Vigorish, Viggerish or Vig The percentage taken by a banking-game operator. It may be either overt or hidden by the mechanics or mathematics of the game.

Vulnerable *Contract Bridge:* Said of a side having won a game toward rubber.

Washy Horse A nervous horse.

Wave (1) To bend the edge of a card during play for identification purposes. (2) The bend itself.

Way Off Very imperfect. "The Roulette wheel is way off."

Welsher One who does not honor a gambling debt.

Wheel Roller *Roulette:* The croupier who spins the wheel and deals the game.

Where's Buster Brown Expression used by members of a dice mob to tell the dice mechanic to switch the crooked dice into the game.

Whip Shot A controlled dice shot in which the two dice are spun from the hand and strike the table surface with a flat spinning motion so that the controlled numbers are on top when the dice stop.

Whipsaw See *Sandbag.*

Window's Open (The) The cheating is being done ineptly.

Wire (1) The finish line at a racetrack. (2) A signal used between two gamblers or cheats. "I sent him a wire." (3) *Stud Poker:* A player who has a pair back to back is said to be *wired.*

With It (To be) To be with a carnival or circus.

Wood Hangers-on, non-players, gamblers without money. Also called *Deadwood.*

Work (1) Crooked cards, or dice. (2) The gaff itself.

Working Points A small share (percentage) of a gambling enterprise bought in order to secure a job with the gambling enterprise. "That floorman has six working points in the casino."

Wrong Bettor, Wrong Player, Wrongie *Craps:* A player who bets the dice to lose.

X (The) The control of all the gambling in town. "The Irish combination has the X on the town."

Yard $100.

Zing It In To bet heavily, particularly to parlay one's winnings.

Zombie (1) A gambler who shows no emotion either when winning or losing big money. (2) A horse which shows no pep.

Index

Combinations and ways
  in Craps, 277
  in two-, three-, four- and five-dice games, 338–39
Come bet, 273, 288
Come-out bet, 274, 280, 293–96
Continental Congress lottery, 150
Continental Press Service, 37
Contract Bridge. *See* Bridge.
Controller, Numbers, 187
Cotton, Charles, 230
Coup in Chemin de Fer, 463, 467
Count stores, 558, 578–79
Cover the Red Spot, 604–7
Crambrook, W.H.M., 616
Craps, 259–336
  ace-deuce standoff, 288
  backboard control shot, 324
  back line, 287–88, 300
  Bahamas double-end layout, 285
  Bank, 241, 265, 281–98. *See also* Bank Craps.
  betting, 272–74, 286–98
    systems, 327–36
  big six and big eight, 288–90
  blanket roll, 324
  bookmaker, 267–68
  boxman, 251
  Caribbean double side dealer, 285
  center bet, 273
  cheating with honest dice, 323–27
  combinations or ways, 277
  come bet, 273, 288
  come-out bet, 274, 280, 293–96
  consecutive passes record, 26
  crooked dice, detection of, 307–23
  dealer, 251
  degenerates, 262–63
  dice used, 260–62. *See also* Dice.
  don't come bet, 273, 288
  English double-end layout, 285
  equipment, 270
  faders, 273
    chances of, 278–79
  field bets, 290–92, 303
  flat bets, 273
  free bets, 300–302
  front line, 286–87, 300
  handle in, 259
  hardway or gag bets, 273–74, 280, 292–93
  horn, Santurce, Miami, or Curaçao bet, 295–96
  hot and cold system, 331–32
  house percentage in, 264, 284, 287–298, 300, 303, 306–7
  hustlers and chumps, 274–76, 318, 335–36
  largest losses in, 263–65
  Las Vegas style, 281–84, 286
  layouts, 284–86
  limits, 330
  lose, don't or don't pass line, 287–88
  luck in, 25–27
  Money (Open), 266, 304–7
  New York, 265, 298
  odds in, 276–81, 289

  one-roll action bet, 274, 280, 293–96
  origin and history of, 266–67
  passing, 273, 277, 280
  place or box number bets, 297–98, 303, 332–33
  play, 270
  players, 270
  point bet, 273
  Private, 265, 270–81, 335–36
  proposition bets, 273
    barring first roll, 826–27
    two-roll, 827–28
  Puerto Rican side dealer, 285
  right bet, 272, 333–34
  Rothstein system, 327–28
  rules, official, 270–74
  in sawdust joints, 227
  Scarne's system, 334–35
  Scarney, 265, 286, 299–302
  sensible gambling rules, 302–4
  shooter's chances, 278–79
  side bet, 273
  spin or whip shot, 324
  table control shot, 325–26
  tables, 282–83, 284
  three-cushion controlled shot, 324–25
  throw, or roll, 271–72
  types of, 265–66
  unfinished hand in, 263–65
  vigorish and, 268–69
  watcher or patience system, 328–31
  win line, do or pass line, 286–87
  wrong bet, 272, 333–34
Crawford, John, xxi–xxii
Credit betting, 85
Credit manager, casino, 249–50
Creepers, 574
Crimping cards, 648–49
Cripple Creek, Colorado, 232
Crockford's Club, 230, 231, 350
Crooked operations, 31. *See also* Cheating.
  basketball games, 131–32
  carnival games, 571 ff.
  casinos, 256–57
  dice, detection of, 307–23
  horse racing, 48–49, 63–66, 88
  lotteries, 155–58
  punchboards, 799–801
  slot machines, 437–40
Crossroader, 641
Croupier
  Chemin de Fer, 463
  Roulette, 401–2
Cuadros, 96, 97
Cuban casinos, 216, 226, 344–48, 475
Culbertson, Ely, 361
Cups and Balls, 616, 617
Curaçao bet, 295
Curaçao Hilton Hotel casino, 271, 299, 344, 407
Cutting cards, 647–52, 656–58, 734
  proposition bet on, 824

Daily double, 40, 84, 86
  in jai alai, 135
D'Alembert system, 411